JUDGE
Richard S. Arnold

JUDGE

Richard S. Arnold

A LEGACY OF JUSTICE ON THE FEDERAL BENCH

POLLY J. PRICE

Foreword by *Justice Ruth Bader Ginsburg*

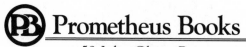

Prometheus Books

59 John Glenn Drive
Amherst, New York 14228–2119

Published 2009 by Prometheus Books

Judge Richard S. Arnold: A Legacy of Justice on the Federal Bench. Copyright © 2009 by Polly J. Price. All rights reserved. No part of this publication may be reproduced, stored in a retrieval system, or transmitted in any form or by any means, digital, electronic, mechanical, photocopying, recording, or otherwise, or conveyed via the Internet or a Web site without prior written permission of the publisher, except in the case of brief quotations embodied in critical articles and reviews.

Inquiries should be addressed to
Prometheus Books
59 John Glenn Drive
Amherst, New York 14228–2119
VOICE: 716–691–0133, ext. 210
FAX: 716–691–0137
WWW.PROMETHEUSBOOKS.COM

13 12 11 10 09   5 4 3 2 1

Library of Congress Cataloging-in-Publication Data

Price, Polly J.
Judge Richard S. Arnold: a legacy of justice on the federal bench/by Polly J. Price.
    p. cm.
Includes bibliographical references and index.
ISBN 978-1-59102-711-9 (cloth:alk. paper) 1. Arnold, Richard S. (Richard Sheppard),
1936-2004. 2. Judges—United States—Biography. I. Arnold, Richard S. (Richard Sheppard),
1936-2004. II. Title.

KF8745.A76P75 2009
347.73'14092—dc22
[B]
2008054573

Printed in the United States of America on acid-free paper

For Philip A. L. Miller

Contents

Foreword by Justice Ruth Bader Ginsburg   7

Introduction   11

Chapter 1.   Beginning the Course of Justice   17

Chapter 2.   William Brennan's Law Clerk   41

Chapter 3.   Law Practice   71

Chapter 4.   The Political Candidate   95

Chapter 5.   Appointment to the US District Court   123

Chapter 6.   Trial Judge for Civil Liberties   145

Chapter 7.   To the Court of Appeals   171

Chapter 8.   Life and Death below the Supreme Court   191

Chapter 9.   Free Speech and the First Amendment   225

Chapter 10.   The Right of Privacy and Abortion   251

Chapter 11.   Desegregation in Little Rock   273

Chapter 12.   "The Intensely Practical Nature of the

                  Political Process"   301

Chapter 13.   Two Opportunities for the Supreme Court   323

Chapter 14.   Open Courts, Public Ethics, and

                  Private Faith   351

Epilogue   377

Acknowledgments   383

Note on Sources   385

Notes   387

Index   453

Foreword

My generation knew no finer federal judge. Richard Arnold was a man of enormous intelligence. He was as kind and courteous as he was wise, the very model of what a good judge should be. He coped with his illness with unrelenting courage. Others, including me, gained strength from his example in our own bouts with cancer. His opinions, speeches, and law journal commentary will continue to inspire legions of jurists to follow in his way.

I wrote those words on September 24, 2004, the day after Richard Sheppard Arnold died, in response to a reporter's request for some lines he could use in composing an obituary.[1] My colleagues expressed similar views on Judge Arnold's character and work. Chief Justice William H. Rehnquist praised his "exemplary service" as long-term head of the budget committee of the US Judicial Conference. Justice John Paul Stevens wrote: "Richard Arnold was a great judge, a true scholar, a wonderful human being." Justice Sandra Day O'Connor spoke of Judge Arnold's efforts "to help other judges around the world improve their own systems." Richard Arnold's classmate at Harvard Law School, Justice Antonin Scalia, acknowledged that Arnold finished ahead of Scalia (Arnold was first in the class) and said, without an ounce of exaggeration: "His carefully reasoned and beautifully written opinions were models of the art of judging." "Splendid," was the word Justice Anthony M. Kennedy chose to describe Judge Arnold, adding that "[h]is intellectual interests were vast, his character upright, and his search for truth and justice unyielding." Justice Clarence Thomas, who was then the Eighth Circuit's "circuit justice," called Judge Arnold "a brilliant, brilliant man," and—uncommon among the best and brightest—"a model of humility." Justice Stephen Breyer said of Judge Arnold's "always clear and intelligent" opinions: "They, like the man who wrote them, showed an understanding of how law is connected to life, how law must work well for those whom law affects."[2]

I am glad Professor Price, once a law clerk to Judge Arnold, has devoted her time and talent to this biography celebrating the life of a prince among jurists and men. I treasure the hours I spent in Richard's bright company—in Washington, DC, and Little Rock, Arkansas, also abroad, participating in exchanges with our counterparts in other countries.

To this day, I try to "follow in his way." When an opinion of his bears on an issue I am attempting to explore or explain, I know I will find important aid. This very term, for example, I found in a Richard Arnold opinion just the right words to convey a basic point about the role of judges in our adversary system. The question presented to the Supreme Court: Should an appellate court, on its own initiative, correct an error disadvantageous to the Government, even though the Government itself did not seek correction of the error. Writing for the Court, I quoted Richard's words, which fit the case to a T:

> [Courts] do not, or should not, sally forth each day looking for wrongs to right. We wait for cases to come to us, and when they do we normally decide only questions presented by the parties. Counsel almost always know a great deal more about their cases than we do, and this must be particularly true of counsel for the United States, the richest, most powerful, and best represented litigant to appear before us.[3]

The matter could not have been put more gracefully.

Richard's brother and colleague on the court of appeals, Morris S. Arnold, captured the mind and spirit of Richard Sheppard Arnold in a statement in which all who prize the federal judiciary would concur:

> He was so careful and fair in his judgments that other judges frequently looked to him for guidance. That's extremely rare given the indepen-

dence of most judges. It wasn't a matter of having personal or political influence, it was just that his thinking was so clear and fair-minded that it carried influence with it.[4]

May Professor Price's well-researched, clearheaded, and carefully composed work serve as an enduring tribute to a man who lived greatly in the law, ever mindful of the people law exists to serve.

Ruth Bader Ginsburg
Associate Justice, Supreme Court of the United States
June 2008

Introduction

I have been fascinated by the administration of the federal courts — how they work and how cases are decided — since I served as a law clerk for Richard Sheppard Arnold on the Eighth Circuit Court of Appeals nearly twenty years ago. Books about the United States Supreme Court are plentiful. Recent books by former Supreme Court law clerks, journalists, and other Supreme Court observers feed a seemingly insatiable public interest in behind-the-scenes stories about the Supreme Court. It is rare, however, to encounter similar writings about the other federal courts. Much of the public and even many lawyers have little idea about the day-to-day work in the United States Circuit Court of Appeals, the court immediately below the Supreme Court.

We study the United States Supreme Court because it has the final word on the very few cases it hears each year. But for ordinary people, and for nearly all civil disputes and criminal prosecutions that end up in the federal court system, another court is far more important. That court — the United States Court of Appeals — consists of nearly two hundred judges spread geographically throughout the United States. While the Supreme Court decides around one hundred cases each year, the judges of the court of appeals decide thousands. The percentage of cases in the federal courts that make it all the way to the Supreme Court is minuscule—less than 1 percent.

Richard Arnold was one of the leading judges of this "other court" until his death in 2004. His career drew comparisons to that of the eminent Learned Hand of an earlier generation. Eight Supreme Court justices took the unprecedented step of issuing public memorials following Arnold's death. Former president Bill Clinton and Senator Hillary Rodham Clinton also issued a joint public statement at Arnold's death, saying, "America has lost one of its greatest jurists, and we have lost a cherished friend."

Unusually for his time, Arnold held great appeal across political lines: both liberals and conservatives supported his rise to the United States Supreme Court. In 1994, more than one hundred federal judges—nearly 20 percent of the entire federal judiciary—wrote President Bill Clinton to endorse Arnold for the seat left vacant by Harry Blackmun's retirement from the Supreme Court. Concerned about Arnold's health, President Clinton instead appointed Stephen Breyer, even though Clinton said he wanted to appoint Arnold and he believed Arnold to be "the most brilliant man on the federal bench." Clinton's hesitation was due to the fact that Arnold had been treated for cancer and his prognosis was not clear. "My Republican predecessors," Clinton said, "had filled the federal courts with young conservatives who would be around a long time, and I didn't want to risk giving them another position."[1]

If the Supreme Court is an unreachable goal for most litigants, it was also unreachable for Arnold because of his ultimately fatal illness. Clinton may have had other concerns beyond Arnold's potential longevity, but in the end Clinton was right according to his criteria: Arnold would have served on the Supreme Court for only ten years, and his seat would have been filled not by a Democrat but by a Republican president.

This book is both a biography and a window into the "hidden" courts of the federal judiciary. I evaluate Arnold's life, judicial philosophy, and significant cases as a contribution to a better understanding of the workings of the lower federal courts, and how they attempt to serve justice in individual cases. One fascination we have with judges is how they decide cases, and the extent to which their political beliefs inform their work. How judges decide cases is inescapably tied to who they are. This, in turn, is dependent on that person's life experiences. Arnold's early life and career before he became a judge were important factors in the judicial philosophy he espoused on the bench.

Journalists need simple explanations for the way judges decide cases, and so they employ terms like *liberal, conservative,* and *judicial activist* when describing judges. Arnold, by contrast, was difficult to classify. Although both liberal and conservative politicians supported his rise to the Supreme Court, both liberal and conservative groups also opposed it. From deeply conservative beginnings, Arnold reached decisions some characterized as "liberal," and his lucid, powerful opinions made him a leader in civil liberties at the close of the twentieth century. Arnold did not always recognize flaws in the system of justice, but he achieved consensus among judges of all political stripes on difficult issues. He articulated a vision of fairness and justice for individuals that set standards for other judges.

For readers unfamiliar with the structure of the federal court system, the US district courts are trial courts, the entry point for both civil and criminal cases. There are nearly seven hundred federal district judges. The next level is the US Court of Appeals, also known as circuit courts. There are thirteen federal circuits with approximately two hundred judges. At the top of the hierarchy is the Supreme Court of the United States, with nine justices. This Court has discretionary jurisdiction over most appeals; that is, the Supreme Court decides which appeals it will hear from the thirteen federal circuits.

Richard Arnold worked for twenty-five years within the second-largest geographical court of appeals—the Eighth Circuit—and served for seven years as its chief judge. For most of his judicial career Arnold supervised the litigation over desegregation in the Little Rock public schools, the longest-running desegregation case in United States history. He considered hundreds of appeals from men facing the death penalty, ninety of whom were executed during his tenure. He decided more abortion cases than any single Supreme Court justice. He rejected a life sentence imposed upon a seventeen-year-old black youth accused of rape. No judge's career better illustrates the critical work of protecting individual rights under the United States Constitution.

Arnold's story illuminates the broad social relevance of civil rights to the American experience as well as for the rule of law in the United States. Arguments about civil rights and civil liberties are never free from controversy. What does it mean to say civil rights are the foundation of the United States Constitution? Where do we fall short of our own aspirations? Arnold's story—including practical manifestations through his judicial work—allows us to examine these issues as an illustration of our recent past and with great relevance for the present.

In a nation in which most citizens say they support the freedoms guaranteed by the United States Constitution, it is unclear how many know what that can mean, and very few experience those guarantees directly. We do not think of the judicial branch as just another government agency with uniformed employees. Yet most Americans are unaware of the day-to-day work of judges in the traditional forum for recognition of civil rights in the United States—the federal courts, where individuals turn to challenge government action.

What a federal appellate judge does on a given day covers a broad spectrum. The day may begin with consideration of handwritten, nearly illiterate petitions from prisoners. The day will certainly include appeals from convicted criminals, because in most federal appellate courts the criminal docket makes up more than half of all the cases coming through the system. On the civil side, the day's encounter can include insurance claims, business disputes, and bankruptcies, as well as appeals from government agency decisions on tax matters or social security benefits. Judges are employed to resolve disputes.

But a significant part of the work involves concrete application of the US Constitution's governing principles in the large category of cases involving "civil rights" and "civil liberties"—the protections and privileges of personal freedom. Among these are freedom of political expression, the right to a fair criminal trial, the right to privacy, the right to redress for injury by the government, the right to vote, the right to personal freedom, and the rights of due process and equal protection. In the United States, civil rights extend beyond government action. Private actors such as employers, restaurant owners, and landlords, for example, may not discriminate against individuals on the basis of race or gender. Richard Arnold considered all judges to be first and foremost public servants of civil liberties. In their responsibility to preserve these rights, Arnold thought federal judges were like Sisyphus—condemned to roll a rock uphill forever.

Who Arnold was and where he came from could also startle. Arnold emerged from a rural region of Arkansas to finish first in his class at both Yale College and Harvard Law School. Calvin Trillin, a classmate at Yale, remembered Arnold's "Ivy Ode" delivered in Latin at commencement, "remarkable," given Arnold's Texarkana roots that "prep-school boys might have considered ridiculous."[2] Arnold was a polymath, learned in Latin, Greek, and Hebrew, and anecdotes abound of the bow tie–wearing Arnold's uncanny recall of classical texts. A newly selected Rhodes Scholar, Rhett Martin, said that the most impressive man he met was Richard Arnold. Arnold, he recalled, had a "most admirable mind"—keen, precise, articulate, humane, learned. During their conversation, Martin mentioned Heraclitus, and Arnold asked what in particular he was referring to. Seeing a chance to impress the judge with his intelligence, Martin rattled off the fragment in Greek. Arnold looked at him thoughtfully and said, "Hmm. I thought that was expressed in the subjunctive." And so it was; the judge was right.[3]

Arnold's career had a Clinton-like trajectory, beginning with his Arkansas roots and including a meteoric rise to the top of his profession. Unlike Clinton, Arnold came from a patrician family. One grandfather was Texas senator Morris Sheppard. The other was a successful, self-educated lawyer, the patriarch of the family law firm. Like his father before him, Richard Arnold attended Yale College and Harvard Law School. This family had many "firsts"—including the first (and likely only) time two brothers would serve together on the same federal court.[4] Richard's younger brother, Morris Sheppard Arnold, was appointed by a Republican president, but despite coming from opposing political parties, the two held very similar views, especially a near absolutism on individual rights. Richard was charmingly shy and retiring, while Morris is comparatively extroverted and gregarious, and no less intellectually gifted.

The Judicial Conference of the United States, the governing body for the federal courts, memorialized Arnold's "great sensitivity for human freedom and dignity."[5] His colleagues on the Eighth Circuit added:

> He was at his best in expounding constitutional rights, particularly as they protect the less fortunate in our society. His contribution to the development of the law in this circuit alone, as well as its impact on the work of the Supreme Court, place him among the very few most significant judges to serve not only on this court, but all the courts of the nation.[6]

What follows is the story of this "other court" through the life of one of its most important judges. Arnold considered himself to be a judicial conservative. He believed in strict enforcement of the Constitution, a statement of governing principles whose details must be worked out in individual cases. He thought the Bill of Rights was the most important part of the Constitution. He gave primacy to the First Amendment. He felt that if the majority of the people vote for something, they should have their way unless faced with a clear constitutional prohibition. He believed that the future depended upon continued public acceptance of the judiciary.

Richard Arnold did not think the judicial process should be hidden from the public. Arnold's private papers, internal court memoranda, and the willingness of numerous judges, politicians, and others to speak with me about Arnold and his work form the basis of this book. This book makes use of internal court documents, interviews with law clerks, diaries, and other nonpublic sources. Prior to his death Arnold granted me access to these items, along with several hours of interviews. My hope is that I present fairly what the record reflects; inevitably, judgments will diverge.

Arnold knew that continued public acceptance of the federal courts was a fragile thing, easily jeopardized by individual behavior. He thought we had a good system of justice, but not a great one. He worked to improve the administration of justice both in individual cases and in the overall operation of the federal courts.

Chapter One

Beginning the Course of Justice

Audacibus annue coeptis.

Look with favor upon a bold beginning. —Virgil[1]

On December 9, 1955, just one year after the Supreme Court's decision in *Brown v. Board of Education*, Yale Law School hosted a discussion titled "The Difficulties Facing Desegregation." The panel discussion, before an overflow crowd in the law school's auditorium, was sponsored by several campus groups including the Yale NAACP and the Civil Liberties Union. The event was billed as a response to a speech given at Yale the day before by Eugene Cook, the staunchly segregationist attorney general of Georgia, called "The Southern View of Segregation."

At the behest of the Yale Law School Conservative Society, Cook had addressed a "public meeting on segregation." Cook opposed desegregation in any form. He declared that the Supreme Court's recent decision outlawing segregated schools was "held in utter contempt by most Georgians and will not be respected or enforced in my State within the foreseeable future."[2] Cook maintained that the NAACP was a subversive, communist organization, and sought to have the organization outlawed in Georgia.[3]

No one denied Cook had presented an extreme view on the subject. The panel discussion at Yale Law School was proposed as a response to Cook "to present both sides of the debate," a pointed jab at the student Conservative Society for refusing requests to pair another speaker with Cook for a debate that would include a pro-*Brown* view.[4]

Members of the audience at the Yale Law School that day heard four speakers. Louis Pollak, a Yale law professor and legal adviser to the NAACP (later a federal district judge), presented the view supporting *Brown v. Board of Education*. He was joined by James Farmer, representing the AFL-CIO. Against this formidable array, the opposing side included Frances Coker, the retired chair of Yale's political science department, and a Yale college student still in his junior year. That college student— Richard Sheppard Arnold—was chosen "for his ability to represent the southern view of desegregation."[5]

Richard Arnold's appearance on the panel was remarkable for several reasons. He was only nineteen years old, the only southerner, and the only undergraduate on a panel of older, more professionally accomplished participants. The sponsoring organizations stated that they had done "everything in their power to assure the best representation to the various approaches to this question," presumably meaning that Richard Arnold was the best representative of the southern view of desegregation, or at least the best one they could come up with.[6]

Although Arnold was headed to Harvard Law School two years in the future, he was not yet trained in law. Louis Pollak, by contrast, taught constitutional law at Yale Law School, after a clerkship with Supreme Court Justice Wiley Rutledge and six years of legal experience in the private sector and with the US State Department. Arnold represented the minority view at Yale at the time—opposition to forced integration of schools in the South. He was already known among his friends in the Yale Political Union as a conservative and an opponent of *Brown*, but with the "respectable" view in opposition rather than Cook's extremism. When Arnold was asked to represent the southern view in this public discussion, he readily agreed.

By 1955, Arnold had already made a name for himself at Yale as a classics scholar, a champion debater, and a conservative thinker in the tradition of William F. Buckley Jr., who had graduated from Yale five years earlier. It was easy to predict that Arnold would have a notable future. Arnold saw himself with a future in politics, and he wanted to be a United States senator like his grandfather, Senator Morris Sheppard of Texas. Although his classmate Calvin Trillin considered Arnold's Texarkana, Arkansas, roots somewhat "absurd,"[7] there was nothing absurd about his prep school record at Phillips Exeter Academy or his record thus far at Yale. In his senior year, Arnold would be elected president of Phi Beta Kappa and would graduate first in his class, collecting numerous academic prizes along the way.

Devout and introspective, Arnold possessed a powerful, curious, and methodical mind. Lean, gangly, and of medium height, Arnold's dark hair and eyes were perpetually accented by a dark coat and tie, which Yale students were then required to wear to dinner. In contrast with most other students, Arnold preferred to wear a coat and tie all the time. Acquaintances who described him at the end of his life noted these remarkable consistencies: Arnold was funny, soft-spoken, and a shy, retiring intellectual. He listened with an intensity others could find unnerving, with his head cocked to the side.

The panel discussion "added four clashing interpretations of the segregation problem" to the views expressed by Eugene Cook the day before. Professor Pollak, the first speaker, argued that *Brown* was correctly decided and had outlawed segregation in the public schools "to confirm the ethical principle of equality." Arnold was the next speaker. He attacked the view that *Brown* was correct as a constitutional matter. He claimed that, as Eugene Cook had maintained the day before, the Supreme Court's decision was based not on law but on "sociology." The alleged "psychological damage to Negroes" upon which *Brown* was based, said Arnold, was a vague concept impossible to prove in a court of law, and insufficient in itself to authorize federal intervention in state affairs.[8] Arnold at times echoed Cook, who had said: "If the Supreme Court could disregard the Constitution today to accomplish a result of which you approve, it likewise can ignore it tomorrow to reach a result of which you disapprove."[9]

Arnold based his response to Pollak on two further grounds. First, Arnold was skeptical that federal intervention could overcome opposition to desegregation as a practical matter. He also believed strongly in a federalism that recognized states' rights in matters of local importance. *Brown* violated fundamental concepts of federalism, Arnold maintained. As he echoed a few months later in a Yale Political Union debate, "it is a state's right to control an institution so much a part of its interests as education."[10]

The third speaker, James Farmer, acknowledged the practical difficulties of implementing *Brown*. He highlighted instances of retaliation against black activists by segregationists, and said that he had "nothing but admiration for the men who risk their livelihoods and even their lives fighting racial intolerance." The final speaker, Francis Coker, had been billed as representing the "opposing" side, but largely supported the grounds of the legal decision. He noted that Eugene Cook's speech represented only the views of a "radical minority" of southern opinion.[11]

Of the four, only Richard Arnold criticized *Brown v. Board of Education* as a matter of constitutional law. But he joined the other three in favor of execution of the ruling on the ground that the Supreme Court had spoken, and its ruling must be followed.[12]

Brown v. Board of Education began a "revolutionary decade" in race relations in the United States.[13] Only a few years after the Yale debate, Arkansas governor Orval Faubus took a public stance against desegregation of the Little Rock public schools. Little Rock would become infamous throughout the world for jarring televised images of angry mobs of whites assaulting young black students, followed a few weeks later by images of the US Army's 101st Airborne approaching the school, ordered there by President Eisenhower in 1957.

Twenty-five years later, Richard Arnold as a federal judge would become a key figure in ongoing federal court litigation over desegregation of the Little Rock public schools. Over that time Arnold had witnessed and helped to shape a transformation of the South as well as the nation. His own transformation from the nineteen-year-old debater at Yale was no less profound.

Much is dependent on the character and philosophy of an individual judge in the American legal system. Compared to other nations, judges in the United States at all court levels are extremely powerful. As a result, judicial candidates often receive intense scrutiny, not only for evidence of high ethical standards, but also for fundamental beliefs about judicial power and how it ought to be exercised. One of the enduring debates today is about ideology in judges, with much interest in predicting the trajectory of new appointees to the bench based on past political affiliation.

But judges are also known to defy predictions about what kind of jurist they would be. At best, there is an uneasy fit between political positions and judicial philosophy, and both may continue to change over a life-time. Richard Arnold is a case in point. His early experiences profoundly shaped him and made him the kind of judge he would become. At the same time, the judge who emerged years later is in many ways not what one might have expected, based on Arnold's beginnings. The young Richard Arnold was profoundly conservative on many issues, but especially on the role of the federal government in matters traditionally left to the states.

The debate at Yale in 1955 is merely one illustration of a developing mind devoted to a wide-ranging engagement in politics and American law. Arnold was very much a twentieth-century figure, and he came of age in the midst of a profound revolution in civil rights and civil liberties. His experiences in the cauldron of a rapidly changing society made Arnold a rather different character than might be anticipated from his early years as a student. Arnold's jurisprudence, decades in the future, both flowed from and contrasted with his beginnings.

Richard Sheppard Arnold was born March 26, 1936, in Texarkana, Texas, where the nearest hospital was located. The family, however, lived on the Arkansas side of this divided city, with a population at that time of around eleven thousand (twenty-five thousand, if the Texas side was included). Texarkana was one hundred and fifty miles from Little Rock by direct rail.

Richard Arnold came from a prosperous south Arkansas family with extensive political ties — "frontier aristocracy," as Jeffrey Toobin described it in his book *The Nine: Inside the Secret World of the Supreme Court*.[14] The *Texarkana Gazette* notice of Richard's birth reported that "his grandparents are Senator and Mrs. Morris Sheppard of Washington, D.C., and Mr. and Mrs. William H. Arnold, of Texarkana."[15] His mother, Janet Sheppard Arnold, was the daughter of Senator Morris Sheppard of Texas, one of the leading senators of the era. Senator Sheppard was first elected to Congress in 1902 to replace his father who had died in office. In 1913 he was elected to the Senate as a Democrat from Texas, holding that office until his death in 1941 at age sixty-five, having never lost an election. Sheppard chaired the Senate Military Affairs Committee and was instrumental in preparing for World War II. Within less than a year after Senator Sheppard's death, Richard's grandmother married the other senator from Texas, Tom Connally, who served in the Senate until 1953. Richard's grandfather and step-grand-father were thus in the US Senate for a continuous forty years.

Richard's father, Richard Lewis Arnold, was the son of William Hendrick Arnold, who founded Arnold and Arnold, the leading law firm of south Arkansas. Born in 1861 at the start of the Civil War, William Hendrick Arnold had been admitted to practice law in 1882 after studying on his own. W. H. had served as mayor of Texarkana, president of the Arkansas Bar Association, a delegate to four Democratic national conventions, and was elected to the 1918 Arkansas Constitutional Convention. He was also a founding member of the American Law Institute in 1923 and the subject of a biography published in 2005.[16]

Late in life, W. H. Arnold published a short book of family history that included a biographical sketch of himself and his sons.[17] He took dozens of copies with him on a tour of Europe in 1935, at age seventy-four. He followed the unusual practice of leaving copies at every hotel and restaurant he visited. W. H. soon attracted the notice of a reporter with the *London Sunday Express*, who termed William "The Man Who Cannot Lose Himself."[18]

Upon his return from the European tour, W. H. resumed his prominent public life. Consistently opposed to many New Deal initiatives of Franklin Roosevelt, W. H. attacked Roosevelt's court-packing plan, writing in a letter to the *Arkansas Gazette*, "Nothing can be accomplished by the addition of six new justices unless the purpose be to have the court overrule decisions unsatisfactory to the president. The proposal is revolutionary, and coming from the White House, its terms excite amazement in the general public."[19]

William Hendrick Arnold died in 1946 in Texarkana, when Richard Arnold was ten years old. He left among his papers a copy of a talk he gave to the Rodeph Shalom Temple in New York City on the history of the Jewish people. He was a man of wide interests and wide travels; his world was surprisingly broad.

W. H. Arnold was a self-educated lawyer with very little formal schooling. Both his mother and father were college graduates, a rarity for south Arkansas in the 1840s. He certainly would have gone to college if the family could have afforded it, but the family had been ruined financially by the Civil War; at the end of the war the family had lost 90 percent of its wealth.

Feeling the loss of educational opportunities, W. H. Arnold saw that his children were educated in grand style. His youngest son, Richard Lewis, attended Phillips Exeter, Yale College, and Harvard Law School. Upon his return to the family law firm, Richard Lewis joined an older brother as two of the seven members of the local Harvard Club. Yet another son, William H. Arnold Jr., was a Rhodes Scholar. Richard S., like his father, Richard Lewis, was destined for Phillips Exeter Academy, Yale College, and Harvard Law School, and would surpass even his father's academic success. All the men on both sides of Richard's immediate family were lawyers, and Richard, too, became a lawyer because his father expected it. He had, in fact, "never really considered being anything else."[20]

The women in his family were also strong, intelligent, and interested in political matters. William Hendrick Arnold's wife, Kate Lewis Arnold, was active in Democratic Party politics within the constraints of her time. She was elected as a national committeewoman for Arkansas in the Democratic primary of 1932. In 1936, a few months after Richard's birth, Kate Lewis played a key role in a visit to the state by Franklin and Eleanor Roosevelt. As head of the committee to plan Eleanor Roosevelt's visit to Hot Springs, Kate Lewis welcomed the First Lady and spoke briefly at a breakfast in her honor at the Arlington Hotel. Franklin, who had spoken in Little Rock, remained on the train during Eleanor's stop in Hot Springs. Both Roosevelts would be joined by Richard's grandfather, Senator Morris Sheppard, for a train tour through Texas.

Arnold's grandmother, Kate Lewis Arnold, delivered a radio address in Miller County in 1938 in favor of John L. McClellan for United States Senate, against the incumbent Hattie Caraway, the first woman elected to the United States Senate from any state. Kate Lewis was Democratic National Committeewoman from Arkansas at that time. The National Committees of both parties were composed of one man and one woman from each state, elected at the Democratic primary.[21]

Kate Lewis Arnold's radio address took place the day before the election. It was not, she urged, "any issue of one woman against another." Kate Lewis said she was "not opposed to a woman for United States Senator if she is capable of giving that type of service we need. And I say frankly, that if Arkansas has a woman with capabilities for the type of service which Arkansas now needs, I do not know who she is." Caraway's only appearance on the floor of the Senate in debate, Kate Lewis noted, was an address of less than five minutes in opposition to an anti-lynching bill.[22] Kate was unwilling to look past Caraway's questionable effectiveness merely because she was a woman.

The senatorial campaign of John McClellan, which Kate Arnold supported, faced a formidable opponent in Hattie Caraway. In 1932, Huey Long, the radical populist governor and later senator from Louisiana, came to Arkansas to assist the Caraway campaign, with the two of them making thirty-one campaign stops in eight days.[23] Even without Huey Long's help, the first woman senator won again six years later against John McClellan, delaying the start of McClellan's thirty-four-year Senate career until 1943. It was the only election McClellan ever lost. Caraway served in the Senate until 1944 when she was defeated by J. William Fulbright.

Of all his accomplished family members, Richard greatly admired his mother, Janet Sheppard Arnold, and probably was most deeply formed by her. His mother, he said, "was interested in everything to do with learning, and everything to do with politics. My interest in religion, study, intellectual pursuits, and reading is something that she transmitted to me."[24] A statement that Richard would often repeat about his mother undoubtedly influenced him. She told her son, "If I were a man, I would be at least a congressman."[25] Father Richard Lewis, on the other hand, was not engaged in political activity, a reaction, perhaps, to the excessively political world of his father and father-in-law. Instead, Richard Lewis devoted his time to law practice at Arnold and Arnold, establishing a reputation as a powerful, successful lawyer for utility companies.

After World War II, Janet Sheppard worked for voting rights for black citizens in Texarkana. Janet Sheppard and Henry Woods, a young lawyer who would later become a federal judge, worked with the local chapter of the NAACP. Arnold later recalled, "Mrs. John J. Jones, the wife of the President of the local chapter, would come to our house to visit my mother. But before she came, Mrs. Jones wished to be assured that she could come in the front door and sit in the living room. 'Of course,' my mother said."[26]

The setting in which Arnold grew up was segregated, but he was influenced by the progressive racial views of his family, especially his mother. Janet published poems in the *Texarkana Gazette* shaming the Ku Klux Klan for their hypocritical Christianity. She would never tolerate racially charged language in the home or in the circles in which she traveled.[27]

A crushing blow was his mother's unexpected death when he was nineteen years old and away at Yale. Janet Sheppard Arnold was forty-three years old when she suffered an aneurism while teaching school, and she died a short time later. Richard's younger brother, Morris Arnold, who was only thirteen years old, was in an adjacent classroom at the time. When she died, the local newspaper editorialized that she was the "most democratic" person they had ever known.[28]

Theological discussions with his mother had been important for Arnold, and his mother's death profoundly affected his religious faith for the rest of his life. She had given him a Bible with a handwritten inscription from Shakespeare. It was Portia's praise of mercy in *The Merchant of Venice*:

> Though justice be thy plea, consider this,
> That in the course of justice, none of us
> Should see salvation.

Morris Arnold, Richard's younger brother, was given a Bible with the scriptural admonition "much is expected from those to whom much is given."[29]

THE EDUCATION OF RICHARD ARNOLD

Richard's kindergarten year corresponded with the American entry into World War II. He attended a small private school for three years, and then Arkansas public schools from grades three through nine. Consistent with the times, all of these schools were racially segregated. Much of his early education came from his own reading. Richard spent hours in his family's library, hurrying to finish his schoolwork so he "could read something interesting." He recalled "wonderful encyclopedias, histories, and law books," staying up at night to read after his parents thought he was in bed.[30]

Young Richard was bookish from an early age and was never viewed by his friends to be particularly athletic. But he regularly joined neighborhood kids, often with his younger brother, Morris, for touch football games in the Arnold family's front yard. One friend, Sam Alston Lee, recalled that Arnold had a "gangly run," in which "his legs kind of flew out to the side."[31] More often, Sam and Richard played poker in Richard's room, looked at *National Geographic* magazines, or worked on merit badges for Boy Scouts. Richard would eventually become an Eagle Scout, always a great point of pride for him.

At thirteen, inside for the summer of 1949 with a bout of malaria, Richard wrote a paper on the topic of the incorporation of the Bill of Rights in the federal constitution. It was a complex and unsettled constitutional problem. After 1937 it was clear that the Supreme Court would incorporate particular Bill of Rights guarantees selectively as limits on the states—a restriction on state and local governments as well as the federal government through the due process clause of the Fourteenth Amendment. *Palko v. Connecticut* explained that some parts of the Bill of Rights were so fundamental that the states were bound to respect them; others were less important, leaving the states free to disregard them.[32]

Just two years before Arnold tackled the question of incorporation as a research project, Justice Hugo Black articulated his dissenting view of "complete" incorporation—the Fourteenth Amendment required states to respect *all* rights articulated in the Bill of Rights because of the privileges and immunities clause, not the due process clause.[33] Black's view never prevailed, but Arnold thought it was the better view and wrote his paper accordingly. The endeavor reflected Arnold's early interest in the profound federalism revolution of the post–Civil War constitutional amendments, an interest abundantly evident in later years. It was certainly not the usual interest for a young teen.

Arnold's religious education was a curious mix of Baptist and Methodist before he settled on St. James Episcopal church in Texarkana, Texas, in his late teens. He left the Baptist church around age nine because of its teachings on the literal age of creation of the earth. Arnold was taught, he said, "that God made the world in six days in 4004 B.C.," but Arnold had challenged his Sunday school teacher that rocks had been found that were a lot older than that. After Arnold talked it over with his parents, they decided he could go to the Methodist church. But within five years, Arnold left the Methodists, early proponents of the "social gospel" in Arkansas, because they were teaching what Arnold thought "was a lot of politics."[34]

His mother's increasing interest in religion was a matter of discussion between her and Richard, and beginning in 1951, Richard joined her in the Episcopal church, where she also taught in the day school. His father only rarely attended services. Richard Lewis was fond of saying that he "was really a Jew" who believed only in the Old Testament. His wife, in turn, was fond of telling him that "if that was all there was to it, that he would be damned, because it was only the New Testament part that would save such a wretch."[35] Richard Lewis often joked that his favorite book of the Bible was Esther, because of the lavish parties described in the opening chapter.[36]

PHILLIPS EXETER ACADEMY: A JEFFERSONIAN VIEW

At age fourteen Richard was sent to Phillips Exeter Academy in Exeter, New Hampshire, for his final three years of secondary school. The school was as famous as any private preparatory school in the country. Founded in 1781, its list of notable alumni was lengthy well before Arnold arrived. Although Exeter drew students from nearly every state, its student population was heavily from New York and New England and overwhelmingly made up of students whose parents were professionals.[37] Arnold joined a class of about two hundred students. With very few exceptions, Exeter students continued on to Harvard, Yale, and Princeton. Placement in an Ivy League college was practically assured for any Exeter student.

At Exeter, and for the following four years at Yale, Arnold experienced an elite, all-male education (Exeter did not admit women students until 1970, one year after Yale). If Arnold was far from his Arkansas roots and homesick, it did not show, and in fact he thrived both in the challenging academic environment and in an endeavor that would become his specialty, debate.

Arnold pursued a classical diploma at Exeter, taking all of the Latin and Greek courses offered in the curriculum. His father had also earned a classical diploma at Exeter and thought his son should do the same. Classical studies became a passion for the son. Reflecting later, Arnold said it had a tremendous influence on his writing ability because of the exercise of understanding the syntax of more complicated languages. He learned to appreciate words and to employ them with precision and brevity. Classical studies, Arnold said, also "helps you to enjoy life. I think about lines of poetry— almost every day something will occur to me."[38] When Richard was home in Texarkana during the summer, he would teach his mother Greek. She wanted to read the New Testament but had never studied Greek in school.[39]

Arnold was frequently featured in the pages of the student newspaper as a prize-winning student and for his leading role on the debate team and in the Phillips Exeter Academy Senate. The senate was a student organization modeled after the United States Senate to deliberate on the issues of the day, ranging from communism in the United States to presidential politics and foreign policy. It met every other Sunday afternoon, and Arnold was a prominent participant. He was elected the group's president for his senior year.

He also wrote an opinion column on a weekly basis for the student newspaper, which he called "A Jeffersonian View." This weekly writing provides a rare glimpse into Arnold's early thinking on political issues and law. Had Arnold received President Clinton's nomination for a seat on the Supreme Court when Arnold later was a serious contender, an enterprising journalist would have discovered a gold mine in the newspaper records of "A Jeffersonian View."

A review of the newspaper columns makes it at once apparent that Arnold's exposition of a southern view of *Brown v. Board of Education* at Yale was a position he had already considered for several years. "A Jeffersonian View" for December 13, 1952, noted that the Supreme Court had just heard arguments in five cases affecting the policy of segregation in the public schools—the cases that would lead to the Supreme Court's opinion in *Brown* two years later. "Hitherto," Arnold wrote, "the Court has accepted the contention that 'separate but equal' facilities satisfy the requirement of the Fourteenth Amendment. But now a radical change in the Court's attitude may occur."[40] Arnold suspected—correctly, as it turned out—that the NAACP's litigation strategy to overturn *Plessy v. Ferguson* would eventually alter the "separate but equal" doctrine in the Supreme Court.

Arnold warned against any such change as "an unwarranted federal intervention in local affairs":

> The "separate but equal" doctrine has been accepted constitutional law since 1896. Why should there be a radical departure from established policy now, especially since such a departure would be extremely difficult to enforce? The management of the schools has always been a matter strictly for the states. The federal government has absolutely no legal justification for intervening; the Fourteenth Amendment nowhere bans segregation, it merely ensures the "equal protection of the laws." The "separate but equal" doctrine conforms both with the letter and the spirit of the amendment. The Supreme Court most certainly has no call to overrule it.[41]

In addition, Arnold wrote, the practical consequences of such a decision "would be appalling." Arnold contended that the majority of persons in the states that would be affected, "both white and colored," are "overwhelmingly opposed to being rudely thrown together by federal fiat," and would not willingly obey it. It would be "far better for the South and for the country as a whole if the Supreme Court refuses to meddle in purely local affairs."[42]

Arnold's "Jeffersonian View" on this topic was especially significant because Thurgood Marshall had spoken the previous year at Exeter. His subject was "race relations in the United States," and at the time, Marshall was special counsel for the NAACP in its litigation over segregated public schools and universities.[43]

In his address to the Exeter students, Marshall recounted several cases in which blacks had been admitted to southern universities and law schools after litigation by the NAACP. He also described the litigation strategy to achieve similar results for public elementary and secondary schools, including psychological tests given to children to show the "terrible effects that segregation leaves in their minds." This would be the litigation strategy of *Brown v. Board of Education*, then working its way through the lower federal courts.[44]

It would be possible to conclude that Arnold sympathized with the Dixiecrats, a group of southern Democratic senators opposed to federal civil rights legislation in the early 1950s. The senators used the filibuster to defeat civil rights measures, and in early 1953, Arnold defended them in a column titled "The Filibuster's Good Points." He noted that the filibuster, a method of debate allowed only in the Senate that allows a minority to prevent a bill's passing "by talking it to death," had been permitted by the rules of the United States Senate for one hundred and sixty years. Arnold believed the filibuster was an important measure to protect minority rights—meaning, for Arnold, a sectional, geographic minority. "It can be used by a minority, in this case a particular section, to prevent the passage of a bill which, although desired by the majority, would be distinctly detrimental to their own interests. In the case of the civil rights legislation, which would be not only detrimental but also unconstitutional, the filibuster is an important bulwark against unjust extension of federal power."[45] It is no surprise that Arnold was engaged in these issues because of who he was (grandson of a senator) and where he came from (a small, segregated southern town).

Both at Exeter and later at Yale, Arnold prominently identified himself with the Republican Party and a party called "The Party of the Right." His opposition to federal intervention in matters of race was of a piece with his views of states' rights generally. His conservatism was not motivated by racial antipathy—his home environment had been very racially tolerant. But the Democrats, "once the party of true liberalism," had introduced a paternalism into American government that was "the bane of true democracy."[46] Supporting Republican Dwight Eisenhower in the 1952 presidential election, Arnold wrote: "The great fundamental issue in this election is the issue of liberty versus the brand of creeping socialism first foisted on the American people by the New Deal policies, and continued by Harry Truman."[47]

Arnold was not sympathetic with the New Deal, calling it an "un-American" philosophy that moved America toward socialism.[48] Arnold's dislike of New Deal federalism, for example, explains his opposition to a bill in the Senate to establish a Federal Fair Employment Practices Commission. Arnold opposed it on the ground that it "impaired freedom of contract." But the bill was intended to protect minority groups from unfair discrimination at the hands of employers, which Arnold suggested would "increase racial strife more than it would stop discrimination."[49]

Arnold addressed segregation, specifically, only once in his column. The communist scare and the cold war were of much greater interest. Of the many speakers brought to campus and topics considered by the debating societies, communism was at the forefront. Frequent topics included Joseph McCarthy and loyalty oaths. The student senate, for example, voted 27 to 18 to repeal the McCarran Security Act of 1950, legislation that required the registration of communist organizations and established a board to investigate persons suspected of being engaged in subversive activities. Supporters of the bill stated, "We must put a stop to witch-hunting acts," which infringed on civil liberties. Senator Richard Arnold, on the contrary, maintained that if the McCarran Act were repealed, it would invite the Communists to plot the overthrow of the government: "If we allow the Reds freedom of speech they would use this privilege to indoctrinate others, and it will mean the destruction of our democratic system."[50]

Arnold was also on the losing side of a vote to abolish the House Un-American Activities Committee. Arnold said, "The Congressional right to investigate any aspect of American life is of the essence of our democracy." He recognized, however, that "innocent people" would necessarily suffer, as "no investigation is perfect."[51]

In an exchange of letters published in the *Exonian*, Arnold was tagged as a "Junior McCarthy" for his objection to what he considered biased political commentary by faculty members. One student wrote: "Rumor has it that two students of this Academy are trying to spread a certain type of homegrown McCarthyism within our walls. They are making wild charges about the political opinions of some of the teachers and alleging that certain members of the English and history departments are 'pinks.'"[52]

One of the two "Junior McCarthys," as the writer termed them, was Richard Arnold. Arnold responded that the selection of new instructors for the history department should secure a more even balance among the number of liberals and conservatives:

> When the Department is composed of six or seven shades of Fair Deal and a moderate or two, the situation is deplorable. It should be easy for every thinking liberal or conservative to see that it is only by conflict in views, secured by a balance in the department, that students will be provoked to serious thinking instead of blind acceptance. The lack of conflict of political opinion in many parts of the school should be a source of anxiety to any genuine Democrat.[53]

What else fueled the charge that Arnold was a "Junior McCarthy"? Arnold opposed a bill to expel Senator Joseph McCarthy from the Senate. Writing about the topic in his column, Arnold did not approve of McCarthy's behavior, but likewise he worried about the continuing threat of communism: "True, the Senator may be abusing his right of congressional immunity in making his violent accusations, but may not the Communists also be abusing their freedom of speech in distributing their pro-Russian propaganda? If McCarthy is to be expelled from the Senate, then by the same token, the teaching of Communist doctrine should be suppressed."[54]

Arnold also supported loyalty oaths for teachers, university professors, and government employees. He wrote, "We have always been amazed to think that any person could consider himself qualified for these jobs after refusing to swear allegiance to the United States. I cannot imagine why anyone would be so touchy that his sensitivity would be offended by being required to declare his loyalty to the government. To require such an oath is not suppression; it is a justifiable precaution which no one should find objectionable."[55]

In light of Arnold's later renown as a judge and as a strident advocate for freedom of speech, it is interesting to consider his early views with respect to the communist issue and, specifically, loyalty oaths for professors:

> The opponents of the oath contend that it abridges the Bill of Rights because it limits the professors' freedom of speech. But it has long been an accepted judicial principle that freedom of speech can be limited when

it offers a "clear and present danger" to the security of the community. What could be a clearer or more immediately present danger to the United States' security than communism? Certainly men should not be allowed to teach communism in the schools. This indoctrination is not an exercise of the right of free speech, it is a dangerously revolutionary tendency, since communism teaches the forcible overthrow of enemy governments.

Why single out teachers? Arnold said it was because a teacher is "most eminently fitted to influence the opinions of others. Especially at the college age is there a great opportunity for unscrupulous professors to take advantage of their position and indoctrinate their students with communism. Teachers, since they are better fitted than most men to influence unduly the thought of others, should be more carefully regulated."[56]

The trip from Exeter to Texarkana by train took the better part of two days. Returning to Arkansas during the term was thus out of the question. Arnold would often spend Thanksgiving holidays with a classmate, either with his friend Alan King in Redding, Massachusetts, or his senior year roommate, Warren Plath, whose parents lived in Wellesley, Massachusetts (and whose sister, Sylvia, was at nearby Smith College).

Warren Plath and Richard Arnold were considered by many classmates to be the two smartest students that year at Exeter, with Plath just edging out Arnold for class valedictorian.[57] It was the only time Arnold did not finish first in his class, as he would at both Yale College and Harvard Law School. The competition was friendly; Plath recalled many poker and Ping-Pong games, and weekly hot dogs or cheeseburgers at Bill's Spa.[58]

As his senior year at Exeter drew to a close, Arnold applied to and was accepted at Yale. Most of his classmates went to Harvard, but Arnold's father, Richard Lewis, had graduated from Yale and "wouldn't hear of" his son going anywhere else.[59]

A YALE MAN

Arnold found Yale to be less challenging academically than Exeter had been.[60] He majored in Latin and Greek and won prizes in both as well as in public speaking. At the end of four years, he was ranked first academically in his class.

Arnold was ahead of his classmates in Latin and Greek abilities, so in fall 1953, his first year at Yale, he added French. The future federal judge Gilbert S. Merritt recalled Arnold's exceptional abilities from their first day at Yale:

> I knew that there was something very special about Richard 45 years ago, not long after we sat down next to each other for our first class as freshmen at Yale College. It was a class in beginning French taught five days a week in a little classroom above Yale's main Gothic gate, looking out over the New Haven green. Within two weeks, he and Monsieur Tofoya, our teacher, were conversing back and forth in French. Within a month, Monsieur Tofoya had put him up in French 20, which required as preparation two good years of high school French. Before the first semester was out, the French Department put Richard into French 30, an advanced class, where they read Baudelaire, Stendhal and other great French writers.[61]

Arnold was nineteen years old and a sophomore at Yale when he received a telegram that his mother had died. The devastated son made the long journey by train back to Texarkana for her funeral. Within a week, he was back at Yale. Introspective and not prone to sharing his feelings with others, Arnold threw himself into his studies and the debate team. He also began a close relationship with the Episcopal church at Yale, becoming the student president of its congregational council by his senior year.

The first summer at home after his mother's death was the most difficult for him. As he did for all of his summer vacations from Yale, Arnold worked at the *Texarkana Gazette*, primarily as a reporter but also, occasionally, as an editorial writer. The managing editor at the time, J. Q. Mahaffey, recalled that Arnold "was very quick to learn, had an outstanding attitude, was very bright, always eager to work, and made an excellent reporter and writer."[62] Mahaffey had known Arnold as a small boy and was intimately acquainted with his family.

By the time Arnold graduated from Yale, he had been tapped to join Elihu, one of Yale's oldest senior societies. In political activities, the same conservative streak evident at Exeter is abundantly present, primarily in reports of speeches Arnold gave in the Yale Political Union. He was also a champion debater on the varsity team. One particular debate became legendary. The Yale team debated Oxford University in New Haven. One of the Oxford debaters quoted a Latin author. In Arnold's response, he said that his opponent had quoted only a part of the piece. He proceeded to quote the rest of it in Latin from memory—and then translated it.[63]

For his senior essay in classics, Arnold wrote a 108-page paper titled "The Emperor Constantine and the Christian Church." It is a well-written, comprehensive study of academic theories to explain the reasons that led Emperor Constantine to recognize and favor the Christian Church. Sources are quoted in the original Greek, handwritten in Arnold's sparse printing style.[64]

But it is also remarkable for the extent to which it reveals Arnold's religious interests. In a prologue, Arnold wrote:

> It is only fair to warn the reader that the author of this paper is himself a Christian, and therefore inevitably biased. The real reason why Constantine did what he did, in my opinion, is that the Holy Ghost told him to. Since this conclusion, however, would be unacceptable to many scholars, and since in any case the Holy Ghost generally works not directly but through the medium of historical circumstance, the opinions here advanced will concern only what Gibbon called the "secondary causes" of historical development.[65]

As part of his evaluation of historical development, Arnold specified that his interpretation was guided by the view "that all human actions are the result of mixed and ever-changing motives, sometimes unknown even to the person who takes these actions, and never derive from any single pure purpose." Arnold closed his preface, beneath his signature line, with the notation "Easter Day, 1957"—the day he completed the work.[66]

At graduation for the class of 1957, Richard Arnold delivered the traditional commencement address at Yale, the "Ivy Ode." The address was in Latin. Arnold's classmate Calvin Trillin recalled the ode in his book *Remembering Denny*:

Dick [Arnold] read the ode after a characteristically modest introduction, which said, in part, "There is virtually no competition for this post, since the number of undergraduates acquainted with an art so arcane as the composition of Latin poetry has dwindled almost to nothing. With due humility, accordingly, I submit the following lines. I hope they are Latin; honesty compels me to admit that they are not poetry."[67]

Denny Hansen, the subject of Trillin's book, was a Yale classmate who had been selected as a Rhodes Scholar and who later committed suicide. After the publication of *Remembering Denny*, Arnold wrote to Trillin, praising the book and speculating whether a religious faith might have helped Hansen. Trillin responded, "I wouldn't quarrel with the proposition that Denny might have been better able to cope with his problems if his life had included a spiritual dimension. I suppose people need some sort of capital to fall back on in truly difficult times—family, faith, the sort of unshakable inner confidence that dates from childhood—and, sadly, he didn't have any capital at all."[68]

Although one of Arnold's uncles had been a Rhodes Scholar, Richard Arnold did not apply for the scholarship. Unlike Denny Hansen, Arnold was not a particularly strong athlete and he may have assumed, probably correctly at the time, that the Rhodes selection committee sought star athletes who were also academically superior. In any event, Arnold had long known he would attend Harvard Law School. He had no choice in the matter, although he said he did not resent his lack of choice. His future, at least through age twenty-five, was planned for him by his father. Arnold would be a lawyer with an elite education, whatever he chose to do with that afterward.

HARVARD LAW SCHOOL

Trouble was brewing in Little Rock when Richard Arnold and his new Harvard Law School classmates were officially welcomed by Dean Erwin Griswold on September 15, 1957.[69] In less than two weeks, nine black students would be denied entrance to Little Rock's Central High School, beginning a standoff between Governor Orval Faubus and President Dwight D. Eisenhower over the enforcement of *Brown v. Board of Education*. The US Army's 101st Airborne Division from Fort Campbell, Kentucky, would arrive in Little Rock, and on September 25 the nine students entered the school with the military escort. As Arnold and his 515 classmates endured the first weeks of law school, Arnold would have seen pictures of the 101st Airborne deployed throughout Little Rock's streets.

The images were shocking—all the more to the home-state boy. The Central High School mob scenes, culminating in the Supreme Court arguments in *Cooper v. Aaron* later that year, caused Arnold great embarrassment. He later wrote:

> When I first arrived at the Harvard Law School in September of 1957, the events at Central High School, including the Governor's obstruction by military force of the order of the United States District Court were in full swing. Most conversations between students who meet each other for the first time include the question, "Where are you from?" I was humiliated to have to answer the question.[70]

It was one thing to oppose *Brown v. Board of Education* as a constitutional matter, as Arnold did. It was quite another to be faced with the chaotic scenes of resistance emanating from his home state, especially when they seemed to bear out the worst of his earlier predictions. Arnold was very much opposed to Faubus's stance because he thought it was clearly illegal. The Supreme Court had spoken, and a federally mandated desegregation of public schools was now the law of the land.

It was an eventful year at Harvard. Desegregation and civil rights were at the forefront of the Supreme Court's docket as well as a consistent topic of high-profile speakers at the law school. Strom Thurmond, US senator from South Carolina and the 1948 "Dixiecrat" candidate for president, addressed the law school forum on the 1957 Civil Rights Act passed by Congress earlier that summer. The first civil rights bill enacted in eighty-two years, the final version, aimed at increasing the number of registered black voters, had little teeth. Nonetheless, before its passage Thurmond had denounced the act in "the longest speech ever heard within the walls of the Senate Chamber," as the law school student newspaper reported.[71] Thurmond accused all three branches of the federal government of blatant violations of the Constitution: The Supreme Court for *Brown v. Board of Education*, the executive branch for use of federal troops in Little Rock, and Congress for the passage of the Civil Rights Bill. Thurmond singled out *Brown* for particular criticism, declaring that "nowhere in the Constitution is the Federal government given any power in the field of public-school education."[72] It was a view that Arnold had endorsed while a student at Yale.

The most eminent speaker of the year was eighty-five-year-old Learned Hand, the famous federal judge from the Second Circuit, who delivered the Holmes Lectures. Hand, frequently said to be the best judge never to sit on the Supreme Court, saw his last opportunity pass in 1942. Franklin Roosevelt gave Hand's age as the reason for choosing Wiley Rutledge instead (Hand was seventy in 1942). Ironically, Rutledge served on the court less than six years before his death in 1949 at age fifty-five. Hand remained an active judge for more than a decade beyond that.[73]

In February 1958, Hand presented a three-part lecture series titled "The Bill of Rights." Hand knew this would likely be his last statement on the jurisprudence of civil liberties, and a large part of the lectures was devoted to the First Amendment. In one lecture, however, Hand attacked *Brown v. Board of Education* on the ground that the Supreme Court had exceeded its constitutional powers.[74] The lectures were published later that year in a book.[75] When Arnold himself became a much-respected federal judge, some compared him to the great Learned Hand for the respect with which he was held in the legal profession.

Whatever personal turmoil the Little Rock events may have caused, Arnold had a very successful academic year. Although he had considered Yale to be less academically challenging than Phillips Exeter Academy, he said that Harvard Law School was "a different order of rigor in intellectual terms." Arnold believed some of his teachers at Harvard, including Paul Freund and Abram Chayes, "were really the most admirable minds that I have been in contact with."[76] At the conclusion of his first year, Arnold was awarded the Sears Prize, a $600 award to the student with the highest grade average in each class. His classmate Herb Dym was also awarded a Sears Prize, one of the few years in which two students had tied for the top grades.

Toward the end of his life, Arnold maintained that Abram Chayes was the "best teacher I ever had."[77] As a first-year student, Arnold wrote the only "perfect" exam ever received by Chayes at Harvard. As one of Arnold's future law clerks related:

> While I was in law school, I kept hearing about Richard Arnold. "Don't worry about trying to write a perfect exam," my civil procedure professor told my class. "It's already been done, but only once." And then my professor told us about a former student, now a federal judge in Arkansas,

named Richard Sheppard Arnold. He wrote his civil procedure exam in a neat, printed handwriting that looked like typing between the lines of the paper. He cited every case by its complete name and correct citation. He addressed every issue thoughtfully and thoroughly. "Perfect," my professor said. "You won't be able to match that." We didn't.[78]

Arnold married Gale Palmer Hussman of Camden, Arkansas, the summer after his first year of law school. Arnold had met Gale at the *Texarkana Gazette*, where they both worked. Gale's father, Walter Hussman, was the principal owner of Palmer Media Group, consisting of daily and weekly newspapers, radio, and television stations in Arkansas, Texas, Louisiana, and Mississippi. The Hussmans were the most prominent media family in South Arkansas, and the Arnolds were the most prominent legal family there.

Richard and Gale moved into an apartment across from the law school at the end of that summer. Richard had been named to the *Harvard Law Review*, a prestigious position available only to the select few students at the top of the class. Gale would later begin work as Professor Paul Freund's secretary, but in the meantime she became an active participant in the Harvard Law Wives' Club. Harvard Law School opened admissions to women beginning in 1953, but only a handful of law students were women during Arnold's years, and none made the *Law Review* in Arnold's class. Ruth Bader Ginsburg, later a Supreme Court justice and close friend of Arnold's, had been a member of the *Harvard Law Review* staff in 1957–1958 before transferring to Columbia Law School to be with her husband.

The *Law Review* dominated Arnold's time. He would be elected as a case editor for his third year. In the *Law Review*'s offices Arnold rubbed shoulders with classmates who would themselves go on to distinguished legal careers. The most famous would become Supreme Court Justice Antonin Scalia. Frank Michelman, Philip Heymann, and David Currie would become distinguished law professors.[79]

In a memorial tribute, Justice Scalia recalled that part of their closeness was due to the fact that they had both studied Latin and Greek: "A close bond of friendship between New York City and Texarkana seems unlikely, but it came to be, particularly during the two years Richard and I worked together on the Harvard Law Review. We had in common two qualities not shared by many of our colleagues: an orthodox Christianity, and a classical education."[80] John French, the law review's president that year, recalled that Arnold and Scalia maintained a running, obscure debate in Latin, on the bulletin board in Gannet House. "The rest of us kept up, if at all," French said, "only by gathering in fours and fives to collaborate on deciphering the posted messages."[81]

Richard Lewis Arnold attended his son's graduation in May 1960. For Richard Lewis, who sported a personalized "HLS 32" license plate denoting the year of his own graduation from Harvard Law School (he had been a classmate of future justice Harry Blackmun), it was a moment of great pride that his son had finished three years at Harvard Law School, ranked first in his class of over five hundred students, and was awarded the Faye Diploma, the faculty's designation of the most promising law graduate. It was an auspicious beginning to a career in the law.

Arnold's early experiences and education started him on a journey from a narrow to an expansive view of civil rights. Arnold recognized that understanding the past—including his own—was crucial to understanding contemporary problems of race in America. Early in his career Arnold took public positions in opposition to forced integration. Yet he came to believe that growing up in segregated southern Arkansas in the 1940s and 1950s helped him to recognize claims of discrimination. A judge's reaction to such claims, he said, related to how often that judge thinks those things happen in general. He had seen it often enough, he thought. Sometimes cases of race or gender discrimination were "as plain as the nose on your face."[82]

Arnold's most important formative experience, however, would come during the year following his graduation from Harvard, when he served as a law clerk for Justice William Brennan on the United States Supreme Court.

Chapter Two

William Brennan's Law Clerk

R ichard Arnold's first job after graduation from Harvard Law School was to serve as one of Supreme Court Justice William Brennan's two law clerks in 1960–1961. Before moving to Washington, however, after graduating in June 1960 Arnold returned to Arkansas to prepare for the bar exam. His study method was to read the Arkansas statutes in their entirety. The method must have been successful—Arnold recorded the highest score since the institution of a written exam for admission to the Arkansas bar.

The clerkship year was pivotal for Arnold. He took the job as a self-described conservative on civil rights and federal court power. But the influence of Justice Brennan, along with Justice Hugo Black, began a critical transformation of his views. Arnold and Brennan developed a close lifelong friendship as a result of that year, and Arnold became a great admirer of Black, an Alabamian who was one of the most strident advocates for the Bill of Rights in United States Supreme Court history. Both Hugo Black and William Brennan became heroes for the politically conservative Arnold.

Not only was it an important episode in Arnold's life, the 1960 Supreme Court term laid the groundwork for the subsequent revolution in the relationship between state and federal law, accomplished by the Supreme Court under Chief Justice Earl Warren. It would be an impor-

41

tant chapter of the story of civil rights in the United States, even if Arnold had not also been a witness to it.

Arnold kept a diary of his year with Justice Brennan, with the thought that he might publish it one day. He never did, although after all the justices who had served during that term had died, Arnold shared portions of it with academic researchers.[1]

When Arnold began his clerkship, Chief Justice Earl Warren met with all of the new law clerks to impress upon them the need for secrecy. "You will learn things, hear things, know things that you will take to your grave with you," Warren said.[2] That standard has become relaxed over the years, with the publication of books by former law clerks describing their very recent experiences.[3] Even before Arnold began his clerkship, William Rehnquist, a law clerk for Justice Robert Jackson (who went on to become chief justice of the Supreme Court), provided the "first signed statement"[4] by a former law clerk describing the role, in a 1957 article titled "Who Writes Decisions of the Supreme Court?"[5]

A Supreme Court clerkship is the ultimate accolade for any law school graduate, and most go on to distinguished legal careers. At the time, to be chosen as a Felix Frankfurter law clerk was the pinnacle for a Harvard Law school graduate.[6] Frankfurter was a professor at Harvard Law School when he was nominated to the Supreme Court by Franklin Roosevelt in 1939. He had served Roosevelt as an informal adviser on many New Deal matters. Frankfurter retained his ties with the Harvard Law School faculty and surrounded himself with its recent graduates as law clerks.

Frankfurter held the deep esteem of many of the Harvard law faculty and was widely considered the Court's most influential member.[7] Arnold's favorite professor at Harvard, Abram Chayes, had been a Frankfurter law clerk. It would be natural for Richard Arnold, first in his law school class academically, to aspire to the position. But Albert Sacks, the Harvard law professor who selected clerks for Felix Frankfurter, deemed Arnold "too conservative" for Frankfurter.[8] Arnold, although first in his class at Harvard and a winner of several academic prizes, was from the South, and he concluded at the time that Sacks "did not like Southerners," a conclusion others found credible.[9] Otherwise, Arnold was by far the most academically qualified member of the Harvard Law School class. That Arnold was "too conservative" for Frankfurter was an ironic judgment, given that he ended up with the far more liberal Justice William Brennan.

Other members of the 1960 *Harvard Law Review* took up Supreme Court clerkships after graduation or in the year immediately following, including Philip Heymann, Frank Michelman, and John French. Antonin Scalia did not. He was awarded a fellowship from Harvard for the year following graduation, allowing him to travel throughout Europe in 1960–1961. At the conclusion of the fellowship year, Scalia joined the law firm Jones, Day, Cockley and Reavis in Cleveland, Ohio.

The Harvard men had traveled to Washington together during their final student year for interviews with some of the Supreme Court justices. Arnold, writing to his classmate Phil Heymann in 2003, remembered their interview with Justice John Marshall Harlan II. "As we came back into his chambers, he said, 'I've asked Heymann to come in.' You may have known that the rest of us were warned that you were going to be the pick."[10] Arnold was also interviewed by Justice Potter Stewart on that day. "'He needs law clerks,' someone said, 'so you may as well take the time to see him.'"[11] Arnold did not receive an offer from either of those justices, and the students returned to Cambridge.

At Harvard, there was a recognized hierarchy of prestige associated with each justice, and for Arnold there was at least one clerkship he would not accept—the clerkship with Justice Tom Clark. Arnold's wife, Gale, had written to his grandmother, Lucille Sanderson Connally, to say that Arnold needed a Supreme Court clerkship. Arnold's grandmother lived in Washington, DC, and her ties with Washington's political and judicial elite were extensive. She had been a senator's wife for about forty years—first as the wife of Senator Morris Sheppard of Texas, and after his death, the wife of Senator Tom Connally, also of Texas. She was well connected with Supreme Court justices, too.[12] His grandmother knew Felix Frankfurter well. As described by Arnold, "She wrote Justice Frankfurter a letter saying, 'Here's my grandson, why don't you hire him?' Apparently he read the letter on the bench and passed it down the row of justices, and when it came to Tom Clark, being from Texas, he knew my grandmother well. He called her up and said, 'I'll give him a job.' This was very embarrassing to me. I didn't want to get a job that way, and Tom Clark was not well-regarded."[13]

Professor Paul Freund selected law clerks for Justice William Brennan, Dwight Eisenhower's recent nominee to the Court. Freund was one of the leading scholars of constitutional law and a native of St. Louis. Arnold's wife, Gale, a graduate of Washington University in St. Louis, had worked as Freund's secretary. One Brennan clerk for the 1960–1961 year had already been selected: Dan Rezneck, a graduate of the Harvard class of 1959, who spent 1959–1960 as a research assistant for Freund on the Holmes Devise history of the Supreme Court.[14]

After the Harvard men returned from their trip to Washington, Freund called Arnold into his office to offer him a clerkship with Brennan. A short time later, Brennan wrote to Arnold, "I am most happy to follow the suggestion of Professor Freund and invite you to accept a law clerkship with me for the 1960 term. It will give me great pleasure if you will accept."[15] Arnold's prompt reply stated that he was "delighted to receive this morning your letter inviting me to serve as your law clerk for the Court's 1960 Term. I view the appointment as a great honor and promise to do my best to justify your confidence."[16] Arnold did not meet Brennan until he started work.

The two Brennan law clerks chosen for that year—Arnold and Rezneck—developed a close relationship with Brennan. On most days they would drive him to and from his home in Georgetown, often discussing the Court's pending cases.[17] Brennan invited the two to his house for holidays and family events. Arnold worked very hard for Brennan's approval. He would note in his diary, with particular pleasure, whenever an opinion he had drafted for Brennan would receive the justice's approval.[18]

The experience with the Supreme Court would be important to Arnold when he later became a judge himself. Arnold learned about collegiality and decision making on a multimember court. Later in his life, Arnold rebutted the view that Justice Brennan molded the Warren Court through the force of his personality:

> Personality, no doubt, is important. Judges are human beings. They live in bodies and react on a personal level. But judges do not cast votes simply because their backs are slapped in a particularly engaging way. What Justice Brennan did, he did as a lawyer and as a judge, and his mastery of the English language, of the history of the Constitution, and of the technical aspects of the law played at least as big a part in his success at constructing majorities as the warmth of his personality and manner.[19]

When Arnold began his clerkship with Brennan, however, Brennan was only in his fourth year on the Court. (He would serve on the Court for a total of thirty-four years.) Brennan's relatively junior status at the time and the ideological divisions on the Court left him frequently on the dissenting side that year. The 1960 term, which Arnold would witness, was particularly note-worthy for the number of 5–4 decisions, with Brennan often in the minority.

What Arnold learned that year about the operation of the nation's highest court would not all be readily transferable to his later experience on the court of appeals. The Supreme Court is the final word. Although the court of appeals is often functionally final, those judges must follow Supreme Court precedent, as best they can interpret it. They are not free to take positions or adopt views that have not received the sanction of a majority of the Supreme Court. An individual Supreme Court justice, on the other hand, might continue to press dissenting views that have never commanded a majority on the Court. Justice Brennan's later opposition to the death penalty is a good example of this.[20]

Furthermore, the Supreme Court has long exercised discretionary jurisdiction—deciding what particular cases and controversies it will consider. The courts of appeal, by contrast, must decide everything that is presented to them. The politics of determining which cases to take, and which to avoid, was an important feature of the 1960 term. The Supreme Court justices weighed priorities for disposition on a weekly basis. The custom at the time was for the justices to hold a weekly conference on Fridays to discuss the cases argued during that week, assign opinions to be written, and also consider which, if any, of the numerous appeals filed during the week to accept for review. On occasion these conferences would carry over to Saturday morning.

It was a busy term for the justices and their law clerks. Throughout the year the Supreme Court heard 146 cases on oral argument out of nearly two thousand petitions for review presented to the Court.[21] An early entry in Arnold's diary notes: "Tomorrow, conference. How can the court dispose of five or six argued cases, most of them of considerable difficulty, and then go on to deal with all the appeals and petitions for certiorari (at least 30 of which are to be discussed)? Who knows?"[22]

THE SUPREME COURT IN 1960

Each Supreme Court era is popularly denoted by the name of the chief justice who served during that time. When Arnold became a law clerk, Earl Warren—appointed by Dwight Eisenhower—had served as chief justice since 1953. The "Warren Court" became synonymous with the liberal exercise of judicial power in favor of civil liberties and civil rights. *Brown v. Board of Education*, decided in 1954, was only the beginning. When driving Justice Brennan to his home in the evenings, Arnold and Rezneck would pass along the way an occasional "IMPEACH EARL WARREN" billboard.[23]

By the end of the Warren Court in 1969, the near-complete incorporation of the Bill of Rights into the Fourteenth Amendment meant that there was no longer any significant difference between rights applicable in federal courts and rights applicable in state courts.[24] The most liberal period of the Warren court—1962 to 1969—came just after Arnold's clerkship with Brennan and was a due process revolution.[25] In the late 1960s, as public concern with crime and violence was a feature of political debate, Richard Nixon ran for president in 1968 as a critic of the Warren court's rulings in favor of criminal defendants, especially the Court's decision in *Miranda v. Arizona*.[26] Immediately after the *Miranda* decision, Congress enacted a statute ostensibly overruling the case to make "voluntary" statements admissible.[27] Nearly all of these later decisions from the Warren Court are still good law, despite later attempts to staff the Court with nominees willing to undo some or all of this legacy. President Lyndon B. Johnson considered Earl Warren "the greatest Chief Justice of them all."[28]

In addition to Earl Warren, Felix Frankfurter, and William Brennan, the other members of the Supreme Court in 1960 were William O. Douglas, Hugo L. Black, Potter Stewart, Charles Evans Whittaker, Tom C. Clark, and John Marshall Harlan II. "Harlan II" was the grandson of the first John Marshall Harlan, who served on the Supreme Court from 1877 until 1911 and who was the only justice to dissent in *Plessy v. Ferguson*.[29]

Arnold was fascinated with the Supreme Court as an institution that was dependent upon the character of the individuals who comprised it. He especially enjoyed the tradition of each justice inviting the other law clerks to lunch during the year, at the Supreme Court dining room usually populated only by the law clerks and staff. Arnold recorded personal characteristics of each justice, along with anything particularly memorable that the justice had said.

One example is Arnold's diary entry for November 22: "The law clerks had lunch today with Justice Black. He intimated that things would have turned out better had the South been required to proceed much more rapidly, instead of 'with all deliberate speed.' He agreed with this formulation in the second round because unanimity was important."[30]

The seventy-five-year-old Black was also a friend of Arnold's grandmother, and he took a special interest in Arnold. Black told Arnold that he had been closest in the Senate to Arnold's grandfather, Senator Morris Sheppard of Texas, and admired him greatly.[31] After Senator Sheppard's death, Arnold's grandmother married Tom Connally, the other Texas senator. Black told Arnold that Senator Connally was a great supporter of his when he was appointed to the Court, but "he doesn't think so much of some of my later votes." Connally, Black said, was "an unreconstructed Southerner." Arnold's diary notes, parenthetically, "This he thought very funny."[32]

Arnold particularly relished Black's recollections of his family. Arnold's grandmother, according to Black, was "like a ray of sunshine when she entered her room." Black also remembered that "Momma," as Arnold referred to his mother, who died when he was nineteen, was "beautiful." Arnold was clearly in awe of Black. Arnold wrote in his diary: "I found him very kind and gracious—he was pleased I was going back to Texarkana. He was perfectly poised and dignified and very acute and bright—not the slightest hint of age. He is truly a great man."[33]

Arnold's relationship with Felix Frankfurter was of a different order. Arnold's wife, Gale, came to lunch one day, and the two ran into Frankfurter just outside the justice's chambers, which were adjacent to Brennan's. Frankfurter told Gale that Richard had "confirmed his earlier impression (gained from watching me walk!) that I had a quality of 'charming arrogance.' As we were leaving he said to Gale, 'There are lots of other things I could say about him.' When we were out in the hall, he bounded to his door and called after us—'Mrs. Arnold—I meant lots of other good things.' I think that he is an uncommonly acute and spry man. He fairly twinkles with vitality. I never feel an equal in his presence."[34]

When Frankfurter invited the other law clerks for lunch, Arnold was taken with Frankfurter's antics: "Frankfurter shouted, gesticulated, flung his silver onto the table, and accused a law clerk of being slippery. Frankfurter literally shouted his disapproval of Senator Fulbright for not taking a more forthright stand on *Brown*."

John Marshall Harlan II, at sixty-two, was substantially younger than either Frankfurter or Black. Arnold's notes from their law clerk lunch with Justice Harlan describe him as "very grandfatherly and judicious, verging on the stuffy, but not without humor. He disagrees with almost everything of importance his grandfather ever said. He does not believe Negroes are an unduly favored class of litigants. He asserted further that he would not restrict congressional investigations of communism with a probable cause showing requirement—everything would be all right up to dragging just anyone off the street and asking him if he were a communist."[35] Harlan was "the soul of dignity," and "deserved the title of 'august' if anyone ever did," Arnold recalled. It amused Arnold greatly that when Justice Brennan saw Harlan in the halls, he would say delightedly, "Hiya, Johnny." Arnold did not believe that anyone else, including Harlan's mother, ever called the justice "Johnny."[36]

William O. Douglas, nominated to the Supreme Court by Franklin Roosevelt, would serve on the Court for nearly thirty-seven years, making him the longest-serving justice in Supreme Court history. Arnold wrote with some surprise that Douglas "was actually rather nice and friendly. He refused to admit that there was any split on the court between two wings or blocks."[37]

Arnold's impression of Justice Charles Whittaker, who, like Clark, was held in relatively low esteem at Harvard, was also improved by the clerks' lunch. "He made a much more favorable appearance than we had expected. He is a simple but tough-minded man, well aware of his own limitations, genuinely humble. He supports *Brown* but thinks *Shelley v. Kraemer*[38] is wrong. He is very sensitive to criticisms of the court as too liberal, procommunist. He was truly a character to inspire affection."[39]

Lunch with a justice other than one's boss was a rare event, occurring by tradition but once during the term. More frequently, Arnold and Rezneck ate lunch with Brennan, especially on Saturdays. On one occasion Arnold met the two retired justices—Harold Burton and Stanley Reed—who still had offices at the Supreme Court. "The Justice and I had lunch in the Methodist building, and Mr. Justice Burton, who is often there, joined us. He is rapidly declining in physical strength. His left hand shakes, and his mental reactions are slow and dull. When we came back to the Court we saw Mr. Justice Reed on the ground floor—he was a model of courtesy and vigor, showing no signs of age."[40]

CIVIL LIBERTIES IN THE SUPREME COURT, 1960–1961

It was an auspicious time for anyone, let alone a southerner, to be present at the Supreme Court. Only two years before Arnold began his clerkship, the Supreme Court handed down its famous decision in *Cooper v. Aaron*.[41] This case was the only instance in which the Supreme Court accepted an appeal involving desegregation in Little Rock, Arkansas. Members of the Little Rock school board, including the superintendent, had succeeded in securing from a federal district court an order to delay integration of the schools for another two and a half years, citing the turmoil created by Governor Orval Faubus's stand against integration and the arrival, for a time, of the United States Army's 101st Airborne division, sent by President Eisenhower.

The Eighth Circuit Court of Appeals had reversed the district court, but the Supreme Court took the case, in an August Special Term, in order to affirm federal judicial supremacy and the mandate of *Brown v. Board of Education*:

> Since the first *Brown* opinion three new Justices have come to the Court. They are at one with the Justices still on the Court who participated in that basic decision as to its correctness, and that decision is now unanimously reaffirmed. The principles announced in that decision and the obedience of the States to them, according to the command of the Constitution, are indispensable for the protection of the freedoms guaranteed by our fundamental charter for all of us.[42]

Justice Brennan was the primary author of *Cooper v. Aaron*, although the decision was signed by all nine justices.[43] While Arnold was clerking for Justice Brennan, he later noted "the memory of *Cooper v. Aaron* was fresh."[44] And the nation still had, in the scheme of things, a fresh memory of *Brown v. Board of Education*. The "Southern Manifesto"—a statement by southern members of Congress that *Brown v. Board of Education* was illegal and illegitimate as a matter of constitutional law—came in 1956. It had been signed by, among others, Arkansas senator J. William Fulbright and congressman Brooks Hays. It was a view with which Arnold held some sympathy.

But the 1960 term was most notable for the steps it did not take in favor of civil rights. Part of the reason for this had to do with the composition of the Court. In his last years on the court, Frankfurter became an outspoken critic of many of the Court's groundbreaking decisions to end racial segregation. He was also the Court's most outspoken advocate of judicial restraint at the time. Frankfurter left the court in 1962 after suffering a stroke, so the 1960 term—when Arnold saw him—was for all practical purposes Frankfurter's last full year.

The fault lines on the Supreme Court are apparent not only in Arnold's diary but also in academic assessments of the 1960 term. In many close cases, Warren, Black, Douglas, and Brennan found themselves together in dissent. Justices Frankfurter and Douglas were the furthest apart; Chief Justice Warren and Justice Brennan agreed more often than any other two justices.[45] Arnold recognized the link between Warren and Brennan, noting on one occasion: "The Chief was in to see the boss today twice—he seems to look to Justice Brennan quite a bit for advice."[46]

There were also stark ideological differences that year in particular, resulting in both unusual techniques for withholding ultimate constitutional adjudication—deciding not to decide—and what one observer termed "deeds without doctrine"—court actions without a rationale sufficient to provide jurisprudential guidance for the future.[47]

In the 1960 term, the most significant cases politically involved prosecutions of Communist Party members and criminal procedure, but there were only a smattering of civil rights cases involving race that the Supreme Court decided to hear. It was a year of retrenchment on racial matters, but the Court's decisions on the Fourteenth Amendment and how it applied to the states would have a significant impact on Arnold, as well as the nation. The Court struggled to articulate what obligations the states must recognize in order to make meaningful a national system of individual rights. The Supreme Court was in the midst of a federalism revolution that Arnold found astonishing.

MAPP v. OHIO: THE EXCLUSIONARY RULE IN STATE CRIMINAL PROSECUTIONS

The most striking and revolutionary decision of the term was *Mapp v. Ohio*,[48] which held that evidence obtained by an unconstitutional search could not be admitted in state prosecutions. The case was handed down on the last day of the term, and Arnold's diary explains why it took until then for the justices to work out a resolution. Robert McCloskey, reviewing the 1960 Supreme Court term in the *American Political Science Review*, said *Mapp v. Ohio* was a development "so spectacularly libertarian" that it must play a major part in any evaluation of the term's results.[49]

Dollree Mapp, an Ohio woman, had been sentenced to seven years in prison for possessing obscene literature, which she claimed she was merely storing for a former tenant who had left it behind along with other belongings. Police officers had searched her home, without a warrant, based upon the allegations of an unnamed informant who claimed that a person wanted for a recent bombing was hiding there, along with gambling paraphernalia. All the police found after an extensive search of the home were allegedly obscene books and pictures. Those materials—evidence that was admittedly seized illegally—were introduced in court and resulted in Mapp's jail sentence.

Mapp v. Ohio came to the Supreme Court seemingly as a First Amendment case. The lawyers had argued it that way before the Court, and the only suggestion that it might turn on another provision of the US Constitution came in an amicus brief filed by the American Civil Liberties Union. In one paragraph, the ACLU suggested instead that Dollree Mapp's conviction was invalid because it was based on evidence from an illegal search.

Arnold's conversations with Brennan reflect little early emphasis on the illegal search. On a drive home from the Supreme Court, Arnold discussed the case with Brennan: "The Justice not only thinks that [the Ohio obscenity statute] is unconstitutional, but went so far as to say the states cannot constitutionally punish a man for reading, in private but with prurient interests, obscene books. Dan and I disagreed, and the Justice labeled us as 'hopeless reactionaries.'"[50]

Arnold also recorded a strategy session between Earl Warren and Brennan: "The Chief came in today to talk over *Mapp* with the Justice. He, too, thinks it must be reversed. [Brennan] and Dan and I argued the matter at some length again this afternoon. The Justice admits he's in an analytical dilemma, but he is 'damn well going to vote to reverse, anyway.'"[51]

The analytical dilemma was this: Three years earlier, in a case known as *Roth v. United States*,[52] the Supreme Court redefined the constitutional test for obscene material. Brennan had written the majority opinion. The First Amendment, he said, protected "all ideas having even the slightest redeeming social importance—unorthodox ideas, controversial ideas, even ideas hateful to the prevailing climate of opinion."[53] But material that would qualify as "obscene" received no such protection: "We hold that obscenity is not within the area of constitutionally protected speech or press."[54] Obscenity, in turn, was determined by "whether to the average person, applying contemporary community standards, the dominant theme of the material taken as a whole appeals to prurient interest."[55]

The problem, then, was that by all accounts the material in Mapp's house *was* obscene, or at least had been determined to be obscene in a state judicial proceeding. There were only three dissenters in *Roth*, so there would be no way Brennan could find enough votes to reverse Mapp's conviction on the basis of the First Amendment while *Roth* — an opinion he had written — was still good law.[56]

This left the possibility that the Court might view the illegal search and seizure at Mapp's house to require reversal of her conviction. But here, again, the analytical dilemma was great. An "exclusionary rule" had long been applied in federal prosecutions where evidence had been obtained in violation of the Fourth Amendment's prohibition of "unreasonable searches and seizures." Such evidence could not be used against the defendant at trial. But the federal exclusionary rule did not apply to state prosecutions, and half the states at that time — including Ohio — still admitted illegally seized evidence in criminal prosecutions. Eleven years earlier, in a case titled *Wolf v. Colorado*,[57] the Supreme Court concluded that the exclusionary rule did not apply to state court proceedings. In *Wolf*, four justices read the Fourteenth Amendment to incorporate all the protections of the Fourth Amendment in state criminal prosecutions, but Frankfurter's majority opinion would not go that far. State officials, Frankfurter wrote, need not apply the exclusionary rule in state court proceedings.[58] Justice Black went even further. In a concurring opinion in *Wolf*, he said that the failure to exclude evidence obtained by an illegal search did not violate the due process clause of the Fourteenth Amendment.

Later conversations reflect Brennan's difficulty with the case: "The Justice is determined to vote to reverse *Mapp*, but he doesn't quite know how. I argued at length with Dan and him that since the First Amendment is out of the case, that the only way to strike down the Ohio statute is to say that to make knowing possession a crime is to use an impermissible means of implementing the state's permissible anti-obscenity policy. Of course, best of all would be to overrule *Wolf* and reverse this case on the Fourth Amendment, but no one thinks there's a chance of that."[59]

This is precisely what would happen. Writing for a bare majority, Justice Tom Clark held that Fourth Amendment protections, incorporated through the due process clause of the Fourteenth Amendment, did require state courts to follow the exclusionary rule, and overturned *Wolf*. The voting was complicated, with the deciding vote falling to Justice Black, who had voted with the majority in *Wolf*.

Brennan made it a regular practice to discuss with his clerks the results of the Friday conferences. Law clerks were never present for any of these conferences, but Justice Brennan would relate the day's events to his clerks. Stories from the justice's conferences, as recorded in Arnold's diary, are from Brennan's explanations. Not all justices favored their clerks with a blow-by-blow of the conferences. Arnold would sometimes find himself in the position of informing other justice's law clerks what had happened there.[60]

At the Friday conference that week, Arnold wrote that "[t]he Chief Justice, Douglas, Brennan, and Clark, were all in favor to overrule *Wolf* (great effort is to be made to get a fifth somewhere for this proposition, to apply the Fourth Amendment exclusionary rule to states through the 14th amendment)."[61] *Mapp v. Ohio* was not decided at the first conference. Instead, that conference began a series of exchanges between individual justices concerning strategies to resolve the case. The most important development was Black's decision on the Fourth Amendment question. Arnold wrote: "Black in to see the Justice before lunch. He has decided to go along with overruling of *Wolf* in *Mapp*. He had just talked an hour with Clark — is convinced that the Fourth Amendment is an empty guarantee without the exclusionary rule. He told Clark he would join him if his opinion applied the Fourth Amendment to the states, as such, as a specific of the Bill of Rights. Naturally the Justice is overjoyed. We are not to speak of it to anyone else within the court for the time being, however."[62]

Justice Clark had been assigned the majority opinion. His opinion, which he circulated to the other justices, overruled *Wolf*, applied the exclusionary rule to the states, and made that the sole ground of reversal. As Arnold noted, Clark held "that the Fourteenth Amendment absorbs or incorporates the Fourth Amendment as such and in full." This was apparently too much for Felix Frankfurter. When Frankfurter received the *Mapp* circulation, Arnold wrote, "he took one look and shot off down the hall in a great hurry, perhaps to see Clark."[63]

Clark received complaining letters from two justices who would end up among those dissenting in the case, "one from Potter Stewart (as *Wolf* was not discussed at conference, and was raised only by ACLU as amicus), one from Harlan (four pages insisting that the exclusionary rule is not a constitutional requirement even in the federal courts)."[64]

Frankfurter took his defeat in *Mapp* as a personal affront and looked for ways to change the result even after Clark's opinion had gained a majority. According to Arnold (as reported by Brennan, whom Arnold referred to as "the Justice" or "the boss"):

> In conference Frankfurter became violent. He shook, almost cried—it is "a death blow for federalism." He demanded reargument—which was voted down, five to four. Most of the tirade was aimed straight at the boss, who said "I've had things said to me today that haven't been said since I was a child." Frankfurter said he would vote against the proce-dure of the decision—question not fully argued, counsel incompetent, no thorough survey of state law, wrong to go on ground which divides court when it unanimously believes the Ohio statute is unconstitutional. Frankfurter wants special counsel appointed to argue the states' case, with a team of experts to study state law. The Justice said he and Clark were the only calm ones there. Brennan told me, "Finally I got fed up and said as calmly as possible, 'I can't help thinking all this furor is directed only to the result in this case, not to the circumstances of reaching it.'" That made Felix furious.[65]

Brennan told Arnold that he had "never seen Harlan so exercised. He's going to write a bitter dissent on the affront to collegial spirit of the court." Stewart and Whittaker also were troubled about "turning *Mapp* into an unexpected vehicle for overruling *Wolf*, but they will join the court on the merits." Arnold records that Harlan, Frankfurter, Stewart, and Whittaker had met privately before the conference to plan their attack. Brennan said, "I would have been more impressed if I hadn't known it was planned." Frankfurter and Harlan would file dissents after the term ended. Frank-furter said it would take him at least ten months to write his dissent.[66]

Along the way, Brennan worried that Black was "getting cold feet" and might ask for reargument. If he did, Arnold wrote, Clark would "with-draw his whole opinion, and rewrite to hold the Ohio statute unconstitu-tional under the First Amendment."[67] Black thought *Mapp* would be "the most damned case of the term."[68]

Mapp became the subject at yet another conference of the justices—the last collective discussion of *Mapp* before the end of the term. "At conference Frankfurter says *Mapp* is the worst tragedy since *Dred Scott*. Justice Brennan says he means it. A note from the Justice in conference says *Mapp* will not come down [on Monday]. The conference was long—lasted until 2:15 p.m. *Mapp* was the subject of much argument."[69]

Justice Black resolved his dilemma over *Wolf* with an explanation in a concurring opinion. In *Wolf*, Black had characterized the exclusionary rule to be merely "a judicially created rule of evidence," not required by the Fourth Amendment. In *Mapp*, Black wrote, "I am still not persuaded that the Fourth Amendment, standing alone, would be enough to bar the introduction into evidence against an accused of papers and effects seized in violation of its commands." Nevertheless, a "more thorough understanding of the problem" led him to conclude that "the Fifth Amendment's ban against compelled self-incrimination" was the true basis of the exclusionary rule.[70] To accept the Black position would have required the Court to "incorporate" the privilege against self-incrimination within the due process protections of the Fourteenth Amendment.[71] The Supreme Court would not take this step until 1964.[72]

The debate between Frankfurter and Brennan (along with Black) over incorporation was of long standing. Arnold recorded an amusing exchange between Brennan and Frankfurter toward the end of the term: "Last night at 11 p.m., the Justice, who had gone to sleep, got a call from Frankfurter. He said 'Potter? Potter Stewart? Potter?' The Justice said, 'This is Bill.' Felix said, 'Oh, all right, I wanted to talk to you, too.'" Frankfurter brought up an opinion Brennan had circulated in a case involving search warrants for allegedly obscene material. Frankfurter told Brennan that his opinion was "substantially all right," but Frankfurter wanted the case to go on the Fourteenth Amendment alone, with no reference to the First. "'You're throwing absorption in my face,' he said. The Justice said he had no such design, and agreed to alter the opinion."[73]

Arnold would favor the view openly expressed by Black, and preferred by Brennan, that "incorporation" of the individual guarantees of the Bill of Rights in the United States Constitution against state action should be total and should result from the privileges and immunities clause. As he described later, "In a sense, I was to the left of Justice Brennan in terms of incorporation of the Bill of Rights. He didn't go as far as Black. He wanted to incorporate only some provisions. And I never did understand how you would decide which you would incorporate and which you wouldn't. And I don't think that anybody has ever answered that question satisfactorily."[74] As a lower court judge himself later in his life, Arnold was never free to adopt this view because the Supreme Court had foreclosed it.

LEGISLATIVE REDISTRICTING: A PREVIEW OF *BAKER v. CARR*

One of the most surprising racial rights decisions of the term, according to contemporary observers, *Gomillion v. Lightfoot*[75] involved gerrymandered city elections in Tuskegee, Alabama, which excluded from voting all but four or five of its four hundred former Negro residents. The Supreme Court held that the legislature had affirmatively acted to deny the vote on racial grounds, specifically forbidden by the Fifteenth Amendment.[76]

Gomillion thus stood for the proposition that electoral apportionment is subject to challenge on the ground of racial discrimination. In the same term the Supreme Court had agreed to hear *Baker v. Carr*,[77] a more general challenge to apportionment schemes that left some populations within a state proportionately less represented.

Arnold closely observed the oral argument, noting in particular the methods used by Robert L. Carter, a New York NAACP lawyer, who argued for the petitioners. "He unfolded a great chart showing how the Alabama Legislature has changed the city's borders, and placed on a high stand directly in front of the bench, with the lectern for arguing counsel in between. He proceeded to illustrate with a pointer how the new boundaries carefully excluded as many Negroes as possible."[78]

The solicitor general of the United States, J. Lee Rankin, also argued the case on behalf of the petitioners and against the state of Alabama. Arnold observed, "The Negroes in the audience were visibly affected during the Solicitor General's ringing plea for equality—they were moved and deeply pleased. The Chief is definitely going for reversal. The boss is still in doubt."[79]

The opinion was assigned to Felix Frankfurter. At Warren's urging, the Court had previously presented a unanimous front on racial cases, most notably in *Brown v. Board of Education* and *Cooper v. Aaron*. But one justice was convinced the Tuskegee case should turn on the equal protection clause. "Charles Whittaker has circulated a short concurrence in *Tuskegee*," Arnold wrote, "in spite of the various Justices' efforts to persuade him not to last night at the Chief's black-tie dinner. The Justice said all the wives were disgusted at the conversations all being taken up with this subject."[80]

Whittaker would not be dissuaded, and his concurrence set out the path the Court would take in *Baker v. Carr*, a case that was argued, but not decided, that year. The following year, after Arnold had entered private law practice, *Baker v. Carr* would be one of Justice Brennan's most important opinions.[81] It would also be Frankfurter's last opinion of any sort—a dissent. Earl Warren called *Baker v. Carr* "the most vital decision" during his service on the Court.[82]

Baker v. Carr would be politically more explosive than the Tuskegee case because it permitted federal courts to examine state apportionment on general equality principles ("one man, one vote"), not solely for overt racial manipulation of elections.

Brennan assigned *Baker v. Carr* to Arnold to prepare a "bench memo," a summary of the facts, precedents, and legal arguments in the case along with Arnold's recommendation for resolution. The case was originally argued that spring. Solicitor General Archibald Cox argued on behalf of the United States, who had intervened as amicus curiae, or "friend of the court." "The Justice liked Archibald Cox's argument in *Baker v. Carr*, but thought some of his subtle distinctions were 'too professorial.' When Cox began elaborating them, Potter Stewart leaned over to the Justice and said, 'God damn it, there he goes again.'"[83]

Felix Frankfurter and Potter Stewart were primarily responsible for the decision to reargue the case in the following year. According to Arnold,

Frankfurter filibustered for 90 minutes before lunch, and it was all directed at Whittaker, who had been openly for appellants at the argument, more than any other Justice, and who had spoken brave words about the plain duty of courts to enforce the Constitution. Frankfurter conducted a parade of horribles, playing on Whittaker's fears. "He scared the hell out of him," the Justice said. "It worked. He certainly knows his man." Whittaker became very nervous, his lip trembled. Frankfurter started out by citing the morning's papers, which recount the U.S.'s horrible blunder in Cuba, caused by lack of foresight. Frankfurter said "Let's not make the same mistake here. Do you realize the terrible difficulties you would place the court in? Look ahead, not just in front of your noses. Look before you act!" He then launched into a very detailed, erudite, and effective lecture on the political question cases. His voice was grave, his arms wildly gesticulating. Harlan and Clark went solidly with Frankfurter. The Chief Justice, Black, Douglas, and the boss were firm to reverse. That left the case up to Whittaker and Potter Stewart.[84]

At the following week's conference, the justices decided *Baker v. Carr* would be reargued, at the request of Potter Stewart. Arnold wrote that Stewart "needs the summer to make up his mind. Whittaker says he's relieved—had grave doubts about his vote to affirm."[85]

In between the two conferences, Frankfurter had worked on Whittaker in particular. Arnold wrote: "Black called the Justice today—he said that Whittaker had called him over the weekend, was very troubled over the position he had taken on *Baker v. Carr* at the conference of April 21, wanted to come see Black. He did so, they had a long colloquy. Whittaker left saying he was solid to reverse. Later in the week Frankfurter had a private meeting of Clark, Harlan, Potter Stewart, and Whittaker, and beat Whittaker down again."[86]

Arnold's report of the machinations in *Baker v. Carr* ended there. When the case was reargued the following fall, Arnold was no longer a law clerk for Justice Brennan. But he followed the case closely. A few years later, when Arnold was running for Congress in Arkansas, he criticized the Supreme Court in *Baker v. Carr* for going "too far."[87]

FIRST AMENDMENT/COMMUNIST ASSOCIATION CASES

In the 1960 term the Supreme Court heard a number of cases related to Communist Party activities—real or imaginary—and the efforts of Congress and the states to stamp out "subversion." In the cases involving the "communist menace," as McCloskey summarized, "[t]he Court, with minor exceptions, held against the individual and in favor of governmental power."[88] Many of the decisions were 5–4, with Brennan often notably in dissent.

In 1960, the McCarthy-era waves of anticommunist prosecutions may have begun to wane, but communism itself was still in the public eye. And the justices would be branded "communists" by some on the basis of some of their rulings. Brennan, for example, received a letter from a high school student in California. According to Arnold, the student's teacher "had said there are many communists high in the government, including Justice Brennan. The boy said he knew some of the Justice's opinions had given the 'edge' to communists, but that he thought the Justice had only been upholding the Constitution. He wants the Justice to send him proof of loyalty so he can convince his teacher. I suggested the Justice tell him he is a Roman Catholic in good standing, but the Justice laughed and said some people might think that was a misrepresentation."[89]

Brennan also reported that "Justice Black teases Charlie Whittaker unmercifully about being listed on one of the lunatic fringe anti-court pamphlets as voting 35% procommunist. 'You can't be half pregnant, Charlie,' he says." Arnold continued, "Whittaker is very upset by this ribbing, even though the tabulation shows him least procommunist of all the Justices. Black is 100%, Douglas 95%, the Chief Justice 92%, the boss 90%, Frankfurter 77%."[90]

One case, although not directly involving Communist Party membership, was a victory for Brennan and Black. An Arkansas case involved the standard by which state statutes might infringe civil liberties—in this case the freedom of association for teachers. In *Shelton v. Tucker*,[91] the Supreme Court struck down an Arkansas statute requiring teachers in the public schools to disclose the names of all organizations to which they had belonged or contributed during the past five years. In the past, laws asking about organizational ties were designed to identify communist sympathizers, but the Arkansas statute seemed specifically intent upon identifying members of the NAACP. The majority opinion, written by Justice Stewart, held that the statute violated the freedom of association protected by the due process clause of the Fourteenth Amendment. It was a close decision, 5–4, with Justice Brennan voting with the majority.

An important element of the majority's decision was the test of constitutionality it used: "Even though the governmental purpose be legitimate and substantial, that purpose cannot be pursued by means that broadly stifle fundamental personal liberties when the end can be more narrowly achieved."[92] The Arkansas statute forced teachers to reveal their ties with any organization, including religious ones that could have no bearing on their professional competence.[93] The Court thus moved closer to what it would later term "strict scrutiny" in reviewing state legislation that is alleged to violate civil rights, requiring less restrictive means that were readily available to accomplish legitimate ends.

UPHAUS v. WYMAN

Willard Uphaus, the head of a pacifist, left-wing organization called World Fellowship, Inc., had refused to produce a list of members when asked for it by New Hampshire's attorney general, Louis C. Wyman. Uphaus was ordered to hand over the list or go to jail. Uphaus chose jail.

Uphaus brought his appeal to the Supreme Court in 1959, the year before Arnold came to the Court. Uphaus lost, but only barely. Five justices turned Uphaus down. Four dissented—Brennan, Warren, Black, and Douglas, who were termed by *Time* magazine as "the court's staunchly civil righteous minority."[94] Brennan wrote the dissenting opinion, terming the New Hampshire investigation of Uphaus to be "exposure purely for the sake of exposure."

The *Uphaus* case returned to the Supreme Court in the fall of 1960. But Brennan believed his hands were tied by the Court's earlier ruling in his case. In a per curiam opinion of one paragraph, the Court's decision simply notes that Uphaus's appeal "is dismissed for want of jurisdiction, in that the judgment sought to be reviewed is based on a non-federal ground."[95]

In an unusual step, Brennan wrote separately—a very short opinion deploring the result but agreeing that the Court did not have federal-question jurisdiction. "In consequence," he wrote, "while I remain of the view that the Court in *Uphaus v. Wyman* incorrectly sustained the previous order of civil contempt made against Dr. Uphaus, that holding, while it stands, also sustains the order challenged on this appeal. Solely under compulsion of that decision, I think that the appeal must be dismissed as not presenting a substantial federal question."[96]

In contrast to Brennan's short concurrence, Justices Douglas and Black filed lengthy and strident dissents, with Chief Justice Warren also joining Black's dissent. Brennan, then, had become the deciding vote not to take the appeal. (Under Supreme Court practice, only four votes are needed to grant review of a case.)

From Arnold's diary entries, it is clear that Brennan agonized over the case. It is also apparent that Arnold sympathized with Dr. Uphaus:

Monday, October 17: *Uphaus v. Wyman*. This is the second appeal. The boss was the deciding vote in August to deny bail. My memo could get Uphaus out of jail—the boss needs only a little push to switch his vote.

But in all conscience, although I deplore Dr. Uphaus's imprisonment, I cannot see my way clear to recommending a note of probable jurisdiction.

Wednesday, October 19: The boss is definitely wavering on *Uphaus* — although he has as yet produced no argument to which I have not had a sound and logical response. The main factor weighing him towards a dismissal is that the judgment will be affirmed again, and Dr. Uphaus sent back to jail for the remaining eight weeks of his sentence.[97]

While Arnold may have sympathized with Uphaus, he was not impressed with Justice Black's dissent in the case when it was circulated to the Court the next month. He wrote: "Hugo Black's dissent in *Uphaus* is a largely irrelevant diatribe likening Dr. Uphaus to John Bunyan and Walter Udall, two famous intellectual martyrs. Douglas's dissent accuses the court of having one law for Negroes in *Bates*,[98] but another less favorable law for subversives. Hugo Black was still hoping the boss would change his mind."[99]

Brennan continued to worry about the case. The Court's decision had been released on November 14. On December 9, Arnold records:

The Justice found out last night that Attorney General Wyman of New Hampshire has filed a motion with the New Hampshire Superior Court to keep Dr. Uphaus in jail until he talks. He became very upset, and slept hardly at all. This morning he was in a very bad mood and quite glum. We discussed ways of recalling his vote to dismiss the appeal, but they all seemed impractical because (we think) they would take five votes. But the Justice thinks that if this case comes up again, Justice Harlan will make the fifth to let Uphaus out. The Justice is convinced that this new move is a significant new fact going to Wyman's vindictive and punitive intent.[100]

Then a few days later, Arnold noted: "The Justice was pleased to see in the papers today and yesterday that Dr. Uphaus is being let out today — 3 days early, in fact. He is much relieved and now feels his vote to dismiss is vindicated. He said that he hopes he never sees the case again."[101]

SIT-IN DEMONSTRATIONS: THE PROBLEM OF STATE ACTION

After *Brown*, for the next several years the Court "moved steadily but not hastily forward against other forms of race discrimination."[102]

Brown had made clear that racial segregation in public schools violated the federal constitution. But what about segregation in other areas of public accommodation? Restaurants, hotels, movie theaters, and public restrooms were still segregated throughout the South, including the nation's capital, Washington, DC. To the extent segregation was required by state law, or occurred in state-run facilities, the logic of *Brown* seemed to dictate that those forms of segregation, too, would ultimately be prohibited by the Constitution. But discrimination by individual business owners—not required by state law or involving government officials—had been outside the Supreme Court's purview since the *Civil Rights Cases* in 1883 determined that the Fourteenth Amendment did not empower Congress to prohibit private discrimination but only discriminatory "state action."[103]

A significant form of social protest known as "sit-ins" occurred in the early 1960s. Led by black college students, individuals and small groups protested the refusal of service at segregated diners by "sitting-in" for lengthy periods. An estimated seventy thousand students participated, with a significant number arrested on a variety of charges including breach of the peace and trespass.[104]

The first sit-in cases to reach the Supreme Court occurred during the 1960 term. The case of *Boynton v. Virginia*[105] involved a black law student who refused to leave a bus terminal restaurant. He was arrested and charged with trespass. The Interstate Commerce Act at the time prohibited "unjust discrimination" in facilities "operated or controlled by a motor carrier." The restaurant in the bus terminal, however, was owned and leased by a local Virginia business. The Supreme Court, then, faced the question of whether private ownership of the restaurant precluded application of the statute.

Brennan assigned the case to Rezneck, but as was Brennan's custom, Arnold shared in conversations about it:

> Driving home, the boss and I went carefully over each aspect of the case. He was most afraid of a holding that the interstate commerce clause could apply to individuals—he thought the Court ought not to hold that no one in interstate commerce could distinguish racially, and he agreed when I

suggested that reversal of *Boynton* under the Commerce Clause might establish that principle. He wished that cert. had never been granted (he and Black, Douglas, and the Chief made the four to grant). He seemed reluctant to apply the 14th amendment to avoid any trespass conviction in this situation. When I pointed out that many more cases would come up raising the point, he agreed and added that he supposed that the "sit-down people" were looking to the court for legal guidance in this case.[106]

In preparation for the Friday conference, where all of the justices would discuss *Boynton*, Brennan continued to debate with his law clerks how the case might be resolved, short of what Arnold feared would be a sweeping extension of the "state action" doctrine:

> The boss said that he had decided that if the issue should be forced, he would vote to reverse under the 14th amendment on the ground that under the narrow facts of this case the state police affirmatively instigated the racial discrimination. Dan pointed out that the police appeared only when called by the owner, and that they simply informed Boynton that under the law he would have to be arrested if he did not leave. The boss was unmoved. Talk about neutral principles! My boss is grasping at straws to aid the Negro social revolution. Apparently he doesn't care how much he has to twist the facts to do it. I have never seen so much conscious, labored straining to reach a preconceived result.[107]

Arnold's view of the case was not ambivalent, as reflected in his record of that Friday's conference:

> The Chief Justice would "go along with any theory to reverse." Brennan, Warren, Douglas, and Harlan, took the position that under Virginia law the petitioner adequately injected the Interstate Commerce Act into the case, and the state failed to prove its inapplicability beyond a reasonable doubt, the theory Brennan had said that morning he would try to "sell" at the conference. But never once during all the discussion of the case did any Justice mention the Constitution! They are even afraid of it in secret![108]

Justice Black was assigned the opinion for the Court. The majority held that the Interstate Commerce Act barred a trespass action against Boynton. The restaurant was subject to the act because the bus company had volunteered to provide terminal facilities, and "the terminal and restaurant have acquiesced in and cooperated in this undertaking." As Arnold predicted, the resolution of the case avoided the constitutional question, and thus limited the significance of the decision for sit-ins in other contexts.

Justices Whittaker and Clark dissented. Arnold heard from another clerk that "the Chief had gone to see Charles Whittaker to try to pressure him into withdrawing his *Boynton* dissent—the Chief is most desirous that the court should present a unanimous face against the South in all race cases."[109] Warren was unsuccessful in this case.

The next spring, another sit-in case arrived, *Steele v. City of Tallahassee*.[110] Brennan was not eager to take it on: "The Justice said, ruefully, 'we'll have to decide this thing sooner or later.'"[111] But the Supreme Court chose not to, in this particular case. As Arnold recorded:

> Sit-in case, first one to reach the court. All nine said deny because the case didn't go to highest court of state in which a decision could be had. Then the Chief said, let's note that we're denying only on the jurisdictional point. Black, the first to comment, shocked everyone by saying, "Chief Justice, I should make it clear right now that I do not believe a general trespass statute, or general common law doctrine of hue and cry, is unconstitutional state action when applied to enforce a merchant's free choice of customers."[112]

The case had been closely watched in the national media. The Court's order stated simply: "Petition for writ of certiorari to the Circuit Court of Leon County of Florida. Denied."[113] Arnold reported that "Tony Lewis of the *Times* almost went wild today trying to find out why *Steele* was denied. He went to the improper extreme of actually asking Dan why—of course he got nowhere with him."[114]

In subsequent years the Supreme Court would take a large number of sit-in cases and side with the demonstrators in all but a few. The main issue in these cases was whether there had been sufficient "state action" to convert discrimination by individuals to the kind of state-sponsored discrimination prohibited by the Fourteenth Amendment.[115]

The problem was ultimately addressed by Congress in the 1964 Civil Rights Act. This act made private discrimination in places of public accommodation, such as restaurants, illegal. The Civil Rights Act resolved what the Supreme Court was struggling with. Congress relied on the federal constitution's commerce clause, rather than the Thirteenth or Fourteenth Amendment, to accomplish what the Supreme Court had felt itself unable to do.

In the 1960 term, however, these developments were in the future. In the meantime, Arnold observed the careful and cautious approach of the justices to matters of race. He recorded, for instance, an anecdote from Brennan about efforts to avoid unnecessary confrontation with segregationists:

> The Justice told me last Saturday that no Supreme Court opinion on schools has ever used the word "integration"—only "desegregation." In the two Brown cases this was pure chance. But not so in *Aaron v. Cooper*. While the Justice was sitting on his porch one day writing the opinion in that case, his next-door neighbor, an NBC-TV news man, came over and told him that at a meeting of the full NBC news staff it had been decided not to use the word "integration" over the air because (it was thought) in the South that word connoted racial intermarriage. So the next day at conference, at the Justice's suggestion, it was decided not to use the word in the opinion.[116]

The agreement not to use the word "integration" did not survive the term. Arnold described a visit from Black to Brennan's office in late February. The purpose was to discuss two cases involving contempt prosecutions by the House Un-American Activities Committee. Black was "most anxious to get the Justice to join his dissents in *Braden*[117] and *Wilkinson*,[118] but the Justice wouldn't budge, although he again asked Dan and me what we thought."[119] Brennan also dissented in those cases, in which the majority narrowly affirmed the convictions, but he would not join Black's dissents, which were far more strident on the First Amendment. Black believed Carl Braden's harassment by HUAC had to do not with alleged communist sympathies but because he had promoted "racial integration" in the South. Arnold later reported: "Black's *Braden* uses the word 'integration.' The justice said he forgot to remind Hugo Black of the court's practice of not using that word."[120]

OUT OF COURT: THE KENNEDY ERA

Although Arnold's diary primarily records the Court's work, Arnold also was interested in proceedings of the other branches of government, and in particular, the succession from President Dwight D. Eisenhower to John F. Kennedy, which occurred in the middle of his clerkship year.

In one entry, for example, Arnold described a gathering of the justices at the White House at the invitation of Dwight Eisenhower, noting it would likely be their last visit to Eisenhower as president:

> The court visited the president this afternoon for the last time in his private quarters at the White House. He was most cordial and gracious, in high spirits indeed. The solicitor General and Attorney General were also there. The food and drink were in lavish abundance, with a number of liveried servants standing about. No one stinted himself regarding highballs, least of all the President (who right after the party went to Walter Reed for a checkup). The president said he had disliked Kennedy greatly before the election, but now, having met and talked with him, was much impressed with his ability and acumen. The whole affair was apparently most impressive to the boss.[121]

Arnold continued, "At the end of the party the president said his farewell to each member of the court, and remarked that he hoped to see them all again. The Justice drove home Frankfurter, Harlan, and Potter Stewart to their Georgetown residences—in that order, the order of seniority!"[122] The justices all lived near each other, and Frankfurter lived right across the street from Brennan.

On John F. Kennedy's inauguration day, the Court met briefly at eleven o'clock for admissions to the bar, and then attended the swearing-in at the Capitol. It was a bitterly cold day. Arnold had a cold and stayed at the Court during the ceremony, watching the event on a television in Whittaker's chambers. "But before hand I went down to the basement to see the Justice off," he wrote. "Each Justice had a chauffeured limousine, and motorcycle policemen led the cavalcade. It was quite a sight—all the judges decked out in morning clothes and high silk hats."[123] The poet Robert Frost provided an enduring image of that day. The following morning, a *Washington Post* headline read "Old Poet Steals Heart of America."

Conversations between Brennan and his clerks were not limited to the Supreme Court's business. Arnold also recorded the successful launch of America's first space astronaut, Alan Shepard, on May 5, 1961. The justices were in conference that morning. "I sent in a note to the Justice about the successful astronaut launching, which we saw on TV in Douglas's office. He said it was the first word the Court had had of the shot—it was the only bright spot of the day."[124]

The Kennedy presidency would bring with it new government officials of great importance to the Court, including a new solicitor general— Archibald Cox—and a new attorney general—Robert Kennedy. Arnold learned to appreciate the role of the executive branch in the Court's work. Brennan understood the Supreme Court could not enforce its own decisions. Discussing Kennedy's possible choices for attorney general, Arnold recorded: "Brennan thinks any attorney general, under existing law, would have to be vigorous in guarding civil rights and enforcing integration, and would become very unpopular in the South."[125]

The year from 1960 to 1961 was a momentous one for the nation as well as the Court. By the end of the term, Brennan's weariness would be apparent to his clerks. It was marked in one respect with Brennan's openness with his clerks about his fears for the Court: "The other day in the car going home the Justice said sadly the court is deteriorating to the point where Justices, especially Black, Frankfurter, and Harlan, are more concerned with maintaining the integrity of their own constitutional positions than with getting a decision in particular cases."[126]

THE 1960 TERM AND ITS INFLUENCE ON A FUTURE JUDGE

Although the Supreme Court's strides in favor of civil liberties that year were small in comparison with the earlier great leap forward in *Brown v. Board of Education*, 1960 to 1961 was still a remarkable year. As Robert McCloskey summarized at the time, "the signs of forward movement in the field of criminal procedure and Negro rights seem unmistakable."[127] The *Mapp* decision, in particular, "stands out like a beacon, perhaps even portending a general erosion of the scruples about federalism that have heretofore retarded movement of this kind."[128]

As was apparent to Arnold, the composition of the Court was an important factor that year. The most liberal of the Warren Court's decisions on criminal procedure and racial equality were in the future, after Felix Frankfurter was no longer a member of the Court.

Arnold's diary indicates that William Brennan, along with Warren, Black, and Douglas, was at times result-oriented in the direction he wanted to go to resolve a case. Brennan, for example, felt strongly in cases such as *Uphaus*, *Ferguson*, and *Mapp* that the individual had been treated wrongly by state government officials. The difficult question was to justify the exercise of federal judicial power, both as a matter of securing a majority on the Court and in terms of conformity with existing precedent and doctrine.

One question is whether Richard Arnold's later decision-making process as a federal judge would reflect Brennan's approach. From the diary, it is clear that cases on civil liberties became real to Arnold for the first time. Arnold's basic instinct in his years on the bench was sensitivity to unfair treatment of individuals by government. Arnold's contribution would be to add intellectual firepower to such "liberal" decisions. Arnold would be known for erudite, convincing, and largely unassailable written explanations of the exercise of federal judicial power in these contexts.

There is evidence of other transformations during that year. At the beginning of the year, Arnold would sometimes note skepticism about Brennan's judicial approach. By the end of the year, the skepticism is less pronounced, and Arnold as an observer of the Court evinces a genuine admiration and affection for the work of his "boss." In part, Arnold gained a better appreciation for the nature of the judicial task. But it also reflected their personal friendship. Brennan and Arnold began a lifelong correspondence, including Arnold's first letter to Brennan after completing his clerkship. Arnold wrote to offer congratulations on the fifth anniversary of Brennan's accession to the bench: "My only wish for the next five years is that you will be more often on the winning side."[129] The two remained close friends until Brennan's death in 1997, at the age of ninety-one.

In a tribute to Justice Brennan at his retirement from the Supreme Court, Arnold wrote: "To watch Justice Brennan, to be in his presence almost every day, and to work under his direction—all of these were priceless opportunities. Hardly a day goes by when I do not think of something he said or did. 'He hath a daily beauty in his life.'"[130]

Arnold also developed an immense respect for Hugo Black. Black had been a member of the United States Senate from Alabama and he was a politician, as Arnold hoped to be. Black believed that the First Amendment enjoyed a "preferred" position in the constitutional hierarchy, a position with which Felix Frankfurter, in particular, disagreed. Arnold was converted to Black's view, and he became a champion of the First Amendment. His later judicial opinions in First Amendment cases establish this reputation, and he would be widely recognized for this.

Arnold admired Black's ability to anchor his decisions in the text of the

Bill of Rights: "Justice Black," Arnold wrote, "is a great one for insisting that the Constitution itself compels his positions."[131] Dan Rezneck, Brennan's other law clerk that year, agreed that Justice Black became a model for Arnold:

> When we were law clerks, in addition to having vast affection for Justice Brennan, we both became great admirers of Justice Hugo L. Black. For us he was the exemplar of a judge dedicated to rigorous legal analysis, mindful of practice concerns and considerations, and yet ever faithful to first principles. I think that model of a judge has remained with Richard ever since. He also shares Justice Black's commitment to civil liberties and the Bill of Rights, while at the same time he has the ability to look at all sides of an argument with discernment and sophistication.[132]

Writing to Hugo Black's biographer, Roger Newman, in 1994, Arnold said: "No one is more worthy of honor than Justice Black. As a Southerner and a constitutionalist, I have a special affinity and admiration for him."[133] Justice Black was someone Arnold "admired immensely, then and now."[134] When Arnold became a judge himself, he kept an autographed picture of Black hung on a wall in his court chambers in Little Rock, next to photographs of William Brennan and Felix Frankfurter. As a judge, Arnold often drafted judicial opinions at a conference table with these justices looking down on him.

There were other ways in which the clerkship year influenced Arnold's actions as a judge. From the legacy of *Cooper v. Aaron*, Arnold learned about the value of unanimity, especially for the Supreme Court in that era facing resistance to its rulings in some parts of the South. He also learned how to operate without unanimity when he believed a principle required it.

Arnold also learned to deal with a high volume of cases, a skill that would become particularly important for federal judges in the closing decades of the twentieth century. He observed how Brennan coped with the relentless parade of controversies to be decided: "The Justice was so tired today when he came out of conference that we went home immediately without discussing the results first, as is our custom. On the way he said he'd die if Mrs. Brennan had invited someone over for the evening. He wants to see 'whatever garbage' there is at the Georgetown [movie theater], 'anything for a soporific.'"[135] In his later years, Arnold learned to appreciate what Brennan and the other justices faced: "Justice Brennan would come back from a conference with his notebook and sit down with us and go over the cases they had discussed, and tell us what the court was going to do. Except on days when he was too tired, and on those days, he'd just give us the notebook. I never did understand why it would make somebody so tired to sit in a room and talk about the law for a couple of hours, until I did it myself with a bunch of other judges. And now I understand it."[136]

The year before Arnold died, he wrote a letter to Phil Heymann, one of Justice Harlan's law clerks that year: "Your remark that when we were in law school there were supposed to be right answers is striking. I still believe that, though the belief makes me a dinosaur. Certainly the Supreme Court doesn't act that way. Maybe they never did."[137]

Chapter Three

Law Practice

As Richard Arnold's clerkship with Justice William Brennan ended, it was clear that a close bond had formed. In later years, Arnold visited Brennan frequently in Washington, DC, and the two maintained a detailed, regular correspondence for the remainder of their lives. Arnold revered Justice Brennan as a father figure and frequently sought his advice.

In 1961 Arnold moved from the rarefied world of a Supreme Court clerkship to private law practice. For the next fourteen years Arnold would represent clients in an astonishing variety of matters. He advised large and small corporations in day-to-day operations and business disputes. In litigation, he represented insurance and electric utility companies, political parties and taxpayers, and criminal defendants, including a death penalty case. He became one of the nation's first environmental lawyers, representing the Environmental Defense Fund in important litigation in Arkansas, Mississippi, and Washington, DC.

Arnold's law practice provided a varied, vital experience for a future judge. He gained firsthand experience of the day-to-day practice of law and the limitations under which lawyers often work. Elihu Root once observed, "About half the practice of a decent lawyer consists in telling

71

would-be clients that they are damned fools and should stop."[1] Arnold was not only a trial lawyer but also a counselor and adviser to his clients.

AN ELITE LAW FIRM EXPERIENCE AT COVINGTON & BURLING

For three years after his clerkship, Arnold remained in Washington, DC, joining the establishment law firm Covington & Burling. With about one hundred lawyers, a premier client list, and a location only a few blocks from the White House, Covington & Burling had become a destination law firm for Harvard graduates as well as former Supreme Court clerks. Firms like Covington valued attorneys who had served as Supreme Court clerks for their insider knowledge of the Court's procedure and personalities, along with their perceived influence in cases the firm might have there.

One of the firm's most prominent partners at the time was Dean Acheson, who had returned to the firm in 1953 after serving as Harry Truman's secretary of state. Acheson was also a former law clerk for Louis Brandeis, the first Jewish Supreme Court justice. Like other leading law firms at that time, Covington & Burling had no female or African American partners. Characteristic with his times, Arnold's educational and career path had thus far associated him almost exclusively with a white male elite.

Arnold's associates at Phillips Exeter Academy, Yale College, and Harvard Law School were all aware that his goal was to become a United States senator representing Arkansas. There was also the tradition of the family law firm in Texarkana, Arnold & Arnold. Why, then, did he not move to Arkansas right away, after completing his clerkship, instead of spending the next three years in Washington? It is clear that Arnold did not expect to stay with Covington through partnership and that he would ultimately return to Arkansas to his family's law practice. His goal at this point seems to have been to gain practice experience in Washington, especially since Covington & Burling was well connected politically and had a significant regulatory practice before the many federal agencies in Washington, DC. For Harvard Law graduates, Covington & Burling was a prestigious destination, and Arnold wanted to learn the Washington business. For someone with a desire to enter national politics, it was important to understand how the federal regulatory agencies functioned in the political structure, and there was no better place for that.

Arnold had been a summer clerk at Covington & Burling in 1959, after his second year of law school. He planned to apply for a Supreme Court clerkship in his third year of law school, but if he did not land one it seems likely he intended to practice law at Covington for a few years anyway, immediately after graduation. The decision to work in Washington, DC, may also have reflected his wife's preference.[2]

While at Covington during the summer of 1959, Arnold developed an interest in antitrust law, one of the staples of the firm's practice. Antitrust as a practice area was primarily federal, in the sense that businesses were regulated by federal statutes and litigation over monopolies took place in federal court.[3]

When Arnold returned to Covington following his clerkship, he worked primarily for Gerhard Gesell, a noted antitrust lawyer and chairman of the Commission on Equal Opportunity in the Armed Forces under Presidents Kennedy and Johnson. Gesell would be appointed to the federal court in 1967 by President Johnson. As a federal district court judge in the District of Columbia, Gesell would go on to preside over landmark cases, including the Pentagon Papers and Watergate prosecutions. He also struck down the district's abortion ban in 1969.[4] Although the US Supreme Court ultimately reversed Gesell's decision, the case would be an important precursor to *Roe v. Wade*.

Arnold worked directly with Gesell on a variety of matters, including representation of General Electric Company in antitrust cases in which the company was accused of price-fixing conspiracies.[5] He also worked for Southern Railway Company in railroad rates matters and the Washington Post Company for libel and antitrust cases.

Arnold would later say that Gesell "taught me how to practice law and gave me an example of a lawyer, a citizen, and a gentlemen," which he strove to follow.[6] Arnold was especially influenced by Gesell's "devotion to the public interest and his willingness to spend his valuable time on pro bono matters." With Gesell, Arnold represented District of Columbia prisoners in matters referred by the American Civil Liberties Union, which Arnold joined at that time. Among other matters, Gesell and Arnold established through litigation that prisoners subjected to disciplinary procedures were entitled to due process of law.[7] With Gesell's oversight, Arnold also helped screen cases for the National Capital Area Civil Liberties Union.

Gesell, in turn, later endorsed Arnold's nomination for his first federal court appointment in 1978, after Gesell had himself served as a federal judge for a dozen years. Gesell remembered Arnold as being very well regarded among his co-workers at the law firm and being an individual who was a highly qualified attorney and wrote extremely well. Arnold, said Gesell, had an almost photographic memory and was highly intelligent.[8]

When he joined Covington in 1961, Arnold shared an office with David Falk, a fellow Harvard Law School and Phillips Exeter Academy classmate. Falk remembered Gesell's reliance on Arnold for the analysis and strategy for many of his cases. And Gesell was one of the "major liberals" at Covington, which undoubtedly influenced Arnold generally, and certainly did in his choice of pro bono work. Falk himself found Arnold to be a congenial, and helpful, office mate: "When you're at a firm like that, you have to go into every little corner of legal research, and follow every avenue. I saved a lot of time on those little corners by asking Arnold, who had encyclopedic knowledge, and at least, at a minimum, would tell me where to go. And he'd more frequently tell me the answer—'Oh, don't worry about that, that really isn't relevant to your problem,' or something like that. So that was very useful for me."[9] Decades later, the story circulated that some of Richard Arnold's original memos, written in the early 1960s, were still in use at Covington & Burling.

Arnold's domestic situation seemed happy. Richard and his first wife, Gale Hussman Arnold, lived in a row house in Georgetown, where they entertained colleagues with elaborate dinner parties.[10] Their first daughter, Janet Sheppard Arnold, was born on July 4, 1963, while Richard was an associate at Covington. Richard and Gale had been married for five years at their daughter's birth.

But it was a turbulent time to be in Washington, DC. Arnold's years in Washington after he graduated from Harvard coincided with John F. Kennedy's presidency and the first year of the Johnson administration. During the Berlin crisis in 1961, Arnold was called to be examined for the military draft. He was rejected on health reasons, apparently for asthma. Arnold was classified 1Y: Qualified for service only in time of war or national emergency.[11]

While Arnold was at Covington, Washington, DC, would be rocked along with the nation when President Kennedy was assassinated in Dallas on November 22, 1963. Arnold's office mate, David Falk, was engaged in the firm's regulatory representations. Falk recalled being on a conference call with a client—the manufacturer of the drug Sominex—in partner

Tommy Austern's office at Covington: "The client said, 'Tommy, do you realize the President's been shot today?' And we didn't know that. And so Tommy hung up the phone and turned to me and he said, 'Well, now you have something to tell your grandchildren. When the President was shot, you were worrying about Sominex.'"[12] Arnold was in the firm's library researching antitrust cases as word spread. Work stopped at Covington, and across the nation, to watch television news coverage.

RETURN TO ARKANSAS: ARNOLD & ARNOLD

Richard Arnold in all likelihood would have been made a partner of Covington & Burling, with a significant income, had he chosen to stay. Instead, just over three years after joining the firm, Arnold left to practice law in Arkansas. The firm presented him with a marble pen holder inscribed "Richard S. Arnold, from his friends at Covington & Burling, August 1964." More significant to Arnold was an agreement from Covington & Burling to be paid an annual retainer of $2,500 dollars should their clients need local counsel in Arkansas.[13] The annual payment was a way to ensure that Arnold would not first be hired by the other side. He received the payment without the necessity of handling any active cases for Covington clients.

The timing of Arnold's return to Arkansas reflected his ambition to become a political player there and the willingness of Gale Arnold to move the young family back to their native region. When Arnold returned to his father's law firm in Texarkana in October 1964, the firm had existed under the name Arnold & Arnold for over forty years. The firm itself was even older. His grandfather, William Hendrick Arnold, had practiced law there since 1883, before his sons joined him after the turn of the century. When Richard returned to Texarkana, Arnold & Arnold was composed of his uncle, William H. Arnold Jr., then the oldest member of the firm, his father, Richard Lewis Arnold, and two cousins, William H. Arnold III and Thomas S. Arnold. Richard's younger brother, Morris, would practice with Richard at the family firm for a brief period a few years later.

Few small firms anywhere could boast the résumé of Arnold & Arnold lawyers. One Arnold had been a Rhodes Scholar; all of W. H. Arnold's sons had received elite educations. Richard's father, Richard Lewis Arnold, was himself a graduate of Phillips Exeter Academy, Yale College, and Harvard Law School. Richard S. added his own stellar academic credentials, a Supreme Court clerkship, and three years at one of the most powerful law firms in the country.

Richard Arnold's ten years of law practice with Arnold & Arnold brought with it a rarity in modern law practice—a sophisticated business law practice with a significant litigation portfolio. Arnold's initial legal work was for existing clients at the firm, including representation of insurance companies and Southwestern Electric Power Company, one of his father's main clients.

Arnold would soon bring in his own clients. On the business side, Arnold's marriage to Gale Palmer Hussman led to his appointment as general counsel for the Palmer Media Group, led by Walter Hussman Sr., Gale's father. It was a multifaceted representation—a great deal of office research, advice, drafting, and counseling, in addition to advice on libel questions and Federal Communications Commission regulations.

Arnold worked closely with Hussman's son (and Gale's brother) Walter Hussman Jr., who would later become the managing editor of the *Arkansas Democrat* (Arnold provided legal counsel for Hussman's purchase of the *Democrat*) and then the owner of the combined *Arkansas Democrat-Gazette*. The younger Hussman relied extensively on Arnold's counsel, particularly in negotiating contracts with the Hussman companies. Arnold also wrote editorials, anonymously, for the family's chain of newspapers.[14] Hussman later recalled that the surprising thing about Arnold was that "even though he was such an intellectual, he was easy to work with and had a surprising understanding of basic business problems. He seemed to be able to talk to all types of people."[15]

On the litigation side, Arnold's practice included a multimillion-dollar will contested by the beneficiaries and a large amount of routine litigation typical of a local practice: divorces, probate proceedings, adoptions, negligence, warranty, and so forth. In a small-town law practice, it was necessary to take, as Arnold said, "whatever comes in the door."[16]

Arnold's most significant cases involved clients who he brought into the firm—a criminal defendant facing the death penalty, taxpayers in lawsuits against corrupt county officials, and the Environmental Defense Fund. These cases reveal an emerging commitment to civil rights and the environment. His work for the Environmental Defense Fund in particular would lead others to label him as a "liberal," even though Arnold's zealous representation of his clients did not require that he personally espouse those causes.

A DEATH PENALTY CASE

In 1969 and 1970, Richard Arnold defended a suspect in a first-degree murder case in which the prosecution sought the death penalty. Arnold was appointed to the case because the murder suspect had no money to pay an attorney. At that time in Arkansas, as in many other states, attorneys appointed to such cases served pro bono—receiving no compensation from the state for the attorney's time spent on the case. Although he was assisted by Victor Hlavinka, another attorney in Texarkana, and his brother Morris Arnold, Richard carried the primary burden at the defendant's trial. Richard Arnold would spend an enormous amount of time, showing the same tenacity in representation that marked his defense of affluent clients. He took the case all the way to the United States Supreme Court, and very nearly had the case reviewed there.

Oddly enough, the judge who first drew the case, the prosecutor, and the defense lawyer all shared the last name "Arnold." W. H. Arnold III, Richard's cousin and former partner at Arnold & Arnold, had recently been elected circuit judge of Miller County. After appointing Richard to defend the murder suspect, a special judge replaced W. H. Arnold for the trial to avoid a conflict of interest. The prosecutor in the case, W. H. "Dub" Arnold, was a very distant cousin, although he shared a surprisingly similar name with Richard's grandfather, William Hendrick Arnold.

It was a particularly ugly murder. On the evening of December 15, 1968, the nude body of Winn Smith was found in the bathroom of his apartment in Texarkana, Arkansas. Smith's bed was saturated with blood, and a trail of blood led from the bedroom to the bathroom where his body was found. Two teeth and fragments of a heavy bronze candleholder were found on the bedroom floor. A broken candleholder and a butcher knife were found in the bathtub. Smith had seventeen stab wounds in addition to head injuries. About midnight the next day, twenty-seven-year-old Kenneth Ray Blanton was apprehended while asleep in Winn Smith's car in a roadside park near Sierra Blanca, Texas. Not only was Blanton in Smith's car, he had Smith's wristwatch and wallet in his possession. Blanton was arrested and returned to Texarkana, where he soon became Richard Arnold's client.

This would be an extremely difficult case to win given the circumstantial evidence against Arnold's client, which extended to the defendant's fingerprints and palm print in the victim's bathroom. Blanton's defense, essentially, was that he might be a thief but was not the murderer. Blanton testified at his four-day trial in late April 1969 that Smith had given him the keys to the automobile for temporary use and that he had used the automobile for about an hour. When he returned to Smith's apartment, he found Smith dead in the bathroom. Once he determined that Smith was dead, he searched Smith's pockets, took some change and his watch, and left for Texas in Smith's automobile. He said he later found Smith's wallet in the glove compartment.

The case was also difficult for Arnold because the prosecution sought, successfully, to put evidence before the jury that Blanton was likely homosexual. The prosecution presented a Little Rock police officer who testified for the state that months before the killing, he and another vice squad officer had stopped an automobile in which Blanton was a passenger, and that Blanton stated on that occasion that he was a homosexual. The prosecution's theory may have been that Blanton was a sexual predator who beat Smith to death for rejecting him. Regardless, introduction of this testimony clearly was an effort to stigmatize the defendant in the eyes of the jury.

During the trial, Arnold attempted to support a theory that a third individual had both the motive and the opportunity to commit the crime. Arnold called Sandy Carter as a witness. Carter, who was a business partner of Smith's, admitted to being in the apartment at 1 p.m. Sunday — when the autopsy indicated Smith was likely already dead — but Carter claimed not to notice anything amiss. Carter testified that he was a homosexual and that he had engaged in homosexual practices with Smith. Blanton had testified that Smith picked him up on the street; that he resisted homosexual advances made by Smith; that he accepted Smith's offer to share Smith's apartment; and that he had gone in Smith's automobile to get some clothes from his own apartment when Smith's murder apparently occurred. Arnold suggested that Carter had committed the murder in a jealous rage. Blanton had merely exercised the poor judgment to abscond with Smith's car and wallet after discovering the body.

Blanton was convicted of first-degree murder in the Miller County Circuit Court, but the jury rejected the death penalty and assessed life imprisonment as the penalty. Avoiding the death penalty was a significant achievement for Arnold, whatever he personally thought of Blanton's guilt or innocence. He never commented publicly on whether he thought Blanton had committed the murder.

The Arnold brothers represented Blanton on appeal to the Arkansas Supreme Court, with Morris writing the brief. The record reflects superb legal work, something that the court was not generally accustomed to receiving on behalf of indigent defendants. The appeal designated a total of eighteen grounds for reversal.[17] Two of these were particularly revealing of the Arnold brothers' zealous representation.

First, the brief argued that the trial court should have granted public funds to pay for investigative, psychiatric, and other services for Blanton's defense. These funds were necessary, they argued, to ensure a fair trial under the federal constitution's Bill of Rights. Yet there was no definitive US Supreme Court precedent requiring this. Arnold hoped to lead the Arkansas court in the direction he thought was suggested by *Gideon v. Wainwright*,[18] a 1963 case in which the United States Supreme Court unanimously ruled that state courts are required under the Sixth Amendment of the federal constitution to provide counsel in criminal cases for defendants unable to afford their own attorneys.

But he not only lacked Supreme Court precedent for what he was asking; no lower federal court had taken this position, either. As Morris Arnold acknowledged in the brief, each of the lower federal courts to address the issue had concluded (erroneously, he thought) that the due process clause did not require that such assistance be provided by the state. Instead, they urged the Arkansas Supreme Court to adopt the view expressed in a dissenting opinion from the Third Circuit:[19]

> As civilization progresses our ideas of fundamental fairness necessarily enlarge themselves. The requirements of due process would not be met by the appointment of a layman as counsel. The appointment of counsel for a deaf mute would not constitute due process of law unless an interpreter also was available. Nor, in our opinion, would the appointment of counsel learned in the law fulfill the requirement of due process if that counsel required the assistance of a psychiatrist in order to prepare an insane client's defense.[20]

At trial, Richard Arnold had sought unsuccessfully to raise an insanity defense for his client. The Arkansas Supreme Court ruled that the state had satisfied its duty to the indigent defendant by providing him with a lawyer (although the lawyer was not paid). It had no further duty to provide any funds for investigation or expert witnesses.

A second issue in Blanton's appeal is equally interesting, because once again the Arnolds asked the Arkansas court to extend recent US Supreme Court precedent. At the trial, Richard Arnold had pressed the judge to select a new jury panel because of racial discrimination practiced in its selection. Arnold argued that Blanton's jury was invalid because the jury commissioners "systematically excluded Negroes." In 1986 in *Batson v. Kentucky*,[21] the United States Supreme Court would reaffirm the principle established over a century earlier, in *Strauder v. West Virginia*,[22] that a state denies a black defendant equal protection under the Fourteenth Amendment when it puts him on trial before a jury from which members of his race have been purposefully excluded.

Blanton, however, was a white man. Arnold argued that the trend of Supreme Court precedent would soon recognize racial exclusion of jurors as a wrong in itself, a wrong to the justice system as a whole. But in a 1947 case known as *Fay v. New York*, the US Supreme Court had suggested that it would not do so. The Arkansas Supreme Court quoted this language: "This court, however, has never entertained a defendant's objections to exclusions from the jury except when he was a member of the excluded class."[23] Arnold had emphasized in his brief that not only was this language from *Fay* "dicta," not essential to the holding of the case, but that it was followed with a sentence leaving the matter open: "Nevertheless, we need not here decide whether lack of identity with an excluded group would alone defeat an otherwise well-established case under the Amendment."[24] But, as the Arkansas court gleefully pointed out, the Supreme Court had cited with approval the Arkansas Supreme Court's earlier rejection of a similar claim, "where a Negro alleged prejudicial error because all white persons were purposely excluded from the jury that indicted him."[25]

Arnold's arguments—and not the Arkansas Supreme Court's view of them—brought Blanton's case within one vote of a hearing before the United States Supreme Court. After receiving the Arkansas court's decision, Richard and Morris Arnold filed a petition for review with the US Supreme Court. That request for review was denied, but three justices— William Brennan, William O. Douglas, and Thurgood Marshall, who had replaced Tom Clark on the Court in 1967—voted to grant certiorari review on precisely the two issues the Arnolds had raised: whether or not a white person could challenge a jury on the ground of exclusion of blacks, and whether an indigent defendant was entitled to state-paid expert assistance, such as psychiatrists and fingerprint experts. Only four votes are needed in order for the Supreme Court to take up an appeal. Justices Douglas, Brennan, and Marshall were all of the opinion that certiorari should be granted, but they could not convince a fourth justice to vote to hear the case.[26]

It would be difficult for Blanton to appreciate, but he was an extremely lucky man to have Richard Arnold as his attorney. Despite his relative youth (Arnold was thirty-three when he took the case), Arnold was probably the best attorney in the state and arguably one of the best in the nation. Although Arnold had never tried a murder case before and worked for no compensation, Blanton escaped the death penalty. Narrowly missing Supreme Court review of his case, Blanton spent the rest of his life in an Arkansas prison, where he died in 1992 at the age of fifty-one.[27]

Arnold's model for his pro bono work in Arkansas was the example set by Gerhard Gesell at Covington & Burling. But for Arnold, the case caused significant financial loss. The huge amount of time expended on Blanton's case could not be billed to paying clients. It is more common now, in most states and in the federal system, for lawyers for defendants facing the death penalty to receive at least a nominal payment from the court for representing indigent defendants. But then, as now, the real problem is the quality of representation supplied to capital murder defendants. Death penalty defense is highly specialized even when the practitioner is competent. John Holdridge, director of the ACLU Capital Punishment Project, said in 2008 that one systemic problem with the death penalty is "poor people getting lousy lawyers."[28] In North Carolina, for example, three death row inmates were released within a six-month period because of poor representation by their trial attorneys, and an early investigation by the *Charlotte Observer* showed that sixteen death row inmates had been represented by lawyers who were later disbarred.[29] When Arnold represented Kenneth Ray Blanton, no such concerns could be raised.

Arnold had more success at the United States Supreme Court in a criminal case one year later. Frank Camp, a hospital administrator in Osceola, Arkansas, was prosecuted for an alleged embezzlement of $20,000. At the first trial, Camp was convicted by a jury and sentenced to a term of years in the state penitentiary, which the Supreme Court of Arkansas affirmed on appeal.[30] At this point Arnold was hired, and he prepared and filed a petition for writ of certiorari in the Supreme Court of the

United States. The petition was based primarily upon claimed impropri-
eties in the closing argument by the prosecuting attorney. The Supreme
Court granted certiorari and reversed summarily, ruling in Arnold's favor
in a short and tersely worded per curiam opinion.[31] On remand, Arnold
tried the case and made the closing argument to the jury. The trial lasted
five days, October 23–27, 1972, and resulted in a hung jury. Camp later
reached a plea agreement with the prosecuting attorney and received a
suspended, or probated sentence, thus avoiding jail time entirely.[32]

POLITICAL CASES

Richard Arnold also became involved in high-profile litigation with political
overtones in Arkansas. One of the first matters Arnold took on after he
returned to Arkansas was a civil suit against an incumbent sheriff and tax col-
lector brought on behalf of a group of taxpayers. Marlin Hawkins, the defendant in the case, was the long time, powerful sheriff of Conway County,
Arkansas. The case was originally filed in 1964 in the Chancery Court of
Conway County, Arkansas, and was eventually tried in 1967 and 1968.[33]
Although the plaintiffs lost the major part of the case in terms of money,
Arnold obtained a judgment in the amount of $8,000, which was affirmed on
appeal to the Arkansas Supreme Court. Despite only a partial victory to
recoup funds, Arnold viewed the case as a substantial victory in establishing
the principle that the sheriff was accountable and showing that he had failed
to account for substantial funds.[34] Arnold viewed the establishment of precedent — principles important for future cases — as important, if partial, victories.

The case was extremely difficult and hard fought, involving complicated issues of fiduciary accounting. It required the marshaling of complex
and voluminous accounting data. Both sides employed certified public
accountants who were examined and cross-examined at length. Sheriff
Marlin Hawkins later complained to the FBI agent conducting Arnold's
background check for nomination to the federal district court that he
thought "Republicans," and specifically the Arkansas Republican Party,
had financed Arnold's representation of the taxpayers, and that Arnold
should have reported the source of the fees.[35]

A few years later Arnold was again called upon to sue another
allegedly corrupt local sheriff on behalf of taxpayers. The trial took place

in January and April 1973. Complex evidentiary questions involving the admission of documents dominated the trial, as well as testimony from certified public accountants. A substantial judgment of nearly $70,000 was obtained and was later affirmed by the Supreme Court of Arkansas on appeal, although by the time the appeal was decided Arnold was no longer in private practice and other attorneys handled the case.[36]

But Arnold's interest in politics reached beyond the legal arena. Arnold was a prominent political player in Arkansas during the time that he was in private practice. As discussed in the next chapter, Arnold's law practice was often secondary to his political activities. But those political activities also brought business to the firm. On one occasion, Arnold represented the Arkansas Democratic State Committee in an emergency hearing in federal court in Little Rock. Only a few days before the 1972 Democratic National Convention in Miami, supporters of George Wallace and the American Independent Party filed a lawsuit seeking to enjoin the Arkansas delegation from attending the convention. They claimed that the selection of Arkansas delegates to the Democratic Convention was unconstitutional because it was based upon a racial and gender quota system.

The chairman of the Arkansas Democratic Party called Arnold the afternoon before the scheduled hearing to ask him to come to Little Rock to try the case. That night and the following morning, Arnold prepared witnesses, including Arkansas governor Dale Bumpers and Ray Thornton, the Democratic nominee for Congress who had just defeated Arnold in a primary election. The trial took place on July 7, 1972, before J. Smith Henley, US district judge for the Eastern District of Arkansas. Henley was a Republican appointee, and, as Arnold said later, Democratic Party officials thought Henley "would be delighted to find a way to turn the knife in a Democratic wound."[37] But Arnold told his clients "that our case would win or lose on its merits, not on politics, and I was right."[38] At the conclusion of the daylong hearing, Judge Henley ruled from the bench for Arnold's side. The case was not appealed, and the Arkansas delegation proceeded to the convention.[39]

Such overtly political cases were the exception rather than the norm in Arnold's practice. A boating accident case, without the political overtones invoked by suing local sheriffs for misuse of funds, was more typical of the varied litigation at a small-town law firm. Generally on the defense side of personal injury litigation, in this case Arnold represented the families of four people killed in a boating accident on the Red River near Texarkana. An associate who first handled the matter thought it was a worker's compensation case. Arnold saw that it was an admiralty case (an obscure area of law for a landlocked state) and filed a lawsuit in federal court. For Arnold, the most striking part of the case was the historical research. It was necessary to establish the navigability of the Red River. To do so, Arnold located and presented the testimony of a witness who actually saw cotton loaded onto barges on the Red River in the 1890s. This case reveals Arnold's penchant for historical scholarship—one that was to be as profitable for his client as it was engaging to him.

Arnold tried the case in federal court without a jury, the protocol for an admiralty case. He won a judgment for the families for $455,000, the largest judgment he ever obtained. The judgment was affirmed on appeal by the Eighth Circuit.[40] Arnold always remembered this argument before the Eighth Circuit because of the presence on the three-judge panel of retired Supreme Court Justice Tom Clark, sitting by designation as a member of the Eighth Circuit. Arnold had known Justice Clark while serving as a law clerk for William Brennan, and Clark not only remembered Arnold but commented on Arnold's service to the Supreme Court at the beginning of Arnold's argument.

ENVIRONMENTAL CASES

Arnold gained national prominence as an attorney through his representation of the Environmental Defense Fund in a series of cases against the US Army Corps of Engineers.[41] Arnold was hired by the Environmental Defense Fund for two projects in Arkansas. The first was to save southwest Arkansas's Cossatot River from a proposed dam. The second was an attempt to halt a channelization project in the Cache River basin. Based on his performance in these two cases, he became the lead lawyer for one of the most significant EDF cases at the time, a challenge to the Tennessee-Tombigbee waterway project that now links the Tennessee River and the Port of Mobile. Arnold took on high-profile environmental cases when there was no trail to follow as one of the first attorneys for the Environmental Defense Fund.

In these cases, Arnold was instrumental in advancing important interpretations of the recently enacted National Environmental Protection Act

(NEPA) of 1969, setting precedent for future environmental litigation. These cases were influential in forcing the federal government to give greater consideration to the effects of its actions on the environment. He would later receive a number of awards for his environmental work. An unexpected result of one of his cases may be the ivory-billed woodpecker, long thought to be extinct but allegedly discovered in recent years in the Cache River area in Arkansas.

THE COSSATOT RIVER AND THE GILHAM DAM

Arnold became the lead lawyer for the Cossatot River effort by invitation of Wellborn Jack Jr., a lawyer in Shreveport, Louisiana. Jack asked Arnold if he would be willing to sue the Corps of Engineers to stop a project known as the Gilham Dam. Arnold said yes; he was not afraid to sue the Corps of Engineers because "my business was suing people, or defending them." At that time Arnold was "not oriented towards the outdoors or towards environmental issues in any particular fashion."[42] It was Arnold's general reputation as a lawyer in the area that led Jack to call Arnold and the EDF to agree to hire him for the case. It would not be an easy task. Arnold was hired to do what seemed, at the time, to be impossible—stop an Army Engineers dam project that was already about two-thirds complete.[43]

Arnold's strategy to halt the project was to challenge the adequacy of the Corps of Engineers' environmental impact statement, a new requirement under NEPA. It would become the first fully litigated NEPA case.[44] The plaintiffs sought to use NEPA and other statutes to enjoin the construction of the Gilham Dam on the Cossatot River in southwest Arkansas. This was the first NEPA case that resulted in a full-scale opinion explicating this statute and holding that it provided a basis for judicial review of agency action. The case was often cited in ensuing years, and the pleadings, which Arnold drafted, were reprinted in a case book on environmental law. Arnold worked extensively with scientific witnesses, including an ecologist, a biologist, and outdoor recreation specialists.

The government did not take the case seriously, Arnold reported: "They thought it was a joke. The U.S. Attorney laughed when we filed the complaint."[45] That, according to Arnold, was not a wise tactic in front of federal judge G. Thomas Eisele: "Judge Eisele was new on the bench, but then as now has a very inquisitive mind. He likes new ideas and new theories and he is not afraid to rule against the United States when the law and the facts indicate that."[46] Arnold argued that the environmental impact statement on the project filed by the Corps of Engineers was biased in favor of the project and ignored significant environmental questions in order to justify construction of the project.

Judge Eisele held a hearing on the motion for preliminary injunction in late 1970, and the trial took place on February 8, 9, and 10, 1971. Arnold won, at least temporarily, by obtaining an injunction halting further construction. It was a major victory for conservationists interested in preserving free-flowing streams because it was one of the first injunctions issued by the federal courts in environmental suits.[47] The opinion of the district court granting an injunction became one of the most-cited cases interpreting the Environmental Protection Act.

Rather than appeal the ruling, the Corps of Engineers undertook a new environmental impact statement in hopes of satisfying Eisele and getting the injunction dissolved. The Corp of Engineers' third environmental study was ultimately deemed sufficient by the district court. The first impact statement, successfully challenged by Arnold, was less than a dozen pages. The revised statement weighed in at twelve pounds.[48] The dam was ultimately completed.

Arnold filed and argued an appeal, but the judgment lifting the injunction was affirmed by the Eighth Circuit. Although he was disappointed with the outcome, Arnold was happy that the court had accepted his argument that the Environmental Protection Act gave citizens the right to file suits over congressional authorization of projects, and that it empowered the courts to overrule agency decisions if the evidence showed that the decisions were arbitrary or capricious. It was the first time any court had interpreted NEPA in this way. "If an agency realizes that the courts can overrule a congressional decision, it will investigate a project with greater care before it presents the project to Congress for authorization," Arnold said.[49] The Supreme Court chose not to review the case, leaving for a later time its first full-scale decision on NEPA. But it was a very important precedent. Eisele's decision to temporarily halt the project had been cited in numerous other environmental suits and became a landmark decision for future environmental cases. The opinion would eventually be cited in every circuit court in the nation.[50]

Arnold's attack on the sufficiency of the corps' environmental impact statement won the day. But he also raised other far-reaching and ambitious arguments, although without success. In all of his environmental cases, Arnold argued that the Fifth and Ninth Amendments protect the environmental rights of citizens. No court had ever recognized such a claim. He also suggested that the idea of a "public trust," an ancient doctrine from Roman law, meant that "there is a public interest even in land that is privately owned and especially land that is owned by the government or any government agency," Arnold told a reporter. Under this doctrine, he said, "the public has a right to see this land dedicated to certain public purposes."[51] All of these arguments would have set precedent if accepted by the courts. But they were not even considered beyond the trial court level. Arnold said at the time, "It's hard to get a District Court to accept because there are two levels of appeals above it and a District judge often feels, quite properly, that he shouldn't be too innovative. I feel that the arguments should be made because this is the way the law grows."[52]

THE CACHE RIVER BASIN AND THE "LORD GOD" BIRD

Impressed with Arnold's legal strategies and results, the Environmental Defense Fund hired Arnold for two other cases. One of these was also in Arkansas, and like the Gilham Dam case, it involved a challenge to a Corps of Engineers project that environmentalists believed endangered the Cache River basin in eastern Arkansas. The project was a $60 million channelization of 232 miles of the Cache River and its tributaries in East Arkansas to stop flooding. The Corps of Engineers' plan did have some meaningful implications for flood control in the area. Environmentalists, on the other hand, argued that the channelization project would have destroyed one of the nation's prime duck wintering areas.[53]

Arnold filed a lawsuit against the Corps of Engineers in 1971 on behalf of the Environmental Defense Fund and several individuals, along with the Arkansas Wildlife Federation and the Arkansas Game and Fish Commission. The Game and Fish Commission's involvement was the first time a state agency had joined private groups in a modern environmental controversy. Arnold's lawsuit raised similar claims about the deficiency of the Corps' environmental impact study.[54] Ultimately, the case resulted in an injunction against the project that remained in effect for some time.

Initially, however, Arnold lost at the trial court level in a hearing before Judge J. Smith Henley. Arnold's contention was that the Corps of Engineers' environmental impact statement—a mere fourteen pages—was too meager. Arnold argued the appeal of Judge Henley's first ruling before the Eighth Circuit on October 18, 1972, in St. Paul, Minnesota. The panel consisted of Judges Lay, Heaney, and Bright. Judge Heaney wrote the opinion reversing the district court, and the case was remanded to that court for consideration of appropriate relief. On remand, another trial was held before Judge Henley on March 18, 1973. At the conclusion of the trial, Judge Henley ruled for Arnold from the bench and entered an injunction stopping the project.

The opinion in the Eighth Circuit was particularly significant for administrative law. It was the clearest and most explicit statement of the nature of judicial review available under NEPA. It also held that the statute created substantive rights. Arnold persuaded the Eighth Circuit that courts have both the authority and the duty to review the substantive decisions of government agencies to determine if they are in accord with the spirit of the Environmental Protection Act.

As in the Gilham Dam case, an injunction would buy time but would not necessarily stop the project. In the case of the Cache River basin, Arnold's actions bought sufficient time for a political solution, working with then Senator Dale Bumpers to halt the project. Delay became victory for environmentalists. The Corps of Engineers abandoned the channelization plan in 1981. With the help of the Nature Conservancy, a large area of land in the region became a national wildlife refuge. Kay Kelley Arnold, Richard Arnold's second wife whom he married in 1980, founded Arkansas's Nature Conservancy in 1983. With the help of other organizations and individuals, Kay and Nancy Delamar, the first two directors of the Nature Conservancy in Arkansas, raised money to buy acreage along the Cache. The Cache River National Wildlife Refuge ultimately preserved 61,000 acres.[55]

The Cache River litigation may also have done more. Less than one year after Arnold's death in 2004, the national press reported the discovery of the ivory-billed woodpecker in the Cache River National Wildlife Refuge. For more than fifty years, the ivory-billed woodpecker was thought to be extinct. Known as the "Lord God bird," so named by John Audubon and Theodore Roosevelt from the exclamations of those who saw the giant woodpecker, the bird is twenty inches long with a wingspan of three feet.

The ivory-billed woodpecker was an inhabitant of dense swamp forests like those preserved in the Cache River basin in eastern Arkansas.

The first glimpse in early 2004 was fleeting, but subsequent video and sound recordings seemed to confirm the existence of at least one ivory bill. In April 2005, the prestigious journal *Science* and a host of scientists from Arkansas, the Cornell University Laboratory of Ornithology, and nine other universities confirmed the sightings.[56] Their findings were announced at a press conference at the Department of Interior in Washington, DC, by John Fitzpatrick of the Cornell Laboratory of Ornithology.[57] The national media quickly picked up the story, including a *60 Minutes* segment by Ed Bradley discussing "one of the most celebrated birds in U.S. history."[58] The *New York Times* provided extensive coverage over a series of months.[59] The *Arkansas Times* reflected on the national jubilation that followed: "Why did grown men and women weep at the news, put on page 1 coast to coast?"[60] Two books about the discovery quickly followed.[61]

After the announcement of the sighting in Arkansas, officials closed off nearly five thousand acres of the Cache Refuge to protect the Bayou DeView area, a swamp full of ancient tupelo and cypress trees. The Nature Conservancy and Cornell raised $10 million in cash and pledges to buy additional acreage for conservation in the area. A federal wildlife director said, "If there is any place in the world to preserve this bird, it's going to be Arkansas."[62]

At the time Arnold filed the lawsuit, the Army Corps of Engineers had proposed a two-hundred-and-thirty-mile ditching project that would have destroyed many of the area's eight-hundred- to thousand-year-old cypress trees. Because of Arnold's speedy appeal to the Eighth Circuit, and its direction to Judge Henley to reconsider the case, Arnold ultimately secured an injunction when only six miles of the proposed channeling had been completed.[63] Even though a 1976 ruling by a federal judge permitted work to resume, the project was never restarted. In the interim, Arnold had gone to Washington as legislative aide for Senator Dale Bumpers, and he worked with Bumpers to create a political solution.

With no additional sighting of an ivory-billed woodpecker since 2005, scholarly doubt about the existence of the bird in the Cache River has increased. If the ivory-billed woodpecker has survived in that part of Arkansas, however, Richard Arnold should share some of the credit for preserving its habitat.

THE TENNESSEE-TOMBIGBEE WATERWAY PROJECT

The alleged sighting of the Lord God bird in the Cache River basin was in the distant future, however. Until that time, Arnold's biggest environmental case was not in Arkansas. Arnold's increasingly national reputation as an environmental lawyer was evident in his selection in 1971 as the lead lawyer for the Environmental Defense Fund's challenge to the huge Tennessee-Tombigbee Waterway navigation project in Mississippi, Alabama, and Tennessee. In a massive undertaking, the Corps of Engineers planned to construct a continuous waterway to provide navigation from the Tennessee, upper Mississippi, and Ohio valleys to the Gulf of Mexico through a tidewater port in Mobile, Alabama. It was one of the largest public-works projects in United States history.[64]

The Environmental Defense Fund filed a suit to enjoin the construction of the Tennessee-Tombigbee Waterway. Arnold was selected because of his track record suing the Corps of Engineers in Arkansas and for his innovative legal arguments about interpretations of the Environmental Protection Act. Moreover, he was already a member of the District of Columbia bar, where the case was first filed, and he had practiced before courts there. Arnold had now become the Environmental Defense Fund's expert lawyer on these cases.

The case was filed in the United States District Court for the District of Columbia in July 1971. On September 15 and 16, Arnold argued a motion for preliminary injunction before Judge John Lewis Smith Jr. Arnold won his motion. The District of Columbia federal court agreed that the government had failed to comply fully with the requirements of the Environmental Protection Act.[65] As the Fifth Circuit summarized in a later proceeding, "NEPA commands 'full good faith consideration of the environment,' not formalistic paper shuffling between agency desks."[66]

The Tennessee-Tombigbee Waterway Development Authority then intervened and asked for a change of venue to the Northern District of Mississippi. Judge Smith granted the motion. The change of venue surprised Arnold: "I thought it was extraordinary. Here you had a case where testimony had already been taken for two days. The party seeking to transfer the case was not involved in it originally. And I think that you will look a long time before you find an instance of a transfer of venue in a situation like that."[67]

After transfer, Arnold tried the case in Aberdeen, Mississippi, before Judge William C. Keady. This was an extremely complex litigation involving technical biological matters and centering on the existence of endangered species. Arnold acted as chief counsel throughout the litigation, even after the case was transferred at the relatively late stage to Mississippi; Arnold was usually the only lawyer appearing in court for the plaintiffs. The trial took ten days, from June 19 to June 28, 1972. At its conclusion, Judge Keady dissolved the injunction and entered judgment for the Corps of Engineers.[68] Judge Keady determined that the corps' environmental impact statement, when considered in its entirety, provided an adequately detailed statement of the environmental impact likely to occur from the navigational project. Or, at least, the statement "was not inadequate" with respect to the likely impact upon endangered species, water quality, and other detrimental effects along the proposed route.[69]

Construction began on the project soon after Judge Keady lifted the injunction. Arnold appealed to the United States Court of Appeals for the Fifth Circuit and argued the case as sole counsel on May 28, 1973, but that court affirmed the Mississippi federal court.[70] Arnold recalled:

I felt that the District Court's opinion and the government's brief in the Court of Appeals really failed to appreciate the points that we had made. And when I say failed to appreciate, I don't mean just disagreed with it. The District Court's opinion read like a different case from the case that had been tried. I never thought that I was going to lose, and I was completely confident in the legal theory. And I still am, which is not relevant, of course, because the court didn't agree with it.[71]

The waterway project, described by the Tennessee-Tombigbee Waterway Development Authority as "unparalleled in the world," was completed in 1984 after twelve years of construction and at a cost of twelve billion dollars.[72] It links fourteen river systems totaling forty-five hundred miles of navigable waterways. The "Tenn-Tom" itself is a 234-mile artificial waterway flowing southward through Mississippi and Alabama.

Arnold's environmental work was featured in a book published by Jeffrey Stine in 1993, when Arnold was a judge on the Eighth Circuit Court of Appeals.[73] Stine concluded that the Environmental Defense Fund decided to take on the Tenn-Tom project because of Arnold's earlier successes in the Gilham Dam litigation in Arkansas: "Arnold had earned a reputation as an extremely talented and articulate litigator. It was on the basis of this accumulated knowledge and Arnold's abundant talent that

EDF selected him to litigate its suit against the Corps on Tenn-Tom."[74] Although the litigation did not achieve all of EDF's aims, Stine reported that "praise of Arnold's competence was unanimous."[75]

Arnold also earned the praise of attorneys for the other side. Twenty years later, Hunter M. Gholson, a Columbus, Mississippi, lawyer who represented the Tennessee-Tombigbee Waterway Development Authority, wrote to President Bill Clinton endorsing Richard Arnold as a candidate for the United States Supreme Court. "Although we were adversaries," Gholson wrote, "Richard and I became good friends and I came to respect (even hold in awe) his magnificent mind, his gracious manner and his uncanny ability to reduce complex issues to understandable basics. He is not only a legal genius, but a person of good humor and impeccable character."[76]

In 1973, Arnold received the Arkansas Conservationist of the Year Award from the Arkansas Wildlife Federation.[77] Arnold's award was based on "his exceptional work as an attorney in the new and important field of environmental law, which has evolved as a result of public concern for preservation of the quality of the environment in this country and the enactment of the Environmental Policy Act."[78] In 1996, the Environmental Law Institute presented Arnold with its annual environmental award. "Judge Arnold's contributions and leadership in shaping environmental jurisprudence as a trial lawyer, legislative draftsman and judge are second to none," said Donald W. Stever, chairman of the organization's board of directors.[79] The president of the Environmental Law Institute, Bill Futrell, recalled seeing Arnold, as a young lawyer in the early 1970s, advance arguments that forged new legal ground. "He was a real precedent setter as a lawyer," Futrell said.[80]

Arnold said later that he had "always considered my time litigating environmental cases as the 'Golden Age' of my law practice. It was not only of great interest intellectually, but I believed, and still do, that my client was on the side of the angels."[81]

ARNOLD AS LEGAL SCHOLAR

Arnold's varied legal experience—a high-powered law firm and a small-town family practice—would be a rarity among federal judges. Not only did Arnold have an unusually diverse legal practice, he was also an accomplished legal scholar. Arnold struggled with the question of what role courts should play in protecting the environment. In an article published in 1973, "The Substantive Right to Environmental Quality under the National Environmental Policy Act," Arnold argued that Congress intended courts to scrutinize the substantive decisions of government agencies to ensure that government actions would not cause undue harm to the environment. Arnold wrote: "It is for the courts to see that the broad policies commanded by Congress are not distorted in individual situations by the agents of Congress. The courts cannot write the tune, but at least they can see that it remains in the same key chosen by the composer."[82]

Arnold's article followed several others that he had published since graduating from law school. He published two articles in premier law journals while he worked at Covington & Burling, the *Yale Law Journal* and the *Virginia Law Review*. Both articles discussed aspects of state judicial power compared to federal. One is often cited in textbooks used in law school courses on the federal courts. That article — "The Power of State Courts to Enjoin Federal Officers"[83] — has had remarkable staying power and is used by some modern legal scholars to argue that federalism should be a two-way street.

Back in Arkansas, amid his law practice and political races, Arnold continued to produce scholarly legal articles. He published an important survey of antitrust cases decided by the United States Supreme Court.[84] For Arnold, this was a way to continue his interest in the field of antitrust. For several years Arnold had taught antitrust as an adjunct professor at the University of Virginia Law School, commuting from Washington, DC, once a week.

He also published an essay on state government in which he urged the adoption of an "ombudsman," a government official who serves as "a sort of governmental complaint department":

> Any citizen who feels himself affronted by any level of government may appeal to the *ombudsman*, who carefully, and without charge, investigates the complaint and, if he finds it well taken, reprimands the delinquent official. He is, in sum, the people's counsel, responsible to no one but them.[85]

In this essay, Arnold outlined the function of the office and the scholarly literature about its use in some other countries. He believed the role should be adapted for use in America, and particularly in Arkansas. He published the piece less than three years after he returned to Arkansas from Washington, DC, and soon after he lost his first race for Congress.

Arnold's scholarly engagement as well as his law practice before he became a judge were critical components in the formation of the judicial philosophy he would demonstrate on the federal bench. But he did not set out to become a judge. Instead, he wanted to serve first in Congress and then in the United States Senate. His life to this point had been lived in preparation for a political career. Arnold's campaigns for office and other political activities, the subject of the next chapter, probably taught him far more about the qualities necessary to serve effectively in the federal judiciary.

Chapter Four

The Political Candidate

Richard Arnold's academic success had placed him among a world of elite figures in Washington, DC. Arnold's return to Arkansas to further his political aspirations meant returning to a very different environment. His friends in Washington—especially Justice Brennan—followed his political engagements with great interest. Brennan predicted Arnold would soon return to Washington as "Mr. Senator."[1] Just after Arnold moved to Arkansas in 1964, Brennan wrote: "We are all particularly intrigued that you are getting your feet wet in politics. We've got bets on how soon they'll be sending you here to Washington, but I won't tell you how we stand until we see who has won."[2]

ARNOLD AS SOUTHERN DEMOCRAT IN THE 1960S

Just back from Washington, Arnold quickly immersed himself in Democratic politics in Arkansas. He worked for the Lyndon B. Johnson–Hubert Humphrey presidential campaign in 1964. In Arkansas, he supported the entire Democratic ticket, which included Governor Orval Faubus in his race against Republican Winthrop Rockefeller. Rockefeller lost that contest, but his good showing energized the Republican Party in Arkansas. Rockefeller would win the governorship two years later, after Faubus decided that six terms in office was enough.

In the 1950s at both Exeter and Yale, and less prominently at Harvard Law School, Arnold identified himself with the Republican Party and the conservative "Party of the Right." He had been considered "too conservative" to clerk for Felix Frankfurter, and William F. Buckley Jr. lauded the rise, at last, of a conservative law clerk on the Supreme Court. Arnold's political affiliation and predilection are less evident in his Washington, DC, years, but he said that he voted for the Republican candidate Richard Nixon against John F. Kennedy in the 1960 presidential election.[3] Upon his return to Arkansas in 1964, however, Arnold publicly identified himself as a Democrat, and a Democrat he would remain.

Did this change in party affiliation reflect a shift in Arnold's political views? After all, he had been quite young when he first called himself a Republican, and that likely resulted from his parent's influence. Or did it merely reflect the reality that Arkansas in 1964 was a one-party state? As had been true for some time, the only political game in town was the Democratic Party. The path to the Senate for any Arkansas candidate at the time would be through the Democrats. Running for public office—and ultimately, becoming a United States senator—was, after all, Arnold's stated reason for returning to his home state and taking up law practice in the family firm in Texarkana.

Southern Democrats at the time were conservative on most social issues. One group of southern Democrats was segregationist, the self-styled "Dixiecrats" originally affiliated with Strom Thurmond in his bid for the presidency in 1948 as the nominee of the States' Rights Democratic Party. Arnold was no Dixiecrat in the 1960s, but he could fairly be described as socially conservative and in favor of states' rights. He was particularly skeptical of intrusions of federal power in state matters. Arnold could identify with the conservative wing of the southern Democratic Party, many of whom would become the so-called Reagan Democrats of a later era.

Whether simply a pragmatic affiliation or representative of a change in political beliefs or priorities, once Arnold returned to Arkansas and campaigned for office, his affiliation with the Democratic Party was prominent. In the political environment he was certainly further removed from the liberal influence of William Brennan and Gerhard Gesell, and it was necessary for Arnold to make compromises to be a political player. Soon after he returned to Arkansas, Arnold allowed his American Civil Liberties Union membership to lapse.[4] It is not clear whether this was a conscious decision to break ties with the ACLU, but ACLU membership would have been a political liability in Arkansas at the time.[5]

On the other hand, in 1967 Arnold would join the Lawyers Committee for Civil Rights under Law, a more politically acceptable organization that had been created by Attorney General Robert F. Kennedy in 1963.[6] Kennedy urged lawyers across the nation to employ the services of the organized bar in the civil rights movement. Committee leaders hoped to encourage lawyers in the south, in particular, to educate the public on civil rights and to provide pro bono representation to victims of discrimination. For the most part the leaders were disappointed in this aim. The committee was most active in Mississippi in the later 1960s, where protesters had focused efforts on voting and many persons were arrested. A few lawyers in Arkansas formed a local committee for the state, but there was little activity publicly evident. Arnold seems to have been a member in name only, but that membership was symbolically important.

Arnold cultivated Arkansas political ties early, even before he moved his family to Texarkana in 1964. On a trip to Arkansas in 1962, for example, Arnold addressed the Texarkana Lion's Club. Arnold chose as his topic an analysis of the US Supreme Court. Arnold told the audience that "liberal" and "conservative" tags were difficult to apply to individual justices. "The issues that appear before the Supreme Court cannot fall into a specific category of liberalism or conservatism," he said. Even worse were accusations that some justices were "communistic."[7]

In response to a question from the audience, Arnold defended the Court's recent decision on prayers in the public schools, *Engel v. Vitale*.[8] Hugo Black had written for the majority that New York public school officials could not promulgate an official prayer, even if nonsectarian, because it was "a practice wholly inconsistent with the establishment clause."[9] Arnold said, "It is my opinion that the Supreme Court had no anti-religious motive in handing down this decision, and was only acting in the interest of the purest interpretation of the Constitution of the United States."[10]

During the same trip to Arkansas, Arnold wrote an editorial published in the *Texarkana Gazette* and four other Hussman-owned newspapers in southwest Arkansas. Titled "The Supreme Court Change," the occasion for the editorial was Felix Frankfurter's retirement after twenty-three years on the Court. "President Kennedy," Arnold wrote, "acting with a speed that can be fairly described as staggering," had already announced Arthur Goldberg as his choice for Frankfurter's successor.[11] "Many will moan that a great 'conservative' has gone, to be replaced by a dangerous 'liberal.'" But, Arnold pointed out, Frankfurter had been "feared as a wild radical" when appointed to the Court in 1939:

> That this fear turned out to be without any justification is a measure of the two most important facts that must be kept in mind when judging a new appointment to the Supreme Court: first, that a man who puts on judicial robes and thus removes himself, to a large degree, from the changes and chances of this mortal political life, often turns out to be quite another man than he had seemed; and second, as Felix Frankfurter himself never tired of pointing out, the terms "liberal" and "conservative" really have very little meaning when applied to the business of judging.[12]

The editorial continued: "In accordance with these principles, we will refrain from joining the national game of speculation over which 'wing' of the court Goldberg will join." But Arnold then endorsed his former professor at Harvard, Paul Freund, who had chosen him for the clerkship with Brennan: "As for the appointment itself, we may perhaps be pardoned if we express passing regret that the seat did not go to a man with a more scholarly and detached background—a man, for example, like Harvard Law School's Professor Paul A. Freund. It would have been more fitting for such a man to succeed Frankfurter, himself a product of the academic world at its best."[13] Arnold sent a copy of his editorial to Brennan.[14] Brennan wrote back to Arnold that the editorial was "splendid."[15]

FIRST RACE FOR CONGRESS: 1966

Richard Arnold made his first bid for elected office in 1966 for an open seat in the US House of Representatives. In July 1965, long time Fourth District congressman Oren Harris announced he would resign to become a federal judge if his nomination by President Johnson was confirmed by the Senate. The contest would be in a Democratic primary election; no Republican could carry Arkansas's Fourth District, made up of twenty counties in southern Arkansas, the largest geographical congressional district in Arkansas. Harris eventually was confirmed as a federal judge, but his resignation from Congress was not effective until February 2, 1966, with the primary election following a few months later.[16] Because Arnold made clear his intention to run for the seat as soon as Harris announced his nomination, it meant a nearly year-long campaign season.

Five candidates entered the Democratic primary, but the contest was between only two—Arnold and David Pryor, a representative in the Arkansas legislature. Arnold had a lot going for him, as a journalist would later remark—financing, political connections, and media endorsements.[17] Arnold was young—merely twenty-nine years old when he entered the race—but so was Pryor, at age thirty-one. "I'm old enough to have gained sound judgment and young enough to gain power for South Arkansas through congressional service," Arnold said at the formal announcement of his candidacy.[18] Electing young men to Congress was something of an Arkansas tradition at the time, and accordingly, many races featured men of relative youth. Bill Clinton was twenty-seven when he entered his first electoral contest, running for Congress in another Arkansas district. Clinton lost that race, but by a much closer margin than did Arnold, and Clinton was successful at his next endeavor—he was elected attorney general of Arkansas at age thirty.

Arnold, like Clinton, chose to start a political career with a race for national rather than state or local office. David Pryor, on the other hand, had run for and been elected to state office and had made a name for himself as a "young Turk" in the state legislature.[19] Pryor had taken on the state's governor, Orval Faubus, then the controlling power in Arkansas's Democratic political machinery, over much of Faubus's legislative agenda. Just as important, Pryor was a graduate of the University of Arkansas, with the opportunity to make contacts that served him well in the rest of his political career. Arnold, by contrast, had an eastern elite education. He had been out of the state except for a few summers from the age of fourteen and had moved back to Arkansas only two years prior to entering the congressional contest.

During his clerkship, Arnold discussed with Brennan his plans to return to Arkansas to run for Congress as a Democrat. Arnold recalled: "I remember Justice Brennan telling me—he gave me some political advice. He said, 'What are you going to do when you get home, politically?' I said, 'I'm going to do everything I can to defeat [Governor Orval] Faubus.' He said, 'Don't do that. He's the leader of the party. You can't beat him. Just be calm about it.' So I tried to follow that advice."[20]

And he did. When he began his campaign for Congress, Arnold went to see Faubus because, as he said later, "Faubus was the leader of the Democratic Party and at that time the most powerful politician in the state."[21] Arnold discussed his candidacy with Faubus, and "the governor said he would take no part in the Fourth District race," a position he later took publicly.[22] Faubus would surely have wanted one of the candidates to beat Pryor, who had been critical of Faubus throughout Pryor's years in the state legislature. Arnold never publicly criticized Faubus, but Arnold could not convince Faubus to endorse him above the other candidates in the race.

After Faubus was no longer governor and held little or no political sway in Arkansas Democratic politics, Arnold said that he had voted "for whoever ran against Faubus" for governor in 1958, 1960, and 1962 (all three times voting by absentee ballot from out of state).[23] But Arnold went to great lengths to inform Arkansas voters that he had supported Faubus in the 1964 and subsequent elections, as his pledge as a Democratic Party candidate required.[24] He seems to have taken Brennan's advice very seriously, and he recognized that Faubus was at that time a powerful political ally to cultivate. Arnold remained appalled at Faubus's earlier defiance of *Brown v. Board of Education*.[25]

Arnold carefully positioned himself as a candidate around several themes: He identified himself as a "conservative," to be against labor unions and closed shops, as an anticommunist and a supporter of the war in Vietnam. He also identified himself as a "Christian." Arnold said he considered "politics a Christian vocation. Public officers are ministers of God just as much as our ordained clergy, but in a different sense."[26]

Arnold's 1966 campaign flyer is revealing. The flyer notes that Arnold was thirty years old, an Eagle Scout, a Sunday school teacher and lay reader, and married with one daughter. The flyer highlights the following "qualifications":

> Lawyer, admitted to practice in Arkansas and Washington, DC.
> Author of articles on State-Federal Relations.
> Three years of Washington law practice before federal agencies.
> First in grades on the Arkansas Bar Examination, and in his college
>   and law school classes.
> Active in 1964 campaign for all Democrats.[27]

The cold war and communism were very much in issue at the time. Speaking to the Miller County Democrats in early October 1965, Arnold received statewide publicity for his strong endorsement of President Johnson's actions in Vietnam and the Dominican Republic. "I think it is time citizens began to speak out in support of the President's efforts to contain communism," he said. "It would be immoral not to have opposed Communism in Vietnam and the Dominican Republic, and international law has always recognized the inherent right of self-defense." He noted the recent burning of draft cards by those opposed to American foreign policy and said he approved making such action a federal crime.[28]

Arnold was openly critical of one aspect of the Supreme Court's 1962 decision in *Baker v. Carr*,[29] an opinion written by his mentor Justice William Brennan in the year after Arnold finished his clerkship. Known as the "one-man-one-vote" decision, in *Baker* the Court ruled that under the Fourteenth Amendment, federal courts could review state reapportionment decisions to determine equality of representation in voting districts. Arnold endorsed the Dirksen Amendment, a proposal to amend the US Constitution introduced by Senator Everett Dirksen to modify the Supreme Court's "one-man-one-vote" decision: "States should be free to apportion one house of their legislature on some basis other than population. The Supreme Court went too far in reading the Fourteenth Amendment to forbid states to model their legislatures after the Federal Congress." The Dirksen Amendment is "really quite a moderate measure," Arnold contended. It would allow states to apportion one house on a nonpopulation basis only after approval by a state wide vote.[30] Arnold's earlier scholarly articles on federal-state relations were not inconsistent with this position—he valued federal legislative supremacy over Supreme Court pronouncements with which he did not agree.

But his criticism of the Supreme Court was balanced. In an address to a civic club in Pine Bluff, Arnold lauded some of the Court's First Amendment decisions. "It is a citizen's right and duty to criticize decisions with which he disagrees. But the criticism should be temperate and informed, instead of emotional. The careless habit of labeling the court 'Communist' or 'atheist' whenever one happens to disagree with them is a poor substitute for thought." Arnold said the Court, like any other human institution, was fallible:

> But let's remember that each case that comes before the court presents a different issue. Disagreement on one point should not be permitted to

sour us on the court as an institution. When the court upheld the Communist Party's refusal to register under the Subversive Activities Control Act of 1950, some people raised the old cry of communism and called for impeachment. The issue in the case was not whether communism is a good thing, but rather whether the Subversive Control Act violates the Fifth Amendment's guarantee against self-incrimination.[31]

Arnold did not think highly of Earl Warren, the chief justice of the United States Supreme Court since 1953 and during Arnold's tenure as a law clerk for Justice Brennan. Arnold did not respect Warren's legal abilities—he termed Warren "not an intellectual or legal scholar."[32] Arnold believed the justices he knew when he worked for Brennan "were mostly far above him [Warren] in intellectual stature."[33] Arnold said Warren's judicial opinions "were good to the extent that the law clerks writing them were good," although he was quick to recognize Warren's qualities as "an affable character, a very friendly man."[34] Warren was a "very dignified, polite, courteous person. You can see why he was elected Governor of California."[35]

On the other hand, Arnold asserted that an "extraordinary expansion" had occurred in the law of criminal procedure, political equality, and racial discrimination under the Warren Court.[36] Arnold recognized that a Supreme Court epoch tended to be referred to popularly by the name of the chief justice, but he pointed out that Warren was not necessarily responsible for all that the Court had done. "It may be," Arnold said, "that if one man's name is to be chosen to describe this period, it should instead be that of the senior Associate Justice, Mr. Justice Black," a man Arnold particularly revered in later years. In any event, Arnold said, under Chief Justice Warren "the Supreme Court's impact on law and life has perhaps been greater during this period than at any time since the tenure of that Jeffersonian devil, Chief Justice John Marshall."[37]

An important part of Arnold's support, he thought, would come from attorneys in his district. In February 1966, Arnold mailed a letter to all of the lawyers in the twenty counties of the congressional district to ask for their vote. In that letter he emphasized his own law experience as well as his family's. "I think you will agree that lawyers bring special skills and talents to the business of writing legislation. In spite of my comparative youth, I have had more legal experience than all the other announced candidates combined, including practice in Washington, D.C., as well as Arkansas. I also served as a law clerk to the Supreme Court of the United

States for one year. And, although I did not always agree with the Court, my service there was informative and educational."[38]

In general, Arnold thought the role of the federal government was too pervasive in American life.[39] But Arnold also spoke eloquently in favor of federal aid for education, so long as federal involvement in Arkansas education remained limited. "We can improve our schools by accepting federal aid while striving to keep interference with local management at a minimum," he told a Fordyce Jaycees political rally, held in front of the Dallas County Courthouse in Fordyce.[40] Before the Shrine Club of Texarkana, Arnold warned against unthinking opposition to all federal programs. "There are those who automatically oppose all federal programs and benefits. They seem to regard the federal government as an enemy to be hated and feared." This view overlooks the fact, he said, that all federal programs are not alike and should be judged each on its own merits. He singled out Operation Head Start as a program particularly deserving of support: "The attraction of this program is that its purpose is to keep children from growing up simply to be added to the welfare rolls. If they can get a head start, which really means only an even start with the average child, they can grow up to useful employment. They can, in President Johnson's words, become tax payers instead of tax eaters."[41]

Arnold was reacting to the "Great Society" social program of President Lyndon Johnson. The social reform programs, aimed at the elimination of poverty and racial injustice, involved new federal spending in education and medical care, among other areas. Federal spending programs certainly had great currency as an issue for politicians at the state level because they came with many strings attached in terms of state compliance. Arnold took a middle ground—federal aid in some circumstances was a good thing, so long as the federal government did not interfere with local self-determination.

None of the five candidates garnered a majority of the votes in the July 26 Democratic primary, forcing a run-off election between the top two candidates—Pryor and Arnold. Arnold ran second, significantly behind Pryor's vote tally. From that point the campaign for both candidates was a relentless whirl of speaking engagements with civic, political, and religious organizations in rural South Arkansas. It was small-town politics at its most basic level. Some events, for example, advertised "free chili and cold drinks." A special guest at a "Rally for Richard" in Pine

Bluff was Lindalyn Edwards of Texarkana, the reigning Arkansas State Dairy Princess, along with "a group of singers from South Arkansas." The Arnold campaign reported that "a busload of enthusiastic supporters" from Texarkana and Miller County followed Arnold to various events.

As the congressional campaign drew to a close, labor became a prominent issue. Arnold favored Arkansas's "right to work" law, providing in general that employees could not be required to join a union as a condition of getting or retaining a job. Right to work laws were a contentious issue for labor, not only in Arkansas but nationally. Arkansas was one of nineteen states with such a law, which was permissible under Section 14b of the 1947 Taft-Hartley Act. A proposal to repeal Section 14b of the Taft-Hartley Act was then before the US Senate. Arnold was against repeal because "a man should be free to decide whether to join a union." He urged the other candidates in the race to state their position on the issue. His own stand against compulsory union membership, Arnold said, was not antiunion or antilabor: "An organization of members with free choice will ultimately become stronger. The issue is a matter of personal liberty, a personal association that cannot be compelled."[42] Arnold's protection of freedom of association was prominent in his later years as a judge, most notably in a judicial opinion concerning whether the Jaycees organization must be required to admit women.[43]

Labor issues became Arnold's primary point of attack against Pryor. Arnold described Pryor's state legislative record as "ineffective" and his voting record as "controlled and dominated by the wishes of union bosses." Pryor had voted "100 percent for the union bosses." Arnold said, "There is a clear-cut choice between my opponent and me. I stand for a conservative, constitutional government and my opponent for liberalism and pro-union policy."[44]

One week before the 1966 run-off election against Pryor, Arnold purchased time for a thirty-minute television speech aired in Little Rock, Pine Bluff, El Dorado, and Texarkana.[45] It was the most confrontational point of Arnold's political career. In his television speech he charged that David Pryor "was controlled by powerful out-of-state union bosses including Jimmy Hoffa," and that Pryor's record in the state legislature was ineffective. He also called attention to what he alleged to be a "strange combination of political bedfellows" in the Pryor campaign. Arnold claimed that he was not antilabor, that he sought the support of the working man, and that he favored reasonable extensions of and increases in the minimum wage. Pryor, on the other hand, had

> voted 100 percent for union labor demands, 100 percent for the wishes of union bosses outside the Fourth District and even outside the State of Arkansas. This record is evidence of domination and control by union bosses, instead of freedom and independence. If you want the Teamsters Union to have a Congressman from the Fourth District, if you want another rubber stamp for Walter Reuther and Jimmy Hoffa in Washington, D.C., then vote for David Pryor on August 9.[46]

Pryor termed Arnold's speech "desperation tactics," an "attempt to gain votes at all costs."[47] The following evening, Pryor aired his own television speech in rebuttal, in which he challenged Arnold to prove a charge that Pryor was linked with national labor interests. Pryor was "deeply shocked" that Arnold "would inject the names of Jimmy Hoffa and Walter Reuther into our campaign, saying in public that they have made large contributions to my campaign. I emphatically declare that this is an outright falsehood."[48]

In response, Arnold repeated the charge to the Associated Press and said that Pryor "had been, in effect, secretly endorsed by the Arkansas AFL-CIO." This endorsement was "kept secret at Pryor's own request," Arnold claimed. Pryor had complained about Arnold's "insinuations." Arnold retorted: "I did not insinuate. I stated plainly and directly that David Pryor is, on his own legislative record, a 100 percent pro-union boss representative. I stated plainly and simply that Jimmy Hoffa's teamsters Union had contributed to Mr. Pryor's campaign." Arnold declared that his information about the Teamsters Union's contributions "is based on statements made to me by two witnesses, prominent in the labor movement."[49]

The evening before the election, Pryor charged that Arnold "has dragged the campaign to its lowest depths."[50] He referred to an anonymous letter circulated in several towns in the district, with a mimeographed picture allegedly depicting Pryor meeting with Stokely Carmichael, a well-known black activist in the civil rights movement who had been arrested many times. There is no evidence that Arnold instigated or knew about the circulation, and he denounced it after the election.

Arnold replied with an emphasis on Pryor's legislative record in the Arkansas General Assembly: of fourteen bills Pryor proposed, only two were enacted. "We need a congressman who can make things happen," Arnold said. "The record shows that my opponent cannot."[51]

The final election results were not close: Pryor won the race with about 65 percent of the vote.[52] Pryor would go on to serve three terms in Congress, as governor of Arkansas, and in the United States Senate for eighteen years. "Pryor Rolls Over Arnold in Race for Congressional Seat" was the *Arkansas Democrat*'s headline the next day.[53] Pryor had run the race as a self-styled "reform" candidate. In his six years in the Arkansas House of Representatives, Pryor voted against many bills sponsored by the administration of Governor Faubus.[54] Arnold, by contrast, did not publicly oppose Faubus. Faubus would soon bow out of Arkansas politics, never to return to elective office. Arnold spent an enormous sum at the time—almost all of it through a personal bank loan of $80,000—only to lose the contest.

David Pryor and Richard Arnold were political adversaries for a time, but the two developed a strong friendship with mutual admiration. Pryor's support as a senator was critical for Arnold's later judicial appointments, and Pryor was an early proponent of the view that Richard Arnold deserved to be on the United States Supreme Court.[55]

Brennan commiserated with his young protégé. In a letter addressed to both Richard and Gale, Brennan wrote: "We read the results in this morning's Post and of course were unhappy with them, perhaps even more than you. But it was a magnificent beginning and I do hope you will look upon it only as that."[56]

Over a decade later, a newly elected Senator David Pryor was invited to a small dinner party in Washington, DC. His seating card for the event placed him next to Marjorie Brennan, the wife of Justice William Brennan. When Pryor introduced himself, Mrs. Brennan responded with a laugh, "Yes, I know who you are, and I don't like you because you defeated our friend Richard."[57]

DEMOCRATIC PARTY INSIDER AND CONSTITUTIONAL CONVENTION DELEGATE

Arnold received substantial press coverage in Arkansas not only for his political activities but also for his endeavors as a lawyer. After his election loss to Pryor in 1966, the *Arkansas Gazette* reported that Arnold had been asked to join the faculty of the Columbia School of Law in New York City, but Arnold had turned the post down. Arnold, who was then thirty, said the invitation to join the law school was extended by William C. Warren, dean of the law school. "I told him that I wasn't interested because I felt that far too many people leave Arkansas seeking opportunities and jobs in large cites," Arnold said. "I believe that more people should stay in Arkansas and help build our state." Arnold also said he would like to get back in politics in future years.[58] It was the second time Arnold had declined an invitation to join a law faculty. He had been invited to teach at Harvard after he finished his clerkship with Justice Brennan.

Arnold's loss to Pryor in his first congressional race focused Arnold's efforts on Democratic state politics, and he quickly solidified his position as an important player. He used the next few years to advance his name recognition and to position himself for another race for Congress in the future. Arnold became a member of the Arkansas Democratic State Committee in 1968 and served as the chairman of its rules committee for the next four years. Arnold believed that people like himself, with education, civic virtue, and "integrity based upon Christian morality," should be in politics, a form of noblesse oblige. He also believed political parties were essentially agencies of government, a view that would be an important component of his pathbreaking voting rights decisions as a federal judge.

Arnold's father, Richard Lewis Arnold, was nonplussed by his son's political involvement. Richard Lewis disliked politicians and believed they were all corrupt—he quit voting after Franklin D. Roosevelt was elected president. His wife, the oldest daughter of Senator Morris Sheppard, had been very interested in politics, and as a conservative libertarian held strongly progressive views on racial equality. The younger Richard Arnold was constantly aware of his own political heritage. His great-grandfather, John L. Sheppard, had been a congressman from Texas, and his grandfather, Morris Sheppard, had been both a congressman (1902–1913) and a senator (1913–1941). William Hendrick Arnold and his wife, Arnold's paternal grandparents, were extraordinarily active in political and civil affairs. With Richard Lewis, this type of engagement had skipped a generation. Richard Lewis reportedly said of his son's campaigns for Congress that it was "all right with him" if his son "wanted to waste the best damn legal mind he ever saw."[59]

In recognition of Arnold's service to the state Democratic Party, Senator J. William Fulbright named Arnold as an Arkansas delegate to the

Democratic National Convention of 1968 in Chicago.[60] In his extensive career in the Senate, Fulbright supported racial segregation, the United Nations, and multilateralism, and opposed the war in Vietnam and the House Un-American Activities Committee. In 1966, Fulbright published *The Arrogance of Power*, in which he attacked the justification for the Vietnam War and the failure of Congress to limit it.[61] Arnold had no public position on segregation, but he openly supported the war in Vietnam, a contrary stance to Fulbright's.

Martin Luther King Jr. and Robert Kennedy had been assassinated earlier in 1968, and protests against the Vietnam War occupied much of the national dialogue. Arnold supported Hubert Humphrey, Johnson's vice president, who indicated, at least in the early days of the campaign, that he would stay on Johnson's course with respect to the war. Humphrey secured the Democratic nomination but lost to Richard Nixon in the general election.

Reflecting on the 1968 convention later, Arnold said it was "devastating to the Democratic party." Humphrey's campaign "could never quite recover from the black eye that the media coverage in Chicago gave him." From Arnold's perspective, what happened at the convention "was nothing like what people around the nation were seeing on television." Arnold claimed he did not know that the media had portrayed the antiwar protests as a riot until he returned to Texarkana.[62] Arnold did not sympathize with the protesters. He believed the Vietnam War was justified, as "an essential part of our foreign policy of containment, to keep the Communists from expanding their domination."[63]

One result of the 1968 Democratic National Convention would be a change in the way many southern states, including Arkansas, selected delegates in the future. The Democratic National Committee issued a mandate following the 1968 convention requiring voters to be given more voice in the selection of delegations to the national convention. It also repudiated the "unit rule." Under the "unit rule," all delegates cast their vote as a block, as dictated by party leadership. It was possible for small groups of state party officials to handpick convention delegates, tell them whom to vote for, and, in effect, choose the party nominee without consulting the voters. A concern particularly for southern delegations was exclusion of racial minorities. Since 1939, an Arkansas law provided that delegates for national conventions would be chosen by the state committees of both the Democratic and Republican parties.

Arnold led the change in Arkansas. The 1968 delegates from Arkansas had been handpicked by Senator Fulbright. In a letter to Arnold, Fulbright wrote: "I have put your name on the list as a delegate. I do not anticipate any problem about this."[64] At the state's Democratic convention in 1969, Arnold proposed that all future delegates to the Democratic National Convention be elected by members of the party at large in a primary, with an equal number of delegates coming from each congressional district. Arnold's resolution requested the state general assembly to enact legislation to provide for popular election of delegates and to recognize that the unit rule had been abolished by the Democratic National Committee, a position the state legislature ultimately took.[65]

He had also written the Speaker of the General Assembly in 1967 "to offer some ideas for the future of our Party." The Democrats had recently lost an election for governor—Winthrop Rockefeller, an heir to the Rockefeller oil fortune, had become the first Republican governor in Arkansas since Reconstruction. Only 11 percent of Arkansas voters considered themselves Republicans before his election. Rockefeller defeated a segregationist Arkansas Supreme Court justice, James D. Johnson. Orval Faubus had chosen not to run for reelection after six terms as governor.

Arnold wrote: "We have never really had a political party in Arkansas. But we must develop one now, to meet the organized opposition."[66] Reflecting upon the gubernatorial defeat, Arnold thought the Democratic nominee's campaign had been "too negative," repelling voters. He also said, "Negroes, traditionally a source of Democratic strength, were driven away, apparently intentionally." Arnold added that he "supported the entire Democratic ticket, and even spoke once for our gubernatorial nominee, but I did so only with the greatest difficulty, because I could not dishonor my pledge." (The pledge Arnold referred to required all Arkansas Democratic Party candidates to support all other Democratic nominees in the general election.)

For the future, Arnold believed the state Democratic Party needed to find "a new, progressive, relatively young face" for a party leader, who would emphasize what Arnold considered to be the progressive 1966 platform adopted by the Arkansas Democratic Convention. Perhaps Arnold was subtly suggesting himself for this role. Arnold also thought the Democratic Party in Arkansas needed greater organization. They needed active Democratic clubs in each county, and Arnold urged replacement of the members of the Arkansas Democratic Central Committee "who are old and uninterested."[67]

Governor Rockefeller, as head of the fledgling Republican Party in Arkansas, found it necessary to work with Democrats to accomplish his legislative agenda, and he enlisted Richard Arnold in some of these efforts. Arnold drafted Rockefeller's tax bills during the governor's second term in office, including proposed income tax and sales tax legislation. Among the tax revisions included a graduated income tax credit for individuals, a bill increasing the percentage rate of the income tax for individuals on a sliding scale based on dollars of income, and an income tax for corporations that would set a flat rate of 7 percent. The sales tax proposal would raise the sales tax to 4 percent from 3 percent and provide a graduated rebate of sales tax for low-income Arkansas citizens, and would extend the sales tax to services.[68] Based on the quality of his work, Arnold was engaged for other statutory drafting of Rockefeller initiatives.

Arnold was also one of ten people appointed by Governor Rockefeller to a study commission to consider a new state constitution. A constitutional convention was called in 1969, and Arnold won an elected position as a representative to the constitutional convention. It wasn't a contest—Arnold was unopposed. Still, he must have savored his election—it was the only time he would ever hold an elected office.

The Arkansas Constitution at the time was largely the one adopted in 1874, when there were only five cities in the state that had a population of more than a thousand. Arkansas voters defeated a new state constitution in 1918, although most of the proposed changes from that effort were put into law through a combination of constitutional amendments and legislation.

The convention drafted what would be presented to the voters as the proposed constitution of 1970. Its major provisions included a reorganization of the executive branch, lowering the voting age to eighteen, and home rule for cities, which would be given the power to enact their own ordinances and to levy additional forms of taxes. The proposed constitution lifted constitutional restrictions on salary levels for governor, attorney general, and other state officers. There was also a provision instructing the General Assembly to enact a comprehensive code of ethics for elected and appointed officials.[69]

The convention's deliberations took place during the summer of 1969. A second session met in January 1970. It included a "Declaration of Rights" section that retained or expanded the protections contained in the

1874 constitution. The important additions included specific prohibition against discrimination on the basis of sex; a guarantee of the right of association; protection against unreasonable invasions of privacy; guarantee of a preliminary hearing in felony cases; expansion of protections of criminal defendants in the areas of right to counsel, change of venue, and double jeopardy; and a broadening of the ability of individuals to file suit against the government when it was alleged that the government had acted illegally.[70] It was one of the first state constitutions to propose an Equal Rights Amendment for women, advocated by the National Organization for Women, a group formed in 1966.

The convention also proposed to replace the system for electing judges with an appointment process. Arnold fully supported appointment, rather than popular election, of state judges. On the first vote, the proposal was defeated 47 to 39, but Arnold was optimistic that he could get enough votes to reverse the position, and he enlisted his father-in-law, Walter Hussman, owner of numerous publishing interests in Arkansas, in his campaign.[71] The second attempt failed by six votes, with a vote of 41 for and 47 against. The proposal to appoint judges rather than elect them ultimately failed at the convention, but the provision for nonpartisan judicial elections would succeed in subsequent legislation.[72] Compensation of all court officials based on fees resulting from convictions was prohibited, and judges were prohibited from practicing law to avoid conflicts of interest. The proposed constitution also called for a judicial ethics commission.

What were some of Arnold's other positions? In letters preserved in his papers, Arnold agreed that the voting age should be lowered to eighteen.[73] He opposed repeal of the Right-to-Work law, a position consistent with his earlier campaign for Congress. As he explained in a letter to the Little Rock Typographical Union, "I simply believe that a person should have the right to make for himself the choice whether to join any organization."[74] The AFL-CIO of Arkansas opposed the proposal to keep Amendment 34, which it termed the "Right to Wreck" law, in the Constitution.[75]

Other letters in the file, from business owners and the Arkansas State Chamber of Commerce, praise Arnold's stance: "We convey the particular gratitude of the business and industrial community for your courageous and effective efforts on the Convention floor in defending Amendment 34.[76] Every person in Arkansas who values the right to work owes you a debt of gratitude which we hereby express on their behalf."[77]

On a local level, in some ways Arnold was the James Madison of the proposed Arkansas constitution. He was on the executive committee and drafting committee, drafted many of its provisions, and engaged in a lobbying campaign to convince Arkansas voters in the 1970 general election that a new constitution was needed. He encouraged his father-in-law to publish in each of his newspapers the full text of the proposed constitution, and wrote separately to other newspapers in the state, asking them to do the same. The state's major newspapers complied and published the proposed constitution in its entirety in special supplements, often with the preamble in large type: "We, the people of the State of Arkansas, grateful to Almighty God for the privilege of choosing our own form of government and for our civil and religious liberty, and desiring to perpetuate and secure these blessings to ourselves and our posterity, do ordain and establish this Constitution."[78]

Arnold also appeared on a live television program on January 5, 1970, on the Arkansas Constitutional Convention, broadcast in Little Rock and carried on other television stations in the state. His speaking tour included Rotary clubs throughout the state.[79] Former governor Sid McMath told Arnold, after reading the draft, that it would be "one of your greater contributions to our State and its people." McMath urged extensive effort toward its passage, acknowledging the "tremendous contribution" Arnold expended in drafting a constitution "that will enable us to grow and prosper in the Twentieth Century."[80]

Arnold enjoyed the work immensely, but the constitution they wrote was defeated by Arkansas voters. It was too much, too soon, for Arkansas voters. G. Thomas Eisele, a convention delegate and later federal judge, believed the constitutional provisions should have been presented to voters not as a package deal but piecemeal over time. The unobjectionable and much-needed reforms in the proposed constitution lost out to a combination of objections, ranging from the labor and usury provisions to the equal rights statement for women. Parts of the 1970 constitution eventually succeeded by legislation and individual constitutional amendment.[81]

In another indication of Arnold's political views, in 1970 he joined nearly two hundred former Supreme Court law clerks in a letter to members of the United States Senate in opposition to Richard Nixon's nomination of Judge Harrold Carswell to the Supreme Court. Carswell was Nixon's second nominee to fill the seat of Abe Fortas. The first, Clement Haynesworth, was rejected by the Senate. Carswell, a Georgia native and a federal judge on the Fifth Circuit, received strong support from southern senators but was criticized for his civil rights record, including his support for racial segregation when he was a candidate for the Georgia legislature.

The law clerks who joined the letter in opposition to Carswell served justices as far back as Oliver Wendell Holmes and Louis Brandeis. The letter did not mention Carswell's civil rights positions but said, "We are all united in our conviction of the importance of the Supreme Court as an American institution and are similarly united in our opposition to the confirmation of Judge Carswell." Carswell, the letter stated, "is not equal to these responsibilities. The record shows him to be of mediocre ability." It concluded with the admonition that "[c]onfirmation of Judge Carswell would be a disservice to the Court and the nation."[82]

Whether the law clerks' letter had any influence is unknown, but in any event Carswell's nomination was defeated by the Senate by a vote of 51 to 45. Nixon then nominated Harry Blackmun, a judge on the Eighth US Circuit Court of Appeals. Blackmun, Nixon's third choice, was easily confirmed. When Arnold was named to the Eighth Circuit in 1980, Blackmun served as its circuit justice, beginning a warm relationship between the two. When Justice Blackmun retired in 1994, Arnold was a prominent contender for his seat on the Supreme Court.

SECOND CONGRESSIONAL RACE: 1972

In his first race for Congress, Arnold raised very little money from campaign contributions. Instead, he largely financed the campaign on his own. He spent about $110,000 on the race and ended up owing $80,000 on a bank loan for which his father-in-law, Walter Hussman, signed the note. Arnold struggled to pay interest on the note, and eventually Hussman bought the note from the bank, extending an interest-free loan to Arnold.[83] Arnold's income from his law practice in 1968 was $31,000—a good year—but that amount varied from year to year.[84] In an interview in 1969, Arnold said he hoped to run for Congress again if Pryor decided not to seek reelection, but he did not know whether he could because he did not have the money and could not borrow $80,000 again.[85] Arnold's debt to Hussman was not fully paid until the beginning of 1978.[86]

Pryor had no opposition in 1968 or 1970 but was considering running for the Senate against the entrenched incumbent, John L. McClellan, in 1972. Arnold said if Pryor sought reelection to the House, he would not oppose Pryor because "one, I think he's doing a pretty good job, and two, I don't think I could beat him."[87] Arnold soon had his opportunity, and somehow he found the money to finance another campaign. In 1972, David Pryor opted to leave his seat in Congress in order to run against McClellan. (Pryor would lose that race, although he would eventually be elected to that seat after McClellan's death and after having served as governor of Arkansas.)

Arnold moved with alacrity to announce for the congressional seat. Six years had passed since Arnold's loss to Pryor. "I've been running for it ever since 1966," Arnold said. "I've always intended to run for it again."[88] He also portrayed himself as having learned something from his prior loss: "Defeat has been a useful experience for me. I learned from it—about myself, about other people, and about the Fourth Congressional District. Since that time, I have consciously and deliberately prepared myself to seek the same office again."[89]

Arnold was thirty-five years old when he ran for Congress a second time. In the interim, Arnold had served in the Arkansas Constitutional Convention in 1969 and 1970, and had established a reputation as one of the leading environmental lawyers in the United States. His main opponent of the three others in the race was Arkansas attorney general Ray Thornton. Thornton had already won a statewide election as attorney general.

Were there any significant changes in Arnold's political positions for this race? The most striking was his advocacy for environmentalism, which made him an early proponent of the environmental movement. Arnold said he supported the conservation of natural resources "and the preservation of natural areas for generations to come."[90] He publicly opposed the construction of the Gilham Dam on the Cossatot River, a cause he was also representing for the Environmental Defense Fund. It was widely known then that Arnold had obtained a federal court injunction temporarily halting the dam. His positions in these cases lost votes for him in some circles, as he acknowledged.[91] He tempered his public campaign statements with the caveat "People unfortunately tend to identify lawyers with their clients. I think this is wrong, but I know people do it. I've always tried to handle controversial cases on a purely professional basis without regard to whether it helps or hurts any political possibilities. I think it's wrong for a lawyer to shrink from representing a client because he fears unpopularity."[92]

Another striking difference was that Arnold now supported a "quick end" to the Vietnam War, but with "a delay of any discussions of amnesty for draft evaders while Americans were still fighting in Vietnam." His position on the war in Vietnam had changed quite a bit since 1966. Was he merely tracking the political winds or had some other happening changed his view? Arnold was at least more consistent with Senator Fulbright's position at this point.

Arnold also told a group at Henderson State College that he did not think President Nixon's proposed moratorium on busing of students to achieve racial balance was a valid approach to the problem. He said the proposal "discriminated against the South." "It appears to leave in effect busing orders that are already in effect in the South while preventing future orders of this type in other parts of the country." But he also questioned imposing limits on the courts. "To me, an independent court system in the long run is much more important than temporary issues like busing. I will not support any legislation that would unduly restrict the independence of the courts, state or federal."[93] Just over one year earlier, on February 20, 1970, an estimated twenty-five thousand people had marched to the Arkansas Capitol in Little Rock against integration and busing.[94] So Arnold's position on busing appears to have opposed the current of sentiment among the white population in Arkansas.

Beyond his position on busing, Arnold did not address issues of school integration arising from *Brown v. Board of Education.* Throughout his campaign Arnold made it clear that he was no segregationist. South Arkansas was also the congressional district with the largest population of African Americans, and it was necessary to seek their votes. For example, although Arnold advocated a law-and-order approach to crime, stating that wrongdoers must be punished "swiftly and surely," he was careful to distinguish his use of "law and order" from George Wallace's use of that term, which Arnold said "meant repression of Negroes."[95]

Arnold was not a glad-handing, outgoing politician as was needed for success at the polls. Once again, his reserved, intellectual manner did not mesh well with the rhetoric he employed in campaign speeches. One illustration of his approach, for example, was his contention: "Too often, the cries of the people do not reach the halls of the United States Congress."[96] To close the gap, Arnold proposed a "home folks hot-line which will enable the people I represent to call me free of charge, and tell me what they feel is needed for our district, our state, and our nation."[97] "Home folks" rhetoric and Arnold's eastern elite education seemed jarring in combination.

A boost for his electoral prospects came from the *Pine Bluff Commercial*, which endorsed Arnold's candidacy in May 1972. The editorial praised Arnold's environmental work, his work on the *Hawkins* case in Conway County, and the state Constitutional Convention. "Richard Arnold ran for Congress last time in 1966. And from the quality of his campaign this time out, it is clear that he has grown in perception, experience and in his apprehension of what is important. Since 1966, Richard Arnold has established his credentials on issues close to home. And he hasn't picked the automatically popular ones, either," especially Arnold's position on the Gilham Dam. "Richard Arnold is no glad-hander, never will be, but there is a depth and understanding behind his competence that the people of this district, and maybe of the country, have need of."[98]

It is not clear where Arnold's campaign funds came from for his second race. It was not a half-hearted campaign, but there were very real financial constraints for advertising. In the few television advertisements in Arnold's campaign, Arnold never apologized for or downplayed his education. One television advertisement for Arnold's campaign that year featured pictures of Arnold at Yale and Harvard Law School and noted he had graduated from both with high honors.[99] The television copy directed "pictures of Arnold's family in outdoor locations, a film of an Arkansas lake with a man fishing," while an Arnold voiceover talked about "the damage of pollution." The script specifies additional pictures of Arnold campaigning: Arnold in office, with "middle aged types, black, farm type, young couple, etc."[100]

Arnold's speeches in the 1972 campaign reveal a more introspective focus. Of his first race, Arnold said: "I was 29 years old then and fired with imaginative ideas for restoring basic virtues to American public life while adjusting rapidly to the change we cannot escape. These basic virtues were then—and still are—respect for an honest day's work, a desire to do the right thing, a surprising capacity for investigation and improvisation, a willingness to live under the rule of law, a willingness to contribute to public welfare, and a kind of naive trust in the destiny of the nation."

The speeches also reflect an interesting focus on the process of historical change. This was first of all apparent in the economy: "At the time of my announcement in 1966 it was almost impossible to convince voters there was any need for a change in our national direction." The reason for this, Arnold said, was that the nation had just experienced a five-year period of economic prosperity. Federal spending was held reasonably in check and the economy benefited. But "storm clouds were already gathering on the horizon in 1966 and the situation soon changed drastically." The worst manifestations of this change, said Arnold, were inflation, job insecurity, and unemployment.

Second, the process of historical change encompassed social and political relations:

> In 1966 you first heard the phrase "Black power." A year later, in 1967, you were confronted by "Burn, baby, burn." Kent State shocked the land in 1970. During these past six years you and I awoke each morning to a daily dosage of unrest and denunciation. We witnessed the rise of an army of extremists with a vested interest in despair. They tried to portray every black American as a loather of white men, and all people under 25 as wreckers of the public order. They painted an ugly portrait of America.[101]

The solution to the problems was "to restore the basic virtues upon which this great nation was founded." Those values included welfare reform: "We should remove the unfair income limitations on Social Security payments," Arnold said. "I think it is wrong to give a person an incentive not to work. And that's what we're doing to people on Social Security." Arnold criticized current social security legislation because "an individual's payments are reduced if he earns money," he said. "That's wrong—both for those people and our nation."[102] But he also viewed poverty to be the greatest problem facing Arkansas at the time.[103] He also called for tax reform because the burden of taxation was "not fairly spread." Arnold wanted a minimum tax because he felt that many high-income people paid no taxes.[104]

In 1972, his second campaign for Congress, Arnold did not even force a run-off election. Thornton's showing, according to press reports, was "a display of surprising strength."[105] Thornton received 67,321 votes compared to Arnold's 39,421. The other two candidates in the race together received about 20,000 votes.[106] Thornton easily won the general election against a Republican challenger and went on to serve six terms in Congress. Later Thornton would become a justice of the Arkansas Supreme Court.

Arnold believed he could win this time because of his strong second-place showing in the earlier race against Pryor. "I was sort of everybody's second choice in 1966," Arnold said in an interview. "Many people tell me: 'You did well before and this is your time.'" He told the reporter before the run-off election, "We're winning. This is my time."[107] The two cadidates receiving the fewest votes had criticized Arnold "because he is the son-in-law of Walter Hussman, owner of the Palmer Media Group, a chain of newspapers and television stations."[108]

Earl Jones, then a thirty-four-year-old Texarkana department store executive, served as Arnold's campaign manager for his second congressional race. Jones recalled when Arnold was campaigning that each Saturday morning Arnold would visit his law firm to go over with his partners questions and problems that had arisen over the past week. Arnold was able to cut through the complex and large stack of work quickly and advise other attorneys there how to handle the finishing touches on the work. This resulted in "a high volume of work Arnold was able to carry on in the campaign at full pace," according to Jones.[109]

Meanwhile, Richard and Gale's second daughter, Lydia, was born in 1969. Along with raising their two young daughters, Gale took an active role in Richard's second campaign. Gale and Earl Jones had disagreements on a number of items during Arnold's political race. Most of the time Arnold sided with Jones, which may have created some ill feelings on the part of Gale Arnold toward him, Jones later recounted. A few years later Richard and Gale would divorce. Jones was called as a witness in those proceedings and was asked by Richard's lawyer whether Gale Arnold had lost the 1972 election for Arnold. Jones said he had to answer no to that question, but he wanted to qualify his answer. In his opinion, Arnold lost the race not because of Gale Arnold, although "she may have lost some votes for him," but because voters mistakenly labeled Arnold as an "eastern liberal" due to nothing more than the fact that Arnold had attended Yale and Harvard.

The "eastern liberal" label was also a common perception for his younger brother, Morris Arnold, who helped with Richard's campaigns for Congress. Although Morris earned a law degree from the University of Arkansas, he had also graduated from Phillips Exeter and Yale. Morris then earned an LLM and an SJD from Harvard before joining the law faculty at the University of Pennsylvania. One attorney told an FBI agent investigating Richard Arnold's background for his appointment to the federal court that Morris Arnold was, he thought, "a law professor teaching somewhere in the East."[110] Another said he believed Morris was "a law professor at some eastern university." Similar to Jones's observation about perceptions of Richard Arnold, these comments reflect a provincial suspicion of the East Coast establishment. Earlier in the 1960s, Arizona senator Barry Goldwater articulated this sentiment for a larger part of the nation when he told a Washington, DC, newspaper, "Sometimes I think this country would be better off if we could just saw off the Eastern Seaboard and let it float out to sea."[111]

ARNOLD MEETS FUTURE SENATOR DALE BUMPERS

One observer of Arnold's race for Congress was Dale Bumpers, who had assumed office as governor of Arkansas in 1971. In the future, Bumpers would be responsible for Arnold's appointment to the federal bench. As Bumpers described meeting Arnold:

> I first met Richard in 1969. He was a delegate to the seventh Arkansas State Constitutional Convention, which was in session at the State Capitol. I had driven the 135 miles from my little hometown of Charleston to Little Rock to lay plans for a trial with my co-counsel, a Little Rock lawyer, who was also a delegate. I went out to the capitol, and as I walked in the same entrance I would later use almost every morning for four years, Richard was coming out. I recognized him from pictures I had seen of him when he had previously campaigned for Congress. I introduced myself and asked if he had seen the lawyer I was seeking. He said he had just seen him and promptly offered to help me find him, which he did. I thanked him, and we parted.[112]

Arnold never considered running against Bumpers after he was elected governor, although some people had suggested that Arnold should run for that office. Arnold was quoted in an Arkansas newspaper as saying Bumpers had done "a brilliant job" in his first months in office. "And I don't mind admitting that I'm surprised. I never dreamed . . . there was as much substance to the man as there is."[113]

Soon after Arnold lost the race for Congress to Ray Thornton, Bumpers enlisted Arnold's help to further his legislative agenda with the

Arkansas General Assembly. Continuing his private law practice for a time, in 1973 Arnold became legislative counsel to the governor. For the next two years Arnold was Bumpers's right-hand man for legislative work. Arnold supervised the drafting of his program of administration bills, supervised lobbying on behalf of the administration with the Arkansas Senate and House, read each bill that passed the General Assembly, advised the governor whether or not to sign the bills, and drafted a veto message if Bumpers decided to disapprove a bill. He also gave Bumpers general legal advice on numerous issues involving the Constitution and laws of Arkansas from 1971 through 1974.[114]

Arnold also helped Bumpers in his race against J. William Fulbright for the United States Senate. He announced in advance of the general election that he would accompany Bumpers to Washington if Bumpers were to win. Speculation about Arnold's decision to go with Bumpers began when legal clients received letters from him, advising that Arnold would be unable to represent them after January 1. Arnold said that Bumpers had asked him in March to accompany him to Washington—before the governor had announced his candidacy for the Senate seat. "I don't know what capacity I'll be there in," Arnold said. "I'll just do whatever he needs me to do."[115]

In August 1974, Arnold wrote to Brennan about his plans to accompany the future senator:

> I will soon be coming back to Washington. Dale Bumpers, with whom I have become close friends during the last two years, is now the Democratic nominee for the United States Senate and, assuming that he survives token Republican opposition in November, will take his seat in January. Soon after he began his campaign he told me that he would not go to Washington without me. This, of course, was an exaggeration on his part, but he nevertheless did quite forcefully request that I become a member of his staff, and I have agreed to do so.[116]

Arnold hoped there would be an opportunity for Brennan to meet Bumpers: "You will agree with me, I am sure, that he is an extraordinary individual, both as a man and as a public servant. It is not too much praise, in fact, to say that he is in a class with you and Gerry Gesell."[117]

The same letter included a handwritten postscript: "P.S. I sued Gale for divorce. A very painful but correct decision. I wanted you to know as a friend. RSA."[118]

A missing topic in the record of Arnold's political activities—striking in retrospect—is any debate or commentary on the most significant transformative event of the 1960s, what author Anthony Lewis described as "The Second American Revolution." As Lewis described in his book *Portrait of a Decade*, this revolution culminated in the passage by Congress of the landmark Civil Rights Act of 1964, followed by the Voting Rights Act of 1965.[119] As a politician, Arnold never commented publicly on what he thought about this fundamental realignment of federal versus state control, or its potential to transform American society.

Arnold's two races for Congress took place in the Arkansas district with the highest percentage of blacks in the state, at least in terms of population. But blacks were a minority of voters compared to the white voters in the district. While Arnold did not ignore them, and in fact took pains to court their votes,[120] none of the candidates in those races seem to have campaigned either for or against racial equality, at least publicly. As Arnold put it later, he was told by older political "experts": "'If you're going to campaign, it's all right to ask for their vote. You go at night, and you go in somebody else's car so you won't be recognized on the way to and from wherever the meeting would be.' The whites knew that you wanted the black vote but they didn't want it thrown up to them. I went all over the district and spoke in black churches, and David Pryor did, too."

Arnold avoided public statements in favor of civil rights. In fact, in the 1966 campaign the Student Non-Violent Coordinating Committee, a group known by the acronym "SNCC," endorsed David Pryor over Richard Arnold. According to Arnold, SNCC sent a newsletter to the black community endorsing Pryor. Pryor was known as a liberal for opposing Faubus. Arnold, by contrast, was viewed with suspicion by some in the black community because of his law firm's representations of business interests, which Arnold thought "terribly unfair."[121] It was emblematic of Arnold's personal quandary at the time. He had not publicly opposed Faubus because he saw that as the route to political success in Arkansas. Pryor chose the opposite tack. But neither candidate explicitly took on the segregationist elite.

More than twenty-five years later, Arnold's two races for Congress would become of great interest to President Bill Clinton's White House staff.

At that time Arnold was very publicly in contention for a seat on the Supreme Court. Researchers in the White House counsel's office pulled newspaper articles about the races from archives and annotated some of them, as part of the vetting process. Presumably, they were looking for potentially controversial stances taken by Arnold in his campaigns.[122]

Arnold's political activities and campaigns for Congress took place alongside his successful and ambitious law practice. Arnold appreciated the legislative role—firmly believing it to be the superior lawmaker—and often deferred to state and federal legislation as a judge. The most striking shift in political views was on the propriety of the war in Vietnam. He maintained his view of federalism and states' rights and exhibited a willingness to criticize Supreme Court actions. He believed his engagement in politics made him a better judge: "I met literally thousands of Arkansas people and became familiar with their personal situations in a way that I never would have as a practicing attorney."[123]

While his political activities may have done little more than that in terms of the core of his judicial philosophy once on the bench, he also made the political connections that were necessary for his appointment as a federal judge. "After my second defeat," Arnold later wrote, "my ideas about public service turned to other branches of government."[124] Arnold put in place a series of relationships he would not have had based solely on his law practice. Arnold's activities in Democratic politics led to his fortuitous association with Dale Bumpers, who would put him on the federal court.

Chapter Five

= *Appointment to the US District Court* =

Those who knew Richard Arnold as a judge have difficulty imagining him in any other career. His demeanor—often described as shy and retiring, intellectually oriented—rarely struck others as that of a natural-born politician, and electoral defeats in two congressional races seem to bear this out. His life's work, instead, became his devotion to the federal judiciary. Arnold himself would say that if he wanted to be in public service, it had become clear to him that he needed an appointed office rather than an elected one.[1]

But seats on the federal judiciary are highly sought after, rarely obtained by most who desire them. A federal judicial appointment is not altogether different from other types of office seeking that occur with each change of party alignment in the White House. Whatever other qualifications one brings to the table, becoming a federal judge is largely dependent upon politically cultivated ties. It also requires being in the right place at the right time, and a great deal of luck.

Because Richard Arnold was identified with the Democratic Party, there was only a narrow window—one presidential term, as it would turn out—between 1969 and 1993 in which he could have been appointed to the federal bench. During that quarter century, the Democrats held the

White House for only four years, from 1977 to 1981, until Bill Clinton became president in 1993. Arnold's confirmation to the court of appeals for the Eighth Circuit, where he would make his most important contributions, occurred on the eve of the Reagan presidency. In his eight years in office, Ronald Reagan did not appoint any person affiliated with the Democratic Party to the court of appeals, and George H. W. Bush followed the Reagan example.[2]

If it took an alignment of stars for Richard Arnold to become a federal judge, that alignment was the confluence of Jimmy Carter's election, a Democrat-controlled Senate, Griffin Bell as attorney general, and, most important, the influence of a freshman senator from Arkansas, Dale Bumpers. And three of these four factors were highly unexpected. Bumpers had served as governor of Arkansas for four years, gaining the post by defeating both former governor Orval Faubus, in the Democratic primary, and Republican incumbent Winthrop Rockefeller. Bumpers then took on the powerful five-term senator J. William Fulbright in 1974. Fulbright had been a leading senator from Arkansas for nearly thirty years and was the longest-serving chairman in the history of the Senate Foreign Relations Committee. Initially a distinct underdog in the Senate race, Bumpers scored a remarkable victory with his defeat of Fulbright in the Democratic primary. Bumpers quickly became a rising political star in the national Democratic Party. He was featured in *Time* magazine in 1974 as "the most promising politician in the South—a region that, as it moderates its once extremist politics, is fast rejoining the mainstream of the Democratic Party."[3] Bumpers would hold his Senate seat until he decided not to seek reelection in 1999.

Richard Arnold's second defeat for a seat in Congress ended his quest for elected political office, but it did not lessen his involvement in politics. He continued to serve in the state Democratic Party leadership, and more important, in 1973 became a key aide to Dale Bumpers, whose race for governor of Arkansas was successful before Arnold's race for Congress had failed. Bumpers knew Arnold and had followed the congressional contest; after Arnold's defeat Bumpers called him to ask for assistance with his legislative agenda as governor.

Arnold had also worked for Bumpers on his 1974 Senate campaign and he readily agreed to accompany Bumpers to Washington to serve as his legislative aide. Arnold's decision surprised some of his friends. Arnold's résumé was vastly superior to that of the typical Senate staffer. Arnold was still a major player in Arkansas politics and had a successful and varied law practice. He had wanted to be in Washington as an elected official himself. Serving in Bumpers's Senate office was perhaps the next best thing, because he could still play an important role in shaping legislation. At thirty-eight, Arnold was still young enough to postpone his own political ambitions for a few years, even if his own childhood dream to be a senator was at least put on hold. After two electoral defeats, another campaign probably no longer appealed to Arnold, and he still owed money to his father-in-law for an election loan to finance his first race for Congress.

In part, Arnold's decision to accompany Bumpers to Washington reflected a need for change in his personal circumstances. He had begun divorce proceedings at about this time. And for both Arnold and Bumpers, a great friendship, with mutual respect, was the driving factor. But there was also a hope that his connection with Senator Bumpers might be turned into a federal judicial appointment. Only a few friends remembered his decision to move to Washington to be connected to an ambition to become a federal judge. Neither Arnold nor Bumpers suggested that they had such an advance agreement or understanding. According to Bumpers, the two did not discuss any "deal" in exchange for Arnold's service. Arnold, he said, did not talk about his ambition to become a federal judge. "That's just something that was a given. I knew Richard well enough to know that anybody with his legal mind would automatically want to be on the federal court. And I wanted him to be there."[4]

Arnold served on Senator Bumpers's staff in Washington, DC, for nearly four years, from 1974 through 1978. Bumpers described Arnold's role as "much more than a Legislative Aide—he was more of a Chief Counsel," his "right arm" on all legislative matters. Arnold drafted all of Bumpers's proposed legislation and amendments. When a piece of legislation required Bumpers's vote, Arnold would read the bill in its entirety and make a judgment about whether particular paragraphs or phrases would accomplish what the bill's author intended. Arnold also read each bill to call attention to parts that he thought were particularly relevant to Bumpers.[5]

Arnold was not only a remarkable scholar of constitutional law and history, according to Bumpers, he was also adept with the procedural rules of Congress. Arcane and difficult, parliamentary procedure in the Senate was often a critical part of the success or failure of a proposed bill. Arnold knew the rules inside and out. Where Bumpers had little interest in Senate rules ("in a sense, they bored me," he said), Arnold knew precisely what he was talking about. "And only somebody with a mind like Richard's could master the rules of the Senate, almost as a side-line," Bumpers said. "He had a remarkable, remarkable mind, in things like that."[6]

Arnold loved the atmosphere of the Senate. He quickly gained a reputation among other senators and their staffs for his knowledge of proposed bills and legislative procedures. The other Arkansas senator at the time, Kaneaster Hodges Jr., said that Arnold was "the most highly respected man that has ever served as an Administrative Aide in Washington. You can't imagine the number of United States senators that would come by Dale Bumpers' desk on the floor of the Senate and ask 'Where is Richard Arnold; I have a question.' They didn't ask Dale."[7]

First a job requirement and then a favorite pastime for the remainder of his life, Arnold read the daily issues of the *Congressional Record*, the official records of proceedings and debates of Congress. Later, when he was a judge, Arnold continued to read the *Congressional Record* almost religiously. He would include the relevant page from the *Record* in congratulatory correspondence to federal appointees whom he knew, especially newly appointed judges, and he would on occasion write to Senator Bumpers about legislative matters Arnold found interesting. Arnold knew the currents of statutory proposals even as he decided cases under existing laws. He also knew keeping close track of legislative matters was important for his later work with Congress to present the annual budget requests for the federal courts, a position Arnold would frankly concede to be lobbying for the interests of the federal judiciary.[8]

Bumpers relied on Arnold to such a great extent that "one of the most difficult things I ever did was to make him a federal judge. He was so absolutely crucial to me and so important to what I thought was my role in the Senate. But I knew that was his lifelong ambition, and I knew once I put him on the federal court that he was on his way to becoming a Supreme Court Justice."[9]

Arnold's potential appointment as a federal judge does not seem to have been a topic of conversation among Bumpers's staff. Robert Brown, later a justice of the Arkansas Supreme Court, also worked for Bumpers and shared a daily ride with Arnold to and from the Senate office building. In the early years of Bumpers's first term in the Senate, Brown "sensed the matter was in the works," but Arnold never mentioned a possible judicial appointment. But the groundwork was being laid, according to Brown, simply because the way one became a federal judge then (and now) is through a United States senator, and "Richard certainly paid his dues." Arnold was no Machiavelli, according to Brown, "but the fact is, that is the way you get an appointment."[10]

Arnold probably did go to Washington with Senator Bumpers with the hope of ultimately receiving a federal judicial appointment. Arnold had discussed the possibility with his Yale classmate Gilbert S. Merritt. When Merritt's nomination for the Sixth Circuit Court of Appeals was proposed in the fall of 1977, Richard called Merritt from Washington. He told Merritt that he was legislative assistant for Dale Bumpers and that he had seen Merritt's nomination and wanted to know if there was anything that he could do to help expedite it. According to Merritt, "He said to me that there was going to be a vacancy in the district court in Little Rock sometime soon, and that he was hopeful that he would be appointed."[11]

CARTER'S PRIORITIES; ARNOLD'S NOMINATION

In later years Arnold would refer to his appointment as a federal judge on the basis of "merit": "My merit was that I worked for a United States Senator." As Arnold told the story, one day in 1978, word came that a vacancy had occurred on the federal district court in Little Rock. "A few days later, the Senator called me into his office, and he said, 'Richard, fix up a letter to the President recommending you to be United States District Judge.'"[12] Arnold would later say that he promptly prepared "a hell of a letter—the finest, most fulsome, most eloquent letter ever sent by a United States Senator."[13]

Arnold referred to the Carter years as "a kinder and gentler time," in which a federal judge could even be effectively confirmed on an elevator. As Arnold related,

> One day when Senator Bumpers and I got on the elevator in the Dirksen Senate Office Building, who should come on with us but the powerful James O. Eastland, chairman of the Senate Judiciary Committee. And so we got on the elevator and Dale said, "Jim, Richard here,"—and he jerked his thumb at me—"Richard here has been nominated to be District

Judge, and I want you to confirm him." And Senator Eastland looked at him, and he said, "Whatever you say, Dale." Then we got down to the bottom of the building and it was time to get off of the elevator. The doors opened up, and Eastland looked at me and said, "After you, Judge."[14]

The next step, as Arnold would relate, was an interview at the Department of Justice. In June 1978, a few days after Bumpers notified the White House that he wished to nominate Arnold for the Little Rock vacancy, Arnold received a call to appear at the Department of Justice. "I thought they would ask me what my judicial philosophy was," Arnold remarked. "I didn't have one. But I was most relieved when only two questions were put to me: 'Was I breathing?' and 'Did I come from the Senator?' Because I was able to answer yes to both of those questions, I was duly nominated by the President for the District Court bench."[15]

Arnold told these stories because he had a great sense of humor and a self-deprecating style. But he also characterized his appointment in this way to deflate the pretensions of some of his colleagues about their own appointment process. Judges, Arnold thought, had a tendency to view their colleagues' nomination process as overtly political, even seeing some as political "hacks" otherwise unqualified to be federal judges, while believing their own appointments to have come about solely because of merit. Arnold would tell these stories about his own appointment to lessen pomposity about such matters.

Judicial appointments were certainly political—a judicial nominee had to have the support of the home-state senators, and at least one of those senators needed to have access to the president and attorney general. But by any criteria, Arnold was an excellent appointment to the bench. Arnold had been an academic star at every institution he attended. He had substantial experience as a lawyer, including both civil and criminal trials. Attorneys who had worked with him, at both Covington & Burling in Washington, DC, and in Arkansas, praised his abilities and his professionalism. Arnold had a publication record that would be the envy of law professors—his articles had appeared in the *Harvard Law Review*, the *Yale Law Journal*, the *Virginia Law Review*, the *Antitrust Law Journal*,[16] and his pivotal article on litigation under the Environmental Protection Act had recently been published in the *Environmental Law Review*,[17] an important source for practitioners.

Arnold's subsequent Senate confirmation looked remarkably easy, and in many ways it was. Arnold's appointment received a unanimously favorable recommendation from the Senate Judiciary Committee, and he was confirmed by the full Senate on a voice vote with no recorded negatives. For the district court appointment, the Department of Justice initiated its background check in July 1978. Just two months later, Arnold had been confirmed by the Senate and had received his commission as a federal district judge.

There was, of course, more to it than that. Richard Arnold was the only judge to be appointed twice during Jimmy Carter's one-term presidency—first to the federal district court in Arkansas and then, within one year, to the Eighth Circuit Court of Appeals. Arnold's two appointments as a federal judge occurred at a time when candidates for the lower federal courts were beginning to receive scrutiny on certain political views from the White House. Moreover, as described below, there was a substantial vetting process that involved the Department of Justice, the Federal Bureau of Investigation, and the Senate Judiciary Committee.

Still, appointments to federal trials and appeals courts were not Supreme Court appointments, historically subject to intense public scrutiny. (Carter had no opportunity during his term to fill a Supreme Court vacancy). Further, in the crush of business resulting from a large number of judicial nominees, the Senate Judiciary Committee could afford relatively little investigation of applicants if the positions were to be filled. In all, Carter appointed 258 federal judges in four years. One reason for this was the creation of 117 new federal trial judges and 35 new appellate judges by Congress in the Omnibus Judgeship Act of 1978.

One feature of Carter's 1976 presidential campaign had been his pledge to place a larger number of women and minorities on the federal courts. Prior to Carter's presidency, only six women had ever been appointed as federal judges. Carter appointed forty women. His record for minority appointments was equally impressive. Carter appointed fifty-five ethnic minorities during his four-year term, dwarfing the number (thirty-three) that had been appointed to the federal bench in all prior administrations.[18] Judicial appointments would be an important aspect of Carter's legacy.

THE CIVIL RIGHTS LITMUS TEST

It is common to chart the beginnings of political litmus tests for judicial candidates in the Reagan era. It is certainly true that the rancor surrounding appointments, especially at lower court levels, increased dramatically after the Senate rejection of the nomination of Robert Bork for the United States Supreme Court. Indeed, the political face of the federal judiciary— including the Eighth Circuit—would undergo a profound transformation with Republican-appointed judges. Under President Clinton, the relationship between the Republican-controlled Senate and the White House over judicial nominees deteriorated to the point that Chief Justice William Rehnquist called attention to the appointments crisis in his State of the Judiciary Address in 1998. Rehnquist singled out primarily the Senate as the "problem" in the large number of court vacancies.[19]

But there was also a "litmus test" of a sort for judges appointed during the Carter years. The criteria became an examination of the candidate's views on civil rights. President Carter was already on record as being interested in the civil rights views of all potential judicial nominees. Combined with Carter's stated preference for women and minorities, some southern senators "saw this as a euphemism for liberal judicial activism."[20]

A question of great interest was the candidate's neutrality on racial issues. By this time, it was clear that an important role for federal courts had become civil rights. This shift in the traditional role of the federal courts followed enactment of the Civil Rights Acts in the 1960s and key constitutional interpretations of the Warren Court. Institutional reform litigation, putting prisons and schools under federal judicial control, became a feature of constitutional work. The question from that point forward would be whether gains in recognition of civil rights as protected by federal courts would continue and solidify or be rolled back.

Whatever arrangements might be made between Attorney General Griffin Bell and the Carter White House, there was still the matter of Senate confirmation, and the first hurdle to clear would be the Senate Judiciary Committee. Edward "Ted" Kennedy would follow Senator Eastland as chair of the Senate Judiciary Committee, and Kennedy was a potential rival to Carter for the 1980 Democratic presidential nomination. The committee questionnaire for nominees included, at Kennedy's insistence, the question "In what specific ways have you demonstrated a commitment to equal justice during your career?"[21]

The Judiciary Committee's questionnaire was not quite the elaborate judicial philosophy survey it would become in later years, but the question about equal rights was pointed. In later years, for example, the Republican-controlled committee inserted into the questionnaire a solicitation of candidates' views on "judicial activism." The contrast with the question-naire from the Carter era is stark. Designed as much to shape the candidate's response as to actually elicit meaningful views, the question is lengthy but makes for an interesting comparison with the relative brevity of Kennedy's question about demonstrated commitment to equal justice:

> Please discuss your views on the following criticism involving "judicial activism."
>
> The role of the Federal judiciary within the Federal government, and within society generally, has become the subject of increasing contro-versy in recent years. It has become the target of both popular and aca-demic criticism that alleges that the judicial branch has usurped many of the prerogatives of other branches and levels of government.
>
> Some of the characteristics of this "judicial activism" have been said to include:
>
> a. a tendency by the judiciary toward problem-solution rather than griev-ance-resolution;
>
> b. a tendency by the judiciary to employ the individual plaintiff as a vehicle for the imposition of far-reaching orders extending to broad classes of individuals;
>
> c. a tendency by the judiciary to impose broad, affirmative duties upon governments and society;
>
> d. a tendency by the judiciary toward loosening jurisdictional require-ments such as standing and ripeness; and
>
> e. a tendency by the judiciary to impose itself upon other institutions in the manner of an administrator with continuing oversight responsibilities.[22]

The Kennedy-led Judiciary Committee in the late 1970s, by contrast, had different priorities. For these reasons Arnold's political views—and especially his views of civil rights—became a matter of scrutiny for his appointment as a federal judge. Good standing on this issue was especially important for Arnold, a white southern male, because of Carter's priorities for diversity on the federal bench.

Richard Arnold, as it would turn out, had a key supporter to back his credentials on civil rights. When visited by an agent from the Federal Bureau of Investigation in 1978, Justice William Brennan described his protégé as holding views on civil rights "exactly like mine."[23] Given Arnold's early history, and some of his more recent statements as a polit-ical candidate, this alignment of the liberal Justice Brennan's views on civil rights with Arnold's was probably something of a stretch—but not a huge one. But it was also no last-minute conversion; rather, it reflected a progression for Arnold that predated his consideration for a judgeship and that would continue throughout his career. If the precise steps in Arnold's transformation are not clear, it is clear these steps began with his work for Justice Brennan as a law clerk in 1960.

President Carter also wished to reform the entire confirmation process to make it less overtly a system of patronage. Carter's campaign platform in 1976 stated that "[a]ll federal judges and prosecutors should be appointed strictly on the basis of merit without any consideration of polit-ical aspects or influence." As he had done while governor in Georgia, Carter wanted to institute a commission or panel nomination process to broaden the number of persons and categories to be considered for an appointment, to reach women and minorities by getting past the old-boy networks. He also wanted to set a "minimum standard of excellence" for those nominations that would be forwarded to the Senate for confirma-tion. Carter established nominating commissions for court of appeals appointments (a process Arnold would encounter), but nominating com-missions were only voluntary for district court positions. The Arkansas senators chose not to use nominating commissions for appointments to Arkansas federal courts.

Prior to Arnold's nomination, Attorney General Griffin Bell, a former judge on the Fifth Circuit, had already encountered resistance from sena-tors to any change in their traditional prerogative of judicial nomination. In the first year of the Carter administration, Bell held a press conference to address "merit selection" of judges and to explain the administration's attempt to shift control of the appointment process from home-state sena-tors to the executive branch. Bell noted that from an early period of Amer-ican history, "the reality became that the Senate nominated and the President confirmed persons to fill those offices. For years, the effective power of nomination has resided in individual senators in the president's political party. A person could not expect to be considered for one of those positions unless he or she knew a Senator personally, knew someone who did, or was owed some political favor by that Senator."[24]

Bell acknowledged that notwithstanding the practice, many excellent judges had emerged through the years from the process. Nonetheless, Bell said, "its deficiencies have been largely that the pool of potential candidates has been very limited and that there has been a general unevenness in the quality of candidates."[25]

Bell recognized, as did Carter, that consultation and cooperation between the two branches was inherent in the process and there was no getting around senatorial prerogative for trial judge appointments. The Constitution and federal statutory law gave the president the responsibility to nominate persons for these offices; the Senate had the ultimate power to consent or to refuse to consent to them. But, Bell said, Senator James Eastland, chairman of the Senate Judiciary Committee, had told him that, although Eastland felt sure that the Senate would accept the new administration's judicial selection commissions for the appointment of judges to the United States Court of Appeals, "it was his judgment that the Senate would not stand for further immediate unilateral intrusions into their historical 'nomination' function."[26] Eastland made clear that senators might be encouraged voluntarily to establish commissions for district judges, but nothing more than encouragement to do so would be tolerated by the Senate.

By the middle of Carter's term, senators from eighteen states had established commissions to nominate candidates for district judgeships, but not in Arkansas.[27] Arkansas's senators—Bumpers, Kaneaster Hodges (filling the unexpired term of Senator John McClellan, who died in office), and later David Pryor—did not use a nominating commission.

Bell said he looked for "Ability—whether or not I thought they had the ability to be a good judge. And I'd been a judge myself so I knew what it would take." He tried to eliminate what he termed "political hacks." Bell also scrutinized a candidate's age: "I wanted to be sure they were going to give at least ten years to the government; after all they're going to get paid for life. And so some of the senators would come up with somebody that was 65-years old, and I had to figure out some way to turn them down. 60 was sort of my deadline, if they'd say they'd work till they were 70."[28]

Bell also looked for evidence of judicial temperament: "I read the whole file. If some of it would indicate they didn't have a good temperament, I'd knock them out on that ground. Temperament is a big thing for a judge." Bell described temperament as even-handedness and the ability to be fair. Bell related a story about one Carter nominee who decided himself that he lacked the requisite judicial temperament: "I once had a judge call me to resign," Bell said. "I told him he did not have to call me to resign. He said, 'I can't control myself. I get into the case. I'm just such an advocate that I'm drawn to one side or the other and I just think it's unfair to the litigants. I just have to say I'm not qualified to be a judge.'"[29]

Other judges, like Bell, understood the necessity of a judicial temperament. Justice William Brennan, in addition to vouching for Arnold's views on civil rights, also told the FBI that Arnold had "an even judicial temperament" and "an ability to maintain a disinterested judicial profile." Brennan said he had "maintained a very close relationship with Arnold and knew him well both personally and from a professional point of view. He is a first-rate lawyer, a first-rate mind, and outstanding in all respects."[30]

Another federal judge, Gerhard A. Gesell, then serving on the United States District Court for the District of Columbia, also told the FBI that Arnold was "a highly qualified attorney, and has an excellent temperament for being a federal judge." Judge Gesell recommended Arnold "most highly" for a federal judgeship. Arnold had worked at Covington & Burling under Gesell's direct supervision before Gesell was appointed to the bench.

What did Gesell, Bell, and Brennan, among others, mean when commenting upon Arnold's prospective judicial "temperament"? Like Bell, Gesell and Brennan knew it had much to do with the appearance of fairness and outward demeanor. "Judicial temperament" was a more general inquiry than Arnold's specific stance on civil rights.

ARNOLD THROUGH THE SYSTEM; BUMPERS WINS; GEORGE HOWARD POSTPONED

Soon after Bumpers assumed his Senate seat, a vacancy occurred on the federal district court in Little Rock.[31] Because Gerald Ford was president at the time, the expectation was that the seat would go to a Republican. The other Arkansas senator, the long-serving John McClellan, was willing to go along with that even though he, too, was a Democrat. Senator Bumpers effectively blocked the appointment of a Republican politician in Arkansas named Edwin R. "Ed" Bethune. One staff member speculated that Bumpers was already thinking about Richard at that time. According to Bumpers, "Senator McClellan wanted to name Ed Bethune. And I liked Ed. I had nothing against him and I thought he'd be a perfectly good judge. But my problem was, I wanted Richard to have that appointment."[32]

Some Republicans in Arkansas were understandably upset about the failure of Bethune's nomination. Bethune, an important figure in the Arkansas Republican Party at the time, had run unsuccessfully for attorney general in Arkansas. Lynn Lowe, a Republican candidate for governor, complained about Arnold's later nomination for a separate federal court vacancy. According to Lowe, Arnold was "too politically oriented since Arnold through his friendship with Bumpers was instrumental in denying Republicans a federal judgeship."[33] Ed Bethune, by then a Republican candidate for Congress, later told the FBI that Arnold was "getting a judgeship that he [Bethune] was blocked from getting by Senator Dale Bumpers." In spite of this, Bethune considered Arnold to be an "outstanding choice."[34] Bethune went on to serve for six years in Congress, but he never received another nomination for the federal judiciary.

When a vacancy occurred on the federal district court in Little Rock in 1978, Bumpers took the opportunity to nominate Arnold. But because the federal court in Little Rock did not yet have a black judge, Griffin Bell went to Bumpers to propose George Howard, then serving on the Arkansas Supreme Court by interim appointment. Midway through Carter's term, Bell was accustomed to the intricate negotiation that might be required: "We had some big fights with Senators over some of them. They all were rated qualified, otherwise I wouldn't put them on the list. I had very good relations with the Senate, and I did all the trading. The Attorney Generals and the Senators would just trade, prior to politicization from the White House."

Bell related the background to his suggestion of George Howard:

> I wanted to see Senator Bumpers appoint a black. President Carter had instructed me to find at least one black district judge in every southern state. I was already working on that anyway. I found a black justice on the Arkansas Supreme Court. So I went to see Senator Bumpers. Senator Bumpers told me right off that he had a nominee of his own. It was

Richard Arnold. I said, "What about Howard?" He said, "Well, he might get it someday but right now Richard is my man." And he just wouldn't discuss Howard.[35]

Bumpers got his way in the first round, according to Bell. "That's all there was to it. If a state had a Democratic senator we would defer to them on a District Judge. But the person had to be qualified. Well of course Richard was totally qualified, there's no problem about that. I struck out on getting a black judge."[36] The problem was not George Howard's negatives, if any, but rather Bumpers's commitment to Arnold. George Howard would be nominated by Bumpers the following year for a newly created seat on the federal district court in Little Rock.

THE ABA COMMITTEE: DISTRICT COURT NOMINATION

Yet another factor in judicial appointments was the American Bar Association. The ABA had long claimed the prerogative to rate federal judicial candidates prior to Senate confirmation.[37] Committee members perform a confidential review, examining a nominee's legal writing, interviewing attorneys, and conducting other research to determine whether the nominee, in the committee's view, is qualified to be a federal judge.

ABA committee chair Thomas Deacey believed one advantage of the ABA's approach to rating applicants was the guarantee of confidentiality for those who were interviewed. The committee destroyed interview notes after its report was prepared. Deacey believed people were more willing to talk to his committee than they would be to the FBI because the ABA was not subject to the Freedom of Information Act, while FBI investigations would be vulnerable to release at a future date.[38]

Griffin Bell agreed with this view, but he did not rely solely on the ABA's evaluation. Bell said, "It's politics in the American Bar, too, and the question in my mind is whether that's a good system or not, to use the American Bar. But there's one advantage to it. They get information that you can't get through the FBI. A lot of people won't tell you anything, they won't tell the FBI, but they'll tell the ABA lawyer."[39]

The ABA committee makes its investigation in confidence and reports the details of the investigation only among its members. The only public report is its conclusion on the candidate—whether they were exceptionally well qualified, well qualified, qualified, or not qualified. The aim, said Deacey, was not to consider any philosophical or political aspects but to consider a person's character, integrity, and his ability as a lawyer and a judge, studying each of these aspects. Only on the latter would the ABA be conducting an inquiry different in purpose from the FBI background check. Deacey worked on many vacancies in Arkansas during the six years he chaired the ABA committee, so he knew many of the attorneys and judges he contacted as part of his investigation of Arnold.[40]

In fact, in the voluminous file of interviews compiled by the FBI, only two attorneys criticized Arnold, and both had been opposing counsel in environmental cases in which Arnold represented the Environmental Defense Fund. One attorney in Jonesboro would not recommend Arnold "because of the applicant's liberalism and involvement in environmental questions." In fact, he termed Arnold "a flaming liberal as far as environmental questions are concerned."[41] The attorney admitted his opinion was somewhat biased because "it is based on his contact in the cases in which he opposed Arnold which involved environmental questions."[42]

John F. Stroud Jr., a lawyer at another Texarkana firm, recalled that six or seven years earlier Arnold had represented a client who was attempting to stop construction of a dam. "This was an unpopular stand for Arnold," Stroud said, because it meant loss of work and jobs in the area during the time the case was being adjudicated. He believed this representation by Arnold "may have cost him some votes when he was running for Congress."[43]

In the ABA's investigation, the only opposition Deacey noted to Arnold's nomination was a perception that he was a better fit for the court of appeals because of his intellectual acumen. Deacey said he would sometimes hear that Arnold "[d]oesn't know a damn thing" about being a trial judge. Arnold had extensive trial practice as an attorney but had never served as a state court judge prior to his consideration for the federal district court. The reservation expressed by some that Arnold was too intellectual to serve as a trial judge was presumably a concern that he would agonize over decisions and bring too much of a cerebral, scholarly approach to a job that is largely about managing dockets, attorneys, and juries. At the trial court level, most of a judge's work is not producing scholarly written opinions but requires ruling on pretrial motions, supervising trials, instructing juries, and sentencing criminal defendants.

THE FBI BACKGROUND CHECK

Background checks of potential judicial nominees by the Federal Bureau of Investigation begin with a request from the Department of Justice. Judicial nominees receive a thorough investigatory review, and Arnold's case was no different. For potential judges especially, the FBI looks for whether a potential nominee is "clean" and whether he or she is likely to become corrupt. Another aim is to uncover anything in the candidate's background that would be potentially embarrassing to the White House. Very little of a private life would not be known prior to confirmation, permitting the White House to pull the nomination rather than let it proceed through the confirmation process. Bumpers, of course, would have known of anything potentially disqualifying because of his long association with Arnold. Had Bumpers thought any problems would come to the surface, he would not have urged Carter to nominate him.

The "usual character investigation" included inquiries about arrests, criminal violations, tax liens, whether an attorney had been sued by a client or had been a party to legal proceedings. The extensive check includes the mundane—confirmation of earned degrees and claimed past employment—to other aspects of honesty that might indicate a susceptibility to being bribed—credit history, financial dealings, property ownership, and general fiscal habits. In Arnold's case, interviewees routinely stated that they thought Arnold was scrupulously honest. A typical observation came from an attorney who had worked with Arnold: "There would not be any way that anyone could ever bribe Arnold or attempt to sway his decisions for any material purposes."[44]

The FBI investigation also tries to ensure that judicial candidates are qualified by soliciting information about trial experience and whether the candidate has good moral standing and is diligent about work ethic. Other questions indicate interest in whether a potential nominee was considered to be "a loyal American"—probably a holdover from the McCarthy days.[45]

An interesting portrait emerges from the series of FBI interviews in July 1978. Arnold is variously described by those who knew him as "low-keyed, even-tempered"; "unassuming and not overbearing, but exudes a quiet confidence"; "an astute listener, has a unique way of pulling things together and responding effectively"; "well-liked and respected on Capitol Hill"; "marvelous sense of humor"; "a congenial man who is not outgoing, but moderately reserved"; and even a "well-groomed appearance." As many as six different agents compiled Arnold's report and conducted interviews in eighteen cities in Arkansas, as well as in Washington, DC, Cambridge, and New Haven.[46]

FBI agents also checked newspaper articles in the *Arkansas Gazette* and *Arkansas Democrat*, looking for, among other things, evidence of Arnold's views on civil rights. The report concluded that "there were no articles located in either paper which indicated Mr. Arnold had made any type of civil rights statements."[47] This is not exactly correct. Because of his two political races, Arnold was on record in news reports addressing various civil rights topics, as noted previously. Arnold's statements were clearly muted, though, reflecting the reality of the conservative Democratic Party in the South at the time. It is not clear for what years the search was conducted.

Attorneys and others were asked about Arnold's stands on civil rights issues. One was asked whether he knew of "questionable organizations" of which Arnold was a member (there were none). That attorney "believed Mr. Arnold would be fair and impartial in all judicial matters, including civil rights."[48] Arnold was also asked whether he had belonged to any group or organization that had discriminated because of race or religion, and Arnold answered in the negative. Interestingly, the question at that time did not include membership in organizations that discriminated against women.

FBI agents also contacted judges and politicians. Congressman Ray Thornton, who had defeated Arnold in his 1972 congressional race, said he "has yet to hear anyone make any adverse comments regarding the applicant's integrity or character and feels that he will make a remarkable judge." Thornton knew Arnold to be one of Bumpers's "most trusted aides."[49]

David Pryor, then governor and the Democratic candidate for the US Senate, told the FBI that "Richard Arnold is the smartest lawyer that he had ever known." Pryor, who had earlier defeated Arnold in a congressional race, said Arnold had "a very high reputation among attorneys" and was "highly regarded because of his contribution in the legislative field." Of the earlier political contest, Pryor said Arnold "ran a very fair and honest campaign" and that he and Arnold were "the closest of friends even though they were political adversaries." Pryor considered Arnold to be "above reproach" and gave him his highest recommendation.[50]

The Arkansas attorney general at the time, Bill Clinton, related the following, as summarized in the FBI agent's report:

He [Clinton] first met the applicant in 1966 and has had a passing relationship with him; however, in the last four years, he has become very
closely associated with the applicant because of his position as an assistant to Senator Dale Bumpers. He knows of no one more qualified for a
position on the bench than the applicant. He described the applicant as a
humanitarian and a supporter of human rights. He felt the applicant
would be completely unbiased and fair in his treatment of all persons.
The applicant comes from a very conservative heritage and is a very loyal
American. He has been extremely impressed in his professional dealings
with the applicant, and he feels he has all the qualities to make an excellent judge. On that basis he would highly recommend the applicant for
that position.[51]

Carter was aware he needed to vet his potential nominees with labor
and minority leaders, and FBI agents also were directed to contact persons
in this category. Even if labor was not a personal priority for Carter, Senator Kennedy had made these priorities clear. Carter may have had a
Democratic super-majority in the Senate, and thus his nominees would be
filibuster proof, yet he had to work with the Senate Judiciary Committee
in order to bring the names forward.

In the "Minority Leaders" category, the FBI interviewed Justice
George Howard, then serving as a temporary appointee on the Arkansas
Supreme Court. Howard said "he has the highest regard for applicant and
was simply delighted that Arnold was being considered for the position."[52]
Justice Howard described Arnold as a very ethical and fair-minded attorney
who conducted himself in the highest standards of his profession, a person
he would highly recommend. One wonders if Howard was aware that the
attorney general was first interested in *him* for the district court vacancy.

The report from labor leaders, however, was not favorable. During his
earlier political career, Arnold ran afoul of labor interests in Arkansas.
Danny De Clerk, president of the Central Arkansas Labor Council, Little
Rock, advised that the council had sent a letter to President Carter
opposing the appointment of Richard Arnold for the federal judgeship.[53]
According to De Clerk, Richard Arnold had promised the labor movement
that he would work at the Arkansas Constitutional Convention on behalf
of their interests with respect to a right to work law. Labor, he said, agreed
to support Arnold as a result of this promise. As far as labor members
could determine, Arnold did not have any effect one way or the other in

connection with the right to work law. Arnold's support never materialized, and for this reason the Labor Council would not support Arnold.[54]

ARNOLD'S DIVORCE: FBI INVESTIGATION

FBI background checks for judicial candidates have been and remain very intrusive. In addition to financial dealings, agents also looked for evidence of alcoholism or drug abuse. All of this would be presented to the Senate Judiciary Committee, and as we know from more recent experience, sometimes these confidential items find their way "leaked" to the press. The point is underscored that few people would voluntarily subject themselves to this sort of interrogation, and it probably dissuades any number of good candidates from seeking a judicial appointment.

Richard Arnold had no hidden vices. A recent divorce was not a scandal sufficient to trouble the president or block the nomination. On his personal data questionnaire provided to the FBI, Arnold noted that he was not married at the time of his application and that he had been divorced three years earlier, in May 1975.[55] Arnold initially filed the suit for divorce; Gale Arnold counterclaimed, and the divorce was granted to her "on the ground of general indignities."[56] Custody of the two daughters was given to Gale. By the time of the divorce Gale was living with the children in Washington, DC, working as a correspondent for her father's newspaper chain, Palmer Media. The marriage had deteriorated for five years or so before the divorce, from 1970 to 1975; stresses had included Arnold's second race for Congress.

FBI concerns in Arnold's background check reflect a more or less perfunctory check of the divorce situation, evident mostly as a recurring theme in questions to others. FBI agents asked acquaintances about the marriage and its dissolution. One interviewee stated that "Arnold was a deeply religious person, and believes this was one reason he remained married to Gale for as long as he did. Arnold did not believe in divorce, hated to think of the family breaking up with the two children involved, and probably stayed married to Gale longer than he should have" because the interviewee felt "both persons had unreconcilable personalities."[57] An FBI agent even asked Justice William Brennan about Arnold's family situation. Brennan reported Arnold's marital difficulties as being "an unfortunate situation," but one that had resulted in "an amicable relationship between the family members involved."[58]

Gale Arnold fully supported Richard Arnold's nomination as a federal district judge and continued to do so when he was under consideration by Clinton for a seat on the Supreme Court. Gale told an FBI agent in 1978 that her ex-husband was "a brilliant individual who came from a very good family." Arnold was "a very fair, broad-minded person, would be a very fair judge." She had "no reason to question his character, associates, reputation or loyalty, and knew of no derogatory information concerning Richard Arnold." Gale Arnold stated that "Richard Arnold would be an excellent judge and recommended him without reservation."[59]

Walter E. Hussman Sr., Gale's father, apparently held no grudges after the divorce. Interviewed by the FBI, he reported "an honest evaluation of Richard Arnold would call for the conclusion that this individual was an outstanding lawyer, an honest, fair, and impartial individual, and an individual with a great deal of legal talent." He described his moral character as "above average" and stated that he "knew of nothing derogatory about this individual." "He concluded with the volunteered statement that Richard Arnold would make an outstanding judge and he supported this nomination."[60]

Hussman's son, Walter Hussman Jr., then the managing editor of the *Arkansas Democrat*, spoke about his work with Arnold as general counsel for the companies owned by his family. He said that relationship "ended primarily due to the fact that Richard Arnold resigned his directorships of some of the companies owned by the Hussman family in order to become an aide to Senator Dale Bumpers, and also because of the pending divorce between Gale and Richard." He said that Arnold "was in no way forced into the resolving of their relationship, that Arnold instituted it on his own."[61]

HEALTH ISSUES

The FBI also conducted an extensive inquiry into Arnold's health. Ominously, this inquiry revealed the beginnings of Arnold's long battle with non-Hodgkin lymphoma. It was not yet fully diagnosed nor was the disease fully developed, but Arnold would serve his entire judicial career—over twenty-five years—with this condition. President Clinton would cite Arnold's health as the reason he could not appoint him to the Supreme Court in 1994. Arnold died from the cancer in 2004.

But in the summer of 1978, Arnold listed the present state of his health as "good,"[62] and by all accounts of his colleagues, it was. The Justice Department questionnaire asked: "Are you currently under treatment for an illness or physical condition? If so, give details." Arnold answered this question with great care. Was he "currently under treatment?" His answer, truthfully, was "No." He added, however: "I am under observation for an enlarged spleen and a condition of the blood that may be related to it. This condition, which has not been definitively diagnosed, does not impair my ability to work and function, physically or mentally. My physician advises me that in his opinion it will not interfere with my ability to render efficient service as a judge in the foreseeable future."[63]

It is evident that Arnold's health crisis had begun. Although the worrisome symptoms were difficult to diagnose, they required no treatment at the time. And with one limited exception, Arnold's health had no impact on his productivity as a judge until the last few months of his life.

In July 1978, Dr. John Lamberg of the National Institutes of Health said Arnold was under his medical supervision for chronic lympho-proliferative disorder, a disease he said was "similar to Chronic Lymphocytic Leukemia." He stated that the disease had not progressed to a state where it necessitated treatment. Dr. Lamberg predicted no decrease in Arnold's stamina "and no decrease in his anticipated life survival." Lamberg told the FBI agent he had already provided detailed information in writing concerning Arnold's physical condition to the US Department of Justice.[64]

The critical factor in Arnold's nomination was not his health, his trial experience, his views on civil rights, or his family circumstances. Instead, the most important factor was the support of the two Arkansas senators.

In a letter dated October 3, 1978, William H. Webster, director of the FBI, wrote to Arnold to "extend congratulations, on behalf of the FBI, to you on your recent confirmation as United States District Judge. The honor of being named to this position by the president must be a source of great pride to you, and I wish you every success as you assume your new responsibilities." As a former Eighth Circuit judge himself, Webster was especially well placed to appreciate both the background and the significance of the position.

Arnold wrote back to Webster: "Your letter of October 3 is much appreciated. It was very kind indeed of you to take the time to write to me, and I am most grateful. This new job is the best thing that ever happened to me, and I am enjoying it immensely. I love the law, and the opportunity to be part of the process of justice is something that I have hoped for for a long time."[65]

Chapter Six

Trial Judge for Civil Liberties

Arnold was forty-two years old when he was sworn in as a federal district judge on October 16, 1978. It had been a remarkably short time since the death of Judge Terry Lee Shell, whom Arnold now replaced, on June 25, 1978. Just one week after Judge Shell's death, the Department of Justice approved initiation of the FBI investigation of Arnold, which was largely completed by the end of July. The Senate Judiciary Committee held its hearings when Congress reconvened that fall. After confirmation by the full Senate, President Carter and Attorney General Griffin Bell signed Arnold's commission on September 22. Arnold immediately began preparations to move his residence to Little Rock. He also hired a staff (two law clerks and a secretary from Arnold & Arnold) and set up his new office and courtroom in Little Rock. His salary was $54,000, the amount Congress had established for all federal district judges.

The swearing-in ceremony took place in Little Rock in the federal courthouse, a five-story building on Capitol Avenue that also housed the post office. Judge G. Thomas Eisele, chief judge of Arkansas's eastern district, administered the oath of office. Arnold's daughters Lydia, nine, and Janet, fifteen, held the Bible used for the swearing in—the Bible had belonged to his mother. His father, Richard Lewis Arnold, held the judicial robe his son put on, a gift from the Texarkana Bar Association. In addition to family members and judges from the court, both United States senators from Arkansas, Dale Bumpers and Kaneaster Hodges, and Arkansas governor David Pryor were there. All the members of the family's Texarkana law firm made the trip for the occasion, and many lawyers from Little Rock were also in attendance.

Senator Dale Bumpers spoke affectionately of his former aide, recalling Arnold's two unsuccessful races for Congress: "We all know that he was not a very successful politician. He was not an eloquent speaker, and he didn't smile like Bill Clinton and I do, but there are many other qualities about him which qualify him much more to be a federal judge."[1] Bumpers expressed what he knew at the time, and others would subsequently conclude about where Arnold's real contribution lay: "It is his ability to understand that some people abuse their power and authority; that some people are born losers; that some people are the hapless unfortunate victims of their upbringing; and that some people are bullies; that some allow their lives to be dominated by greed and avarice. Every nation ought to be judged by the degree of personal freedom it provides its people."[2]

The Arkansas attorney general at the time was a thirty-two-year-old holding his first elected office, Bill Clinton. Ten years Arnold's junior, Clinton was elected as attorney general in 1977, serving one term before running successfully for governor. Clinton was not originally on the program. Arnold ran into Clinton a few days earlier on Capitol Avenue in Little Rock and asked him if he would like to speak at Arnold's inauguration. Clinton explained to the audience why his name was not listed on the program and joked about his last-minute addition: "I feel that I have a right to be here because for nearly a decade, as long as I have been active in some capacity in Arkansas politics, people have been coming up to me with this kind of compliment, 'You know, you're almost as smart as Richard Arnold.'"[3]

Clinton commented upon the job facing Arnold: "A federal judge really brings the law of this country to the hard and complicated and often contradictory context of life's conflicts. The federal courts have given in the last decade, especially, a great opportunity for our people to become more decent and just. But in order for that to happen we need men like Richard Arnold on the bench who will not shirk from using power, nor will they be tyrants in abusing it."[4] Clinton invoked the eminent jurist Learned Hand, a judge with whom Arnold would be compared later in his career. He hoped Arnold would approach "this hard job" with the same attitude expressed by Judge Hand: "I like to think that the work of a Judge is an art. It's a bit of craftsmanship, isn't it? It's what a poet does. It's what a sculptor does. He has some vague purposes and he has an indefinite number of what you might call frames of reference, among which he must choose. For choose he has to, and he does."5

Judge Gerald Heaney, representing the Eighth Circuit, had traveled to Little Rock from Minnesota. Heaney was appointed to the Eighth Circuit in 1966 by Lyndon Johnson. Born in 1918, Heaney was a decorated World War II veteran who had been one of a first wave of military men to land on Omaha Beach. More than half of his unit was killed. Heaney had joined the war effort following his graduation from the University of Minnesota Law School in 1941. He returned from the war to practice law in Duluth, where he was also a Democratic-Farmer-Labor Party activist.

Judge Heaney became one of the longest-serving members of the Eighth Circuit, and Arnold and Heaney would serve there together for many years.6 Heaney was already an important figure in school desegregation cases in Little Rock, St. Louis, and Kansas City, Missouri. He would play a leading role with Arnold in the supervision of the Little Rock school desegregation effort after Arnold joined the Eighth Circuit. Heaney was more outspoken about civil rights than Arnold would be, reflecting perhaps the political climate of Minnesota compared to Arkansas, although the two would largely agree on civil rights matters as they served together. In 2001, for example, Heaney told a graduating class at the University of Minnesota in Duluth: "In 1964, the Congress, under the leadership of Minnesota's Senator Humphrey, passed the Civil Rights Act, an act that for the first time prohibited discrimination based on race in broad areas of human conduct. The acknowledgment of the dignity and promise of all humans is the most important change that has occurred in my lifetime — more important than the artificial heart, the computer, the internet and space exploration."7

Judge Heaney also addressed the audience that day at Arnold's swearing-in ceremony. Heaney was very much aware that the Eastern District of Arkansas faced the largest backlog of civil rights cases in the country.8 He pointed out that Arnold's share of the pending case load would be at least four hundred civil and criminal cases:9 "The Judges of this Court have attempted under almost impossible circumstances to handle the pending case load during the time that they have been without the judicial manpower that they have needed." Heaney mentioned the pending judiciary act that would create new judgeships: "Perhaps with the new bill that has been passed, we will get some additional relief which will enable this Court to fulfill its historic function."[10] Heaney also looked forward to an additional judge for the Eighth Circuit as a result of the bill — ironically, that judge would be Richard Arnold.

As Judge Eisele presided, Arnold repeated the traditional oath of office: "I, Richard Sheppard Arnold, do solemnly swear that I will administer justice without respect to persons and do equal right to the poor and to the rich, and that I will faithfully and impartially discharge and perform all of the duties incumbent upon me as United States District Judge for the Eastern and Western Districts of Arkansas, according to the best of my abilities and understanding, agreeably to the Constitution and laws of the United States."[11]

Arnold told those gathered for the ceremony that it is "presumptuous for anyone to agree to be a judge," because the Bible instructed "judge not, lest ye be judged," an enduring characteristic of his attitude.[12] Judging other people was difficult: "Those who exercise that power should keep in mind that it does not belong to us for ourselves. It belongs to another, the United States, and is exercised for another's benefit, the people of the United States. We must remember that the power is temporary. It is enjoyed day to day with the knowledge that we will be called to account before the judge of us all."[13] Arnold added: "A judge, it seems to me, bears a particularly heavy burden when he comes to make that account. I hope that it is not a violation of the First Amendment to ask each of you to say a prayer for me from time to time. It won't do any harm and it might do some good."[14]

Arnold remembered both his mother, Janet Sheppard Arnold, and his paternal grandmother, Kate Lewis Arnold. He often spoke with pride of his grandmother's political activities within the limited context of her times. He recalled that his mother read bar exams; she was not a member of the Examining Committee (his father was), or even formally a lawyer. Arnold said this was one of his earliest memories of his mother, who died when he was nineteen years old. He added, "It is her Bible upon which I took the oath today, and I remember so particularly one of the things that she wrote on the flyleaf, which is something that every Judge should remember. It's a quotation from a famous jury speech made by a famous lawyer, Portia, and she said this: 'Though justice be thy plea, remember this: that in the course of justice none of us should see salvation.' And that is something that we, I hope, all have in mind."[15]

The trial judge is the only figure in the judiciary who really acts individually, as opposed to the collegial votes of the higher courts. Once he joined the Eighth Circuit, Arnold would have to persuade at least one other judge in order to prevail on a position—he would have to persuade a majority of all other active Eighth Circuit judges if the case was before the entire court sitting en banc. It is especially instructive, then, to examine Arnold's year as a federal district court judge because we learn about what he was willing to do when solely responsible. As he said about a life in the judiciary, "The joy of it is that we have a small part, case by case, in doing justice."[16] This is especially true at the district court level.

Although he spent only a short time on the district court, Arnold compiled a notable record there. He worked especially hard to clear the backlog of cases that had accumulated. After a mere three months on the bench, the *Arkansas Democrat* reported Judge Arnold had already established himself as an admired judge and had drawn "praise of attorneys" for his expeditious handling of the overwhelmed docket. "He rarely grants a continuance in a case while other federal judges appear to do so as a matter of course. Arnold appears to have a passion for being expeditious. A day hardly passes without his filing a stack of orders in the clerk's office."[17] It was a busy and productive year, at the end of which his fellow judges would lament his loss to their court upon his nomination to the Eighth Circuit.

Arnold probably felt that he had to overcome the perception of his overtly political appointment. If there were any doubts about Arnold's stance on civil rights, his year as a district court judge resolved them convincingly. It was a remarkable year in many ways.

Three cases were particularly significant that year. One was a criminal case from a state prisoner who alleged that racial discrimination had resulted in a life sentence in prison in violation of the federal constitution. Two cases had to do with discrimination in other government contexts: the hiring practices of the Arkansas National Guard and the rules for high school girls' basketball.

EQUAL PROTECTION AND GIRLS' BASKETBALL:
DODSON v. ARKANSAS ACTIVITIES ASSOCIATION[18]

One of the best examples of Arnold's views of civil rights is a little-known case on the rules of girls' high school basketball. *Dodson v. Arkansas Activities Association*,[19] a dispute about the rules for girls' basketball in Arkansas, was an early indication of Arnold's judicial method and temperament.

Arnold frequently said there was "no such thing as a little case."[20] By this he meant that every case brought into a federal court is important to the litigants. Large sums of money are not always at stake. Not all cases involve sweeping institutional reforms or even important constitutional questions. Nonetheless, Arnold believed such cases are part of the "highest calling" of a judge: "There really isn't such a thing as a little case. A case is always a controversy between two or more citizens, or non-citizens maybe, who have a claim for justice based on the facts. The important job of the court is to listen to the parties and decide where justice lies. It's our job to do the ordinary work of the grist of the mill day in and day out and make sure that the individual citizen gets his or her due."[21]

Litigants deserve to be heard and to feel assured that they have been heard, however trivial the issue may appear or however routine or repetitious the case may seem. As Arnold noted, an individual's lawsuit "may be the most important thing in that person's life."[22] He treated *Dodson v. Arkansas Activities Association* with this sort of respect, and in a manner that revealed much about his judicial beliefs.

The litigation began well before Richard Arnold assumed his duties as a United States district judge in October 1978. Diana Lee Dodson,[23] then a fourteen-year-old student in the Arkadelphia public school system, filed a lawsuit in January 1977 against the Arkansas Activities Association, the governing body of Arkansas school athletic programs, asking that girls be permitted to play under the same full-court basketball rules as those under which Arkansas boys played. Arkansas schools at that time required that basketball for girls be played under "half-court" rules. The state required that girls compete under an archaic form of the grade-school girls' game that survived in only three other states and was not played in college-level competition. In this game, which had been played in Arkansas and some other states since at least the World War II era, girls' teams had six players. Three players were forwards, the scorers for the team who stayed on one end, and three others were guards, defenders who stayed at the other end of the court. No player could cross the center line in the middle of the court. Arkansas boys played the "full-court," or "five on five" game, consistent with today's standard game of basketball.

Prior to the litigation, coaches of Arkansas schools were divided on the desirability of changing the rules for the girls' game to match those of women's college teams in the United States and most other high schools (except for Iowa, Oklahoma, and Tennessee). In response to requests from some of the larger schools, the AAA had twice asked its members whether to change to full-court basketball for junior high and senior high girls. Both times a majority of the member schools voted to retain half-court basketball for Arkansas girls.

The federal court lawsuit followed. Diana Lee Dodson, who was then a junior high school student and a good basketball player, claimed through her lawyer that differences in girls' and boys' junior high and senior high basketball rules mandated by the Arkansas Activities Association deprived girls of equal protection under the Fourteenth Amendment and violated Title IX of the Education Amendments of 1972.[24] In particular, it deprived girls in Arkansas of the opportunity to compete for college scholarships. Because of Title IX, scholarships had emerged as a meaningful issue in the mid-1970s for college women's basketball.

The case was tried in 1977 in Little Rock before Judge Terry L. Shell. For many months no decision was forthcoming. The case was still under advisement when Judge Shell died the following year. Replacing Judge Shell on the district court, Arnold inherited *Dodson* among other pending cases. Judge Arnold sought the agreement of the parties to submit the case for his decision based upon the trial transcript and briefs, avoiding the necessity to retry the case. After the hearing transcript was prepared, a matter that had lingered for nearly two years came to conclusion in a matter of weeks. It took some work to sort through the numerous cases pending before Judge Shell to determine which ones could be moved forward in this way, but Arnold proved efficient at the task.

In what has been called "probably the most significant step for female athletes in the state of Arkansas,"[25] Judge Arnold ruled in favor of Diana Lee Dodson and declared that Arkansas's half-court rules for girls violated the equal protection clause of the Fourteenth Amendment. Judge Arnold determined that tradition alone, without supporting gender-related substantive reasons, was not a sufficient reason to justify the fact that such rules placed girl athletes who aspired to college scholarships at a substantial disadvantage to boy athletes. Arnold cited testimony in the record that college women's basketball teams all played the full-court game, and recruiting for those teams centered upon athletes who had played full-court basketball and thus were prepared to play that game. Even the University of Arkansas—today the state's premier women's basketball program—focused its primary recruitment efforts out of state. Dodson wanted the opportunity to compete for a basketball scholarship at the collegiate level. Arnold cited testimony from the hearing that the disadvantage to Arkansas girls schooled in the half-court game was "tremendous" for college scholarship competition.[26]

The decision was surprising because the only other courts to address this specific claim had ruled that half-court basketball rules for girls did not violate any constitutional right. The Sixth Circuit Court of Appeals, reversing a Tennessee district court, had stated in a per curiam (unsigned) opinion that distinct differences in physical characteristics and capabilities justified not only separation of girls' and boys' sports teams by gender but the rules for those games as well.[27] In addition, a federal district court in Oklahoma had dismissed a similar claim under the theory that no fundamental constitutional rights were implicated, and even if an equal protection claim could be stated for the case, any injury to girls was de minimis.[28]

These courts had trivialized the claim that half-court rules for girls' basketball violated equal protection. The Sixth Circuit, for instance, had written that the plaintiff "has succeeded in procuring the order of a federal court which imposes her own personal notions as to how the game of basketball should be played."[29] Further, the court stated, "It must be apparent that its basis is the distinct differences in physical characteristics and capabilities between the sexes and that the differences are reflected in the sport of basketball by how the game itself is played. Since there are such differences in physical characteristics and capabilities, we see no reason why the rules governing play cannot be tailored to accommodate them without running afoul of the equal protection clause."[30] Similarly, the Oklahoma district court wrote that such a claim did not "merit the attention of the court."[31]

The language Judge Arnold chose for his opinion in *Dodson*, however, never demeaned the interest at stake, as these other courts had done. Consistent with Arnold's respect for people generally, he made an effort to understand interests with which he could not personally identify. He carefully read the testimony presented at the hearing, noting its details. Golf, not basketball, was his sport. Presumably he did not identify with the game of basketball, given that he once said of a legal standard articulated in a constitutional case, "If that's a legal test, I'm a basketball player."[32]

Arnold distinguished the earlier cases politely but without apology: "This Court is aware that the two precedents most closely in point are to the contrary. To some degree the record here appears different, because here tradition alone is offered to support the sex-based distinction. To the extent that the reasoning of those cases is contrary to this opinion, this Court respectfully disagrees. They are not binding authority here, and their reasoning seems, with deference, unpersuasive."[33] Simply because the game had always been played that way in Arkansas was not a sufficiently compelling interest to overcome the economic inequity. As Arnold noted, girls historically had been prohibited from playing the more rigorous full-court game of basketball because with their "bustles, long trains, and high starched collars," they could not "get up and down the court fast enough."[34]

To allay the concerns of those who might view his decision to require that girls be allowed to play on boys' teams, Arnold also wrote: "It is proper to add a word about what this case is not about. It is not about whether girls could or should play against boys. The question is whether girls are entitled to play full-court against each other. The point here is that Arkansas boys are in a position to compete on an equal footing with boys elsewhere, while Arkansas girls, merely because they are girls, are not."[35]

Judge Arnold's decision in the case was fully consistent with the policy animating Title IX of the Education Amendments of 1972,[36] but it was not, then, a Title IX case. Although the complaint also alleged a violation of Title IX, Arnold dismissed that claim in a footnote.[37] Instead, Arnold's decision turned on his analysis of the plaintiff's equal protection claim. As an initial matter, Arnold had no difficulty determining that the Arkansas Activities Association's mandate of rules for its voluntary members constituted state action: "The Association, although not itself a governmental body, is supported in large part by dues paid by public school districts. [It] in effect exercises a delegated governmental power. It is, at least for present purposes, subject to the equal protection clause of the Fourteenth Amendment."[38]

Further, *Dodson* was among the earliest cases to apply the intermediate standard of constitutional scrutiny suggested by the US Supreme Court in *Craig v. Boren.*[39] To withstand constitutional challenge, classifications by gender must serve important governmental objectives and must be substantially related to achievement of those objectives. Because tradition alone supported Arkansas's continued requirement of half-court basketball for girls, Arnold held that this justification—as an outdated and overbroad generalization about the differences between males and females—did not constitute an important governmental objective. Arnold wrote, "Simply doing things the way they've always been done is not an 'important government objective,' if indeed it is a legitimate objective at all. Change for its own sake is no doubt to be avoided, and tradition is a healthy thing. But tradition alone, without supporting gender-related substantive reasons, cannot justify placing girls at a disadvantage for no reason other than their being girls."[40]

The Arkansas Activities Association's decision not to appeal Arnold's decision came after polling its member schools. The AAA sent letters to each of its 500 schools, and of the 419 that responded, the great majority (303) did not want the ruling appealed.[41] One hundred and sixteen school districts thought that the decision should be appealed.

The following season all Arkansas schools complied with the ruling.[42] Full-court basketball competition for junior high and senior high school girls in Arkansas was played for the first time in the fall of 1979, leaving only two states—Iowa and Oklahoma—still playing the half-court girls' game. Tennessee's school activities association, although the Sixth Circuit had ruled in its favor on the issue of half-court rules for girls, voted to switch to five-on-five basketball anyway.[43]

Diana Lee Dodson's lawsuit was filed when she was in the ninth grade. Judge Arnold's decision came at the conclusion of her junior year in high school, meaning that Dodson's senior year basketball team would play under full-court rules. Unfortunately, Dodson seriously injured her knee before that year and never had the opportunity to compete for a scholarship or to play college basketball. She attended college, but later, a tragic event claimed her life. Diana Lee Dodson was shot and killed in 1991.[44] Some years later Judge Arnold mentioned both her career-ending injury and her later death with sadness, even though he had never met Diana Lee Dodson.[45]

The opinion in *Dodson*, among the first cases Arnold encountered, reveals several features of his approach to judicial work that would stand out over his career. It exemplifies three characteristics that Arnold himself would later suggest to be essential for the continued public acceptance of the justice system. In the day-to-day business of judging, Arnold said that it was important to avoid delays in resolving cases, to decide cases boldly, and to show respect for litigants and their lawyers.

Judge Arnold was concerned about delays in the judicial system. In a tribute to Judge Henry Woods, Arnold wrote: "He was decisive, which, after all, is an indispensable quality for a judge. The job of a judge is to decide cases, not to dither over them. Cases do not normally improve with age."[46] In *Dodson*, after the two-day hearing, the parties had waited nearly eighteen months for a ruling. The delay was occasioned in part by Judge Shell's death, but the case had lingered in his court for over a year. Once on the bench in Judge Shell's place, Arnold wasted no time resolving the matter. Arnold issued his opinion in the case in less than three weeks after receiving the prepared trial transcript. The litigants deserved an answer and deserved no further delays or the additional expense of a rehearing before a new judge. And yet Arnold decided the case and wrote his opinion with great care. His notes from the hearing transcript and briefs of the case are meticulous.[47]

Arnold emphasized speedy, yet careful, resolution of cases as necessary to the continued acceptability by the public of the judicial branch: "You have to get the case out the door, because there are other cases waiting on it. Then you have to try to get it right, [and] write an opinion which is intelligible, which explains the result, and which we hope, is acceptable to the losing side. And that takes time. I worry that sometimes our opinions are not living up to that standard."[48] Over the course of his career, Arnold was increasingly concerned about the volume facing the federal courts and whether without additional judgeships the federal courts could continue to produce quality work at an acceptable pace.[49]

A conscientious judge should keep the wheels of justice moving: "People want to know the answer. They want a result. It's important to them of course that the result be in their favor, but if they're going to lose anyway, it's important for them to know quickly. The virtue highlighted here is quickness, promptness, no agonizing over these matters, but just deciding them."[50] In *Dodson*, in fact, it appears that the Arkansas Activities

Association preferred the decision to be in the hands of the courts because its members had been relatively evenly divided on the issue. The AAA's decision not to appeal was ratified by a vote of nearly two to one among all member schools.[51] The issue was resolved, and all Arkansas schools made the transition to full-court basketball in the following season.

Arnold believed it was important for judges to be bold—to have courage in the exercise of power. He once said, "After you are convinced that you have jurisdiction, after you have given to the state courts and to the other branches of government the deference and respect that is their due, after you have satisfied yourself that you really are, if there is a statute involved, enforcing the will of the legislature, after all of those hurdles have been gotten over, then the greatest error that a judge can make is to pull your punches because you're afraid that the majority of your neighbors are not going to like what you decide."[52]

Dodson is a good example. No doubt Judge Arnold was sensitive to the likely response of critics that the rules of a game of basketball could not possibly implicate the federal constitution. In fact, an Arkansas basketball coach wrote to the *Arkansas Gazette* that it was "beyond my comprehension how courts have jurisdiction over the rules of a game."[53] Arnold said later that he expected the decision would be reversed by the Eighth Circuit Court of Appeals, given the prior decision by the Sixth Circuit. Nonetheless, he believed it was the right decision, whether or not he was to be reversed.[54]

In an address before the Judicial Conference at Duluth, Minnesota, Judge Arnold later said: "There is probably more danger in the courts from an excess of timidity than from an excess of boldness in decision, and yet the timid among us may get reversed less."[55] Whether a judge is affirmed or not "is not really a true measure of judicial prowess. The decision that is reversed today may be the law of tomorrow."[56] By "boldness of decision," Judge Arnold meant that momentary popularity or public acceptance is not the guide. "But if by public opinion we mean the shifts of popular emotion that occur from day to day, if that is the beat to which the courts should march, then we will not long have courts worthy of the name. Our courts will be blown about by every wind of doctrine, and the security we have found in a Constitution that restrains government even, or especially, when it acts to carry out the majority will, will soon be gone."[57]

Later, as a judge on the US Court of Appeals, Arnold reflected upon the constitutional decision-making process.[58] That process, he said, involves several steps. First, and most important, a judge looks to the words of the Constitution.[59] Second, to the extent those words are not clear, a judge should try to ascertain the intent behind the document, either from historical research or reasonable inferences from the structure.[60] Third, judges look to precedent, and for lower-court judges the US Supreme Court's precedent is decisive.[61] But the really difficult cases, he said, are those that are not answered by any of the above, and in those cases, the greatest danger lies in the influence of a judge's own personal preferences.[62]

Constitutional law questions, Arnold would say, require a judge to avoid putting personal preferences into law. For Arnold, he would still of necessity "come to it with, I guess, some feeling about American history, [and] some presumption about personal liberty."[63] A judge should bring to constitutional decisions "the best knowledge you can get of American history and tradition, your sense of our system, your sense of the American ideal of worth of the individual."[64]

Judge Arnold's notes of the *Dodson* case show that he carefully considered the determinations in other jurisdictions that the equal protection claim in the rules of girls' basketball presented, at best, a de minimis injury. Nor did he follow the Oklahoma district court's argument that the equal protection claim in this context was not worthy of recognition because it did not implicate a fundamental right such as free speech or the right to vote. Arnold's opinion in *Dodson* dealt with constitutional uncertainty in a decisive way.

In *Dodson*, Arnold never trivialized the claim of a fourteen-year-old girl. Henry Morgan recalled a conversation with Arnold some years after the case: "He remembered who I was. I talked to him about that 'silly' basketball case, thinking he might not remember. He said, 'Oh I remember that case, and it was not silly. It was my first case.'"[65] Arnold himself later told the *Arkansas Democrat-Gazette*: "[*Dodson*] was an important case to people interested in basketball, which includes everyone. I've had people come up to me and say you shouldn't be involved in anything that trivial. Basketball is not trivial. And it isn't trivial that the girls were being made to play an inferior form of the game either. Aside from other things, it put them at a disadvantage in getting scholarships. Women's basketball is growing and a lot more people are interested in it."[66]

Although a handful of courts have cited the *Dodson* opinion on related questions of gender discrimination in sports,[67] on the particular issue — the constitutionality of half-court basketball rules for girls — only three other states continued to play the game after the *Dodson* decision, and in all of those states the change came about through each state's athletic association rather than by court order. In Tennessee, where the Sixth Circuit had ruled half-court basketball rules did not violate the federal constitution,[68] the Tennessee Secondary Schools Athletic Association nonetheless voted to change to the full-court game. Some schools in Oklahoma continued the half-court game through 1995.[69]

In Iowa, like Oklahoma, the state's athletic association voted to allow individual schools to choose between the two games, providing two separate state competitions.[70] But Judge Arnold's opinion seems to have influenced the outcome in Iowa. The Iowa Girls High School Athletic Union voted to allow full-court competition only after three players sued in 1984. The lawsuit was based on *Dodson*'s premise that female students were not able to compete for scholarships on the same terms as male players. United States District Judge Donald O'Brien rejected the Athletic Union's motion to dismiss and scheduled the lawsuit for trial.[71] Judge Arnold was then sitting on the Eighth Circuit, of which Iowa is a member, no doubt giving the *Dodson* precedent added weight.

More than a dozen journal articles[72] also mention Judge Arnold's opinion in *Dodson*, including one that portrays *Dodson* as among the "revolutionary" decisions interpreting the equal protection clause of the Fourteenth Amendment to mandate equal athletic opportunities for high school females.[73] One judge's decision, then, can have a far-reaching effect in ways measured other than by the number of subsequent court citations.

A HIRING QUOTA FOR THE ARKANSAS NATIONAL GUARD

Although in his career Richard Arnold would on numerous occasions uphold claims of racial and gender discrimination in employment,[74] only once did he impose a racial quota as a remedy. The case involved the Arkansas National Guard. At the time of its infamous deployment by Governor Orval Faubus during the Central High School crisis in the 1950s, the Arkansas National Guard had no black members. The first black member of the guard was enlisted in 1965, well after the guard's intervention at Central High School. The guard's first black employee was not hired until 1971. Although by the end of the 1970s blacks made up 23 percent of guard membership (skewed toward high percentage units from largely black regions in the Arkansas delta), they held only 2 percent of its full-time civilian jobs.

The case before Arnold was about race discrimination in the Arkansas National Guard's civilian employee positions. Corenna Taylor, a black woman, cited three instances of racial discrimination in her federal court lawsuit. First, she alleged that she had been terminated as a recruiter, a position she held only briefly, because of her race. Second, she was then demoted from recruiter to mail-room clerk. Finally, Taylor alleged that the environment of racial harassment in the National Guard caused her to quit that job. She claimed she had been effectively discharged from her position as mail-room clerk because of her race.

The case was initially tried in Richard Arnold's court in February 1980, a mere few weeks before Arnold would be sworn in as a court of appeals judge. Arnold ruled in Taylor's favor, labeling the guard's racial atmosphere "in a word, dismal," and finding that "discrimination in the Guard has been pervasive."[75] Arnold found that her employment as a National Guard recruiter had been terminated because of her race. He also found that her resignation as mail-room clerk was in fact a constructive discharge on account of race. Taylor had stayed, according to Arnold, "as long as any self-respecting black person would." The Arkansas National Guard, Arnold said, had intentionally discriminated on the basis of race over a long period of time. The actions in Taylor's case violated both Title VII of the Civil Rights Act of 1964, as amended in 1972 to include state employees, and 42 U.S.C. section 1983. He ordered further briefing and a separate hearing on the question of remedy. The United States government then asked to intervene to present its view of the matter.

In the interim, Arnold assumed duties on the Eighth Circuit but continued to sit as a district judge by designation on Taylor's case through its conclusion. Following a five-day hearing in May and June 1980, Arnold ordered the guard to hire one black for every three white employees it hired, until blacks made up 16 percent of the guard's civilian workforce. (Sixteen percent reflected the proportion of the black population of Arkansas.) Arnold's bench notes from the hearing, written in his characteristic small print, ran thirty-three legal-size pages.

In his final opinion in the case, issued in August 1980, Arnold affirmed his finding of intentional racial discrimination against Taylor, and further, that the racial conditions of the Arkansas National Guard were "appalling."[76] Arnold agreed with the US Department of Justice that Title VII did not apply to National Guard employment. But he upheld his original view that Taylor had a claim under the 1866 civil rights statute, popularly referred to as Section 1983 for its place in the United States Code.[77] The Department of Justice, although at that time typically a proponent of civil rights in employment, in this case had intervened to argue against recognition of a civil rights claim for National Guard employment, on the ground of interference with military objectives.

A substantial portion of Arnold's August opinion was devoted to a justification for the broad remedy Arnold had ordered. The plaintiff had asked Arnold to impose a hiring plan for its civilian employees. They had asked that one out of every two employees hired by the defendant must be black until a certain ratio was reached. Arnold modified it to one out of three but otherwise granted the precise relief sought. In his justification, Arnold noted among other things that Taylor was entitled to reinstatement. Reinstatement to a pervasively racist work environment, however, seemed to Arnold to miss the point of employment discrimination laws: "The racial atmosphere in the Arkansas National Guard is still far below that civilized and decent respect for co-workers that both the State and its citizens are entitled to."[78]

Not only was Taylor entitled to reinstatement, she was entitled "to be reinstated in a work place where all people are treated with decency and respect. The court finds that this goal will be materially impeded unless the Arkansas National Guard is required to step up its employment of qualified black persons."[79] Arnold preferred not to order a hiring quota. "Racial quotas," he wrote, "are philosophically abhorrent to the Court, but the proof here leaves no choice. There is simply no other way to ensure that the law will be complied with in the future."[80]

Arnold's sweeping remedy was affirmed in its most important respects by the Eighth Circuit, in an opinion written by Judge Gerald Heaney. Ongoing oversight of the remedy fell to newly installed district judge George Howard Jr., who was appointed to fill the seat vacated by Arnold. Howard's oversight continued for another six years, until the guard had satisfied the hiring quota set by Judge Arnold. By all accounts, Arnold's ruling transformed the Arkansas National Guard. John W. Walker of Little Rock, one of Taylor's attorneys, said the effect of the ruling "changed the whole system" in Arkansas but was even broader in that it had an effect on National Guard systems in other states.[81]

In 1992, Arnold exchanged letters with Taylor's attorney, John Walker. Walker had written to both Arnold and Heaney to inform them that Corenna Taylor had died after a sudden illness, at the age of forty-six. Walker termed the case "perhaps the most successful employment discrimination case in the state. The one for three hiring ratio resulted in great and prompt benefits to thousands of African American citizens in this state. The National Guard in Arkansas is now a stunning success because of that."[82]

Arnold's response to Walker revealed views Arnold rarely expressed in public, outside of his judicial opinions:

> I deeply appreciate your thoughtfulness in letting Judge Heaney and me know about Ms. Taylor. She was an impressive person in the courtroom. What you have to say about the order in *Taylor v. Jones* is most heartening. People who attack the concept of affirmative action should be told about this case. I firmly believe that without a sharp and drastic break with the past, the Arkansas National Guard would have continued without significant change. The great point is that not only African Americans, but the whole body of the citizenry, is uplifted and improved when an institution is opened up in this way. I feel very lucky to have been part of this, and the same goes for the voting rights act cases of recent years—another example, I think, of successful affirmative action. In a perfect world where everybody was born with an equal chance, this kind of thing wouldn't be necessary, but that's not the kind of world we have, nor has it ever been.[83]

As his letter to Walker makes clear, Arnold had changed significantly from the views he had expressed as a young man about the propriety of federal intervention in most state affairs.

A LIFE SENTENCE FOR RAPE

One of the most significant criminal cases Arnold encountered as a district judge was the case of a black teenager who had been sentenced to life imprisonment, without the possibility of parole, for rape. Harold Eugene Rogers, seventeen years old at the time of the crime, was convicted by an Arkansas jury for the rape of a twenty-one-year-old white woman in 1973. The jury imposed a sentence of life imprisonment, a sentence not subject to parole because of a separate Arkansas statute. Under Arkansas law, the only way in which Rogers's sentence could become subject to parole would be if the Arkansas governor should commute it to a term of years by executive clemency.

Rogers's case gained the attention of the national NAACP. James Meyerson and Nathaniel Jones of the NAACP's New York office joined George Howard Jr., a noted civil rights lawyer from Pine Bluff, Arkansas, who had recently completed an interim appointment on the Arkansas Supreme Court for one year, from 1977 to 1978. Howard would soon be appointed to fill Richard Arnold's district court seat when Arnold was nominated to the Eighth Circuit, becoming Arkansas's first black federal judge. George Howard was the man Griffin Bell originally proposed for the judicial position Arnold occupied.

Attorneys for Rogers brought his case to the federal courts by way of a petition for habeas corpus. In a habeas corpus proceeding in federal court from a state conviction, a prisoner alleges that his federal constitutional rights were violated by the state justice system. Habeas corpus is a civil, not criminal, proceeding in which a court inquires as to the legitimacy of a prisoner's custody. The United States Congress granted all federal courts jurisdiction to issue writs of habeas corpus to release prisoners held by any government entity if the person is in custody in violation of the Constitution or laws or treaties of the United States.[84] In the 1950s and 1960s, decisions by the Warren Court greatly expanded the use and scope of the federal writ. The most publicized use of habeas corpus in modern times has been to allow federal courts to review death penalty proceedings; however, far more noncapital habeas petitions are reviewed by the federal courts.[85]

Arnold had served on the district court about three months when he was assigned Rogers's case. In his first opinion in the case, Arnold upheld the validity of the conviction.[86] Arnold was troubled, though, about unfairness—and especially the possibility of racial bias—in the sentence. Rogers alleged that the life sentence violated the Eighth Amendment's prohibition against cruel and unusual punishment, and the Fourteenth Amendment's due process clause. While Arnold's first opinion did not reach that question, Arnold believed the claim might have merit. Rogers, however, had not exhausted his state remedies with respect to that issue. In general, before a federal court will rule on a habeas petition from a state prisoner, the state courts must first have had an opportunity to correct the alleged mistake. Arnold directed Rogers's attorneys to file an application for post-conviction relief with the Supreme Court of Arkansas, and Arnold retained jurisdiction for possible further action pending the outcome at the Arkansas Supreme Court.

The Arkansas Supreme Court, predictably, upheld the life sentence as not unconstitutionally excessive. That court said the Eighth Amendment's ban on cruel and unusual punishment did not help Rogers because it was directed "toward the kind of punishment, not its duration."[87] The Eighth Amendment, according to the Arkansas court, simply did not apply to the length of a prison sentence, distinguishing it from cases involving the death penalty because "the death penalty is unique." It also denied that the question was one for the judiciary: "If the penalty assessed against petitioner is too severe under the facts of the case, it is a matter that addresses itself to executive clemency and not to this court."[88]

The Arkansas Supreme Court issued its opinion on June 11, 1979. Rogers then returned to Arnold's court. After the last brief on the issues was filed on September 5, Arnold issued his opinion three weeks later, ruling in favor of Rogers. Although Arnold made clear he did not view a life sentence for rape to be per se unconstitutional, Arnold reduced Rogers's sentence to thirty years in prison (the minimum penalty for first-degree rape in Arkansas) unless the state chose to conduct a new sentencing trial for Rogers.

Just a year before, in 1977, the Supreme Court declared in *Coker v. Georgia*[89] that applying the death penalty in rape cases was unconstitutional because the sentence was disproportionate to the crime. *Coker* resulted in the removal of twenty inmates—three whites and seventeen blacks—awaiting execution on rape convictions from death rows around the country. But nowhere had the Supreme Court indicated that a life sentence could be similarly disproportionate. Arnold, in fact, accepted the possibility that life sentences for rape could be "just": "Rape is a violation of the person that must be abhorrent to everyone, and it is deserving of the severest censure. There are cases of rape for which life imprisonment is entirely appropriate, even required by justice."[90]

This case, however, was not one of them. Arnold believed that Eugene Rogers's life sentence for rape violated the Eighth Amendment's ban against cruel and unusual punishment as well as the Fourteenth Amendment's due process clause, because the jury was not given standards or instructions to guide its sentencing discretion. Arnold worried—with good reason—that racial bias had influenced the jury's decision: "Here, the jury was given a range of punishments from which to choose. It was given no guidance on how to make the choice. The petitioner's rights not to be sentenced on the basis of racial factors, and not to be subjected to a cruel and unusual punishment, were thus in jeopardy."[91]

Arnold noted that the Arkansas legislature did not view all rapes as equally reprehensible and that it obviously thought that some rapes were more blameworthy than others by providing a range of punishments up to life imprisonment. "The rub is that the jury in this case was given no guidance in making these distinctions. The jury simply announced its verdict as to punishment, giving, of course, no reasons." It could give no reasons because the legislature had provided no standards. "We cannot know, and the jury could not know, what weight, if any, the General Assembly might have assigned to the defendant's youth, the fact that he did not use a gun, the absence of aggravated injury, the lack of a prior record, or any other aggravating or mitigating circumstances. We do not know that petitioner could have received no greater punishment had he been of full age, had the victim been maimed for life, and had petitioner been guilty of previous rapes." In Rogers's case, none of these aggravating circumstances occurred.

Arnold's reasoning process is instructive and shows his concern with interpretation of unclear Supreme Court precedent. Little of the analysis in Arnold's opinion came directly from the NAACP briefs. Instead, Arnold seems to have relied upon his own knowledge of the breadth of Supreme Court precedent. The problem Arnold faced was that there was no clear Supreme Court precedent that required guidance of jury sentencing discretion in rape cases. The closest analogy, which Arnold invoked, was the Supreme Court's recent death penalty decision in *Gregg v. Georgia*.[92]

Gregg was one of three related cases, from Georgia, Florida, and Texas, presenting newly revised legislation tailored to satisfy the Supreme Court's objections to arbitrary imposition of death sentences. *Gregg* indicated that juries must be provided with "guided discretion" if they are to impose a death sentence. Although there was no majority opinion of the court but merely a plurality for the judgment, Arnold noted that lower courts could properly look to the opinion for guidance, and the opinion was significant because it discussed in full the question of sentencing discretion: "where discretion is afforded a sentencing body on a matter so grave as the determination of whether a human life should be taken or spared, that discretion must be suitably directed and limited so as to minimize the risk of wholly arbitrary and capricious action."[93]

Arnold thought the same reasoning applied to life sentences. Discretion, Arnold noted, must be exercised in an informed manner. "This is especially necessary when juries have the sentencing power, because jurors are not trained in such matters and may never before have made a sentencing decision. Guidance should be given the jury about the factors that the State deems relevant to the sentencing decision."[94]

But did this Supreme Court guidance have any relevance to a case involving life imprisonment and not the death penalty? Arnold acknowledged the issue was uncertain and that there was some reason to think otherwise. He quoted a sentence from the plurality opinion in another case, *Lockett v. Ohio*,[95] by Chief Justice Burger, that "if read broadly and literally, would give a clear answer of 'no' to that question."[96] The chief justice had written that "legislatures remain free to decide how much discretion in sentencing cases should be reposed in the judge or jury in noncapital cases. We recognize that, in noncapital cases, the established practice of individualized sentences rests not on constitutional commands, but on public policy enacted into statutes."[97]

Arnold, however, was not convinced the answer to that question was clearly "no." Arnold pointed out that this passage of the opinion was not joined by a majority of the court, and that it was dicta (a statement by the court not necessary to the resolution of the capital case before it). He also believed the statements were not meant to have full literal force: "There are surely some kinds of exercise of discretion in noncapital cases that States could not validly allow their sentencing authority. If a judge or jury, for example, explicitly imposed a sentence because of the race of the defendant, or the victim, or both, no one would argue that the sentence should stand, no matter how broad the sentencing authority's discretion in general."[98]

This was the best Arnold could do. He believed race had infected the sentence. In this case there could be no proof of that, so Arnold sought to frame the issue as one of lack of sentencing guidance for the jury, an issue that had carried the day with the Supreme Court in death penalty cases. He believed the procedures used in Rogers's case created "a high risk of an erroneous determination." This was because the jury was given no guidance whatever on the question of punishment, by contrast with the careful instructions the jury was given on the issue of guilt or innocence. Accordingly, the jury, Arnold wrote, could have considered anything, even forbidden racial factors. Feeling in the community was understandably high. The sentence meted out was the most severe available under the law, although the individual circumstances of the case seemed to place it at the lower end of the spectrum of culpability. Statutory sentencing standards, communicated to the jury by the court, could have substantially reduced the risk of error. The jury could still have secretly disregarded them, but the whole premise of the system of trial by jury . . . is that jurors are conscientious and make a genuine effort to obey instructions. The instructions could at least have given the jurors a framework for deliberation and debate in the jury room. The jury might still have returned a life sentence, but at least the defendant and the public would have had some assurance that it was based on intelligible and neutral principles.[99]

The sentence, according to Arnold, was therefore unlawful under both the Eighth Amendment and the Fourteenth Amendment's due process clause. Arnold ordered Rogers to be released "on the expiration of 30 years from the date of his conviction, the minimum penalty prescribed by law for the crime of first-degree rape when this crime was committed. If the State of Arkansas wishes to retry the issue of petitioner's punishment in order to seek a longer sentence, it may do so, but only if this new trial is conducted according to constitutionally permissible procedures, and only if it is commenced within 90 days."[100]

Arnold was sensitive to the relationship between federal and state courts. He wrote, "It is with reluctance that this Court differs from the Supreme Court of Arkansas. That Court conscientiously interpreted and applied its view of the law to this case. This Court must do the same. Under the Act of Congress giving this Court jurisdiction to review the federal constitutional validity of the confinement of state prisoners,[101] the duty cannot be avoided. The relief granted will keep interference with the State's administration of criminal justice to the minimum required to satisfy the Constitution of the United States."[102]

Harold Eugene Rogers's seeming victory—the possibility of release after thirty years of prison—was short-lived. A panel of the Eighth Circuit reversed Arnold unanimously, holding that the federal constitution did not require sentencing guidance in noncapital cases. A defendant's due process rights, it said, are unimpaired by the complete absence of sentencing guidelines.[103]

As Arnold had done, the Eighth Circuit also rejected Rogers's claim under the equal protection clause that black rape defendants received disproportionately harsh sentences because of invidious racial discrimination. They affirmed Arnold's holding that Rogers had failed to prove racially discriminatory sentencing. A showing of disproportionate impact on black defendants was insufficient under Supreme Court precedent. Instead, Rogers had to show a discriminatory purpose in his sentencing. Rogers claimed that black convicted rapists in Arkansas had tended to receive stiffer sentences than their white counterparts. The statistics presented by Rogers's attorneys "did tend to bear out this proposition," but the divergence between white and black "is not so stark as to bespeak the existence of discriminatory purpose."[104] The more telling statistic depended upon the race of the victim: When the victim of a rape was white, the sentence imposed by an Arkansas court was significantly harsher than when the victim was black. The Eighth Circuit, however, held that Rogers had no standing to raise the claim. If anything, the court said, it was a claim for black women to raise, which the court doubted could be maintained.[105]

But this was precisely why Arnold was so concerned about the unguided jury discretion in imposing a sentence. Even if the Arkansas jury in Rogers's case was motivated by racial animus, there would be no way to prove it, as Arnold noted, because jurors were not required to give reasons for the sentence they chose. Hence, for Arnold, the absence of any guidelines for jurors when imposing a sentence within a broad range needed a remedy. The proof, however, could not come from Rogers's statistical evidence of racial disparity in sentencing, according to Supreme Court precedent, because it did not prove anything one way or another with respect to his case.

Arnold believed the Supreme Court's recent decision in *Gregg* meant that the constitutional mandate of guided discretion for juries imposed in death penalty cases should be extended even to cases where the death penalty was not a possibility. The Eighth Circuit panel disagreed: "We decline so to extend the rule."[106] They did so on the ground that state sovereignty was the controlling interest, and it overrode the concerns motivating the Supreme Court in death penalty cases. "In moving from capital to non-capital cases, the especially compelling concerns originally motivating the guided discretion rule are no longer operative. As a result, the values promoting deference—diversity, federalism—gain predominance. Whatever may be the benevolent purposes of a rule of guided discretion—and we do not deny them—they are generally not of sufficient weight to justify displacing Arkansas' preference on this matter."[107] In effect, the Eighth Circuit weighed state sovereignty more heavily than federal constitutional rights.

Additionally, the Eighth Circuit rejected Arnold's finding that the lack of sentencing guidelines violated substantive due process rights under the Fourteenth Amendment. Arnold had urged that a still-more recent Supreme Court decision, *Mathews v. Eldridge*, also indicated a criminal defendant had a basic due process right to guided jury discretion in sentencing.[108] In *Eldridge*, the Supreme Court dictated an interest-balancing approach to determine whether the government's interest in unbridled jury discretion at sentencing outweighed the defendant's private interest. The Eighth Circuit noted that *Eldridge* was initially developed for use in the administrative context, "and apart from the action of the lower court in this case, has not yet been expressly employed by a federal court to test the procedures used at a criminal trial." Nonetheless, the panel found Arnold's reasoning persuasive: "We perceive no doctrinal obstacle to extending Eldridge and view it as a useful specification of factors to be considered in any case raising procedural due process questions."[109]

Proceeding to its "balancing" test, however, the Eighth Circuit panel disagreed with Arnold's conclusion. "Overall, we do not find that the balancing of relevant factors favors Rogers. We certainly could not agree that Rogers' private interest substantially outweighs the governmental interest of Arkansas." Thus, the court concluded that neither the Eighth Amendment, nor procedural due process, required sentencing guidelines to be constitutionally mandated for non–death penalty cases. As the court stated tersely, "They are not."[110]

Arnold was ahead of the field on this issue. Although it is still true that the Supreme Court has not extended the protections of the Eighth Amendment to require sentencing guidance for noncapital cases,[111] the trend became in both state and federal systems to establish sentencing guidelines to limit the sentencing discretion of judges and to seek more uniformity in sentences.

Had Arnold's view prevailed, Harold Eugene Rogers would have been released from prison in 2003, the year before Arnold's death, when Arnold was still serving as a senior appeals court judge. Rogers would have been forty-seven years old, after serving the thirty-year prison sentence Arnold ordered in lieu of a retrial by the state of Arkansas. Instead, as of 2008, Rogers was still in prison in Arkansas, in his thirty-fifth year of confinement.

If there were any doubts about Arnold's stance on civil rights, his year as a district court judge showed him to be a staunch proponent of federal court protection. In light of his earlier views, Arnold was surprisingly receptive to civil rights claims. One might conclude that his bold positions in the Harold Eugene Rogers, National Guard, and girls' basketball cases were an attempt to prove himself the equal of George Howard, the black civil rights lawyer from Arkansas who had been Carter's and Bell's preferred nominee for Arnold's position.

All cases before Richard Arnold in his year as a district court judge were not as memorable as these three, perhaps, but all were vital to the litigants. If Arnold resolved these three cases with the view that such civil rights positions would be the trend of the future, he would have been wrong. Arnold had mixed success even in these three rulings: He was reversed in one case and likely would have been in *Dodson* if the matter had been appealed. The third case—the Arkansas National Guard—was affirmed in an opinion written by Judge Heaney, then the strongest proponent of civil rights on the Eighth Circuit.

Chapter Seven

To the Court of Appeals

In 1979, Richard Arnold had been on the federal district court in Little Rock for less than one year when he came under consideration for a newly created seat on the Eighth United States Circuit Court of Appeals. The American Bar Association had deemed Arnold "well qualified" for the district court position, its second-highest rating. When its Judiciary Committee undertook another investigation one year later for Arnold's appointment to a newly created seat on the Eighth Circuit Court of Appeals, the committee viewed Arnold to be "exceptionally well qualified," its highest rating. In just over one year, Arnold had proven himself to be an exceptional district court judge.

Less than eighteen months had elapsed from Arnold's appointment as a trial judge to his Eighth Circuit confirmation. Some other judges then serving on the Eighth Circuit reacted with surprise at Arnold's quick elevation, with the view that such rewards usually followed more time in the trenches. Donald P. Lay, who had become chief judge of the Eighth Circuit prior to Arnold's nomination to that court, said that Arnold was known as "the new kid on the block." The feeling, according to Lay, was that Arnold had not yet paid his dues on the district court. Lay said some of his fellow judges were skeptical of Arnold's abilities: "I don't think people at that point appreciated the quality of writing and just where he fit in his judicial philosophy—it took a while for that to grow upon the other members of the court."[1]

With Arnold's recent confirmation by the Senate to the district court in Arkansas, his candidacy for the Eighth Circuit would come with a presumption among the Senate Judiciary Committee that Arnold was "qualified," possessed the requisite judicial temperament, and had no scandals or other difficulties in his record. Arnold's second confirmation should have been easy to justify, but in some ways it was not. The Eighth Circuit had no women members, and Arnold's appointment to that court delayed the addition of one. The Eighth Circuit would be nearly the last federal court of appeals to gain a female judge, with President Clinton's appointment of Diana E. Murphy in 1994, beating the First Circuit for this "last" distinction by a matter of months.[2]

Further, Arnold's health was explicitly a concern, and a health crisis Arnold experienced in late 1980 would likely have prevented his appointment had it occurred a few months earlier.

CARTER'S MERIT SELECTION COMMISSIONS

At a press conference in late October 1978, around the time Arnold was sworn in as a district judge in Arkansas, President Carter reiterated his goal for more diversity on the federal bench. He called on the Senate, which he said had "historically played an important role in judicial selection, particularly at the district court level," to work with him "to achieve a more representative judiciary." To further this goal, he said, Carter would not nominate any judges in a Circuit "until I have had an opportunity to review *all* candidates for that Circuit."[3] In answer to a question about specific goals, Carter replied:

> My goal is to have black judges in Georgia, Florida, the Carolinas, Mississippi, Alabama, Louisiana, indeed throughout the country. We are working with every Senator in the government to encourage their submission to me of names selected by commissions which include both women and minority representatives. And I can't give you an exact number yet, but whenever possible, we will have a representative number of blacks, those who speak Spanish and women.[4]

President Carter continued the theme in early 1979: "We have tried to induce the members of the Senate to do two things: One is to choose a list of potential judge appointees on the basis of merit, but also to take into consideration the fact that for many years there have been discriminatory practices in the appointment of judges against minority groups . . . and also against women."[5]

President Carter wanted both to raise the quality of federal judges and to increase the number of women and minorities on the federal bench. The effort to add minorities and women to the ranks of federal judges was at least part of the reason Carter attempted to put in place what he called "merit selection" committees for all federal judicial appointments. By executive order, Carter established nominating commissions for all court of appeals appointments. But for the district judge level, traditionally a prerogative of each state's senators, nominating commissions were only voluntary.

One year into the Carter administration, Attorney General Griffin Bell, a former judge on the Fifth Circuit, issued a statement on the selection of federal judges. His purpose was to address "merit selection" and to explain the Carter administration's attempt to shift control of the appointment process from home-state senators to the executive branch.

In his first press conference as attorney general, Griffin Bell had said, "[W]e expect to put in merit selection commissions, to select the federal courts of appeals judges, before too long."[6] In fact, these commissions were established within the first month of President Carter's term of office. In that same period, Carter wrote to each individual senator urging the use of a nominating commission for select candidates for district judge nominees.

The court of appeals nominating commissions were established by executive order on February 17, 1977.[7] Each panel was charged, upon the request of the president, to recommend for nomination as circuit judges "persons whose character, experience, ability, and commitment to equal justice under law" fully qualified them to serve in the federal judiciary. All members would be appointed by the president, with no more than eleven members for each circuit. Each panel was to include members of both sexes, members of minority groups, and approximately equal numbers of lawyers and nonlawyers, with membership of each panel to include at least one resident of each of the states within the geographic area of the circuit. Attorney General Bell later charged that the White House wanted to appoint nominating commission members based on political patronage. The compromise with Bell was that Bell could appoint the chairman of each commission.[8]

When notified by the president of a vacancy, the panel was required to give public notice of the vacancy within the relevant geographic area; invite suggestions as to potential nominees; conduct inquiries to identify potential nominees; conduct inquiries to identify those persons among the potential nominees who are "well-qualified to serve as a United States Circuit Judge"; and provide a confidential report to the president with its recommendations of five persons whom the panel considered best qualified to fill the vacancy. Commission members received no pay but were allowed some travel expenses.

Potential nominees on this list of five had to meet five criteria:

1. be a member in good standing of at least one state or the District of Columbia bar (and in good standing with any other bars of which they may be members);

2. that they possess, and have reputations for, integrity and good character;

3. that they are of sound health;

4. that they possess, and have demonstrated, outstanding legal ability and commitment to equal justice under law; and

5. that their demeanor, character, and personality indicate that they would exhibit judicial temperament if appointed to the position of United States Circuit Judge.[9]

It was the first time a president stated by executive order the criteria he intended to apply to lower federal court appointments. The criteria for being a good judge thus explicitly included a "commitment to equal justice under law," "judicial temperament," "reputation for integrity and good character," and, of significance for Arnold, that the candidate be "of sound health." The last was not unreasonable since federal judges receive lifetime appointments with the ability to retire at full salary.

Despite resistance from the Senate, at the end of 1979 all of President Carter's appointments for judgeships on federal courts of appeals had been through nominating commissions. The nominating commissions for the court of appeals are particularly significant because Carter's appointees became the pool from which Clinton would choose his two Supreme Court nominees, Justices Ruth Bader Ginsburg and Stephen Breyer. Further, senators from eighteen states had by then established commissions to nominate candidates for district judgeships.[10] When Carter was defeated after one term in office, President Ronald Reagan dropped the nominating commissions, and no subsequent president reinstated the practice.

THE THREE-WAY DEAL: GEORGE HOWARD, HENRY WOODS, AND RICHARD ARNOLD

A deal between Attorney General Griffin Bell and Senator Dale Bumpers allowed Arnold's name to be put forward for the Eighth Circuit in exchange for the appointment of George Howard as Arkansas's first black federal judge. Journalists seemed well aware that Arnold's promotion was the result of a political compromise within the executive branch. The *Arkansas Democrat* and *Arkansas Gazette* both reported in November 1979 that an agreement had been worked out between the administration and Arkansas's senators for a black to be appointed to fill the vacancy created "when Judge Arnold leaves to go to the Eighth Circuit."[11]

The vacancy on the Arkansas district court that would be created if Arnold were named to the Eighth Circuit coincided with a second vacancy: under the 1978 Judiciary Bill, a new seat had been created in the Eastern District of Arkansas. Bumpers had recommended Henry Woods, a noted Little Rock lawyer and close associate of Bumpers, for the newly created seat. But that nomination had been held up for months by the White House because Woods was white, and Arkansas still did not have a black federal district judge.[12] Carter and Bell held firm after their earlier capitulation on Arnold. This was now a second chance to appoint George Howard to the district court, and it would be successful.

As the *Arkansas Gazette* reported, both Woods and Judge Arnold were nominated by the White House in December 1979 as part of a package designed to ensure the appointment of George Howard to the federal bench in Arkansas. The confirmations of Woods and Arnold on the same date "marked the end of a long and controversial battle that began years ago as an effort to get some assistance to the overburdened federal bench in the Eastern District of Arkansas."[13]

The opposition to Woods was ironic. Woods was known in the 1950s for his involvement in civil rights causes, including work for the NAACP. As Senator David Pryor would testify before the Senate Judiciary Committee, Woods had been a prominent liberal voice during the 1957 integration crisis in Little Rock: "Henry displayed courage when he spoke out for social justice when it was not a popular stand in our state."[14]

Still, Bumpers's earlier proposal of Woods had upset some black leaders in the state.[15] Woods was prominent in the early campaigns of Dale Bumpers, beginning with the first campaign for governor in 1970. Woods and Arnold worked together "almost daily" on Bumpers's first campaign for Senate.[16] For that and other work for the Democratic Party, Woods was rewarded by Senators Bumpers and Pryor with a federal judgeship. Woods would go on to be one of the most liberal judges on civil rights matters in Arkansas, surpassing Arnold's brief record on that court. For many years, Woods was the key figure in the Little Rock school desegregation litigation. Woods would eventually quit the case in frustration after several key reversals in opinions written by Arnold.[17]

At the joint confirmation hearing, Senator Howell Heflin of Alabama called Woods "one of the great lawyers of America." Former Arkansas governor Sid McMath, who served from 1948 to 1952, was in the audience to support his former protégé Woods. Senator Heflin pointed to McMath and said "the McMath administration was recognized across the South" as progressive and as having "sanity in racial matters."[18]

Arnold and Woods were confirmed on the same day, February 20, 1980, by voice vote of the Senate. A few months later, George Howard Jr. was confirmed to fill Arnold's seat on the district court, where he would serve until his death in 2007. As Bumpers later said: "Griffin Bell and I worked out the arrangement for Richard to go to the Eighth Circuit. I told Griffin Bell that I wanted Richard to have that appointment. And he was amenable to it. They had somebody they wanted on the District Court. And I agreed to that, in exchange for Richard going to the Eighth Circuit."[19] Writing to Arnold a few years later, Griffin Bell would say, "I am very proud to have played a small part in your having become a judge on two occasions."[20]

THE ABA COMMITTEE: A WOMAN FOR THE EIGHTH CIRCUIT

Bumpers had expected the confirmation of Arnold to take place more quickly than it did. Ultimately, Arnold would be confirmed in February 1980; Bumpers had predicted it would occur by December 1979. The delay came from the circuit nominating commission, the FBI background investigation, and the Senate Judiciary Committee. Whatever "deal" Bumpers thought he had concluded, there was still the issue of the nominating commission, which was charged with presenting five names for that position to President Carter.

The deal on behalf of George Howard was necessary for Arnold's promotion — Bell had seen to that. But it did not resolve the question of a woman on the Eighth Circuit. There was already a black judge on the court, since Carter had appointed Theodore McMillian of St. Louis in 1978. The Eighth Circuit, however, continued to be an all-male court.

The Eighth Circuit Nominating Commission, which would pass on to Carter Arnold's name in 1979, was put together by the Democratic National Committee and the White House. Initially, a member from Arkansas was overlooked, but in August 1977 that was remedied with the nomination of Sid McMath, a former governor of Arkansas and a prominent trial lawyer in the state. McMath was recommended by Arkansas attorney general Bill Clinton.[21]

The nominating commission had put forward the name of one woman — Joan M. Krauskopf, a law professor at the University of Missouri at Columbia. Krauskopf was four years older than Arnold. An honors graduate of Ohio State's Law School, Krauskopf soon thereafter had embarked on a career as a law professor. At the time of her consideration for the Eighth Circuit seat, Krauskopf had recently moved from a law school in Colorado.[22] Carter presumably would have preferred Krauskopf's appointment to Arnold's because of his stated preference for adding women to the federal judiciary.

Indeed, during the early months of 1979 it appeared that President Carter had decided to nominate Krauskopf for the Eighth Circuit seat. Michael Egan, associate attorney general in the Carter administration, wrote to Arnold's friend Gilbert Merritt in March 1979 in response to Merritt's recommendation of Arnold for the Eighth Circuit. Egan wrote, "The President and the Attorney General have tentatively agreed on another candidate."[23] Egan did not name Krauskopf as the preferred choice, but Arnold seems to have learned that she was. Arnold wrote to Justice William Brennan in April to let him know that "the President has decided to nominate Joan Krauskopf, a Law Professor at the University of Missouri, to the existing vacancy on the Court of Appeals for the Eighth Circuit." Arnold was pleased, he told Brennan, "to have gotten on the short list of five."[24]

But there was also the matter of the American Bar Association rating committee. That committee rated Krauskopf "not qualified" for the court of appeals. The ABA Judiciary Committee's stated criteria to evaluate nominees was "integrity, professional competence and judicial temperament."[25] The committee adopted the view that ordinarily a nominee to the federal bench should have at least twelve years' experience in the practice of law, including substantial courtroom experience.[26]

According to a member of the committee, Krauskopf received a "not qualified" rating because she lacked trial practice, except for a single domestic relations case in Colorado. Further, she was not a member of the bar of any state within the Eighth Circuit. Arnold wrote to Brennan in August that "the woman law professor whom the President had initially settled on didn't make it." The Bar Association had "rated her unqualified (lack of trial experience), and Judge Bell went along with them."[27]

Judge Donald P. Lay of Minnesota, who had just become chief judge of the Eighth Circuit in 1979, called the committee to support Krauskopf. According to the committee member, Lay said: "We'll see that she gets educated, and in the meantime we won't assign her to any important cases." An editorial in a Kansas City, Missouri, newspaper blasted the ABA rating of Krauskopf as gender discrimination. Had she been a man, the editorial charged, the committee would have approved her.

The rating "not qualified" would be rare for the ABA Judiciary Committee. When the ABA in 2006 deemed a Connecticut judge who was nominated to the federal bench by President Bush "not qualified" for the post, that judge was only the sixth nominee (out of 445) since 1999 to be so rated.[28]

Ironically, the ABA committee in later years would be accused of "liberal" bias. In 1996, Senator Orrin G. Hatch, a Utah Republican who was chairman of the Judiciary Committee, charged that "Most Republicans believe the A.B.A. leans much too far to the left."[29] Probably the opposite was true during the Carter era. Eventually, Carter asked Griffin Bell to ignore the ABA ratings of potential nominees.[30]

By contrast, the ABA reported Arnold to be "exceptionally well qualified" for the newly created Eighth Circuit position. A committee member said the only earlier opposition to Arnold for the district court position had been the perception that Arnold was a better fit for the court of appeals because of his intellectual acumen. When the ABA received the request to investigate Arnold for the court of appeals, Arnold had cleared the backlog and it was "obvious that Arnold was a superstar trial judge." Trial judges who served with Arnold objected to his leaving the district court for the Eighth Circuit because he was "the best district court judge we've ever had."[31]

Griffin Bell read every FBI file on every nominee himself, before rating each candidate for President Carter. Because of Arnold's selection to the Eighth Circuit, Bell said, "I had to go back to the commissions and tell them to start looking harder for women." At that time, Bell said, the American Bar wanted all nominees to have practiced law for fifteen years. Bell recognized that most women lawyers would have difficulty fulfilling this requirement because "we were just beginning to get a lot of women lawyers. I had to make a special effort to get that done. If we could find a qualified woman or a qualified black we would recommend them over anybody else, to create diversity. And we had some big fights with Senators over some of them. They all were rated qualified, otherwise I wouldn't put them on the list."[32]

While the Eighth Circuit nominating commission was at work to fill the newly created seat, Carter spoke on judicial reform at the annual Law Day reception at the White House:

> I am also concerned about equality of opportunity and a representative group of federal judges. It is time for women to be adequately represented, those who speak Spanish, and blacks. And for a Senator or for a selection committee of the most distinguished citizens to choose district judges to say, "Well, I cannot find a qualified black because there are none who serve in the State court system, or there are none who have had 20 years' experience in a distinguished law firm," this in itself is no reason to perpetuate a travesty of justice, because basing present discrimination on past discrimination is obviously not right.[33]

And yet the Eighth Circuit nominating committee was accused of doing just that.

Four years later, Arnold wrote about the experience in response to a questionnaire from the Association of Women Lawyers of Greater Kansas

City. Arnold reported that the strongest and most influential support for his nomination came from "politicians or party" and secondarily from "other lawyers." Arnold volunteered an additional insight:

> The purpose of the Commission was to assess candidates on the basis of merit, as opposed to personal or political connections. The Commission sent a list of five candidates to the President, who in the end selected me. I believe the Commission chose the five people it considered best qualified. The list included a Republican District Judge who was superbly qualified [fellow Arkansan G. Thomas Eisele]. As to the choice among the five, certainly political factors played a part. This is not improper, in my opinion. Sometimes it is hard to tell where merit leaves off and politics begins.[34]

Intense lobbying for the newly created seat on the Eighth Circuit had taken place not only from the two Arkansas senators but also from Missouri and South Dakota. Vice president Walter Mondale, a Minnesotan, was also alleged to have lobbied on behalf of various judge candidates.[35] An *Omaha World Herald* editorial described Arnold's appointment as one that "was apparently dealt from the bottom of the political deck."[36]

Donald Lay, the incoming chief judge of the Eighth Circuit, responded with a vigorous defense of Arnold's qualifications: "As chief judge of the Eighth Circuit, I am concerned that someone would get the impression that we do not have distinguished people coming on the court. It is important that the people in this region have confidence in our court system. We don't build that kind of confidence if the impression is left that we have a bunch of political hacks being appointed."[37] Lay defended Arnold's appointment not only by pointing out his stellar qualifications but also by explaining that his name had come from a nominating commission, a process that had sifted through an initial field of twenty-three applicants and sent five names, including Arnold's, to the president. Lay said he had been told informally by some members of the nominating commission that Judge Arnold "was the most outstanding and had the finest credentials of the five they recommended."[38]

Part of the criticism of the selection process, Lay said, was that it involved efforts by the Carter administration to place more blacks and more women in federal judgeships. Newspapers throughout the Eighth Circuit had reported the compromise that allowed George Howard to be appointed, noting pointedly that it included a seat for Arnold on the

Eighth Circuit. Hence, the nominating commission seemed to be merely a rubber stamp for a decision already reached by the White House. President Carter, Lay said, "should be commended and not criticized for putting minority members on the bench."[39]

Concerned with the reactions of his fellow judges to his statements to the press, Lay sent a memo to all active judges of the Eighth Circuit on January 2, 1980. In it he included the recent articles in the *Omaha World Herald* about the Arnold nomination. One quotation he called an "error": "I did not attempt to rate Judge Arnold as being the best of the five. You will note that this language is lifted from the last paragraph in the same column. In any event, I hope none of you are offended by my response."[40] Lay would say later that he had responded to the charges of political cronyism because it "really made me mad." Arnold, in any event, was grateful, according to Lay: "Richard always said that I was his friend for life for telling them off."[41]

The Eighth Circuit would not have a woman judge until 1994, when President Clinton's nominee Diana E. Murphy was confirmed to the court by the Senate. Judge Murphy remains the only woman of eleven active judges and seven senior circuit judges, and in the history of the Eighth Circuit is the only woman of fifty-seven judges.

EXCLUSIONARY CLUBS ISSUE

Having emerged from the "deal" between Bumpers and the White House, the ABA rating committee, and the Eighth Circuit nominating commission, Arnold still faced a hearing by the Senate Judiciary Committee and confirmation by the full Senate. One important change had occurred since his previous confirmation hearing. Senator James Eastland was no longer chair of the Senate Judiciary Committee. That job had devolved to Senator Edward Kennedy. Senator Eastland was the most senior member of the Senate when he resigned at end of 1978. He had served as chair of the Senate Judiciary Committee for an unprecedented twenty-two years.

Senator Kennedy had different priorities. Kennedy and then the Republican chairs who followed him hired their own investigators for candidates.[42] Kennedy made it clear that he would closely scrutinize the civil rights record of each nominee. He also sent the message that membership in male-only clubs would potentially be disqualifying. There was no such requirement under Senator Eastland, although nominees were required to list membership in any clubs that excluded on the basis of race. Arnold had kept his membership in the Metropolitan Club of Washington, DC, a male-only institution, after his district court appointment.

Arnold was confronted with this issue at his hearing before the Senate Judiciary Committee:

> **Senator Baucus:** What is your reaction to the questions I have asked prior nominees with respect to membership in clubs which, according to some standards, discriminate on the basis of sex or race? What should the standard of this committee be in passing upon those nominees? Should sitting judges resign their memberships in any clubs which may or may not discriminate?

> **Judge Arnold:** When I went on the district bench, I was a member of clubs that fall in that category. No question was raised about it, and it frankly never occurred to me that a question would be raised. I did not personally feel that the memberships impaired my functioning or affected my mental attitude toward litigants. No one indicated to me that they thought my impartiality would be questioned because of it.

> After a while, I began to be conscious of the positions that the committee was taking. I can see that there are circumstances in which the impartiality of a judge or the apparent impartiality might be questioned because of that type of membership. So eventually, I divested myself of all those memberships, feeling that if a question is raised, it is better to have it resolved in favor of eliminating appearances of impropriety.[43]

Arnold's statement makes it clear that he had not resigned because he, personally, had come to the conclusion it was the right thing to do; instead, it was a pragmatic, compelled decision. Arnold later said it was clear the Senate would not approve him unless he resigned his membership in the Metropolitan Club of Washington, in particular. In 1988, after the club had admitted women, Arnold wrote to request reinstatement, explaining his earlier resignation: "I was elected a resident member of the club in 1978. Later that year, I was appointed a United States District Judge and moved to Little Rock. At that time, I became a non-resident member. Then, in December of 1979, the president nominated me to be a United States circuit judge for the Eighth

Circuit. I was informed, before being nominated, that I would need to resign from the club because of its men-only policy. I complied with this request. I understand that the membership policy has now changed, and the purpose of this letter is to request reinstatement as a non-resident member."[44] Arnold was promptly reinstated to membership in the club.

In his questionnaire submitted to the Senate Judiciary Committee, Arnold had also told them he belonged to a club in Little Rock that excluded female members from its "Men's Grill," but he discounted that fact as significant discrimination. The Little Rock Club "has both black and female members, but women are not permitted in the 'Men's Grill' at lunchtime," Arnold wrote. "I have not been involved in efforts to change these policies," he added. But he also told the committee a substantial part of his practice of law in the past was devoted to demonstrating a commitment to equal justice to all persons, and he reminded them that "[e]very day in my work as a U.S. District Judge I strive to do equal justice to the poor and the rich."[45]

The issue of all-male clubs would come before him later in his career on the Eighth Circuit. He would uphold the right of the Jaycees to exclude women as an expression of their First Amendment rights, a position that would be reversed by the Supreme Court in an opinion written by his mentor, Justice William Brennan.[46]

ANOTHER FBI INVESTIGATION

The Senate Judiciary Committee also had the results of another FBI investigation of Arnold. Even though Arnold's nomination to the court of appeals came less than one year after the conclusion of the initial FBI investigation, an extensive check was repeated, this time including attorneys who had appeared in his court in the short time he served as a federal district judge, in addition to judges of that court and the Eighth Circuit, as well as the laborious process of reinterviewing nearly everyone contacted before. The FBI was vigilant about the possibility of bribery of a judge. Bribery was especially a concern at the trial-court level. It was less so for the court of appeals, because a judge there is rarely in a position to influence a case on his or her own.

The FBI background investigation for the court of appeals nomination began in December 1979. Importantly, there was also a new inquiry on Arnold's medical condition. Dr. John Lamberg, one of Arnold's doctors at the National Institutes of Health, stated on December 4, 1979, that Arnold's prognosis "in view of his medical problem was survival without treatment of greater than 10 years." Dr. Lamberg described Arnold as "having a problem with his spleen, which was diagnosed as lymphoproliferative disorder."[47]

Dr. Everard Hughes, also with the National Institutes of Health, stated that he had seen Judge Arnold approximately every three months for the last eighteen months. Dr. Hughes reported that Arnold had "an enlarged spleen, which is thought to be due to a medical condition known as lympho-prolific leukemia." Dr. Hughes said that "this is a benign form of leukemia, which is not serious," and noted that "this condition has improved without any medical treatment of Judge Arnold." In less than one year from these opinions, Arnold would have to have his spleen removed.[48]

In addition to Arnold's doctors, the list of interviewees is again impressive in number. A cover memo in the FBI report to the Senate Judiciary Committee concludes: "Judge Arnold is highly recommended by his fellow judges in the eastern and western districts of Arkansas and is considered an ideal appellate judge. He is also highly recommended by state and local judges; minority, religious, and labor groups; law enforcement officials; and Arkansas Bar Association officials." Justice Brennan was contacted again, and the report states that "Mr. Justice Brennan continues to hold Judge Arnold in very high esteem and was extremely pleased to learn that President Carter intends to appoint Judge Arnold to the position of circuit judge." Brennan described Arnold as being "an absolutely brilliant jurist, who by every standard is eminently qualified for appointment to the U.S. Court of Appeals."[49]

The FBI also interviewed current judges of the Eighth Circuit. Judge Gerald W. Heaney reviewed a number of Arnold's district court opinions and "found them knowledgeable and scholarly." Heaney believed Arnold "enjoys an excellent reputation" and "is open-minded on racial issues."[50]

Judge Eisele was interviewed a second time. Eisele had previously told the FBI that Arnold would make an outstanding judge, and "now his belief has been fulfilled." Eisele described Arnold as hardworking, diligent, intelligent, practical, and an exceptional judge: "Judge Arnold has done an outstanding job, has developed a tremendous relationship with his fellow judges, and he is highly respected by his fellow judges. Judge Arnold is extremely fair in all matters and does not become involved emotionally in his cases." Eisele said Arnold not only would make an outstanding Eighth Circuit Court of Appeals judge "but is Supreme Court caliber material."[51]

Judge Elsijane Trimble Roy, a contemporary of Arnold's on the Arkansas federal district court bench and its first woman judge, said that Arnold "has been the light for his fellow judges in his brilliance, his concern for others, and his practical approach to matters." Arnold, she said, had the "unique ability of being extremely fair, and always takes an impartial stance on all matters regardless of the emotional aspects of the issues." She described Arnold as being "very religious" and told the FBI agent that she was "distressed at the fact that he is leaving because it will be a substantial blow to the quality of the work that is being done in the Eastern District of Arkansas." Judge Roy said Arnold "is the type of individual who could go to the U.S. Supreme Court."[52]

Judge William Overton, another federal district court judge, said he considered Judge Arnold "to be a genius, who knows how to use his brain, and uses it very practically and very responsibly." Henry Jones, a US magistrate judge, said "one thing he has noted in particular is that Judge Arnold has immediately taken control of his docket and has cleared it up to a good extent, primarily by being considerate of the attorneys involved and also making them settle cases that should be settled and to get moving on the cases that should be moving."

One large category in this report consists of interviews of attorneys who appeared before Judge Arnold in the year that he had served as a federal district judge. All but one attorney advised they would "recommend" that Arnold be appointed to the Eighth Circuit. The attorney who chose not to endorse Arnold based his choice on a disagreement with some of his decisions.

The observations of the attorneys are noteworthy and descriptive of Arnold's style as a trial judge. Arnold listened to lawyers and witnesses with total concentration, a characteristic of individual conversations as well as a courtroom demeanor consistently commented on throughout his life. Arnold cocked his head to the side and looked intently at the speaker. The effect could be unnerving, although unintentionally so.

Philip Lyon, a Little Rock attorney, recalled that Arnold was one of the few judges that he had been in contact with who had read all of the depositions and thoroughly prepared for the trial. In one instance, the trial lasted all day with very few breaks, and after the attorneys had finished, the judge immediately made a ruling on the case. Judge Arnold summed up the testimony that had been given during the day in a very articulate manner. He considered Arnold to be "the old classic Southern gentleman type." Other attorneys, including Michael Moore, noted "that judge Arnold is Supreme Court material."[53]

James Roy Jr., an attorney from Springdale, said that he considered Richard Arnold to be the best judge he had ever appeared before. One of the things that fascinated him about Arnold was that sometimes other attorneys would cite cases out of context, but "Arnold would immediately pick up on the case and advise the attorney citing the case that he was citing the case out of context and that it really stood for the following point. Then judge Arnold would go on to describe a case that would fit into the particular issue." Roy said Arnold "was absolutely brilliant because of his thorough knowledge of the law."[54]

Philip Anderson said that Arnold "is not an emotional person and shows remarkable self-control and patience in dealing with others." Lawyers that have practiced before Judge Arnold had told Anderson, a longtime personal friend, that "Arnold brings great dignity to the court and makes people feel they are participating in something important."[55]

Some attorneys addressed specific issues that had arisen in Arnold's courtroom, including attorneys in the Harold Rogers rape case. Joseph Purvis, then deputy attorney general for the state of Arkansas, felt that Judge Arnold "arbitrarily made a ruling in this case since there was no statutory basis toward the ruling." (The ruling, in fact, had been on constitutional, not statutory, grounds.) Purvis "felt that the judge had no precedent for such a ruling" and the case at that time was on appeal to the Eighth Circuit. Purvis advised the agent that while he had no objection to Arnold's serving on the court of appeals, "he does not wholeheartedly endorse him."

The FBI report included one attorney's critical remarks. H. Clay Moore complained about what he considered unfair treatment from Judge Arnold in a case involving a bank loan. As recorded by the agent, Moore's statement seems to reflect Arnold's commitment to moving the docket expeditiously:

> At the outset of the trial, Judge Arnold became upset with Moore for not notifying a party to the case that it was set for trial. He threatened to hold Moore in criminal contempt at the outset of the trial. Moore stated he did not feel judge Arnold gave him the benefit of the doubt or the opportunity to explain what had occurred. Judge Arnold did not want to grant a continuance, and the Judge implied that Moore's actions in failing to notify the party was an attempt by Moore to obtain a continuance. He felt the judge's attitude was reflected throughout the trial in his demeanor, but he could not point to any errors on the part of the judge in the trial.

In chambers, Arnold asked for an apology and Moore apologized for his failure, according to the FBI report. Moore was "personally a little shocked that Judge Arnold acted so strongly toward him at the outset of the trial, and he questioned the Judge's demeanor and judicial temperament as a result of his actions."[56] The jury returned a verdict against Moore's client. Perhaps predictably, attorneys who found themselves on the losing side of Arnold's rulings were more critical.

One update for the FBI file was Richard's marriage to Kay Kelley on October 27, 1979, at Heber Springs, Arkansas. Richard, forty-three, and Kay, twenty-six, had been introduced by mutual friends. Kay was an administrative liaison for Governor Bill Clinton and she was also completing her law degree at the University of Arkansas at Little Rock (the degree was awarded in 1980).

Kay Arnold would continue her political affiliation with Clinton, and in some ways her ties with both Bill and his wife, Hillary, were more extensive than Richard's through the White House years. Kay was a member of Governor Clinton's staff from 1979 to 1980 and served as a member of his cabinet from 1986 to 1987. She would later serve as a vice president of Entergy Corporation. Kay joined Entergy (then Arkansas Power & Light Co.) in 1988 as general manager of corporate communications before going to Washington as director of federal governmental affairs. President Clinton later nominated Kay as a member of the board of directors of the Inter-American Foundation, where she served beginning January 2000.

Arnold was sworn in as a court of appeals judge on March 7, 1980, in Judge Elsijane Roy's courtroom in Little Rock. The oath of office was administered by Judge J. Smith Henley, Arkansas's only other member of the Eighth Circuit. "The position will give me an opportunity to study law and reflect that trial judges don't always enjoy," Arnold said. He would retain his docket until his successor on the district court was confirmed, and also retain jurisdiction over some cases in which he had invested substantial work.[57]

In late August 1980, Arnold experienced his first real crisis associated with the underlying diagnosis of lympho-prolific leukemia. With persistent abdominal pain, while still completing district court cases and before he had yet sat with the Eighth Circuit for hearings, in late August 1980 Arnold underwent surgery for the removal of his spleen at the National Institutes of Health at Washington. At that point, his physicians expected a ten-day hospital stay followed by a short recuperation period, which the *Arkansas Gazette* reported would require limitation to working only half days.[58]

Arnold developed an infection, however, and the infection kept him hospitalized in Washington, DC, much longer. At times his survival was in real doubt. Arnold was hospitalized for nearly two months, followed by recuperation in Little Rock when he was able to return. There he received a letter from Chief Justice Warren Burger in mid-November wishing a speedy recovery. "What is most important is that you recover your health fully. You must not let concern for court work interfere with a complete recovery."[59] Some time later he also received a letter from Donald P. Lay, the new chief judge of the Eighth Circuit, telling Arnold that he had worried that Arnold's close call with his health would mean the newly inaugurated Eighth Circuit judge would never actually join the court.

Had Arnold's health crisis occurred six months earlier, it would undoubtedly have delayed his nomination to the Eighth Circuit, if not prevented it altogether because of Reagan's Republican victory in 1980 and the ensuing change in appointment prerogative. Once Reagan was elected, said Senator Bumpers, "Senator Pryor and I had virtually no say-so with these judgeships. We might try to block a nomination from somebody that was just totally unacceptable. As it turned out, there were pretty good nominees. And then he was succeeded by George H. W. Bush. And so the Republicans had the most say about who these judges would be. And while I had no objection to any of them, and I learned to like all of them, one of the things that was really difficult to accept was that the thing I enjoyed most was picking judges. And the Republicans were in control virtually all the time I was there."[60]

LIFE ON THE EIGHTH CIRCUIT: A PREVIEW

It had been a busy, tiring week of court hearings in St. Paul, Minnesota, for the Eighth Circuit judges. Judge Arnold, two law clerks, and secretary Brenda King left the Warren Burger Federal Courthouse late that Friday afternoon for the Minneapolis airport. It would be close whether they could make it in time for the first leg of the return flight to Little Rock. But the imperturbable Arnold drove the rental car with his usual deliberate speed, both hands loosely at the top of the steering wheel.

A few miles from the airport, Arnold stopped at a railroad crossing as a train approached. The train was *long* and moving slowly. No one spoke as the minutes ticked by. Just as the last train car cleared the crossing, another train from the opposite direction approached the intersection. It, too, was moving slowly and had every sign of being equally long. The clerks stared in disbelief. "Well," Arnold said, "that will take our minds off the first train."[61]

With his new role as a court of appeals judge, Arnold traveled one week out of every month to either St. Paul or St. Louis, the two seats of the Eighth Circuit. There he would join the other judges from this geographically broad circuit for oral argument in cases set for review. Usually those hearings were before panels of three judges; occasionally the entire court would assemble in a process known as en banc review. At the conclusion of the week, the judges returned to their home states with the task of preparing written opinions for those cases, in addition to other court business.

Unlike his experience as a trial judge, Arnold was now a member of a collegial court, where outcomes were decided by majority vote. Here he would make his name, serving for nearly twenty-five years.

There were other differences ahead for Arnold. As a trial judge for only a short time, Arnold had not encountered some of the more contentious issues in the modern federal courts. What he faced in the future, that he had not on the district court, included death penalty and abortion cases as well as the long-running litigation over desegregation of the Little Rock schools. The caseload for the Eighth Circuit would increase dramatically in the next decades. Arnold would serve as chief judge of the Eighth Circuit for seven years and serve in an important administrative capacity for the entire federal judiciary. In 1993 and 1994, Arnold would be subject to the spotlight of a potential Supreme Court nomination.

Chapter Eight

Life and Death
below the Supreme Court

Richard Arnold thought the government should live up to a high standard, and nowhere did he feel this was more true than in death penalty cases. The death penalty is one of the most contentious and time-consuming matters within the federal courts. In his career, Arnold considered far more death penalty appeals than any single Supreme Court justice because his court did not have discretion to deny review. Unlike in the rarified world of the Supreme Court, appeals court judges do not choose their cases. The great majority of executions, in fact, take place without any prior substantive review by the Supreme Court, and the Supreme Court does not give reasons when it refuses to hear an appeal. Thus, lower federal courts—and especially Arnold's court, the Eighth Circuit—perform the bulk of the judiciary's work in death penalty cases. The usual denial of certiorari by the Supreme Court effectively left Arnold's work as the final word.

Death penalty appeals were the most personally difficult cases Arnold faced. During his years on the bench, ninety men were executed within the Eighth Circuit, most of those in Arkansas and Missouri. Arnold considered nearly two hundred appeals related to death sentences and wrote fifty opinions in those cases, several in dissent. Although Arnold affirmed most of the death sentences he considered, he would have granted stays of execution or new trials to eight prisoners who ultimately were executed.[1] Based upon his written opinions alone, in one out of every four cases Arnold believed the prisoner's death sentence was problematic. Indeed, prior to his death in 2004, Arnold's last major death penalty decision granted a new trial to the condemned Missouri prisoner Vernon Brown, but the en banc Eighth Circuit reversed Arnold and reinstated Brown's death sentence.[2] Brown was executed a few months later.

In his brief career as a trial judge, Arnold encountered many criminal defendants, but none of those cases involved the death penalty. After Arnold joined the court of appeals in 1980, a steady stream of emergency petitions and habeas corpus appeals from condemned prisoners occupied his attention. Four of the seven states within the Eighth Circuit impose the death penalty for some crimes. Of these, Arkansas and Missouri produce the highest number of executions. Nebraska imposes the death penalty, as does South Dakota. North Dakota, Minnesota, and Iowa do not have a death penalty, but executions can take place even in those states under federal law: Congress added a number of death penalty crimes to federal statutes throughout the 1980s and 1990s. Although some federal death sentences were imposed within the Eighth Circuit, Arnold's most significant opinions concerned state prisoners on death row, whose appeals to the federal system through habeas corpus challenged the constitutionality of state criminal proceedings. In all death penalty matters, Arnold believed there was no "graver or more important judicial function."[3]

Death penalty cases take a number of years to resolve, working first through state court appeals systems followed by sometimes multiple trips through the federal court hierarchy. As a general requirement for a federal habeas appeal, a prisoner must first have presented his claims in state courts in order to obtain review of his case in the federal courts. Arnold once noted, "Delay, in large part, is a function of the desire of our courts, state and federal, to get it right, to explore exhaustively, or at least sufficiently, any argument that might save someone's life."[4] Federal courts are the last to rule on state inmates' claims of constitutional violations, and often the court of appeals, rather than the US Supreme Court, is the last stop, meaning that Arnold's court was effectively the last hope for prisoners facing imminent execution. Yet as executions increased in the Arnold years, federal courts intervened in death cases only rarely.

Death penalty cases raised pressing and vexing questions of civil rights throughout the latter part of the twentieth century. The United States Supreme Court effectively halted state-sponsored executions in 1972 when it decided, in *Furman v. Georgia*, that the system of capital punishment as then implemented violated the Eighth Amendment prohibition against cruel and unusual punishment.[5] In *Furman*, the Supreme Court split five to four in overturning the imposition of the death penalty in each of the consolidated cases, but the majority could not agree as to a rationale and produced not an opinion but merely a short statement announcing the result. As a result, every state's death penalty statute was invalidated, and 631 death sentences were vacated.[6]

Thirty-eight states, including Arkansas, quickly revised their death penalty sentencing procedures to address *Furman*'s concern with arbitrary imposition of the death penalty. In 1976, another fractured Supreme Court upheld Georgia's amended sentencing code, and juries across the nation were invited once again to impose the death penalty for some criminal defendants.[7] In 2007, New Jersey became the first state in more than forty years to abolish executions; currently, thirteen states currently do not have a death penalty. But with an increasing number of federal crimes now subject to the death penalty, government-sponsored executions are a possibility in every part of the United States.

Arnold's tenure as a federal judge coincided with the resumption of executions in the United States and efforts by both the Rehnquist Court and Congress to speed up the appeals process in death penalty cases. One goal of the Republican Party, beginning with President Ronald Reagan and continuing through the Bush presidencies, was to limit the number of appeals from condemned inmates, and by the turn of the century it had succeeded. Over this time period, both Congress and the Supreme Court engaged to limit the appeal process in death penalty cases. By 2004, 944 persons had been put to death in the United States since the resumption of executions in 1977.[8]

When Arnold began his judicial career, the immediate body of precedent from the Supreme Court was mostly a legacy of the Warren Court, with that Court's expanded definition of "due process." The majority of Arnold's years as a federal judge were spent under the supervision of the Rehnquist Court. Chief justice William Rehnquist opposed what he considered "last-minute obstructionism" by lawyers for convicted defendants.

A condemned inmate was rarely successful in obtaining a reprieve of exe-cution from the Rehnquist Court. Yet Arnold's mentor, William Brennan, along with Thurgood Marshall, adhered to the view that the death penalty in all circumstances was unconstitutional. It was, they believed, a violation of the Eighth Amendment's prohibition against cruel and unusual punish-ment. They were fighting a rearguard action against the Rehnquist majority. Harry Blackmun also came to hold this view late in his career.

Arnold did not think the death penalty was per se unconstitutional, but in any event this view, publicly expressed by a few Supreme Court jus-tices, was not an option for him. Arnold and his colleagues were effectively the last resort for the numerous condemned inmates from Arkansas and Missouri, but they were without power to alter the laws to be applied to each death penalty appeal. Arnold never strayed from the view that lower court judges are strictly bound by whatever the Supreme Court has said is the law, although he recognized that lower courts have to sort out and apply to concrete cases an often fractured (and therefore confusing) Supreme Court precedent. For most legal questions, the available options were circumscribed. If precedent required, Arnold scrupulously abided by it, even if this resulted in the execution of an inmate whose constitutional claims were never considered by the federal courts.

Once on the bench but before any executions had taken place within the Eighth Circuit, Arnold said: "I don't like it. I don't like the death penalty, but I know that it is not unconstitutional."[9] He rarely spoke of his personal views of the death penalty. Arnold was circumspect in public statements; he believed his job as a judge was to mask personal beliefs in the interest of public neutrality. His job, he said, required that he swear an oath to uphold the Constitution. Even if he personally was opposed to the death penalty, the Supreme Court, or at least a majority of it, had said that in most instances the death penalty was perfectly constitutional.

In 2001, Sandra Day O'Connor, a Republican appointee to the Supreme Court, made headlines when she told a Minnesota lawyers' group that the United States had a capital punishment system that "may well be allowing some innocent defendants to be executed."[10] DNA exon-erations of death row inmates would become a prominent issue only in the last years of Arnold's life (as of 2008, fifty-three men convicted of murder had been exonerated through DNA evidence nationwide)[11], but he never doubted the possibility that a death penalty sentence could be mistakenly applied to the innocent. Arnold was above all a proponent of fair process, fair juries, effective representation by counsel, and proper government conduct in all aspects of criminal proceedings. But privately Arnold abhorred the death penalty, even as he supported the right of legislatures to allow it and of juries to impose it. Shortly after the 1989 mail bomb killing of his friend Robert Vance, a judge on the Eleventh Circuit, Arnold told his wife, Kay Arnold, that should he ever be murdered, he did not want the murderer to be executed in return. When faced with a death penalty appeal, he also said that he did not "feel qualified to decide it, particularly."[12] But, he added, he did not feel less qualified than anyone else.

Arnold's religious faith—he was an Episcopalian with Catholic leanings—intensified his concern about executions. According to his wife, Kay, he would seclude himself in his study at home to pray throughout execution evenings, even in those cases in which he had voted to allow the execution to proceed. Prayer for Arnold, in fact, was a daily routine. Diary entries often include notations of "M.P." (morning prayer), "E.P." (evening prayer), readings and devotionals, and attendance at mass, but these activities had an added solemnity on a "death watch" evening.

Although he did not wear his religion on his sleeve, Arnold's pursuit of Catholicism also meant that he would have respected the Church's stance on the death penalty. The Catholic Church had maintained that the death penalty was never warranted, in any circumstance. John Paul II visited St. Louis in January 1999 and called for an end to the death penalty in the United States. Arnold had been in St. Louis hearing cases only the week before and no doubt followed the pope's visit there with interest.

Arnold's first death penalty case, portentously, was also his first dissent. This case was not from Arkansas or Missouri but from Georgia, where he sat as a visiting judge with Robert Vance on the Eleventh Circuit. Ivon Stanley was a mentally retarded young black man convicted of robbing, kidnapping, and killing Clifford Floyd, an insurance agent, in Decatur County, Georgia, in 1976. Stanley alleged that his defense attorney was constitutionally ineffective during his capital murder trial. Arnold agreed. In the penalty phase, Stanley's counsel introduced no evidence, even though relatives and friends of Stanley could have testified that he was perhaps worthy of compassion, as Arnold wrote, a "uniquely individual human being."[13] Because it was a death case, Arnold was especially wary of concluding that the attorney's failure was inconsequential:

"The more serious the consequences of a wrong decision, the more one wants to be careful to make the right one. It is not asking too much, when life is at stake, to require the State or counsel himself to explain a choice to present *no* evidence in mitigation."[14] Arnold's lengthy dissent—disagreeing with Judge Vance—refused to presume that the problems at Stanley's trial made no difference in the outcome. Stanley was electrocuted on July 12, 1984, shortly after the Supreme Court refused to hear his case.

DEATH WATCH: STAY REQUESTS AND SCHEDULED EXECUTIONS

An execution is a formal government ceremony and is preceded by an official proclamation from the governor setting an execution date. Arnold was never present in the death chamber for the last minutes of any condemned prisoners, but he was certainly aware as the clock ticked. Arnold asked to be called by his law clerk when the wait was over—either the execution had taken place or, very rarely, the United States Supreme Court had intervened at the last moment. Each year he sent his law clerks to tour the Arkansas penitentiary system as guests of the prison warden. He wanted his clerks to see for themselves conditions at the prison and especially the area set aside as "death row."

No executions took place within the Eighth Circuit during the first few years after Arnold joined the court, but already appeals from condemned inmates were working their way through the system. Tiny Mercer and Gerald Smith were executed in Missouri in 1989, the first within the Eighth Circuit since the resumption of executions in 1976. These were followed in quick succession by four more executions in Missouri and two in Arkansas in 1990. The first executions in Arkansas since 1964 took place in June 1990. John Swindler had been convicted of murdering an Arkansas policeman and two teenagers. Ronald Gene Simmons had killed sixteen people in and around Russellville, Arkansas, mostly members of his own family. Then-governor Bill Clinton "didn't have qualms" about executing either of them.[15]

The appeals before Arnold and his colleagues included a steady stream of emergency applications for stays of execution. A stay of execution, when issued, allows judges more time to consider the merits of a prisoner's claim. Often there was a strikingly quick time between the lifting of a stay and the execution of the condemned prisoner. George "Tiny" Mercer, for example, Missouri's first executed prisoner since 1965, had been scheduled to be executed on October 20, 1988. Arnold, along with Chief Judge Lay and Judge Theodore McMillian, entered a stay of execution the day before. When the same judges lifted the stay two months later, after hearing the case and deciding that Mercer had no meritorious appeal, the state immediately set another execution date and carried it out within three days.[16]

A "death watch" evening meant long hours in chambers for both law clerks and judges, and full readiness in the clerk's offices in St. Louis to accept and distribute last-minute court filings. All court personnel wanted to avoid either of two scenarios that might come about if a judge could not be reached before a scheduled execution. The worst scenario would be a prisoner's execution before his appeal to the federal courts could be considered for the simple reason that one or more judges could not be located. Second, the court might issue a stay of execution unnecessarily, meaning that the elaborate execution procedure begun by a state would be disrupted for no reason other than failure to locate one of the judges.

For death watch, the clerk of court for the Eighth Circuit followed scrupulous procedures for contacting the judges. Hoping to avoid surprise and to plan in advance for appeals by inmates, the court's rules required the state attorney general to notify the clerk promptly, by telephone or fax, when a warrant for execution was issued. The clerk would then contact counsel for the inmate to determine any litigation plans. All pleadings filed after the issuance of a warrant for execution were to be treated as emergency matters.[17]

As late as 1995, the Eighth Circuit was still dependent upon fax machines to distribute emergency appeals to its judges. On the evening of Larry Griffin's execution, Michael Gans, clerk of the court, fed four fax machines in St. Louis to distribute last-minute legal documents to the twelve judges in their various home states. While those faxes went out, Richard Arnold drafted a dissent to his court's decision to permit the execution. The dissent was prepared in time to accompany the condemned inmate's last-minute appeal to the US Supreme Court. The last appeal for Griffin was filed at 11:20 p.m., minutes before the scheduled midnight execution. Arnold's dissent convinced Justices Ginsburg, Stevens, and Breyer that Griffin's execution should be postponed, but they needed two more votes from the other justices, which were not forthcoming. The Supreme Court turned down Griffin's appeal at 2:40 a.m., and Griffin was promptly executed.[18]

The process for conveying emergency appeals to members of the Eighth Circuit received a sharp rebuke from some Supreme Court justices in the case of Winford Stokes, convicted of strangling and stabbing a waitress in St. Louis in 1978. Stokes originally was scheduled to die at 12:01 a.m. on May 11, 1990, under a warrant for execution that would expire at midnight on that same date. United States District Judge George Gunn granted a stay of execution two days before Stokes's scheduled execution. State officials immediately appealed Gunn's decision to the Eighth Circuit. The matter was assigned to a panel consisting of Arnold, Theodore McMillian, and Pasco Bowman. The panel did not rule until midday of the scheduled execution. Over a dissent by Judge Bowman, Arnold and McMillian voted to keep the stay in place pending fuller review of Judge Gunn's action. The state then asked the Eighth Circuit to vacate the panel's stay, but a quick poll of the full court did not garner sufficient votes to lift the stay in order to allow the execution that day. Expecting this result, Missouri officials immediately appealed to the Supreme Court asking that it be permitted to carry out the execution before midnight.

Within hours the Supreme Court in a contentious 5–4 decision lifted the stay of execution, and Stokes was almost immediately executed.[19] Officials at the Missouri prison had continued throughout the day their readiness to execute Stokes by lethal injection, despite their knowledge that a stay of execution had been issued from a federal district court. Dale Riley, a director of the Department of Corrections, informed the press that "[t]he execution must be carried out before midnight or it would have to go back to the Missouri Supreme Court for another execution date."[20] Winford Stokes was kept in a holding cell adjacent to the execution chamber throughout that time, as his attorneys responded to the state's appeals to be allowed to execute Stokes that same day.

Three members of the Supreme Court wrote a separate opinion criticizing the Eight Circuit panel, of which Arnold was the lead judge, for its delay in lifting the stay. A news article in the *St. Louis Post-Dispatch* claimed the Supreme Court had used "an unusually acid pen" in its sharp criticism of the panel's delay in handling the last-minute appeal.[21] Justices Kennedy, Rehnquist, and Scalia wrote that the more than twenty-four-hour delay meant that the Eighth Circuit found itself unable to rule on the state's motion until hours after the scheduled execution. Instead, the court should have made certain that three active judges were available to act upon emergency stays of this sort in order to provide a timely ruling.[22] Justice Kennedy's opinion invited states to take the extraordinary step of circumventing federal appeals courts entirely "if the Court of Appeals fails to act in a manner sufficiently prompt to preserve the jurisdiction of the court and to protect the parties from the consequences of a stay entered without an adequate basis."[23]

The 5–4 Supreme Court decision generated a vigorous dissent from Arnold's mentor, William Brennan, joined by Justices Marshall and Blackmun, about the "unseemly and indefensible" rush to justice.[24] Brennan noted that the Eighth Circuit was "closer to this case than we could hope to be in the few hours we have had to consider the matter." Defending its actions, Brennan wrote, "When a person's life is at stake we cannot tolerate such facile judgments."[25] The Supreme Court's order permitting the execution was issued before the release of the opinions supporting it. By the time those opinions were publicly available, Stokes was dead. Arnold shook his head when he was informed that the Supreme Court had lifted the stay of execution. "They are not wasting any time to kill this man," he said.[26]

The problem had been that the St. Louis clerk's office had been unable to contact Judge McMillian one evening, delaying the Eighth Circuit's decision until the following day. (Judge McMillian had traveled from his office to speak before a lawyers' association.) McMillian almost always voted for stays of execution, and the other judges entered the stay in his absence to allow time for his input. After the Supreme Court's rebuke, the circuit judges were provided with cell phones and fax machines for their homes.[27]

The drama of legal maneuvers preceding a scheduled execution usually did not end in the condemned man's favor. Jonas Whitmore and Edward Charles Pickens were both executed in Arkansas on the evening of May 11, 1994. The day before, one Eighth Circuit panel had denied Whitmore's request for a stay, but another panel had granted a stay of execution for Pickens. In Pickens's case, the panel directed a lower court to consider whether Arkansas governor Jim Guy Tucker should have recused himself from Pickens's clemency request because Tucker, as state attorney general, had participated in Pickens's prosecution. The full Eighth Circuit, within twenty-four hours, reversed the panel and reinstated Pickens's execution by a vote of 6 to 4. Richard joined his brother Morris Arnold in the futile effort to stay the execution. Both had voted for a stay of execution for Pickens, but their views did not prevail.

At the same time the Eighth Circuit reinstated the death penalty,

Pickens's lawyers filed an emergency appeal before the Supreme Court. At 8 p.m. on May 11, the time of the scheduled execution, Pickens was already strapped to the gurney in the execution chamber when prison officials received word that the Supreme Court had rejected Pickens's appeal.[28] Three justices—Harry Blackmun, Ruth Bader Ginsburg, and John Paul Stevens—had voted to grant a stay but needed two additional votes that were not forthcoming. Within one hour, Pickens was executed by lethal injection. Pickens had been through four sentencing trials, and his eighteen years on death row was the second longest of any Arkansas inmate.

On occasion, Arnold exercised his authority as a single judge to issue a stay of execution on an emergency basis. Such stays remain in place until other judges assigned to the case can be consulted. In the case of Thomas Winford Simmons, Arnold conducted a one-hour emergency hearing in his chambers in the Little Rock courthouse, after which he entered a temporary stay of execution. "In most cases of doubt," Arnold said, "the doubt should be resolved in favor of life."[29] Simmons was convicted of killing four people, including a Fort Smith, Arkansas, police detective. His attorneys had raised what Arnold viewed to be possibly substantial issues that Arnold believed the full court should consider, even if it ultimately rejected them. The judges assigned to hear that appeal were Theodore McMillian and District Judge Morris Arnold, Richard's brother, sitting on the case by designation. The court ultimately upheld Simmons's death sentence but left the stay in place so Simmons could ask the Supreme Court to review his case. Simmons was unsuccessful there. One year later, while awaiting execution on death row, Simmons killed himself in his cell, at age forty-seven.[30]

BARRY LEE FAIRCHILD

One of the most significant death penalty cases to arise in Arkansas involved Barry Lee Fairchild. This case illustrates the many legal maneuvers, stays, near-death experiences, and public debate that accompany a state-sponsored execution. Barry Fairchild was a poor, mentally handicapped African American living in Pulaski County, Arkansas, when a jury sentenced him to death for the 1983 murder of a twenty-two-year-old white nurse, Marjorie Mason. Mason had been abducted, robbed, raped, and shot twice in the head in a rural area near Little Rock.

Some estimates of Fairchild's IQ were in the low sixties. Without a lawyer present, Fairchild gave a statement to the police in which he acknowledged participating in the kidnapping and rape but denied involvement in Mason's death, saying he had not known that those with him would kill her. He steadfastly refused to name anyone who was with him that night. At his trial, Fairchild recanted and insisted he had no connection to the crimes.

Evidence discovered since his trial revealed that he was the last of a number of black men to have been brought into the Pulaski County sheriff's office in the investigation of the Mason murder. Each suspect was told there was proof he had done it, and some were beaten in an attempt to extract a confession. Fairchild claimed that he, too, had been beaten and also had been rehearsed for twenty minutes on what to say. After Fairchild allegedly was beaten and instructed what to say, the officers set up a videotape for a confession. At one point on the videotape he is asked how many times Mason was raped. He paused, looked behind the camera, waited with his mouth open, then finally raised two fingers. He looked back at the camera and said, "Two, two times."

On three different occasions, Fairchild narrowly avoided execution through last-minute stays from the federal courts. In March 1989, Fairchild came within five days of being executed when his lawyers obtained a stay of execution from the Eighth Circuit based on testimony that he might be mentally retarded. That appeal took more than a year to resolve. The following year, Governor Bill Clinton set an execution date of September 5, 1990. Fairchild was moved from death row at Tucker Maximum Security to the execution facility at Cummings, Arkansas. But the Eighth Circuit issued a stay the day before his scheduled execution, based on new witness testimony of police beatings in the hunt for Mason's killer.

Arnold and the Eighth Circuit then affirmed a lower-court ruling by Judge G. Thomas Eisele, a federal district court judge in Little Rock. Eisele ruled that Fairchild was not retarded and had received a fair trial, noting, "Our confidence in this verdict remains unshaken." Arnold kept the stay of execution in effect but added that if Fairchild's attorneys did not act quickly to seek a higher review, the stay would be dissolved. The US Supreme Court declined to review the case, setting the stage for a third last-minute stay of execution issued on September 4.

The September 4 stay followed a hearing that morning in Arnold's chambers in Little Rock. Fairchild's attorney at the time was John Wesley

Hall, who had argued before the court more than eighty times, often before Judge Arnold.[31] According to Hall, Arnold's questioning of attorneys was on an intellectual par with Justice Antonin Scalia, but without Scalia's famous tone of sarcasm in his voice when he disagreed with counsel or thought an argument was silly.

Hall attempted to present a third petition for habeas corpus. The Eighth Circuit had already denied two such petitions when Judge Eisele dismissed the third one on August 31, leading to the September 4 hearing before Arnold. Hall argued the discovery of new evidence—the alleged abuse of Pulaski County inmates in the early 1980s. The new evidence included seven witnesses, four of whom had come forward to say they were beaten by Pulaski County sheriff's officers in an attempt to coerce confessions to murdering Mason. The other three described similar treatment in the investigation of other crimes. Federal courts had earlier rejected Fairchild's argument that his confession was coerced. But the evidence presented at the hearing in Judge Arnold's chambers resulted in a unanimous stay of execution pending an evidentiary hearing. Sheriff Tommy Robinson, later a member of Congress, denied any allegations of beatings and said that "even the ivory-tower jurists on the appeals court" will at some point "realize what a charade this case has become."[32]

Fairchild smiled when he was told that afternoon about the stay of execution. Because the state planned to appeal the decision on an emergency basis to the Supreme Court, prison officials kept Fairchild in the cell next to the death chamber. A spokesman declared that "[i]f the stay is dissolved before midnight tonight we would be bound to carry out the execution."[33] But that stay remained in place.

A second execution date was set by Governor Jim Guy Tucker for September 22, 1993. Earlier that month, Human Rights Watch wrote to Governor Tucker of Arkansas, urging him to grant a stay of execution to Fairchild, citing his low mental capacity and reports that officers investigating the murder may have coerced his confession through physical abuse. On the day Fairchild was to be executed, September 22, Judge Eisele vacated his death sentence and directed that the sentence of death be reduced to life imprisonment without parole. Eisele read his findings of fact and conclusions of law from the bench to expedite the state of Arkansas's probable appeal.

The state immediately filed an appeal with the Eighth Circuit, asking the court to summarily reverse Judge Eisele's ruling and to allow the scheduled execution to take place that evening. Members of the Eighth Circuit panel assigned to the case received the motion, along with Judge Eisele's opinion, by fax from the clerk's office.

On that day, Arnold was in Washington, DC, for the Judicial Conference, at work on the federal judiciary's budget requests at the administrative office of the United States Courts. Arnold had a scheduled lunch with Mark E. Middleton, an Arkansas friend of President Clinton. Middleton worked at the time in White House chief of staff Mack McLarty's office as an aide to the president. (There was no Supreme Court vacancy at the time, but Justice Harry Blackmun had announced a few months earlier that he was not likely to stay on the Court much longer, and Arnold knew he was a strong contender for Blackmun's seat.) Arnold also had arranged a meeting with Justice Harry Blackmun at his Supreme Court chambers. There, in the early afternoon, he received a message from one of Justice Blackmun's staff asking him to call Judge Pasco Bowman II, one of the panel members assigned to the Fairchild case.[34]

The panel had only about two hours to consider the state's motion, conferring by telephone before denying the motion for summary reversal. The result, effectively, was to leave in place for the time being Judge Eisele's stay of execution. The panel asked for a full briefing schedule so that the case could be argued on the merits before the panel during the October court week in St. Paul, Minnesota.[35]

Although it is not clear whether Arnold worked on the case in Justice Blackmun's chambers or at another location in Washington, DC, he managed to write an 1,100-word concurring opinion to explain the panel's actions. In his opinion, Arnold wrote:

> We considered it our duty to give the State an answer tonight. In the end, I am simply not certain enough, one way or the other, to reverse the judgment of a United States District Court in a matter involving human life, without at least some more time for reflection.[36]

Arnold wrote that Fairchild "probably did not kill Marjorie Mason."[37] But that fact, if true, would not prevent his execution, because Fairchild qualified as an accomplice to the murder and thus under the "felony murder" rule could be punished as if he had pulled the trigger himself.

The issues raised before Judge Eisele had not been presented in any of Fairchild's prior habeas petitions and therefore were subject to dis-

missal as procedurally barred and as an abuse of the writ, "unless some
reason for avoiding these defenses appears." Arnold mapped possible
responses as if to guide Fairchild's counsel concerning positions to espouse
at the coming hearing in October. He noted, in particular, that the Court
could consider Fairchild's claim only if he could bring himself within the
"actual innocence" or "miscarriage of justice" exception to the normal rules
of procedural bar. Judge Eisele believed this test had been met and that
under existing Supreme Court precedent Fairchild's mental state was not
blameworthy enough to deserve the death penalty. No evidence in the
record supported that Fairchild killed Marjorie Mason himself, intended
that she be killed, or even that he expected that she would be killed.

But, according to Arnold, this point was probably raised too late:

> Thus, the fact—and it is a fact—that Fairchild's jury did not find that
> Fairchild himself had any particular mental state with respect to Ms.
> Mason's killing, cannot be a ground for relief at this late date. This point,
> if it had been raised in a proper and timely manner, would apparently
> have had merit, and it seems that Fairchild's life could have been saved,
> pending a new penalty proceeding in the state courts. Rather, Fairchild
> must now show, by clear and convincing evidence, that no reasonable
> jury could find that he "knowingly engaged in criminal activities known
> to carry a grave risk of death."[38]

Arnold set out the issue for both sides to address prior to the upcoming
oral argument. No doubt this was to save time—to clarify that the court of
appeals by refusing the state's motion for summary reversal was not necessarily endorsing Judge Eisele's opinion.[39] That Arnold could prepare
the September 22 concurring opinion in a mere few hours indicated both
his understanding of Supreme Court precedent and his intimate familiarity
with the facts of Fairchild's case. Moreover, it indicates his desire to provide reasoned elaboration for a denial order that for most courts would
have been issued per curiam with no explanation.

Fairchild's lawyers immediately filed an appeal with the Supreme
Court, but ultimately Fairchild lost this appeal as well. The Supreme
Court denied certiorari; a new execution date was set for August 31, 1995.
Soft-spoken and courteous throughout his years on death row, Fairchild
worried about the effect his execution would have on his mother. Yet he
seemed resigned: "If it's gonna happen, there ain't no reason to be upset.

STATE OF ARKANSAS
EXECUTIVE DEPARTMENT

PROCLAMATION

TO ALL TO WHOM THESE PRESENTS SHALL COME. . . . GREETINGS:

WHEREAS,   Barry Lee Fairchild, SK - 893, was duly presented under proper proceedings to the Circuit Court of Lonoke County, Arkansas, on a charge of Capital Murder and, after being tried in that Court by a duly empaneled jury, was found guilty and his sentence and punishment fixed at death; and

WHEREAS,   The conviction having been appealed to the Supreme Court of Arkansas and a writ of habeas corpus having been sought from the United States District Court for the Eastern District of Arkansas; and

WHEREAS,   Upon review of this case, the judgment and sentence of the Circuit Court of Lonoke County, Arkansas, was affirmed, the petition for writ of habeas corpus was denied, and all avenues of appeal or review of those decisions have been exhausted and all stays have been dissolved; and

WHEREAS,   A successor petition for writ of habeas corpus having been sought from the United States District Court for the Eastern District of Arkansas, and that Court having dismissed that petition and having dissolved the stay of execution previously issued on that petition; and

WHEREAS,   It has become my duty pursuant to law and official policy to fix the date and day for carrying into effect the sentence and the judgment of the Lonoke County Circuit Court as affirmed;

NOW, THEREFORE,   I, Bill Clinton, by virtue of the power and authority vested in me by law, as Governor of the State of Arkansas, do hereby set May 10, 1989, as the date upon which the Commissioner (Director) of the Arkansas Department of Correction will carry into effect the judgment and sentence of the Lonoke County Circuit Court by executing Barry Lee Fairchild at the place and in the manner prescribed by law.

IN WITNESS WHEREOF, I have set my hand and caused the Great Seal of the State of Arkansas to be affixed. Done in office this fourteenth day of April, 1989.

Bill Clinton
_____
GOVERNOR

_____
SECRETARY   OF   STATE

An execution warrant for Barry Lee Fairchild. Fairchild was executed August 31, 1995.

That's life."[40] Each time Fairchild was transferred to the execution chamber holding cell, he gave away his personal possessions, including a watch and high-top basketball shoes, to other prisoners.

Fairchild received one last round of consideration from the federal courts in the spring and summer of 1995. On August 3, Judge Eisele denied Fairchild's last habeas petition. On August 23, an Eighth Circuit panel consisting of Judges Magill, Ross, and Loken summarily denied a stay request and affirmed Judge Eisele's order. (Arnold was out of the country but had made prior arrangements for his substitution on the Fairchild case should action be required in his absence.) Michael Gans in St. Louis immediately sent copies of Fairchild's motion for stay and his brief on the merits to each active judge, in anticipation of a petition for en banc rehearing, reminding the judges that Fairchild's execution was set for one week later.

On the eve of Fairchild's scheduled execution, Gans informed Judge Arnold that the Supreme Court's death penalty coordinator, Cynthia Rapp, called to report that Fairchild's motion for stay and petition for a writ of certiorari had both been denied, with no dissents. Gans reported that Fairchild's attorneys had assured both the Supreme Court and him that they would not make any further federal court filings and that all efforts would be directed to convincing the governor to grant Fairchild clemency. Governor Tucker, however, had already stated publicly that he would not grant clemency in Fairchild's case.

On August 11, the Arkansas Board of Pardons and Paroles declined to recommend a change of sentence to Governor Tucker by a vote of four to three. Days later, a former chaplain for the state department of correction wrote Governor Tucker that the actual killer was not Barry but his brother Robert: "The information I want to share with you is that as a result of counseling and contact with Barry and his brother, I have been informed that Barry did not murder the nurse, but he did cover for his brother, who did murder the woman."[41] Robert Fairchild, Barry's only brother, was at the time serving a forty-year sentence on a variety of charges. When Robert was questioned, he steadfastly maintained that he knew nothing of the crime. Robert Fairchild was never tried in the Mason case.[42]

Shortly after 9:00 on the evening of August 31, 1995, the state of Arkansas carried out the execution of Barry Fairchild. At the time of his execution, Fairchild was either forty-one or forty-three years old (his date of birth seems to have been uncertain), and he had been on death row for twelve years. Fairchild's case had been one of the "most publicized and contentious death penalty cases in modern Arkansas history."[43] The Fairchild case received more public attention than any other in Arnold's experience to that point, including the involvement of the National Coalition to Abolish the Death Penalty, NAACP Legal Defense Fund, the Southern Christian Leadership Conference, Christian Ministerial Alliance, and Amnesty International.

On the day of the scheduled execution, the *New York Times* ran a story about the Fairchild case titled "Execution of Retarded Man Is Fought."[44] Fairchild's attorneys contended through the years that he was retarded, although the findings on Fairchild's IQ were "mixed." It was only after Barry Fairchild was sentenced to die that mental retardation became a factor in his case. Two psychologists evaluated him and both IQ estimates were in the low sixties. However, the state's psychologist testified that Fairchild malingered in his presentation, while the defense expert stated that Fairchild could not have faked on two separate IQ tests and still have such a similar profile. These mattered because of an Arkansas law prohibiting the execution of anyone with an IQ of 65 or below. Judge Eisele ruled, after a long hearing, that Fairchild was not retarded. The Arkansas Supreme Court reached the same conclusion in 1993 on the basis of Eisele's opinion.

Whether Arnold agreed that Fairchild deserved the death penalty, ultimately he had no doubts about what the law required. In his last opinion in Fairchild's appeal, Arnold wrote that this case had been "more carefully examined than any other habeas proceedings I have seen in 14 years on the federal bench."[45] He noted, pointedly, that Fairchild "probably did not kill Ms. Mason," that the actual killing "was probably done by his confederate," and that "Fairchild may not have intended or even expected this to happen." These facts, Arnold wrote, could have been the basis of a well-founded attack on the sentence of death. "Fairchild chose otherwise," he wrote.

Was Fairchild's confession to the rape and kidnapping coerced? Like Judge Eisele, Arnold did not believe so, even though he took pains to chastise the Pulaski County sheriff's department about its behavior. Arnold believed investigators had physically abused some suspects in the course of investigating the Mason murder. That fact did not change the result in Fairchild's case. "But it is still disgraceful," Arnold wrote. "This is an affront to justice which the citizens should not tolerate."[46]

In 2002, too late for Barry Fairchild, the US Supreme Court declared the execution of persons with mental retardation to be unconstitutional.[47] A few years later, the Supreme Court held that the Eighth Amendment also prohibits execution of juveniles under the age of eighteen at the time of their crime.[48] Prior to these Supreme Court decisions, states within the Eighth Circuit had executed people in both of these categories. In Arkansas in 1992, Ricky Rector, who had effectively been lobotomized by a self-inflicted gunshot wound after he shot four people, killing one, had virtually no comprehension of his situation but was nonetheless executed. The forty-year-old left the dessert from his last meal waiting in his cell for "when he returned." The prison chaplain subsequently went into psychiatric care and referred to Rector's execution as a crime in itself, saying, "We're not supposed to execute children."[49]

PROSECUTORIAL MISCONDUCT: NO "QUICK AND EASY DEATH"

In Barry Lee Fairchild's case, Arnold had made it a point to excoriate the behavior of sheriff's officers in detaining and beating black suspects, although this "affront to justice" was not enough to keep Fairchild alive. Arnold generally held the government to high standards. He was particularly intolerant of prosecutorial misconduct. His face would carry a look of bewildered concern and exasperation when an attorney tried to defend outrageous behavior.

Steve Hawke, a lawyer who represented the state of Missouri in many death penalty cases, remembered arguing a case in the late 1980s before a panel that included Judge Arnold. Arnold asked Hawke whether the penalty phase argument in the death penalty case was "the worst you have ever seen." Fifteen years later, Hawke argued another death penalty case before Judge Arnold, and Arnold again reflected on whether it was the worst argument he had ever seen. Of course, Arnold told Hawke, he remembered one from fifteen years before that might have been worse.[50]

In one of his most-cited death penalty opinions, Arnold vacated the death sentence of Calvert Antwine because the prosecutor had told the jury that Antwine's gas-chamber death would be painless and that executing him would save the taxpayers money.[51] Michael Shaffer told the jury that Missouri's gas chamber was merely "a pellet dropped into acid," which, when inhaled, would cause Antwine's death "instantaneously."[52] There was no clear Supreme Court precedent prohibiting prosecutors from using these types of arguments to the jury.

Writing for a unanimous panel, Arnold explained that this misconduct violated Antwine's due process rights because it "was so inflammatory that it rendered the entire sentencing proceeding fundamentally unfair." He added, "So where is the harm in this vision of a quick and easy death? The danger is that the jurors, faced with a very difficult and uncomfortable choice, will minimize the burden of sentencing someone to death by comforting themselves with the thought that the death would at least be instantaneous, and therefore, painless and easy."[53] The "cost" argument, even if it were a proper consideration for the jury, was simply wrong: a recent study "demonstrated that the cost of sentencing someone to death greatly exceeds the cost of sentencing him to life imprisonment."[54] The jury might have chosen a life sentence for Antwine, Arnold said, "if the prosecutor had not fed their fears of economic burden while easing their conscience with the idea of a quick, humane death." Arnold ordered the state of Missouri to sentence Antwine again. The state petitioned the full court for rehearing; only Judge C. Arlen Beam of Nebraska voted to reconsider Arnold's opinion. The Supreme Court subsequently denied a writ of certiorari on Missouri's appeal.

The *Antwine* panel included Judges Theodore McMillian and Judge Thomas M. Reavley. McMillian readily concurred with Arnold's opinion when he circulated his proposed opinion to the panel. Arnold's notes reflect that McMillian, known as a liberal on death penalty issues, voted to affirm on everything except the final argument to the jury. The prosecutor's argument to the jury was "so flagrant the court should have stepped in."[55] Unlike McMillian, however, Arnold was also willing to reverse on two additional theories raised by the defendant: the prosecutor had exhibited racial bias in excluding potential jurors, and evidence suggested the defendant suffered from bipolar disorder that was not investigated by his original trial counsel.[56] Arnold did not get agreement from the other judges on these additional grounds, so he did not include them in the opinion he later circulated.

Judge Reavley, sitting by designation from the Fifth Circuit, disagreed with Arnold, but chose not to record a dissent. He wrote to Arnold: "I have your thorough opinion and Judge McMillian's concurrence. I disagree, as I said at our opinion conference. I think counsel's performance satisfied reasonable standards, and the argument was objectionable only in the query involving the jurors working to support Antwine for 50 years. I regard that one inquiry as harmless beyond any doubt. So I would affirm [Antwine's death sentence]. I see nothing to be gained by writing a dissent, and I will not note a dissent without giving reasons. So you may take this as a concurrence in your opinion."[57] Arnold, in turn, responded: "I appreciate the position you are taking on this case. It actually gave me a great deal of trouble, and I am not certain that my opinion is right, but it is where I came out after a lot of thought. I am grateful for your allowing us to file the opinion without a recorded dissent."[58] The exchange with Judge Reavley is revealing about the respect with which other judges held Arnold.

On another occasion, Arnold struck hard at racial bias in the selection of a jury. Eddie Lee Miller, a black man, was convicted in 1979 of the murder of W. F. Bolin, a white man. Before the trial began the prosecutor in the case had used ten peremptory strikes to remove ten potential black jurors. (In the jury selection process, a peremptory strike permits each side to exclude a certain number of jurors without giving a reason.) In addition, during the trial the prosecutor asked the jury to consider the cost of keeping Miller in prison for life as opposed to executing him. He also commented on Miller's failure to take the stand or to ask for mercy in the penalty phase of the trial, referring to Miller as a "mad dog"—"you don't do but one thing with a mad dog. You put him to death."[59] The jury sentenced Miller to die in the electric chair.

The prosecutor's closing arguments had violated Miller's due process rights, but even more important, the jury selection process exhibited racial bias and thus violated Equal Protection. Judge Eisele, who heard the case first, reversed the death sentence and ordered a new trial. Arnold readily affirmed, adding his own strong criticism of the prosecution's conduct in Miller's case. The original trial had taken place in 1979. At that time, the Supreme Court had not yet issued its landmark decision in *Batson v. Kentucky*,[60] forbidding prosecutors to use peremptory challenges to remove prospective jurors because of their race. Arnold respected jury verdicts, but those juries had to be fairly made up of a cross section of the community, and the prosecutor had to behave in line with what the constitution required. Applying the Supreme Court standard retroactively to a 1979 trial was no stretch for Arnold or for Eisele.

For Arnold, prosecutorial misconduct was especially bad if it injected race into the jury's deliberations. Arnold knew that race may affect everything from arrest to voir dire (jury selection) to sentencing. He was also entirely aware that racial disparity in death sentences was, and is, a problem nationwide—not just within the Eighth Circuit. According to Amnesty International, even though blacks and whites are murder victims in nearly equal numbers of crimes, 80 percent of people executed since the death penalty was reinstated in 1976 have been executed for murders involving white victims. More than 20 percent of black defendants who have been executed were convicted by all-white juries.[61] In 2007, 42 percent of death row prisoners were black, although blacks make up only 12 percent of the US population.[62]

NOT "HARMLESS ERROR"?

Death penalty trials do not have to be perfect to comply with constitutional standards. "Harmless error," as the doctrine is known in the federal courts, will save the proceedings from reversal later on, even though particular aspects of the trial violated rules or clear constitutional prohibitions. A trial procedure could be flawed, or some evidence could be illegally obtained, and a guilty verdict could still stand if the mistake was merely a harmless error that did not outweigh all the other evidence of the case. Some mistakes are never harmless error, such as the admission of a coerced confession. The "harmless error" rule requires judges to weigh the evidence to decide whether a particular mistake—even an intentional one by the prosecution—would have made a difference in the outcome. Arnold was particularly wary in this task and was inclined to view significant errors as *not* harmless. He recognized that the standard gave a great deal of leeway to the views of individual judges. His first opinion in a death penalty case (also his first dissent) disagreed with the Eleventh Circuit over whether an error had been "harmless."

In his last major death penalty decision before his death, Arnold ruled in favor of Vernon Brown, who was convicted of strangling a nineteen-year-old St. Louis woman in 1985. Arnold believed the penalty phase of Brown's trial was "fatally flawed" because of the exclusion from evidence of a letter written by Brown's brother, a sergeant in the US Army serving in Saudi Arabia at the time of Brown's sentencing. That exclusion, according to Arnold, was not harmless error. The letter was an attempt to show that Brown's life was worth saving and therefore should have been presented to the jury.[63] Subsequently, the full Eighth Circuit reversed Arnold's decision. Brown was executed in May 2005, although not for the strangulation death. Brown had also been sentenced to death for the unrelated murder of a nine-year-old girl, Janet Perkins.[64]

Often federal courts in death penalty cases confront the litigation strategies of the NAACP's Legal Defense Fund and the American Civil Liberties Union.[65] Both groups frequently petitioned to file friend-of-the-court briefs in death penalty cases from Arkansas and Missouri. Due to both his keen interest in individual constitutional rights and his respect for neutrality in the judicial function, Arnold read each brief with care. In one memorable dissent, Arnold chided his own court for its refusal even to consider those briefs:

> This is a death case. Such cases command our attention and careful study in a unique way. Life—anyone's life—is a transcendent value, and there is no graver or more important judicial function than deciding matters of life and death. In this situation, we ought not close our ears to any responsible voices, whether or not we agree with what they are saying. Here, the voices are unquestionably responsible. The NAACP Legal Defense and Educational Fund, the American Civil Liberties Union of Western Missouri, and the Missouri Capital Punishment Resource Center all have substantial experience and expert knowledge in the field of death penalty law. We are not required to accept their arguments on the merits, but we should give them respectful consideration. Refusing them leave even to file briefs is inconsistent with this duty.[66]

With the increasing caseload in all federal courts, judges often feel pressure to decide cases quickly and not revisit them once a decision was made. At least in death penalty appeals, Arnold tried to resist the pressure to run through cases quickly. In one instance, Arnold took the unusual step of vacating his own decision because he had misunderstood a legal question. Eric Clemmons had been sentenced to death for killing another inmate at the Missouri State Penitentiary. Clemmons claimed another inmate actually committed the murder. Although the state had wrongfully withheld some exculpatory evidence at the trial, Clemmons was now barred from raising the issue in federal court. He had not properly presented the claim first to Missouri courts. "The state courts are and must be the primary forum for the administration of the criminal law," Arnold wrote.[67]

But Arnold was receptive to the idea that he had been wrong when Clemmons's attorneys filed a petition to rehear the case. Arnold not only granted that petition, he reversed himself and vacated Clemmons's conviction and death sentence.[68] Arnold had overlooked a key piece of evidence that had, in fact, been presented to the Missouri courts, and he had not properly understood Missouri evidence law. In a detailed and lengthy opinion, Arnold described how both errors caused the analysis of Clemmons's case to be flawed. Missouri retried Clemmons, and at this retrial the jury acquitted him of the murder. Clemmons remained in custody in any event because of his convictions for other crimes. Clemmons escaped the death penalty after serving thirteen years on death row because Arnold was willing to consider the possibility that his judicial ruling had been wrong.

Eric Clemmons's case is an example of the seriousness with which Arnold regarded claims of innocence, as Arnold wrote, one of the "extraordinary circumstances in which justice requires the rehearing of a decided case."[69] Death row petitioners, like Eric Clemmons, were almost never sympathetic characters. Rarely was the issue in doubt whether the prisoner had, in fact, committed the crime. In spite of this, Arnold believed the "duty to search for constitutional error with painstaking care is never more exacting than it is in a capital case."[70]

ARNOLD AND THE SUPREME COURT: FREDERICK LASHLEY AND LLOYD SCHLUP

Typically, death penalty litigants within the Eighth Circuit received no further action by the Supreme Court, but for Arnold two exceptions are significant: the cases of Frederick Lashley and Lloyd Schlup.

The *Schlup* case was a resounding triumph for Arnold. Lloyd Schlup, sentenced to death for the murder of a fellow inmate in Missouri, argued that he was innocent of the crime and that evidence of such "actual innocence" was sufficient cause to permit the federal courts to review his case, which would otherwise not be reviewable there because it was his second habeas petition. Arnold dissented from the full court's refusal in 1993 to rehear a panel's decision and denial of Schlup's motion for stay of execution.[71] Schlup had attempted to provide several affidavits and statements from present or former prisoners, which he characterized as newly discovered evidence that he was not present at the scene of the murder. He also relied on videotape, offered at trial as part of an alibi defense, showing his presence in the dining room near the time of the murder. Some of these claims were not raised in his first habeas petition, and he attributed this failure to ineffective assistance of counsel.

Arnold's very short dissent raised two points. First, he believed that "a question of great importance in habeas corpus jurisprudence"—confusion among lower courts about proper interpretation of prior Supreme Court precedent on a particular point—deserved the court's en banc time. Second, Arnold believed that a majority of Supreme Court justices had come to recognize that compelling evidence of actual innocence might serve as its own justification for granting a habeas petition, and that this was a plausible case for invoking the actual innocence exception.[72]

Missouri governor Mel Carnahan intervened in November 1993, just eight hours shy of Schlup's scheduled execution, to allow time for Schlup's attorneys to appeal to the US Supreme Court. Subsequently, the Supreme Court agreed to hear the case and directed the Eighth Circuit to hold an evidentiary hearing on the new evidence.[73] Importantly, the Supreme Court majority (in a 5–4 decision) agreed with Arnold on all points, including support for Arnold's assertion that compelling evidence of actual innocence might serve as a freestanding ground to overcome a procedural bar to habeas review.

As a result, the state of Missouri was required to retry Lloyd Schlup, fourteen years after his death sentence had been imposed. Schlup entered a plea bargain with prosecutors opting for life imprisonment against the possibility of another death sentence.

Arnold's ruling in Frederick Lashley's case, however, received a very different reaction from the Supreme Court. Frederick Lashley was sentenced to death by a Missouri jury for murdering his foster mother in a particularly brutal fashion. In 1981, while Janie Tracy was living in St. Louis, Lashley broke into her home, and when she returned later that evening he struck her over the head with a cast-iron skillet with enough force to break the skillet into two pieces. Lashley then plunged a butcher knife into her skull.

On appeal to the federal courts, Lashley contended that his trial counsel was ineffective and that the trial court judge violated his Eighth Amendment rights by refusing to give a mitigating-circumstance instruction that his attorney requested — that Lashley had no significant history of prior criminal activity. Initially, the Eighth Circuit panel, including Arnold, George Fagg, and H. Franklin Waters (sitting by designation from the Western District of Arkansas), voted to affirm the lower court's dismissal of Lashley's habeas petition. In late October 1991, however, Arnold drafted a proposed dissent to Judge Fagg's majority opinion on the Eighth Amendment issue. In a memo to the other two judges, Arnold explained his difference with Judge Fagg's reasoning on the issue whether Lashley's attorney had waived an argument in earlier proceedings (Arnold believed he had not).[74] Originally the memo to the judges, first drafted by a law clerk, summarized the issue and stated, simply, "I disagree." Arnold changed this, writing instead: "I feel differently, and would like to explain why." This is a good example of Arnold's low-key effort to "lobby" other judges for his position on a case. The memo, with Arnold's draft dissent, was hand-delivered to Judge Fagg when the judges gathered for court week.

Although it is rare for one judge to persuade a panel to change its view through writing a dissent, Arnold did it more often than others. And in this case, Arnold's view prevailed. Judge Waters — a Reagan appointee — changed his vote to agree with Arnold, and thus Arnold's proposed dissent became the majority opinion with Judge Fagg now in dissent. Arnold held that the Missouri trial court violated the Eighth Amendment by refusing to give mitigating-circumstance instructions requested by Lashley.[75] Arnold believed due process, and prior Supreme Court precedent, supported a presumption that a defendant is innocent of other crimes at the sentencing phase, even though the Supreme Court had never explicitly considered the question. Arnold ordered the state of Missouri to either conduct a new sentencing procedure or reduce Lashley's sentence to life imprisonment.[76]

Judge Waters later may have regretted changing his vote at Arnold's persuasion. The state of Missouri appealed the ruling, asking the Supreme Court to review the case. In a 7–2 decision, the Court granted certiorari and, dispensing with briefs and argument, summarily reversed Judge Arnold.[77] In an unsigned opinion, the Court stated that the Eighth Circuit majority (Arnold's opinion) "plainly misread our precedents." The Missouri trial court had not erred in refusing the instruction, contrary to what Arnold believed to be the requirements of an earlier Supreme Court decision known as *Lockett*.[78] "In short," the opinion reads, "until the Court of Appeals' decision in this case, it appears that lower courts consistently applied the princi-

ples established by *Lockett* and its progeny."[79] The opinion continued:
"Today we make explicit the clear implication of our precedents: Nothing in
the Constitution obligates state courts to give mitigating circumstance
instructions when no evidence is offered to support them. Because the jury
heard no evidence concerning Lashley's prior criminal history, the trial
judge did not err in refusing to give the requested instruction."[80]

Justices Stevens and Blackmun dissented (Justice Brennan was no
longer a member of the Court), agreeing with Judge Arnold that the state
was uniquely situated to prove whether or not Lashley had a significant
prior criminal history, and for this reason, it was error to refuse the miti-
gating-circumstances instruction, "The defendant has no significant history
of prior criminal activity." With Arnold, the dissenters believed that an erroneous ruling by the trial judge "unquestionably explains why the record contains no specific testimony about respondent's prior criminal history. Even
though due process may not *automatically* entitle a defendant to an instruction that he is presumed innocent of other offenses at the penalty phase of
the trial, the instruction should certainly be given when a trial court error is
responsible for the absence of evidence supporting the instruction."[81]

The Lashley case became an issue in Arnold's opportunity for a seat on
the US Supreme Court in 1993. At that time Arnold's opinions were under
scrutiny by journalists, interest groups, and advocates of other potential
nominees. Two editorials in the *Washington Times* tried to make an issue of
the Frederick Lashley decision in consideration of Arnold's potential nomination. In an editorial titled "Looking for a Supreme," the *Times* suggested
Judge Arnold "may have a bit of explaining to do" over the case.[82] The
ediorial claimed the Supreme Court's recent reversal in *Lashley v. Delo* was
"extremely unusual," employed only in cases in which "the lower court has
badly erred in applying the law." The reversal was "a sharp rebuke, a true
black eye for an appeals court judge. The question for Judge Arnold is
whether this summary reversal goes either to his competence as a jurist or
to his willingness as an appeals court judge to be bound by precedents
established by the Supreme Court."[83] At Ruth Bader Ginsburg's confirmation hearing before the US Senate only a few months earlier, Senator Orrin
Hatch posed questions about the constitutionality of the death penalty,[84]
and no doubt Arnold would have faced the same.

Frederick Lashley was executed July 28, 1993, about three months
after the Supreme Court's reversal of the Eighth Circuit. Arnold did not

believe Lashley was innocent of the crime. But Arnold would have required Missouri to conduct another sentencing trial, remedying the constitutional problem Arnold believed had occurred. In another irony, Lashley was a juvenile at the time of the crime. He was put to death before the Supreme Court decided in 2005 that executing juveniles who committed crimes under the age of eighteen violates the federal constitution.[85]

INFLUENCE OF JUSTICES BRENNAN AND BLACKMUN

William Brennan was a lifelong friend and mentor. From 1961 through Brennan's death, a period of nearly forty years, the two corresponded regularly about family, politics, and legal issues. In 1963, just two years after Arnold finished his clerkship, William Brennan wrote one of the Supreme Court's most expansive habeas decisions. *Fay v. Noia*[86] was a notable instance of the expansion of federal court power to review state criminal proceedings during the Warren Court era.

In that case, a felony murder conviction in a New York court, the state conceded that the defendant's confession had been coerced and that it had been introduced in the trial in violation of the due process clause of the federal constitution. The state contended, however, that Noia could not raise this claim in federal court through habeas corpus because he had failed to follow the proper state appeals procedures to raise the claim, and he was now barred from doing so. The Supreme Court, in a 6–3 decision, held that Noia had not waived his right to seek federal review. Brennan wrote that there was no higher duty than to maintain unimpaired the right to seek a writ of habeas corpus, whose "root principle is that in a civilized society, government must always be accountable to the judiciary for a man's imprisonment."[87]

In a later case, Brennan would write one of his most stirring dissents in a death penalty decision. The case addressed the racial disparity among those executed. Brennan believed that even if capital punishment were constitutional in principle but not in practice, this could hardly be so where it was demonstrably biased against members of a particular race:

> It is tempting to pretend that minorities on death row share a fate in no way connected to our own, that our treatment of them sounds no echoes beyond the chamber in which they die. Such an illusion is ultimately corrosive, for the reverberations of injustice are not so easily confined. The

way in which we choose those who will die reveals the depth of moral commitment among the living.[88]

Brennan, in turn, was often impressed with Arnold's turn of phrase in defense of individual rights. Brennan was particularly fond of Arnold's stirring defense of the Bill of Rights in a case called *Williams v. Nix*:

> A system of law that not only makes certain conduct criminal, but also lays down rules for the conduct of the authorities, often becomes complex in its application to individual cases, and will from time to time produce imperfect results, especially if one's attention is confined to the particular case at bar. Some criminals *do* go free because of the necessity of keeping government and its servants in their place. That is one of the costs of having and enforcing a Bill of Rights. This country is built on the assumption that the cost is worth paying, and that in the long run, we are all both freer and safer if the Constitution is strictly enforced.[89]

Chief Judge Donald P. Lay later told Arnold these words "sounded like Brennan." Arnold relayed this story to Brennan in a letter: "After I wrote these words, Don Lay told me they 'sounded like Brennan.' I told him that was exactly what I was trying to do!"[90]

Arnold also admired Justice Blackmun. Blackmun was the supervising circuit justice for Arnold's court for the majority of his tenure, and thus Blackmun and Arnold were intimately connected, especially after Arnold himself became chief judge. Harry Blackmun originally came from Arnold's court—the Eighth Circuit—and remained its circuit justice throughout his years of active service. Brennan, Blackmun, and Arnold also shared the Harvard Law School bond. Arnold admired Blackmun's willingness to change his views of the death penalty, because it was "more important to be right than consistent."[91] Blackmun's much-noted change of heart with respect to the constitutionality of the death penalty was, for Arnold, evidence that "the Justice was not afraid to change, and what is more, was not afraid to admit publicly that he had changed and to explain why. This is maturity, not vacillation. Consistency is a virtue, but not the only virtue."[92] He also wrote of his admiration for Blackmun's ability to set aside his personal beliefs about the death penalty.[93] In 1994, Blackmun would publicly support Arnold to be his replacement on the Supreme Court.

As Blackmun's views on the death penalty changed, he paid increasing attention to death penalty appeals coming from the Eighth Circuit. In 1989, Blackmun engineered an emergency stay of execution in a case in which a divided Eighth Circuit had voted to allow it to proceed. Leonard Marvin Laws alleged he had received ineffective assistance of counsel at his death penalty trial. Among other things, he claimed that his attorney failed to tell the jury of his decorated service in Vietnam or the possibility of post-traumatic stress disorder in returning Vietnam veterans. In a 5–4 vote, the full Eighth Circuit overturned an opinion by Judge McMillian that had granted Laws a new penalty trial. Arnold agreed fully with McMillian, and helped to strengthen McMillian's dissenting opinion by helping to write it (although his name does not appear as an author).[94]

Although at Blackmun's referral the Supreme Court had voted to temporarily stay Laws's execution, the Court ultimately turned down the appeal. Blackmun did not file a dissent to this denial of certiorari, but Justices Brennan and Marshall did. Typically, a Brennan and Marshall dissent to denial of certiorari in a death penalty case consisted of one sentence: "Adhering to my view that the death penalty is in all circumstances cruel and unusual punishment prohibited by the Eighth and Fourteenth Amendments, I would grant the petition for certiorari and vacate the death sentence in this case." In this instance, however, the dissent is lengthy — detailing the reasons they believed Arnold and the other Eighth Circuit dissenters were right.[95] Marvin Laws was executed in 1990.

During Arnold's tenure on the Eighth Circuit, both the US Supreme Court and Congress limited the role of the lower federal courts in capital cases arising under habeas corpus. First, in *McCleskey v. Zant*,[96] the Supreme Court limited defendants on death row to a single course of appeals at the federal level except in extreme instances, a ruling attorney John Wesley Hall said "makes sure they get packed off to the death chamber right away."[97] Warren McCleskey had received a last-minute reprieve from a federal court when his lawyers discovered that prosecutors had planted an informant in a cell adjoining McCleskey's, a violation of the Sixth Amendment right to counsel for which a federal judge ordered a new trial.

The Supreme Court reinstated the conviction, holding that McCleskey should have raised the issue earlier. The Supreme Court's decision in the case of Warren McCleskey led Justice Anthony Kennedy to write for the majority: "Perpetual disrespect for the finality of convictions disparages the entire criminal justice system." Marshall, Blackmun, and Stevens dissented, calling the ruling an "unjustifiable assault" on the long tradition of habeas review. Arnold believed the Eighth Circuit was already consistent with the Supreme Court's ruling in *McCleskey*. "We were already applying that rule," he noted.[98] McCleskey was executed in Georgia shortly after the Supreme Court's decision in his case.

The effort to speed up executions included Congress. In 1996, Congress enacted the Antiterrorism and Effective Death Penalty Act. That act set a one-year time limit to file a petition for federal habeas review, with the clock running from the moment review of the prisoner's case was complete in the state courts. The title of the act itself—"effective death penalty"—indicates the intent of Congress. If an inmate was unable to secure a lawyer for this federal appeal, or if that lawyer made any mistakes in raising his claims, the one-year limit could expire without any review of a death sentence by the federal courts. For those states willing to provide lawyers for death row inmates, however, the time period is reduced to a mere six months. The increasing number of executions each year following the passage of the Effective Death Penalty Act meant that, for its sponsors at least, the measure was a success.

Delays in the Eighth Circuit occurred at the federal trial court level—there were simply too many appeals from prisoners, and too few district judges, to process them quickly. As a result, in Arkansas and Missouri death penalty habeas cases were backed up in the district courts, and they needed help from other districts. As chief judge of the court, Arnold recruited other federal judges to go to Arkansas and Missouri to help with the caseload.[99]

Arnold remained intensely interested in the habeas jurisdiction of the federal courts throughout his life. Arnold once said: "A judge of an inferior federal court, as the Constitution describes, is in the worst possible position to do anything systematic about habeas corpus, because policy is set by Congress and interpreted by the Supreme Court."[100] After he was appointed by Chief Justice Rehnquist to chair the Committee on the Budget for the federal branch, Arnold had a new platform. For nine years, from 1987 to 1996, Arnold presided over important changes in the judiciary's budget and had much to say to Congress about habeas jurisdiction and especially the tremendous cost of administering the death penalty.

Arnold's appearances before Congress to present the budget requests for the federal courts became a common feature of the 1990s. In 1992, fed-

eral court habeas corpus jurisdiction in death penalty cases assumed a central role in these hearings. As Arnold wrote to Blackmun after his presentation that year:

> Today was my day to testify before the House Appropriations Subcom-
> mittee on the courts' budget request. Mr. Rogers of Kentucky, the
> ranking minority member, gave us a good wooling around on *habeas*
> *corpus* in death-penalty cases. The subject was hardly a budgetary one.
> The hearing was the most contentious I have attended. There is bad
> feeling between the two political parties, and crime is at the top of
> everyone's list of issues. Almost the whole hearing was taken up by Mr.
> Rogers's attack, quoting a letter from Henry Hyde of Illinois, on the
> Judicial Conference position on *habeas corpus*. The experience was
> intensely interesting if not altogether pleasant.[101]

Representative Harold Rogers of Kentucky articulated his concerns
about the matter with Justices Antonin Scalia and Sandra Day O'Connor,
who appeared on behalf of the Supreme Court's budget request. He asked
the justices "to comment on the impact that the use of the habeas statute
in capital cases has had on the Judiciary."[102] Rogers clearly opposed multiple appeals to the federal courts and he exhibited some antagonism
toward required funding for the federal Death Penalty Resource Centers.[103] O'Connor noted the increasingly large numbers of applications to
individual justices relating to capital cases in the state courts. Particularly
for last-minute applications and successive habeas petitions, the practice
"does not reflect well on the system that we have in place."[104] Rogers's
exchange with Arnold was similarly confrontational, and Arnold wanted
Blackmun to know about it.

Death penalty appeals were time consuming and personally upsetting for
Arnold. Although Arnold often voted in favor of new trials for condemned
inmates, most death row appeals did not succeed before the Eighth Circuit. His scorecard—which he would not have kept himself—was probably even, in the number of cases in which his views led to a reprieve, further review, or exoneration of a prisoner. Other judges noted, privately,
that Arnold seemed to have deep reservations about the death penalty,

even though in a majority of the cases before him he nonetheless voted to uphold the execution.[105]

Despite an increasing caseload, Arnold struggled to give priority to appeals in death cases. His philosophy in these cases went beyond merely ensuring the fairness of the trial. He also believed that no one should be eligible for the death penalty unless there was no dispute that the defendant had murdered the person killed. Sometimes, the issue of whether the defendant actually committed the murder was hotly disputed. The Supreme Court's precedent for "actual innocence" as a criteria for reversal by federal courts was quite stringent. Arnold instead adopted a pragmatic approach in cases of possible innocence, an approach more evident in conference with the other judges of the Eighth Circuit than apparent in any written opinion. Judge Arlen Beam, for example, described Arnold's philosophy: "In cases in which the issue of whether the defendant actually committed the murder was hotly disputed, and where there was decent evidence on both sides, we should not take the chance that we had convicted somebody who maybe hadn't committed the murder."[106] It was a philosophy he shared with other judges as they discussed cases in closed chambers. It was a difficult philosophy to implement in specific cases, but Arnold looked for ways to rule in favor of prisoners when he believed there was real doubt about their guilt.

Arnold never took the view of Brennan and Marshall that the death penalty was unconstitutional in all circumstances; in fact, it is unlikely that he believed it to be so despite his personal opposition to it. Arnold believed the death penalty was largely a matter for the legislature. In his numerous opinions on death penalty matters, Arnold showed more respect for state judges and juries, at least in form, than did Brennan, and he was less strident in tone. Arnold always publicly thanked attorneys for death row inmates by name, in published opinions, even when he disagreed with them.

Arnold disliked the death penalty but permitted most executions to proceed. The best he could do was to ensure a fair trial had taken place and that other judges would take these appeals seriously. Some judges seem to give serious scrutiny in death penalty cases only to instances of arguable innocence—the prisoner might be the wrong man. Arnold worried as much about constitutional purity in the process of the death penalty, even if that meant lengthy delays in the resolution of death penalty cases.

Arnold never commented further when someone was executed whom he thought should have lived. Although in a number of death penalty cases

Arnold found himself in dissent in favor of the condemned, when he lost the votes in those cases he seemed to close his mind on the matter and, at least after a while, did not dwell on the case. He moved on, because other cases were waiting.

Chapter Nine

Free Speech and the First Amendment

Richard Arnold was probably most noted for his First Amendment opinions. He believed that freedom of speech and association and the right to participate equally in the political process were linked. As he once said, "The First Amendment is and should be first. It is the cornerstone of all our liberties and, together with the Legislative Article, the most important part of the Constitution."[1] This statement is revealing of Arnold's deeply held beliefs because it links the First Amendment with an entire section of the US Constitution creating the legislative power of Congress. Arnold believed in the supremacy of the legislature, both state and federal, within constitutional limits. One job of the federal judiciary, as he saw it, was to ensure that robust political debate, including particularly the right to criticize government, was unfettered.

One sign of Arnold's renown in this area is the Richard S. Arnold Prize for Scholarship in Free Speech, awarded annually by the Speech Communication Association's Commission on Freedom of Expression. The prize is named for Arnold as "a jurist noted for his outstanding opinions in Constitutional and First Amendment Law."[2] In addition, the First Amendment Center, with offices at Vanderbilt University and Washington, DC, bestows a major award named for Arnold on one law student each year in its national First Amendment moot court competition.[3]

In a 1993 tribute to Arnold, Justice William Brennan singled out Arnold's First Amendment opinions as among his most courageous. Brennan wrote: "Judge Arnold has consistently vindicated the First Amendment guarantees of freedom of the press and freedom of speech, even in cases in which the protected expression was controversial, distasteful, or hateful."[4]

Arnold's views of the First Amendment, in fact, owed much to William Brennan. As Brennan's law clerk in the 1960 Supreme Court term, Arnold had been impressed with his boss's approach to free speech cases, particularly those involving the House Un-American Activities Committee. While Arnold was a first-year law student at Harvard, Brennan, then a new member of the Supreme Court, wrote the opinion in *Roth v. United States*, an obscenity case invoking the memorable language: "All ideas having even the slightest redeeming social importance—unorthodox ideas, controversial ideas, even ideas hateful to the prevailing climate of opinion—have the full protection of the guarantees."[5]

A few years later, after Arnold had returned to Arkansas to practice law and run for Congress, Brennan wrote the pivotal decision in *New York Times v. Sullivan*.[6] It was the first case to invoke the First Amendment's guarantee of freedom of speech and the press to limit an award of damages in a libel action brought by a public official against critics of his conduct. In a passage quoted often, Brennan wrote: "We consider this case against the background of a profound national commitment to the principle that debate on public issues should be uninhibited, robust and wide-open, and that it may well include vehement, caustic, and sometimes unpleasantly sharp attacks on government and public officials."[7]

New York Times v. Sullivan established the principle that public officials may not recover damages for speech related to their official conduct unless they can prove actual malice, "that the statement was made with . . . knowledge that it was false or with reckless disregard of whether it was false or not."[8]

Perhaps more important in Arnold's developing views about the First Amendment was the example of Justice Hugo Black. Justice Black was a near absolutist on the First Amendment. Black was known for his famous aphorism "No law means no law," echoing the language of the First Amendment, "Congress shall make no law respecting an establishment of religion, or prohibiting the free exercise thereof; or abridging the freedom of speech, or of the press."[9] Justice Black first used "No law means no law" in a dissent to a Supreme Court opinion allowing California to deny bar admission to a candidate who refused to answer questions about Communist Party affiliation. Arnold was Justice Brennan's law clerk at the time and was one of the first to read Justice Black's draft. Brennan also dissented in that case but wrote a separate opinion. Black's more strident language left a lasting impression with Arnold.[10]

Arnold also admired Justice Black's Madison Lecture, given at New York University in 1960. Black said, "It is my belief that there are 'absolutes' in our Bill of Rights, and that they were put there on purpose by men who knew what words meant, and meant their prohibitions to be 'absolutes.'"[11] In *New York Times v. Sullivan*, Justice Black had written a separate concurring opinion to emphasize the distinctiveness of his view: "An unconditional right to say what one pleases about public affairs is what I consider to be the minimum guarantee of the First Amendment."[12]

Arnold came closest to Black's view of the Bill of Rights in First Amendment cases, even to the extent that some termed him "Justice Black revived."[13] As a Supreme Court law clerk, Arnold had encountered some of the last few communist prosecutions, and Justice Black's (as well as Brennan's) handling of them left a lasting impression. Arnold had come to the Court already keenly interested in the issue of free speech:

> At that time [1960], there was a theory called "preferred position," which I still kind of like. And that is that certain provisions of the Bill of Rights are better than others, and roughly it corresponds to what we now use strict scrutiny on—free speech, freedom of religion, and so forth. I spent an awful lot of time reading to get a theoretical grounding. My father gave me a book called *The Bill of Rights*. It was a compilation of opinions, with a heavy emphasis on Black's and Douglas's dissents. I read the book in the early 50s. So maybe that was the beginning of my thought about the First Amendment.[14]

The history of the First Amendment in the Supreme Court is engagingly recounted in Anthony Lewis's book *Freedom for the Thought That We Hate*.[15] As a court of appeals judge, Arnold worked under Supreme Court precedent, much of it significantly shaped by Brennan and Black. For lower federal courts, if a clear Supreme Court authority governs the outcome of a case, there is virtually no need for an extended written opinion. But Arnold would encounter a number of questions that were not clearly answered by Supreme Court precedent. In such instances the values of a judge inevitably come to the fore. Arnold would have to fill in the gaps, and he did so with a commitment close to Justice Black's position of "primacy" to which he was always attracted.

BURNING CROSSES IN MINNESOTA

Two prosecutions for cross burning in Minnesota in the early 1990s brought attention to the conflict between threatening, hateful behavior toward racial groups and the First Amendment. One of the two cases gave Arnold a forum to assert First Amendment protection for expressive conduct. The other case, in which Arnold did not participate, was decided by the United States Supreme Court. In a sharply divided opinion, the majority of justices sided with Arnold's view that cross burning could be protected by the First Amendment, a significant affirmation of Arnold's stance.

In 1989 Bruce Roy Lee constructed a cross and burned it on property adjacent to a racially mixed apartment building in Coon Rapids, Minnesota. Lee explained to a tenant that his intent was to try to "get rid of some of the bad blacks that were there."[16] The local United States Attorney charged Lee with conspiracy against civil rights under a federal statute.[17] The statute was not directed specifically at cross burning but rather to conspiracies of all kinds to threaten or intimidate others in the exercise of a federal right. A jury convicted Lee and sentenced him to five years in prison.

On appeal to the Eighth Circuit, Lee contended that the First Amendment was a bar to his conviction because he had been engaged in "expressive conduct," which could not be criminally punished. Two judges on the panel assigned to the case rejected Lee's First Amendment claim. Arnold, however, believed the First Amendment protected Lee's actions. In a dissent to the panel opinion, Arnold wrote: "The act of cross burning, as it occurred in this case, was expressive conduct. It was intended to convey a message, an idea: 'We do not like black people, and we want them to move out,' or something of the sort. This kind of communication, no matter how hateful, is 'speech' within the meaning of the First Amendment. It is entitled to protection from governmental sanction just as much as speech of which we might approve."[18]

Arnold acknowledged that evidence supported the prosecutor's contention that burning a cross in full view of the apartment complex was intended to, and did in fact, cause fear for at least some of the black residents. "Still," Arnold wrote, "something is lacking, in my opinion, to justify the application of the statute, as against a First Amendment challenge, on this record."[19]

Arnold explained that the government's interest in a case such as this was to ensure its citizens of the right to be free of physical force, or threats of physical force. But in this case, it appeared that Lee had done more than forcefully state a view that was considered "revolting or appalling." The law established by the Supreme Court, Arnold wrote, "seems to be this: even speech that advocates violence is protected by the First Amendment, unless the likelihood of actual violence crosses some constitutionally derived line." That line had not been crossed in this case, Arnold contended. The burning cross was nearly four hundred feet away, on another's property.[20]

Arnold's dissent in *United States v. Lee* attracted the attention of the full Eighth Circuit, and the court agreed to rehear the case en banc. At about the same time, the United States Supreme Court agreed to hear another Minnesota cross-burning case, this one from St. Paul. The appeal went directly to the US Supreme Court from the Supreme Court of Minnesota, so the Eighth Circuit did not participate in this case. But the Supreme Court's resolution of this case, *R.A.V. v. City of St. Paul, Minnesota*,[21] effectively endorsed Arnold's *Lee* dissent and would affect the outcome of that case before the full Eighth Circuit.

In June 1990, a group of white teenagers burned a crudely constructed cross inside the fenced yard of a black family in St. Paul. One of the teenagers challenged the constitutionality of the St. Paul bias-motivated crime ordinance with which he had been charged. That ordinance provided:

> Whoever places on public or private property a symbol, object, appellation, characterization or graffiti, including, but not limited to, a burning cross or Nazi swastika, which one knows or has reasonable grounds to know arouses anger, alarm or resentment in others on the basis of race, color, creed, religion or gender commits disorderly conduct and shall be guilty of a misdemeanor.[22]

All nine justices of the US Supreme Court agreed that the St. Paul ordinance was unconstitutional. But the rationales varied sharply. Writing for a five-justice majority, Antonin Scalia held that the First Amendment prohibited the government from "silencing speech on the basis of its content." Cross burning, wrote Scalia, was nonverbal expressive activity protected by the First Amendment, so the St. Paul ordinance specifically barring the cross burning was unconstitutional on its face.[23] Scalia's opinion was not approval of the conduct: "Let there be no mistake," Scalia wrote, "about our belief that burning a cross in someone's front yard is reprehensible. But St. Paul has sufficient means at its disposal to prevent such behavior without adding the First Amendment to the fire."[24]

Other justices expressed different views about the constitutional problem with the St. Paul ordinance. The larger issue, for them, was to preserve the possibility that a properly drafted "hate crime" law could be upheld under the First Amendment.[25] Justice Blackmun, for example, wrote: "I see no First Amendment values that are compromised by a law that prohibits hoodlums from driving minorities out of their homes by burning crosses on their lawns, but I see great harm in preventing the people of St. Paul from specifically punishing the race-based 'fighting words' that so prejudice their community."[26] The majority's decision, some justices feared, would not only invalidate other hate crimes legislation but also many of the speech codes adopted at public universities.[27]

The Supreme Court's ruling in *R.A.V.* dealt with a different statute than the Eighth Circuit faced in the *Lee* case. Nonetheless, the ruling was especially significant as an endorsement of Richard Arnold's earlier dissenting view that the act of burning a cross could be expressive conduct and thus protected by the First Amendment.

When the full Eighth Circuit court reheard *United States v. Lee* in 1992, four judges sided with Arnold to reverse Bruce Roy Lee's conviction and remand the case for a retrial, if the US Attorney chose to try the case again. Three more judges, including Richard's brother, Morris Arnold, agreed the defendant's conviction should be reversed but would have gone further to hold that there was insufficient evidence to sustain a retrial on the conspiracy count. Two judges—McMillian and Lay—would have affirmed the conviction on the ground that the cross burning was *not* protected speech under the First Amendment.[28] The US Supreme Court declined to review the Eighth Circuit's decision.

Arnold's view of the matter carried the day in the Eighth Circuit, but the divided opinion among the Eighth Circuit judges, as in the Supreme Court, reflected the difficulty of applying "free speech" principles for cross burning.

The difficulty was less pronounced in the flag-burning context, where the Supreme Court had earlier protected flag burning as a form of symbolic speech.[29] Flag-burning cases, however, did not present the problem of harassment, threats, and intimidation against an identifiable group.

After the Eighth Circuit handed down its decision, Lee's attorney, John W. Lundquist, summarized the cross-burning case this way: he said the opinion "reaffirms an individual's right to engage in expression no matter how hateful when there's no accompanying force or threat of violence."[30] A decade later, the US Supreme Court would rule that states may ban cross burning that is meant to intimidate, so long as such a law clearly places on the prosecution the burden of proving that the cross burning was intended as a substantial threat and not merely as a form of symbolic expression.[31]

FREEDOM OF THE PRESS AND THE GOVERNOR OF SOUTH DAKOTA

One of Arnold's most high-profile First Amendment cases involved William Janklow, at that time the Republican governor of South Dakota. Janklow filed a $10 million libel lawsuit against *Newsweek* for a story alleging that Janklow, as state attorney general, had pursued the prosecution of Dennis Banks, an American Indian activist, for seeking to bring rape charges against Janklow in a tribal court. The allegation that Janklow had raped a teenaged Indian girl five years earlier was later acknowledged to be false. Janklow's lawsuit centered on one paragraph of the *Newsweek* article, which referred to Banks's initiation of tribal charges of assault against Janklow in 1974.[32] According to the governor, the article defamed him by implying that he began prosecuting Banks in revenge.

A federal judge in South Dakota had dismissed the libel suit in 1984. The judge concluded that the basic facts reported by *Newsweek* were true. Further, the judge characterized the suggestion of the revenge motive as an expression of "opinion" and applied the rule that statements of opinion do not constitute libel. As the Supreme Court articulated in *Gertz v. Robert Welch, Inc.*, "Under the First Amendment there is no such thing as a false idea. However pernicious an opinion may seem, we depend for its correction not on the conscience of judges and juries but on the competition of other ideas."[33]

On appeal, however, a panel of the Eighth Circuit reinstated the suit over Arnold's dissent. Judges Pasco Bowman and George Fagg believed that the meaning that could be drawn from the article—that Janklow was prosecuting Banks for revenge—amounted to a statement of fact, not an expression of opinion.[34] As such, Janklow would be entitled to submit his case to a jury if he could establish "actual malice" on the part of *Newsweek*, a standard applied to public figures that requires "a high degree of awareness of probable falsity" of the story.[35] If Janklow could establish this, *Newsweek* would not have a First Amendment privilege against Janklow's suit for defamation.

Arnold disagreed. He believed the statement was an "opinion about the motives of a public official and should be absolutely privileged" under the First Amendment.[36] "Until today," he wrote, "I had thought that one of the undisputed rights of every American, including the much-discussed 'media,' was to question the motives of public servants. Such personal criticism may be abusive, and perhaps we would have a better country if there were a lot less of it, but it is, in my opinion, no part of the business of government, including the Judicial Branch, to tell the people that they cannot criticize the motives of their own employees."[37]

Arnold admitted that this kind of public discussion had its costs— persons may be deterred from public office. "Federal judges are no strangers to this sort of attack," he wrote. "But the only restraint that should be imposed on this sort of discussion is self-restraint, either of the individual citizen or of the press itself. The Framers of our Constitution long ago struck the balance in favor of speech, and judges ought not to reweigh-it, however much we might desire to elevate the level of public discourse."[38] The full Eighth Circuit granted *Newsweek*'s petition for rehearing on the question of whether the article should be read as fact or opinion. On appeal to the full Eighth Circuit, Arnold's previous dissent prevailed in a 6–3 decision. Now writing for the majority, Arnold announced, "We now hold it to be opinion, absolutely protected by the First Amendment." Arnold wrote, "Courts must be slow to intrude into the area of editorial judgment, not only with respect to choices of words but also with respect to inclusions in or omissions from news stories. Accounts of past events are always selective, and under the First Amendment the decision of what to select must almost always be left to writers and editors. It is not the business of government."[39]

Arnold also noted the importance of the First Amendment protection of such speech:

It is vital to our form of government that press and citizens alike be free to discuss and, if they see fit, impugn the motives of public officials. Here we have criticism of the conduct of a state attorney general who now serves as governor, as well as questions about the actions of three other governors of two other states, all involving an issue of national importance, the treatment of Indian people. Few other discussions of public concern could make a greater claim for *First* Amendment protection.[40]

The Supreme Court refused to hear the case; Richard Arnold's opinion was the final word.[41]

Despite losing this case, Governor Janklow continued his successful political career. Although term limits prevented him from running for a third consecutive term in 1986, he did successfully run for a third term in 1995, and a fourth term following that, to become South Dakota's longest-serving governor. Following his departure from office again because of term limits, he won South Dakota's only seat in the House of Representatives in 2002. His service in Congress was cut short after his involvement in a car accident led to the death of a motorcyclist. Janklow had been speeding at the time, though he blamed the accident on a bout of hypoglycemia. He was convicted of second-degree manslaughter and sentenced to one hundred days in jail. He then resigned his seat in the House.[42]

PUBLIC TELEVISION AND POLITICAL DEBATES: A SUPREME COURT REVERSAL

Arnold's commitment to protect an open arena for political debate came through again in *Forbes v. Arkansas Educational Television Commission*, although the Supreme Court would later reverse his decision.[43]

In 1992, a public television network in Arkansas, AETN, sponsored a debate for candidates in Arkansas's third congressional district. Ralph P. Forbes, a perennial contender for political office, qualified for the ballot as an independent candidate for the congressional seat. But Forbes was excluded from the televised debate by AETN on the ground that he had little popular support and thus was not a "viable" candidate.

Forbes lost the 1992 congressional election by a wide margin. He had lost most of his political races in the past by similarly wide margins, although he was a serious contender for lieutenant governor of Arkansas only two years before the 1992 congressional campaign. In the primary race for the Republican nomination for lieutenant governor, Forbes had forced a run-off election and had garnered nearly 47 percent of the votes statewide. He had also carried all but one of the sixteen counties within the Third Congressional District by absolute majorities.[44] There was, therefore, some circumstantial evidence suggesting Forbes to be a potentially viable candidate for the 1992 congressional seat.

Two months before the scheduled debate, AETN informed Forbes he would not be allowed to participate. Forbes sued the Arkansas Educational Television Commission, a state agency whose members are appointed by the governor, under both the First Amendment and a federal statute that provides political candidates a limited right of access to television airtime. He sought a federal court order requiring AETN to allow him to participate in the debate, along with money damages if he were to be excluded.

The federal district court denied Forbes's request for an injunction, which the Eighth Circuit affirmed in an appeal before Judges Arnold, McMillian, and Gibson. But the panel believed Forbes had a potentially meritorious claim for money damages against AETN, so it remanded the case to the district court to consider Forbes's First Amendment claim.

The Arkansas public television commission appealed to the full Eighth Circuit. In a 6–5 decision, Arnold affirmed that a public television station was a "state actor" and thus was subject to First Amendment constraints, and that AETN did not have an absolute right to determine which of the legally qualified candidates for a public office it would put on the air. Instead, it must prove that the justification for the decision was both "rational and viewpoint-neutral."[45] It was a closely divided decision.

Although the public television debate had long since taken place, and indeed the congressional election had been decided, Forbes at last presented his First Amendment claim in a trial. A jury found that the decision to exclude Forbes from the debate was not the result of political pressure nor based on opposition to his political opinions. Accordingly, the district court entered judgment in favor of AETN and the other defendants, dismissing Forbes's lawsuit. The jury agreed that the decision had been, as AETN argued, an exercise of standard journalistic judgment.

The case then came before the Arnold, McMillian, and Gibson panel a second time. They reversed the district court and sent the case back for another trial, on the ground that the trial judge had applied an incorrect legal standard for the First Amendment. Writing for the court, Arnold held that even if there was no bias against Forbes's viewpoint in the decision to exclude him from the debate, the stated reason, that Forbes was not a "viable" candidate, was not a legally sufficient rationale under the First Amendment. While private journalists could offer their opinions on the viability of certain candidates, government journalists were still government employees and therefore could not.[46]

One key to the case, as Arnold wrote in his opinion for the court, is that a decision about whether a person lacked sufficient political support is a subjective ground that "would place too much faith in government."[47] Arnold believed that whether Forbes was viable was "ultimately a judgment to be made by the people of the Third Congressional District," not by officials of the government in charge of channels of communication. The state of Arkansas, by statute, already determined political viability by its statute governing ballot access: Forbes had complied with this statute by gathering enough signatures to appear on the ballot.[48] Forbes was not only entitled to his views (which had been extreme — he was a former member of the American Nazi Party)[49] but also to a podium on the stage of public debate.

Not only did the other two judges on the panel agree with Arnold; Judge McMillian wrote to concur in Arnold's "excellent analysis" and added, "hopefully we have given *Forbes v. Arkansas* a decent burial."[50] Judge Gibson agreed it was "an excellent opinion" but disagreed with Judge McMillian only to the extent that he thought the Eighth Circuit would see the case again, "once the jury determines the amount of damages in this case."[51] Interestingly, Gibson expected a second jury trial to come out favorably for Forbes.

Importantly, at about the same time another panel of Eighth Circuit judges decided a similar case from Iowa, Jay B. Marcus of the Natural Law Party asked to be part of a series of formal debates on Iowa Public Television. Marcus was told no by the producers, with the justification that political candidates were presented on the basis of their "newsworthiness." Marcus sued, citing the *Forbes* precedent to argue that his exclusion on the basis of a judgment of "newsworthiness" violated the First Amendment.

Marcus lost this case. Judge Frank Magill, writing for himself and Judge George Fagg, distinguished Arnold's opinion in *Forbes*:

> *Forbes* cannot be read to mandate the inclusion of every candidate on the ballot for any debate sponsored by a public television station. Nor does

Forbes suggest that public television station administrators, because they are government actors, have no discretion whatsoever in making broadcast determinations. Rather, *Forbes* held that there was no compelling interest in excluding statutorily-defined viable candidates from a debate based on the viability of the candidate. Unlike "viability," which is ultimately for the voters to decide, "newsworthiness" is peculiarly a decision within the domain of journalists.[52]

Judge Arlen Beam dissented. In his view, Arnold's opinion in *Forbes* required the court to rule in favor of Marcus: "In my view, there can be no realistic argument advanced that a subjective opinion by a government employee that a candidate is or is not 'newsworthy' is different from a subjective conclusion that he or she is or is not 'politically viable.' The inquiry involves two peas from the same analytical pod. *Forbes* requires us to grant the emergency injunction requested in this case."[53] The split among the judges in the Iowa case reflected the larger split within the Eighth Circuit over the Ralph Forbes case—that one decided by the narrowest of margins, a six-to-five vote.

Meanwhile, the Arkansas Educational Television Commission appealed Arnold's latest ruling in *Forbes* to the United States Supreme Court, and the justices agreed to hear the case. They took the matter, Justice Anthony Kennedy wrote, because of a conflict with a decision from the Eleventh Circuit on a similar issue, and because of "the manifest importance of the case."[54] Six justices voted to reverse Arnold's opinion. Writing for the majority, Justice Anthony Kennedy stated simply that "[t]he broadcaster's decision to exclude the candidate was a reasonable, viewpoint-neutral exercise of journalistic discretion."[55] Kennedy's opinion focused on Forbes's perennial candidate status and affirmed AETN's right to exclude him.

The majority were also concerned that Arnold's ruling could limit speech. Kennedy wrote, "In addition to being a misapplication of our precedents, the Court of Appeals' holding would result in less speech, not more. In ruling that the debate was a public forum open to all ballot-qualified candidates, the Court of Appeals would place a severe burden upon public broadcasters who air candidates' views."[56] Kennedy's concern was that a public broadcaster would forgo the venture entirely rather than present a debate with an unmanageable number of participants.

Justice John Paul Stevens dissented, joined by David Souter and Ruth Bader Ginsburg. They believed Arnold's opinion should be affirmed on the First Amendment principles Arnold had employed. "Well-settled constitutional principles," Stevens wrote, together with "the standardless character of the decision to exclude Forbes from the debate" were key to the case. Stevens did not necessarily agree with Arnold that all candidates who qualified for ballot access were entitled to debate, but he did agree that government-owned media must employ preexisting standards for such political activities.

THE FIRST AMENDMENT IN PUBLIC UNIVERSITIES

A case involving funding to a gay student group at the University of Arkansas brought national headlines and applause from gay rights advocates who termed it "a major victory."[57] The Gay and Lesbian Students Association (GLSA), an officially recognized student group at the University of Arkansas, petitioned the student senate for funds without success for several years, including a request for $165 to hold a program on discrimination against homosexuals. The student senate denied each request, and appeals to university administrators were unsuccessful.[58]

The Gay and Lesbian Students Association brought a civil rights suit, assisted by the American Civil Liberties Union, arguing that funding was denied solely on the basis of the group's message. It had been the only officially recognized student organization to be denied money. The university claimed that funding had been denied due to a lack of educational merit and benefit of the planned activities. But statements from members of the student senate clearly indicated the vote was based upon disagreement with the goals of the organization.

The key to the case would be the university's "public" status. Although federal courts had ruled a decade earlier that gay student groups are entitled to official recognition at public universities, no court had yet extended that principle to the right to receive public money.[59]

A federal district judge in Fayetteville ruled against the gay students. Judge Franklin Waters held that the denial of funding to the group did not unduly interfere with the association's rights of free speech and free association, and that the denial of funding was not discriminatory because of the university's legitimate interest in distributing its funds in a "manner that was beneficial to the campus as a whole."[60]

Arnold disagreed. The record, he said, was replete with evidence that the senate's action was based on viewpoint discrimination. This denial of funding for content-motivated reasons violated the First Amendment. While no student group at a public university has an automatic right to funding, when funds are made available to any group, they must be distributed in a viewpoint-neutral manner. The GLSA met all the objective criteria for funding, yet was denied funds twice, and in the latest action on the matter, the student senate had voted never to fund the group again.

As Arnold explained:

> It is apparent that the GLSA was denied funds because of the views it espoused. Nor is there a compelling state interest justifying the Senate's denial of funds. The University provides no argument, and we can think of none. True, sodomy is illegal in Arkansas. However, the GLSA does not advocate sodomy, and, even if it did, its speech about an illegal activity would still be protected by the First Amendment. People may extol the virtues of arson or even cannibalism. They simply may not commit the acts.[61]

In short, Arnold held that a public body that chooses to fund speech or expression must do so evenhandedly, without discriminating among recipients on the basis of their ideology:

> The University need not supply funds to student organizations; but once having decided to do so, it is bound by the First Amendment to act without regard to the content of the ideas being expressed. This will mean, to use [former justice Oliver Wendell] Holmes's phrase, that the taxpayers will occasionally be obligated to support not only the thought of which they approve, but also the thought that they hate. This is one of the fundamental premises of American law.[62]

The university chose not to press its case further, either to the entire Eighth Circuit or to the Supreme Court. Nan Hunter, director of the American Civil Liberties Union's Lesbian and Gay Rights Project, lauded Arnold's decision: "It extends the principle that the state can't discriminate against particular messages."[63]

Another case involving First Amendment rights of college students came from Minnesota. A student newspaper at the University of Minnesota's Twin Cities campus lost its funding when officials objected to an "extremely provocative" issue of the newspaper that satirized Jesus

Richard (*left*) and his younger brother, Morris ("Buzz"), with their mother, Janet Sheppard Arnold, in 1948. Janet was the oldest daughter of Senator Morris Sheppard of Texas. She died in 1955, when Richard was nineteen years old.
Photograph courtesy of Arnold family.

Harvard Law Review officers in 1959 included future law professors and a Supreme Court justice. *Left to right, front row:* Nathan Lewin, Richard S. Arnold, John D. French, Antonin Scalia, and Fletcher Yarbrough. *Second row:* Frank Michelman, Herbert Dym, Daniel K. Mayers, David Currie, and Philip Heymann. *Photograph courtesy of Special Collections, Harvard Law School Library.*

Justice William Brennan swore in Arnold as a member of the Arkansas Bar in August 1960, shortly after he began his tenure as a Supreme Court law clerk. *Photograph courtesy of Supreme Court Historical Society.*

Richard Arnold on graduation from Harvard Law School in 1960. Arnold graduated first in his class and received the prestigious Faye Diploma. *Photograph courtesy of Arnold family.*

As Richard Arnold began his clerkship with Justice William Brennan, "Impeach Earl Warren" billboards could be seen throughout the United States, but primarily in the South. Warren was the chief justice of the Supreme Court from 1953 through 1969. The billboards, erected by the John Birch Society, were a reaction to *Brown v. Board of Education* and other liberal decisions of the Warren Court. *AP Photo.*

Richard Arnold as a young attorney at Arnold & Arnold in Texarkana, Arkansas, circa 1966.
Photograph courtesy of Arnold family.

Campaign flyer from Arnold's first race for Congress in 1966. *Courtesy of Arnold family.*

Members of Arnold & Arnold at the Texarkana, Arkansas, firm in 1968. *From left to right:* Morris Sheppard Arnold, Thomas Saxon Arnold, Richard Lewis Arnold, William Hendrick Arnold Jr., William Hendrick Arnold III, and Richard Sheppard Arnold. The portrait in the background is of William Hendrick Arnold. *Photograph courtesy of Arnold family.*

Richard Arnold is sworn in as a federal district judge in Little Rock, Arkansas, on October 16, 1978. With Arnold are his daughters, Janet and Lydia. Seated to the left of Arnold is Hillary Rodham Clinton, wife of then–Arkansas attorney general Bill Clinton. *Photograph courtesy of* Arkansas Democrat-Gazette.

Richard Arnold with two campaign volunteers, Stroud Kelly and Susan Webber Wright, during his 1966 race for Congress. Susan Webber Wright was later appointed to the federal district court in Arkansas by George H. W. Bush. *Photograph courtesy of* Texarkana Gazette.

Richard Arnold is sworn in as a member of the Eighth US Circuit Court of Appeals, March 7, 1980. Arnold is pictured with his daughter Lydia.
Photograph courtesy of Arkansas Democrat-Gazette.

Hearing before the Senate Judiciary Committee, February 7, 1980, for Henry Woods and Richard Arnold. Arnold was later confirmed by the Senate to a newly created seat on the Eighth US Circuit Court of Appeals, and Woods was confirmed to a seat on the federal district court in Little Rock. *From left to right*: Henry Woods, Senator David Pryor, Senator Dale Bumpers, and Richard Arnold.
Photograph courtesy of office of Senator Dale Bumpers.

Richard Arnold as a member of the Eighth Circuit, sporting a trademark bow tie, in 1993. *Photograph courtesy of* Arkansas Democrat-Gazette.

Richard Arnold in undated photo.
Photograph courtesy of Arnold family.

Funeral of Justice William Brennan, July 29, 1997, at St. Matthew's Cathedral in Washington, DC. Brennan's former law clerks served as pallbearers. Richard Arnold is pictured at top left. *AP Photo (J. Scott Applewhite).*

Chief Judge Richard Arnold greets Justice Clarence Thomas at the Eighth Circuit Judicial Conference in 1997. *Photograph courtesy of Eighth Circuit Library.*

Former president Bill Clinton and Richard Arnold in Little Rock, March 2003. *Photograph courtesy of* Little Rock Soirée *magazine.*

Richard Arnold with fellow Eighth Circuit judges Frank Magill (*left*) and John R. Gibson. The photograph was taken in the St. Paul, Minnesota, courthouse on May 13, 1994. Handwritten on the photograph are the words "Between the vetting and phone call!" indicating it was taken on the day Arnold would later learn that President Clinton had chosen Stephen Breyer rather than him for the Supreme Court. *Photograph courtesy of Eighth Circuit Historical Society; chambers of Frank Magill.*

Richard Arnold's chambers in Little Rock, Arkansas.
Photograph courtesy of US District Court for the Eastern District of Arkansas.

Richard Arnold with his brother, Morris Sheppard Arnold, and grandchild, Evan Hart, in 1998. The Arnolds are the only two brothers to be appointed to the same federal court of appeals. *Photograph courtesy of Gail K. Arnold.*

Watercolor rendering of the Richard Sheppard Arnold United States Courthouse in Little Rock, Arkansas, dedicated on September 28, 2007. *Watercolor rendering by David Walker and provided courtesy of the General Services Administration.*

Former law clerks and members of Richard Arnold's staff standing below Arnold's portrait at the dedication of the Richard Sheppard Arnold United States Courthouse on September 28, 2007, three years after Arnold's death. *Photograph courtesy of Lindsley Smith.*

Portrait of Richard Arnold by Jason Bouldin of Oxford, Mississippi. This portrait hangs in the Richard Sheppard Arnold United States Courthouse in Little Rock, Arkansas. A second portrait, depicting Arnold standing, hangs in the Thomas F. Eagleton Courthouse in St. Louis, the largest courthouse in the United States. *Photograph from oil painting by artist Jason Bouldin.*

Christ, the Roman Catholic Church, ethnic groups, and public figures.[64] The newspaper issue had generated predictably vehement criticism from church leaders, citizens, legislators, and students, expressed among other ways through letters to the board of regents. The regents unanimously passed a resolution stating that they were "compelled to deplore the content" of that issue of the *Minnesota Daily*. In another resolution passed unanimously the next month, the regents stated that the issue in question was "flagrantly offensive" and established an ad hoc committee "to review with the President the concerns expressed and the recommendations of the President regarding the Minnesota Daily." Among other things, the regents directed the special committee to consider the "appropriate mechanism for circulation and financial support for the *Minnesota Daily*." Subsequently, the student newspaper found its financial support reduced.[65]

Editors of the student newspaper sued the president and regents of the University of Minnesota system over the newspaper's loss of financial support. They lost in federal district court but continued to press their case on appeal to the Eighth Circuit. By random assignment, Arnold—a devout Christian and admirer of the Roman Catholic Church—was among the three judges to draw the case. Arnold would sympathize with those who found the publication offensive, among other reasons, because of what he described as "a blasphemous 'interview' with Jesus on the Cross that would offend anyone of good taste, whether with or without religion."[66]

Writing for a unanimous panel, Arnold ruled in the students' favor. The reduction in funds available to the newspaper was motivated at least in part by the offensive issue of the newspaper, a result Arnold said was forbidden by the First Amendment. A public university may not constitutionally take adverse action against a student newspaper, such as withdrawing or reducing the paper's funding, because it disapproves of the content of the paper.

It was clear to Arnold, at least, that one motivation for the university's action had been to prevent a recurrence of the offensive publication. As such, Arnold bypassed what he viewed as needless further proceedings in the district court. The existence of an improper motive was clear—no judge, Arnold believed, could find to the contrary. Arnold thus remanded the case to the district court only for issuance of an appropriate injunctive order. As DC Circuit Court of Appeals Judge Patricia Wald described, "here lay the vigor and fearlessness of Judge Arnold's ruling," displaying "courage in a hostile setting."[67]

ARNOLD IN DISSENT: "DON'T ASK, DON'T TELL"

Arnold's view of the First Amendment did not always prevail with his colleagues on the Eighth Circuit. Indeed, some of his most important statements about the meaning of the First Amendment came in dissenting opinions. An important example was Arnold's dissent in a constitutional challenge to the US military's "Don't Ask, Don't Tell" policy for homosexuals.

In one of the first cases to test the constitutionality of the "Don't Ask, Don't Tell" policy, Arnold dissented from the majority's conclusion that the policy was constitutionally valid as applied to the case of Richard F. Richenberg Jr. Richenberg was an air force captain who had been discharged for an alleged violation of the policy.[68] "Don't Ask, Don't Tell," as the policy is popularly known, prohibits military officials from inquiring about the sexual orientation of any member of the military. But members of the military who engage in "homosexual conduct" may be discharged. As interpreted by the military, "A statement by a service member that he or she is homosexual or bisexual creates a rebuttable presumption that the service member is engaging in homosexual acts or has a propensity or intent to do so."[69]

Richenberg had served in the air force since 1985, including a tour in the Gulf War. In 1993, after the "Don't Ask, Don't Tell" policy went into effect, Richenberg told his commanding officer that he was homosexual. Although Richenberg had admitted that he was a homosexual, he also stated under oath that he did not intend to violate military law by acting upon those feelings. He was nonetheless discharged from the military. Richenberg took the matter to federal court, claiming that his discharge under the policy violated both his due process rights and the First Amendment.

Writing for the majority, Judge James Loken found no constitutional violation in Richenberg's discharge, in part from his deference to the role of other branches of government in governing the military. Arnold disagreed. Richenberg had not engaged in any "homosexual conduct," Arnold emphasized; he had merely admitted his orientation. Arnold wrote:

> The statute, however, blurs the line between status and conduct by making a service member's admission that he or she is a homosexual sufficient grounds for presuming that the service member is likely to or intends to engage in prohibited conduct. If this presumption were irrebuttable, the statutory scheme would raise serious First Amendment

problems. Accordingly, it is our job to review the record with great care to ensure that Captain Richenberg had a proper opportunity to rebut the presumption. After reviewing the evidence submitted to the Board of Inquiry, it is my view that Captain Richenberg met his burden and should not have been discharged.[70]

Arnold insisted that the failure to permit Richenberg to rebut the presumption that, because he is gay, he would necessarily engage in prohibited conduct, effectively and unconstitutionally punished him for his thoughts, not his actions: "To assume automatically that he would [violate the military's policy] is to disadvantage him simply for who he is and not for what he has done or will do. Our whole constitutional heritage rebels at the thought of giving government the power to control men's minds."[71] The First Amendment, Arnold believed, "does not allow the government to make this assumption without at least affording Captain Richenberg some realistic opportunity to show that the assumption is erroneous in his particular case."[72]

The US Supreme Court declined to review the case. Arnold's opinion in *Richenberg v. Perry* is still the lone dissent on this issue.

A RIGHT OF ASSOCIATION FOR THE MINNESOTA JAYCEES

The First Amendment not only protects freedom of speech and thought, it has long been viewed to protect freedom of association. The "right of the people peaceably to assemble" is specifically guaranteed in the First Amendment. No specific mention is made of a "right of association," but the Supreme Court has held it to be an essential part of freedom of speech because groups, like individuals, have a right to collective expression. In a number of cases in the twentieth century, the US Supreme Court defined the parameters of a freedom of association, especially in a series of cases involving the NAACP.[73]

Arnold's appreciation of freedom of association was at its height in cases involving political speech. The commitment was forged over decades but most notably as a reaction to the communist cases he encountered as a Supreme Court law clerk. Groups, as well as individuals, had a fundamental right to be free from government interference, so long as those groups did not transgress the fundamental rights of others.

This commitment led Arnold into what was probably the most controversial judicial opinion of his career. Arnold had been on the Eighth Circuit a mere few years when he was assigned to a panel facing a novel and complicated issue. The issue was whether the Junior Chamber of Commerce, a national organization with seven thousand chapters and nearly three hundred thousand members at the time, had to admit women.[74]

The case came from Minnesota. A 1972 state law banned discrimination on the basis of sex in "places of public accommodation." Regular membership in the Jaycees, a civic and service organization, was open only to men between the ages of eighteen and thirty-five. Women were allowed to be "associate members," according to the national charter, but they could not vote or hold office. The Minnesota Supreme Court interpreted the 1972 state law to include the Jaycees, and the Minnesota Department of Human Rights ordered the Jaycees to admit women to full membership in its local chapters in Minnesota.

After that ruling, the Jaycees brought suit in federal court claiming that the statute, as applied to them, was unconstitutional as a violation of the rights of speech, petition, assembly, and association guaranteed by the First and Fourteenth amendments.

Judge Diana Murphy, then a federal district judge but later to be appointed to the Eighth Circuit, rejected the Jaycees' claim. She believed that the Jaycees' "practice of distinguishing the rights and privileges of men and women members" was "not afforded affirmative constitutional protection" by the First Amendment. Even if it were, the state had shown a compelling interest in "preventing discrimination in public accommodations on the basis of sex."[75] Judge Murphy found the Jaycees to be a place of public accommodation, similar to hotels and restaurants that were required to be open to both sexes.

In an opinion written by Richard Arnold, the Eighth Circuit reversed, ruling in favor of the Jaycees.[76] Arnold believed the Jaycees' decision to exclude women was not one that the state of Minnesota could override. The reason, he said, was that the Jaycees were more of a "private" organization than a "public" one, and much of the Jaycees' activities was in the expression of political beliefs and advocacy of legislation. This gave them a right of freedom of association, protected by the First Amendment. "This is not to say that no state law could be written to redress this kind of nongovernmental discrimination," he wrote. "But if, in the phrase of Justice

Holmes, the First Amendment protects the thought that we hate, it must also, on occasion, protect the association of which we disapprove."[77]

The Minnesota law was thus unconstitutionally vague because it supplied no ascertainable standard for the inclusion of some groups as "public" and the exclusion of others as "private," yet the Jaycees clearly engaged in activities that were both "political and ideological."[78] It was a stark confrontation for Arnold. He was always hesitant to strike down a state statute in the name of the federal constitution unless clearly compelled to do so. His strong opinions about the careful exercise of federal jurisdiction in matters of state sovereignty dated back many years, reflected in articles he published in the 1960s.

But for Arnold, political association rights were paramount. Quoting from the Supreme Court's decision in *NAACP v. Alabama*, Arnold wrote: "It is beyond debate that freedom to engage in association for the advancement of beliefs and ideas is an inseparable aspect of the 'liberty' assured by the due process clause of the Fourteenth Amendment, which embraces freedom of speech."[79]

Arnold stressed that the decision was "a narrow one":

> The law will continue to apply with full vigor to all business and commercial activity in the usual sense of those words—to businesses, for example, that sell goods and services to the public. It will also apply to those non-membership activities of the Jaycees and other groups that affect the public at large, including the sale of goods, the dispensing of charitable donations, the organization of sporting events, and the like. It is only the law's interference with an organization's choice of its own members that we hold invalid under the First and Fourteenth Amendments.[80]

For his resolution of the case, Arnold was bound by an earlier ruling by the Minnesota Supreme Court that the public accommodations statute applied to the Jaycees.[81] In a six-to-three decision, that court held that the organization was "a business facility whose goods, privileges, [and] advantages are sold or otherwise made available to the public."[82] The Minnesota court distinguished the Jaycees from "private organizations" such as the Kiwanis. Arnold specifically noted that a dissent by the Minnesota chief justice, joined by two others, questioned this determination. It was a curious construction of the statute, but Arnold had no choice but to proceed with it. Pointedly, though, Arnold quoted from that dissent:

> Although the result reached in the majority opinion is felicitous, I cannot believe that the members of the Minnesota legislature who voted for the law we have been called upon to construe thought the Junior Chamber of Commerce, a service organization, to be "a place of public accommodation." The obligation of the judiciary is to give that meaning to words accorded by common experience and understanding. To go beyond this is to intrude upon the policy-making function of the legislature.[83]

The national president of the Jaycees interpreted Arnold's decision to "reaffirm our members' rights to decide who should belong to their organization."[84] There was, in fact, considerable contention within the ranks of the organization on the issue. Local chapters in Minneapolis, St. Paul, and Cedar Rapids, Iowa, and elsewhere, had flouted the national organization's rules by admitting women to full membership.[85]

Donald P. Lay, then chief judge of the Eighth Circuit, dissented. Lay believed Arnold had applied what he considered to be an "outdated rationale of our jurisprudence, one which relegated women to a status inferior to that of men."

Minnesota attorney general Hubert H. Humphrey III appealed the decision to the US Supreme Court. Announcing his decision, Humphrey said, "This case involves significant constitutional and public policy issues. The issues of equal opportunity and nondiscriminatory use of public accommodations raised in this case deserve to be resolved."[86] Clay Moore, a Minneapolis lawyer representing the Jaycees, noted that lawsuits over the issue were pending elsewhere, but that Minnesota's would likely be the leading case.

The case made national headlines when the Supreme Court justices agreed in early 1984 to hear Minnesota's appeal. The Minnesota Jaycees' case, wrote Linda Greenhouse in the *New York Times*, was "likely to become a focal point for the debates now taking place in many parts of the country over discrimination by private clubs."[87] Numerous advocacy groups filed "friend of the court" briefs with the Supreme Court. Many service clubs, private associations, and other voluntary organizations saw their "right of association" at stake. But many state and local governments were equally concerned about efforts to eradicate discrimination.[88]

As Greenhouse noted, the potential reach of the Supreme Court's action on the matter was difficult to predict. As a preliminary matter, the justices would decide whether the Minnesota law was impermissibly vague as applied to the Jaycees, as Arnold had ruled. If they agreed with Arnold, they could then avoid the broader question whether private membership groups had a constitutional right to discriminate on the basis of sex in their choice of members. But if it did reach that question, the case "could have far-reaching implications, extending beyond sex discrimination to discrimination based on race or ethnic background."[89]

When the Supreme Court heard arguments in the case in April 1984, Jaycees attorney Carl D. Hall Jr. said the organization needed to remain all male because admitting women would change its purpose and its positions on public issues. "We have a constitutional right to promote just the interests of young men," Hall said. Asked for examples of how women members would change the Jaycees' beliefs and ideas, Hall responded that the Jaycees had taken positions in favor of constitutional amendments requiring a balanced budget and organized prayer in public schools. "It shouldn't be necessary to take positions against the proposed Equal Rights Amendment and abortion to show that we exist for young men," Hall pressed.[90] But several justices doubted whether those or any other public issue presented substantially different beliefs between men and women. "Young men are developed by running projects. They learn by doing," Hall said. Justice Sandra Day O'Connor, the Supreme Court's first woman justice and only in her third year on the Court, responded, "And women do too, don't they? They learn in exactly the same way." At another point, Justice Thurgood Marshall asked, "Aren't you just afraid that women will take over?" "That's a legitimate fear," Hall replied.[91]

The Supreme Court, without dissent, reversed the Eighth Circuit, ruling against the Jaycees. The vote was 7–0; Chief Justice Warren E. Burger, who at one time was president of a local Jaycees chapter in Minnesota, did not take part in the ruling. Harry Blackmun, also from Minnesota, and a former judge on the Eighth Circuit, also chose not to participate in the appeal.

Even worse for Arnold, the opinion was written by his friend, mentor, and former boss, Justice William Brennan. The Court agreed that the First Amendment's protections included safeguards for expressive association and that the state of Minnesota had infringed upon the Jaycees' freedom in this regard. But the Court was "persuaded that Minnesota's compelling interest in eradicating discrimination against its female citizens justifies the impact that application of the statute to the Jaycees may have on the male members' associational freedoms."[92] The Jaycees, Brennan wrote, had failed to demonstrate that the Minnesota law imposed "any serious burdens on the male members' freedom of expressive association."

Justice O'Connor wrote a separate opinion concurring in the Court's judgment. In her opinion, the Court's approach was "both overprotective of activities undeserving of constitutional shelter and under-protective of important First Amendment concerns." She believed the Jaycees to be essentially a "commercial" organization. For other organizations, however, O'Connor was uneasy with what she termed the "membership-message" connection: "Whether an association is or is not constitutionally protected in the selection of its membership should not depend on what the association says or why its members say it."[93]

The issue of private organization membership would become an enormously complex field of Supreme Court jurisprudence over the ensuing decades. Sixteen years after the Jaycees case, the Supreme Court overturned a similar New Jersey antidiscrimination statute as applied to the Boy Scouts of America. Ironically, the Supreme Court relied heavily on its opinion in *Roberts v. Jaycees* to uphold the right of the Boy Scouts to exclude homosexuals as part of its right of "expressive conduct."[94] It was a closely divided 5–4 decision.

Years later, Justice Sandra Day O'Connor reflected on the difficulty Richard Arnold faced, given the Supreme Court's prior precedent:

> In that area it is not easy. It is not fair, I think, to look at a judge's work on the basis of the position at the end of the line. What you have to do is look at all the precedents then in place, with the understanding that he has to follow them, and that it's not what he would prefer. It is what the precedents dictate. And probably he thought they went the other way. He was being what he should be — a judge who felt bound by what had been decided.[95]

Arnold understood at the time that the question was novel and was "not controlled by precedent." In the absence of controlling Supreme Court authority, he said, lower court judges must look "to principle and reason" based upon broader First Amendment concerns.[96]

Arnold did believe he had followed the law. The Supreme Court's opinion in Jaycees, Arnold said later, read "almost like a different case" from the one he had decided.[97] Many of the rationales in Brennan's opinion were not arguments that had been raised before the Eighth Circuit. Almost twenty years after the Supreme Court reversed his decision, Arnold still believed that "the stronger side was the side of liberty, liberty of association." He was fully aware at the time that his decision was "not good politics," and by this time he knew his position had likely undermined his chances of serving on the Supreme Court.[98]

Other prominent court of appeals judges also agreed with Arnold at the time. Judge Richard A. Posner of the Seventh Circuit wrote to Arnold: "I read your opinion in the *Jaycees* case with great interest and enjoyment. You did a terrific job. The dissent was perfunctory."[99] Similarly, Sixth Circuit Judge Gilbert S. Merritt wrote Arnold in support of his *Jaycees* opinion. In reply, Arnold wrote: "I suppose it is one of the hardest cases I have ever written, and to know that someone else approves of it is a great help."[100]

Including the *Jaycees* case, during the summer of 1984 Arnold would be reversed by the Supreme Court an unprecedented three times. Reversal by the Supreme Court would be a rare occurrence for Arnold, but the combined vote against Arnold in these three cases was twenty-three to two. Years later, Arnold quipped to some of his law clerks, "no one can be *that* wrong."[101]

RELIGIOUS EXPRESSION

The First Amendment, of course, protects more than freedom of speech, thought, and association. The first clause of the amendment states that "Congress shall make no law respecting an establishment of religion, or prohibiting the free exercise thereof." Religious freedom loomed large in Arnold's thinking about the First Amendment, and he was equally committed to it. He would many times face complicated issues of the appropriate line between a government-established religion and its free exercise. Two examples from Nebraska and Iowa are instructive of Arnold's views.

The case of *McCurry v. Tesch* arose out of a long-standing dispute between the state of Nebraska and the Faith Baptist Church of Louisville, Nebraska, concerning the church's operation of a school without complying with several Nebraska laws.[102] The state obtained an injunction against the school, which was affirmed by the Nebraska Supreme Court.

Some time later, the state trial court in the matter determined that the school was still in operation in violation of the injunction. That court authorized the local sheriff to enforce the order forbidding the use of the church for a school. Sheriff's deputies entered the church on a Monday morning and ejected those who were gathered there for a "prayer vigil." No schoolchildren were present, and no classes were being held. The deputies padlocked the church to prevent reentry except for scheduled religious services on Saturday, Sunday, and Wednesday evenings, as they had interpreted to be the requirement of the trial court's order.

Arnold held that the deputies' actions violated the church members' right to the free exercise of religion. As he wrote:

> The right to worship free from governmental interference lies at the heart of the First Amendment. It embraces not only the right to free exercise of religion, but also the right to freedom of expression. This principle applies with particular force to places, such as church buildings, which have a special spiritual significance to the persons who wish to worship there. It is no part of the business of government in this country to decide when people may go to church. The First Amendment protects prayer at six o'clock on Monday morning just as much as at eleven o'clock on Sunday morning.[103]

The difficulty of the case was not the conclusion that the First Amendment had been violated; rather, the question was whether the state officials involved in the incident were immune from the church members' claim for damages. A federal district court judge believed they were. That judge interpreted the state court order to mean that the deputies should invade the church, remove the plaintiffs, and padlock the church. Thus, the court found that the law enforcement officers were following a court order in good faith, and dismissed the lawsuit against them.

Arnold disagreed. He wrote:

> We hold that the state-court orders did not authorize the law-enforcement officers' action here. If the orders are ambiguous, they should be construed against the authority asserted by the state, because orders conferring such authority would be unconstitutional. Thus, there is no ground for the application of absolute "quasi-judicial immunity," though, as we make clear later, those defendants against whom damages are sought may have a defense of qualified immunity.[104]

In other words, deputies handed a court order must make sure it does not violate the US Constitution, if it is so obviously flawed. The officers might yet win the case on a qualified immunity defense, but there was no guarantee.[105]

Judge George Fagg wrote a dissenting opinion. Fagg believed the terms of the state court order clearly stated the sheriff was to secure the building on days other than Saturday, Sunday, and Wednesday and accused Arnold of an erroneous interpretation of the state court's order. He concluded, "It would be anomalous for the court to punish obedient law enforcement officers by exposing them to civil damage liability based upon the shortcomings of orders drafted by absolutely immunized state judges."[106]

Who was right? Judge Patricia Wald, then serving on the US Court of Appeals for the District of Columbia, believed what was important about Arnold's decision was "its reaffirmation of the worshippers' unreserved right of free exercise in their own church and on their own time." Arnold's interpretation sent a strong message that law enforcement officials must act carefully, even with a state court order, before disrupting religious worship. "That signal," Judge Wald wrote, "was an important one for civil liberties in the heartland."[107]

The Eighth Circuit also encountered numerous lawsuits over religious displays on public property, as did other federal courts throughout the nation. In one such case, Arnold found himself in dissent. In Des Moines, Iowa, Rabbi Moishe Kasowitz requested to display a twenty-foot-tall menorah on the grounds of the Iowa Statehouse during Hanukkah. When he was denied permission, Kasowitz brought suit in federal district court asking for a preliminary injunction to allow its placement. He argued that the state's action was discriminatory because of two Christmas trees on the capitol grounds. Those Christmas trees, he argued, were Christian symbols and promoted religion as much as a menorah.[108]

The federal district court sided with state officials, who had decided that placing the menorah on the capitol grounds would violate the constitutional separation of church and state. The rabbi brought his appeal to the Eighth Circuit. Because of the urgency of the matter (Hanukkah was already under way by this point), the Eighth Circuit responded rapidly. But the court ruled in favor of the state. In a one-paragraph per curiam opinion, two judges—Magill and Gibson—upheld the district court and declined to rule on the constitutionality of the Christmas trees.

Arnold was the third member of the panel. It would have been easy for Arnold to join the two-sentence majority opinion that stated, simply, "The order of the District Court, denying plaintiffs' motion for preliminary injunction, is affirmed. We find no abuse of discretion in the District Court's action." But Arnold disagreed. In a dissenting opinion, Arnold wrote:

> A Christmas tree owned by the State of Iowa has been erected in the rotunda of the state capitol. Another Christmas tree, also owned by the state, has been erected on the capitol grounds. The ornaments on the tree in the rotunda of the state capitol include angels. The state is obligated to treat all religions evenhandedly. Allowing the placement of these Christmas trees, while at the same time denying permission for the Menorah, appears to be a discrimination against the Jewish religion. So long as Christian symbols are permitted, other religions should be given equal treatment.[109]

Arnold would have granted the injunction sought by Rabbi Kasowitz but would also leave to the state the option of removing the Christmas trees from the state capitol grounds, "in which event the state would be free" not to allow the menorah.[110]

Rabbi Kasowitz did not appeal. Kasowitz said he was disappointed in the panel's ruling, but it was "too late" to appeal the decision. "We feel that our First Amendment rights are being abused," Kasowitz said. "We are not being allowed freedom of expression and freedom of religion."[111]

Balancing the First Amendment's "free exercise" of religion clause with the prohibition against an "establishment" of religion has generated numerous Supreme Court opinions ranging from holiday displays in public arenas to displays of the Ten Commandments in courthouses. The lower federal courts must then implement these pronouncements in the varied local circumstances where the cases arise throughout the nation. The litigation in Des Moines pitting a menorah against Christmas trees was merely one illustration.

But the many other cases Arnold faced in his career also illustrate how important First Amendment issues reach the Supreme Court in the first place—from a federal trial court and through one of the federal courts of appeal. Arnold was often in the paradoxical position of having to apply Supreme Court rules where they exist, while reconciling the results with his often strongly held views of the First Amendment. That Arnold left such a vivid footprint in this area is the more significant achievement when measured against the inherent limitations of the "subordinate" courts.

Chapter Ten

The Right of Privacy and Abortion

In the closing decades of the twentieth century, the duties and constraints of lower court federal judges received perhaps their greatest test in questions related to abortion. Beginning in the late 1980s, the Supreme Court gradually moved away from an expansive view of *Roe v. Wade* but did not overturn it. Lower court judges were left to interpret and apply constitutional principles from Supreme Court opinions in which the justices were sharply divided. The rules to be applied by the lower federal courts proved to be a moving target.

Issues related to abortion arose within every state of the Eighth Circuit, including ongoing attempts by states to regulate abortion on demand. The Eighth Circuit became, as one journalist termed it, "the legal epicenter for the battle over abortion."[1] Arnold was frequently left to observe, as he would in more than one opinion, "We cannot know how the Supreme Court will ultimately resolve this issue, but we must now decide it for ourselves."[2]

Arnold wrote opinions in more than a dozen cases involving questions related to abortion. With one limited exception, the Supreme Court affirmed Arnold's work, although the Supreme Court would change course in later years on some of the issues Arnold confronted. In that one case, Arnold was "far ahead of the Supreme Court" in his view that statutes forbidding the use of public facilities, employees or funds to encourage or counsel abortion were "flatly inconsistent with the First Amendment," a view the Supreme Court would later reject.[3]

"PRIVACY" AS A CONSTITUTIONAL RIGHT

Prior to *Roe v. Wade*, the Supreme Court recognized a fundamental right of privacy for individuals with respect to contraception, in large part because decisions related to "family" are intensely personal. This sphere, the Supreme Court stated, is to be free from unwarranted governmental intrusion—a classical view of individual freedom from state control now translated into personal decision making in intimate matters. The year before *Roe* was decided, for example, Justice William Brennan wrote, "If the right of privacy means anything, it is the right of the individual, married or single, to be free from unwarranted governmental intrusion into matters so fundamentally affecting a person as the decision whether to bear or beget a child."[4]

An important precursor to the recognition of a right of privacy was *Poe v. Ullman*, which appeared on the Supreme Court's docket in 1960 while Arnold was a law clerk for Justice William Brennan.[5] In a five-to-four decision, the Supreme Court dismissed a challenge to a Connecticut law that prohibited the use of contraceptives. The court dismissed the challenge because no evidence was presented that the statute was likely to be enforced. A strong dissent by Justice John Marshall Harlan argued that the Court should hear the case on the merits, and he took a broad view of the "liberty" protected by the Fourteenth Amendment. As David Garrow described in his book, *Liberty and Sexuality: The Right of Privacy and the Making of Roe v. Wade*, Justice Brennan, following his law clerk Richard Arnold's recommendation, agreed with the majority that the case did not present an adequate controversy or full record for review.[6]

Four years later, the Connecticut contraception statute was challenged again in the Supreme Court, in a case known as *Griswold v. Connecticut*. This time, the Supreme Court invalidated the contraception law with the Court's first articulation of a sphere of privacy subject to constitutional protection.[7]

Whatever Arnold's personal views of the existence of a right of privacy in the federal constitution, he subscribed to full recognition of the right in numerous cases outside of the abortion context where he believed

Supreme Court precedent permitted. This larger view of the right of privacy led to one of Arnold's most celebrated dissents in a 1990 case involving the right of a parent to select her child's name. A writer in the *New York Times* described it as "a wise dissent" in favor of family privacy.[8]

In *Henne v. Wright*, two mothers wanted to choose last names for their daughters that were prohibited by a Nebraska statute restricting the choice of surnames that parents could enter on an infant's birth certificate.[9] Debra Henne wanted to give her daughter the last name "Brinton," the surname of the child's father. Brinton also wanted the child to have his name and he had acknowledged paternity of the child. At the time, however, Debra's divorce from Robert Henne was not yet final. Nor had there been any judicial determination of paternity, even though Robert Henne did not contest the designation of Brinton as the father. But under Nebraska law, the child's surname could not be Brinton.[10] The statute required that every child's surname must have a legally established connection to the surname of one parent.

In the second case, Linda Spidell wanted to give her daughter the last name "McKenzie," the same surname as her other two children who were born in California. Spidell had chosen the surname McKenzie simply because she liked that name, not because of any family relationship. Spidell wanted all of her children to share the same last name, but she was informed by Nebraska hospital officials that she could not enter McKenzie on her child's birth certificate.

The mothers challenged the statute as a violation of the Fourteenth Amendment, and a federal district court agreed. On appeal to the Eighth Circuit, however, Judge Myron Bright and Judge Frank Magill believed the statute violated no constitutional right. The ability to choose a surname for one's child, they believed, did not implicate a fundamental right of privacy. Instead, they applied the Supreme Court's "rational basis" test to conclude that the Nebraska name statute was constitutional. As the state had argued, records are easier to keep and use if every person has the surname of "at least one legally verifiable parent."[11]

Arnold, however, dissented from the panel's view of the case. He believed the parents' choice of surnames in these cases was constitutionally protected: "The fundamental right of privacy, in my view, includes the right of parents to name their own children, and the State has shown no interest on the facts of these cases sufficiently compelling to override that right."[12] Why? As the most quoted sentence from Arnold's dissent explained: "There is something sacred about a name. It is our own business, not the government's."[13]

Arnold's dissent in this case is revealing of Arnold's deeply held views about the federal constitution. Arnold believed the case "could well be analyzed" as a First Amendment issue. "What I call myself or my child is an aspect of speech. When the State says I cannot call my child what I want to call her, my freedom of expression, both oral and written, is lessened. And if the First Amendment is at stake, everyone would concede that the State could not win without showing a compelling interest."[14] But, Arnold noted, the parties had not presented the case in First Amendment terms. Thus, he wrote, "it would be unfair for an appellate court to decide the case on that basis, at least without a chance for additional briefing."[15]

But he also took the opportunity to explain the uneasy position of the right of privacy in the Constitution. Viewing the case in terms of a right of privacy, Arnold said, was "trickier ground" than the First Amendment:

> There is a "Speech Clause," but no "Privacy Clause" as such. The right of privacy is not the beneficiary of explicit textual protection in the federal constitution. It is an unenumerated right. There are such things in constitutional law, however. We know that much (if we know little else) from the Ninth Amendment. The Founders of this Nation deeply believed that the individual took primacy over government. People existed, and had rights, before there was such a thing as government. Government might protect or recognize rights, but rights, some of them anyway, existed before government and independently of it, and would continue to exist after government had been destroyed. The source of rights was not the State, but, as the Declaration of Independence put it, the "Creator."[16]

Arnold provided a forthright explanation of the source of "privacy" according to earlier Supreme Court decisions. But no Supreme Court privacy case had addressed the question of a right to choose a name. Nonetheless, Arnold thought the right of privacy was broad enough to include it: "The real question is, not whether there is a right of privacy but how do you tell what it includes? The limits of the right remain controversial, and no doubt they will continue to be tested by litigation. Precedent tells us at least this much, though: family matters, including decisions relating to child rearing and marriage, are on almost everyone's list of fundamental rights."[17]

Arnold acknowledged the state's interest in preventing false implications of parentage. At the oral argument of the case, for example, Arnold used himself as an example: "I would have an interest in keeping a stranger from naming her child 'Richard S. Arnold, Jr.,' and the state would have an interest in defending my reputation against such a false implication." But nothing of the sort was present here. Debra Henne, Arnold pointed out, wanted to give her daughter the surname of the girl's father. Neither the father nor the man to whom she was married when the baby was born had any objection. Linda Spidell's choice of McKenzie, which was neither her name nor the name of the child's father, was "not so eccentric as it seems," Arnold wrote, because of her "quite natural desire that all of one's three children have the same surname."[18]

Arnold could not convince either Judge Bright or Judge Magill, both from North Dakota, to adopt his view, although Bright wrote to Arnold, "I liked your dissent even if I disagree with it as a matter of constitutional law."[19] Arnold's Eighth Circuit colleague in Arkansas, J. Smith Henley, weighed in on the matter even though he was not assigned to the case. Henley wrote to the other Eighth Circuit judges: "The majority opinion written, and joined, by our folks from Fargo displays neither concern for the ancient common law tradition nor the zeitgeist of the current era." Henley by then had taken senior status; only active judges could participate in en banc proceedings unless they had been one of the judges on the case under review. A simple majority vote of active judges is necessary for hearing before the full court, a proceeding usually reserved for cases involving "a question of exceptional importance" or to reconcile conflicting panel opinions.[20]

Judge Henley urged an active judge to seek rehearing en banc in *Henne v. Wright*, even if the parties did not.[21] Arnold himself requested a poll of the Eighth Circuit judges. The effort failed, narrowly, by a vote of six to four. Judges McMillian, Gibson, and Beam agreed with Arnold that the entire Eighth Circuit should reconsider the panel's decision, but the case ended without further review.[22]

Another dissent illustrates Arnold's essential libertarianism on matters of personal privacy, but in the very different context of the right to be free from unreasonable search and arrest in an airport. In 1989, Arthur

Weaver was stopped, questioned, and arrested by a police officer at the Kansas City airport. The officer testified that he stopped Weaver because of a variety of factors, including the fact that he was black, had come from Los Angeles, was of a young age, and because of his style of dress. The officer searched Weaver and found cocaine. Weaver sought to suppress the cocaine evidence, claiming that the detention and search were illegal under the Fourth Amendment.[23]

A federal district court ruled the search had not violated any constitutional right. On appeal to the Eighth Circuit, a majority agreed with this conclusion. Arnold, however, dissented. One of Arnold's concerns was the obvious fact that Weaver had been stopped because he was a young black male. Arnold wrote that "use of race as a factor simply reinforces the kind of stereotyping that lies behind drug-courier profiles. When public officials begin to regard large groups of citizens as presumptively criminal, this country is in a perilous situation indeed."[24] Harvard law professor Randall Kennedy singled out Arnold's dissent in *Weaver* as appropriately rejecting the common practice of using race as an indicator of suspicion on the specious ground that, proportionally, blacks engaged in certain sorts of criminality at higher rates than whites.[25]

What is even more revealing in Arnold's dissent was his extrapolation from the unfairness of targeting people based upon race to a more general point about freedom of movement and personal privacy. Arnold acknowledged that it was "hard to work up much sympathy for Weaver," because the cocaine found on his person meant Weaver was "getting what he deserved, in a sense." But what was missing, Arnold wrote, was "an awareness that law enforcement is a broad concept. It includes enforcement of the Bill of Rights, as well as enforcement of criminal statutes. Cases in which innocent travelers are stopped and impeded in their lawful activities don't come to court." Arnold believed airports were "on the verge of becoming war zones," where anyone was liable to be stopped, questioned, and searched without reasonable basis. "The liberty of the citizen," Arnold wrote, "is seriously threatened by this practice."[26]

Quite apart, then, from the specific context of abortion, Arnold exhibited a willingness to question government actions that he believed intruded into a constitutionally protected sphere of private decisions, actions, and beliefs. It is easy to see how Arnold's views of the right of privacy, like the Supreme Court's, were influenced by the more specific prohibitions on government action in the Bill of Rights, especially the Fourth Amendment's admonition that "[t]he right of the people to be secure in their persons, houses, papers, and effects, against unreasonable searches and seizures, shall not be violated."

These two dissenting opinions also show Arnold's insistence that constitutional limits on government be adhered to. Although not specifically linked to the right of privacy, freedom of speech and association under the First Amendment would be one such constitutional limit that Arnold would defend in the abortion context. Arnold recognized the First Amendment implications of *Griswold v. Connecticut*, a landmark Supreme Court decision recognizing a right to privacy protected by the US Constitution. Arnold referred to *Griswold*, for instance, in the Minnesota Jaycees case:

> *Griswold v. Connecticut* contains perhaps the broadest statement of the right of association, though it may be dictum. "The association of people is not mentioned in the Constitution nor in the Bill of Rights," Justice Douglas said for the Court. "Yet the First Amendment has been construed to include" that right.[27]

Abortion protests and picketing implicated both free speech rights and privacy interests of abortion providers and others. Within the states of the Eighth Circuit, abortion protests raised nearly as many significant cases for Arnold as did state legislation imposing restrictions on access to abortion.

PROTESTING ABORTION

One of the more high-profile abortion protest cases involved the arrest and prosecution of Regina Dinwiddie, a frequent protester outside of Planned Parenthood of Greater Kansas City. Beginning in 1994, Dinwiddie verbally threatened a physician outside the facility, often through a bullhorn, and warned him, "Remember Dr. Gunn [a physician who was killed in 1993 by an opponent of abortion]. This could happen to you. He is not in the world anymore. Whoever sheds man's blood, by man his blood shall be shed."[28]

Dinwiddie also threatened and, on at least one occasion, used physical force against other members of Planned Parenthood's staff and some of its patients. She told the executive director of Planned Parenthood, "You have not seen violence yet until you see what we do to you." She also physically obstructed patients from entering the clinic. At least one doctor began wearing a bulletproof vest, and an armed guard was placed at the clinic's entrance.[29]

The local United States Attorney's office charged Dinwiddie with violating the Freedom of Access to Clinic Entrances Act, legislation passed by Congress in 1994. The act made it a federal crime to intimidate or use physical force to prevent people from gaining access to a reproductive health facility. Prior to its passage, Attorney General Janet Reno had urged Congress to enact the measure because antiabortionists had "increased the intensity of their activity, from picketing to physical blockades, sabotage of facilities, stalking and harassing abortion providers," as well as arson, bombing, and the murder of a physician, Dr. David Gunn.[30]

Prior to her trial in Missouri, Dinwiddie had also traveled to Florida to attend the death penalty trial of Paul Hill, an abortion opponent and former minister charged with killing an abortion provider, Dr. John Britton, and his escort. As the trial judge read the death sentence to Hill, Dinwiddie shouted, "This man is innocent, and his blood will be on your hands, the hands of the people of the state of Florida and on the jury!" before deputies forcibly removed her from the courtroom.[31]

The federal district court in Missouri issued a permanent injunction ordering Dinwiddie not to violate the Freedom of Access to Clinic Entrances Act and not to be within five hundred feet of the entrance of any reproductive health services clinic. She could enter the five-hundred-foot perimeter only if she was engaging in "legitimate personal activity," which could include "peacefully" carrying a placard or distributing literature "in a manner that would not constitute intimidation, interference, or physical obstruction." She could also speak within the five-hundred-foot perimeter only if she spoke "unamplified" and did not intimidate or obstruct patients or clinic staff.[32]

Dinwiddie appealed to the Eighth Circuit, challenging both the injunction and the constitutionality of the Freedom of Access to Clinic Entrances Act. Arnold had little difficulty upholding the statute. For Arnold, the government's interest was significant: The act "furthers the government interest in protecting women who obtain reproductive-health services and ensuring that reproductive-health services remain available."[33]

Although Arnold found the allowance for "legitimate personal activity" to be too vague and instructed the district court to modify the injunction, he otherwise upheld the trial court's action in all respects. With Arnold's imprimatur, Dinwiddie became the first person in the United

States to be subjected to a federal injunction concerning protests at abortion clinics.[34] The two other judges on the panel, Myron Bright and George Fagg, joined Arnold's opinion without dissent. Judge Fagg termed Arnold's work "a powerhouse opinion."[35] Judge Bright agreed that it was nothing short of "a great opinion."[36]

Another abortion protest presented a more difficult case for Arnold, pitting his strong views in favor of free speech against the rights of religious worshippers. The city of Lincoln, Nebraska, had enacted an ordinance to restrict picketing of churches and other religious premises thirty minutes before, during, and after any scheduled religious activity.[37] The ordinance was a response to abortion protesters who for the past year had picketed in front of a Presbyterian church where an abortion physician served as deacon and church elder. The protests included multiple five- to six-foot-posters showing gruesome images alleged to be of aborted fetuses. The signs would be held in parishioners' faces, and protesters made statements about fetuses being murdered, killed, and butchered by a member of their church. Church members and pastors described a "siege-like atmosphere." A pastor testified that children who attended the church, in particular, were vulnerable to this abusive atmosphere.[38]

Even though an important aspect of the ordinance was an attempt to protect the rights of religious worshippers, Arnold struck down the ordinance as a violation of the free speech clause of the First Amendment. The ordinance was overly broad, he wrote, and thus was not narrowly tailored to protect legitimate interests, the constitutional standard applicable to the case. The ordinance banned all signs, regardless of their content, and that was far broader than what was required to protect children.

Furthermore, even if the signs did contain disagreeable content, the First Amendment would still protect such displays. "Expressive communication is frequently upsetting," Arnold wrote. "The protection of such robust debate is at the core of the First Amendment." The protesters were not on church property, and so long as those protests remained peaceful, the city could not ban them in such broad fashion.[39]

Arnold was sympathetic to the claim that the ordinance was necessary to allow Lincoln's citizens to exercise their religion freely. "Such an interest," he wrote, "is undoubtedly substantial and important." If, for example, antiabortion protesters were to attempt to enter a church without permission, or to interrupt church services with their own speech, the city would be within its rights to prosecute them either as a trespass, for disturbance of the peace, or under a more narrowly tailored ordinance. But the ordinance in this case "goes beyond the church building and church property, and seeks to forbid peaceful communication on property belonging to the public," and there was no physical interference with access to the church.[40]

This time, Judge Bright disagreed with Arnold, and in his separate opinion specified, "I strongly dissent." Bright saw the case as one of religious freedom for churchgoers, which government may reasonably protect from unwanted messages. Bright believed the "minor limitation" to the protesters' activities required by the ordinance "pales in comparison to the incivility, invasion of tranquility, and intimidation tactics visited upon those seeking to enter the church of their choice. That interference should not be countenanced." Bright believed the government's interest was substantial—churchgoing parents and children "should not be required to face such a gauntlet," he wrote.[41] Bright could not convince Arnold that this type of abortion protest should not be protected by the First Amendment.

THE "GAG RULE" AND USE OF PUBLIC FACILITIES FOR ABORTIONS

In another instance, Arnold's understanding of the requirements of the First Amendment favored abortion rights. Arnold took the view that a statute forbidding the use of public facilities, employees, or funds to counsel abortion was "flatly inconsistent with the First Amendment."[42] Arnold thought a "gag rule"—attempts to prevent physicians from giving patients information about abortion—was unconstitutional.

The case arose in Missouri. Public healthcare providers and private physicians practicing in public hospitals challenged that state's 1986 abortion statute. The statute prohibited the use of public employees and facilities to perform or assist abortions not necessary to save the mother's life, and made it unlawful to use public funds, employees, or facilities for the purpose of "encouraging or counseling" a woman to have an abortion.

The case came before a panel consisting of Arnold, Chief Judge Donald P. Lay, and Theodore McMillian in 1988. Writing for the court, Lay struck down those provisions, among others, and enjoined their enforcement, as a violation of the right to choose an abortion as announced in *Roe v. Wade*.[43]

Arnold wrote a short separate opinion. He agreed that these provisions were unconstitutional, but he would have invalidated the prohibition on use of public facilities, employees, or funds to counsel certain abortions as a violation of the First Amendment, not as a restriction on the right of access to abortion. "These statutes," Arnold wrote, "sharply discriminate between kinds of speech on the basis of their viewpoint: a physician, for example, could discourage an abortion, or counsel against it, while in a public facility, but he or she could not encourage or counsel in favor of it." Such a result was "flatly inconsistent" with the First Amendment.[44]

Arnold disagreed, however, with the majority's holding that the statute's preamble was unconstitutional. The preamble included a statement by the legislature establishing three "findings": (1) The life of each human being begins at conception; (2) unborn children have protectable interests in life, health, and well-being; and (3) the natural parents of unborn children have protectable interests in the life, health, and well-being of their unborn child.[45] Judge Lay's opinion struck that section as unconstitutional, on the ground that the statement of when life begins was not a permissible government position to justify abortion regulations. Lay took this position on the basis of the Supreme Court's earlier statement that "a State may not adopt one theory of when life begins to justify its regulation of abortions."[46]

Arnold agreed that a governmental declaration about when life begins, insofar as it was used to justify regulation of abortion, was unconstitutional. But he believed that section of the statute should be upheld as it related to subjects other than abortion. "The statute," Arnold wrote, "may mean that the negligent killing of a fetus gives rise to a state-law tort action for wrongful death." Such a change in the common law, if limited to non-abortion situations, would not violate the federal constitution, Arnold believed. The statute could also specify the property rights of the unborn and extend protection to them by the criminal law against violence by others. Legislation on these subjects, "wise or unwise, is within the purview of state legislatures," Arnold wrote, recording his disagreement with the majority on this issue.

The following year, in *Webster v. Reproductive Health Services*, the Supreme Court reversed the Eighth Circuit.[47] The Court upheld the portion of the Missouri law that prohibited the use of state funds in performing or assisting with abortions. Prior to this decision, many legal scholars and federal courts had believed such legislation to be forbidden by *Roe*.

The opinion for the Court by Chief Justice William Rehnquist first addressed the Missouri statute's preamble. The majority agreed with Arnold that the statute's language might be used to interpret other state statutes or regulations, and because that was a matter for the courts of Missouri, the preamble could not be invalidated as unconstitutional. Rehnquist quoted from Arnold's dissent in a significant affirmation of Arnold's view.[48]

The state of Missouri had chosen not to appeal the Eighth Circuit's invalidation of the sections of the statute restricting the speech of public employees or persons in public healthcare facilities. In noting this, Rehnquist also highlighted Arnold's separate opinion with respect to the First Amendment. Rehnquist used Arnold's opinion to clarify that the Court would accept the state's claim that the statute was "not directed at the conduct of any physician or health care provider, private or public" but was "directed solely at those responsible for expending public funds."[49] Thus, as the case was presented to the Supreme Court, Arnold's view was again singled out, and the Court's opinion constituted a limited victory for Arnold on the "gag rule" issue.

Arnold's limited First Amendment victory in *Webster*, however, ended with *Rust v. Sullivan* in 1991, in which a bare majority of the Supreme Court upheld federal regulations prohibiting the use of public funds in programs "where abortion is a method of family planning," including counseling. Rehnquist also authored that majority opinion and he specifically rejected the view that any free speech rights were violated.[50]

RESTRICTIONS ON MINORS

In the years following *Roe*, states enacted a number of abortion regulations, including restrictions on access to abortion by minors. Initially, the framework for lower courts to evaluate these regulations was set by *Roe*, which permitted a balance between the state's interest in protecting a woman's health and the potential life of the fetus against the woman's right to decide whether or not to carry her pregnancy to term. *Planned Parenthood v. Casey*, decided by the Supreme Court in 1992, affirmed that before viability of the fetus, "the State's interests are not strong enough to support a prohibition of abortion or the imposition of a substantial obstacle to the woman's effective right to elect the procedure."[51]

Importantly, however, the plurality opinion lowered the standard for analyzing restrictions of that right. Rather than apply the standard of "strict scrutiny" to state abortion laws, the Court considered whether the specific abortion regulations in question created an "undue burden." A regulation that "has the purpose or effect of placing a substantial obstacle in the path of a woman seeking an abortion of a nonviable fetus" creates an undue burden and is invalid.[52]

One Eighth Circuit case led to the Supreme Court's first significant foray into the regulation of access to abortion by minors, and although the Supreme Court affirmed Arnold's position in the case, his vote would generate opposition from abortion rights groups when his name surfaced as a possible Supreme Court nominee. A Minnesota statute required notification of both parents forty-eight hours before any abortion could be performed on a girl under eighteen. Although the statute accommodated minors with only one living parent or with legal guardians, it required notification of both the custodial parent and the noncustodial parent in situations of divorce or separation.

A physician and other individuals challenged the law on the ground that this requirement placed an unconstitutional burden on the exercise of the right to decide whether to terminate or continue a pregnancy. After various earlier proceedings, the case, *Hodgson v. Minnesota*, came before the full Eighth Circuit in 1988. In a seven-to-three decision, the Eighth Circuit upheld the parental notification requirement, but only because the statute provided a process for "judicial bypass." A teen wishing to avoid notifying her parents could go to a Minnesota court for a determination that she was mature enough to make the decision or that an abortion without parental consent would be in her best interests.[53] If the teen received special approval from a state judge, she could proceed with the abortion without notifying her parents.

Arnold did not write the majority opinion, but he joined it without writing a separate opinion. He was the only Democratic appointee to do so, a fact noted by the *New York Times* in a front-page story about the Eighth Circuit's decision. By 1988, when the Reagan administration had appointed almost one-half of the sitting federal bench, the makeup of the Eighth Circuit had changed dramatically. Six of the seven judges in the *Hodgson* majority were Reagan appointees; Arnold was the lone Carter appointee to vote in favor of the consent requirement. All three dissenters had been appointed by Democrats, creating a vote the *New York Times* described as "a vivid example of the effect that the Reagan Administration's push to appoint more conservative judges has had on some Federal appeals courts."[54]

Writing for the majority, Judge John R. Gibson recognized the significant authority of parents in the upbringing of their children. Notification was a lesser burden than consent, and the statute did not require the parents to approve of the procedure. Gibson acknowledged that the need to notify *both* parents could place an undue burden on a woman's right to have an abortion, but the existence of the judicial bypass procedure provided a constitutionally sound alternative.[55]

The dissenters were Donald Lay, Gerald Heaney, and Theodore McMillian. They argued that the Supreme Court had never addressed a statute that required both parents to be notified. Minnesota's parental notification law was unique in the nation, they said, because it required that both parents be notified even in cases of divorce, separation, or desertion by the father. In the absence of a clear statement from the Supreme Court that such a requirement was valid, the dissenters would strike down the statute on the ground that it was not narrowly tailored to address the state's important interests.[56]

When the Supreme Court announced it would review the *Hodgson* case, a total of twenty-five states then had laws requiring minors seeking abortions to notify or to obtain consent from at least one parent.[57] In 1990, the Supreme Court affirmed the Eighth Circuit's decision in *Hodgson*.[58] But the resulting opinions expressed differing rationales. A conservative wing of the Court would have gone even further to hold that the dual-parent notification would be constitutional even without a judicial bypass.[59] By contrast, the liberal wing dissented in part, arguing that the judicial bypass procedure did not save the statute.[60]

Justice Scalia explained the fractured nature of the Supreme Court's ruling:

> As I understand the various opinions today: One Justice holds that two-parent notification is unconstitutional (at least in the present circumstances) without judicial bypass, but constitutional with bypass; four Justices would hold that two-parent notification is constitutional with or without bypass; four Justices would hold that two-parent notification is unconstitutional with or without bypass, though the four apply two dif-

ferent standards; six Justices hold that one-parent notification with bypass is constitutional, though for two different sets of reasons; and three Justices would hold that one-parent notification with bypass is unconstitutional.[61]

The result, nonetheless, was that the Minnesota statute was constitutional, as the Eighth Circuit majority had said it was. Justices O'Connor, Stevens, Brennan, Marshall, and Blackmun believed that the two-parent notice requirement was unconstitutional. O'Connor joined the Court's conservatives, however, to form a majority for upholding the law because it provided for judicial bypass.[62]

Five years later, the Eighth Circuit was presented with a new question about the extent to which states might regulate the access of minors to abortion. A South Dakota law required physicians to notify only one parent of a minor seeking an abortion, but it provided no judicial bypass mechanism. The state argued that parental notice laws did not need a bypass procedure to be constitutional, as four justices had suggested in *Hodgson*. Furthermore, the state argued, if a bypass provision was necessary, the South Dakota statute provided a limited "doctor bypass" for "abused and neglected minors."[63]

Writing for a unanimous three-judge panel, Arnold struck down the statute as constitutionally insufficient because it lacked a bypass procedure for a minor to show either that she was sufficiently mature to make an independent decision or that an abortion without parental notification was in her best interest. The Supreme Court had already stated in *Bellotti v. Baird* that parental *consent* requirements for minors were an undue burden without the availability of judicial bypass.[64] Arnold believed that such a bypass was required for parental *notification* as well, even if the statute required that only one parent be notified. The bypass option allowing a physician to sanction an abortion for an "abused or neglected" minor was insufficient, Arnold said, because it did not include "mature" or "best interest" minors who were not abused or neglected. Arnold recognized that the Supreme Court in *Hodgson* had not provided guidance on this question.[65] The two other Eighth Circuit judges on the case, John Gibson and George Fagg, agreed with Arnold that the South Dakota statute was unconstitutional.

The Supreme Court declined to hear an appeal from the case. As the *Washington Post* noted, although the refusal to hear an appeal does not carry the same significance as a Supreme Court opinion, the Court's action in this case was significant because the South Dakota statute was the only one of its kind in the nation. Thus, the "practical effect of the court's action is to eliminate this kind of regulation for the foreseeable future."[66]

An earlier case involving Missouri's judicial bypass procedure for minors provided Arnold with an opportunity to recognize the ethical dilemma of some judges. The case provoked a sharp response from Arnold to a state court judge whom Arnold believed had been biased against elective abortion. A seventeen-year-old pregnant girl appeared before a juvenile court judge in Missouri seeking a determination that she was of sufficient maturity to elect to terminate her pregnancy without the consent of one parent. The juvenile court judge said that she was not and refused to permit an abortion. According to transcripts, the judge told the girl: "This is probably the most important case that I've ever sat on since I've been a circuit judge, because depending upon what ruling I make, I hold in my hands the power to kill an unborn child. In our society, it's a lot easier to kill an unborn child than the most vicious murderer. The issue then is this: The court firmly believes that the killing of an unborn fetus is murder."[67]

Arnold did not name the judge who made the statements, but he made clear that judges who were unable "with a clear conscience" to enforce federal court decisions on abortion should remove themselves from such cases. Arnold wrote:

> This Court can sympathize with the ethical conflict which judges must experience when their legal duty is to act contrary to deeply held personal beliefs. The question of elective abortion arouses passionate opinions. But the law on this subject cannot be disputed in the lower courts, including the Juvenile Courts of Missouri and this Court. The Supreme Court has announced that it is a woman's right to control the issue of her body up until the time that issue can live separately. The decision is the law of the land. Regardless of personal discomfort with the law, it is the duty of judges to apply it.[68]

After her experience in the Missouri juvenile court, the seventeen-year-old had challenged the Missouri court's denial in federal court. A federal district judge issued an injunction against the state, and the teenager (who was two months away from attaining the age of majority) legally obtained an abortion. The case thus became "moot," and she lacked standing to maintain her challenge to ongoing Missouri court practices.[69]

Nonetheless, Arnold believed it important to state clearly the duty of state court judges to respect federal law. The juvenile court judge involved in the case soon returned to private practice. He was critical of Arnold's suggestion that he should have taken himself off the case: "And Scott Wright [a federal district judge] shouldn't have taken himself off the case? He's one of the most liberal judges. I don't place any credence in what federal judges say. I couldn't care less."[70] Clearly, Arnold's instructions about supremacy of federal law were necessary.

PARTIAL-BIRTH ABORTION

Arnold's most significant abortion case, *Carhart v. Stenberg*, was decided in 1999.[71] The state of Nebraska enacted a statute that made it a crime to perform an abortion procedure referred to as "partial-birth" abortion. The target was a procedure known medically as dilation and extraction, or D&X. The Nebraska law defined this type of abortion as "an abortion procedure in which the person performing the abortion partially delivers vaginally a living unborn child before killing the unborn child and completing the delivery."[72] The procedure was rarely used to terminate a pregnancy during the first sixteen weeks, but the description fit other forms of abortion more commonly used in later stages of a pregnancy.

Dr. LeRoy Carhart brought suit challenging the statute on two grounds. First, he argued that in some cases, D&X was the safest abortion procedure and that outlawing it placed an undue burden on a woman's right to abortion. He also argued that the statute's language could be read to ban another, more commonly used procedure, known as dilation and evacuation (D&E).

Arnold agreed with Carhart's second contention. The statute created an undue burden, he concluded, because in many instances it would ban the most common form of legal abortion in pre-viability instances, D&E. The statute made it a crime to intentionally bring "a substantial portion" of a living fetus into the vagina for the purpose of performing an abortion. The problem for Arnold was that the term "substantial portion" was nowhere defined in the statute. Arnold believed it could include an arm or a leg of a fetus, which can occur during D&E. Arnold wrote, "What the term means for the purposes of the statute has been debated at length, both in the record before us and on the floor of the Nebraska Legislature.

But if 'substantial portion' means an arm or a leg—and surely it must—then the ban created by the statute encompasses both the D&E and the D&X procedures."[73]

The state argued that the Supreme Court had left open the option for states to protect the "partially born." Arnold wrote that "the phrase 'partially born' is new to us":

> Apparently the State uses it to describe a process in which the fetus is killed when it is more outside the womb than inside. If we assume that there is such a legal category, and that, as the State argues, the rule of *Roe v. Wade* does not apply to it, the argument is still unavailing on the record before us in this case. As we have explained, the Nebraska statute is violated when an arm or a leg of a fetus that is still alive is pulled out of the womb as part of the D&E abortion procedure. In such a situation, although a substantial part of the fetus, as defined by the Nebraska law, has been extracted from the uterus, it cannot be said that the fetus as a whole is more outside the uterus than inside. In addition, we think that the word "born" refers most naturally to a viable fetus, one that is capable of surviving outside the mother. The Nebraska statute is not limited to viable fetuses. So if there is a separate legal category for the "partially born," and we express no view on that question, we do not see how it could be relevant to the present case.[74]

Arnold's decision, joined by Roger Wollman and Paul Magnuson, also affected other "partial-birth" statutes within the Eighth Circuit. On September 24, 1999, when Arnold's opinion in Carhart was released, the Eighth Circuit also filed two additional Arnold opinions striking down similar statutes in Iowa and Arkansas.[75] Indeed, throughout the nation, an additional fourteen states had enacted similar laws.

A newspaper editorial lauded Arnold's opinion as "unbiased," something that had "not happened often since Reagan-Bush appointees seized control." Calling Arnold "the best and brightest of the Eighth Circuit judges," the editorial writer believed "good sense could prevail in St. Louis" because of his work. "Any time Richard Arnold is on the case, the chance of achieving justice increases astronomically."[76]

When the Supreme Court announced in late 1999 that it would hear the case, it marked the first time since 1992 the Court had reentered the abortion arena. The Court affirmed Judge Arnold's ruling by a vote of five to four. The majority not only agreed with Arnold that the statute was invalid because it covered common procedures other than D&X but also because the statute lacked a health exception for the mother for late-term abortions. Prohibiting D&X even in instances in which it was the safest procedure available for late-term abortions created an unconstitutional burden. Justice Stephen Breyer, who joined the Court after President Bill Clinton decided not to advance Arnold's nomination as a Supreme Court justice, wrote the opinion for the majority. Breyer declared: "A State cannot subject women's health to significant risks . . . where state regulations force women to use riskier methods of abortion. Our cases have repeatedly invalidated statutes that in the process of regulating the methods of abortion imposed significant health risks. They make clear that a risk to a woman's health is the same whether it happens to arise from regulating a particular method of abortion, or from barring abortion entirely."[77]

In a dissenting opinion, Justice Clarence Thomas sharply disagreed with striking down the statute because it might include D&E procedures. He wrote that "the majority speculates that some Nebraska prosecutor may attempt to stretch the statute to apply it to D&E. But a state statute is not unconstitutional on its face merely because we can imagine an aggressive prosecutor who would attempt an overly aggressive application of the statute."[78]

The Supreme Court's decision, as expected, drew praise from pro-choice advocates and criticism from abortion opponents. An editorial in the *St. Louis Post-Dispatch* said the Supreme Court's decision could be "summed up in two words: Women won." But the "narrowest of margins"—a five-to-four decision—was duly noted.[79]

Seven years later the Supreme Court would reverse course. In 2007, the Court accepted for review another Eighth Circuit opinion on partial-birth abortion, this time involving a federal statute, the Partial-Birth Abortion Ban Act of 2003. Arnold died in 2004 and never participated in any constitutional challenge to the federal act. Dr. LeRoy Carhart, who had successfully challenged the Nebraska statute, also brought suit against the federal ban. The federal statute had been more carefully phrased to avoid the problem of the Nebraska statute. But the Eighth Circuit held the federal statute unconstitutional on the basis of the Supreme Court's decision in *Carhart v. Stenberg* because it did not include an exception for the health of the mother.[80]

The Supreme Court upheld the federal Partial-Birth Abortion Ban Act, reversing both the Eighth and Ninth Circuits. The majority opinion written by Justice Kennedy distinguished its earlier decision in *Carhart v.*

Stenberg on the ground that the language of the federal statute was different from the legislation at issue from Nebraska. The Court did not overtly overrule *Stenberg*.[81] But the composition of the court had changed in the meantime; Justice Sandra Day O'Connor had retired from the Court and had been replaced by Justice Samuel Alito. Chief Justice John Roberts had also replaced William Rehnquist. Justice Alito voted with Kennedy, Scalia, Thomas, and Chief Justice Roberts to uphold the federal ban. The dissenters this time — Justices Ginsburg, Stevens, Souter, and Breyer — believed the federal act was unconstitutional for precisely the reasons they had expressed earlier.

Did the Supreme Court's decision mean that states could now ban the "partial-birth abortion" procedure, even without an exception for the life of the mother? The question was significant because, despite the majority's claim that it had not overruled *Stenberg*, new state statutes waited in the wings. In 1999, for example, Missouri had enacted a statute known as the "Infant's Protection Act" over then-governor Mel Carnahan's veto. The statute classified "partial-birth abortion" as infanticide and made it a felony. The Eighth Circuit had struck down the statute as unconstitutional in 2005, but the Supreme Court vacated that opinion and remanded it to the Eighth Circuit for further consideration in light of its ruling on the federal Partial Birth Abortion Act.[82] It is clear that since Arnold's decision in the first *Carhart* case, some state legislators continued to look for ways around the constitutional deficiency Arnold had identified.

CONTROVERSY OVER ARNOLD'S JUDICIAL RECORD ON ABORTION

In a tribute to Richard Arnold in 1993, Judge Patricia Wald said of his decisions involving reproductive rights that "Orthodox feminists must recognize that his position is in most respects far more expansive than the present Supreme Court's."[83] Nonetheless, some women's groups would oppose Arnold's possible nomination to the Supreme Court on the basis of an alleged record in abortion cases that they viewed to be detrimental. Press reports alluded to these as "opinions that could cause controversy within women's groups."[84] Another article alleged that Arnold's "opinions on abortion rights would cause him problems."[85]

The objection of the National Abortion Rights Action League to Arnold's record on reproductive rights seemed to be based solely upon *Hodgson v. Minnesota*, which the Supreme Court had affirmed. Although the Supreme Court's affirmation of *Hodgson* was narrowly divided, the case indicated that the Eighth Circuit, and Arnold, had correctly gauged the direction of the Supreme Court on the matter.[86]

Some judges in recent years have expressed strong opposition to, or support of, the Supreme Court's decision in *Roe v. Wade*. It is notable that nowhere in the historical record is there any indication of Arnold's view of *Roe* as a matter of constitutional law, or, for that matter, of his personal views on abortion. Arnold was circumspect in his judicial opinions in abortion cases. Neither did he mention the subject of abortion in his diaries or correspondence. This reticence apparently held true in conversations with other judges and acquaintances. It may be that Arnold discussed such personal views with family or close friends, but if so, they respected Arnold's desire for public neutrality on this volatile issue. Arnold's reticence also illustrated his professionalism—he would refrain from public comments on issues practically guaranteed to come before him.

What is clear is Arnold tried for evenhandedness and he had a great awareness that his personal views were not relevant and should not be publicly expressed. Arnold was certainly aware of the position of the Catholic Church on the issue of abortion. He would have known, for instance, of a march led by the Catholic archbishop of St. Louis on the anniversary of *Roe v. Wade* in 2000. The archbishop led a march of an estimated two thousand people from St. Louis Cathedral to Planned Parenthood, six blocks away, which he had characterized during the Mass as "an evil that needs conversion."[87] A deeply devout Episcopalian for a substantial period of his life, Arnold considered becoming a Catholic. But if Arnold found a conflict between his religious views and the cases he considered, it is nowhere evident. We are simply left to speculate what those views might have been.

Although we do not know what Arnold felt personally about abortion or any possible conflict with his religious views, we have an ample record of his take on privacy rights and the shield that the courts interpose between individuals and overly intrusive government. His abortion jurisprudence was worked out in the small and evolving space between those predispositions, on one side, and the constraints imposed by the Supreme Court, on the other.

Chapter Eleven

Desegregation in Little Rock

A s an aspiring politician, one of Richard Arnold's earliest appearances on a prominent public stage was his defense of a moderate white southern approach to desegregation while a student at Yale in 1955.[1] Beginning at Harvard Law School in 1957, he found the violent uproar at Central High School in Little Rock both distressing and personally embarrassing. Ironically, when he reached the Eighth Circuit two decades later, Arnold found himself a central figure in the ongoing Little Rock school desegregation cases. After *Cooper v. Aaron*,[2] the Supreme Court did not involve itself again in the Little Rock school cases, leaving final resolution of numerous appeals exclusively to the Eighth Circuit. Beginning in 1982, the most critical and controversial decisions concerning desegregation in Little Rock by the Eighth Circuit bore Arnold's signature, or at least reflected his significant influence. Arnold's last opinion in the Little Rock school cases, written a few months before his death in September 2004, seemed to signal the close of nearly fifty years of federal court involvement. By then, the Little Rock schools had been under federal court supervision longer than any other school system in the nation.[3]

When Arnold joined the Little Rock cases, "desegregation"—elimination of the use of government power to enforce segregation—had been largely accomplished. The remaining, intractable question was the extent to which "integration" could be achieved in the face of white flight and an urban school district with a majority-black student enrollment. To the extent that integration aims to remedy the lingering effects of historical forced segregation through separate school systems, it has proven to be an elusive goal, not only in Little Rock, but in most urban school systems.

Richard Arnold sat on twenty-eight appeals of school desegregation issues and would write sixteen opinions in these cases. These opinions never simply rubber-stamped district court actions. Indeed, Arnold and the panel frequently reversed district court orders.[4] Arnold himself was never reversed on a school desegregation issue, either by the Eighth Circuit sitting en banc or by the United States Supreme Court.

The membership of the panel assigned to the Little Rock school cases—including Judges Gerald W. Heaney and Roger L. Wollman—remained consistent for almost twenty years.[5] Other Eighth Circuit judges seem to have deferred to Arnold's views not only because of his intellectual prowess but perhaps also because he was viewed as a "representative" of Arkansas on the court—closest to the ground among the appellate judges, with an extensive background in Arkansas politics. "Everybody knows Judge Arnold," the *Arkansas Democrat* reported in 1987, maintaining that Arnold was "as well known to many Arkansans as they will ever know a federal judge."[6] The lore, although apparently not the reality, was that Arnold had been selected for the panel specifically for an "Arkansas" presence.[7]

Richard Arnold profoundly shaped the Little Rock desegregation litigation. Because of his long and deep involvement, the Little Rock school cases provide unique insight into the development and application of his judicial method and philosophy. Although he was described as a "powerful liberal-leaning intellectual,"[8] it is not easy to characterize Arnold as either a "liberal" or a "conservative" in the Little Rock desegregation cases. Arnold refused to order consolidation when that seemed, to some at least, an appropriate remedy under United States Supreme Court precedent at the time. Instead, he preferred a political solution in a state that had demonstrated political resistance in the past. Arnold recognized that a court-imposed solution, as distinct from a remedy to which local parties subscribed, had an excellent chance to fail.

Arnold's opinions in these cases anticipated directions taken by the Supreme Court in school desegregation in the 1990s, characterized by the move to end extensive federal judicial oversight of desegregation efforts at the local school district level.[9] Judge Arnold's actions in the Little Rock school cases generated both praise and criticism, but they exhibit a unifying theme. Arnold adopted a particular view of public law litigation and the role of parties in working out remedies for constitutional violations in institutional reform cases. Arnold worked out his own synthesis, driven largely by pragmatism. Arnold showed a strong preference for settlement by the parties rather than court-imposed constitutional criteria.

THE EARLY HISTORY

Before Richard Arnold's involvement, Little Rock schools had been under federal court superision for nearly twenty-five years.[10] Following the Supreme Court's 1954 decision in *Brown I*,[11] and before its "all deliberate speed" direction of *Brown II*,[12] the Little Rock Board of Education announced a plan to gradually desegregate its schools. On May 22, 1954, five days after the announcement of *Brown I*, the Little Rock school board stated that it would comply with the Supreme Court's decision. Over the next year, the school board developed a plan for gradual integration, starting with the high schools in 1957. The board planned to integrate the remaining grades over a seven-year period. One week after the board announced its plan, the Supreme Court instructed in *Brown II* that desegregation should be implemented "with all deliberate speed."[13]

In February 1956, Wiley Branton, Thurgood Marshall, and Robert Carter of the NAACP Legal Defense Fund filed suit in federal district court in Little Rock challenging the pace of the Little Rock school board's desegregation plan.[14] The plan included construction of three new high schools and six new junior high schools, financed by a four-million-dollar bond issue approved in 1953. The plan specified integrating high schools first, followed by junior high schools, and completing integration of elementary schools by 1963. The board stated: "Since our school system has been segregated from its beginning until the present time, the time required in the process as outlined should not be construed as unnecessary delay, but that which is justly needed with respect to the size and complexity of the job at hand."[15] Further, the board maintained that "the plaintiffs unreasonably insist on a hasty integration which will be unwise, unworkable, and fraught with danger; that would prove detrimental to the personal interest of plaintiffs and the educational needs of both races, and would unnecessarily and inevitably hinder and retard the accomplishment of integration of the schools of the defendant District."[16]

The 1956 plan for integration, for only one high school with only a few minority students, was minimal. The district court nonetheless refused the plaintiffs' requested relief, and entered an order approving the plan and retaining jurisdiction to ensure compliance.[17] A panel of the Eighth Circuit Court of Appeals affirmed the district court.[18]

The notorious events at Central High School occurred soon after Richard Arnold entered Harvard Law School. It was a dramatic confrontation between state and federal powers, a constitutional crisis that played out on national television. Nine black students were to begin the integration of Central High School as the school term opened on September 3, 1957. Governor Orval Faubus ordered the Arkansas National Guard to surround the school to deny entrance to the nine black students, claiming the action was necessary to prevent violence. Soon thereafter, the federal district court enjoined the governor and the Arkansas National Guard from interfering with integration.[19] A few weeks later, the nine students entered the school but were removed later in the morning because of the presence of a growing mob of whites outside the school. President Dwight D. Eisenhower federalized the Arkansas National Guard and sent members of the United States Army's 101st Airborne to ensure integration at Central High School. Military forces were still present at the end of that school year.

During that year, the Little Rock school board petitioned the district court to postpone integration for an additional three years. The district court granted the request, finding that implementation of the original desegregation plan had become impossible due to public opposition.[20] The Eighth Circuit Court of Appeals sitting en banc overturned the court's decision.[21] Three weeks later, the United States Supreme Court unanimously affirmed the Eighth Circuit. This famous case, *Cooper v. Aaron*,[22] would be the only instance in which the Supreme Court heard an appeal involving desegregation in Little Rock. The justices wrote:

> As this case reaches us it raises questions of the highest importance to the maintenance of our federal system of government. It necessarily involves a claim by the Governor and Legislature of a State that there is no duty on state officials to obey federal court orders resting on this Court's con-

sidered interpretation of the United States Constitution. Specifically it involves actions by the Governor and Legislature of Arkansas upon the premise that they are not bound by our holding in *Brown v. Board of Education*. Since the first *Brown* opinion three new Justices have come to the Court. They are at one with the Justices still on the Court who participated in that basic decision as to its correctness, and that decision is now unanimously reaffirmed. The principles announced in that decision and the obedience of the States to them, according to the command of the Constitution, are indispensable for the protection of the freedoms guaranteed by our fundamental charter for all of us.[23]

The Little Rock school board was ordered to proceed with its original integration plan for September 1958, but instead, the defiant Governor Faubus ordered the Little Rock schools closed. The Little Rock schools remained closed throughout the 1958–1959 school year, despite a ruling by a three-member federal court invalidating the legislation on which Faubus's order was based.[24]

The Little Rock schools reopened in the fall of 1959. In the next years, desegregation proceeded in Little Rock with more deliberation than speed. A new lawsuit was filed in 1965, once again alleging that black children were being denied admittance to predominantly white schools in Little Rock. In 1966, only 17 percent of black students in Little Rock attended schools with white students. Seven schools remained all white, and twelve schools were still all black. At that point, the Little Rock school board abandoned use of the Arkansas pupil placement laws and proposed a freedom-of-choice plan.[25] The board proposed several plans over the next years, while the plaintiffs, in *Clark v. Board of Education of LRSD*, or *Clark*, as it came to be known, alleged that freedom-of-choice plans failed to meet constitutional standards.[26] The district court retained jurisdiction in the *Clark* case and issued several decisions over the next fifteen years.

The most important development in the *Clark* litigation came when the Eighth Circuit held the freedom-of-choice approach to be unacceptable from a constitutional standpoint, and required the Little Rock School District to implement a plan to achieve racial balance in all of its schools.[27] Elsewhere, other courts also rejected "freedom of choice" plans and instead required school districts to attain "racial balance," in accordance with the Supreme Court's directions in *Green v. County School Board of New Kent*

County[28] and *Swann v. Charlotte-Mecklenburg Board of Education*.[29] Busing became the primary tool to achieve racial balance in Little Rock, as it did in other parts of the country. In 1977, about ten thousand students in the Little Rock school district rode buses to and from their assigned schools.[30]

By the 1980s and 1990s, consensus about the desirability of desegregation proved easier to sustain than agreement on how best to remedy past segregation. In the Eighth Circuit, as in other parts of the country, the most intractable problems of school desegregation arose from the urban school districts. In Kansas City and St. Louis, as well as Little Rock, Arnold and the other judges of the Eighth Circuit oversaw and tried to manage the conflicts.

KEY DECISIONS OF THE ARNOLD COURT

When Richard Arnold was first assigned to the Little Rock school cases, the paradigm for federal court supervision of school desegregation included a number of features.[31] The federal district court retained jurisdiction "more or less indefinitely — until the vestiges of the old dual system had been rooted out and a unitary system had been achieved." Racial "balance" was required in school districts with a history of segregation required by state law. Busing had become the primary tool to neutralize segregated housing patterns and populate schools in approved ratios. In Little Rock, as elsewhere, courts experimented with compensatory programs for disadvantaged students, magnet schools, and majority-to-minority interdistrict transfer programs.[32]

During Arnold's tenure in the Little Rock school cases, three important developments shaped the course of the litigation and the ultimate resolution of partial unitary status for the Little Rock School District: (1) a 1985 en banc decision rejecting the district court's order of consolidation;[33] (2) a 1990 panel opinion rejecting the district court's modifications of a settlement agreement;[34] and (3) a 2004 opinion, Judge Arnold's last in these cases, affirming a finding of partial unitary status over the objection of the NAACP Legal Defense and Education Fund.[35]

A COURT-ORDERED CONSOLIDATION

From 1959 until 1982, the Little Rock School District operated under successive desegregation plans, the details of which were frequently litigated.

In 1982, however, the Little Rock School District adopted a new strategy to achieve integration. The district filed a lawsuit against two neighboring school districts—the North Little Rock School District ("NLRSD") and the Pulaski County Special School District ("PCSSD")—as well as the state of Arkansas and the state board of education, asking the federal district court to order interdistrict relief. Although all three school districts operated under federal court desegregation decrees,[36] the Little Rock School District sought to force consolidation of the three districts as the only feasible resolution of the problem of segregation. This lawsuit became the main strategy for desegregation of the Little Rock schools.

By the close of the 1970s, the Little Rock area schools had come to resemble northern urban schools with a self-contained, inner-city, majority-black school district, surrounded by suburban school districts that were predominantly white. Throughout the 1970s, increasing white flight compounded the district's problems in attaining nonracially identifiable schools. The Little Rock School District was completely surrounded by the Pulaski County Special School District, which also completely surrounded the separate North Little Rock School District. Both suburban school districts featured predominantly white schools and a predominantly white student population. Thus, the Little Rock schools faced a situation similar to the status of the Detroit schools that led to the Supreme Court's *Milliken* decisions. In *Milliken v. Bradley* (*Milliken I*),[37] the Court reversed an order to consolidate the Detroit inner-city school system with fifty-two contiguous suburban school districts. Before such interdistrict relief may be imposed, the Court wrote: "[I]t must first be shown that there has been a constitutional violation within one district that produces a significant segregative effect in another district. Specifically, it must be shown that racially discriminatory acts of the state or local school districts, or of a single school district have been a substantial cause of interdistrict segregation."[38]

The Little Rock School District made precisely this claim in its suit against the state and its neighboring school districts. But unlike the Detroit schools, the Little Rock School District offered evidence that satisfied the *Milliken I* standards for an interdistrict remedy. Along with other evidence, the district court had found discriminatory intent in extensions of City of Little Rock boundaries to encompass residential sections in which many white families lived or subsequently moved into, while those areas remained within the Pulaski County Special School District.[39] If the boundaries of the city and its school district had remained coterminous, the black-white ratio in the Little Rock schools would have been sixty-forty, rather than more than 70 percent black. In other words, the district court found that the boundaries between the two school districts had been maintained to keep Little Rock schools predominantly black and Pulaski County Schools predominantly white.[40] The district court also pointed to the existence of segregated housing in the Little Rock area and attributed a causal role to both the state of Arkansas and the Pulaski County Special School District in creating and perpetuating this condition.

A majority of the Eighth Circuit, sitting en banc, agreed with most of the district court's findings of interdistrict violations. In a thirty-page opinion for the court, Judge Gerald W. Heaney sustained the findings of interdistrict violations by all of the defendants. He wrote:

> The state's actions which originally segregated LRSD and then forestalled its desegregation for over twenty years are not too remote in time to be relevant for this appeal. Rather, the long history of concurrent actions on the part of the state, PCSSD, and NLRSD exerted an unmistakable interdistrict effect on the schools of the metropolitan area by singling out LRSD as the school district which provided some educational opportunities for black students and by identifying PCSSD and NLRSD as white districts.[41]

Nonetheless, the Eighth Circuit rejected Judge Henry Woods's order mandating consolidation of all the school districts in and around Little Rock,[42] a decision Richard Arnold supported in his separate concurrence. Arnold wrote that he "approved completely" of the court's decision not to order consolidation of the three school districts. Although he noted that consolidation was within the judicial power of the United States and that upon proper proof he would support it, he believed the extent of the interdistrict violations did not require consolidation as a remedy. Arnold wrote, "Consolidation would mean destruction of three popularly governed units of local government, and substitution in their stead of one judicially created and judicially supervised school district." Arnold believed consolidation to be "a drastic step that should be reserved for clearer cases." Instead, Arnold wrote, "Our task as judges is not to force these school districts to do what we think is right or socially good, but to apply the law to the facts and announce the result, whatever it may be."[43]

While Judge Arnold agreed that consolidation should not be ordered, he wrote separately to make two points. He quarreled with the court's extended analysis of the record and adoption of a detailed remedial decree. The proper course, instead, would have been to remand the case for the district court to craft a new remedy, because that was in line with his view of how the courts should operate. The majority ordered a re-drawing of the Little Rock School District's boundaries to include areas subsequently annexed by the City of Little Rock, along with other forms of interdistrict relief. It also imposed a forty-five-minute cap on the length of one-way bus rides for students in the PCSSD, whose schools covered the largest geographical area among the three districts. Concerning the majority's imposed remedy, Arnold stated that it was a "decree that will, I dare say, startle all the parties to this case, including even those (if there are any) who like what they see."[44]

Arnold also disagreed with the notion of historical guilt as represented in the majority opinion. The majority held that the state of Arkansas had committed constitutional violations that produced substantial interdistrict effects, and awarded interdistrict relief in the form of financial support to the school districts for future desegregation efforts against the state. Arnold wrote: "I quite agree that the state of Arkansas has been, in this field, a persistent violator of constitutional rights. I cannot agree that these violations (with one exception) are responsible for the racial disparity now existing between PCSSD and LRSD, or that they justify (again with an exception) interdistrict relief against the State."[45] The exception, according to Arnold, was the assistance of the state, "with a racially discriminatory motive in the movement of school children across district lines," especially in the 1958–1959 school year in which the Little Rock schools were closed.[46] On the basis of this history, Arnold would "agree that the State should pay for any voluntary majority-to-minority transfers between PCSSD and LRSD. That would be a fair recompense for what it did in the late fifties."[47]

Although Arnold was unable to persuade the majority that the state of Arkansas's compensatory funding should be more limited, he played the pivotal role in the decision to reject consolidation of the three school districts. He did so by citing the *Milliken I* Court's dicta that "[n]o single tradition in public education is more deeply rooted than local control over the operation of schools,"[48] and by concluding that *Milliken I* counseled that "no particular degree of racial balance is required by the Constitution."[49] *Milliken I*, however, involved no finding of interdistrict segregative effects, whereas in the Little Rock metropolitan area, Arnold acknowledged some interdistrict violations and allowed that in an appropriate circumstance the federal courts had authority to require consolidation. However, Arnold believed these were not the appropriate circumstances. He opted for a less intrusive remedy, one that preserved a degree of political self-determination for the existing school districts.[50]

On the other hand, Arnold's view was instrumental in supporting the interdistrict relief ordered by the majority, despite his view that the court should not undertake such an order without remand to the district court. Arnold agreed with the finding that there was evidence of discriminatory location of public housing as well as annexation decisions that had an unmistakable impact on the racial makeup of the respective school districts. A dissenting opinion joined by two other judges, in fact, criticized Arnold's support for the change of boundaries because it was based on his "speculation, belief, and fair approximation" of the evidence of racial effect in maintaining the PCSSD's boundaries in the face of the City of Little Rock's annexations. The dissent maintained that Arnold "improperly relies upon his own factual conclusions based on an overly generous interpretation of the record to justify the remedy ordered today."[51]

Interestingly, in a footnote to his opinion, Arnold indicated that he did not subscribe to the notion that all-black schools are "necessarily educationally inferior." An editorial in the *Arkansas Gazette* noted, "Federal Judge Richard S. Arnold of the Eighth Circuit Court of Appeals at St. Louis resides at Little Rock and knows something of the schools in the area. It's not surprising that it was he among the appellate judges who remarked on an irony of the Little Rock school consolidation case."[52] Arnold wrote, "The 'blacker' Little Rock School District, ironically, appears by all accounts to produce more scholars of note and to offer a broader selection of courses, than the 'whiter' districts with which it wishes to merge."[53] The Little Rock School District had the highest number of National Merit Scholarship semifinalists in the state—nearly three times as many as the much larger Pulaski County Special School District.

If the Eighth Circuit's ruling pleased Pulaski County and North Little Rock school and government officials,[54] it nonetheless received criticism elsewhere. Skip Rutherford, former president of the Little Rock school board and a longtime friend of Arnold's, believed that the only lasting answer to the problems of segregation in the Little Rock metropolitan area was a court-ordered consolidation of the three districts.[55] Similarly, a 222-

page report on desegregation in the Little Rock School District prepared by the University of Arkansas at Little Rock in 1997 concluded:

> With the benefit of hindsight, it can be said that any realistic hope of having a desegregated school district in Little Rock—if desegregated is defined as racial balance in schools across the district—came to an end with the Eighth Circuit Court's reversal in 1985 of the district court's consolidation order. However, the experience in other cities suggests that the initial racial balance of a consolidated district would have been short-lived. Indeed, the growth in recent decades of bedroom communities outside Little Rock and Pulaski County supports the view that consolidation would have provoked white flight beyond the borders of a countywide district. Nonetheless, by broadening the geographical area and lengthening the time-frame, the district judge's consolidation order might have had more beneficial effects than the solution of the Eighth Circuit Court of Appeals.[56]

The Eighth Circuit's compromise ordered most Little Rock School District boundary lines to coincide with city limits. As a result the LRSD gained nearly seven thousand students and fourteen schools from the PCSSD. Nonetheless, today blacks now outnumber whites in the LRSD by three to one.[57]

Judge Gerald Heaney, author of the thirty-two-page majority opinion reversing Judge Woods's consolidation order, attributed the majority's decision to reverse the consolidation order largely to Arnold's influence. Two decades later, Judge Heaney stated:

> Richard was not only a great judge but a great human being. And we all had such respect for him that I think we gave an awful lot of weight to his views on the matter. It was his feeling that we really didn't have the precedent in our favor in terms of adopting Judge Woods's view that the school districts should be consolidated, even if that might have been the most effective and in the long run probably the best chance of having a long term integrative effect. But I agreed with Richard and I didn't do so unwillingly, partially because I had such great respect for him as a person and as a judge.[58]

Judge Roger Wollman, who would soon become a member of the panel assigned to the Little Rock school cases, agreed that Arnold had a "tremendous influence" on the court's decisions and that he became the "intellectual leader of the court."[59]

The most difficult issue for the court, according to Heaney, was whether Judge Woods was correct in concluding that the only way to achieve a reasonable degree of integration was to consolidate the schools:

> We all agreed at that time. We thought that Judge Woods had gone further than he ought to have gone. But in retrospect, I don't know whether we were right or whether we were wrong. Obviously it was very difficult to achieve any high degree of integration within the Little Rock School District because you had such a high percentage of black kids. So I think Judge Woods was very disappointed in our decision. We thought we were doing the right thing at the time. If ever a district would have been well served by consolidation, that might have been the district. But the opposition to consolidation from the point of both North Little Rock and Pulaski county was very strong.[60]

Ultimately, under the parameters set down by the Eighth Circuit in this decision, all of the parties, including the class of plaintiffs represented by the NAACP Legal Defense and Education Fund known as the "Joshua Intervenors,"[61] would reach an agreement to settle the litigation in 1989. In the interim, however, the litigation continued but now under settled school district boundaries. When the City of Little Rock annexed additional land in 1986, the district court ordered that this additional territory become part of the Little Rock School District, rather than the Pulaski County Special School District. The Eighth Circuit panel reversed this ruling, stating that the change of boundaries ordered by the appeals court in 1985 did not require automatic boundary extensions for subsequent city annexations.[62]

The continuation of separate districts generated other problems that reached Arnold's court. In a 1988 opinion written by both Judge Heaney and Judge Arnold, the Eighth Circuit panel again reversed Judge Woods on several issues, including whether the Pulaski County Special School District's student assignment plan met constitutional standards. The Little Rock School District sought invalidation of the Pulaski County plan approved by Judge Woods. Arnold and Heaney wrote that Judge Woods had acted improperly by rejecting a proposed plan without a hearing, and reversed Woods's subsequent approval of another plan because it allowed "a constitutionally impermissible continuation of a dual educational system" in the county.[63]

The Little Rock School District also sought more money from the state of Arkansas for remedial programs in its racially identifiable elementary schools. Judge Woods had rejected this request, consistent with his view that the Little Rock schools should not have any racially identifiable schools in its plans. The Eighth Circuit panel reversed this ruling as well. The panel defined a "racially identifiable black elementary school in [the] LRSD as any elementary school that is 81% or more black" and held that the state of Arkansas was "obligated to fund remedial and compensatory programs" in these schools.[64] At that point in the litigation, the state had paid about $8.5 million for magnet schools for the 1987–1988 school year alone, and it would now be required to pay even more through the mid-1990s.[65]

THE INTERDISTRICT SETTLEMENT AGREEMENT

With consolidation ruled out as a resolution to the desegregation of Little Rock area schools, the three school districts negotiated a settlement among themselves and the state of Arkansas. As part of this agreement, the state legislature would authorize $109 million to fund desegregation programs, primarily in the Little Rock School District. This agreement would limit the state's liability to a finite amount and dismiss it from the case. In addition, the Little Rock School District was permitted to maintain seven elementary schools with essentially all-minority enrollment. These schools would receive double funding, paid for in part out of the state's settlement, and would be known as "incentive schools." Interdistrict and magnet schools would continue, and focus would shift from achieving racial balance in each school to improving achievement levels of minority children. The parties agreed that the district court would retain jurisdiction to oversee compliance with the settlement plans.[66]

Federal District Judge Henry Woods rejected the proposed settlement. He did so on the ground that it did not go far enough to achieve desegregation in the LRSD, and that the state's funding would prove inadequate to justify dismissing it from the case. The plans, he wrote, were "facially unconstitutional and do not even purport to be within the mandates of the Court of Appeals."[67] Judge Woods then entered a modified consent decree to which all the parties to the litigation objected. Among other things, the decree created the Office of Metropolitan Supervisor with management powers over all three school districts. Judge Woods also reduced the amount of attorneys' fees specified in the settlement, objecting in particular to the LRSD's agreement to pay the Legal Defense Fund $2 million in attorneys' fees.[68]

In his opinion for the panel, Judge Arnold rejected the district court's modifications and held that Judge Woods should have approved the settlement plan, even though it proposed eight initially all-black elementary schools, and even though it called for more than $3 million in attorneys' fees. Arnold began his opinion with a note of weariness: "We have before us another chapter in the Little Rock school desegregation case, in the form of ten separate appeals from various orders of the District Court."[69]

Arnold first noted that the Office of Metropolitan Supervisor as established by Judge Woods amounted "virtually to a de facto consolidation of these entities."[70] The parties had not asked for this kind of supervision and indeed had presented a settlement plan that did not require it. Arnold expressed a fundamentally different attitude toward the proposed settlement than had Judge Woods:

> The most important fact about the present appeals is that they arise out of settlements agreed to by all parties in the District Court. The law strongly favors settlements. Courts should hospitably receive them. This may be especially true in the present context—a protracted, highly divisive, even bitter litigation, any lasting solution to which necessarily depends on the good faith and cooperation of all the parties, especially the defendants. As a practical matter, a remedy that everyone agrees to is a lot more likely to succeed than one to which the defendants must be dragged kicking and screaming.[71]

Arnold's more favorable disposition toward settlement is evident in the language he chose to describe the case's history. He termed the settlement agreement "a sharp departure from the adversary bitterness that had marked this controversy for over thirty years." In the settlement process, "counsel for all parties engaged in intense and difficult negotiations," efforts that "bore fruit."[72] Furthermore, Arnold extended great deference to the wishes of the NAACP Legal Defense and Education Fund. He noted that it had "vigorously prosecuted" the Little Rock school case for more than thirty years, and "absent an extremely good reason—and we have been given none—we are reluctant to disregard their judgment as to what is best for their own clients."[73] Although the court need not automatically approve anything the parties set before it, "any remedy will necessarily require some judicial supervision—monitoring, at least—for a long time. A court has a strong interest in not involving itself, along with the prestige of the law, in an ongoing equitable decree which is either manifestly unworkable or plainly unconstitutional on its face."[74] This settlement posed neither problem, Arnold wrote, and thus should have been accepted as proposed. John Walker, lead attorney for the Joshua Intervenors, publicly expressed his support for the agreement, stating, "we believe the settlement approach was beneficial."[75]

No party to the case, in fact, supported the district court's ruling on appeal. The court of appeals allowed a group of parents to intervene in the case in support of Judge Woods's decision and the work of the metropolitan supervisor.[76] Otherwise, the ten separate appeals from Judge Woods's rulings would have had no opposing argument before the Eighth Circuit.

Arnold seemed particularly happy with the state legislature's decision to fund its share of the settlement agreement, even though he had previously disagreed with the concept of "historical guilt" as the sole justification for requiring the state to fund desegregation efforts in the Little Rock School District. "We hope the state of Arkansas will get enough credit out of this to counterbalance past evils," Arnold said at the hearing.[77] Previously, while acknowledging that the state had a responsibility, he had declared that much of the history cited by the lawyers and his fellow judges was "simply irrelevant."[78] Over Arnold's objection, the Eighth Circuit had essentially ruled that all the state's current taxpayers were responsible for the state's actions in the 1950s. Nonetheless, Arnold quit fighting that issue. The state's liability had become the law of the case, and in any event an agreed-to settlement was far preferable to Arnold than continuing to mandate payments from the state by court order.

The Arkansas legislature and Governor Bill Clinton provided funds "without being ordered by any court" to do so, Arnold noted.[79] "Enactment of the settlement bill, without precedent so far as we know in any other state, was a significant step towards erasing the legacy of lawlessness that had marked the State of Arkansas's initial reaction to the constitutional requirement of equal, integrated education."[80] Arnold hoped that the panel's ruling could "lead to a period of calm in this case, perhaps even bringing the parties a happy issue out of all their afflictions." With the settlement recognized by the court, the parties "should be able to devote more energy to education, and less to litigation."[81]

Donald P. Lay, soon to be succeeded by Arnold as chief judge of the Eighth Circuit, later reflected on Richard Arnold's actions: "Judge Arnold disagreed with Judge Woods as to how it should be carried out. My own personal belief, and I didn't sit on the case, was that if Judge Woods's plan had been adopted, I think that maybe we would have gotten that matter settled a lot quicker and more expeditiously than we did. But that's speculation on my part."[82] Judge Lay also stated:

> Judge Arnold and Judge Woods both had the same interest at heart in trying to obtain complete integration. I guess I supported Judge Woods more in terms of how he was on the ground and knew the situation such that it should have been enough for Judge Arnold. But Richard Arnold wrote his own analysis. And I don't know—Judge Arnold may have been right and Judge Woods's way may have been a harder case. It's hard to say. But I never saw a case where Richard Arnold backed away from the primary purpose of integration. And I sat with him on many integration cases.[83]

Following the Eighth Circuit's second major reversal, Woods removed himself from the school cases. Woods said that the appeals court "had blocked any substantial progress toward a solution of the manifold problems of these school districts."[84] Woods wrote in his recusal order, "Whatever the plan finally mandated by the Court of Appeals, those who take as their part delay and obstruction will have won. I am unable to successfully implement a plan to bring equity to the children of this county under the restrictions imposed by the Court of Appeals. Perhaps the application of a fresh mind and the perspective of another judge can find hope in a situation which I perceive as hopeless."[85] The case was reassigned to Judge Susan Webber Wright, who had been on the bench less than two months.[86]

Jack Bass, in his book *Unlikely Heroes*, wrote about "the creative force of a single district judge" as an important element in the successful desegregation of many southern school districts.[87] Judge Woods certainly believed this. In many ways he is a tragic figure, as the self-portrayal in his recusal order reflects. The order is worth an extended quotation to show the depth of disagreement as a personal matter between Woods and Arnold. Woods wrote:

> A hold has now been placed by the Court of Appeals on the development
> of additional magnet schools and the construction of any new schools

"absent agreement of all parties." From past experience I can state that an agreement will never be reached for additional magnet schools.

It has been my intention to oversee a progressive educational plan to serve the children of these districts into the twenty-first century. Such a plan would bring peace to a community long plagued with a worldwide reputation for racial problems in its public schools. However, I have steadfastly resisted the notion of peace-at-any-price. In the words of Martin Luther King, Jr., what the children in this community, black and white, need and deserve is "not a negative peace which is the absence of tension, but a positive peace, which is the presence of justice."[88]

In his lengthy recusal order, Judge Woods also recalled the Eighth Circuit's decision five years earlier to reverse his order of consolidation:

I still believe that the solution which makes common sense for the children in this community is consolidation of the school districts. I believe that, had the Court of Appeals affirmed that decision in 1984, we would now be several years into a productive workable plan. Instead, the Appellate Court, while affirming each of the one-hundred-five findings of fact in the 1984 decision, reversed the remedy and mandated a remedy of its own which turned primarily on redrawing boundary lines. In the five years since consolidation was rejected by the Court of Appeals, all efforts to untie this Gordian knot have inevitably resulted in one-year, stop-gap measures instead of sensible long-term plans.[89]

Judge Arnold, it will be recalled, agreed with the majority that the consolidation order should be reversed. He disagreed, however, that the Eighth Circuit should adopt its own remedy, without remand to the district court.[90]

Judge Woods did not limit his criticisms to the Eighth Circuit. He also chastised the attorneys in the case:

Thus we are now in the throes of another of the many appeals perfected in this case, some of which have accomplished nothing but enrichment of the participating attorneys. On this subject the time has come to speak frankly. Lawyer fees paid by the three districts in this litigation have been grossly exorbitant. This is a principal reason for the poor financial situation in which the schools find themselves. The office of the Metropolitan Supervisor has requested a national accounting firm to ascertain just how much the three districts have paid out in legal fees since this litigation began. I am sure the figures will be shocking.[91]

Judge Woods had previously rejected a portion of the settlement agreement that required payment of $3 million from the Little Rock School District to the Legal Defense Fund, whose attorneys, along with John Walker, represented the Joshua Intervenors. Judge Woods rejected this part of the settlement agreement because, in part, the fees included "work done in litigation long since terminated" involving the Little Rock schools, including more than thirty years of litigation.[92] Under the agreement, the NAACP Legal Defense and Educational Fund would distribute the payment among the various counsel, both past and present, in proportions that it judged appropriate.[93]

This ruling, too, was reversed in Arnold's panel opinion. Consistent with his views of party control of the settlement, Arnold wrote that Judge Woods should not have rejected the $3 million fee agreement, $2 million of which was to be paid by the Little Rock School District. "Certainly the amounts are large. Lawyer-bashing is popular in some quarters, and some lawyers deserve criticism, but the efforts of counsel in this case are worthy of substantial recognition," including efforts first begun in *Cooper v. Aaron* in 1956.[94]

The Eighth Circuit panel later declined the parties' request that the most scathing comments in Judge Woods's final order be stricken from the record because the remarks were irrelevant to the subject of Woods's decision to step down from the case. "The district court is entitled to its own opinion," Arnold wrote. "Our job is to review judgments, not to rewrite the opinions of district courts."[95]

Henry Woods and Richard Arnold enjoyed a professional relationship and personal friendship for many years preceding their involvement in the Little Rock school cases. Arnold and Woods worked closely together in then-governor Dale Bumpers's successful campaign for the Senate in 1974. Later, the two appeared at a hearing together for confirmation to federal judgeships—Henry Woods to the district court and Richard Arnold to the Eighth Circuit Court of Appeals. Both were confirmed on the same day.[96] Of Woods's service as a federal judge, Arnold remarked:

He became a great judge, renowned for humanity as well as learning. He was decisive, which, after all, is an indispensable quality for a judge. Moreover, he had passion. It may surprise the reader to hear that judges ought to have passion. But judging is not a bloodless exercise. It involves real people in real causes, and the end product, at least the desired end product, is justice under the law. No goal is more deserving of passionate devotion, and no judge ever showed that devotion more clearly than Henry Woods.[97]

To soften the blow of each major reversal, Arnold referred to Woods as a "scholarly and distinguished judge,"[98] who had worked for the "cause of quality desegregated education in Pulaski County, Arkansas, with zeal and devotion."[99] Nonetheless, Judge Woods's stormy response indicates that their interactions in the Little Rock school cases were probably difficult for both men. There is no evidence, however, that the dispute disrupted their friendship.

"ABANDON HOPE ALL YE WHO ENTER HERE":
TOWARD UNITARY STATUS

Judge Henry Woods was not the only voice of frustration with the long-running Little Rock school cases. A newspaper editorial in 1994 suggested that "Little Rock's eternal school desegregation case should come with a little warning label pasted on the file folder—perhaps a quote from Dante to lend a little class: Abandon Hope All Ye Who Enter Here."[100]

Any hope that the settlement agreement would end the litigation was quickly abandoned when proposed modifications to the 1989 agreement were rejected by Judge Wright, Judge Woods's replacement. Wright believed the modifications would fundamentally alter the settlement that had been approved by the Eighth Circuit.[101] On appeal, attorneys asked the Eighth Circuit panel to apply a legal standard under which changes agreed to by the parties would be accepted more or less automatically. Once again, however, no party to the litigation defended the district court's order. At this point, the parties still maintained a remarkable agreement about desegregation measures.

In this opinion also written by Arnold, the panel vacated Judge Wright's orders and remanded the case. Noting that the "desegregation obligations undertaken in the 1989 plan are solemn and binding commitments," Arnold wrote that "even changes that go beyond the level of detail could be approved if the parties affirmatively establish good reasons" and the modifications were not disputed.[102] The court's 1990 opinion established a benchmark for future action in this case. Any changes, Arnold wrote, should relate to details and not to the substance of the plan. Changes going beyond mere details could also be approved if the parties established good reasons for them, but an asserted lack of funds in the school districts would not justify a reduction in the commitment to desegregation represented by the 1989 plan.

Although noting that generally the standard for court approval of proposed modifications to the consent decree was the same one the court had applied to the 1989 settlement plan — "the parties' agreement should be upheld if it is constitutional, workable, and fair to class members" — Arnold stated that the test now had a different procedural context. "Although changes can be made," Arnold wrote, "the District Court and we must take into account the potential for confusion, even chaos, that constant change creates. The parties and the public deserve a period of stability."[103]

There are many indications in this opinion, as well as other opinions following the 1989 settlement agreement, that Arnold preferred final resolution of the desegregation cases by the parties themselves. His opinions encouraged such a result by reversing district court orders that disregarded points agreed to by all of the parties. He also treated the 1989 settlement as an agreement in the nature of a binding contract. At one oral argument, Arnold also questioned why the attorneys were changing the settlement. "There can't be that every year or six months, the parties make substantive changes. I hope that you and your clients, when you make those decisions, weigh in the balance the costs, not just in money but in energy and irritability."[104]

At another hearing, this time to consider an injunction entered by Judge Wright prohibiting a teacher strike in Pulaski County as hindering desegregation efforts, Arnold said: "It seems to me that the job of the District Court is to enforce the settlement agreement, period."[105] Expressing frustration, Arnold criticized the PCSSD's petition to the district court to stop the strike: "If anything goes wrong, things that ordinary school districts would have to cope with, [the district] goes to the court, and the court fixes it, even though there is no specific provision in the consent decree that has anything to do with the subject."[106] To the extent possible, Arnold preferred a hands-off approach by the court.

Writing for the panel, Arnold reversed the district court's order to end the teacher strike, noting, "The fact that the case has been settled does not make the three school districts involved wards of the Court."[107] He added: "We understand the concerns that led the District Court to protect PCSSD and its school children from the effects of a teachers' strike. But we cannot agree that the settlement agreement, even by implication, took away the right to strike, assuming such a right exists under state law, nor can we find any other source of authority for the action the District Court took."[108]

Like Democratic appointee Judge Woods, Republican appointee Judge Wright also experienced reversal in an Arnold opinion; he was an equal-opportunity reverser. Reversals occurred primarily in disputes about interpretation of the settlement agreement. But Arnold and the panel affirmed Judge Wright in several key cases, including Judge Wright's rejection of a Voting Rights Act claim brought by black parents against the Little Rock school board in 1995.[109] Despite the rejection of the Voting Rights Act claim, as of 1996 three of seven Little Rock school board members were African American and one was its president. An African American also served as superintendent during this period.[110]

In 2001, the Little Rock School District petitioned the district court for unitary status, a move that would release it from further court supervision. The Joshua Intervenors, representing the class of black students in Pulaski County schools, opposed the petition. The Joshua Intervenors contended that the Little Rock School District had not met its goals under the settlement agreement in several areas and thus was not in "substantial compliance" with the consent decree.[111]

In his final written opinion in the Little Rock school cases, Arnold affirmed a grant of partial unitary status to the Little Rock School District by Judge William R. Wilson Jr., the third district judge to preside over the interdistrict litigation begun by the LRSD in 1982.[112] The district court determined that the Little Rock School District had substantially complied, in good faith, with its obligations under the settlement agreement. Some monitoring of student achievement would continue, hence the designation of "partial" unitary status. But the practical effect was an end to the interdistrict litigation. Affirming the district court judgment, Arnold wrote, "It goes without saying, but we say it anyway, that LRSD remains fully subject to the Constitution and all other applicable laws, and that these obligations are enforceable by appropriate legal action."[113]

This was one of the very few opinions in which Arnold did not agree with the Legal Defense Fund's position. Recounting the history of the case since 1982, which Arnold termed "complex to say the least,"[114] Arnold addressed the Joshua Intervenors' contention that racial disparities still existed in extracurricular activities, advanced placement courses, and student discipline. The Joshua Intervenors contended that the LRSD did not act in good faith and alleged that Central High School was still functionally segregated, although the building itself had been integrated.[115]

Arnold found no clear error in any of the district court's findings of fact. The Intervenors argued, for example, that discrimination occurred in extracurricular activities because many of those activities did not have a proportionate share of African American participants. Rejecting this contention, Arnold cited the parties' prior agreed-to plan, in which "LRSD undertook to promote the participation of African-American students and to eliminate barriers to participation," and stated that "this provision does not make LRSD an insurer."[116] Arnold firmly enforced the agreement by its own terms, as a matter of contract interpretation, and not by reference to an external constitutional standard. The agreement of the parties may have broken down, but according to Arnold, the original settlement proposal determined the scope of relief to which the Intervenors were entitled.

RESEGREGATION?

With substantial court supervision of the Little Rock schools nearing an end, it is likely that few will agree on what the litigation accomplished or on the significance of Arnold's role. Considering only numeric ratios, Little Rock schools have experienced resegregation. The Little Rock School District has seen a complete reversal in its student makeup since 1957, with African Americans representing the majority of students in the school district today. This phenomenon is consistent with developments in many other urban school districts. Some scholars attribute this general tendency to the United States Supreme Court's retreat from *Brown*: "Resegregation is the unmistakable pattern over the last fifteen years. This is a consequence of the Supreme Court relaxing standards of judicial oversight, and federal courts dissolving more desegregation plans."[117] They note that "between 1990 and 2000 public school segregation in the South *increased* even though residential segregation decreased during the same period."[118] Other scholars have also attributed to the Supreme Court the failure to achieve greater pupil mixing and the recent increases in racial isolation.[119]

However one views the Supreme Court's decisions in school desegregation, Arnold's opinions seem to fit squarely within them and in some respects even anticipated their direction. For example, the 1990 decision rejecting Judge Woods's modifications to the proposed settlement presaged the Supreme Court's 1992 decision in *Freeman v. Pitts*.[120] In *Freeman*, the Supreme Court indicated that so long as any racial imbalance was a function of unintentional geographic segregation, the federal courts had no role in trying to fashion remedies through court orders. The Court's specific mandate was to return schools to the control of "local authorities," allowing easier findings of unitary status so long as good-faith integration efforts had been made.[121] Arnold was not troubled by the maintenance of racially identifiable schools in the Little Rock School District under the parties' proposed settlement, whereas Judge Woods had found these provisions unacceptable from a constitutional standpoint.[122]

Further, in the 1991 decision of *Board of Education of Oklahoma City Public Schools v. Dowell*, the Supreme Court indicated that court-ordered plans were "not intended to operate in perpetuity," allowing districts to be released from desegregation once obligations were fulfilled.[123] Student achievement, not student ratios, became the focus of the Little Rock School District's efforts toward desegregation.[124] Prior to *Dowell*, Arnold had already ensured that this changed goal would be pursued in Little Rock by reversing district court orders that he believed interfered with the parties' agreed-upon aims. There is no doubt that under many measures, the Legal Defense Fund's fifty-year effort in the federal courts has had a significant impact in the Little Rock schools. Richard Arnold's role in the last decades of this litigation was also highly significant.

PUBLIC LAW LITIGATION IN ARNOLD'S COURT

District of Columbia Circuit Judge David Tatel, in his 2004 Madison Lecture at New York University, spoke about judicial methodology in the context of school desegregation.[125] To explore the current debate about judicial "activism," Tatel identified methodological constraints that distinguish judging from policy making. Among the questions to include:

Is the decision consistent with principles of stare decisis—that is, does the decision follow precedent, or, if not, does it either explain why otherwise controlling case law does not apply or forthrightly overrule that case law on principled grounds? Is the decision faithful to constitutional and statutory text and to the intent of the drafters? Does it appropriately defer to the policy judgments of Congress and administrative agencies? Does it apply the proper standard of review to lower-court fact findings? Are the issues it resolves generally limited to those raised by the parties? Does it avoid unnecessary dictum? And finally, are its results openly and rationally explained?[126]

Arnold's votes and opinions in the Little Rock school cases, in some respects, seem profoundly conservative. Arnold gave the parties much latitude to determine the shape of desegregation efforts in Little Rock. He also believed court-ordered school district consolidation was not appropriate for this case. Arnold has been characterized as more moderate than liberal, compared to the other Carter appointee to the Eighth Circuit, Theodore McMillian, and also to Johnson appointees Gerald Heaney and Donald Lay.[127]

In 1982, when Arnold first joined the panel hearing appeals from the Little Rock school desegregation cases, he was already known as a strong proponent of individual civil liberties. As a district judge, Arnold had ordered the integration of the Arkansas National Guard.[128] Arnold reluctantly imposed a strict hiring quota (the only time he ever imposed a racial quota), which was a remedy that was subsequently affirmed by the Eighth Circuit.[129] In response to an equal protection claim brought by a fourteen-year-old basketball player, he also ordered the Arkansas Activities Association (the governing body for public and private school athletics) to permit girls to play full-court basketball.[130]

But in 1982, Arnold's views of federal court involvement in desegregation were untested. His personal history was important. Earlier in his life he had taken many public positions on desegregation-related issues. Arnold was a freshman at Yale when *Brown I* was handed down.[131] He was opposed to it as a constitutional matter. Arnold finished his studies at Yale first in his class, which undoubtedly gave his views some weight with his fellow students. The events in Little Rock subsequent to *Brown* seem to have caused some evolution in his views.

Once on the bench, Arnold's attitude toward federal court oversight of desegregation evinced an independent mind. Arnold's particular view of the appropriate supervisory role of the courts explains many aspects of his decisions. Except in one respect, Arnold's view was very much in line with the public law litigation model described earlier by Abram Chayes and others.[132] But the one exception—the degree of responsibility given to the parties, rather than more direct district court supervision—is important, and it shows Judge Arnold's independent thinking about institutional reform litigation in the federal courts. He brought to the table more than mere political preferences for outcomes.

Arnold cited one of Chayes's articles on public law litigation in his 1990 opinion requiring the district court to accept the terms of the settlement as negotiated by the parties.[133] Chayes's framework for "public law litigation" expressed his concern to accommodate the reality of judicial power to the theory of representative government, especially in civil rights cases.[134] Writing in 1976, Chayes stated, "We are witnessing the emergence of a new model of civil litigation and, I believe, our traditional conception of adjudication and the assumptions upon which it is based provide an increasingly unhelpful, indeed misleading framework for assessing either the workability or the legitimacy of the roles of judge and court within this model."[135] Chayes noted that this new model in the federal courts meant fact finding was principally concerned with "legislative" rather than "adjudicative" facts: "The whole process begins to look like the traditional description of legislation. Indeed, if, as is often the case, the decree sets up an affirmative regime governing the activities in controversy for the indefinite future and having binding force for persons within its ambit, then it is not very much of a stretch to see it as, pro tanto, a legislative act."[136]

Chayes also articulated a preference for decrees formulated through good-faith bargaining by the opposing parties and enforced by the court, and this point was perhaps the most influential for Arnold. Chayes noted that the decree process forces the courts to rely on the parties' negotiations to minimize the need for judicial resolution of remedial issues. Other reasons supported resolution by the parties as well: "The interest in a decree that will be voluntarily obeyed can be promoted by enforcing a regime of good faith bargaining among the parties."[137] Arnold echoed this sentiment when he wrote: "As a practical matter, a remedy that everyone agrees to is a lot more likely to succeed than one to which the defendants must be dragged kicking and screaming."[138]

In a regime that relies upon parties' agreement with respect to remedies for a constitutional violation, adequacy of the representation is of primary importance. Although the "negotiating process ought to minimize the need for judicial resolution of remedial issues," Chayes wrote, federal courts must scrutinize the settlement to ensure that the interests of absentees are adequately accommodated.[139] Arnold strongly favored settlement of the Little Rock school cases, and many of his opinions were intended to make settlement an easier process. He probably believed agreement would be a better resolution than a court-imposed decree. But the extent to which enforcement of good-faith bargaining was a priority for Arnold, as Chayes argued was necessary, is unclear. At no point did Arnold address the adequacy of representation for the class of black plaintiffs, nor did he point to instances in which fairness of the settlement for this class had been examined by the district court.

This is potentially important because the public law litigation model relies to a great extent on individual bargaining for constitutional remedies.[140] Institutional remedies for an entire class require some degree of assurance that all "class" interests are adequately represented. Arnold may have simply deferred to the district court on the issue of adequacy of representation in order to determine fairness of the settlement to the entire class. The district court conducted a fairness hearing for the settlement on May 7, 1989.[141] Notice of the settlement terms was provided to the class, along with an opportunity for objection. Apparently no objections emerged—the objection hearing was later canceled.[142] Although it is not entirely clear what happened here, the fairness hearing may have been relatively encompassing, even if it did not bring out disagreement among the class about the best course to pursue for desegregation remedies.

For Arnold to interject on the terms of the settlement would be equivalent to stating that the NAACP Legal Defense Fund and the class represented by the Joshua Intervenors did not know what was in their best interest, something he was unwilling to do. Many of the appeals from district court orders included the Joshua Intervenors in opposition to the district court's rulings. The Legal Defense Fund was a genuine participant in a negotiated resolution that brought about the best result possible under the circumstances, Arnold believed.

Nonetheless, the degree of compromise by any minority group raises questions about the adequacy of the remedy. Scholars have critiqued the reliance on settlement in institutional reform cases on the ground that no true bargaining power exists for discrete and insular minorities, particularly if these parties believe a settlement is the only path to a remedy. Is the role of the district court merely one of "peace maker," or to protect an insular minority?[143]

Arnold seems to have taken the preference for party control of the remedial order even further than would Chayes. Such a view is consistent with a public address Arnold later gave in which he discussed settlement in constitutional litigation.[144] In this address, Arnold specifically mentioned an article by Owen Fiss, "Against Settlement," published in the *Yale Law Journal* in 1984.[145] In this article, Fiss criticized the "drive for settlement" in class actions, particularly in institutional reform cases.[146] Like Abe Chayes, Owen Fiss was a friend whom Arnold greatly admired.[147] Arnold said: "I want you to know, I am neither against settlement, nor do I think that people should be coerced into settling their cases—and some lawyers feel that they are being coerced."[148] Arnold was at least sensitive to the issue, even if he largely rejected Fiss's cautions in his enforcement of the settlement of the Little Rock school litigation.

Arnold's pragmatism was also informed by his deference to legislative determinations in the democratic process. As Chayes and others noted, all public law litigation to some degree reflects legislative failure. But for Arnold, that was of itself an insufficient reason for the federal court to intervene. He sometimes favored democratic responsibility over judicial pronouncements, reflecting a great respect for the democratic process.

As an example, Arnold wrote of the court's reversal of Judge Henry Woods on the consolidation issue:

> Some have characterized our decision as holding that consolidation was forbidden. This is a misunderstanding of the nature of this lawsuit. Consolidation may be, in terms of educational quality and racial fairness, a good thing. It is unquestionably permissible, given the proper circumstances, under state law. And the General Assembly, if it saw fit, could require consolidation, or relax the state-law requirements for achieving it. Nothing we have said or held is inconsistent with these propositions. We have held only that the Constitution does not compel consolidation. What the parties might choose to do of their own volition is, in general, their own business.[149]

In Arnold's years on the Eighth Circuit, he heard twenty-eight appeals from the Little Rock school desegregation cases. Unlike the prominent national stage in 1957, however, these cases never again centered specifically on Central High School. Arnold, it seems, was not even sure where in Little Rock the famous high school was located. On the occasion of a visit to Little Rock by Justice Sandra Day O'Connor, Arnold asked if there was anything in Little Rock she would like to see before he drove her back to the airport. "Yes," she said, "I would like to see Little Rock Central High School." Central High School had become a nationally known battleground for school desegregation in 1957. Arnold readily complied with O'Connor's request, but during the drive he had to call his secretary for directions, a story Justice O'Connor later recounted with some amusement.[150]

As an appellate judge on the Eighth Circuit, Richard Arnold did not take a deferential approach to district court orders in the Little Rock school desegregation cases. He did, however, defer to the views of the class represented by the NAACP Legal Defense Fund with respect to what constitutional remedies were appropriate. One could characterize the Eighth Circuit's role as profoundly conservative in two respects, and Arnold was key to both. He was a leader in the formulation of the rulings even for those opinions he did not personally author. These cases illustrate Arnold's resolution of the tension between his own ideas of federalism and judicial restraint, and a more activist approach associated with his friend and mentor, William Brennan.

Chapter Twelve

"The Intensely Practical Nature
of the Political Process"

Richard Arnold's political experiences before he became a judge served him especially well in two endeavors. The first was his leading role in election law cases, especially in application of the Voting Rights Act of 1965 in Arkansas. In one of those cases, Arnold's decision became an important national precedent, at least for a time, and changed the face of Arkansas politics. The case required Arnold to examine "the intensely practical nature of the political process," as he termed it—a political process that he had experience with firsthand as an unsuccessful candidate for Congress.[1] It was part of the background of knowledge he brought to the task of judging.

The second area in which Arnold's political knowledge was called into play was his work as chairman of the budget committee for the Judicial Conference. He was appointed to this position by Chief Justice William Rehnquist in recognition of his diplomatic skills and his familiarity with the Senate, stemming from his years as a legislative aide for Senator Dale Bumpers. For nearly a decade Arnold presented the federal judiciary's annual budget requests to Congress. Rehnquist's appointment of Arnold was especially meaningful because the chief justice for years was a firm advocate of more resources for the judiciary, and Rehnquist lauded Arnold for his "exemplary service for the judiciary."[2] It was in this work, as a representative of the federal judiciary before Congress, that Arnold believed he made his most important contributions as a judge.[3]

Arnold, then, was both a judge of the political process in election cases and a participant in the political process as a leading spokesman for the judicial branch in Congress. Arnold's pragmatic understanding of political realities informed his work in both instances.

JEFFERS v. CLINTON:
A "TRULY EXTRAORDINARY VOTING RIGHTS OPINION"[4]

As a judge, Richard Arnold was difficult to classify along "liberal" and "conservative" lines. One case in particular, though, placed Arnold squarely in the liberal tradition. Acclaimed as a "landmark" opinion,[5] *Jeffers v. Clinton* (then-governor Bill Clinton was a named defendant) was the most notable and far-reaching of all the election law cases Arnold decided. Arnold's opinion in this case was affirmed unanimously by the United States Supreme Court. But as the Supreme Court's membership changed over the ensuing years, so did its view of cases like *Jeffers*. As a bold step of affirmative action for black voters, *Jeffers*, was in some ways the first and last of its kind.

In 1989, a group of seventeen black plaintiffs challenged Arkansas's 1981 apportionment plan for elections to the state legislature. At issue was a large section of the state's electoral map. The plaintiffs claimed that the black population of the state, then around 16 percent of the total population, was sufficiently large to make possible the creation of a number of compact, contiguous legislative districts having a black voting-age majority. Instead, with very few exceptions, the plan had been drawn in such a way to dilute black voting strength.

At the time the suit was brought, there were only six black legislators out of a total of one hundred and thirty-five (five black members of the state house of representatives, and one black member of the state senate). None of the black legislators was from the Delta, the region along the Mississippi River where the largest number of African Americans lived. East Arkansas elected its first black legislator in 1988, only after a three-judge federal court in a separate case, again with Arnold writing the opinion, ordered the creation of an all-black district within what had been a single-member white-majority district.[6]

The *Jeffers* case was more than an attack on legislative district boundaries. It also claimed that the state had been guilty of widespread, continuous, and intentional racial discrimination in elections, a violation not only of the Voting Rights Act but also of the Fifteenth Amendment. As a consequence, the plaintiffs claimed, Arkansas should be subjected to the remedy of "preclearance," a special procedure created by the Voting Rights Act of 1965. "Preclearance" means that a state may not change any electoral practice, law, or procedure without the permission either of the attorney general of the United States or of a special three-judge court.

The Voting Rights Act of 1965, a watershed in American history, outlawed numerous practices that had prevented the equal exercise of voting rights for African Americans, including poll taxes and literacy tests. Congress designated a number of states, mostly in the South, for preclearance. The purpose was to bypass a potentially obstructionist judiciary and the case-by-case litigation approach that would inevitably take place if southern governments came up with "an unending series of inventive new ways to deny blacks the vote."[7] As one legal scholar put it, the preclearance regime of the Voting Rights Act replaced adjudication with "an administrative regime designed to deter as well as to remedy denials of the right to vote."[8] When a state or local government must justify its changes, "and bear the burden of justifying those changes, it is likely to think hard" before doing so.[9]

Arkansas was *not* one of the states originally designated for "preclearance." Its record of voting rights for African Americans, while by no means exemplary, was at least judged by Congress not to require oversight by the United States attorney general for changes in its voting laws. Indeed, within the Eighth Circuit as a whole, only one section of South Dakota fell under the preclearance provisions of the 1965 Voting Rights Act.

Eventually, Arnold would require Arkansas to be subjected to the remedy of "preclearance," but only in a limited way.[10] Any changes to laws concerning majority vote requirements in general elections (but not in primaries), statewide or local, would be subject to approval by the court or the Department of Justice. Although this part of the case was significant in that it was the first (and still the only) time an entire state was placed under preclearance by federal court order, it was especially significant for Arkansas, as one editorial writer put it, because "Arkansas for the first time joins the 16 states that have been found guilty of discrimination and that for 25 years have had their elections supervised by the federal government."[11]

The most significant effect of the *Jeffers* litigation, however, would be Arnold's ruling that the state must redraw its electoral districts. *Jeffers* was a "vote dilution" case. The gist of the claim was that even if the district lines had been drawn with no intent to dilute black voting power, the result was still a violation of the Voting Rights Act and should be remedied by a federal court. The Board of Apportionment could have drawn up to sixteen majority-minority legislative districts, but it did not, in effect restricting the number of black candidates that could be elected. This, the plaintiffs argued, was a violation of their right to an equal vote.

Since *Baker v. Carr* was decided in 1964, citizens could challenge the apportionment of voting districts on the "one man, one vote" principle. Legislative districts, whether for state or federal elections, must serve roughly equal populations. As populations change, states must reapportion, and like Arkansas, they typically do so every ten years based on US census figures. But no case before *Jeffers* addressed the specific claim that states *must* draw majority-black single-member districts when they can readily do so, as a requirement of the Voting Rights Act.

For states like Arkansas, the most important section of the 1965 act was the following provision, in relevant part:

> No voting qualification or prerequisite to voting or standard, practice, or procedure shall be imposed or applied by any State or political subdivision in a manner which results in a denial or abridgement of the right of any citizen of the United States to vote on account of race or color.[12]

Congress enacted an important amendment to this section in 1982. The amendment explicitly prohibited "vote dilution" of minorities as a wrong. It also provided that the wrong need not be proved by an intent to discriminate but could be proved through its "effects." Vote dilution, according to an earlier Supreme Court decision, occurred when minorities "had less opportunity than did other residents in a district to participate in the political processes and to elect legislators of their choice."[13]

Four years later, the Supreme Court handed down its first interpretation of the amended Voting Rights Act in *Thornburg v. Gingles*.[14] *Thornburg* required, Arnold believed, "a rather uncompromising structure for the application of the law in vote-dilution cases."[15] Under *Thornburg*, a showing that minority voters have less opportunity to elect candidates of their choice would suffice to establish their claim: "The essence of a § 2 claim [under the Voting Rights Act] is that a certain electoral law, practice, or structure interacts with social and historical conditions to cause an inequality in the opportunities enjoyed by the black and white voters to elect their preferred representatives."[16]

What followed were hundreds of vote dilution suits throughout the nation.[17] But *Thornburg* involved vote dilution in multimember districts; not the single-member districts at issue in *Jeffers*. An open question was whether a state had denied the right to vote on account of race by its failure to create majority-black single-member districts. The question for Arnold was what the amended Voting Rights Act now meant in this context. Was it intended to increase minority representation?

Jeffers v. Clinton was heard by a special district court of three judges, as provided by the Voting Rights Act. Two federal district judges from Arkansas, G. Thomas Eisele and George Howard, were designated for the case along with Richard Arnold, the sole member from the Eighth Circuit.

Judge Eisele joined Arnold and Howard as a last-minute substitution for Federal District Judge Stephen Reasoner. Surprisingly, two weeks before the trial was set to begin, Reasoner recused himself from hearing the *Jeffers* case because one of his law clerks was married to a state senator whose district potentially would be affected if district lines were redrawn.

Reasoner told Arnold and Howard that he should have recognized the issue earlier. He hoped that Chief Judge Donald Lay could appoint someone "to replace me in time to salvage the scheduled hearing."[18] Arnold replied, "I am not certain that a similar circumstance would cause me to disqualify myself, but it's your decision, and I understand your reasons. If it is any comfort, the same late realization of grounds for disqualification has happened to me a couple of times."[19]

Within a few days, Lay appointed Eisele to replace Reasoner. Eisele moved with alacrity to get up to speed on the case. Eisele had a full trial calendar in the weeks leading up to the trial, but he, Howard, and Arnold met for preliminary discussions of how to handle the voting rights case during breaks in Eisele's trial schedule.[20]

The trial took twelve days in early October 1989. The first hurdle for the plaintiffs was the problem of delay. The apportionment plan they challenged was drawn in 1981. It would be redrawn again after only one more election, in line with the 1990 census. The plaintiffs had waited eight years before challenging the 1981 plan, and if they were successful, the state would have to undertake a massive redrawing of legislative districts in a very short time and for only one election. The state argued that the case should be dismissed on this ground of unreasonable delay; the plaintiffs could bring a new challenge, if necessary, after the next census. The plaintiffs contended that the suit could not be brought before the 1986 amendment to the Voting Rights Act, and it took several years to prepare after that.

Arnold thought it was a close question, but as "essentially one of judgment and degree," Arnold sided firmly with the plaintiffs:

> In part, the expense and disruption that will undeniably occur are nothing but a consequence of the wrong that has been done. To the extent that electoral confusion and disruption exceed what they would have been if the case had been filed earlier, we think that fairness and equal opportunity in voting are worth it. We will not say to these plaintiffs, "Wait for another census. The time is not yet ripe." They have heard these words too many times in the past.[21]

Arnold then held that the state's failure to create more majority-black districts was a violation of the Voting Rights Act. Even though the 1981 plan included five black-majority districts, Arnold said it did not go far enough. The test was not whether the discrimination was intentional but whether it had the effect of denying blacks equal political opportunity. Arnold embraced the theory that minority voters are most effectively represented when they can actually elect candidates of their choice.

The key for Arnold was the stark fact that minorities were vastly underrepresented in public office. No black legislator had been elected from a majority-white district in the twentieth century. "For the foreseeable future," Arnold wrote, "the present location of legislative district lines will make it very difficult to elect more than six black legislators, out of a total in both houses of 135 members." The black population, Arnold noted, was 16 percent of the Arkansas population. "In this situation, black citizens have less opportunity than other members of the electorate to elect representatives of their choice."[22]

Arnold's lengthy opinion cataloged some of this history. With the exception of Reconstruction, no black candidate was elected to the Arkansas General Assembly until 1972, seven years after passage of the Voting Rights Act.

No black candidate had won statewide or countywide office since Reconstruction. There had also been instances of racially charged advertising during elections and intimidation and harassment of black voters and candidates.

It was also significant for Arnold that blacks in the region suffered disproportionately from poverty. He recognized the "tremendous amount of white poverty, especially in the Delta," but poverty among blacks was "more nearly the rule than the exception."[23] This fact, a result of past discrimination, made it that much more difficult for blacks as a group to exercise proportionate political power. The extent to which a racial group had suffered the effects of discrimination in employment, education, and health, in turn, hampered their ability to participate in the political process.

A final factor for Arnold was the existence of racially polarized voting, a relevant factor identified in *Thornburg*. In the region in question, in fact, Arnold concluded that "the white voting majority is powerful enough, and consistent enough, to defeat black voters' preferences for black candidates almost without exception." Arnold deplored the racial polarization, but recognized its reality: "The fact is that there is a strong tendency for white voters to vote for white candidates when there is a black candidate in the race. Black voters behave in exactly the same fashion. This is not a particularly admirable commentary on the voting behavior of either race, but it is a fact in present-day Arkansas politics, and there is no reason to suppose that it will change substantially in the near future.[24]

Arnold ordered the state board of apportionment, consisting of then-governor Bill Clinton, the secretary of state, and the attorney general, to redraw the electoral map in time for the 1990 elections. Districts with a 60 percent black voting-age majority should be created if possible. Past discrimination—social, economic, and legal—had placed black voters at such a disadvantage that giving them a simple majority, Arnold believed, was not sufficient to create a fair chance as a practical matter. Arnold required no set number of new majority-black districts, but he emphasized that the state could have created as many as sixteen after the 1980 census.

Arnold recognized that his decision was precedent setting because none of the Supreme Court's prior decisions could automatically be applied to the single-member context. Nonetheless, Arnold wrote, "the basic principle is the same. If lines are drawn that limit the number of majority-black single-member districts, and reasonably compact and contiguous majority-black districts could have been drawn, and if racial cohesiveness in voting is so great that, as a practical matter, black voters' preferences for black candidates are frustrated by this system of apportionment," then a claim under the Voting Rights Act is established.[25] Arnold would later characterize his action in *Jeffers* as one of affirmative action for black political rights.[26]

Arkansas appealed the ruling to the United States Supreme Court, arguing that Arnold had incorrectly interpreted the Voting Rights Act. The Department of Justice took the position that the *Jeffers* opinion should be summarily affirmed. It was the first ruling of its kind to reach the Court. Civil rights lawyers had feared that the Supreme Court might use the case to retreat from the 1986 ruling.[27] Instead, the Supreme Court by a unanimous decision summarily affirmed, without a written opinion. A lawyer for the NAACP Legal Defense and Educational Fund applauded the Supreme Court's action for its likely effect on voting district apportionment in the following year, saying it sent "a strong message to state and local governments that their 1991 redistricting plans must not shortchange African Americans and other minorities."[28] As the *New York Times* noted, the Supreme Court's ruling in *Jeffers v. Clinton* had force as a precedent despite the absence of a formal opinion.[29]

Arnold's opinion made national headlines because of its far-reaching implications.[30] The remedy meant creating an electoral system that ensured that black voters could elect representatives in numbers more nearly resembling their percentage of the population. An editorial in the *Arkansas Democrat* applauded the ruling as "long overdue" and as one that "sent a shiver through some white legislators from these areas."[31]

The state board of apportionment then carried out the court's order. The board used the drawings devised by the plaintiffs as a start for redrawing district boundaries, and it held public hearings in the Delta region before submitting its reapportionment plan to the court.[32] Arnold and Howard rejected two districts as having insufficient black voting-age majorities, even though the state had proposed majorities of 56 and 58 percent.[33] Ultimately, the court approved twelve new majority-minority House districts and three for the Senate in those areas of the state with substantial black populations, adding only slight modifications to the plan submitted by the state. Once again, Arnold's opinion was affirmed by the Supreme Court.[34]

JUDGE EISELE'S DISSENTS: A DIFFERENCE OF IDEOLOGY

The court's decision in *Jeffers*, however, was not unanimous. Judge Howard agreed with Arnold on all points, but Judge Eisele wrote a lengthy dissent, one of several that he would write in the case. As an initial matter, Eisele believed the plaintiffs had waited too long to challenge the 1981 apportionment, and he would have dismissed the case on that ground.

But the most significant difference with Arnold was the decision to order the creation of majority-black voting districts. Eisele wrote a passionate 158-page dissent, warning that the *Jeffers* decision would lead toward "a political structure that can only be described as 'separate but equal.'"[35] Eisele believed that the court's interpretation of the Voting Rights Act would change "the political landscape of America in fundamental ways without legislative mandate, redefining the nature of our democratic form of government, contrary, I believe, to the Constitution."[36]

The dissent is a fascinating discourse not only on the Voting Rights Act but also on the American political system and how best to obtain equality for racial minorities. "In one sense," Eisele wrote, "majoritarian democracy always discriminates against political minorities," whether they are racial or religious minorities, or Republicans in an overwhelming Democratic county.[37] It could not be the case, Eisele believed, that super majorities for black voters would be required following every census, everywhere in the United States, to guarantee that minorities would be elected. So long as there were no other obstacles in the way, the failure of blacks to elect candidates of their choice is a function of the democratic process of majority rule. Eisele wrote his dissent in detail, he said, "not only to explain the law as I understand it but also to help open up the issues to legal, scholarly, popular and political debate, keeping in mind, as we must, that we are here dealing with the heart and soul of democratic government."[38]

Arkansas Gazette editorial writer Robert McCord agreed with Eisele. He, like Eisele, believed that Arnold's opinion "stretched the Voting Rights Act out of shape." The intent to have more minority representation in the legislature was "laudable" but would result in an affirmative action program for legislative bodies — supervised by the courts — moving the country toward a proportional representation system. "The people who wrote the Constitution knew that perfect equality was not achievable, but they adopted the republican form of government in order to avoid something worse, such as the system in India that sets aside seats in parliament for members of social castes."[39]

McCord also noted that Eisele was a Republican; Arnold and Howard were Democrats. But any charge of racism against Eisele, McCord wrote, would be from those "with short memories." Eisele had been the architect of Winthrop Rockefeller's successful campaign to become Arkansas's first Republican governor since Reconstruction, at a time when the Republicans were the most racially progressive party in the state. Like Arnold, Eisele was a graduate of Harvard Law School and was a courageous and uncommonly able federal district court judge.

Eisele's disagreement did not end there. A few months later, Arnold issued a third opinion in the *Jeffers* case, this time ordering a limited remedy of "preclearance" for some Arkansas voting laws. The most important part was Arnold's decision to retain jurisdiction over the 1991 reapportionment, to permit the *Jeffers* plaintiffs to challenge the state's new district lines without the need to file a new lawsuit. The court clearance of the 1991 apportionment was one of the key goals of the plaintiffs, according to their attorney.[40]

Eisele again disagreed, writing:

> While throughout the world the people of nation after nation are rejecting the idea of minority rule, we today find a United States district court holding that the State of Arkansas may be punished for its perceived motive in adopting laws which give expression to that most basic of democratic principles: majority rule.
>
> As I see it, my brothers, in their construction and application of the law and the Constitution, are unconsciously leaning over backward in their sincere effort to help those believed to be the victims of racial discrimination. And when one leans over backward, one is likely to fall, and, when one falls, others in the way will likely be hurt. That is what I see happening here.[41]

Eisele believed assisting minority groups in this way violated the voting rights of whites. The ideological difference with Arnold was stark. Eisele did not say so, but he probably viewed Arnold's decision as the "political" one.

Several years later, when Eisele wrote to then-president Bill Clinton to endorse Arnold's nomination to the Supreme Court, he recalled the *Jeffers* case: "You are acutely aware that Richard and I have had our disagreements over the law—some *big* disagreements, such as in the *Jeffers* proceedings in which you were a party. But my experience in dealing with him on those occasions has only reinforced my admiration and respect for him as a judge. (I have told him that everyone is entitled to be wrong on occasion. He graciously returned the sentiment.)"[42]

Arnold and Eisele had "a great personal relationship," Eisele said, despite their disagreements in *Jeffers*. "He was a charming guy, a man of grace, and one who really was concerned about the underdog, and felt that the judicial process ought to keep an eye open to the inequalities that exist in our society. I think he's right, but sometimes we get too short sighted, in terms of the realities to those."[43]

Despite Eisele's many strident dissents in the various *Jeffers* proceedings, Arnold was reversed only once, on a question of the appropriate attorneys' fees the state must pay the plaintiffs. Over Eisele's view that the fee was excessive, Arnold and Howard approved an award of just over one million dollars in 1993. That decision was vacated by the Eighth Circuit, in light of a Supreme Court decision changing the law on that issue two months after the original award.[44] On remand, Arnold reduced the award of attorneys' fees by three hundred thousand dollars.[45]

Ultimately, however, Eisele was right about the future direction of the Supreme Court in this area. Although *Jeffers* had been summarily affirmed by the Supreme Court, and in the next few years would be cited in more than seventy-five other cases around the country, beginning in 1993 the Supreme Court decided a series of cases that cast doubt on the constitutional validity of state districting plans drawn with race as a predominant factor, even if the intention was to benefit a racial minority. In *Shaw v. Reno*, for example, Justice Sandra Day O'Connor, writing for the majority, believed where district lines were drawn solely on account of race, even if intended to help minorities gain representation, the result was unconstitutional.[46] More recently, in *Easley v. Cromartie*, Justice Breyer wrote, "The Court has specified that those who claim that a legislature has improperly used race as a criterion, in order, for example, to create a majority-minority district, must show at a minimum that the legislature subordinated traditional race-neutral districting principles to racial considerations." If race was "the predominant motivating factor" in drawing district boundaries, that act could be challenged in federal court.[47] Congress presumably ratified the Supreme Court's interpretations of the Voting Rights Act when it reauthorized the 1965 act, without significant change, in 2006.

Thus, even a few years later, Arnold's decision in *Jeffers*, requiring the state to draw super-majority districts for minority voters, would likely have been reversed by the Supreme Court. But in the meantime, the 1990 election made history in Arkansas politics. The Delta region elected its first black state senator and a total of ten black state representatives. By the mid-1990s, black representation in the Arkansas General Assembly had increased markedly, tripling the number of blacks in the Senate and more than doubling the number in the House.[48]

As Representative Ben McGee, an African American from Marion, Arkansas, said following the 1990 elections, "The more the Legislature resembles the overall population of our state, the better off we are. That's the simple fact. The result of these lawsuits is that the Legislature has become more like Arkansas — some black, some white; some richer, some poorer. You get a truer picture of the diversity of our state, and a stronger realization that our diversity is also our strength."[49] McGee was elected following Arnold's ruling in another voting rights case that created single-member districts from one multimember district. McGee was elected from one of those districts in 1988, defeating a longtime incumbent who had twice defeated McGee in the old multimember district.[50]

After *Shaw v. Reno* was handed down in 1993, P. A. "Les" Hollingsworth, the lead lawyer for the black voters in the *Jeffers* case, said that the districts redrawn by the state's board of apportionment would now be "subject to challenge." But he defied any criticism of the *Jeffers* decision, reportedly saying in an interview: "To you all, we're all just a bunch of niggers who don't deserve to have the representation that we choose. My ancestors were bought and sold and brought here by force. They weren't allowed the benefits of all these noble constitutional principles you're talking about."[51]

The original lawsuit itself remained in Arnold's court for five years, through a change in the named defendant from Governor Bill Clinton to Jim Guy Tucker, who replaced Clinton after his successful presidential campaign. In the last ruling in the case, the court upheld Arkansas's 1991 redistricting plan against the challenge that it failed to create a sufficient number of majority-black districts. Writing for the court, Arnold recognized that *Shaw v. Reno* had undercut the rationale he had used in ordering the creation of super-majority districts in 1990.[52] *Shaw* held that plaintiffs stated a cognizable claim when they challenged, on equal-protection grounds, North Carolina congressional redistricting "so extremely irregular on its face that it rationally can be viewed only as an effort to segregate the races for purposes of voting, without regard for traditional districting principles and without sufficiently compelling justification." *Shaw* stated that redistricting legislation that is "so bizarre" that it is "unexplainable on grounds other than race," is subject to strict scrutiny under the equal protection clause.[53]

Although the state had created four majority-black House districts and one majority-black Senate district in the Delta region, the plaintiffs argued that it should have created one more of each. Rejecting this claim, Arnold wrote that in essence the plaintiffs' proposals for more super-majority districts would violate the same voting rights principles that the original case accused whites of violating. This time, Eisele largely agreed with Arnold. He wrote, "The plaintiffs are the ones who are insisting on a race-conscious gerrymander aimed at creating additional black majority districts. Clearly, if the board had drawn district lines as suggested by the plaintiffs, then the board's decision could have been challenged on equal protection grounds."[54] The state's plan retained most of the super-majority districts in the Delta it had put in place in 1990. In the 1991 elections a total of twelve blacks were elected to the Arkansas General Assembly, compared to only four in 1980.[55] Arnold's court-ordered redrawing of legislative districts tripled black representation in the state.

Jeffers was far from the only momentous decision on Arnold's plate at that time. The exhibits, trial record, and briefs in *Jeffers* alone took up a table and two file carts in Arnold's chambers. Next to it, though, were equally voluminous records in the Little Rock school desegregation case, awaiting decision in various matters on appeal. The Barry Lee Fairchild death penalty case was also back on appeal—a momentous one for Fairchild, who would soon face execution.

These cases were high profile, but they made up only a fraction of the relentless number of cases awaiting decision. Arnold's share of the 2,681 cases filed in the Eighth Circuit in 1990 meant that by the end of that year he would write 113 opinions and direct the entry of an additional 78 administrative orders.[56]

Arnold wrote the opinions in *Jeffers* himself, as he would for the Barry Lee Fairchild death penalty case and the various appeals concerning school desegregation in Little Rock. With reluctance, Arnold had to rely on law clerks and staff attorneys for the more routine matters. The simplest cases, as well as the most difficult, Arnold drafted himself because he could write them much faster than any of the clerks. Cases in between would be divided for first draft purposes among his law clerks. Few clerk drafts survived serious rewriting by Arnold. As Arnold would say to his staff, "The clerks may draft a lot of the opinions, but I write all of them." Opinions with initial drafts by law clerks were, Arnold said, "50 percent yours and 100 percent mine."[57] In *Jeffers*, a law clerk assisted with footnotes and fact checking, but Arnold mastered the facts of the case and wrote the opinions accordingly.

Arnold's law clerks, in fact, usually learned early of their limited value in comparison with their boss's capabilities. In the first court week for a brand new crew of law clerks, the three clerks attended a morning session of oral argument at the courthouse in St. Louis. As Price Marshall described,

> We noticed the Judge was staring at us. We weren't doing anything, and we didn't know why he kept staring at us. Finally he beckoned one of us to the bench and handed me a note. Am I supposed to go back to chambers to write an order holding this lawyer in contempt? Does he need *Marbury v. Madison* because he is about to pronounce some constitutional judgment, and I need to go to the library to fetch it for him? When I opened the note, it said, "Get me a tuna fish sandwich for lunch."[58]

Where did Arnold's politician hat show in his judicial opinions? He was no politician in robes, as judges are sometimes characterized. But in election law cases and, most notably, in *Jeffers v. Clinton*, Arnold's prior experience as a political candidate was critical to his decision and is notable in the opinions.

Arnold drew on his campaigns in south Arkansas, for example, to conclude that a black lawyer who was running for state senate had been intimidated by government officials. Roy Lewellen, a black lawyer in Marianna,

Lee County, ran for the state senate in 1986 against a white incumbent. At about the same time, the sheriff and the prosecuting attorney instituted a well-publicized criminal prosecution against Lewellen for witness bribery. Lewellen testified in some detail before Arnold's court, giving a number of reasons for his belief that the prosecution was designed to discourage him in particular and black political activity in general. Arnold found this testimony "entirely credible," even though defendants had offered no witnesses to rebut it. Arnold wrote, "We do not think that a white lawyer, even one who opposed the political powers that be, would have been treated this way."[59]

Even more important, it required understanding the political layout of the Delta, which Arnold did because the congressional district in which he campaigned twice encompassed some of this area. He also understood the point of political engagement: "If I can vote at will but never elect anyone," Arnold wrote, "my political ability is less than yours. Elections, and winning them, are the whole point of voting."[60]

But perhaps Arnold's political thinking was most notable in how he handled the preclearance issue. He left the primary election system alone, ruling that the majority-vote requirement in party primaries had not been maintained in Arkansas to discriminate against the black minority.[61] "It reflects a deep-seated attachment to the principle of majority rule, one of the cardinal pillars of democracy," he said. In many parts of the state, Arnold noted, winning the Democratic nomination in the primary was tantamount to election because of a lack of Republication opposition. Requiring a runoff in the primary system "ensures that the election will not be determined by a mere plurality of those who vote in a party primary."[62] A similar rule was unnecessary for general elections because there were almost never more than two substantial candidates. Arnold knew this territory well—he lost in a runoff primary race for Congress against David Pryor and failed to make a sufficient showing to force a runoff in his second bid.

And that practical, pragmatic side is particularly evident in his belief that the court should retain jurisdiction over the 1991 redistricting. Plaintiffs would have sixty days to challenge a new districting plan, but if no challenge was forthcoming, the plan would go into effect. Arnold believed this federal court review of the 1991 districting plan would actually "work to the advantage of the state, because if the plan adopted in 1991 survives this hurdle, the chances of its being allowed to govern undisturbed until the census of 2000, will be, as a practical matter, greatly enhanced."[63]

Arguably, a judge with less political experience might not have been as sensitive to these practical concerns.

BUDGETING JUSTICE: FINANCING THE FEDERAL COURTS

As a young man, Richard Arnold had wanted to be a United States senator. As he gained renown within the federal judiciary, an unexpected opportunity arose for Arnold to have regular contact with members of both the Senate and the House of Representatives in a political capacity. Chief Justice William Rehnquist appointed Arnold in 1987 to present the annual budget request of the federal judiciary before Congress, a job Arnold carried out for nine years. Arnold was the political face of the judicial branch before Congress for most of the 1990s, a critical period for the federal judiciary.

Rehnquist picked Arnold because of his familiarity with Congress, his experience as a senator's aide, and, equally important, because Senator Dale Bumpers, Arnold's former boss and the man most responsible for his appointment to the federal bench, was a member of the Senate appropriations subcommittee responsible for the federal courts.[64]

The institutional ties between the federal courts and Congress are substantial. As summarized by Robert A. Katzmann, later appointed by President Clinton to the Second Circuit, Congress "creates judgeships; determines the structure, jurisdiction, procedures (both civil and criminal), and substantive law of the federal courts; passes laws affecting such disparate areas as judicial discipline and sentencing policy; and sets appropriations and compensation. The legislative branch adds to the judiciary's responsibilities whenever it enacts laws that result in court cases arising under the statutes."[65]

Arnold appreciated the relationship of the federal judiciary with the executive and legislative branches of government. As he pointed out in a speech at the St. Louis University Law School, "The Federal Courts have neither the power of the purse nor that of the sword. This is why the courts are thought to be, by ourselves at least, the least dangerous branch of government." The courts, he said, have no substantial money of their own, except for filing fees and admission fees from lawyers. The money must come from Congress "if the judges are to be compensated, if the lights are going to turn on in the courtroom, if the doors are going to open, and if the rent is going to be paid. That is the major source of Congress' power and a major function of any legislative body in the democratic form of government."[66]

Arnold was clearly in his element on Capitol Hill. He had enjoyed his years as a legislative aide to Senator Dale Bumpers, and Bumpers, in turn, recognized Arnold's political skills at the time: "To me, he was much more than an aide. Even his political advice was almost always flawless. He was a master craftsman of legislation, and I never sent our legislation to the Legislative Council to be drafted. Richard did it all."[67] Thomas Eisele, his colleague on the federal bench in Little Rock, noted these political skills as well, but thought they were best employed as Arnold primarily used them as a judge: "I think he would have loved to have served in the legislative branch, but the truth of the matter is he belonged in the judicial branch."[68]

The job as chair of the budget committee for the federal courts entailed frequent trips to Washington, DC, to testify before various committees in hearings on matters concerning the federal courts. In Arnold's years overseeing the federal courts' budget requests, the amount needed to fund the courts grew significantly. In 1987, the budget was about $1.3 billion. By 1996, the budget request was $3.1 billion.[69] The request had to be renewed every year.

Arnold was especially adept at pointing out the critical role the federal courts played in law enforcement—law and order being a perennial interest for politicians of all stripes. In 1996, for example, Arnold told the House Appropriations Committee, "The judiciary is an integral part of the criminal justice system, and as such, has a direct impact on public safety. As Congress continues to expand the role of the Justice Department, it increases the caseload and workload in the courts and the need for additional resources."[70] In the closing decades of the twentieth century, Congress created an extraordinary number of new federal crimes, resulting in more work for federal prosecutors and federal courts, and larger populations in federal prisons.

In the same hearing, Arnold pointed out that the Justice Department increased funding for US attorneys by 7 percent, the Drug Enforcement Agency by 18 percent, and the Immigration and Naturalization Service by 25 percent. The federal courts had no choice whether to accept the accompanying rise in their workload. "Every case that is filed, whether criminal or civil, must be handled, and ultimately disposed of by the courts. Every indigent defendant charged in a criminal case must be provided court appointed counsel. Every felon released from prison must be supervised." Arnold told the committee, "We are making every possible effort to make the courts as efficient and cost-effective as possible. The Congress and the Executive Branch have more control over the judiciary's workload than we do. As long as we comply with our constitutional and statutory mandates, and as long as the Congress and President continue to make fighting crime a high priority, our workload will increase. Increased workload means increased costs."[71]

Arnold would also put into perspective the comparative amount of the judiciary's request. In 1996, for example, Arnold noted that the requested budget for the operation of the federal court system for the coming year was $3.47 billion, which represented just two-tenths of 1 percent of the entire federal budget. "We have been successful in holding down our request by deferring or delaying expenses where possible, and by implementing a large number of management innovations, improvements, and economy measures," Arnold said in Senate budget hearings.[72]

The year 1993 had been a particularly difficult one for the judiciary's budget. In a C-SPAN interview in March 1993, Arnold said, "We are going to run out of money to pay lawyers to represent criminal defendants" if the judiciary did not receive a supplemental budget from Congress. Arnold noted also that in a couple of months the federal courts would no longer be able to pay juries for their service.[73] The crisis had come about from a dramatic and unexpected increase in the federal courts' criminal docket and a budget cut from the prior year. Congress did make a supplemental appropriation, but it took substantial lobbying on Arnold's part.

The judiciary had asked Congress for an additional $70.8 million to pay court-appointed lawyers and an additional $7.5 million to pay jurors in civil cases. The situation was familiar because it was the third year in a row that the federal judiciary found itself running out of money. The year before, the judiciary borrowed money from other budget items to fund the shortfall, but Arnold noted the shortfall was "too great and the excess funds too few" to do that again in 1993. The year's budget request had been cut by $370 million—they were "cut to the bone," Arnold said.[74]

During the Clinton administration, Arnold also capitalized on his friendship with the president to push the budget requests for the federal courts. Arnold wrote to Clinton in May 1994 about a budget amendment transmitted to Congress by White House chief of staff Leon Panetta that had erroneously subtracted $285 million from the budget request for the federal judiciary. As Arnold informed Clinton, that development was contrary to an earlier agreement that "had occurred solely on account of your personal intervention." Now, however, Arnold wrote Clinton that "the train has gone off the track," and he asked once again for Clinton's assistance with the judiciary's budget request.[75]

Arnold wrote Clinton again in June 1994. It seems the matter was not yet resolved to Arnold's satisfaction. He wrote, "It alarms me to hear our Subcommittee Chair say that you have targeted the Judiciary for cuts. I am confident this is not your intention, but it is clear that the situation will not change without personal intervention from you." Arnold's request was for Panetta to make it clear "on the Senate side that you are not proposing a decrease in the Judiciary's budget request, and that you are asking that all parts of the budget as transmitted by you be given equal and fair consideration."[76]

In response, Clinton wrote Arnold that he hoped to avoid "some of the confusion of the past" and that he intended "to carefully track funding for the Judiciary during the development of the FY 1996 budget." Clinton also reported to Arnold he was "pleased that in a discretionary budget that's virtually frozen for FY 1995," the recently passed Senate version of the appropriations bill "provided the Judiciary with an eight percent increase over FY 1994."[77]

In the following year, Arnold once again called on Clinton for his assistance with the federal judiciary's funding. Arnold worried about a recurrence of the problem they had experienced in the past: the Office of Management and Budget wanted to cut the judiciary's request before transmitting it to Congress. Arnold wrote Clinton,

> I am writing to you immediately because I know this is occurring without your knowledge. The governing statute expressly provides that the President is to send to Congress "without change" the budget request of the Judicial branch. You made a decision at the time that OMB would not be allowed, in the future, to reduce our budget request. It surprises me to learn that we are, potentially anyway, facing a recurrence of this problem. Obviously someone in OMB is unaware of the decisions that you have made.[78]

Arnold later described the issue and President Clinton's response:

> In our view, this was a clear violation of the statute, as well as the almost uniform practice among the three branches of Government. Because I

was Chairman of the Budget Committee, it was my job to correct it. I called everybody I knew in the Executive Branch, including a lot of people in the White House. Finally, I called the President, who knew nothing about it. Granted, you would not expect him to be acquainted with the matter to that level of detail, but eventually he corrected it. It was actually one of the most satisfactory meetings I have ever had on budget matters. It took about three minutes, and he told me "yes" before I had even made my speech. I said, "thank you, Sir," and that was the end.[79]

Arnold worked with alacrity to stay on top of the budget proceedings through both the White House and Congress. But at the same time he fulfilled Rehnquist's expectation about his political sense — he was extremely "politic" in all his public statements about the relationship between Congress and the courts. For example, he said in an interview that Congress had always looked very favorably on budget requests coming from the judiciary, and that the judiciary committee staff was very knowledgeable and easy to work with.[80]

Arnold also described his past relations with both the House and Senate:

> Interestingly, the two houses of Congress are very different. For about the first five or six years of my work, the Chairman of the House Subcommittee was the wonderful Neal Smith of Iowa. He gave us almost exactly what we asked for, to the extent that he could. From the House, one must go to the Senate which, under Senator Hollings, except for the last year, would always cut our requests. This year will be interesting because we have a new majority in both Houses. The House Chairman, Harold Rogers from Kentucky, has been a ranking member for a number of years and is very knowledgeable. I am sure he will do the best he can for us. The Senate Chairman is Senator Gramm of Texas. I went to see him, and he said he would be the most supportive Chairman we have ever had for civil and criminal justice. He further assured me that he would do his best to get for us whatever we genuinely, reasonably needed. I was very encouraged.[81]

In the nine years Arnold presented the judiciary's budget request to Congress, he carefully emphasized a key factor that distinguishes the federal courts' request from the budget of other parts of the government that rely on Congress for funding. "We do not determine our own workload," he said.

"In this respect, we are really a passive instrument of government. We do the work that Congress gives us to do. As new federal statutes are enacted, the workload of adjudication goes up." Arnold worried about suggestions by some members of Congress that the federal judiciary raise its filing fees to cover funding shortfalls. "Justice should not be for sale," Arnold said. While the courts should be open to the use of certain fees, those fees should not "raise unreasonable barriers to a citizen's access to justice."[82]

When Arnold stepped down as chief judge of the Eighth Circuit, Chief Justice Rehnquist and other members of the Supreme Court honored him in March 1998 with a dinner at the Supreme Court celebrating his work for the judicial branch. The nearly one hundred guests included Supreme Court Justices Antonin Scalia, Ruth Bader Ginsburg, David Souter, and Clarence Thomas. The Judicial Conference's resolution honoring Arnold lauded him for "his gifted intellect, integrity, and statesman-like demeanor" and for his leadership on the budget in which he "demonstrated unwavering good judgment and has earned our utmost respect and gratitude."[83]

Richard Arnold had wanted to be a political actor before he became a federal judge. Arnold's appointment to the Eighth Circuit gave him two chances to continue his interest — one he must have anticipated and one he probably did not.

Arnold knew he was likely to encounter a number of election law cases and especially lawsuits brought under the Voting Rights Act of 1964. In these instances he became a judge of the political process, although he recognized the close constraints of his judgment based upon governing law.

In his work representing the federal judiciary in budget matters, it is not likely Arnold had anticipated an opportunity to engage so directly in setting national policy. This work entailed a merger of "politics" with practical governance. In this way, perhaps Arnold's hopes about being a political mover were realized, although not in the way that he had first imagined.

Chapter Thirteen

Two Opportunities
for the Supreme Court

The election of Bill Clinton in 1992 presented the Democrats with their first opportunity to appoint a justice of the United States Supreme Court since Lyndon Johnson named Thurgood Marshall in 1967. When Clinton assumed office, Byron White was the only sitting justice appointed by a Democratic president, having been named by John F. Kennedy in 1962. Clinton would name two Supreme Court justices during the next eight years—Ruth Bader Ginsburg and Stephen G. Breyer—both during his first term. There were no vacancies on the Supreme Court during Clinton's second term.

Clinton spoke of wanting judicial nominees to have a broad view of the Bill of Rights and the right of privacy in particular. He also believed that "the narrow judicial appointments of George Bush," as he wrote just before the November 1992 election, "have resulted in the emergence of a judiciary that is less reflective of our diverse society than at any other time in recent memory. I strongly believe that the judiciary thus runs the risk of losing its legitimacy in the eyes of many Americans."[1] The *Washington Post* speculated that a Clinton presidency "is likely to mean more women and minorities on all courts," given that Clinton complained in campaign speeches that there was a lack of diversity among judges appointed by

Bush and that they failed to meet "high standards of excellence."[2] Clinton was looking for "a progressive on social policy, civil rights and privacy issues," along with a "conciliator" along the lines of former Justice William J. Brennan Jr.[3]

Some of Clinton's views on the ideal Supreme Court justice were known before he ran for president. While Clinton served as governor of Arkansas, he had criticized Robert Bork's restrictive view of the Constitution in testimony submitted to the Senate Judiciary Committee during Bork's confirmation hearing in 1987. Bork was ultimately rejected for the Supreme Court by a vote in the Senate of 52–48. Clinton believed Bork, who had been his constitutional law professor at Yale, "would set back progress on civil rights in the South by seeking to overturn precedents of the liberal era under Chief Justice Earl Warren."[4] "That is why Supreme Court appointments are so important," Clinton wrote in his prepared statement. "They keep our Constitution and its guarantees of liberty alive."[5]

Circuit judges of the United States Courts of Appeal were a natural pool of experienced jurists with proven records. For more than a decade, though, these positions had been staffed by Republican presidents Ronald Reagan and George H. W. Bush with avowedly ideological aims. Many of the remaining Carter appointees were beyond the age range for consideration, in light of the recent trend to nominate relatively young justices to the Supreme Court. Arnold, however, had been one of the younger appeals court judges appointed by Jimmy Carter, at age forty-three. Stephen Breyer, a judge on the First Circuit, was forty-one years old when he was named to the bench. Ruth Bader Ginsburg, a judge on the District of Columbia Circuit, was forty-seven when she was appointed by Carter. She was sixty when she later joined the Supreme Court.

Richard Arnold was prominently in contention for both Clinton-era Supreme Court vacancies. He was among the handful of circuit judges appointed by the last Democratic president, Jimmy Carter, who was both young enough and sufficiently well regarded as a jurist to be a likely contender. As Jeffrey Toobin recounted in his book *The Nine*,[6] Arnold was "a leading ornament of the federal judiciary—a scholarly moderate respected by colleagues across the political spectrum."[7] An Arnold nomination "would have been greeted with something close to acclamation."[8]

Speculation began early—soon after Clinton's successful election campaign—that Arnold would be a likely nominee. James J. Kilpatrick, reporting on admitted "gossip" at the Supreme Court in November 1992, wrote in his syndicated column: "By general agreement, Judge Arnold would be Clinton's first choice for a vacancy on the high court."[9] The *New Republic* also noted Arnold's likely appointment. In an article by Jeffrey Rosen, *New Republic* readers learned that "[i]n addition to being Clinton's closest friend on the federal bench, he is, objectively, a star."[10]

Potential opponents as well as supporters of Richard Arnold had ample time to line up their positions because speculation emerged so early that Arnold would be a contender. Similar to Breyer and Ginsburg, Arnold was a federal circuit judge with a national reputation. He also had a close connection to Clinton and notable bipartisan support. Chief Justice William Rehnquist, for example, relied on Arnold extensively to secure annual appropriations from Congress for the federal judiciary. Arnold was viewed as a moderate liberal, although his opinions were sometimes difficult to classify. One editorialist characterized Arnold as "not so much of the right or of the left as above."[11]

ATTORNEY GENERAL CONTENDER: AN EARLY INDICATION OF WHITE HOUSE CONCERNS

There was no Supreme Court opening in January 1993 when Clinton took office. Instead, filling the Department of Justice's top position was Clinton's first priority. Even before Clinton assumed office, *Newsweek* magazine had speculated that Judge Arnold might be President Clinton's attorney general.[12] Such speculation preceded any conversations between Arnold and White House staff. Arnold told his law school classmate Robert Joost on January 23 that "he doesn't want the job," but he would accept it "if Bill asks me."[13]

Arnold traveled to Washington on February 7, 1993, at the request of the White House for discussions with Bernard Nussbaum, White House counsel, and Vincent Foster, deputy White House counsel and a former law partner of First Lady Hillary Rodham Clinton. The request came after the nomination of Zoe Baird, Clinton's first nominee for attorney general, was withdrawn following revelations that she had hired undocumented aliens as domestic workers. After Baird's withdrawal, federal judge Kimba Wood, said to be Clinton's next choice, withdrew from consideration following revelations that her babysitter had also been an illegal immigrant.[14] Arnold read about the second withdrawal on February 6. That same day, Arnold would be contacted about the position. As Arnold remembered: "One Saturday afternoon, there was a note under my door from Lisa Foster to 'call her husband Vince [Foster] right away' which I did. He said, 'Would you have any interest in being Attorney General?' And I said, 'Well, I won't say no, but I'm not running for it.'"

Foster asked Arnold to fly to Washington the next day for a meeting at the offices of the law firm Swidler & Berlin, some of whose lawyers served the incoming administration as "vetters" of potential appointees.[15] In addition to two members of the firm, James Hamilton and Lester Hyman, Vince Foster and Walter Dellinger, head of the Department of Justice's Office of Legal Counsel, were also present for the meeting. As Arnold recalled:

> I spent maybe three hours with them. I answered everything to the best of my ability, and about five o'clock, I said, "Well, I need to go to church." It was Sunday. Vince and Walter had a White House car, and they took me to St. Mathew's Cathedral. One of my political difficulties was that I was trying to become a Roman Catholic, which I never succeeded in doing because of divorce and remarriage. But that was regarded as making me politically suspect on abortion.[16]

After the church service, Vince Foster was waiting for Arnold in the White House car. Arnold thought he would be taken to the White House for the appointment to be announced. Instead, Foster went with him to Arnold's hotel, the Washington Court. There the two ran into Stephen Breyer, who was in town for a conference of federal court of appeals judges. Breyer encouraged Arnold to take the job. As Arnold related, Breyer said, "'You've got to do this. You've got to take this.' I said, 'Steve, you know, they haven't offered it to me.'"[17]

The vetting process included a search for any skeletons in each candidate's past—especially to avoid more surprises such as hiring illegal aliens as domestic servants. An undated memo, apparently referring to Arnold as "X," was prepared in the vetting for the attorney general position. "X apparently had a very stormy relationship with his ex-wife," the memo reported. One section of the memo provides "LSH comments" (likely Lester S. Hyman, one of the founding partners of Swidler & Berlin, who Arnold said was at the meeting): "The real question here is whether the ex-wife is sufficiently vituperative that she either would appear in opposition to X's nomination or would leak allegedly derogatory information to the press or to women's rights groups. It would be essential for the White House to know the answer to this question before sending up the nomination."

If this document indeed referred to Arnold, any concerns were allayed by his former wife, Gale Arnold. Gale later wrote a letter to the White House affirming her support for Richard Arnold and urging his nomination to the Supreme Court.[18]

Upon returning to his hotel room, Foster told Arnold they needed to "talk to the doctors." Arnold gave him the names of his doctors, and the White House operator got the doctors on the phone:

> I told them, "I'm being considered for a job that may be short-term. And so I want your medical advice to me personally. If I'm offered this job, is it dumb of me to take it? Should I be concerned?" And the doctors, every one of them said, "No. Go ahead, take it. No problem." And I told Vince [Foster] that.

> About two hours later, he called me and said that I was not going to be appointed Attorney General and I could relax, which I gratefully did. He didn't tell me why. He said, "We have to have a cover story." He said, "You can say that you asked not to be considered." I said, "Vince, that's not true. I'm not going to say that. But if you and Bernie [Nussbaum] make a public statement on it, I will not contradict you in public."[19]

Women's groups continued to advocate for a female nominee for attorney general, and the Clinton administration seemed determined to appoint a woman. Among others contacted about the position were federal judges Rya Zobel and Patricia Wald. Judge Wald told Arnold she had been interviewed for the job but that she did not want to be considered. She was sixty-four years old and she would have given up all her senior status entitlement, a prospect, she said, that did not make any sense for her personally.[20] Janet Reno was ultimately named to the position. Clinton announced her nomination on February 11, less than one week after Arnold's interview with Nussbaum and Foster.

When Arnold was later a prominent contender for two Supreme Court vacancies, some women's groups targeted Arnold's 1983 decision in *United States Jaycees v. McClure*.[21] As discussed earlier, Arnold's ruling that the

Minnesota Jaycees could not be forced by state law to admit women was reversed by the Supreme Court, in an opinion written by Justice Brennan. That decision may have been one factor in the choice to bypass Arnold for attorney general. One journalist, at least, concluded that Arnold was taken out of consideration "when the review process found one of his rulings that said the Jaycees of America had the right to restrict its membership to men only." It was not the time "to push a white male with that potentially controversial ruling on his unofficial resume."[22]

FIRST SUPREME COURT VACANCY

The first Supreme Court vacancy occurred when Justice Byron White announced his retirement on March 19, 1993, to be effective at the end of the Court's term in June. Although appointed by a Democrat, White had been a reliable conservative on many issues, including abortion, beginning with his dissent in *Roe v. Wade*.[23] White was seventy-five years old and had served on the Court for thirty-one years.

The search process for White's replacement was summarized in a mid-April memo from Ron Klain, associate counsel to the president and a former Justice White law clerk, to White House counsel Bernard W. Nussbaum, a law school classmate of Arnold's. The memo recapped the process they had discussed earlier that day. First, the president would "narrow the list from the current 22 names, to a small group of 2–4 potential candidates." The memo then described the review process for those finalists, including literature reviews, phone calls, and interviews, culminating with the candidates to see Attorney General Reno and the president on the same day. The last step would be for the president to "consult with key Senate Democrats ([Joe] Biden and [George] Mitchell), make his final decision, give advance notice to key Republicans ([Bob] Dole and [Orrin] Hatch), and make a public announcement."[24]

Richard Arnold's name was frequently mentioned in media reports as a likely contender for that opening, but another circuit judge — Ruth Bader Ginsburg — would receive the president's nomination. Arnold, and other potential nominees, were said to suffer from the "white male" problem. An editorial in the *Arkansas Democrat-Gazette* in the early days following Justice White's announced retirement believed Arnold was "already disqualified on the basis of his sex and race." The editorial cited one unnamed source close to the White House to state "The odds against a WASP male are at least 10 to 1."[25]

But it was also during the process of naming Justice Ginsburg that speculation arose—and was confirmed by a member of Clinton's staff—that White House wariness toward Arnold's appointment to the Supreme Court had more to do with the fact that he was from Arkansas and was a friend of the Clintons. Several weeks before Clinton announced his choice, media reports stated that Richard Arnold was off the list of possibilities because Clinton was "worried about the appearance of cronyism" should he pick a judge from Arkansas.[26]

A number of Arkansans went to Washington with Clinton to fill key White House and agency positions, including Thomas F. "Mack" McLarty III (White House chief of staff), Webster "Webb" Hubbell (associate attorney general), Vince Foster (deputy White House counsel), William Kennedy (associate White House counsel), Bruce Lindsey (senior adviser, Office of Presidential Personnel, and later deputy counsel to the president), Rodney Slater (first African American director of the Federal Highway Administration, later secretary of transportation), and Jocelyn Elders (first African American surgeon general). The Washington stint ended badly for a few of them. Vince Foster, suffering from depression, committed suicide on July 20, 1993, in Fort Marcy Park in Virginia. Webb Hubbell resigned from his post as associate attorney general (the number three post at the Department of Justice) on March 14, 1994, after independent counsel Robert Fisk opened a criminal probe into charges that Hubbell had overbilled clients while practicing law at the Rose Law Firm in Little Rock. (Hubbell eventually served eighteen months in a federal prison.) Jocelyn Elders, surgeon general of the United States, was fired by President Clinton in December 1994 following controversial remarks she had made. Further, "Travelgate" had become a contentious issue in mid-1993, when the White House travel staff was fired to be replaced with World Wide Travel, a company based in Little Rock.

The charges of "cronyism" also coincided with a golf club membership issue concerning the Country Club of Little Rock. Webb Hubbell, nominated as associate attorney general, resigned his membership from the club in anticipation of opposition from the Senate Judiciary Committee after reports spread that the club had long excluded black members.

Within hours of Hubbell's resignation, three members of the White House staff—Vince Foster, Thomas F. "Mack" McLarty, and William Kennedy —also resigned from the club.[27]

By the early 1990s, the lack of black members seemed to have less to do with any intentional exclusion than the difficulty, despite efforts by Arnold and others, to recruit blacks for the club. At the time of Hubbell's resignation from the club, it had recently added its first black member, Dr. Howard Reed, whom Arnold was instrumental in recruiting.[28] Dr. Reed joined the club in 1992 just after Clinton's election. The club's previous all-white membership had become an issue during the presidential campaign after Clinton played golf there the previous spring.[29]

Because of his resignation, the club's racial history did not become an issue at Hubbell's confirmation hearing. But because Richard Arnold was also a member of the club, the issue likely played a role in White House concern for the "appearance of cronyism" should Arnold be nominated for the first Supreme Court vacancy. At least this was the conclusion of the *Arkansas Democrat-Gazette*: "The controversy and the ensuing resignations reduced Arnold's chances of being named to replace White on the Supreme Court."[30]

The response to the "cronyism" charge from judges and others included a letter campaign urging the president that Arnold was a national figure and that his state of origin should have no bearing on his decision. Nussbaum himself thought calling Richard Arnold a crony was "incredible—he was one of the most distinguished people in the world."[31]

But there were also indications that a serious push for Arnold would result in opposition from abortion rights groups.[32] Nina Totenberg, for example, reported on National Public Radio that Arnold was one of the names in consideration, but "women's groups view a number of his decisions as hostile," she claimed.[33]

Ironically, it was not one of Arnold's written opinions but a vote in a recent case that abortion rights supporters chose for their attack. Arnold joined a majority on the appeals court in upholding a Minnesota law requiring minors under eighteen to notify both parents forty-eight hours before receiving an abortion unless judicial bypass was granted. The opinion was subsequently affirmed by the Supreme Court. But Arnold had been the only Democrat-appointed judge to vote with the six Eighth Circuit Republican appointees in the decision. The other Democratic appointees, Lay, Heaney, and McMillian, dissented. Lynn Paltrow of the

Center for Reproductive Law and Policy said Arnold's vote "gives us grave concern" that he "does not support abortion rights."[34]

Arnold's decision in the *Minnesota Jaycees* case also became an issue.[35] Arnold first learned that case might be a stumbling block when contacted by the White House about the attorney general position. Before he was interviewed by White House vetters, Vince Foster had called Arnold at home. According to Arnold, Foster "read to me from some sort of legal memorandum. He said, 'This was prepared outside.' I gathered he meant outside the White House. And it was a critique about the *Jaycees* opinion. Someone had thought enough about me or had been fearful enough of me to start gathering ammunition to be used against me if I were nominated for something or other. Anyway, he read me a passage from this legal memo and I gave him the answer as best I could. He said, 'Okay, that sounds good.'"[36]

Arnold also received support from prominent media figures, including Jeffrey Rosen's column in the *New Republic* lauding Arnold's "legal sophistication, graceful writing, warmhearted gregariousness, self-restraint and the ability to persuade by intelligent argument."[37] But it would be frustrating for Arnold when he had no public forum to respond to mischaracterizations of his record. At least for the "cronyism" charge, Arnold would respond with good humor: "You know, it's just much too late to move."[38]

Two months into the search for Justice White's replacement, Clinton was said to be unhappy with the selection of Supreme Court candidates sent to him by his staff and asked for more names. No name proposed thus far had struck Clinton as "a brilliant suggestion," said one administration official. "Find me somebody who when the name is heard people say, 'Yes. Wow. A home run. That person belongs on the Supreme Court.'"[39] Those thought to be on the list at the time, besides Arnold, included US District Judge Jose Cabranes and appeals court judges Ruth Bader Ginsburg, Amalya Lyle Kearse, Stephanie K. Seymour, Patricia M. Wald, and Mary Schroeder.[40] By this time, Mario Cuomo, whom Clinton had called to discuss the vacancy, had withdrawn from consideration. Court observers surmised, correctly as it turned out, that Clinton would select a woman, the Supreme Court's second.

President Clinton announced his choice of Ruth Bader Ginsburg on June 15. She would be the first Jewish justice to serve since Abe Fortas resigned from the court in 1969.[41] Many had expected Stephen Breyer to be named. Breyer reportedly had been the choice of many senior aides in the White House.[42] Introducing Judge Ginsburg at the announcement,

Clinton said: "I believe that in the years ahead she will be able to be a force for consensus-building on the Supreme Court, just as she has been on the Court of Appeals, so that our judges can become an instrument of our common unity in the expression of their fidelity to the Constitution."[43]

According to Nussbaum, ultimately Clinton did not want his first Supreme Court nominee to be from Arkansas, and he expected to have at least one and possibly two more appointments to make.[44] Arnold understood this, and in any event was delighted that his friend Ruth Bader Ginsburg had received the nomination. He traveled to Washington to attend her formal swearing-in ceremony at the Supreme Court on October 1, 1993. Arnold believed Ginsburg was "the best lawyer on the Supreme Court" because of her earlier, pathbreaking work in women's rights litigation. A few months before her nomination, Arnold had run into Ginsburg when he was in Washington. He had just been interviewed for attorney general. Ginsburg thought Arnold would be superb for the position. Arnold recounted later: "Ruth said she thought it was silly for anybody to hold the *Jaycees* case against me."[45]

REPLACING JUSTICE BLACKMUN

The letter campaign in support of Arnold intensified just after Supreme Court Justice Harry Blackmun announced in late 1993 his intention to retire.[46] Blackmun had served on the Court since 1970. Blackmun's resignation was not unanticipated—he was eighty-four years old when Clinton assumed the presidency. When Blackmun's retirement was officially announced on April 6, 1994, a thirty-seven-day process began before the president's choice for a replacement would be announced.

In some circles, at least, there was an expectation that Blackmun's replacement would come from the same geographic region. Blackmun had served on the Eighth Circuit before his elevation. Supreme Court appointments in the past had at times been consciously geographic, in order to seek a balanced representation on the Court. Arnold, of course, was from the same circuit as Blackmun—the Eighth. Arnold was fifty-eight years old when Blackmun announced he would retire.

Harry Blackmun had become one of the Court's most publicly well-known and, in some circles, "infamous" figures. Only a few months before his retirement, for example, Blackmun changed his position on the death penalty, writing in *Callins v. Collins*[47] in February 1994, "I no longer shall tinker with the machinery of death." Years after his former colleagues William Brennan and Thurgood Marshall had done so, Blackmun decided that the death penalty was unconstitutional in all circumstances.

Perhaps overstating the matter, the *New York Times* in 1993 wrote that Blackmun was "the most vilified member of the Supreme Court in history" due to his opinion for the Court in *Roe v. Wade*.[48] When the court later cut back on access to abortions in *Webster v. Reproductive Health Services*,[49] a 5–4 decision, Blackmun was in dissent.

Because Arnold was mentioned prominently as a possible replacement for Blackmun, interest groups looked hard at Arnold's judicial record in abortion cases. The National Abortion Rights Action League said in a press release that Arnold would be a "poor choice" for the Supreme Court.

It was difficult for Arnold's supporters to overcome the NARAL attack, despite the fact that the great majority of his prior decisions on abortion were fully within the liberal line and had even received the endorsement of NARAL's Missouri chapter. The Missouri chapter of NARAL issued a statement supporting Arnold's opinion in *T.L.J. v. Webster*,[50] which involved a Missouri statutory process for obtaining court approval for abortion for minors. A state court judge had said he would never approve an application by a minor for an abortion, because it was "murder." Arnold wrote a strongly worded opinion that a judge in such circumstances was obligated to recuse from the case if unwilling to follow the law.[51] Arnold was criticized for that statement by abortion opponents in Missouri.[52]

Frank Susman, a St. Louis lawyer and abortion rights advocate, came out resolutely in Arnold's favor. Susman had litigated many abortion cases before Arnold and had argued for the pro-choice side in the *Webster* case in the Supreme Court. Susman stated: "I personally would have no qualms about Judge Arnold when it comes to women's rights in general or reproductive rights specifically."[53]

A DIFFICULT YEAR FOR AN ARKANSAN: CLINTON'S SELECTION PROCESS, ARNOLD'S SUPPORT

The recurring charge of "cronyism" in connection with a possible Arnold appointment reared its head again in 1994—this time with the Whitewater investigation in its early stages. Although Arnold never served in Clinton's gubernatorial administration and was in no way involved in the Whitewater affair, Arnold was still from Arkansas and was a Clinton friend. As Steve Umin, a Washington lawyer and Yale classmate of Arnold's, facetiously characterized the issue, "A friend of the President is bad enough, but a friend from Arkansas is a 'crony.'"[54]

Arnold was held in high regard by other federal judges, and they undertook an unprecedented effort to inform the White House of their support for Arnold specifically to counteract the cronyism charges. Not only was the letter campaign by federal judges in full swing, Arnold also received important endorsements from major media outlets and notable public figures. Jeffrey Rosen, for example, wrote a lengthy article supporting Arnold in the *New Republic*. Arnold, Rosen wrote, "is one of the most respected appellate judges in the nation. Of the current candidates, he seems the best prepared to articulate an energetic, principled liberal vision." Clinton was said to want to nominate Arnold but, "in the wake of Whitewater, considers it politically implausible because of the appearance of cronyism." Because Arnold "was the best person for the job," according to Rosen, "it would be unfortunate, not to say perverse, if his Arkansas roots kept him off the Court."[55]

In addition, Stuart Taylor Jr. wrote an article published in the *Legal Times*, an influential Washington, DC, lawyers' publication, assessing Arnold's career and concluding he was "the class of the field" of the rumored short list of Clinton's potential nominees.[56] Amalya Kearse and Stephen Breyer, Stuart wrote, "may be in Arnold's league in terms of intellectual horsepower—but neither has his reputation for warm, unpretentious humanity and gentle persuasiveness." Arnold faced a succession of divisive issues on the Eighth Circuit, Taylor noted, especially dealing with the First Amendment. Arnold, he wrote, had vigorously protected the free-speech rights of people ranging from "a gay-students association at the University of Arkansas, to a white-supremacist group, from abortion clinics to an iconoclastic student's newspaper at the University of Minnesota and *Newsweek*."[57]

Of the supposed political liability that Arnold was from Arkansas, Taylor wrote:

> It is a sad commentary on the superficiality of political discourse in the television age to hear people—including me, in some sound bites I'd like

to rephrase—downplaying Arnold's Supreme Court prospects for reasons such as this. Well-connected Democrats tell us it's potentially crippling—not because Arnold has anything to do with any of the activities grouped under the "Whitewater" rubric, but simply because of geographical guilt by association. Isn't this ridiculous?[58]

Also in circulation was a set of tributes to Arnold by noted jurists recently published in the *Minnesota Law Review*. Third Circuit Judge Leon Higginbotham, appointed in 1964 as the first African American federal judge in the Eastern District of Pennsylvania, called Arnold "one of the firmest supporters of civil liberties generally and equal rights specifically of any judge on the bench." Patricia Wald, a longtime judge on the District of Columbia circuit and recently its chief judge, praised Arnold's courage, compassion, and "persistent, ornery refusal to rely on hyper-technicalities to dismiss individual rights claims with uncomfortable consequences." His mentor, Justice William Brennan, said Arnold was "undoubtedly among the most gifted members of the federal judiciary."[59]

Arnold received public endorsements from Utah senator Orrin Hatch, who after the 1995 midterm elections would become chairman of the Senate Judiciary Committee but was then its ranking Republican. Senator Hatch, when asked on April 13 whom President Clinton should appoint to the Supreme Court, strongly endorsed Richard Arnold.[60] Arnold was also endorsed by other Republican senators, including Thad Cochran of Mississippi, who wrote the White House on Arnold's behalf in April and followed up with a telephone call in May.[61] Republican senator Larry Pressler also wrote to the president urging the appointment of Arnold.[62] If Republican support for Arnold raised eyebrows in Democratic circles, there was no public comment.

Perhaps surprising on the surface, William F. Buckley Jr. wrote an editorial urging Arnold's appointment to the Supreme Court. "Quality," Buckley wrote, "is nowhere more resplendent than in Richard Arnold." Buckley offered that it would be just as offensive to discriminate against Arnold because he came from Arkansas "as it would be to hold his race or religion against him."[63]

After Senate majority leader George Mitchell withdrew his name from consideration in early April, the search focused more specifically on Arnold. The conservative *Washington Times* published a lengthy article on Arnold as the "gutsy" choice for the Supreme Court.[64] The article noted Arnold's praise came from both sides of the political spectrum, "from conservative writer William F. Buckley to liberal former Supreme Court Justice William Brennan Jr." But it described, based on unnamed White House sources, the administration's dilemma in nominating a judge from Arkansas.

"Arnold's credentials are unassailable," according to a senior White House official. "But we don't operate in a world without politics." The article described a growing campaign by prominent judges and lawyers, calling the White House and members of the Senate to urge his nomination. As the *Washington Times* put it, the quiet campaign to "nationalize" Arnold's candidacy "provides a rare glimpse at the backstage jockeying that goes into the making of a high court candidate."[65] Arnold's opinions "have a generally liberal cast, particularly on civil rights and civil liberties issues." The article highlighted in particular *Jeffers v. Clinton*, a voting rights case in which Arnold wrote a sweeping order directing Arkansas to redraw its state legislative and congressional voting-district lines.[66]

DOCUMENTS FROM THE CLINTON LIBRARY

It is clear from voluminous files at the Clinton Presidential Library that Arnold was the subject of a substantial vetting process, with significant research into Arnold's past. Most of the important documents, ostensibly showing specific communications between White House counsel and the president concerning Arnold, are not yet available to researchers. The Clinton Presidential Library withheld 954 documents—a total of 1,882 pages—under various restrictions of the Presidential Records Act and the Freedom of Information Act. Most of the pages withheld were categorized "relating to the appointment to federal office," and "confidential advice to the President from his advisors, or between such advisors," two exemptions under the Presidential Records Act. Those provisions allow the Clinton White House to withhold such documents until 2012.[67]

Some of the withheld documents, and much of the story of the Supreme Court nomination process, can nonetheless be pieced together from other sources. There is known to be, for example, a forty-six-page memo titled "Opinions of Chief Judge Richard S. Arnold of Special Concern to Women."[68] This memo analyzes thirty-six Arnold opinions. The authorship is unknown, but most likely the document was prepared by former Arnold law clerks and other supporters to be provided to the White House. The memo attempts not only to explain Arnold's *Minnesota Jaycees* and the abortion decisions, but also describes numerous other Arnold decisions that were favorable to women's rights.

White House attorneys focused on the abortion question, including communication early in Clinton's first term about Arnold between the NOW Legal Defense and Education Fund and Bernard Nussbaum.[69] In another file labeled "Richard Arnold," a handwritten note to "Rick" from "Carter," undated, states: "I pulled abortion consent decisions only. If you want more, call."[70]

The great majority of available documents at the Clinton Library are letters of support for Arnold's appointment from members of the legal profession, including well over one hundred federal judges. Many of these judges signed a joint letter to President Clinton:

> We, the undersigned federal judges are fully aware that you are well acquainted with Judge Richard Arnold. However, we are not sure you are aware of the respect and support he has around the country and the universal acceptance his appointment to the Supreme Court would receive.[71]

The letter cites Arnold's "unequaled academic and intellectual credentials," his experience as a federal trial and appellate judge, and his "exceptional service to the judiciary" in his administrative roles. The letter concludes:

> Mr. President, you have made it clear that you advocate basic fair play and equal opportunity. We respectfully submit that a person with such unsurpassed credentials should not be excluded because of his geographical roots.

The ninety-one signatures are a mixture of Republican and Democratic appointees from throughout the nation. Many other judges wrote separately. Clinton himself estimated that more than one-eighth of the federal bench had written to him in support of Arnold. The effort was surely unprecedented, as one judge pointed out. That judge wrote to inform the president that he would not sign the letter of support because he believed that federal judges should not be involved in the president's choice.[72]

Another federal judge defended the letter-writing campaign by members of the judiciary: "Federal judges are entitled to defend the integrity of other judges who are wrongly attacked. I guarantee that the federal judges in this country will defend Richard Arnold against any such silly charges."[73] The effort was to convince Clinton that Arnold would "sail through the confirmation process."[74]

Other federal judges weighed in on the issue in the final weeks of the selection process. One such letter suggested to the president that "if you select Richard Arnold you will be proud of the fact for the remainder of your days."[75] Judge Thomas P. Griesa, chief judge of the Southern District of New York, wrote that "Judge Arnold has gained a degree of respect in the federal judiciary which is absolutely remarkable."[76]

Judge G. Thomas Eisele, a Republican appointee, wrote to Clinton: "What I think you are finding, or will find if you inquire, is that Judge Arnold is the overwhelming choice of *all* federal judges across this nation, regardless of their pre-appointment political affiliations."[77] Recall that Judge Eisele filed strong dissents to Richard Arnold's opinions in *Jeffers v. Clinton*, making this a particularly gracious recommendation.

But it was not only Republican-appointed judges who contacted Clinton in favor of Arnold. Mike Huckabee, the then Republican lieutenant governor of Arkansas (later governor and presidential candidate), wrote to Clinton:

> Since I am a Republican, my strong support for Judge Arnold might surprise some, but would not surprise those who know Judge Arnold personally or who know him from his distinguished legal career. It's my heartfelt belief that Judge Arnold would continue his enviable record on the bench as one who judged according to the law instead of prevailing politics or public opinion. I assure you that I would do all possible to encourage the support of the Republican Senators for his swift confirmation.[78]

At least one judge's letter was brought specifically to President Clinton's attention, according to a note in Victoria Radd's files.[79] The letter was from the highly respected federal judge Louis H. Pollak. Pollak was senior United States district judge for the Eastern District of Pennsylvania, appointed by Jimmy Carter, with a long and distinguished judicial career. A former dean of Yale Law School, Pollack had worked with the NAACP beginning in 1950 in desegregation suits, including *Brown v. Board of Education.* Arnold participated with Pollak in the discussion of desegregation held at Yale Law School nearly forty years earlier, while Arnold was a college junior.[80] The two took different sides of the issue, with Arnold defending the "southern" view of *Brown.*

Pollak's letter to Lloyd Cutler, he said, was sparked by reading in the *New York Times* that Arnold's Arkansas roots were considered a disqualifying factor. "As I am sure I hardly need argue to you, Arnold is superbly qualified for a place on the Court. To fail to nominate him because he comes from the same state as the President would be an unfairness not only to Arnold but—more important—to the Court and to the people of the United States."[81]

The three-page letter contains advice to Cutler about how the president could handle Arnold's nomination with the press, especially that the president should "point out that his estimate of the nominee's qualifications is shared by a host of qualified observers who are not Arkansas friends of the President or of Judge Arnold." He continued, "I really find it hard to believe that a large cohort of senators would risk making fools of themselves by fighting Arnold's nomination on grounds of geography or otherwise."

Pollak also recounted Franklin Roosevelt's decision not to appoint Learned Hand and the tactical implications of that episode for Arnold's situation. The irony of Roosevelt's choice of the forty-eight-year-old Wiley Rutledge, rather than the seventy-year-old Hand, is that Rutledge died six years later. Hand remained active on the Second Circuit for almost twenty more years and became one of the most prominent judges in American history.

Pollak concluded his letter by saying that he was "*not* contending that Richard Arnold is the only person highly qualified for appointment. There certainly are others." (Pollak mentioned Stephen Breyer, Amalya Kearse, and Jon Newman.) "My only plea is that Richard Arnold not be denied consideration on grounds so fecklessly irrelevant as his Arkansasness."[82]

There were also a substantial number of letters from attorneys and law professors, including a joint letter signed by thirty-three professors of environmental law urging the president to consider Arnold's work as an environmental advocate before he was appointed to the bench.[83] "Beyond his highly regarded judicial record and supreme analytical and educational credentials, we believe that Judge Arnold would bring needed experience in environmental law to the Court. As an increasing number of environmental cases come before the Court, it is vitally important that the Court include a Justice well-versed in the complexity of environmental issues and sensitive to the concerns underlying the nation's environmental laws."[84]

Other letters came from women in the legal profession, defending Arnold's record on the Eighth Circuit. One such letter came from a prominent woman attorney who had represented several national women's organizations in equality litigation. While she did not agree with Arnold's opinion in the *Jaycees* case, she wrote, "What is important to me is the body of a judge's work, viewed as a whole and from the perspective of its evolution. Viewed in that light, I believe Judge Arnold to be firmly committed to the principles of equal protection for all persons, including women. His decisions affecting women in the workplace are evidence of that commitment as are the several other important women's rights cases he has decided."[85]

Another letter came from the president of the Women's Bar Association of the District of Columbia.[86] "I believe that those who would oppose Judge Arnold's selection based solely upon his *Jaycees* opinion are shortsighted and are engaging in precisely the sort of stereotyping we have fought so long to eliminate." Those who opposed Arnold on the basis of that one opinion, she wrote, "are reasoning—incorrectly—that if Judge Arnold *ruled* against women, he must *be* against women. They also forget that a circuit judge has only limited ability to set precedent, constrained as he is by his duty to follow the Supreme Court's guidance."

The correspondence, while overwhelmingly in support of Arnold, was not completely so. There were also several letters in opposition. A Democratic fund-raiser from California wrote, "I believe it would be a mistake to appoint Richard Arnold to the Supreme Court. I say this predicated upon his record on abortion and other issues important to a liberal democrat, which is the category I fall into."[87] This was another example of the generic charge that Arnold was not sufficiently protective of abortion rights—a charge that was apparently uninformed of Arnold's record.

CLINTON CHOOSES A JUSTICE

White House counsel Lloyd Cutler told reporters in mid-April 1994 to expect the president's announcement in two weeks.[88] That prediction was wrong, by an additional two weeks.

On May 5, the *Wall Street Journal* reported in a headline, "Clinton Has Supreme Court Short List; Judge Arnold of Arkansas Is a Favorite."[89] At a press conference the same day, a reporter asked Clinton about Arnold's prospects:

> Mr. President, the *Wall Street Journal* says that Judge Richard Arnold is now your favorite to become the next Supreme Court justice. Should he be penalized because he's from Arkansas? Is he your favorite?

> THE PRESIDENT: Well, first of all, I have no comment on whether I have a favorite or not. And, secondly, he shouldn't be penalized because he's from Arkansas. He was first in his class at Harvard and Yale. He's the Chief Judge of the Eighth Circuit, and he's been head of the Appellate Judges Association. So I don't think anyone would question—it would be difficult to find, just on terms of those raw qualifications, an appellate judge with equal or superior qualifications. I don't think any American would expect someone to be disqualified because they happen to come from my state.[90]

Earlier that week, Clinton and White House Chief of Staff McLarty discussed women senators who had expressed concern about Arnold's nomination, reportedly Dianne Feinstein and Barbara Boxer of California, Barbara A. Mikulski of Maryland, Patty Murray of Washington, and Carol Moseley Braun of Illinois.[91]

Ultimately, though, Clinton's decision turned on estimates of Arnold's health rather than any potential opposition from women's groups. White House officials had long known of Arnold's underlying lymphoma. Only a few months after the nomination of Ruth Bader Ginsburg for Byron White's seat on the Supreme Court, Arnold was informed that he had a cancerous tumor in his mouth.[92] A routine visit to his dentist in late July uncovered a lymphoma above his front teeth, intruding into a sinus cavity. Physicians at the National Institutes of Health, where Arnold met with doctors after the discovery of the tumor, prescribed low-level radiation treatment for two weeks. His doctors said, according to Arnold, that "the treatment would be effective and [they] were not equivocal about it."[93]

A few weeks later, Arnold began daily radiation treatments in Little Rock. As Arnold was quick to tell the press, he would not receive treatment for any other type of cancer. He continued to work every day, and he had full confidence in the medical care he was receiving.[94] As he wrote to Justice William Brennan, the fourteen-day regimen of low-level radiation treatment was "not a big deal—no significant side effects and an excellent prognosis. What I am going through is simply a mild manifestation of the underlying disorder that caused me to have my spleen out in 1980. People who have not had similar experiences tend, unfortunately, to exaggerate the gravity of the situation."[95]

Arnold had been diagnosed two decades earlier with a form of non-Hodgkin lymphoma. It was said to be a type that could flare up from time to time and would remain with him the rest of his life. But as Arnold would say, "you will die of other causes."[96]

The week of May 9, 1994, sealed Arnold's fate. Clinton wanted more and better assurances of Arnold's potential longevity. At Steve Umin's suggestion, White House staff arranged a telephone call from Clinton to Dr. Lee Nadler, a leading expert on Arnold's disease at the Dana Farber Cancer Institute. Clinton wanted Dr. Nadler to review Arnold's medical records to provide a prognosis. Nadler was willing to do so but first required Arnold's consent.[97]

Arnold was then contacted by White House staff. A handwritten note from Victoria Radd to "L" (presumably Lloyd Cutler) described the conversation: "I spoke with Judge Arnold. He himself has decided to: (1) authorize the doctor to send us the letter; and (2) authorize the doctor to speak with the President. Judge Arnold hopes to get this done in the next 30 minutes. He will call me (and fax the letter) ASAP after making these calls."[98] Arnold had previously arranged for his medical files to be shipped to Nadler.

At the time, Arnold was in St. Paul, Minnesota, where he was hearing cases with other Eighth Circuit judges. On Thursday evening, Arnold received a call from Dr. Nadler. As Arnold reported, "I had the impression that he had been in touch with the White House, and he may have even talked to the president already. He said that he was going to prepare a letter, an opinion letter for me." Nadler told Arnold that he would call him the next morning, Friday, to read the letter.[99]

The same evening, Lloyd Cutler called Arnold to schedule a "vetting" session. Just before midnight, Arnold's phone rang at his hotel room. On the line with Cutler were Bruce Lindsey, Vickie Radd, Mack McLarty, and Joel Klein. As Arnold reported, McLarty said, "We're going to have to make some decisions." McLarty was vague, according to Arnold, but

Arnold believed McLarty "had learned somewhere that I was going to need more treatment." There was an "awful lot of communication between doctors and the White House" that Arnold did not know about, he said, but he had "given his consent" for his doctors to speak with the White House. The telephone conversation lasted for half an hour.

At seven o'clock the next morning, Dr. Nadler called Arnold and read his letter over the telephone. Arnold recalled: "His letter said that I wasn't fit to sit on the Supreme Court at that time, which was manifestly untrue. The letter was very harshly phrased. And I've gotten to know him pretty well since then. He has told me that the letter was too harshly phrased. The last sentence said, 'I cannot assure you that Judge Arnold will be able to sit on the Supreme Court *at this time*'—underscored."[100]

The letter from Nadler, who had never met Arnold in person, told Clinton that Arnold needed a new regime of aggressive treatment. Arnold said later: "Dr. Nadler's letter contained an opinion somewhat different from what I have been told by my physicians. I want to make it clear that I believe Dr. Nadler gave me his genuine and honest view. But doctors are like lawyers, they don't always agree." Arnold's other doctors, he said, all "adhered to their opinion that they did not agree with Dr. Nadler."[101]

After the phone call, Arnold went to the federal courthouse in St. Paul where oral arguments were scheduled for that morning. Before Arnold went on the bench for the first case, White House staff reached him by telephone. "We understand you have a letter," he was told. Arnold replied, "Well, I don't have the letter and I haven't read it, but I have had it read to me." Arnold said, "I didn't have any choice but to give them the letter. So I called Lee Nadler and said, 'Fax the letter.' At that point I knew that I was not going to be appointed."[102]

Arnold received another call from the White House sometime later that morning, with the message that he was to expect a call from President Clinton. Arnold left the bench, and the other two judges on the panel heard the remaining cases. Arnold "took refuge," he said, in Judge George Fagg's chambers, "because you couldn't answer all the calls that came to my number."

Around one thirty, Arnold left the courthouse with his law clerks and secretary for the airport, for an already scheduled return flight to Little Rock. Members of the media saw Arnold leave. Arnold waved as he drove from the underground parking garage, but he did not stop to speak with them. Arnold had been told before he left the courthouse to call the White

House when he arrived in Cincinnati to change planes for the flight to Little Rock. A reporter from ABC traveled with them because, Arnold said, "they believed I was going to be appointed, and they thought I was going to Washington, not Little Rock," despite Arnold's protestations about his travel plans.

When he arrived in Cincinnati, Arnold called the telephone number he had been given, and Vickie Radd answered. She told Arnold, "The president wants to talk to you." Arnold recalled the conversation: "When I talked with the president, he was very considerate of me. He said, 'Well, you can get properly treated. I certainly want to consider you next time.' And I told him that having read the letter I realized that he couldn't nominate me. And I got on the airplane and came home to Little Rock. The ABC reporter gave up at that point because he saw me get on the Little Rock airplane."

Prior to Clinton's late afternoon announcement on May 13, Lloyd Cutler earlier that day held a press briefing, in which he stated the necessity of appointing a justice who could "serve in the span of 15 to 20 years as Justice Blackmun had done." As Arnold already knew, this was a signal that Arnold would not be the president's choice.

A few hours before speaking with Arnold, President Clinton reached Senator Dale Bumpers by telephone. Bumpers and the other Arkansas senator, David Pryor, were on the same flight from Washington. Bumpers recalled, "The flight attendant came back to me and said, 'Aren't you Senator Bumpers? You have a call from the President.'" Clinton told Bumpers that he was going to appoint Breyer to the Court in light of Dr. Nadler's letter. Bumpers, hoping to delay Clinton's decision, asked if he could call Clinton again when they landed in Nashville. As Bumpers related, "David and I went to a room in the airport that they furnished us, and I called the President back and tried to talk him into waiting a bit. I didn't try to talk him into appointing Richard. I just said, 'You know, you don't have to make that decision now.' He felt he did—he's the President. And I understood precisely why. It had been hanging for some time and he felt that he had to do it."[103]

The final decision was made by President Clinton that afternoon. Clinton had struggled with the decision, alone, for the prior hour. At six o'clock, after he had been able to speak with Arnold, Clinton stepped out of the Oval Office for a press conference to announce his choice.

Described as "a ceremony so rushed that his nominee was absent,"[104] Clinton ended the suspense immediately: "Good afternoon. Today I am proud to nominate Judge Stephen Breyer to serve on the United States Supreme Court."[105] Before describing Breyer, Clinton spoke of two contenders who had "made this decision a difficult one for me." Clinton briefly mentioned Bruce Babbitt, his secretary of the interior and a former presidential contender. But he focused most of his remarks on Richard Arnold:

> Judge Richard Arnold, the chief judge of the Eighth Circuit, has been a friend of mine for a long time. I have the greatest respect for his intellect, for his role as a jurist and for his extraordinary character. I think a measure of the devotion and the admiration in which he is held is evidenced by the fact that somewhere around 100 judges—one-eighth of the entire federal bench—wrote me endorsing his candidacy for the Supreme Court.

> But as has been widely reported in the press, Judge Arnold has cancer and is now undergoing a course of treatment. I have every confidence that that treatment will be successful. And if I am fortunate enough to have other opportunities to make appointments to the Court, I know I will be able to consider Judge Arnold at the top of the list.[106]

Stephen Breyer also had very powerful supporters, including Senator Edward Kennedy, with whom Breyer had worked closely as chief counsel to the Senate Judiciary Committee in the 1970s. Breyer was the preferred choice of Lloyd Cutler, who replaced Nussbaum as White House counsel at a critical stage. Nussbaum, although he believed Breyer was a fine appointment and a great choice, had preferred Arnold. Once he left, Nussbaum said, he was no longer "in a position to really push this over the goal line." If he had been there, Nussbaum said, "I really believe Arnold would have been on the Supreme Court. This wasn't a favor to a friend from Arkansas. This would have been a great thing for the United States and for the Supreme Court."[107]

Arnold was not upset with Clinton—indeed, he said often that Clinton's decision was reasonable—"I think it is reasonable for a president to consider longevity when he makes judicial appointments. And I guess I was hoping at one point at least that the conclusion reached would be different. But I think that the conclusion that he reached is one that a reasonable person could reach, based on the information that he had available to him. And I don't fault him for it. And I told him that on the phone."[108] But Arnold still believed Dr. Nadler's prognosis had been incorrect.

The president received several indignant letters in the weeks following his announcement of Breyer's nomination, taking him to task for allegedly discriminating against Arnold because of his health condition. One writer, for example, said: "Discussions like those you held with Judge Arnold's doctors are both illegal and actionable in the private sector. In the spirit of that law, it seems to me unconscionable that you would adopt a procedure which so clearly violates the intent of the Americans with Disabilities Act."[109]

Two officials of the Kansas Commission on Disability Concerns wrote to Clinton that he had "lost sight of some of your promises" to disability rights leaders during his presidential campaign. The letter reminded Clinton of his earlier statement that "[w]e must continue to voice our conviction that it is morally wrong to deny equal rights to citizenship to Americans with disabilities." They wrote, "Is the fact that he has a disability that currently requires treatment rightful justification for denying him the opportunity to fulfill what might perhaps be his lifelong dream? We understand, Mr. President, that your office is exempt from the ADA, but we would like you to understand that many employers in this nation will refer to your example of not nominating Judge Arnold because of his cancer as their justification for not hiring job candidates with disabilities."[110]

Tony Mauro's column in the *Legal Times* — "Disqualified by Cancer: Is That Legal?" — called Arnold a "victim of discrimination on the basis of disability."[111] Mauro pointed out that in the context of private employment, there is little doubt that the White House's actions in Arnold's case would be illegal under the Americans with Disabilities Act. The judicial branch and judicial appointments, however, are not covered by the ADA, and White House officials justified consideration of Arnold's condition on the special nature of a Supreme Court vacancy that made it appropriate to consider life expectancy. As one official put it, according to Mauro, "Clinton did not want to name a successor to liberal Harry Blackmun who would serve only a few years and then be replaced with 'another Clarence Thomas' by a Republican president."[112]

Frank Rich also wrote a column on the subject in the *New York Times*. "All the Monday-morning quarterbacking" about President Clinton's choice "may miss the point," he wrote. The "lost runner-up" for the Supreme Court seat was not Bruce Babbitt but Arnold, "a highly-regarded chief judge on the Federal Court of Appeals who has been under treatment for lymphoma since 1978":

> The political reasons that a President wants Supreme Court appointees with longevity are obvious. But there may be higher reasons for choosing a man or woman who has been forced to confront mortality by coping daily for 16 years with a serious illness. Were Judge Arnold to live only 14 more years—taking him to 72, the average life expectancy of white American men—or even considerably less, his facing down of his own death might make those limited years of service an extraordinary asset to American jurisprudence, not a liability.

> His experiences would have an immense practical value—and no doubt a humanizing effect—in deliberations where the very definition of life and death can be up for grabs. More important than his firsthand knowledge of clinical issues of illness, medicine and dying, however, would be his depth of perspective on life before the grave. A man who has been forced into sustained contemplation of his own end is likely to have a firmer fix on what really matters than many of us do.[113]

Arnold thought references to discrimination on the ground of disability were "silly," he said, and he did not think much of the suggestion that someone suffering from cancer had any special claim to judicial insight. Instead, Arnold thought it was perfectly reasonable for the president to take into account a candidate's health status. He just thought the information provided to the president was wrong.

In an extensive interview with Stuart Taylor Jr. a few months later, published in the *American Lawyer*, Arnold's public reaction downplayed his personal disappointment. It was a great honor, Arnold said, to be considered for the Supreme Court: "And if I came close, I am certainly flattered by that. People have asked me if I'm disappointed. It isn't really something that you can be disappointed about, because it's so unlikely to happen to any given individual that it either happens or it doesn't. I didn't really feel disappointed. I felt relieved for the decision-making process to be over."[114]

The relief came from an end to the press speculation and the "rumors" he would hear about himself. As a sitting judge, Arnold felt he must follow the conventions about not making public statements. Arnold said he never successfully solved that problem, how to correct misinformation. He had heard, for example, that a senator thought that a certain opinion he had written was wrong and she had serious reservations about it. Arnold could not, he said, simply call her on the phone: "At least I didn't think that I could."[115]

It had clearly hurt Arnold deeply to have opponents question his devotion to individual rights and the Constitution, particularly that he was hostile to women's rights.[116] He did "not mind people disagreeing with my opinions," he said. "That's part of the process":

> I would hope that, if the occasion ever arose again, that an effort would be made to look at the whole record, instead of just picking out two or three things that someone disagreed with. And if they look at the whole record and say, "Well, we still don't think that he's sufficiently sensitive to our concern," then they have a right to say that. But I would rather that the judgment be made on that basis, than simply on the basis of disagreement with two or three opinions or votes that I cast.[117]

But Arnold also valued much of the process. He appreciated the efforts of his friends and colleagues. "You know, whether I got picked or ever would be, it's really a priceless experience for me to have people support me in that way."[118] Arnold knew of some of these letters sent to Clinton supporting his nomination because the authors sent copies to him. Most he would never know about. Of those he did, he wrote thank-you notes to the senders in the weeks following Breyer's nomination to the Supreme Court.[119]

It was still possible another vacancy would occur on the Supreme Court while Clinton was in office, and Clinton had said publicly that he would like to consider Arnold for another seat if his health situation should improve. The health situation did improve, at least in the sense that the initial assessment by Dr. Nadler was inconsistent with what other doctors had previously stated. Dr. Nadler himself later said he regretted the severity of his wording in the letter, that it had been "too harshly phrased."[120]

But the "next appointment" never came for Clinton, and indeed there was not another new Supreme Court Justice until 2006. Arnold served ten more years on the federal bench, "ten good years" lost to the Supreme Court, as one editorialist wrote following Arnold's death in 2004. "Never mind that ten years, or even five years, or just one year, of opinions by a

Richard Arnold would have been worth infinitely more," editorialist Paul Greenberg wrote. "Much like Learned Hand before him, Richard Sheppard Arnold was the greatest American jurist of his time not to serve on the Supreme Court of the United States."[121]

If those ten years were lost to the Supreme Court, they were not lost to the Eighth Circuit. Some of Arnold's most significant work as a federal judge would take place in the next decade, including landmark decisions in abortion rights, school desegregation, and a remarkable tax case, *Anastasoff v. United States*, that would set off a nationwide debate on the work of federal courts.[122]

Chapter Fourteen

Open Courts, Public Ethics, ═══════ *and Private Faith* ═══════

O ne theme of Arnold's years on the bench was his concern for transparency and public accountability in the judiciary, a concern rooted in his faith's emphasis on humility. While many members of the United States judiciary hold the view that they are admired around the world, Arnold was not sure they had fully earned it. He believed the American justice system was "good," but not great. He was especially concerned about public perception of the work of federal courts. He knew that most of the work of federal courts occurred out of the press spotlight, and it was this work, he said, that "affects the public more than they know."[1]

Judge Richard Posner, a friend of Arnold's from the Seventh Circuit, commented on the potential for bad behavior from judges appointed with life tenure, removable only by impeachment. Posner wrote:

> A federal judge can be lazy, lack judicial temperament, mistreat his staff, berate without reason the lawyers and litigants who appear before him, be reprimanded for ethical lapses, verge on or even slide into senility, be continually reversed for elementary legal mistakes, hold under advisement for years cases that could be decided perfectly well in days or weeks, leak confidential information to the press, pursue a nakedly polit-

ical agenda, and misbehave in other ways that might get even a tenured civil servant or university professor fired; he will retain his office.[2]

Fortunately such instances are rare. During Arnold's tenure, he did not believe that any judge on the Eighth Circuit merited such an indictment, or at least he never recorded those thoughts.

Arnold believed that judges, like other government officials, were "public servants" who "work for the people."[3] He understood, and said publicly, that the ongoing operation of the federal courts was fully dependent upon the consent of the governed: "If the day comes in this country when the people cease to give general consent to the exercise of judicial power, that's the day we will have no more courts, and that's the day we shouldn't have any more courts."[4]

AN UNDERGROUND BODY OF LAW

One practice bothered Arnold in particular. Federal courts of appeal issue over 80 percent of their decisions in what they term "unpublished" form. An opinion bearing the notation "Not for Publication" means that the court has not authorized it for official publication in the *Federal Reporter*. Often these opinions are unsigned ("per curiam") and relatively short. In some instances, the decision is merely one word: "Affirmed." For the rest, these opinions seldom contain an extensive recitation of facts or analysis of the applicable law.

"Unpublished" is a misnomer. Although designated "not for publication," these opinions have long been readily available from the court itself or through electronic databases for a fee. An opinion sent for "official publication," by contrast, would appear in the *Federal Reporter*. Officially published opinions typically contain extensive recitation of the facts of the case and apply those facts to a usually more extensive evaluation of the relevant law.

Defenders of the practice—almost all of them federal appellate judges—say that it is necessary because the federal judiciary could otherwise not cope with the caseload. Unpublished, non-precedential opinions are reserved for cases in which the judges agree that no new issues are presented. Both the facts of the case to be decided and the law applicable to it are routine in the court's experience. The decisions are merely uncontroversial applications of established legal doctrine that do not make new law. Dealing with such cases in an abbreviated opinion that does not form precedent for future cases, the argument goes, frees judges to devote more time to matters of greater legal urgency.[5]

Most opinions designated "not for publication" are unanimous. But one study revealed that 24 percent of unpublished decisions issued by appeals courts are not only not unanimous but also that "various judges disagree so much that one writes a dissenting opinion."[6]

The federal courts of appeal increased their use of this practice in the closing decades of the twentieth century (from 37 percent of all cases decided in 1977, to over 80 percent by 2000). This dramatic rise in the phenomenon of the unpublished opinion brought with it increasingly vocal discontent from outside the judiciary. Federal courts now dispensed "justice in the dark," an article in *Forbes* charged. "Judges can be sloppy. They are not accountable for illogic or inconsistency in the rulings."[7] Other critics call it "a black mark against the legal system," one that shields the judiciary from public scrutiny.[8] Further appeals are for all practical purposes precluded. The Supreme Court almost never accepts a case if there is no published opinion to consider.

The most serious problem with unpublished opinions—especially when those opinions may not be cited to a court as potential precedent— is the risk of inconsistent rules of law. *Forbes* recounted an example from the Ninth Circuit Court of Appeals, terming it "proof that unpublished decisions mask plenty of inconsistency."[9] The Ninth Circuit had affirmed the conviction of an undocumented alien who had returned to the United States after being deported. As *Forbes* reported, "His lawyer found that the court had in the past issued twenty-seven separate unpublished decisions applying three different rules to the same immigration issue."[10]

One of the most cited academic criticisms came from an empirical study in which the authors concluded that unpublished opinions were "dreadful in quality." In a 1996 article published by William M. Richman and William L. Reynolds, they wrote: "It is not difficult to understand why unpublished opinions are dreadful in quality. The primary cause lies in the absence of accountability and responsibility; their absence breeds sloth and indifference."[11] Unpublished opinions also found a critic in Supreme Court Justice John Paul Stevens, who called them "decision-making without discipline."[12]

By 1999, the number of such "unpublished" decisions accounted for an astounding 80 percent of all cases decided by federal appeals courts—four out of every five appeals. Arnold worried that increasing use of unpublished opinions meant the judiciary could avoid responsibility for outcomes, and he was not alone in his concern. Judge Posner, also a prolific legal scholar, stated that unpublished opinions are "a formula for irresponsibility."[13] A North Carolina state supreme court justice, whose state appellate courts also issue opinions not for publication, said: "The unpublished opinion constitutes a great temptation to be less than fully accountable. It allows a judge to resolve an important case by making it disappear, rather than going on record on a matter that may be controversial."[14]

One of Arnold's objections was that such abbreviated decisions ran the risk of not fully representing the decision process or properly explaining to the losing party why he or she had lost the case. Arnold had well-known views about how all judicial opinions should be written. Most important, he believed opinions should be written for the losing side of the case, so that the person (not the lawyer) could understand the reasons for losing. "I think about losing litigants a lot," Arnold once said. "Those are the people who need to understand that they have been heard—that a reasoning creature of some kind has evaluated their argument and come to some sort of defensible conclusion about it. They won't like it; they won't enjoy losing, but I hope that they will have a sense that they have been heard. And so it's important how opinions are written. I worry that sometimes our opinions are not living up to that standard."[15]

A former law clerk recalled Arnold's admonition: "When you draft an opinion, always write to the losing side. Write to those most difficult to persuade." An opinion should address as many of the losing side's arguments as necessary to convince them that the arguments had been considered. (An exception would be if a party raised an excessive number of clearly frivolous matters. These could be disposed of together without necessarily writing separately and thoroughly on each one.) Arnold believed that "the art of judging well, and an opinion's precedential power, rely on the ability to persuade others of the rightness of a decision rather than on the gun behind the pen." His opinions were intricately and solidly built. He said no more than was necessary. "Despite his extraordinary learning," the law clerk recalled, "he spoke directly, wrote simply, and never condescended."[16]

Arnold's "unpublished" opinions were longer than most unpublished opinions. One reason he thought unpublished per curiam opinions were such a bad practice is that they were often merely one sentence, without any explanation of the court's reasoning. He didn't necessarily think opinions should be long, but even a second sentence explaining that the decision was based upon precedent, and naming the precedent, would be preferable to a one-word affirmance.

Arnold recognized that his court received some frivolous appeals. As Arnold wrote for a proposed American Bar Association report, "There are some cases, not many, but some, that really do not deserve oral argument." He believed that some pro se appeals (from persons not represented by a lawyer) fell into this category. "Occasionally," he said, "even a civil case in which lawyers appear on both sides deserves only cursory treatment. I do agree that the present system places too much emphasis on quantity and speed. These are important values, but they are not the only values."[17]

In 1995 in a lecture at the University of Missouri–Columbia School of Law titled "The Future of the Federal Courts," Arnold identified the most pressing problem facing the federal courts to be the increase in the volume of cases. He said, "I'm afraid that the volume is just about on the brink of swamping us."[18] Judicial statistics bear out a dramatic increase in cases filed in the Eighth Circuit. In 1984, for example, Arnold wrote 149 opinions, including 63 signed opinions for the court, 17 published per curiam opinions, 60 unpublished per curiam opinions, 5 dissents, and 4 concurrences.[19] From 1990 to 1997, the number of filings in the Eighth Circuit increased by nearly 25 percent. Even though 1997 saw 3,388 appeals filed, the court's median disposition time to terminate appeals was still less than ten months, better than the national average of just over eleven months.[20]

At the time, the Eighth Circuit had only ten active judges to handle these appeals. Like other circuits, the Eighth relied heavily on its seven senior judges as well as visiting judges from other courts. The court also had the assistance of fifteen staff attorneys in St. Louis, in addition to each judge's "chambers" clerks. Many opinions designated "per curiam, not for publication" are initially drafted by staff attorneys. One report estimated that the staff attorneys work on approximately 40 percent of the cases filed with the court.[21]

But what Arnold really objected to was the rule followed in most federal courts of appeal, including the Eighth Circuit, that prevented parties from citing to unpublished opinions. The Eighth Circuit's rule read: "Unpublished opinions are not precedent and parties generally should not cite them."[22] In other words, any opinion not officially "published" was unimportant beyond that individual case.

Lawyers, however, rely on court opinions to advise their clients and to predict how a court will rule in the future. Arnold was fully aware that lawyers and judges feel an obligation to read all relevant judicial decisions, including those not available for citation. In other circuits, lawyers had been sanctioned by courts for making "creative attempts to circumvent the prohibition."[23] In response, the American Bar Association issued a formal opinion stating it is "ethically improper for a lawyer to cite to a court an unpublished opinion . . . where the forum court has a specific rule prohibiting any reference in briefs to an opinion marked 'not for publication.'"[24]

From nearly the moment Arnold joined the Eighth Circuit, he sought to change the court's rule on non-precedential opinions. Beginning in 1983, Arnold raised the issue before the Eighth Circuit judges by way of a motion to change the rule in order to allow the parties to cite to such opinions. For the next ten years, his motions never received a second. As he wrote to a fellow judge: "There is absolutely no justification for unpublished opinions, unless we abolish the rule that they cannot be cited as precedent. It's not so much a concern to me whether they are mailed to West [a legal publisher], as whether they are available to the bar and the public to remind the courts of what they have done in the past. As I have said in public several times, the rule of our courts on the subject is an abomination."[25]

In one early illustration of this sentiment, Arnold delivered an address to the Sixth Circuit Judicial Conference in 1982 in which he identified the "vice" of unpublished opinions to be rules that do not permit citation. The potential for arbitrariness was real: "The result may be that a judge who writes, and the panel which files, an unpublished opinion holding one way on a certain point of law can, so far as the rules of court are concerned, feel perfectly free to decide the other way the next day. That is not the kind of behavior that we as judges, I am sure, would consciously engage in, and not the kind of behavior that we conceive of as being consistent with the judicial function."[26]

Speaking at the Drake University Law School in Iowa in 1999, Arnold was said to be "less genteel" than his "Old South school of courtly manners" usually required. According to a newspaper account,

> Arnold was asked about a story in the *New York Times* reporting that because of crushing workloads, some federal appeals courts are resorting to perfunctory one-word rulings—"Affirmed" or "Denied"—with no

written opinion giving the court's reasoning. The practice is an "abomination," Arnold said. He told of participating recently in a court session where more than 50 cases were decided in two hours. "We heard many, many cases with no opinions or unpublished opinions," Arnold said. "I felt dirty. It was a . . . betrayal of the judicial ethos. It makes me feel terrible."27

Arnold had also published a law review article that year further describing his objection to the practice. Arnold expressed his concern that a court could issue an opinion, stamp it "unpublished," and have the ability to disregard it entirely in the future. Arnold wrote the article to "venture a few personal comments from one who has produced probably hundreds of unpublished opinions, but has always felt uneasy about it."28

Arnold identified the beginning of the "unpublished opinion" phenomenon to be the recommendation in 1964 by the Judicial Conference of the United States that judges publish only those appellate opinions "which are of general precedential value."29 The problem, as Arnold saw it, was that "[i]f we mark an opinion as unpublished, it is not precedent. We are free to disregard it without even saying so. Even more striking, if we decided a case directly on point yesterday, lawyers may not even remind us of this fact. The bar is gagged. We are perfectly free to depart from past opinions if they are unpublished, and whether to publish them is entirely our own choice."30

Unpublished opinions create an underground body of law. Arnold seems to have been looking for a case to make precisely this point. In the early months of 2000, he found it.

A CHALLENGE TO ALL FEDERAL COURTS

Anastasoff v. United States was a small tax case. It did not involve Arnold's great cause—the Bill of Rights—and in fact was later dismissed as moot when the government agreed to refund the amount the taxpayer had claimed she had overpaid—$6,436.31 But Harvard Law professor Frank Michelman, who had been a classmate of Arnold at Yale and Harvard, termed it Arnold's "single, boldest stroke of constitutional interpretation," reminiscent of John Marshall, the first great chief justice of the Supreme Court.32

The case itself was one of many routine taxpayer lawsuits for a relatively small amount of money. Faye Anastasoff sued the Internal Revenue Service in federal district court because the IRS refused to consider her claim for a tax refund. The IRS received her claim one day after the three-year claim period expired, but Anastasoff had mailed the refund request *before* the end of the claim period. The IRS took the position that the date of receipt by the IRS, and not the date of mailing (the so-called mailbox rule), determined whether the claim had been filed on time.

A federal district court agreed with the IRS. Eight years earlier, in an unpublished ruling in the case of *Christie v. United States*,[33] an Eighth Circuit panel had held in favor of the IRS on this precise question. It was the only case in the Eighth Circuit to have considered the question. The Supreme Court had not addressed the issue—an illustration of the numerous questions of law on which lower federal courts can and do diverge, without Supreme Court oversight.

Christie was an unpublished opinion, although it should have been officially published because it was the first time the Eighth Circuit had decided that particular question. Thomas Walsh, Faye Anastasoff's lawyer, claimed he could not find the *Christie* opinion "to save our lives." He continued: "The government had it because they keep a bank of favorable unpublished opinions. If it's an unfavorable precedent, of course, no one will ever know it exists."[34]

On appeal to the Eighth Circuit, the case was argued before Arnold and Gerald Heaney, with Paul Magnuson, sitting by designation from the Minnesota federal district court, as the panel's third member. Walsh conceded *Christie* was clearly on point. But he contended that the panel was not bound by *Christie* because it was an unpublished decision and thus was not precedent within the Eighth Circuit. The attorney for the IRS, by contrast, cited to *Christie* and suggested to the court that the decision in *Christie* was the correct outcome and should be followed.

As usually stated, the doctrine of precedent at its core is that the holding of a case must be followed in similar cases, until overruled. "Binding" precedent—from factually similar cases in the common law setting and from prior interpretations of statutes in the area of legislation, such as in *Anastasoff*—must be followed, distinguished, or overruled. It is often said that a case is squarely on point only if the facts of the case are sufficiently similar and the general principles necessary to the decision correspond to the present case. If not, the prior case may be "distinguished," and there is then said to be no precedent to follow.[35]

The problem Judge Arnold faced was that the Eighth Circuit followed the practice that no panel of three judges could overrule a prior case.[36] If a precedent were to be overruled, that action required the full Eighth Circuit sitting en banc. Arnold was revolted by the notion that he need not be bound by what the Eighth Circuit had done in the past on the exact question.

Instead, Arnold ruled in favor of the IRS because, he said, the court was bound to follow the *Christie* case, even though it was "unpublished" and the Eighth Circuit rule specified that it was *not* precedent. Faye Anastasoff lost the appeal because *Christie* had previously decided the same question. But Arnold needed a justification to disregard his court's rule on non-precedential opinions. He resolved the problem by holding that the Eighth Circuit rule "insofar as it would allow us to avoid the precedential effect of our prior decisions, purports to expand the judicial power beyond the bounds of Article III, and is therefore unconstitutional. That rule does not, therefore, free us from our duty to follow this Court's decision in *Christie*."[37]

According to Arnold, the portion of the rule that specified that unpublished opinions are not precedent violated Article III of the Constitution, thus issuing a great challenge to all federal courts.[38] That article, which confers "judicial power" on United States courts, was understood by the framers to include the then long-standing tradition that a court's prior decisions are a necessary starting point for judicial decision. When a court departs from this core idea, it violates the essential function of the judiciary to treat like cases alike or explain the difference. The bulk of Arnold's opinion was devoted to a lengthy review of historical evidence to support his theory for the invalidity of the Eighth Circuit's non-citation rule.

Arnold was careful to state that the practice of designating opinions "not for publication" was not itself the problem:

> We wish to indicate what this case is not about. It is not about whether opinions should be published, whether that means printed in a book or available in some other accessible form to the public in general. Courts may decide, for one reason or another, that some of their cases are not important enough to take up pages in a printed report. Such decisions may be eminently practical and defensible, but in our view they have nothing to do with the authoritative effect of any court decision. The question presented here is not whether opinions ought to be published, but whether they ought to have precedential effect, whether published or not.[39]

Arnold was aware that judges designated many of their opinions "not for publication" because of a crushing workload. In the opinion, he wrote:

It is often said among judges that the volume of appeals is so high that it is simply unrealistic to ascribe precedential value to every decision. We do not have time to do a decent enough job, the argument runs, when put in plain language, to justify treating every opinion as a precedent. If this is true, the judicial system is indeed in serious trouble, but the remedy is not to create an underground body of law good for one place and time only. The remedy, instead, is to create enough judgeships to handle the volume, or, if that is not practical, for each judge to take enough time to do a competent job with each case. If this means that backlogs will grow, the price must still be paid.[40]

Arnold also explained that the court was not "creating some rigid doctrine of eternal adherence to precedents." Cases can be overruled and, according to Arnold, "sometimes they should be. If the reasoning of a case is exposed as faulty, or if other exigent circumstances justify it, precedents can be changed. When this occurs, however, there is a burden of justification. The precedent from which we are departing should be stated, and our reasons for rejecting it should be made convincingly clear. In this way, the law grows and changes, but it does so incrementally, in response to the dictates of reason, and not because judges have simply changed their minds."[41]

Judge Gerald Heaney filed a separate concurrence in Arnold's opinion. He described the decision as a "great public service," but he called for the full Eighth Circuit to hear the case on the tax question, believing *Christie* had been wrongly decided.

The lawyers in the case did not raise or discuss the constitutional question in the briefs submitted to the panel. This fact was not remarkable for Arnold because he routinely considered appeals in which attorneys for both sides failed to locate controlling legal precedent. Arnold would supply the missing law himself from his nearly encyclopedic knowledge of Supreme Court, Eighth Circuit, and legislative precedent. A former law clerk, Price Marshall, described one such instance. Discussing a pending appeal with Judge Arnold one afternoon, a fellow clerk summarized an immigration case about a question of extradition:

"Do they cite *Ker v. Illinois?*" the Judge asked.

"No, sir."

The Judge got up, went to his set of United States Reports, and pulled down a volume. He opened the table of contents and said quietly to himself, "I thought the name was spelled with one 'r,' not two." Flipping to the case as he walked back, he said, again only to himself, "Oh, it was a typographical error." Handing the book to my co-clerk, the Judge explained the holding in *Ker* to us and why this decision from 1886 controlled the case he was about to hear.[42]

Arnold's opinion in *Anastasoff* quickly set off a national debate.[43] Academics, judges, and lawyers soon filled the pages of law journals and legal publications with arguments for and against Arnold's ruling, and many called for courts to change the restriction on citation. The reaction to Arnold's bold step engendered such national debate that it threatened to overshadow Arnold's other landmark decisions in the memory of the legal community.

The immediate response in the media expressed both approval and disapproval. *Forbes* wrote: "At last, one federal appeals court has declared war on the practice."[44] A *Legal Times* headline, on the other hand, stated "Judge Richard Arnold of the 8th Circuit Has Taken Aim at Unpublished Opinions, But Missed His Mark."[45] The *San Francisco Chronicle* said that although Arnold was "no flake" and was "highly respected by judges and lawyers," that had not stopped other judges from the Ninth Circuit "wondering if he's off his rocker."[46] A colleague reported to Arnold that his opinion was "the talk of the Ninth Circuit Conference when I was out there. Most of the judges seem to think you are on the right track," despite the article questioning Arnold's sanity.[47]

Judge Alex Kozinski of the Ninth Circuit became Arnold's most vocal critic in the unpublished opinion debate. Judge Kozinski has been characterized as a "high-flying conservative" and "the most controversial judge on our most controversial court."[48] Typically outspoken, Kozinski told a reporter: "As a matter of constitutional doctrine it's hogwash. It's total nonsense, and I expect it to have a very short life. I have been surprised at how much attention people are paying to this opinion."[49] Kozinski later wrote essays supporting the practice of unpublished opinions, and he testified before Congress on the issue.

Judge Kozinski also expressly disagreed with the *Anastasoff* holding in *Hart v. Massanari*, a Ninth Circuit opinion in which a lawyer who had cited an unpublished opinion, contrary to the circuit's rule, was required to "show cause" why he should not be disciplined for that action. Judge Kozinski upheld the Ninth Circuit's non-citation rule, but he decided that the lawyer's violation of the rule did not merit sanctions.[50]

Harvard Law School professor Laurence Tribe, a noted scholar of constitutional law, had a "mixed reaction" to the decision. Arnold had raised the stakes in the unpublished opinion debate by calling it a constitutional issue. But Arnold's novel approach to "judicial power" as a constitutional constraint may have been "apocalyptic," even if Tribe sympathized with Arnold's view that non-precedential decisions are "inconsistent with the very notion of what the judicial power under the Constitution presupposes and means."[51]

Shortly after Arnold issued the panel opinion in the case, he wrote to Judge Gilbert S. Merritt of the Sixth Circuit: "I'm sure many judges are dismayed, and it remains to be seen whether I will get away with this. If the case stands up, my guess is that the world will go on pretty much as it was: we will still decide a lot of cases without extended reasoning, some lawyers will cite some of them, and most of the time it won't make much difference to the outcome. As you say, some of our colleagues don't seem to be following even the published opinions."[52]

What many critics missed is that *Anastasoff* did not require publication of opinions. It merely said an Eighth Circuit panel of judges should consider as precedent *any* prior adjudication by the court. But while in subsequent years numerous law review articles carried on the debate, few sided with Arnold's constitutional interpretation. Law professor Arthur Hellman said, "It would be unfortunate if criticism of Judge Arnold's constitutional holding were to deflect attention from the very real issues raised by non-citation rules."[53] Perhaps Arnold's purpose was not to convince others on the constitutional issue but to raise the issue in a way that could not be ignored.

Some judges, lawyers, and law professors have suggested that any rule prohibiting the citation of opinions violates the First Amendment.[54] There also have been suggestions that due process and equal protection theories better support Arnold's point than his reliance on Article III's "judicial power." Under these theories, a court must consider the precedential value of prior unpublished opinions to ensure that it is treating persons equally — applying the same law to all.[55] No court has yet agreed. But it is clear that the potential to dispense uneven justice was Arnold's primary concern.

A few months after Arnold's opinion in *Anastasoff* garnered national headlines, the full Eighth Circuit granted Anastasoff's motion for rehearing en banc and the case was set to be reargued in St. Louis. In the interim, however, the IRS changed its position on cases like Faye Anastasoff's. It had recently lost a similar case in the Second Circuit Court of Appeals, *Weisbart v. United States*, a published decision disagreeing with *Christie*.[56] After it lost the *Weisbart* case, the IRS announced it would follow the "mailbox rule" to determine whether a refund claim met the statutory deadline.[57]

The IRS also acknowledged Anastasoff's entitlement to the refund she had claimed. The tax division of the Department of Justice told the Eighth Circuit that the case was now "moot." Federal courts may take jurisdiction only of "cases and controversies" under Article III, section 2 of the Constitution. Only those disputes "appropriate for judicial determination" may be considered.[58] A controversy that has been settled no longer presents an issue appropriate for court consideration.

The full Eighth Circuit agreed the case was now moot, and Arnold wrote the opinion dismissing the case:

> There is no longer any dispute over whether the taxpayer will get her money. She has received it in full. Nor is there any dispute over whether *Weisbart* or *Christie* is a correct interpretation of the Internal Revenue Code. The government now unequivocally adopts the *Weisbart* rule. The controversy over the status of unpublished opinions is, to be sure, of great interest and importance, but this sort of factor will not save a case from becoming moot. We sit to decide cases, not issues, and whether unpublished opinions have precedential effect no longer has any relevance for the decision of this tax-refund case.[59]

Arnold's pathbreaking panel opinion was now officially "vacated." As Arnold noted, "The constitutionality of that portion of Rule 28A(i) which says that unpublished opinions have no precedential effect remains an open question in this Circuit."[60] Not all "moot" cases must be dismissed — courts can decide that a particular case presents issues of vital public importance or injuries that may be repeated yet evade review. Instead of pursuing the vital-issue exception, however, Arnold exercised restraint. He cared deeply about the non-citation issue, yet he wrote the opinion vacating his own prior work in this case.

In some ways Arnold's panel opinion in *Anastasoff* was a parting shot. A few months later, in a letter to President George W. Bush in early 2001, Arnold announced he would retire from regular active service to assume senior status.[61] Senior status allows judges more control over their caseload, although they are excluded from participation in en banc hearings. In his letter, Arnold informed President Bush of his "intention to continue to render substantial judicial service as a senior judge." And he did. For the next three years, until his death in 2004, there is little discernable decrease in Arnold's productivity. Indeed, several important judicial opinions—in death penalty cases and in the Little Rock school desegregation litigation—lay in the future.

Perhaps Arnold had decided to take senior status even before he wrote the opinion in *Anastasoff*. If so, the realization that he would soon step down from active service may have freed him for bolder steps. In 2001, it was clear to Arnold that there was no longer any possibility he would be considered for a Supreme Court vacancy. George W. Bush, a Republican, had prevailed in the disputed 2000 election. When Bush's first term of office would end, Arnold would be sixty-eight—probably too old for a Supreme Court nomination even if a Democrat were to win the next presidential election.

The timing of Judge Arnold's resignation from active service was unusual in one respect. Arnold relinquished his seat on the Eighth Circuit at the beginning of the George W. Bush presidency, meaning that his replacement on the Eighth Circuit would be appointed not by a Democrat, as Arnold had been, but by a Republican president. Arnold was not unduly troubled by health issues at that point, but he did not feel the need to time his move to senior status to benefit the Democratic Party. Arnold's seat on the Eighth Circuit was filled by Lavenski R. Smith, whose nomination drew opposition from the Alliance for Justice, NARAL, the National Abortion Federation, and Planned Parenthood. Smith had earlier published a number of statements in opposition to abortion characterized in the media as "passionate."[62] Despite some liberal opposition, Smith was confirmed by the Senate in 2002 without Democratic opposition.

Arnold was unhappy with the characterizations of judges as "liberal" or "conservative," and he did not like the notion that judges were so closely identified with the political process of appointment that they should be considered Democrats or Republicans. It was important to him that judges appear to be above the political process. The terms "conservative" or "liberal," Arnold said, "simply do not fit the process of judging."

In a memorial tribute to fellow Eighth Circuit Judge J. Smith Henley, Arnold wrote: "I defy anyone, even with thirty-nine years of judicial service as a criterion, to say that Judge Henley was either 'conservative' or 'liberal' and to defend the answer with reason. The job of judges is to find the facts and apply the law, not their own wills, and Judge Henley understood that well."[63] Judge Henley, a Republican before his appointment to the federal bench by President Eisenhower, was most noted for reforming the Arkansas state prison system. In 1970, he had been the first federal judge in the nation to declare an entire state penitentiary system in violation of the Eighth Amendment. Henley could hardly be called "conservative" on that issue.

Beginning with the failed nomination of Robert Bork for the United States Supreme Court, rancorous Senate confirmation hearings also disturbed Arnold. Arnold wrote to Bork to say that he had not been treated fairly. He later sent encouraging letters to Justice Clarence Thomas and Charles W. Pickering, a federal district judge in Mississippi twice nominated by President George W. Bush for the Fifth Circuit Court of Appeals.[64] Pickering had two Senate hearings at which he maintained his opposition to abortion. He served briefly on the Fifth Circuit via a recess appointment by President Bush, but ultimately Pickering withdrew his name from consideration and announced his retirement from the federal bench.[65]

Arnold was not certain Supreme Court appointments were any more controversial than in the past. In a book preface in 2003, for example, Arnold pointed out that before 1984, the Senate had refused to confirm more than one-fourth of all Supreme Court nominees. But, he added, "We may be returning to the level of conflict characterized by this earlier period."[66]

In that same preface, Arnold also wrote:

> Are there not at least some neutral principles that could be agreed upon for judging the judges? Some examples might be craftsmanship, promptness in decisionmaking, regard for colleagues, and clarity of writing. A judge's reputation should be based not merely on whether his or her views seem to accord with contemporary values 20 years, or even 100 years, later. Instead, judges ought to be evaluated in the context of their own times and for broader qualities.[67]

Many of these "broader qualities" underlay his concern about unpublished opinions. Coming less than one year before Arnold's death, these reflections on the ideal judicial legacy are a poignant reminder of his views of judicial legitimacy in *Anastasoff*.

Richard Arnold was vindicated in 2006 when the Supreme Court mandated a rule change for all federal appellate courts, requiring that they allow citation of unpublished opinions. Although all unpublished decisions issued after January 1, 2007, may now be cited, the rule does not take any position as to whether an unpublished decision has precedential value. Tony Mauro of the *Legal Times* attributed the new rule largely to Arnold: "Though the propriety of an essentially secret judicial process has been debated for years, the catalyst for change was Judge Richard Arnold's opinion in *Anastasoff*."[68]

Arnold died in 2004, three years before the Supreme Court's rule change went into effect. But he knew the debate had continued.[69] The Department of Justice and a US Judicial Conference advisory committee had recommended in 2003 the enactment of a rule to allow lawyers to cite unpublished opinions in all appeals courts.[70] The House Judiciary Committee held oversight hearings on the question, and in the interim, several circuits modified their own rules in various respects.[71] As these developments were under way, the *National Law Journal* acknowledged that Richard Arnold's opinion in *Anastasoff* had "pushed the judiciary toward a rule change," an article Arnold carefully preserved in a scrapbook.[72]

A MODEL FOR JUDICIAL BEHAVIOR

As noted in the introduction to this chapter, Richard Arnold frequently spoke and wrote about how he believed judges should behave and why it was important for judges to uphold high standards. "Next to doing right," Arnold said, "the great object in the administration of justice should be to give public satisfaction." How? In addition to "doing right," one should also "strive to appear to be doing right, to do right in such a way as to command the public's respect."[73] Arnold was especially concerned with the public's perception of judges. He believed judges "ought to be polite. We ought to be reminded that our powers derive from the continuing consent of the governed, and if we lose that consent for very long among a very large percentage of those who are 'the governed,' then we are in deep trouble."[74]

Arnold did not mind criticism from other judges, although Judge Alex Kozinski's public statement that Arnold's opinion in *Anastasoff* was "hogwash" likely tested his limits. But Arnold objected to arrogant and bullying behavior by judges toward lawyers or members of the public.

A judge's character is not fully revealed solely from a reading of his or her judicial opinions. Other actions and behaviors, apart from the record of judicial decisions, fill the gap. Arnold was known for being scrupulously polite and courteous to lawyers who appeared before him. Lawyers consistently lauded his courteous demeanor during hearings: Arnold, for example, was said to have "probably the highest I.Q. on the court," and he was "an active questioner, so counsel had better be prepared." Yet he was regarded as a "polite gentleman" as well as the "brightest judge on the bench."[75]

Arnold also behaved with notable courtesy toward members of the public. He asked that all telephone calls for him should be forwarded with no screening. Staff should not ask, "Who is calling?" before putting the call through. "I work for the public," he would say.[76] Arnold would on occasion answer the phone himself, much to the surprise of many unsuspecting callers.

Eighth Circuit Judge Pasco Bowman recalled "Judge Arnold's unfailing courtesy to everyone with whom he came in contact." Walking to the courthouse in St. Louis, Bowman and Arnold passed a beggar "almost every morning." Judge Arnold not only knew the man's name, he "always spoke kindly to him, and always put something into his cup." Arnold could be firm when the situation called for it, said Bowman, "but his firmness never took the form of an attack on another person's dignity."[77]

Judge Gilbert Merritt of the Sixth Circuit said Arnold was a hero and a model, not only because he was "a high achiever with a great capacity for work," but also because of his "enlarged capacity for sympathy and the ability to put himself into the shoes of another."[78] Merritt related a similar anecdote about an encounter the two had with a homeless person: "Even though pressed for time, he could not pass a beggar by or allow a genuine request for aid to go unanswered. One such time, after he gave the beggar a little money, I said, 'Richard, that guy is probably an alcoholic or a dope addict.' He responded in good humor, 'You never know, he may be an angel.' In his mind, the guy was just one of God's children in need."[79]

Arnold was an unusually open judge in other ways. He responded to press inquiries when he could do so without commenting on a pending case, and he even wrote unsolicited letters to journalists. He wrote to Joan Biskupic, for example, to compliment her for her series in the *Washington Post* on the federal sentencing guidelines. "You have made a great contribution to public understanding of very important issues. Please accept my thanks and congratulations on such a fine job."[80] Arnold was a staunch advocate for better press-bar relations so that the public would be better informed about the work of the federal courts.

Arnold would also meet when requested with citizen groups interested in law reform. In 2002, for example, Arnold met with Dr. Jakob Roginsky and others from a group known as "A Matter of Justice Coalition." That group hoped to raise the awareness of the public "about the shortcomings of the federal legal system," and sought dialogue with judges throughout the country.[81] After the meeting, Arnold wrote to Dr. Roginsky that he "enjoyed meeting with you and your colleagues. Your concerns are entirely legitimate, and I share many of them. I will have in mind what you have said. In addition, please call or write to me any time you wish."[82]

Most revealing of Arnold's character, however, were his responses to letters he received from members of the public who wrote to him. In one example, an elderly South Dakota couple wrote to Arnold concerning their son's imprisonment. They did not have a lawyer and did not know how to raise their son's claims before a federal court. Arnold wrote back, patiently explaining the process:

> I have read and considered your letter. As I understand it, your claim is that your son was convicted and sentenced to a lengthy prison term as a result of the illegal acts of South Dakota police and prosecutors. Further, you claim that the South Dakota Supreme Court has thoroughly misrepresented the law in addressing your son's challenge to his conviction and sentence. I have no authority to investigate state officials or to review the merits of the South Dakota Supreme Court's decisions. The proper remedy, once your son has exhausted his avenues of appeal in the state court system, is to file a *habeas* petition in federal district court. I hope this information will be of assistance to you.[83]

Few judges would go to such lengths to inform a member of the public of the complicated processes of habeas jurisdiction.

In another example, Arnold responded to a letter about a criminal case that was still on appeal within the Arkansas state courts. He understood that most non-lawyers had difficulty understanding when and how federal courts might review state criminal convictions. So he took the time to explain it:

The case you refer to is in the state courts. My court, which is a federal court, has only limited authority to review state-court convictions, and we cannot exercise even that authority until the conviction becomes final in the state courts. If the Arkansas Supreme Court affirms the conviction, it is possible for the defendant to file a petition for habeas corpus in a federal district court. Assuming certain procedural requirements are met, the federal courts will then review any federal constitutional issues raised with respect to the conviction. That's about all I can properly say at this point. I am sorry this letter is not more helpful.[84]

Arnold's brief letters to citizens were masterpieces of clarity in the spirit of Strunk and White. In another instance, a member of the public had written Arnold about the seemingly stalled progress of a criminal case. Arnold responded:

I am disappointed in the fact that the case was docketed in our court on January 7, 1997, but has not yet received any action. I have investigated the matter and have determined that the case is now being actively worked on. I am grateful to you for calling this case to my attention. It has taken altogether too long, and for that I apologize on behalf of the Court. Victims of crimes have rights, and one of those rights is that courts act promptly. I deeply regret that this has not occurred in this case.[85]

On one occasion, Arnold was moved to take action after he received a letter from Fred L. Zimmerman, a Catholic priest who served as director of Dismas House in St. Louis, a halfway house for prisoners on supervised release. Zimmerman wrote to Arnold about a problem with social security benefits for these former prisoners. Inmates who had been eligible for social security were cut off when they went to Dismas House and could not apply for reinstatement of the benefits until after their final release date. At that point, it would take three to four months longer to start their payments again.[86]

Zimmerman wrote to Arnold about the problem after he read a newspaper article describing an opinion written by Arnold in a case concerning eligibility for social security benefits. The article, titled "Court Upholds Inmate in Social Security Case," described an Eighth Circuit opinion, *Peeler v. Heckler*.[87] Zimmerman told Arnold that with over fifty residents, Dismas House quite frequently ran into the same problem. "We have four or five cases at the present time whose release date is approaching and they have no home or job or the means to pay for themselves. It seems to me that the Bureau of Prisons should consider some remedy for the only source of income the men have been deprived of when incarcerated. If we want to help prevent crime, we must see that these men have a means of support when they are released."[88]

Arnold wrote to the director of the Federal Bureau of Prisons, Norman A. Carlson, to ask what could be done about the problem. He enclosed the letter he had received from Father Zimmerman as well as his opinion in *Peeler v. Heckler*.[89] Arnold wrote:

> We have taken a cursory look at some of the social-security regulations, and they seem to contain no prohibition against the filing of an application by an inmate who is about to be released. It seems to me that some arrangement might be reached under which inmate applications would be received and kept on file. There should be a way for the Bureau of Prisons and the Social Security administration to work together to try to avoid the time lag described by Father Zimmerman.[90]

In closing, Arnold added: "No doubt there are problems and complexities here that I do not see, but I commend the issue to your consideration and would be grateful for whatever help you feel able to give."

Arnold, who had not met Father Zimmerman, wrote to him, enclosing his letter to the Bureau of Prisons. "I was glad to receive your letter. The problem you mention, I should think, could be solved if the Social Security administration could be prevailed upon to entertain applications for reinstatement of benefits shortly before the actual release date is reached." Arnold added, "I appreciate hearing from you and want to assure you that we in the courts desire to cooperate in every appropriate way."[91]

Arnold's intervention worked. Norman Carlson addressed the problem at the Bureau of Prisons and reported back to Arnold and Zimmerman. Carlson wrote: "Based on a recent decision by Judge Richard Arnold, we initiated a policy which requires staff to assist eligible inmates in applying for Social Security benefits four to six months prior to their release from confinement. Hopefully, these new procedures will permit eligible inmates to begin receiving Social Security benefits immediately following their release, which should enhance their transition into the community."[92]

It was an unusual step for a federal judge to take. But the cause of destitute former prisoners and the religious organization requesting help were of deep interest to Arnold. He wrote to Father Zimmerman, "When we return to St. Louis to hold court, I would enjoy coming out for a visit." Arnold's concern was completely in character for him because his life centered around a deep religious faith that informed his public work.

DIVINE MERCY AND JUSTICE: ARNOLD'S CHRISTIANITY

Many of Richard Arnold's friends concluded that his courteous treatment of others, both in his court work and in his private life, sprang from his lifelong religious faith. Humility, respect for others, and a high sense of ethical obligation, as Arnold possessed, can exist quite apart from any religious origin. But for Arnold one cannot readily separate his faith from his public demeanor. To Arnold, all people were created in God's image, and a duty to treat all persons with dignity followed.

Throughout his life Arnold remembered the inscription his mother had written on a Bible she had given him—a quotation from Shakespeare known as Portia's "Quality of Mercy" speech: "Though justice be thy plea, remember this: that in the course of justice none of us should see salvation."[93] That quotation was linked, for Arnold, with a passage in the book of Micah asking, "What doth the Lord require of thee?" The answer from the Hebrew Prophet: "To do justly, and to love mercy, and to walk humbly with thy God."[94] Mercy is an important part of divine justice in the Christian and Jewish tradition. Arnold often said he relied on God's love and mercy in his life.

Arnold thought deeply about the difference between divine justice and the justice he dispensed in civil society. A college student in a political science class once wrote to Arnold with the question "Do judges use a 'higher law' perspective in deciding cases?" Arnold's reply is instructive about how he negotiated potential conflicts between his religious beliefs and his oath to uphold the laws of the United States:

> The question presupposes that there is a "higher law than the Constitution," to use the slogan made popular by William H. Seward, later Secretary of State, before the Civil War. I personally believe that such a higher law exists. Some call it natural law, some the moral law, and some God's law. Of course, judges have no commission to decide cases according to their own personal religious or moral views. But when the

positive law, either in the form of an Act of Congress or a constitutional provision, is unclear, judges cannot help but be influenced to some degree by their own moral or religious feelings.[95]

Arnold added, "Judges should use this sort of approach with great care and circumspection. There are as many views of morality as there are people, and a judge has no right to impose his or her moral views on the community."

Arnold's was not a religion worn on his sleeve. He did not make a show of his daily church attendance or note it to his staff or other judges. Judge John Gibson recalled many occasions in which Arnold would quietly excuse himself following a dinner with a group of judges, only to find out later that Arnold had gone to a church to pray.[96]

Although Arnold readily spoke about his Christian faith when asked, he rarely volunteered information. Arnold carefully avoided public statements about what his religious beliefs meant for his judicial work. One of the few public appearances of a religious capacity was his reading of the New Testament at the National Prayer Breakfast, a yearly event in Washington, DC, hosted by members of the United States Congress.[97]

Arnold also spoke at a gathering of lawyers and judges on Law Day in 1998 to celebrate a "Red Mass," hosted by the Catholic Diocese of Little Rock and the Arkansas Bar Association. Held annually in England since the Middle Ages, the "Red Mass" draws its name from the color of the vestments worn by those officiating. The purpose of the Mass is to evoke God's blessing and guidance in the administration of justice. At an address following the Mass, Arnold spoke about spirituality, urging that it goes hand in hand with justice. "What we do transcends the merely human," Arnold said. "We're called upon to sit in judgment of other people, and it's not possible to do that properly without the guidance of the Holy Spirit." But even with spiritual guidance, Arnold said, not all decisions will be correct ones: "Some of them may be in error, but they will be done in the proper spirit and attention." Arnold added, "I personally have never heard a voice telling me 'reverse,' or even 'affirm,'" drawing laughter from the crowd. "But I'm not saying I never will, either."[98]

Arnold's diaries reflect that he attended daily services, often in Catholic churches, although he was officially, by church membership, an Episcopalian. His personal diary listed persons prayed for and theological works he had studied. He read daily the Anglican Book of Common Prayer (the 1928 version, which he preferred) and carried it with him on his frequent travels for court work. Among other passages from the Book of Common Prayer, Arnold prayed the Litany, "That it may please thee to bless and keep the Magistrates, giving them grace to execute justice, and to maintain truth."[99]

Arnold's Christianity is evident from his school years. Arnold had been president of the Episcopal student organization at Yale for his last two years there. After law school, Arnold joined St. Paul's Episcopal Church in Washington, DC, and over the years that he lived in Washington, Arnold served as an acolyte, a vestryman, and a warden of the church. Likewise in Arkansas, Arnold served in various Episcopalian church offices in Texarkana and in Little Rock after he became a judge.

For a number of years, Richard Arnold seriously considered seeking to enter the Catholic Church, but he came to the decision that he would not do so. As of 1988, Arnold said in an oral history interview, he attended the Roman Catholic Church "most of the time," although he also attended Episcopal services. He did not regard his Catholic interests "as much of a change." He did not think the Eucharist was "sufficiently emphasized" at Trinity Episcopal Cathedral in Little Rock. He recognized the issue was "very subjective"—"I haven't come to any theological conviction that Anglican orders are invalid or anything like that. It occurred to me that if I like the Roman Church better, at least in Little Rock, and if I was more comfortable there, why shouldn't I go there?"[100] About becoming a Catholic, Arnold said, "Actually, I've only thought about this for about 35 years, so it seems I have had a rather slow process of making up my mind."[101]

Arnold was what some term an "Anglo-Catholic," or high-church Episcopalian. He liked the Latin Mass. Many acquaintances might have assumed Arnold was Catholic, from his occasional references in personal letters. For example, Arnold's correspondence with Justice Brennan, who was Catholic, frequently included remembrance cards from various Catholic churches Arnold had visited, including the Immaculate Conception Monastery in Jamaica, New York, and the National Shrine of the Immaculate Conception in Washington, DC.[102] In other letters Arnold would tell Brennan, "I have been praying for you—an activity guaranteed, at least, to do no harm."[103] In one letter, Arnold humorously noted that his swearing in to the district court on October 16, 1978, was also the date of the election of Pope John Paul II: "There must be some favorable collocation in the heavens," he wrote.[104]

Arnold was not embarrassed to share his religious beliefs with Brennan. When Justice Brennan was ill in the late 1970s, Arnold wrote: "Each day at Morning and Evening Prayer I pray for you and Mrs. Brennan that God will restore you to health and preserve you from pain. Illness and misfortune some times seem to be the rule rather than the exception, but I am persuaded that the love and grace of God will be suf- ficient to sustain us, and to go before us into every place where we are called."[105] Brennan had been diagnosed with a squamous carcinoma of the vocal cord. Arnold had written to Brennan during his period of radiation treatment. The treatment was successful, and at Arnold's suggestion, Brennan later wrote to encourage Eighth Circuit Judge Floyd Gibson, who had been given the same diagnosis.[106]

SAINT LOUIS ABBEY

In the last decade of his life, Arnold developed a close relationship with the monks at Saint Louis Abbey, and especially Abbot Thomas Frerking. Frerking and Arnold shared a deep interest in classical learning. Frerking, a scholar of the works of Thomas Aquinas, had been a Rhodes Scholar and a professor of theology and philosophy at Notre Dame before joining Saint Louis Abbey as a Benedictine monk. Arnold visited the abbey when he was in St. Louis for court work and on occasion made separate trips to stay in the abbey's guest wing for spiritual retreat.

Arnold had been introduced to Frerking by Jordan B. Cherrick, a St. Louis lawyer who had become friends with Arnold through meetings of the Eighth Circuit Judicial Conference. Cherrick, a religious Jew with a strong background in Jewish theology and philosophy, shared with Arnold a deep interest in ecumenical theological studies. Cherrick, Frerking, and Arnold met every few months at Saint Louis Abbey for what Arnold called "the study group." The books they studied ranged from the Bible to the works of Christian theologians but with an emphasis on texts from the Jewish tradition, including works of Maimonides and Rabbi Judah Lowe of Prague.

A few years earlier Arnold had taken up Hebrew, a reflection of his love of learning and languages. As he once wrote to Cherrick, "Judaism combines the love of God and the love of scholarship in a manner exceeded by none. Someday I hope to have time to pursue my dabbling in elementary Hebrew. I did get as far as reading the book of Jonah, with a lot of help, and large portions of the Song of Songs."[107] (When his brother, Morris, asked him why he was learning Hebrew, Richard replied that he "wanted to understand what they were talking about in Heaven!")[108]

In addition to his meetings with the study group, Arnold also enjoyed the larger community of Benedictine monks at Saint Louis Abbey. He had previously made spiritual retreats at the small Benedictine monastery in the Episcopal Church, Saint Gregory's Abbey in Michigan. Saint Louis Abbey was also a Benedictine monastery, but in the Catholic Church. Located on bucolic acres in the St. Louis suburb of Creve Coeur, Saint Louis Abbey is a monastery that operates a highly regarded boys' school and has the care of a parish of the Archdiocese of St. Louis. The guest-wing rooms overlook a small garden, woods, and meadow, providing an atmosphere of deep reflection.

Saint Louis Abbey became a congenial spiritual home for Arnold. He was attracted to the Benedictines because of their way of life and form of devotion: the Benedictine order places a high value on theological study and scholarship and it also values personal humility, respect of others, and quiet contemplation. At Saint Louis Abbey, Arnold shared these interests especially with Frerking but also with many other monks. It was one of the few environments in which Arnold could speak Latin, Greek, and Hebrew.

Evening meals were silent, but Arnold also joined the brothers for lunch. Seated around wooden tables, Arnold and the monks would converse on politics and current events, or theological issues such as whether anger is ever a proper emotion (Arnold said there was a place for indignant response).[109] Each table in the monastery's dining room seated eight; other monks not seated with Arnold routinely greeted him when going in and out. The brothers remembered Arnold's "wonderfully clear and precise mind, great learning," humility, and sense of humor.[110]

Arnold always referred to Frerking as "Father Abbot." His affection for Abbot Thomas is evident in Arnold's invitation to him to give the invocation at a court ceremony in Little Rock unveiling two portraits of Arnold. One portrait would hang in the newly named Richard S. Arnold Federal Courthouse in Little Rock, the other would be placed in the Thomas F. Eagleton Federal Courthouse in St. Louis. By tradition in most federal circuits, a portrait is officially presented by the court on the occasion of a judge's accession to senior status. The portrait presentation in Little Rock, on June 28, 2002, featured twelve Eighth Circuit judges—the most ever to assemble in Little Rock. The ceremony was attended by about three hundred people, including Senator Dale Bumpers, federal district court and state judges, and twenty-nine former law clerks.[111]

Chief Judge David R. Hansen of Cedar Rapids, Iowa, introduced Abbot Thomas Frerking for the invocation. Abbot Thomas included in his invocation a quotation from the Book of Wisdom, "Love justice, you who judge the earth. And justice, justice shalt thou pursue."[112]

Writing later to his friend, Arnold told Abbot Thomas, "Your presence at the portrait ceremony in Little Rock made the occasion very special indeed." It raised the proceedings, Arnold said, "to a level higher than the merely civic":

> Your excellent prayer underscored the fact that we all depend on God. All must be done to His glory, though we in government are (properly) reticent about that, lest we offend any citizen's individual conscience. I was very happy indeed that in this instance, the sort of occasion on which it is proper for a judge to make a personal expression of belief, you were there to give us a proper beginning.[113]

Such expressions by Arnold of the potential for conflict between personal belief and public duty were rare. By virtue of his position as an Eighth Circuit judge, Arnold had a very public exterior life. Inwardly, he was a very devout Christian. Even with his closest friends, Arnold never seems to have discussed whether, in the details of his court work, he faced a conflict between teachings of the church and his oath to uphold the law.

What his public life represented, though, was surely informed by his religious beliefs. Upholding the law of the land was an oath Arnold had taken, and one that he scrupulously adhered to as a matter of religious obligation. His further devotion to "open courts"—publicly accountable and transparent judicial institutions with judges as public servants—bears this out.

Epilogue

Richard Arnold's health deteriorated rapidly in 2004. He had been diagnosed with lymphoma nearly thirty years earlier but over that time had experienced remarkably few debilitating periods. With a recurrence of his underlying lymphoma in the early spring, Arnold spent several weeks in a Little Rock hospital, "in jail," as he would describe it, undergoing treatments and battling infections. His secretaries, Brenda King and Becky Fitzhugh, or one of his law clerks, would visit Arnold each day to take court work and retrieve Arnold's memoranda, orders, or drafts of judicial opinions.

Despite his health struggles and hospitalizations, during the first half of 2004 Arnold wrote a number of significant judicial opinions, including an abortion case from South Dakota[1] and a dissent in a death penalty case.[2] He also wrote an opinion that upheld a lower court ruling largely releasing the Little Rock School District from nearly fifty years of federal court supervision of its desegregation efforts.[3] Arnold's friend Philip S. Anderson, a former president of the American Bar Association, called it "an opinion of historical significance."[4] The repeated hospitalizations and additional treatments made Arnold's work more difficult, but the quality of his work was undiminished.

377

Colleagues remarked that Arnold's spirits were up throughout that summer. Arnold was sufficiently confident about his prognosis that he made plans to hire more law clerks for the following year. In May, Arnold wrote Frank Michelman, who, along with his other classmate Philip Heymann, helped select promising students at Harvard Law School to be Arnold law clerks. He told Michelman that he wanted to hire law clerks for the court term beginning fall 2005: "My tentative answer now is yes—I would like for you or Phil to pick one law clerk for me from the Harvard Law School."[5]

But by the end of August, Arnold's failing health had made it too difficult for him to take on any new case assignments. Arnold opted for an experimental treatment at the Mayo Clinic in Rochester, Minnesota. He left Little Rock for the last time on September 13. Accompanied by his wife, Kay, Arnold was flown to Rochester in a corporate airplane owned by his former brother-in-law, Walter Hussman Jr. Before Arnold left Little Rock, he dictated a letter to Thomas Frerking, who was soon to travel to Rome for a conference of abbots at the Vatican. Arnold expected to return to his regular activities. He wrote, "I will cherish your letter, which brings me love and support. My ambition is to get back up there [to St. Louis] and resume our studies, but just now I am confined to quarters."[6]

Arnold began a course of treatments at the Mayo Clinic but by September 19 had developed an infection that proved insurmountable for him. He died in Rochester, Minnesota, on the evening of September 23, 2004, at the age of sixty-eight.

On September 28, hundreds of mourners from across the nation crowded into Trinity Episcopal Cathedral in Little Rock, Arkansas, for his funeral. Eight justices of the US Supreme Court took the unprecedented step of issuing public memorials following Arnold's death, including Justice Antonin Scalia, who asserted that Arnold was "one of the great federal judges of our time."[7] Former president Bill Clinton and Senator Hillary Rodham Clinton also issued a joint public statement at Arnold's death, saying, "America has lost one of its greatest jurists, and we have lost a cherished friend."[8]

Serving justice, for Arnold, had been a calling of public service. He often said that "the courts should be places of mercy as well as justice, whenever the law would allow."[9] At his funeral, as Arnold had requested, his favorite quote about the quality of justice was read—from Portia's praise of mercy in *The Merchant of Venice*: "Though justice be thy plea, consider this, that in the course of justice, none of us should see salvation." It was the same quotation, inscribed in the Bible given to him by his mother, that Arnold had read at his investiture in 1978—the beginning of his judicial career.

DEDICATION OF THE RICHARD SHEPPARD ARNOLD COURTHOUSE

In 2003, Congress renamed the federal courthouse in Little Rock the "Richard Sheppard Arnold United States Courthouse." Construction of a 169,000-square-foot annex, under way before Arnold's death, was finally completed in 2007. At the dedication ceremony in September of that year, former president Bill Clinton, appearing on large-screen video, told the audience:

> Richard Arnold was one of the best on the bench, one of the most brilliant people I met, and one of the finest. It is no surprise that this courthouse is named in his honor. Richard was an inspiration to me personally and professionally. And I am very proud to have the chance to honor him today. His death was a great loss to all of us, but I know that he would be so proud that through this courthouse, his love of the law and public service will be carried on through the next generation of jurists. This courthouse is a fitting and permanent reminder of a brilliant man, a great judge, a patriotic American, and a cherished friend.[10]

More than three hundred people gathered for the ceremony, including a number of Eighth Circuit judges who had traveled to Little Rock from their home states. Former US senator Dale Bumpers, one of several speakers to remark on Arnold's brilliance and humor, told about receiving a phone call from Arnold a few years back, reporting the good state of his health. Arnold had told Bumpers, "I should be serving my eighth year on the Supreme Court."[11]

"A LIGHT IN THE LAW"

The significance of a judge's career on the bench often is fully revealed only after the passage of time marks the endurance value of the judge's work. One early summation of Arnold's career, however, was particularly revealing. In an editorial titled "A Light in the Law," Paul Greenberg, a Pulitzer Prize-winning columnist, said Arnold was, "like the best of judges, apart. Much like Learned Hand before him, Richard Sheppard Arnold was the greatest American jurist of his time *not* to serve on the Supreme Court of the United States."[12] Greenberg explained:

> The whole course of American law might have been clarified and elevated if Richard Arnold had served on that court, but we'll never know. And just what was Richard Arnold's law like? Was it conservative or liberal, to the right or left? None of the above. Like the best law, it was apart. It had no ideology. It was law from the inside out, casting a new light that immediately sounded like old wisdom once pronounced.[13]

Arnold himself believed that his most important contributions may have been in administrative work for the federal judiciary. In an obituary that Arnold drafted, in the third person, he wrote: "When Judge Arnold first went on the bench, he expected that he would leave his mark, if at all, in published opinions deciding cases. He did write and publish hundreds of opinions during his 26 years on the bench. But perhaps his most significant service was in various administrative capacities."[14] Arnold singled out his nine-year service as chairman of the Budget Committee of the Judicial Conference of the United States for nine years, a position to which he was appointed by Chief Justice William H. Rehnquist. "As budget chair," Arnold wrote, "it was the judge's job to submit to Congress each year the funding request for the entire Judicial Branch of the federal government, except for the Supreme Court, which handles its own budget. The judge was heard to remark how much he enjoyed this service: 'It has a little touch of politics about it,' he said, 'and I have always enjoyed politics.'"[15]

Richard Arnold's early ambition to be a United States senator was transformed into a significant judicial career. Arnold was proud of his ancestry, particularly for roles his relatives had played in national politics. His own first cousin, Connie Mack, also a grandson of Senator Morris Sheppard, served in both the House and the Senate, completing his two terms in the Senate in 1999. When Mack's son, Connie Mack IV, was elected to Congress in 2004, Arnold wrote to him, "Hooray for you! You will become the fourth generation in the family to be a United States Representative. I am very proud of you."[16]

Arnold understood that the course of justice was a continuing process. In his lifetime he did not see final resolution of sharply debated legal issues, including school desegregation, rules for administering the death penalty, or the boundaries of abortion. Yet Arnold resolved many hundreds of individual disputes, and Arnold's judicial opinions continue to be cited in other courts. His speeches and writings, often about the attainment of justice in the federal court system, continue to receive notice.[17]

Arnold had a certain resiliency deep within that allowed him to contribute to the federal judiciary in remarkable ways, despite living with lymphoma for the entire duration of his career on the bench. He is remembered, as Justice Scalia said, as "the liberals' favorite conservative and the conservatives' favorite liberal."[18]

Acknowledgments

A project of this type incurs many debts along the way. I am grateful to the Emory University Research Committee for providing financial support at an early stage. I also benefited from a fellowship at the Bill and Carol Fox Center for Humanistic Inquiry at Emory University. Emory Law School made a research leave possible and provided two summer research stipends.

My thanks to the many judges, court staff, and Arnold friends and family who allowed me to record interviews with them for this biography. They are acknowledged in "A Note on Sources," and while their names are not repeated here, the book could not have been completed without their assistance.

Many others also deserve recognition. At risk of omitting important contributors, I thank the following: Judge Morris S. Arnold, Kay Kelley Arnold, William Bader, Becky Fitzhugh, Michael Gans, Brenda King, Bobby Looper, and D. Price Marshall Jr. Many of Richard Arnold's sixty-two law clerks shared their experiences and provided editorial suggestions. Crata Castleberry, branch librarian, Eighth US Circuit Court of Appeals, Little Rock, provided cheerful assistance in matters large and small over several years.

Members of my family were enlisted often and from time to time: Marlene H. Boen, Bobby J. Price, Kevin Price, and Amy M. Wills. My niece Ashton Wills met Judge Arnold at age three. Two nephews under five years old at the beginning of the project, Andrew and Alan Price, might be difficult to classify in the "help" category, but they had their own input.

Walter E. Hussman Jr. and the *Arkansas Democrat-Gazette* provided many of the photographs reprinted in this book. Other institutions to thank include the *Arkansas Times*, the *Texarkana Gazette*, the Phillips Exeter Academy Library (especially the assistance of Edouard DesRochers), the Yale University Library, the *Yale Daily News*, the Harvard Law School Library, and personnel at the archives listed in "A Note on Sources."

Several Emory Law School students assisted with research at various points: Noor Abdel-Samed, Nicholas Bedford, Andrew Fedder, Alexandra Gallo-Zelaya, Joseph Gordon, Rachel Elizabeth Green, Michaela Kendall, and Vincent Russo. Brandon Goldberg provided especially resourceful support and pursued many thankless tasks. Other research assistants included Robert W. Hartle Jr., Elizabeth Sykes, and Lindsey Sykes.

Edward Shoemaker, JD, PhD, and Philip A. L. Miller read the entire manuscript and provided invaluable suggestions. Other Emory colleagues read various chapters, and I benefited from my association with Emory's biography group, coordinated by Amy Benson Brown. The Emory Law Library staff as usual provided great support, with special recognition for Terry Gordon and Will Haines.

This is a long list. The work remains mine, however, along with any errors. I welcome your comments and reactions at my book blog, http://blogs.law.emory.edu/price.

February 12, 2009

A Note on Sources

The following manuscript and reference collections were key sources for this book:

PRIVATE COLLECTIONS

"Arnold papers" refer to the Richard S. Arnold private collection. An archives designation is pending.

"FBI File" designations (I, II, and III) refer to Freedom of Information Act releases in response to author requests.

PUBLIC LIBRARIES AND ARCHIVES

Clinton Presidential Library
Carter Presidential Library
Eighth Circuit Library, St. Louis
Arkansas History Commission Manuscript Collection (Richard S. Arnold Campaign Collection, 1966, 1972)

Library of Congress (William Brennan and Harry Blackmun papers)
University of Central Arkansas Archives, Torreyson Library (Morris
S. Arnold Papers, Arkansas Constitutional Convention 1969 Oral History)

Richard S. Arnold Oral History, 1989. Frances Ross, Department of
History, University of Arkansas at Little Rock, completed this oral history
as part of the Arkansas Federal Judicial History Project. A transcript is on
file at the Circuit Library, Eighth US Circuit Court of Appeals, St. Louis.

INTERVIEWS

Richard Arnold participated in six hours of recorded interviews in 2004
for this biography. In addition, the following individuals allowed me to
record interviews. All of them informed the work even if I did not quote
from the interview directly. I am grateful for their participation: Philip S.
Anderson, Gale Hussman Arnold, Kay Kelley Arnold, Judge Morris S.
Arnold, Judge C. Arlen Beam, Griffin Bell, John Billheimer, Judge
Myron Bright, Justice Robert L. Brown, Senator Dale Bumpers, Jeremy
E. Butler, Jordan B. Cherrick, Thomas E. Deacy Jr., Judge G. Thomas
Eisele, David Falk, Frances Fendler, Becky Fitzhugh, John French,
Abbot Thomas Frerking, Michael Gans, Judge John R. Gibson, Janet
Hart, Judge Gerald W. Heaney, Thaddeus Holt, Walter Hussman Jr.,
Gregory T. Jones, Allan King, Brenda King, Judge Donald P. Lay,
Richard Lee, Sam A. Lee, Judge D. Price Marshall Jr., William L.
Massey, Edward W. McCorkle, Judge Gilbert S. Merritt, Frank
Michelman, Henry Morgan, Bernard W. Nussbaum, Justice Sandra Day
O'Connor, Hugh Peterson, Warren J. Plath, Senator David Pryor, Daniel
A. Rezneck, Lydia Turnipseed, and Steve M. Umin.

Notes

FOREWORD

1. See Tony Mauro, "Supreme Court Justices Remember 8th Circuit Judge Richard Arnold," *Legal Times*, September 28, 2004.

2. Letter from Justice Stephen Breyer to Circuit Judge Gilbert Merritt, May 24, 2007.

3. *Greenlaw v. United States*, 128 S. Ct. 2559 (2008), (quoting *United States v. Samuels*, 808 F. 2d 1298, 1301 (8th Cir. 1987)).

4. "Richard Arnold, 8th Circuit Judge, Dead at 68," First Amendment Center Online staff, September 27, 2004.

INTRODUCTION

1. William Jefferson Clinton, *My Life* (New York: Knopf, 2004), p. 592.

2. Calvin Trillin, *Remembering Denny* (New York: Farrar Straus Giroux, 1993), p. 37.

3. Gary Borjesson, e-mail to author, July 10, 2008. Borjesson related the story as told to him by Rhett Martin, a Rhodes Scholar who met Judge Arnold in 2002.

4. 28 U.S.C. §458, enacted in 1998, prohibited future appointments of relatives to the same court. The statute specifies: "No person shall be appointed or

employed in any court who is related by affinity or consanguinity within the degree of first cousin to any justice or judge of such court." The statute was not a reaction to the Arnold brothers serving together on the Eighth Circuit, but rather was a reaction to the nomination of William Fletcher to serve on the Ninth Circuit, where his mother, Betty Fletcher, already served. Robert Schmidt, "Fears of Gridlock on Judicial Nominations Dispelled," *Legal Times*, November 2, 1998, p. 1.

5. Memorial Resolution, Judicial Conference of the United States, March 15, 2005 (Chief Justice Rehnquist presiding).

6. Resolution presented by the judges of the Eighth Circuit, adopted January 10, 2005.

CHAPTER ONE

1. Virgil, *Georgics* no. I, l. 40. Quoted with translation in Fred R. Schapiro, *The Yale Book of Quotations* (New Haven, CT: Yale University Press, 2006), p. 791.

2. *Yale Daily News*, December 9, 1955, p. 1.

3. Ibid., p. 9.

4. *Yale Daily News*, December 5, 1955, p. 2.

5. *Yale Daily News*, December 8, 1955, p. 1.

6. Ibid.

7. Calvin Trillin, *Remembering Denny* (New York: Farrar Straus Giroux, 1993), p. 37.

8. *Yale Daily News*, December 12, 1955, p. 1.

9. *Yale Daily News*, December 9, 1955, p. 9.

10. *Yale Daily News*, February 28, 1956, p. 1.

11. *Yale Daily News*, December 12, 1955, p. 1.

12. Ibid.

13. Anthony Lewis, *Portrait of a Decade: The Second American Revolution* (New York: Random House, 1964), p. 5.

14. Jeffrey Toobin, *The Nine: Inside the Secret World of the Supreme Court* (New York: Doubleday, 2007), p. 76.

15. "Births," *Texarkana Gazette*, March 28, 1936. Newspaper clipping in Morris S. Arnold papers, University of Central Arkansas Archives.

16. Mari Serebrov, *The Life and Times of W.H. Arnold of Arkansas: Reconstructing the Southern Ideal* (Infinity Publishing, 2005).

17. W. H. Arnold, *The Arnold Family* ([Texarkana, AR:] West Publishing Co., 1935).

18. Serebrov, *The Life and Times of W.H. Arnold of Arkansas*, p. 333.

19. Letter to the editor, *Arkansas Gazette*, February 19, 1937. Newspaper clip-

ping in Morris S. Arnold papers, University of Central Arkansas Archives.

20. Interview with Richard S. Arnold, June 30, 2004.

21. "Address by Mrs. W.H. Arnold, Texarkana, Arkansas, Favoring the Candidacy of John L. McClellan for United States Senator," Kate Lewis Arnold file, Box 1, Series 1, Arkansas Women's History Collection, Archives and Special Collections, Ottenheimer Library, University of Arkansas at Little Rock.

22. Ibid.

23. Interview with Senator David Pryor, July 23, 2008.

24. Frances Ross, interview with Richard S. Arnold, February 8, 1988, pp. 9–10. This oral history transcript is on file at the Circuit Library, Eighth US Circuit Court of Appeals, St. Louis.

25. Ibid., p. 9.

26. Richard S. Arnold, "Judge Henry Woods: A Reminiscence," *University of Arkansas at Little Rock Law Review* 25 (2003): 229.

27. Interview with Morris S. Arnold, August 26, 2008.

28. Ibid.

29. Morris Sheppard Arnold, "A Tribute to Richard S. Arnold," *Arkansas Law Review* 58 (2005): 484.

30. Frances Ross, interview with Richard S. Arnold, February 8, 1988, p. 10.

31. Interview with Sam A. Lee, March 4, 2005.

32. *Palko v. Connecticut*, 302 U.S. 319 (1937).

33. *Adamson v. California*, 332 U.S. 46, 89 (1947) (Black, J., dissenting).

34. Frances Ross, interview with Richard S. Arnold, February 8, 1988, pp. 16–18.

35. Ibid., p. 22.

36. Interview with Jordan B. Cherrick and Abbot Thomas Frerking, July 16, 2008.

37. *Exonian*, September 17, 1952, p. 1.

38. Frances Ross, interview with Richard S. Arnold, February 8, 1988, p. 28.

39. Ibid., p. 30.

40. Richard Arnold, "A Jeffersonian View," *Exonian*, December 13, 1952, p. 2.

41. Ibid.

42. Ibid.

43. Arnold likely attended Marshall's address; his friends from that period recalled that he rarely missed the notable speakers Exeter was able to attract, which, while Arnold was there, included Senator Robert A. Taft (then a leading contender for the Republican presidential nomination), Margaret Mead, Paul Tillich, and President Harry S Truman, who spoke from the rear platform of a train in Exeter in October 1952.

44. *Exonian*, November 3, 1951, p. 1.

45. "A Jeffersonian View," *Exonian*, January 10, 1953, p. 2.

46. "A Jeffersonian View," *Exonian*, September 27, 1952, p. 2.

47. "A Jeffersonian View," *Exonian*, November 1, 1952, p. 2.

48. *Exonian*, November 5, 1952, p. 1.

49. *Exonian*, March 5, 1992.

50. *Exonian*, October 24, 1951, p. 1.

51. *Exonian*, February 6, 1952, p. 1.

52. *Exonian*, May 10, 1952.

53. Ibid., p. 2.

54. *Exonian*, October 22, 1952, p. 2.

55. Ibid., p. 2.

56. "A Jeffersonian View," *Exonian*, December 6, 1952, p. 2.

57. Interview with Alan King, August 31, 2005.

58. Interview with Warren Plath, August 29, 2005.

59. Interview with Alan King, August 31, 2005.

60. Frances Ross, interview with Richard S. Arnold, February 8, 1988, p. 31.

61. Gilbert S. Merritt, "Upon the Death of Richard Arnold, A Tribute," *Arkansas Law Review* 58 (2005): 538.

62. FBI File I. Designations to a numbered "FBI File" refer to documents from Freedom of Information Act requests delivered to the author. For more explanation, please see "A Note on Sources" at the conclusion of the book.

63. Interview with Hugh Peterson, March 11, 2008.

64. Richard S. Arnold, "The Emperor Constantine and the Christian Church," Senior Essay: Classics, Yale University, May 1, 1957. Arnold papers.

65. Ibid.

66. Ibid.

67. Quoted in Philip S. Anderson, "Richard Sheppard Arnold," *Arkansas Law Review* 58: 487–88.

68. Calvin Trillin, letter to Richard Arnold, September 17, 1992. Arnold papers.

69. *Harvard Law Record*, September 26, 1957, p. 1.

70. Richard S. Arnold, "In Memoriam: William J. Brennan, Jr.," *Harvard Law Review* 111 (1997): 5, 7.

71. "South Carolina Senator to Discuss Civil Rights," *Harvard Law Record*, December 5, 1957, p. 1.

72. "Thurmond Claims Rights Act Product of Practical Politics," *Harvard Law Record*, December 12, 1957, p. 1.

73. Gerald Gunther, *Learned Hand: The Man and the Judge* (New York: Knopf, 1994).

74. Ibid., pp. 662–64.

75. Learned Hand, *The Bill of Rights* (Cambridge, MA: Harvard University Press, 1958).

76. Frances Ross, interview with Richard S. Arnold, February 8, 1988, p. 31.

77. Interview with Richard S. Arnold, June 30, 2004.

78. Price Marshall, "Tribute to the Honorable Richard S. Arnold for His Service as Chief Judge of the United States Court of Appeals for the Eighth Circuit," *Journal of Appellate Practice and Process* 1 (1999): 200.

79. "Law Review Elects New Officers," *Harvard Law Record*, March 5, 1959, p. 4. Other officers that year included John D. French, who was elected as president; Herbert Dym, Daniel K. Mayers, Nathan Lewin, and Fletcher Yarbrough.

80. Antonin Scalia, "A Tribute to Chief Judge Richard Arnold," *Arkansas Law Review* 58 (2005): 540.

81. John D. French, "Remembering Richard," *Arkansas Law Review* 58 (2005): 506

82. Frances Ross, interview with Richard S. Arnold, December 2, 1988, p. 276.

CHAPTER TWO

1. See, for example, David J. Garrow, *Liberty and Sexuality: The Right to Privacy and the Making of Roe v. Wade* (Berkeley: University of California Press, 1994), pp. 184–85. Richard Arnold also gave me access to the diary prior to his death.

2. Interview with Dan Rezneck, December 12, 2005.

3. See, for example, Edward Lazarus, *Closed Chambers: The Rise, Fall, and Future of the Modern Supreme Court* (New York: Penguin Books, 1999); David Margolick, Evgenia Pertz, and Michael Shnayerson, "The Path to Florida," *Vanity Fair*, October 2004, pp. 310–20.

4. William D. Rogers, "Clerks' Work Is 'Not Decisive of Ultimate Result,'" *U.S. News & World Report*, February 21, 1958, p. 114.

5. William H. Rehnquist, "Who Writes Decisions of the Supreme Court?" *U.S. News & World Report*, December 13, 1957, p. 74. In this article, Rehnquist charged that the Court was staffed with an overabundance of liberal, left-wing law graduates.

6. David Halberstam, *The Fifties* (New York: Ballantine Books, 1994), p. 661.

7. Robert O'Neil, "Clerking for Justice Brennan," *1991 Journal of Supreme Court History*: 3.

8. Interview with Richard S. Arnold, July 2, 2004.

9. E-mail message from Morris S. Arnold, January 29, 2008.

10. Richard S. Arnold, letter to Philip B. Heymann, November 7, 2003. Arnold papers.

11. Ibid.

12. Arnold's mother kept an autographed picture of Chief Justice Harlan Fiske Stone, which hung in their Texarkana house. Stone had been a friend of Arnold's grandmother. Richard S. Arnold, letter to Bennett Boskey, April 30, 2001. Arnold papers.

13. Interview with Richard S. Arnold, July 1, 2004.

14. Interview with Dan Rezneck, December 12, 2005.

15. William Brennan, letter to Richard S. Arnold, December 14, 1959. Brennan papers, Library of Congress.

16. Richard S. Arnold, letter to William Brennan, December 17, 1959. Brennan papers, Library of Congress.

17. Richard S. Arnold, "A Remembrance: Mr. Justice Brennan," *1991 Journal of Supreme Court History*: 6.

18. For example, here is Arnold's diary entry for *Polites v. United States*, 364 U.S. 426 (1960): "Wednesday, November 16: I drafted the *Polites* dissent this morning. It was typed and sent in to the Justice on the bench. He sent it back with a note that it was 'splendid,' and directions to have it printed."

19. Richard S. Arnold, "In Memoriam: William J. Brennan, Jr.," *Harvard Law Review* 111 (1997): 5.

20. Justices Brennan and Thurgood Marshall, and later Harry Blackmun, adhered to the view that the death penalty violated the Eighth Amendment prohibition on cruel and unusual punishment. Brennan and Marshall in the 1980s would frequently record their dissent from denials of certiorari in death penalty cases on this ground. This topic is discussed in greater detail in chapter 8.

21. "Supreme Court, 1960 Term," *Harvard Law Review* 75 (1961): 85.

22. Richard S. Arnold, personal diary, October 13, 1960.

23. John D. French, "Remembering Richard," *Arkansas Law Review* 58 (2005): 506.

24. D. Grier Stephenson Jr., review of *Justice for All: Earl Warren and the Nation He Made*, by Jim Newton, *Journal of Supreme Court History* 33 (2008): 212.

25. Stephenson, review of *Justice for All*, p. 212.

26. Jim Chen, "Come Back to the Nickel and Five: Tracing the Warren Court's Pursuit of Equal Justice under the Law," *Washington & Lee Law Review* 59 (2002): 1249; Jack Harrison Pollack, *Earl Warren: The Judge Who Changed America* (Upper Saddle River, NJ: Prentice Hall, 1979), p. 269.

27. 18 U.S.C. §3501. In 2000, the US Supreme Court ruled that *Miranda*, not this statute, governs statements made during custodial interrogations in both state and federal courts. *Dickerson v. United States*, 530 U.S. 428 (2000).

28. *New York Times*, June 23, 1969, p. 1.

29. *Plessy v. Ferguson*, 163 U.S. 537 (1896). *Plessy v. Ferguson* was a landmark decision upholding the doctrine of "separate but equal" in public accommodations, later repudiated in *Brown v. Board of Education* (1954).

30. Richard S. Arnold, personal diary, November 22, 1960.

31. Richard S. Arnold, personal diary, February 27, 1961. "I sent Black a happy birthday note today, giving him my and Mom-Mom's best wishes. He told the Justice he wanted to see me. He was closest in the Senate, he said, to grandpa and to Senator Norris."

32. Richard S. Arnold, personal diary, February 28, 1961.

33. Ibid.

34. Richard S. Arnold, personal diary, November 22, 1960.

35. Richard S. Arnold, personal diary, April 11, 1961.

36. Richard S. Arnold, "A Remembrance: Justice Brennan," *1991 Journal of Supreme Court History*: 7.

37. Richard S. Arnold, personal diary, March 14, 1961.

38. *Shelley v. Kraemer*, 334 U.S. 1 (1948). *Shelley v. Kraemer*, a case from Missouri, was argued by Thurgood Marshall. The Supreme Court held that restrictive covenants excluding sales of property on the basis of race could not be enforced by states as a violation of the Fourteenth Amendment.

39. Richard S. Arnold, personal diary, May 16, 1961.

40. Richard S. Arnold, personal diary, April 1, 1961.

41. *Cooper v. Aaron*, 358 U.S. 1 (1958).

42. *Cooper*, 358 U.S. at 19–20.

43. Richard Arnold wrote about this episode in a tribute to Justice Brennan: "It is well known that Justice Brennan wrote the Court's opinion in *Cooper v. Aaron*, or most of it, at any rate. (The Justice told me that Justice Black wrote the opening paragraph, and that Justice Harlan inserted into the last paragraph the statement that the three new Justices who had come to the Court since the first opinion in *Brown v. Board of Education*, Justices Harlan, Brennan, and Whittaker, were fully persuaded of the correctness of the opinion.)" Richard S. Arnold, "In Memoriam: William J. Brennan, Jr.," *Harvard Law Review* 11:6–7.

44. Richard S. Arnold, letter to Bennett Boskey, April 30, 2001.

45. "Supreme Court, 1960 Term," p. 92.

46. Richard S. Arnold, personal diary, October 19, 1960.

47. Compare Alexander M. Bickel, "The Supreme Court 1960 Term Foreword: The Passive Virtues," *Harvard Law Review* 75 (1960): 80, with Robert G. McCloskey, "Deeds without Doctrines: Civil Rights in the 1960 Term of the Supreme Court," *American Political Science Review* 56, no. 1 (March 1962): 71–89.

48. *Mapp v. Ohio*, 367 U.S. 643 (1961).

49. McCloskey, "Deeds without Doctrines," p. 81.

50. Richard S. Arnold, personal diary, October 18, 1960.

51. Richard S. Arnold, personal diary, March 30, 1961.

52. *Roth v. United States*, 354 U.S. 476 (1957).

53. *Roth*, 354 U.S. at 484.

54. *Roth*, 354 U.S. at 485.

55. *Roth*, 354 U.S. at 489 (citations omitted).

56. Justice Brennan would later abandon this view of obscenity under the First Amendment. By the time the Supreme Court abandoned the *Roth* test in *Miller v. California* (1973), Brennan argued all obscenity was constitutionally protected unless involving minors, or distributed to minors or unwilling third parties.

57. *Wolf v. Colorado*, 338 U.S. 25 (1949).

58. Thomas Y. Davies, "Mapp v. Ohio," in *Oxford Companion to the United States Supreme Court*, edited by Kermit L. Hall et al. (New York: Oxford University Press, 1992), p. 520.

59. Richard S. Arnold, personal diary, March 29, 1961.

60. Arnold's diary for Saturday, October 15, notes that Arnold had lunch with Chief Justice Warren's law clerks. Arnold "told them the news of what went on at the conference. Apparently the Chief tells them very little about what happens."

61. Richard S. Arnold, personal diary, March 31, 1961. The conference notes also described indecision on the part of other justices about whether the case could be decided on First Amendment grounds (a decision ultimately rejected): "Two—Black, also Douglas—to overrule Roth. Two—Harlan, Frankfurter—say it violates substantive due process to forbid mere possession. Five—The Chief Justice, Brennan, Clark, Whittaker, and Potter Stewart—say the First Amendment forbids prohibition of mere possession; *Roth* distinguished as involving only possession for purposes of sale."

62. Richard S. Arnold, personal diary, April 12, 1961.

63. Richard S. Arnold, personal diary, April 28, 1961.

64. Richard S. Arnold, personal diary, May 2, 1961.

65. Richard S. Arnold, personal diary, May 5, 1961.

66. Ibid.

67. Richard S. Arnold, personal diary, June 8, 1961.

68. Richard S. Arnold, personal diary, June 5, 1961.

69. Richard S. Arnold, personal diary, June 9, 1961.

70. *Mapp*, 367 U.S. at 661, 665.

71. Francis A. Allen, "Federalism and the Fourth Amendment: A Requiem for Wolf," in *Supreme Court Review: 1961*, edited by Phillip B. Kurland (Chicago: University of Chicago Press, 1961), p. 25.

72. *Malloy v. Hogan*, 378 U.S. 1 (1964).

73. Richard S. Arnold, personal diary, June 1, 1961. The case Frankfurter referred to was *Marcus v. Search Warrants of Property, Kansas City, Missouri*, 367 U.S. 717 (1961). That case presented a challenge to Missouri's procedures authorizing the search for and seizure of allegedly obscene publications. Brennan's opinion

held that the search procedure lacked adequate safeguards required by due process under the Fourteenth Amendment, and avoided a discussion of the First Amendment, as Frankfurter had suggested.

74. Interview with Richard S. Arnold, July 1, 2004.

75. *Gomillion v. Lightfoot*, 364 U.S. 339 (1960).

76. McCloskey, "Deeds without Doctrines," p. 84.

77. *Baker v. Carr*, 364 U.S. 898 (1960), prob. juris. noted.

78. Richard S. Arnold, personal diary, October 18, 1960.

79. Richard S. Arnold, personal diary, October 19, 1960.

80. Richard S. Arnold, personal diary, November 3, 1960.

81. *Baker v. Carr*, 369 U.S. 186 (1962).

82. Jack W. Peltason, "Baker v. Carr," in *Oxford Companion to the Supreme Court of the United States*, edited by Kermit L. Hall (New York: Oxford University Press, 1992), p. 57.

83. Richard S. Arnold, personal diary, April 19, 1961.

84. Richard S. Arnold, personal diary, April 21, 1961.

85. Richard S. Arnold, personal diary, April 28, 1961.

86. Richard S. Arnold, personal diary, May 1, 1961.

87. Arnold's views of *Baker v. Carr* are discussed in chapter 4.

88. McCloskey, "Deeds without Doctrines," p. 86.

89. Richard S. Arnold, personal diary, December 10, 1960.

90. Richard S. Arnold, personal diary, April 5, 1961.

91. *Shelton v. Tucker*, 364 U.S. 479 (1960).

92. *Shelton*, 364 U.S. at 488.

93. "Supreme Court, 1960 Term," p. 128.

94. "Truer Course," *Time*, Monday, June 22, 1959.

95. *Uphaus v. Wyman*, 364 U.S. 388 (1960).

96. *Uphaus*, 364 U.S. at 389 (Brennan, J., concurring).

97. Richard S. Arnold, personal diary, entries for October 17, 1960, and October 19, 1960.

98. The reference is likely to *Bates v. Little Rock*, 361 U.S. 516 (1960), decided in the year preceding Arnold's clerkship. In *Bates*, officials of local branches of the NAACP were convicted of violating occupational licensing ordinances for refusing to furnish to city officials the names of their members. The Supreme Court reversed the convictions on the basis of the due process clause of the Fourteenth Amendment, as an unjustified interference with the members' freedom of association.

99. Richard S. Arnold, personal diary, November 11, 1960.

100. Richard S. Arnold, personal diary, December 9, 1960.

101. Richard S. Arnold, personal diary, December 12, 1960.

102. McCloskey, "Deeds with Doctrines," p. 83.

103. *Civil Rights Cases*, 109 U.S. 3 (1883).

104. Joel B. Grossman, "Sit-In Demonstrations," in *Oxford Companion to the United States Supreme Court*, edited by Kermit L. Hall (New York: Oxford University Press, 1992), p. 785.

105. *Boynton v. Virginia*, 364 U.S. 454 (1960).

106. Richard S. Arnold, personal diary, October 11, 1960.

107. Richard S. Arnold, personal diary, October 13, 1960.

108. Richard S. Arnold, personal diary, October 14, 1960.

109. Richard S. Arnold, personal diary, November 28, 1960.

110. *Steele v. Tallahassee*, 365 U.S. 834 (1961).

111. Richard S. Arnold, personal diary, February 21, 1961.

112. Richard S. Arnold, personal diary, March 3, 1961.

113. *Steele v. Tallahassee*, 365 U.S. 834 (1961).

114. Richard S. Arnold, personal diary, March 3, 1961.

115. Grossman, "Sit-In Demonstrations," p. 785.

116. Richard S. Arnold, personal diary, November 22, 1960.

117. *Braden v. United States*, 365 U.S. 431 (1961).

118. *Wilkinson v. United States*, 365 U.S. 399 (1961).

119. Richard S. Arnold, personal diary, February 27, 1961.

120. Ibid.

121. Richard S. Arnold, personal diary, December 14, 1960.

122. Ibid.

123. Richard S. Arnold, personal diary, January 22, 1961.

124. Richard S. Arnold, personal diary, May 5, 1961.

125. Richard S. Arnold, personal diary, November 16, 1960.

126. Richard S. Arnold, personal diary, June 10, 1962.

127. McCloskey, "Deeds without Doctrines," p. 86.

128. Ibid. *Mapp v. Ohio*, in bringing state law in line with the federal exclusionary rule, made the United States the only country to take the position that some police misconduct must automatically result in the suppression of physical evidence. The unique position of the United States on this subject remained true more than fifty years after *Mapp* was decided. Adam Liptak, "U.S. Stands Alone in Rejecting All Evidence When Police Err," *New York Times*, July 19, 2008, p. A1.

129. Richard S. Arnold, letter to William Brennan, October 14, 1961. Brennan papers, Library of Congress.

130. Richard S. Arnold, "A Remembrance: Justice Brennan," *1991 Journal of Supreme Court History*: 8 (quoting Shakespeare, *Othello*, act V, scene I, 19).

131. Richard S. Arnold, personal diary, November 22, 1961.

132. Daniel A. Rezneck, letter to Lloyd Cutler, April 8, 1994. Clinton Presidential Library.

45. Stine, Arnold interview, p. 5.

46. Ibid., pp. 5–6.

47. "Started with Gilham Dam."

48. James Fullerton, "Arnold Garners Honors for Work on Environment," *Arkansas Democrat-Gazette*.

49. Rick O'Neal, "Lawyer Sees Victory in Midst of Defeat on Suit: Judges Rule Citizens, Courts Can Review Congress' Decisions," *Arkansas Democrat*, November 30, 1972.

50. *Environmental Defense Fund, Inc. v. Corps of Engineers*, 325 F. Supp. 749 (E.D. Ark. 1971).

51. Ginger Shiras, "Arnold Gets Results in Ecology Lawsuits," *Arkansas Gazette*, November 7, 1971.

52. Ibid.

53. Michael B. Dougan, *Arkansas Odyssey: The Saga of Arkansas from Prehistoric Times to Present* (Little Rock, AR: Rose Publishing, 1994), p. 597.

54. *Environmental Defense Fund, Inc. v. Froehlke*, 473 F.2d 346 (8th Cir. 1972).

55. "Lord God! Good News," *Arkansas Times*, June 9, 2005; John W. Fitzpatrick, "The View from Sapsucker Woods," *Birdscope* 19, no. 3 (Summer 2005), Cornell Lab of Ornithology, http://www.birds.cornell.edu/Publications/Birdscope/Summer2005/view_sapsucker-summer2005.html (accessed July 9, 2008).

56. "Lord God! Good News," p. 1.

57. "Excerpts from the Ivory-Billed Woodpecker Press Conference," April 28, 2005, http://www.birds.cornell.edu/Publications/Birdscope/Summer2005/ib_press_conference.html (accessed July 9, 2008).

58. "Finding the Lord God Bird: Ed Bradley Reports on the Rediscovery of the Ivory-Billed Woodpecker," *60 Minutes*, October 16, 2005. A transcript of the show is available at http://www.cbsnews.com/stories/2005/10/13/60minutes/main940587.shtml (accessed June 9, 2008).

59. See, for example, James Gorman, "Ivory Bill or Not? The Proof Flits Tantalizingly Out of Sight," *New York Times*, August 30, 2005, p. D1.

60. "Lord God! Good News," p. 1.

61. Tim Gallagher, *The Grail Bird: The Rediscovery of the Ivory-Billed Woodpecker* (Boston: Houghton Mifflin, 2006); Jerome A. Jackson, *In Search of the Ivory-Billed Woodpecker* (New York: HarperCollins, 2006). A new epilogue disputes the April 2005 discovery in Arkansas.

62. Sam Hamilton, regional director for US Fish and Wildlife, Atlanta, Georgia, quoted in "Lord God! Good News," *Arkansas Times*, June 9, 2005.

63. Jack Schnedler, "Pratt Cates Remmel Jr. Looking for a Rare Bird," *Arkansas Democrat-Gazette*, July 31, 2005.

64. A history of the project, along with current information and navigability is available at http://www.tenntom.org (accessed July 9, 2008) and http://tenntom.sam.usace.army.mil (accessed July 9, 2008). See also Jeffrey K. Stine, *Mixing the Waters: Environment, Politics, and the Building of the Tennessee-Tombigbee Waterway* (Akron, OH: University of Akron Press, 1993).

65. *Environmental Defense Fund v. Corps of Engineers*, 331 F. Supp. 925 (D.D.C. 1971).

66. *Environmental Defense Fund v. Corps of Engineers*, 492 F.2d 1123, 1129 (5th Cir. 1974).

67. Stine, Arnold interview, p. 22.

68. *Environmental Defense Fund v. Corps of Engineers*, 348 F. Supp. 916 (D. Miss. 1972).

69. Ibid.

70. *Environmental Defense Fund v. Corps of Engineers*, 492 F.2d 1123 (5th Cir. 1974).

71. Stine, Arnold interview, p. 41.

72. http://www.tenntom.org/MAINPAGES/ttwhome.html (accessed July 9, 2008).

73. Stine, *Mixing the Waters: Environment, Politics, and the Building of the Tennessee-Tombigbee Waterway.*

74. Ibid., p. 110.

75. Ibid., p. 278, n.4.

76. Hunter M. Gholson, letter to President William Clinton, April 13, 1994. Clinton Presidential Library.

77. "Ecology Awards Planned," *Arkansas Democrat*, October 31, 1973.

78. "Texarkana Lawyer Wins Conservationist Award," *Arkansas Gazette*, November 2, 1973.

79. Jane Fullerton, "Arnold Garners Honors for Work on Environment," *Arkansas Democrat-Gazette*, November 15, 1996, p. 4B.

80. Ibid.

81. Richard S. Arnold, letter to Nicholas Churchill Yost, April 9, 2004. Arnold papers.

82. Richard S. Arnold, "The Substantive Right to Environmental Quality under the National Environmental Policy Act," *Environmental Law Reporter* 3 (1973): 50028.

83. Richard S. Arnold, "The Power of State Courts to Enjoin Federal Officers," *Yale Law Journal* 73 (1964): 1385; Richard S. Arnold, "State Power to Enjoin Federal Court Proceedings," *Virginia Law Review* 51 (1965): 59.

84. Richard Arnold, "The Supreme Court and the Antitrust Laws, 1953–1967," *Antitrust Law Journal* 34 (1967): 2.

85. Richard Arnold, "An Ombudsman for Arkansas," *Arkansas Law Review* 21 (1968): 327. Richard Arnold retained his collegiate love of classical literature and

the Latin language. An introductory quote from Juvenal's *Satires*—"*Sed quis cus-todiet ipsos custodes?*" (But who will guard the guardians?)—graces the beginning of this article. Morris S. Arnold was editor-in-chief of the *Arkansas Law Review* that year and solicited the article from his brother.

CHAPTER FOUR

1. William Brennan, letter to Richard S. Arnold, September 10, 1962. Brennan papers, Library of Congress.

2. William Brennan, letter to Richard S. Arnold, November 9, 1964. Brennan papers, Library of Congress.

3. Waddy W. Moore, interview with Richard S. Arnold, June 17, 1969, Arkansas Constitutional Convention Oral History Project, p. 24. University of Central Arkansas Archives.

4. In his questionnaire submitted to the Department of Justice for nomination to the federal district court, Arnold lists membership in the ACLU for the years "1961(?)–1965(?)." Question marks appear in the original. Arnold papers.

5. As one example, the 1972 campaign for state attorney general featured Republican Ed Bethune's attack on his Democratic challenger, Jim Guy Tucker, as "weak" on the issue of crime. Bethune charged that Tucker was a member of the American Civil Liberties Union, which he denounced as "an ultraliberal organization that is soft on criminals, drugs, and sex offenders." "Ed Bethune," http://en.wikipedia.org/wiki/Ed_Bethune (accessed July 10, 2008). Bethune lost that race, but the ACLU affiliation probably cost Tucker some votes.

6. The organization's history is described in an article by Charles T. Lester Jr., "The History of the Lawyers; Committee for Civil Rights under Law 1963–2003," available at http://www.lawyerscommittee.org/2005website/aboutus/history/history.html.

7. "'Liberal' or 'Conservative' Tag Won't Stick on Justices," *Texarkana Gazette*, August 28, 1962.

8. *Engel v. Vitale*, 370 U.S. 421 (1962).

9. *Engel*, 370 U.S. at 424.

10. "'Liberal' or 'Conservative' Tag Won't Stick on Justices."

11. Editorial comment, "The Supreme Court Change," (no date), enclosure in letter from Richard Arnold to William Brennan, September 5, 1962. Brennan papers, Library of Congress.

12. Ibid.

13. Ibid.

14. Richard S. Arnold, letter to William Brennan, September 5, 1962. Brennan papers, Library of Congress.

15. William Brennan, letter to Richard S. Arnold, September 10, 1963. Brennan papers, Library of Congress.

16. John R. Starr, "Texarkana Lawyer Aims for Congress Post," *Arkansas Democrat*, January 21, 1966.

17. Mike Trimble, "Arnold's '66 Loss to Pryor May Be High Court's Gain," *Arkansas Democrat-Gazette*, March 21, 1993, p. 1A.

18. John R. Starr, "Texarkana Lawyer Aims for Congress Post," *Arkansas Democrat*, January 21, 1966.

19. The characterization is Arnold's—see Trimble, "Arnold's '66 Loss."

20. Interview with Richard S. Arnold, July 1, 2004.

21. Waddy W. Moore, interview with Richard S. Arnold, June 17, 1969, Arkansas Constitutional Convention Oral History Project, p. 48. University of Central Arkansas Archives.

22. John R. Starr, "Political Candidate Shoots for Congress," *Arkansas Democrat*, January 26, 1966, p. 14.

23. Moore, interview with Richard S. Arnold, p. 24.

24. Press release and speech notes, Richard Arnold Campaign Collection, Arkansas History Commission.

25. John P. Frank and A. Leon Higginbotham Jr., "A Brief Biography of Judge Richard S. Arnold," *Minnesota Law Review* 78 (1993): 7.

26. Press release, Richard Arnold Campaign Collection, Arkansas History Commission.

27. Campaign flyer, Richard Arnold Campaign Collection, Arkansas History Commission.

28. "Lawyer, Eye on Harris' Seat, Praises Johnson on Vietnam," *Arkansas Gazette*, October 5, 1965.

29. *Baker v. Carr*, 369 U.S. 186 (1962).

30. Press release, Arnold Campaign Collection, Arkansas History Commission.

31. "Arnold Says Criticism Should Be Responsible," undated newspaper clipping, Arnold papers.

32. Moore, interview with Richard S. Arnold, p. 19.

33. Ibid., p. 21.

34. Ibid., p. 19.

35. Ibid.

36. Richard S. Arnold, "The Supreme Court and the Antitrust Laws, 1953–1967," *Antitrust Law Journal* 34 (1967): 2.

37. Ibid.

38. Richard Arnold campaign collection, Arkansas History Commission (February 1966).

39. Moore, interview with Richard S. Arnold, pp. 22–23.

40. Press release, Richard Arnold Campaign Collection, Arkansas History Commission.

41 "Some Federal Spending Said Worthwhile," *Arkansas Democrat*, November 19, 1965.

42. "Arnold Backs 14b; Seeks Others' Views," *Arkansas Democrat*, February 9, 1966.

43. The case, *United States Jaycees v. McClure*, 709 F.2d 1560 (8th Cir. 1983), rev'd, *Roberts v. United States Jaycees*, 468 U.S. 609 (1984), is discussed in chapter 9.

44. Press release, Richard Arnold Campaign Collection, Arkansas History Commission. The press release notes that the speech was carried on Little Rock, Texarkana, and El Dorado television.

45. Associated Press, "Pryor Calls Arnold Attack 'Desperation,'" *Arkansas Democrat*, August 2, 1966.

46. The speech is recapped in a press release marked "Palmer Bureau, AP, Gazette, Commercial, UPI, Times." Press release, Richard Arnold Campaign Collection, Arkansas History Commission (no date).

47. Associated Press, "Pryor Calls Arnold Attack 'Desperation.'"

48. Associated Press, "Pryor Challenges Foe on Labor Accusation," *Arkansas Democrat*, August 3, 1966.

49. Press release, Arnold Campaign Collection, Arkansas History Commission.

50. Associated Press, "Pryor and Arnold Swap Charges Election Eve.' *Arkansas Democrat*, August 9, 1966.

51. Ibid.

52. In the 1966 run-off election, David Pryor received 72,986 votes and Arnold received 40,091.

53. Associated Press, "Pryor Rolls Over Arnold in Race for Congressional Seat," *Arkansas Democrat*, August 10, 1966.

54. Ibid.

55. Interview with David Pryor, July 14, 2004.

56. William Brennan, letter to Mr. and Mrs. Richard Arnold, August 10, 1966. Brennan papers, Library of Congress.

57. Interview with David Pryor, July 21, 2008.

58. "Arnold Refuses Teaching Post," *Arkansas Gazette* (undated clipping). Arnold papers.

59. John A. Fogleman, letter to Richard S. Arnold, October 23, 1991. Arnold papers.

60. J. William Fulbright, letter to Richard S. Arnold, June 24, 1968. Arnold Campaign Collection, Arkansas History Commission.

61. J. William Fulbright, *The Arrogance of Power* (New York: Random House, 1966).

62. Jack Schnedler, "'68 Flashbacks," *Arkansas Democrat-Gazette*, August 22, 1996, p. 1E.

63. Moore, interview with Richard S. Arnold, p. 34.

64. J. William Fulbright, letter to Richard S. Arnold, June 24, 1968. Arnold Campaign Collection, Arkansas History Commission.

65. Maurice Moore, "Arnold Wants Election of Convention Delegates," *Arkansas Democrat*; September 12, 1968, "Party Panel Plans Study on Delegates," *Arkansas Democrat*, November 12, 1969; "Arnold to Propose Presidential Primary," *Arkansas Democrat*, July 27, 1970.

66. Richard S. Arnold letter, February 27, 1967. Arnold Campaign Collection, Arkansas History Commission.

67. Ibid.

68. Bobbie Forster, "Texarkana Lawyer Is Drafting Tax Bills," *Arkansas Democrat*, January 7, 1969.

69. Ernest Dumas, "2 Defeated 'Constitutions' Still Affect the State's Law," *Arkansas Gazette*, March 28, 1971, p. 5A.

70. Harry A. Haines, memo to delegates, Public Information Committee (no date on original). Arnold Papers, Constitutional Convention File.

71. Richard S. Arnold, letter to W. E. Hussman, August 12, 1969, Arnold papers, Constitutional Convention File.

72. Waddy W. Moore, interview with Garnett Thomas Eisele, February 18, 1970, Arkansas Constitutional Convention, Oral History Project, p. 43. University of Central Arkansas Archives.

73. Richard S. Arnold, letter to Bishop Paul V. Galloway, July 14, 1969, Arnold papers, Constitutional Convention File.

74. Richard S. Arnold Papers, letter to Harold J. Bowers, July 15, 1969, Arnold papers, Constitutional Convention File.

75. Richard S. Arnold, pamphlet titled "Arkansas State AFL-CIO Delegate Voting Record," no date given, Arnold papers, Constitutional Convention File.

76. This refers to Freedom to Work Constitutional Amendment #34 of 1944, retained in the proposed constitution of 1970.

77. Arthur M. Smith, letter to Richard S. Arnold, August 13, 1969, Arnold papers, Constitutional Convention File.

78. Proposed State Constitution, *Arkansas Democrat, Special Sunday Magazine Supplement*, October 5, 1969.

79. "Arnold Says Constitution Needs Push," *Arkansas Democrat*, October 1, 1969.

80. Sidney S. McMath, letter to Richard S. Arnold, October 6, 1969, Arnold papers, Constitutional Convention File.

81. Interview with G. Thomas Eisele, October 1, 2007.

82. Letter to "Dear Senator," with names of law clerks appended, March 31, 1970. Arnold papers.

83. Moore, interview with Richard S. Arnold pp. 46–47.

84. Ibid., p. 17.

85. Ibid., p. 47.

86. Richard S. Arnold, letter to Mark Bradham, March 30, 1998. Arnold papers.

87. "Pryor's Foe Considering Another Bid," *Arkansas Gazette*, July 7, 1971.

88. Ibid.

89. *Pine Bluff Commercial*, May 18, 1972, p. 4.

90. Ibid.

91. Ginger Shiras, "Arnold Gets Results in Ecology Suits," *Arkansas Gazette*, November 7, 1971. "If these preliminary victories delighted environmentalists, 'they're losing me votes,' said Arnold." In all of Sevier County, Arkansas, the location of the Cossatot River project, Arnold received only four hundred votes. A local newspaper, the *DeQueen Bee*, opined that Arnold "must have gotten those by mistake." Interview with Morris S. Arnold, July 13, 2008.

92. Ibid.

93. "Arnold Hits Bus Measure," *Arkansas Gazette*, April 20, 1972, p. 7A.

94. Moore, interview with G. Thomas Eisele.

95. Moore, interview with Richard S. Arnold, p. 19. In response to the question "What does the law and order phrase mean to you?" Arnold replied: "What it means depends on who says it. As it was used in the Wallace campaign, it meant repression of Negroes, at least it was intended to and did communicate that idea. To me it means obedience to law which is a good thing."

96. "Texarkana Lawyer Enters Contest for Pryor's Seat," *Arkansas Democrat*, March 12, 1972.

97. Ibid.

98. *Pine Bluff Commercial*.

99. Script for television copy, "Arnold Listens." Arnold Campaign Collection, Arkansas History Commission.

100. Faulkner and Associates, Inc. Television/Radio Copy, May 10, 1972, Arnold Campaign Collection, Arkansas History Commission.

101. Campaign speech. Arnold Campaign Collection, Arkansas History Commission.

102. Press release, "Arnold Calls for Social Security Reform," May 23, 1972.

103. Moore, interview with Richard S. Arnold, p. 40.

104. May 17, 1972, press release. Arnold Campaign Collection, Arkansas History Commission.

105. Rick O'Neal, "Unofficial Count Seats Thornton in Congress," *Arkansas Democrat*, May 31, 1972.

106. Ibid.

107. Rick O'Neal, "4th District House Seat Run-off Seen," *Arkansas Democrat*, May 21, 1972.

108. O'Neal, "Unofficial Count Seats Thornton in Congress."

109. FBI File II, Earl Jones interview.

110. FBI File I, Interview of Damon Michael Young, July 7, 1978.

111. Barry M. Goldwater, "Washington Star," December 3, 1961, quoted in *The Yale Book of Quotations*, by Fred R. Schapiro (New Haven, CT: Yale University Press, 2006), p. 317.

112. Dale Bumpers, "A Tribute to Richard S. Arnold," *Arkansas Law Review* 58 (2005): 497–98.

113. "Started with Gilham Dam: He Became Environmental Attorney," *Arkansas Democrat*, September 18, 1971.

114. FBI File I, questionnaire.

115. "Arnold May Quit Practice: Says If Bumpers Wins Election He'll Go with Him," *Arkansas Democrat*, June 30, 1974.

116. Richard S. Arnold, letter to Justice Brennan, August 7, 1974. Brennan papers, Library of Congress.

117. Ibid.

118. Ibid.

119. Anthony Lewis, *Portrait of a Decade: The Second American Revolution* (New York: Random House, 1964).

120. Arnold later recounted the following anecdote: "The first time I ever went to Malvern to campaign, I went to see a black preacher. The reason I went to see him was that my friends in Texarkana, my black friends, told me he was a person of influence and obviously should be somebody that I would talk to. I went to see him and he said 'Let's go eat lunch.' I said 'Fine.' We went to lunch at a place in Malvern which was 'for white people.' There was no problem. Everybody was perfectly courteous about him but it was not something that happened a lot in Malvern in 1965. But later on, when I went back to see other people in Malvern, I was really bitterly attacked for this. They said this was the stupidest thing they had ever heard of. 'Why would you come up here, and instead of talking to us, why would you go to that Black? I don't think they said 'Black.' And they said 'Why would you go to a restaurant with him that way?' Apparently, it was all over town that I had come in there and not seen any white people." Frances Ross, interview with Richard S. Arnold, November 29, 1988, pp. 121–22. This oral history transcript is on file at the Circuit Library, Eighth US Circuit Court of Appeals, St. Louis.

121. Ibid., pp. 122–23.

122. FOIA response, Request 2006-0188-F, Clinton Presidential Library.

123. Trimble, "Arnold's '66 Loss to Pryor May Be High Court's Gain," p. 7A.

124. Richard S. Arnold, letter to Mark Bradham, March 30, 1998. Arnold papers.

CHAPTER FIVE

1. Interview with Richard S. Arnold, July 1, 2004.

2. Sheldon Goldman and Elliot Slotnick, "Picking Judges Under Fire," *Judicature* 82, no. 6 (1999): 282.

3. "Bumpers: Watch That Killer Smile," *Time*, November 18, 1974.

4. Interview with Dale Bumpers, June 29, 2004.

5. Ibid.

6. Ibid.

7. Transcript, "Investiture of the Honorable Richard Sheppard Arnold as United States District Judge for the Eastern and Western Districts of Arkansas," October 16, 1978, p. 14. Arnold papers.

8. Richard S. Arnold, "Money, Or the Relations of the Judicial Branch with the Other Two Branches, Executive and Legislative," *St. Louis University Law Journal* 40 (1996): 22–23.

9. Interview with Dale Bumpers, June 29, 2004.

10. Interview with Robert Brown, August 23, 2004.

11. Interview with Gilbert S. Merritt, March 17, 2008.

12. Richard S. Arnold, "The Federal Courts: Causes for Discontent (Irvin R. Goldberg Lecture)," *SMU Law Review* 56 (2003): 767–68.

13. Ibid., p. 767.

14. Ibid., pp. 767–68.

15. Ibid.

16. Note, "Consequences of Abstention by a Federal Court," *Harvard Law Review* 73 (1960): 1358; Richard S. Arnold, "The Power of State Courts to Enjoin Federal Officers," *Yale Law Journal* 73 (1964): 1385; Richard S. Arnold, "State Power to Enjoin Federal Court Proceedings," *Virginia Law Review* 51 (1965): 59; Richard S. Arnold, "The Supreme Court and the Antitrust Laws 1953–1967," *Antitrust Law Journal* 34 (1967): 2.

17. Richard S. Arnold, "The Substantive Right to Environmental Quality under the National Environmental Policy Act," *Environmental Law Review* 3 (1973): 50028.

18. Elliot Slotnick, "Federal Judicial Selection in the New Millennium: Prologue," *University of California, Davis, Law Review* 36 (2003): 592.

19. "Cushman, Senate Imperiling Judicial System, Chief Justice Says," *New York Times*, January 1, 1998, p. 1.

20. Slotnick, "Federal Judicial Selection in the New Millennium: Prologue," p. 591.

21. Ibid., p. 592.

22. United States Senate Committee on the Judiciary, "Questionnaire for Nominee for the Supreme Court of the United States (public version released for Samuel Alito)," http://i.a.cnn.net/cnn/interactive/us/0511/alito.questionnaire/SAA .Questionnaire.pdf, p. 60 (accessed July 24, 2008).

23. FBI File I, interview with Justice William Brennan, July 17, 1978.

24. Press conference, Statement of Attorney General Griffin Bell, February 1978, p. 1. Carter Presidential Library, Collection JC-DPS: Records of the Domestic Policy Staff (Carter Administration), 1976–1981. File unit: Judicial Merit Selection. Box: 23.

25. Ibid., p. 2.

26. Ibid., p. 3.

27. Ibid., p. 8.

28. Interview with Griffin Bell, October 11, 2007.

29. Ibid.

30. FBI File I, summary of interview with William Brennan, July 17, 1978.

31. Ultimately, Elsijane Roy filled this seat, making her the first woman to serve as a federal judge in Arkansas. Carter and Bell were thus able to fulfill some of their objectives with this first vacancy. Lisa Hammersly, "Richard Arnold Sworn in as Federal Judge," *Arkansas Democrat*, October 16, 1978, p. 1: "Arnold was rumored to be Bumpers' candidate for a federal judgeship in 1977 after Judge Harris, of El Dorado, retired. Judge Roy was finally named to that position after Bumpers held up in committee the nomination by then-president Gerald Ford of Ed Bethune, a Searcy lawyer."

32. Interview with Dale Bumpers, June 29, 2004.

33. FBI File I, July 7, 1978.

34. FBI File 1, July 13, 1978.

35. Interview with Griffin Bell, October 11, 2007.

36. Ibid.

37. William H. Neukom, "The Broad Reach of the Unsung ABA," *ABA Journal* (March 2008): 9.

38. Interview with Thomas Deacey, March 4, 2005.

39. Interview with Griffin Bell, October 11, 2007.

40. Interview with Thomas Deacey, March 4, 2005.

41. FBI File I, interview with G. D. Walker, July 12, 1978.

42. FBI File I, agent interview report.

43. FBI File I, July 7, 1978.

44. FBI File I, agent interview with Wellborn Jack Jr., July 12, 1978.

45. The agent summary states: "Arnold is a loyal American citizen without prejudice for race, color, creed or religion." FBI File I, Michael W. Palmer, July 12, 1978.

46. The FBI file table of contents lists: "Employments, Federal Judges and Magistrates, U.S. Attorneys, State and Local Judges, Bar Memberships, Opposing Attorneys, Co-Counsels and Fellow Attorneys, state officials, minority leaders, community leaders, law enforcement officials, opposing political party, political party activities, labor leaders, members of religious groups."

47. FBI File I, Investigation at Little Rock, Arkansas, July 12 and 13, 1978.

48. FBI File I, Julian B. Fogleman, July 14, 1978, W. Memphis.

49. FBI File I, July 13, 1978.

50. FBI File I, July 12, 1978.

51. FBI File I, July 14, 1978. Federal District Judge G. Thomas Eisele said in his interview that he was "very excited about having a fellow Harvard graduate on the bench with him" (interview date July 11, 1978).

52. FBI File 1, July 13, 1978.

53. FBI File I, S.A. report, July 27, 1978.

54. Chapter 4 describes Arnold's position on this issue in the 1966 campaign and again at the Constitutional Convention.

55. The Arnolds were married at Camden, Arkansas, on June 14, 1954.

56. The chancery court divorce file is sealed and not accessible to the public by agreement of the parties. However, Arnold provided the contents of the file to the FBI, portions of which were included in the FBI report forwarded to the Department of Justice and the Senate Judiciary Committee.

57. FBI File I, interview with Jack Lessenberry, July 13, 1978.

58. FBI File I, interview with William Brennan, July 17, 1978.

59. FBI File I, interview with Gale Arnold, July 12, 1978.

60. FBI File I, interview with Walter E. Hussman Sr., July 12, 1978.

61. Ibid.

62. FBI File I, questionnaire, p. 17.

63. Ibid., p. 18.

64. FBI File I, interview with John Lamberg, July 12, 1978.

65. Richard S. Arnold, letter to William H. Webster, November 6, 1978. FBI File I.

CHAPTER SIX

1. Transcript, "Investiture of the Honorable Richard Sheppard Arnold as United States District Judge for the Eastern and Western Districts of Arkansas," October 16, 1978, p. 8.

2. Ibid., pp. 8–9.

3. Ibid., p. 16.

4. Ibid., pp. 16–17.

5. Ibid., p. 17.

6. Heaney assumed senior status in 1988. He retired on August 31, 2006.

7. "Weight of Wisdom," *Magazine of the University of Minnesota Duluth* 18, no. 2 (Summer 2001). (Heaney received an honorary degree from the University of Minnesota, Duluth, in 2001.)

8. "Woods, Arnold Confirmed on Voice Vote by Senate," *Arkansas Gazette*, February 21, 1980, p. 7A. The article reports that as of July 1980, the Eastern District faced a backlog of 761 cases, some of them three years old.

9. Transcript, "Investiture of the Honorable Richard Sheppard Arnold," p. 28.

10. Ibid., p. 29.

11. Ibid., pp. 26–27.

12. Ibid., p. 37.

13. "Texarkana's Richard Arnold Takes Oath as New U.S. District Judge," *Arkansas Gazette*, October 17, 1978.

14. Transcript, "Investiture of the Honorable Richard Sheppard Arnold," p. 38.

15. Ibid., p. 36.

16. C-SPAN, interview with Richard S. Arnold, March 17, 1993.

17. John McAnulty, "Arnold Draws Praise of Attorneys," *Arkansas Democrat*, February 4, 1979.

18. Portions of the following originally appeared as Polly J. Price, "Lessons from Small Cases: Reflections on Dodson v. Arkansas Activities Association," *University of Arkansas Little Rock Law Review* 27 (2005): 367–85. The author gratefully acknowledges permission to use parts of that article here.

19. *Dodson v. Arkansas Activities Ass'n*, 468 F. Supp. 394, 398 (E.D. Ark. 1979).

20. Richard S. Arnold, "Mr. Justice Brennan and the Little Case," *Loyola of Los Angeles Law Review* 32 (1999): 669.

21. Ibid., p. 668.

22. Ibid., p. 669.

23. Diana Lee Dodson was represented in the complaint by her mother, Diana R. Dodson, then a professor at Henderson State University in Arkadelphia, Arkansas.

24. 20 U.S.C. § 1681 et seq.

25. The quotation is attributed to Alvy Early, athletic director, University of Arkansas-Monticello, in "The Century in Sports: 6 Girls Switch to 5-On-5," *Arkansas Democrat-Gazette*, July 25, 1999, p. C11.

26. Ibid., p. 398.

27. *Cape v. Tennessee Secondary School Athletic Ass'n*, 563 F.2d 793, 795 (6th Cir. 1977).

28. *Jones v. Oklahoma Secondary School Activities Ass'n*, 453 F. Supp. 150, 155–56 (W.D. Okla. 1977)

29. *Cape*, 563 F.2d at 795.

30. Ibid.

31. *Jones*, 453 F. Supp. at 155, 156.

32. Richard S. Arnold, "Remarks at a Symposium on the Judiciary Sponsored by the Arkansas Bar Association Committee for the Bicentennial of the Constitution," July 2, 1983. Arnold papers.

33. *Dodson*, 468 F. Supp. at 398–99 (citations omitted).

34. Ibid.

35. *Dodson*, 468 F. Supp. at 398.

36. 20 U.S.C. § 1681 et seq.

37. Ibid., p. 396, n.1 (citing 20 U.S.C. § 1681(a)).

38. *Dodson*, 468 F. Supp. at 396.

39. *Craig v. Boren*, 429 U.S. 190 (1976).

40. *Dodson*, 468 F. Supp. at 398.

41. "AAA Plans No Appeal of Basketball Ruling," *Arkansas Gazette*, April 24, 1979.

42. "The Century in Sports: 6 Girls Switch to 5-On-5," p. C11.

43. See "AAA Plans No Appeal of Basketball Ruling."

44. "LR Woman Who Won Girls Basketball Suit Killed; Roommate Held," *Arkansas Democrat-Gazette*, November 11, 1991, p. 8B.

45. Interview with Richard Arnold, July 5, 2004. When I first learned to play basketball in Russellville, Arkansas, girls still played under half-court rules. My junior high career culminated in a district championship for the Gardner Junior High Whirlwinds. At the end of the season, our coach told us that we needed to learn a different game. All girls' basketball games in Arkansas would henceforth be played according to the boys' rules. Not particularly aware of civic affairs at that time, I did not think much about the reason for the change in rules. I played college basketball at Emory University and St. Andrews University, Scotland.

Many years later, at work in Judge Arnold's chambers as his law clerk, I came across an opinion he had written as a district court judge. The case, of course, was *Dodson*. It was then that I realized I had learned to play full-court basketball as a high school student because the judge for whom I was clerking had ordered that it be done. I searched for and found my first high school yearbook. The yearbook noted that the Russellville Cyclones girls' basketball team, of which I was a member, had been district champions that year (1980). It also noted that we had played full-court basketball for the first time, the same as the boys' team. I showed the yearbook pages to Judge Arnold and I told him about my former teammates who had gone on to win college scholarships to play basketball. These potential scholarships had been an important element of Diana Dodson's claim that playing under half-court rules disadvantaged Arkansas female athletes because all college women's teams played full-court basketball. Judge Arnold later returned the yearbook with a smile and the words "I guess I did some good."

46. Richard S. Arnold, "Judge Henry Woods: A Reminiscence," *University of Arkansas Little Rock Law Review* 25 (2003): 230.

47. *Dodson* case file, Arnold papers.

48. Richard S. Arnold, "The Future of the Federal Courts," *Missouri Law Review* 60 (1995): 536.

49. See, for example, Richard S. Arnold, "The Federal Courts: Causes of Discontent," *SMU Law Review* 56 (2003): 767.

50. Arnold, "Justice Brennan and the Little Case," p. 667.

51. "AAA Plans No Appeal of Basketball Ruling."

52. Richard S. Arnold, "Improving the Public's Perception of Federal Judges," *Society of Barristers Quarterly* 17 (1982): 324.

53. Jim Yeager, letter to the editor, *Arkansas Gazette*, April 10, 1979.

54. Interview with Richard Arnold, July 5, 2004.

55. Richard S. Arnold, "The Art of Judging," address before the Eighth Circuit Judicial Conference, Duluth, Minnesota, August 8, 2002, p. 21. Arnold papers.

56. Ibid., pp. 21–22.

57. Ibid., p. 22.

58. See, for example, Richard S. Arnold, "Remarks at a Symposium on the Judiciary Sponsored by the Arkansas Bar Association Committee for the Bicentennial of the Constitution," July 2, 1983.

59. Ibid., p. 3.

60. Ibid., pp. 4–5.

61. Ibid., p. 5.

62. Ibid., pp. 5–6.

63. Ibid., p. 7.

64. Ibid., p. 8.

65. Telephone interview with Henry Morgan, December 7, 2004.

66. Phyllis D. Brandon, "Richard Sheppard Arnold," *Arkansas Democrat-Gazette*, March 23, 1997, p. 1D.

67. See, for example, *Ridgeway v. Montana High School Ass'n*, 633 F. Supp. 1564, 1580 (D. Mont. 1986), aff'd, 858 F.2d 579, 582 (9th Cir. 1988).

68. *Cape*, 563 F.2d at 793.

69. Penny Soldan, "Records Broken as Curtain Falls on 6-on-6 Basketball," *Daily Oklahoman*, June 4, 1995, 1995 WL 6291219. In "Deep Six-On-Sixed," *Sports Illustrated*, March 20, 1995, the author described Clara Baer, a physical education instructor at Newcomb College in New Orleans, as the creator of the six to a side, three on offense, three on defense game that persisted among high school girls in Oklahoma through 1995.

70. See Chuck Schoffner, "6-Player Basketball Strong in Two States," *Houston Chronicle*, August 19, 1990, 1990 WL 2953844 (Iowa permitted full-court basketball in 1984; Oklahoma did the same in 1987). The half-court game was voted out of existence entirely in Iowa schools in 1993. "6-Player Basketball Voted Out in Iowa," *Omaha World-Herald*, February 4, 1993, 1993 WL 7176143.

71. "Dismissal Motion Denied: Judge Decides to Hear 6-Girl Basketball Suit," *Omaha World-Herald*, April 27, 1984, 1984 WL 2516596.

72. See, for example, Neena K. Chaudhry and Marcia D. Greenberger, "Seasons of Change: Communities for Equity v. Michigan High School Athletic Association," *UCLA Women's Law Journal* 13 (2003): 41; Patricia A. Cain, "Women, Race, and Sports: Life Before Title IX," *Journal of Gender, Race, and Justice* 4 (2001): 350; "Does Gender Equity in College Athletics Entail Gender Equality?" *Southern California Law Review* 7 (1997): 1466; Diane Heckman, "Women and Athletics: A Twenty-Year Retrospective on Title IX," *University of Miami Entertainment and Sports Law Review* 9 (1992): 1; Carolyn Ellis Staton, "Sex Discrimination in Public Education," *Mississippi Law Journal* 58 (1988): 348; Comment, "Half-Court Girls' Basketball Rules: An Application of the Equal Protection Clause and Title IX," *Iowa Law Review* 65 (1980): 766.

73. Arline Schubert, George Schubert, and Cheryl Schubert-Madsen, "Changes Influenced by Litigation in Women's Intercollegiate Athletics," *Seton Hall Journal of Sport Law* 1 (1991): 244–45.

74. As one example as a district court judge, Arnold concluded that Westinghouse Electric Corporation in Little Rock demoted an employee for racial reasons. His ruling was subsequently upheld by the Eighth Circuit. *Christine Vaughn v. Westinghouse Electric Corp.*, 702 F.2d 137 (8th Cir. 1983). See "Ruling Upholds Decision in Bias Case," *Arkansas Gazette*, March 13, 1983.

75. *Taylor v. Jones*, 489 F. Supp. 498, 500 (E.D. Ark. 1980).

76. *Taylor v. Jones*, 495 F. Supp. 1285, 1294.

77. 42 U.S.C. § 1983.

78. *Taylor*, 495 F. Supp. at 1293.

79. Ibid., p. 1294.

80. Ibid., p. 1296.

81. George Wells, "Black Sued Guard, Improved Conditions," *Arkansas Democrat-Gazette*, July 3, 1989.

82. John W. Walker, letter to Richard S. Arnold and Gerald Heaney, June 19, 1992. Arnold papers.

83. Richard S. Arnold, letter to John W. Walker, June 22, 1992. Arnold papers.

84. 28 U.S.C. § 2241.

85. Chapter 8, "Life and Death below the Supreme Court," contrasts the expansive habeas corpus practices of the Warren Court with later congressional and Rehnquist Court narrowing.

86. *Rogers v. Britton*, 466 F. Supp. 397 (E.D. Ark. 1979).

87. *Rogers v. Britton*, 476 F. Supp. 1036 (E.D. Ark. 1979), at 1037, rev'd, *Britton v. Rogers*, 631 F.2d 572 (8th Cir. 1980), cert. denied, 451 U.S. 939 (1981).

88. *Rogers v. State*, 265 Ark. 945 (1979), 961 (per curiam).

89. *Coker v. Georgia*, 433 U.S. 584 (1977).

90. *Rogers v. Britton*, 476 F. Supp. 1036 (E.D. Ark. 1979), rev'd, *Britton v. Rogers*, 631 F.2d 572 (8th Cir. 1980), cert. denied, 451 U.S. 939 (1981).

91. *Rogers*, 476 F. Supp. at 1043.

92. *Gregg v. Georgia*, 428 U.S. 153 (1976).

93. *Gregg*, 428 U.S. at 189

94. *Rogers*, 476 F. Supp. at 1039–40.

95. *Lockett v. Ohio*, 438 U.S. 586.

96. *Rogers*, 476 F. Supp. at 1040.

97. *Lockett*, 438 U.S. at 603, 604–605.

98. *Rogers*, 476 F. Supp. at 1040.

99. Ibid., pp. 1041–42.

100. Ibid., p. 1043.

101. Arnold here refers to the federal habeas corpus statute, 28 U.S.C. § 2254.

102. *Rogers*, 476 F. Supp. at 1043.

103. *Britton v. Rogers*, 631 F.2d 572, 577 (8th Cir. 1980), cert. denied, 451 U.S. 939 (1981).

104. Ibid.

105. *Britton*, 631 F.2d at 577 n.3.

106. Ibid., p. 579.

107. Ibid.

108. *Mathews v. Eldridge*, 424 U.S. 319 (1976).

109. *Britton*, 631 F.2d at 580.

110. Ibid., p. 581.

111. See, for example, *Harmelin v. Michigan*, 501 U.S. 957 (1991). Writing for the Court, Justice Scalia explained that imposition of mandatory sentence of life in prison without possibility of parole, without any consideration of mitigating factors, such as fact that petitioner had no prior felony convictions, did not constitute cruel and unusual punishment; severe, mandatory penalties may be cruel, but they are not unusual in the constitutional sense.

CHAPTER SEVEN

1. Interview with Donald P. Lay, May 11, 2005.

2. Judge Diana E. Murphy was appointed by President Clinton to the Eighth

Circuit in 1994, making her the first woman to serve as a judge on that court. The First Circuit gained its first female judge in early 1995, when Clinton appointed Sandra Lea Lynch.

3. Presidential Statement, October 20, 1978, Collection JC-1002; Records of the White House Office of Counsel to the President, 1977–1981. File unit: Judicial Appointments, 02/1980–08/1980. Box: 96. Carter Presidential Library.

4. Ibid.

5. Press Conf. #43, January 26, 1979. Carter Presidential Library.

6. Statement of Attorney General Griffin Bell, February 1978, p. 3. Carter Presidential Library, Collection JC-DPS: Records of the Domestic Policy Staff (Carter Administration), 1976–1981. File unit: Judicial Merit Selection. Box: 23.

7. Executive Order, February 17, 1977. Carter Presidential Library, Collection JC-1005, Office of the Chief of Staff Files, 1977–1980. File Unit: Circuit and Appeals Judges. Box: 42.

8. Interview with Griffin B. Bell, October 11, 2007.

9. Executive Order, February 17, 1977. Carter Presidential Library, Collection JC-1005, Office of the Chief of Staff Files, 1977–1980. File Unit: Circuit and Appeals Judges. Box: 42.

10. Bell statement, p. 8.

11. "Investigations to Start Soon in Plan to Promote Arnold to 8th Circuit," *Arkansas Gazette*, November 9, 1979, p. 7A. See also "Arnold Expected to Be Appointed," *Arkansas Democrat*, November 9, 1979, p. 12A.

12. "Woods, Arnold Confirmed on Voice Vote by Senate," *Arkansas Gazette*, February 21, 1980, p. 7A.

13. Ibid.

14. "Selection and Confirmation of Federal Judges—Part 5." Senate Judiciary Committee hearing, February 7, 1980, pp. 454–55.

15. "Arnold Expected to Be Appointed."

16. Richard S. Arnold, "Judge Henry Woods: A Reminiscence," *University of Arkansas Little Rock Law Review* 25 (2003): 230.

17. This subject is discussed in detail in chapter 11, "Desegregation in Little Rock."

18. "Nominees Meet Senators," *Arkansas Gazette*, February 8, 1980, p. 3A.

19. Interview with Dale Bumpers, June 29, 2004.

20. Griffin Bell, letter to Richard Arnold, January 10, 1984. Arnold papers.

21. Carter Presidential Library papers, JC-1005, Office of the Chief of Staff Files, 1977–1980. File Unit: Judicial Nominating Commission, Eighth Circuit. Box: 105. Memo to Laurie Lucy from Harriet Peppel, August 3, 1977.

22. Krauskopf would also hold teaching positions at North Carolina, Arizona, and West Virginia, before rejoining her alma mater as a chaired professor in 1987.

23. Michael J. Egan, letter to Gilbert S. Merritt, March 22, 1979. This letter

was produced by the US Department of Justice in response to a Freedom of Information Act request, OLP/05-R00863.

24. Richard S. Arnold, letter to William Brennan, April 12, 1979. Brennan papers, Library of Congress.

25. The ABA Standing Committee on the Federal Judiciary, "What It Is and How It Works," p. 3, http://www.abanet.org/scfedjud/federal_judiciary07.pdf (accessed August 30, 2008).

26. Ibid., p. 4.

27. Richard S. Arnold, letter to William Brennan (undated). Brennan papers, Library of Congress.

28. Stacey Stowe, "Rell's Choice for U.S. Judge Is Termed 'Not Qualified,'" *New York Times*, May 6, 2006, p. B4. Of the earlier five, three were later confirmed by the Senate and two withdrew. The committee forwards the results of its investigation to the Senate Judiciary Committee, which does not release information other than its rating. Ibid.

29. Neil A. Lewis, "Senators Question Bar Association's Role in Selecting Judges," *New York Times*, May 22, 1996.

30. Griffin Bell remarks from "National Seminar for Circuit Judges," Washington, DC, October 24, 1988, Richard S. Arnold (notes of speech), Arnold papers.

31. FBI File II, statement of Judge Elsijane T. Roy.

32. Interview with Griffin Bell, October 11, 2007.

33. Remarks of Jimmy Carter, Law Day Reception, May 1, 1979. Carter Presidential Library.

34. Richard S. Arnold, letter to Kathleen K. Jenkins, August 2, 1984. Arnold papers.

35. "Arkansan's Credentials 'Finest': U.S. Court Nominee Defended," *Omaha World Herald*, December 1979.

36. "How Not to Select a U.S. Judge," *Omaha World Herald*, undated newspaper clipping. Arnold papers.

37. "Arkansan's Credentials 'Finest.'"

38. Ibid.

39. Ibid.

40. Donald P. Lay, memo to "All Active Judges," January 2, 1980. Arnold papers. (A stamp on the memo indicates Arnold received the copy from Judge Floyd R. Gibson.)

41. Interview with Donald P. Lay, May 11, 2005.

42. Griffin Bell remarks from "National Seminar for Circuit Judges," Washington, DC, October 24, 1988, from Arnold's notes from the event.

43. "Selection and Confirmation of Federal Judges—Part 5," Senate Judiciary Committee hearing, February 7, 1980, pp. 454–55.

44. Richard S. Arnold, letter to Board of Governors, Metropolitan Club of the City of Washington, June 30, 1988. Arnold papers.

45. John Bennett, "Judge Lists Assets with Senate Committee," *Tri-State* (Memphis, TN), January 4, 1980, p. 9B.

46. This case is discussed in chapter 9, "Free Speech and the First Amendment."

47. FBI File II.

48. Ibid.

49. FBI File II, interview date November 20, 1979.

50. FBI File II, December 3, 1979.

51. FBI File II, interview date November 16, 1979.

52. FBI File II.

53. Ibid.

54. FBI File II, interview date November 15, 1979.

55. FBI File II. Philip S. Anderson would later serve as president of the American Bar Association.

56. FBI File II.

57. "They're Ready to Go, Arnold, Woods Say after Getting News," *Arkansas Democrat*, February 21, 1980.

58. "Judge Undergoes Spleen Surgery," *Arkansas Gazette*, August 29, 1980, p. 9A.

59. Warren Burger, letter to Richard Arnold, November 14, 1980. Arnold papers.

60. Interview with Dale Bumpers, June 29, 2004.

61. Interview with Brenda King, June 29, 2004.

CHAPTER EIGHT

1. This list includes Robert O'Neal, Marvin Laws, Larry Griffin, Edward Charles Pickens, Vernon Brown, Darryl V. Richley, Ivon Stanley, and Jonas Whitmore.

2. *Brown v. Luebbers*, 371 F.3d 458, 471 (8th Cir. 2004) (Arnold, J., dissenting), cert. denied, 543 U.S. 1189 (2005). Brown was executed in 2005.

3. *Williams v. Armontrout*, 912 F.2d 924, 942 (8th Cir. 1990) (Arnold, J., dissenting).

4. *Chambers v. Bowersox*, 157 F.3d 560, 570 (8th Cir. 1998), cert. denied, 527 U.S. 1029 (1999).

5. *Furman v. Georgia*, 408 U.S. 238 (1972).

6. Welsh S. White, *Litigating in the Shadow of Death: Defense Attorneys in Capital Cases* (Ann Arbor: University of Michigan Press, 2006), p. 1.

7. *Gregg v. Georgia*, 428 U.S. 153 (1976).

8. Source: Death Penalty Information Center, www.deathpenaltyinfo.org/executions-united-states.

9. Oral History, Arkansas Federal Judicial History Project, interview by Frances Ross, December 2, 1988, p. 281. This oral history transcript is on file at the Circuit Library, Eighth US Circuit Court of Appeals, St. Louis.

10. Crystal Nix Hines, "Lack of Lawyers Blocking Appeals in Capital Cases," *New York Times*, July 5, 2001.

11. Fernanda Santos, "Vindicated by DNA," *New York Times*, November 25, 2007, p. A1.

12. Oral History, Arkansas Federal Judicial History Project, interview by Frances Ross, December 2, 1988, p. 283.

13. *Stanley v. Zant*, 697 F.2d 955, 973 (11th Cir. 1983) (Arnold, J., dissenting), cert. denied, *Stanley v. Kemp*, 467 U.S. 1219 (1984).

14. *Stanley*, 697 F.2d at 974–75 (Arnold, J., dissenting).

15. Bill Clinton, *My Life* (New York: Knopf, 2004), p. 359.

16. Jim Mosley, "New Execution Date for Convicted Killer," *St. Louis Post-Dispatch*, January 4, 1989, p. 7A.

17. Eighth Circuit Local Rule 22A.

18. William H. Freivogel, "Death Watch for Griffin Ended Late Appeals Stretch Time, But Result Is as Usual," *St. Louis Post-Dispatch*, June 22, 1995, p. A1.

19. *Delo v. Stokes*, 495 U.S. 320 (1990) (per curiam).

20. "Missouri Planning for Execution Despite Appeal," *New Orleans Times-Picayune*, May 12, 1990, p. A3.

21. William H. Freivogel, "Death Row Appeals May Speed Up Here," *St. Louis Post-Dispatch*, May 16, 1990, p. 1B.

22. *Stokes*, 495 U.S. at 322 (Kennedy, J., concurring).

23. Ibid., p. 323.

24. Ibid., p. 327 (Brennan, J., dissenting).

25. Ibid., pp. 325–26.

26. Interview with Price Marshall, September 28, 2007.

27. Interview with Judge C. Arlen Beam, November 6, 2007.

28. Ray Pierce and Patricia Manson, "State Executes Murderers Whitmore, Pickens," *Arkansas Democrat-Gazette*, May 12, 1994.

29. George Wells, "Halt Ordered to Execution in '81 Killings," *Arkansas Democrat-Gazette*, May 25, 1988.

30. Holly Clark, "Death Row Inmates' Art to Be Shown by Coalition," *Arkansas Democrat-Gazette*, March 24, 1991.

31. Hall later parted company with the NAACP Legal Defense Fund on this case because of their characterization of Judge Eisele as "racist." Interview with John Wesley Hall, April 1, 2005.

32. Anne Farris, "Fairchild Wins a Stay," *Arkansas Democrat-Gazette*, September 5, 1990.

33. Ibid.

34. Blackmun papers, Library of Congress, Richard Arnold file. September 22, 1993, note to Mr. Justice Blackmun from "dsp" asking that he give a message to Arnold to call Judge Bowman "upon his arrival in your chambers" (Pasco M. Bowman II). "It concerns the Fairchild case."

35. *Fairchild v. Norris*, 5 F.3d 1124 (8th Cir. 1993).

36. Ibid., p. 1125 (Arnold, J., concurring).

37. Ibid., p. 1124.

38. Ibid., p. 1125 (citations and quotation omitted).

39. Ibid.

40. Phoebe Wall Howard, "Calm Fairchild Talks of Death," *Arkansas Democrat-Gazette*, September 5, 1990.

41. Ray Pierce, "Chaplain Says Fairchild's Brother Pulled Trigger," *Arkansas Democrat-Gazette*, August 30, 1995, p. 6B.

42. Ibid.

43. John Brummett, "The Fairchild Issues Won't Die," *Arkansas Democrat-Gazette*, August 29, 1995, p. 7B.

44. *New York Times*, August 31, 1995.

45. *Fairchild v. Lockhart*, 979 F.2d 636, 643 (Arnold, J., concurring).

46. *Fairchild*, 979 F.2d at 643 (Arnold, J., concurring).

47. *Atkins v. Virginia*, 536 U.S. 304 (2002).

48. *Roper v. Simmons*, 543 U.S. 551 (2005).

49. Death Penalty Focus, *The Monster Test*, http://www.deathpenalty.org/index.php?pid=editorial1.

50. Memorial Session in Honor of Richard Sheppard Arnold, United States Court of Appeals for the Eighth Circuit (St. Louis, Missouri, January 10, 2005), at 14 (remarks of James Layton).

51. *Antwine v. Delo*, 54 F.3d 1357 (8th Cir. 1995), cert. denied, *Bowersox v. Antwine*, 516 U.S. 1067 (1996).

52. Tom Jackman, "Appeals Court Says Sentencing Faulty in Brother's Slaying," *Kansas City Star*, May 13, 1995, p. C3.

53. *Antwine v. Delo*, 54 F.3d at 1362.

54. Ibid., p. 1364.

55. Arnold papers, case file *Calvert L. Antwine v. Paul Delo* (No. 94-1890WM).

56. Ibid.

57. Judge Reavley, e-mail to Richard S. Arnold, May 8, 1995, Arnold papers.

58. Richard S. Arnold, e-mail to Judge Reavley, May 8, 1995, Arnold papers.

59. *Miller v. Lockhart*, 65 F.3d 676, 679 (8th Cir. 1995).

60. *Batson v. Kentucky*, 476 U.S. 79 (1986).

61. Amnesty International, *Death by Discrimination: The Continuing Role of Race in Capital Cases* (2003), http://web.amnesty.org/library/index/engamr510462003.

62. Source: National Statistics on the Death Penalty and Race, Death Penalty Information Center, http://www.deathpenaltyinfo.org/article.php?scid =5&did=184#defend.

63. *Brown v. Luebbers*, 344 F.3d 770 (8th Cir. 2003), opinion vacated in part on rehearing en banc, 371 F.3d 458 (8th Cir. 2004), cert. denied, 543 U.S. 1189 (2005).

64. Donna Walter, "Federal Court Reinstates Man's Death Sentence," *Daily Record*, June 17, 2004; Peter Shinkle, "Court Throws Out Death Penalty in 1985 Murder Case," *St. Louis Post-Dispatch*, September 20, 2003.

65. Two books provide a detailed history of the death penalty in the United States and litigation strategies employed by death penalty opponents. These are Stuart Banner, *The Death Penalty: An American History* (Cambridge, MA: Harvard University Press, 2003) and Herbert H. Haines, *Against Capital Punishment: The Anti-Death Penalty Movement in America, 1972–1994* (New York: Oxford University Press, 1999).

66. *Williams v. Armontrout*, 912 F.2d 924, 942 (8th Cir. 1990).

67. *Clemmons v. Delo*, 100 F.3d 1394, 1403 (8th Cir. 1996).

68. *Clemmons v. Delo*, 124 F.3d 944 (8th Cir. 1997).

69. Richard Arnold, "Why Judges Don't Like Petitions for Rehearing," *Journal of Appellate Practice and Process* 3 (2001): 34–35.

70. *Clemmons v. Delo*, 100 F.3d 1394, 1401 (8th Cir. 1996), opinion vacated on rehearing by *Clemmons v. Delo*, 124 F.3d 944 (8th Cir. 1997), cert. denied, *Bowersox v. Clemmons*, 523 U.S. 1088 (1998).

71. *Schlup v. Delo*, 11 F.3d 738, 754 (8th Cir. 1993) (Arnold, C. J., dissenting from denial of suggestion for rehearing en banc and of motion for stay of execution), vacated, *Schlup v. Delo*, 513 U.S. 298 (1995).

72. Ibid.

73. Ibid.

74. Richard S. Arnold, memo to Judge Fagg and Judge Waters, November 1, 1991. Arnold papers.

75. *Lashley v. Armontrout*, 957 F.2d 1495 (8th Cir. 1992); rev'd, *Delo v. Lashley*, 507 U.S. 272 (1993).

76. *Lashley*, 957 F.2d at 1501–1502.

77. *Delo*, 507 U.S. 272 (1993).

78. *Lockett v. Ohio*, 438 U.S. 586 (1978).

79. *Delo*, 507 U.S. at 277.

80. Ibid.

81. Ibid., p. 285 (Stevens, J., dissenting).

82. "Looking for a Supreme," *Washington Times*, April 9, 1993, p. F2.

83. Ibid.

84. Ruth Bader Ginsburg's confirmation hearing is described in Benjamin Wittes, *Confirmation Wars: Preserving Independent Courts in Angry Times* (Lanham, MD: Rowman & Littlefield, 2007), p. 79.

85. In 1988, the Supreme Court held the death penalty unconstitutional for those who had committed crimes under the age of sixteen. *Thompson v. Oklahoma*, 487 U.S. 815 (1988).

86. *Fay v. Noia*, 371 U.S. 391 (1963).

87. *Fay*, 371 U.S. at 402.

88. *McCleskey v. Kemp*, 481 U.S. 279 (1987) (Brennan, J., dissenting).

89. *Williams v. Nix*, 700 F.2d 1164, 1173 (8th Cir. 1983), rev'd, *Nix v. Williams*, 467 U.S. 431 (1984).

90. Richard S. Arnold, letter to Justice Brennan, August 24, 1993. Brennan papers, Library of Congress, Richard Arnold files.

91. Richard S. Arnold, "A Tribute to Justice Harry A. Blackmun," *Harvard Law Review* 108 (1994): 9.

92. Ibid.

93. Richard S. Arnold, "Mr. Justice Blackmun—A Tribute," *Creighton Law Review* 28 (1995): 590.

94. Case file (various memoranda) Leonard Marvin Laws. Arnold papers.

95. *Laws v. Armontrout*, 490 U.S. 1040 (1989) (Marshall, J., dissenting from denial of certiorari).

96. *McCleskey v. Zant*, 111 S. Ct. 1454 (1991).

97. Phoebe Wall Howard, "Appeal Limit in Death Cases Stirs Debate: Ruling to Speed Up Executions," *Arkansas Democrat-Gazette*, May 20, 1991.

98. Ibid.

99. Interview with C. Arlen Beam, November 6, 2007.

100. Richard. S. Arnold, "Money, or the Relations of the Judicial Branch with the Other Two Branches, Legislative and Executive," *St. Louis University Law Journal* 40 (1996): 19.

101. Richard S. Arnold, letter to Justice Blackmun, February 20, 1992, in Blackmun papers, Library of Congress.

102. Hearing before the Subcommittee of the Committee on Appropriations, House of Representatives, 102d Congress, 2d sess., February 18, 1992, p. 39.

103. Ibid., p. 41.

104. Ibid., p. 39.

105. Interview with John R. Gibson, November 6, 2007; interview with C. Arlen Beam, November 6, 2007.

106. Interview with C. Arlen Beam, November 6, 2007.

CHAPTER NINE

1. Quoted on the Web site of the First Amendment Center, http://www .firstamendmentcenter.org/news.aspx?id=14893 (accessed February 8, 2009).

2. Press release, "Arnold Prize Announcement," April 15, 1994. Arnold papers.

3. David L. Hudson Jr., *First Amendment Moot Court Honors Judge Arnold*, First Amendment Center, February 28, 2005, http://www.firstamendmentcenter.org/ news.aspx?id=14893 (accessed August 6, 2008).

4. William J. Brennan Jr., "Preface, A Tribute to Chief Judge Richard S. Arnold," *Minnesota Law Review* 78 (1993): 1–2.

5. *Roth v. United States*, 354 U.S. 476, 484 (1957).

6. *New York Times Co. v. Sullivan*, 376 U.S. 254 (1964).

7. Ibid., p. 270.

8. Ibid., pp. 279–80.

9. *Konigsberg v. State Bar*, 366 U.S. 36, 61 (1961) (Black, J., dissenting). Two years earlier, in *Smith v. California*, 361 U.S. 147, 157 (1959), Justice Black wrote in a concurring opinion, "I read 'no law . . . abridging' to mean no law abridging."

10. Richard S. Arnold, "Diary for Supreme Court 1960 Term." Arnold papers.

11. Hugo Black, "The Bill of Rights," *New York University Law Review* 35 (1960): 865.

12. *New York Times v. Sullivan*, 376 U.S. 254, 297 (1964) (Black, J., concurring).

13. Richard W. Garnett, "Tribute to the Honorable Richard S. Arnold," *Journal of Appellate Practice and Process* 1 (1999): 211. The original attribution of Arnold as "Justice Black revived" appears in John P. Frank and A. Leon Higgenbotham Jr., "A Brief Biography of Judge Richard S. Arnold," *Minnesota Law Review* 78 (1993): 23.

14. Interview with Richard S. Arnold, July 1, 2004.

15. Anthony Lewis, *Freedom for the Thought That We Hate: A Biography of the First Amendment* (New York: Basic Books, 2007).

16. *United States v. Lee*, 935 F.2d 952, 954 (8th Cir. 1991).

17. 18 U.S.C. § 241 (1988).

18. *Lee*, 935 F.2d at 958 (Arnold, J., dissenting).

19. Ibid., p. 959.

20. Ibid., p. 960.

21. *R.A.V. v. City of St. Paul, Minnesota*, 505 U.S. 377 (1992).

22. St. Paul Bias-Motivated Crime Ordinance, St. Paul, Minnesota, Legis. Code § 292.02 (1990).

23. *R.A.V.*, 505 U.S. at 390–93 (1992).

24. Ibid., p. 396.

25. Linda Greenhouse, "High Court Voids Law Singling Out Crimes of Hatred," *New York Times*, June 23, 1992, p. A1.

26. *R.A.V.*, 505 U.S. at 416 (Blackmun, J., concurring).

27. Greenhouse, "High Court Voids Law," p. A1.

28. *United States v. Lee*, 6 F.3d 1297 (8th Cir. 1993), cert. denied, *Lee v. U.S.*, 511 U.S. 1035 (1994).

29. See, for example, *United States v. Eichman*, 496 U.S. 310 (1990) (striking down the federal Flag Protection Act of 1989), and *Texas v. Johnson*, 491 U.S. 397 (1989) (a decision that invalidated laws in forty-eight states).

30. Quoted in Margaret Zack, "New Trial Ordered in 1989 Cross Burning," *Minneapolis Star-Tribune*, October 8, 1993, p. 7B.

31. *Virginia v. Black*, 538 U.S. 343 (2003).

32. *Janklow v. Newsweek, Inc.*, 788 F.2d 1300, 1301 (8th Cir. 1986) (en banc).

33. *Gertz v. Robert Welch, Inc.*, 418 U.S. 323, 339–40 (1974).

34. *Janklow v. Newsweek, Inc.*, 759 F.2d 644, 649 (8th Cir. 1986).

35. Ibid., p. 653.

36. *Janklow*, 759 F.2d at 656 (Arnold, J., dissenting).

37. Ibid.

38. Ibid., p. 657.

39. *Janklow v. Newsweek, Inc.*, 788 F.2d 1300, 1306 (8th Cir. 1986).

40. Ibid., p. 1305.

41. *Janklow v. Newsweek, Inc.*, 479 U.S. 883 (1986) (denial of petition for certiorari).

42. T. R. Reid, "Janklow Sentenced to 100 Days in Jail," *Washington Post*, January 23, 2004, p. A3; "Janklow's Mixed Legacy of Good Deeds and Harsh Methods," CNN.com, January 22, 2004, available at http://www.cnn.com/2004/US/Central/01/20/janklow.legacy.ap/index.html (accessed August 8, 2008).

43. *Forbes v. Arkansas Educational Television Commission*, 93 F.3d 497 (8th Cir. 1996), rev'd, 523 U.S. 666 (1998). *Forbes* is described in Richard W. Garnett, "Tribute to the Honorable Richard S. Arnold," *Journal of Appellate Practice and Process* 1 (1999): 213–15.

44. *Arkansas Educational Television Commission v. Forbes*, 523 U.S. 666, 684–85 (1998) (Stevens, J., dissenting).

45. *Forbes v. Arkansas Educational Television Commission*, 22 F.3d 1423, 1429–30 (8th Cir. 1994) (en banc).

46. *Forbes v. Arkansas Educational Television Commission*, 93 F.3d 497, 504–505 (8th Cir. 1996).

47. Ibid., p. 500.

48. Ibid., pp. 504–505.

49. Editorial, "Public Journalism: What Is It, Anyway?" *Arkansas Democrat-Gazette*, March 23, 1997, p. 4J (noting Ralph Forbes was a former member of the American Nazi Party).

50. Theodore McMillian, memo to Chief Judge Richard S. Arnold, August 15, 1996. Arnold papers.

51. John R. Gibson, memo to Chief Judge Arnold, August 16, 1996. Arnold papers.

52. *Marcus v. Iowa Public Television*, 97 F.3d 1137, 1142 (8th Cir. 1996).

53. Ibid., pp. 1144–45 (Beam, J., dissenting).

54. *Arkansas Educational Television Commission v. Forbes*, 523 U.S. 666, 672 (1998).

55. Ibid., p. 669.

56. Ibid., pp. 680–81.

57. Linda Greenhouse, "Appeals Court Extends Rights of Gay Groups," *New York Times*, June 24, 1988, p. A10.

58. *Gay and Lesbian Students Ass'n v. Gohn*, 850 F.2d 361 (8th Cir. 1988).

59. Greenhouse, "Appeals Court Extends Rights of Gay Groups," p. A10.

60. *Gay and Lesbian Students Ass'n v. Gohn*, 656 F. Supp. 1045 (W.D. Ark. 1987), rev'd, 850 F.2d 361 (8th Cir. 1988).

61. *Gohn*, 850 F.2d at 367–68.

62. Ibid., p. 362.

63. Greenhouse, "Appeals Court Extends Rights of Gay Groups," p. A10.

64. *Stanley v. Magrath*, 719 F.2d 279, 280 (8th Cir. 1983). This case is discussed in Patricia M. Wald, "Judge Arnold and Individual Rights," *Minnesota Law Review* 78 (1993): 42–43.

65. *Stanley*, 719 F.2d at 280–82.

66. Ibid., p. 280.

67. Wald, "Judge Arnold and Individual Rights," pp. 42–43.

68. *Richenberg v. Perry*, 97 F.3d 256 (8th Cir. 1996), cert. denied, *Richenberg v. Cohen*, 522 U.S. 807 (1997).

69. Policy on Homosexual Conduct in the Armed Forces, 1 Pub. Papers 1111 (July 19, 1993).

70. *Richenberg*, 97 F.3d at 264 (Arnold, J., dissenting).

71. Ibid., p. 264 (quotation omitted); Garnett, "Tribute to the Honorable Richard S. Arnold," pp. 212–13.

72. *Richenberg*, 97 F.3d at 264 (Arnold, J., dissenting).

73. For example, see *NAACP v. Alabama*, 357 U.S. 449 (1958).

74. Mary Sandok, "Appeals Panel Says National Jaycees Can Exclude Women," Associated Press, June 8, 1983 (available on LexisNexis database).

75. *United States Jaycees v. McClure*, 534 F. Supp. 766, 770–71 (D. Minn. 1982), rev'd, 709 F.2d 1560 (8th Cir. 1983), rev'd sub nom. *Roberts v. United States Jaycees*, 468 U.S. 609 (1984).

76. Arnold's *Jaycees* decision is ably described and analyzed in greater detail in Richard W. Garnett, "Jaycees Reconsidered: Judge Richard S. Arnold and the Freedom of Association," *Arkansas Law Review* 58 (2005): 587–609. I am indebted to Garnett for some of the views expressed here.

77. *Jaycees*, 709 F.2d at 1561.

78. Ibid., p. 1570.

79. Ibid., p. 1566 (quoting *NAACP v. Alabama*, 357 U.S. at 460).

80. Ibid., p. 1573.

81. *United States Jaycees v. McClure*, 305 N.W.2d 764 (Minn. 1981).

82. Quoted in *Jaycees*, 709 F.2d at 1564–65.

83. Quoted in ibid., p. 1565.

84. Mary Sandok, "Appeals Panel Says National Jaycees Can Exclude Women," Associated Press, June 8, 1983 (available on LexisNexis database).

85. John Carlson, "Jaycees Push Bias Complaint on Membership," *Des Moines Register*, January 8, 1984; Margaret Zack, "High Court to Hear State Jaycee Case," *Minneapolis Star and Tribune*, January 10, 1984, p. 3B.

86. "State to Appeal Jaycees Ruling to Supreme Court," *Minneapolis Tribune*, August 19, 1983.

87. Linda Greenhouse, "Justices to Hear Jaycees Sex Discrimination Case," *New York Times*, January 10, 1984, p. 11.

88. J. S. Banbridge Jr., "Can Women Be Kept at the Back of the Jaycees Bus?" *American Bar Association Journal* 70 (June 1984): 78.

89. Greenhouse, "Justices to Hear Jaycees Sex Discrimination Case," p. 11.

90. "Jaycees' Attorney Asks Supreme Court to Uphold Male-Only Membership Rule," *Arkansas Gazette*, April 19, 1984.

91. A summary of the oral argument before the Supreme Court with quotations is in Steve Berg, "Jaycees Present All-Male Argument to Supreme Court," *Minneapolis Star-Tribune*, April 19, 1984, p. 1B.

92. *Roberts v. United States Jaycees*, 468 U.S. 609, 623 (1984).

93. Ibid., pp. 632–33 (O'Connor, J., concurring in part and concurring in the judgment).

94. *Boy Scouts of America v. Dale*, 530 U.S. 640 (2000).

95. Interview with Sandra Day O'Connor, February 19, 2008.

96. *Jaycees*, 709 F.2d at 1576.

97. Interview with Richard S. Arnold, June 30, 2004.

98. Ibid.

99. Richard A. Posner, letter to Richard S. Arnold, June 24, 1983. Arnold papers.

100. Richard S. Arnold, letter to Gilbert S. Merritt, July 14, 1983. Arnold papers.

101. Garnett, "Jaycees Reconsidered," p. 587.

102. *McCurry v. Tesch*, 738 F.2d 271 (8th Cir. 1984), cert. denied, 469 U.S. 1211 (1985). Arnold would, on occasion, preside at a wedding for a friend or colleague, and he presided at the author's wedding. Although deeply religious himself, he wanted no appearance of religion in his public performance. He used a photocopy of the Episcopalian wedding ceremony but had blacked out religious terms, e.g., "holy matrimony" became "matrimony."

103. Ibid., pp. 275–76.

104. Ibid., p. 275.

105. Patricia M. Wald, "Judge Arnold and Individual Rights," *Minnesota Law Review* 78 (1993): 41.

106. *McCurry*, 738 F.2d at 278 (Fagg, J., dissenting).

107. Wald, "Judge Arnold and Individual Rights," pp. 41–42.

108. United Press International, "Rabbi Loses Bid to Erect Statehouse Menorah," December 25, 1986 (available on LexisNexis Wire Service Stories database).

109. *Lubavitch v. Walters*, 808 F.2d 656 (8th Cir. 1986) (Arnold, J., dissenting).

110. Ibid.

111. Quoted in United Press International, "Rabbi Loses Bid to Erect Statehouse Menorah."

CHAPTER TEN

1. Marshall H. Tanick, "Eighth Circuit Looms Large in Abortion Battle," *Daily Record* (St. Louis), August 19, 2006.

2. *Planned Parenthood v. Miller*, 63 F.3d 1452, 1457 (8th Cir. 1995), cert. denied, *Janklow v. Planned Parenthood, Sioux Falls Clinic*, 517 U.S. 1174 (1996).

3. John P. Frank, "A Tribute to Chief Judge Richard S. Arnold," *Minnesota Law Review* 78 (1993): 16. The case Frank referred to is *Reproductive Health Services v. Webster*, 851 F.2d 1071 (8th Cir. 1988) (Arnold, J., concurrent and dissenting), rev'd, *Webster v. Reproductive Health Services*, 492 U.S. 490 (1989), discussed in this chapter.

4. *Eisenstadt v. Baird*, 405 U.S. 438, 453 (1972).

5. *Poe v. Ullman*, 367 U.S. 497 (1961).

6. David J. Garrow, *Liberty and Sexuality: The Right of Privacy and the Making of Roe v. Wade* (Berkeley: University of California Press 1998), pp. 184–85.

7. *Griswold v. Connecticut*, 381 U.S. 479 (1965).

8. Zick Rubin, "A Rose Isn't a Rose, Some Judges Say," *New York Times*, July 13, 1990, p. A27.

9. *Henne v. Wright*, 904 F.2d 1208 (8th Cir. 1990), cert. denied, 498 U.S. 1032 (1991).

10. The relevant Nebraska statute is as follows:

(1) If the mother was married at the time of either conception or birth of the child, or at any time between conception and birth, the name of such mother's husband shall be entered on the certificate as the father of the child and the surname of the child shall be entered on the certificate as being (a) the same as that of the husband, unless paternity has been

determined otherwise by a court of competent jurisdiction, (b) the surname of the mother, (c) the maiden surname of the mother, or (d) the hyphenated surname of both parents; (2) If the mother was not married at the time of either conception or birth of the child, or at any time between conception and birth, the name of the father shall not be entered on the certificate without the written consent of the mother and the person named as the father, in which case and upon the written request of both such parents the surname of the child shall be that of the father or the hyphenated surname of both parents; (3) In any case in which paternity of a child is determined by a court of competent jurisdiction, the name of the father shall be entered on the certificate in accordance with the finding of the court and the surname of the child may be entered on the certificate the same as the surname of the father; (4) In all other cases, the surname of the child shall be the legal surname of the mother; and (5) If the father is not named on the certificate, no other information about the father shall be entered thereon.

Neb. Rev. Stat. §71-640.01 (1990).

11. *Henne*, 904 F.2d at 1215.

12. Ibid., p. 1216 (Arnold, J., dissenting).

13. Ibid., p. 1217.

14. Ibid., p. 1216.

15. Ibid.

16. Ibid., pp. 1216–17.

17. Ibid., p. 1217.

18. Ibid.

19. Myron H. Bright, memo to Judge Arnold, May 15, 1990. Arnold papers.

20. Federal Rule of Appellate Procedure 35(a).

21. J. Smith Henley, memo to All Circuit Judges, June 6, 1990. Arnold papers.

22. Chief Judge Donald P. Lay, memo to All Circuit Judges, July 31, 1990. Arnold papers.

23. *U.S. v. Weaver*, 966 F.2d 391 (8th Cir. 1992), cert. denied, 506 U.S. 1040 (1992).

24. *Weaver*, 966 F.2d at 397 (Arnold, J., dissenting).

25. Randall Kennedy, "Is All Discrimination Created Equal?" *Time*, October 16, 1995, p. 72.

26. Ibid.

27. *United States Jaycees v. McClure*, 709 F.2d 1560, 1567 (8th Cir. 1983), rev'd, *Roberts v. United States Jaycees*, 468 U.S. 609 (1984) (citing *Griswold*, 381 U.S. at 482).

28. *United States v. Dinwiddie*, 76 F.3d 913, 917 (8th Cir.), cert. denied, *Dinwiddie*

v. United States, 519 U.S. 1043 (1996).

29. *Dinwiddie*, 76 F.3d at 917–18.

30. Adam Clymer, "Reno Urges Senate to Curb Anti-Abortion Violence," *New York Times*, May 13, 1993, p. A21; Tanya Melich, "The War on Abortion Clinics," *New York Times*, September 9, 1993, p. 9.

31. Associated Press, "Killer of Abortion Doctor Is Sentenced to Die," *New York Times*, December 7, 1994, p. A16.

32. *Dinwiddie*, 76 F.3d at 918.

33. Ibid., p. 924.

34. Richard A. Serrano, "'94 Federal Law Is Making Anti-Abortion Protests Scarce," *St. Louis Post-Dispatch*, December 10, 1996, p. 5B.

35. George G. Fagg, memo to Chief Judge Arnold, February 8, 1996. Arnold papers.

36. Myron H. Bright, memo to Chief Judge Arnold, February 8, 1996. Arnold papers.

37. *Olmer v. City of Lincoln*, 192 F.3d 1176 (8th Cir. 1999).

38. *Olmer*, 192 F.3d at 1182–82 (Bright, J., dissenting).

39. Ibid., p. 1180.

40. Ibid., pp. 1180–81.

41. Ibid., p. 1188.

42. *Reproductive Health Service v. Webster*, 851 F.2d 1071, 1085 (8th Cir. 1988) (Arnold, J., concurring in part and dissenting in part), rev'd, 492 U.S. 490 (1989).

43. *Roe v. Wade*, 410 U.S. 113 (1973).

44. *Webster*, 851 F.2d at 1085 (Arnold, J., concurring and dissenting).

45. Quoted in *Webster*, 851 F.2d at 1075.

46. *Akron v. Akron Center for Reproductive Health, Inc.*, 462 U.S. 416, 444 (1983).

47. *Webster v. Reproductive Health Services*, 492 U.S. 490 (1989).

48. Ibid., pp. 505–506.

49. Ibid., p. 512.

50. *Rust v. Sullivan*, 500 U.S. 173 (1991).

51. *Planned Parenthood v. Casey*, 505 U.S. 833, 846 (1992) (joint opinion).

52. *Casey*, 505 U.S. at 877.

53. *Hodgson v. Minnesota*, 853 F.2d 1452 (8th Cir. 1988), aff'd, 497 U.S. 417 (1990).

54. Stuart Taylor Jr., "Curbs for Minors Seeking Abortion Upheld on Appeal," *New York Times*, August 9, 1988, p. A1.

55. *Hodgson*, 853 F.2d at 1463–66.

56. Ibid., pp. 1466–67 (Lay, C.J., dissenting).

57. Stuart Taylor Jr., "Curbs for Minors Seeking Abortions Upheld."

58. *Hodgson v. Minnesota*, 497 U.S. 417 (1990).

59. *Hodgson*, 497 U.S. at 481 (Kennedy, White, Scalia, and Rehnquist concurring in part and dissenting in part).

60. *Hodgson*, 497 U.S. at 472 (Marshall, Brennan, and Blackmun concurring in part and dissenting in part).

61. *Hodgson*, 497 U.S. at 479–80 (Scalia, J., concurring in part and dissenting in part).

62. Linda Greenhouse, *Becoming Justice Blackmun* (New York: Times Books, 2005), pp. 196–97.

63. *Planned Parenthood v. Miller*, 63 F.3d 1452, 1458 (8th Cir. 1995), cert. denied, *Janklow v. Planned Parenthood*, 517 U.S. 1174 (1996).

64. *Bellotti v. Baird*, 443 U.S. 622 (1979).

65. *Miller*, 63 F.3d at 1459.

66. "Abortion: Completing the Picture," *Washington Post*, May 2, 1996, p. A28.

67. William C. Lhotka, "U.S. Court Warns Judges on Anti-Abortion Bias," *St. Louis Post-Dispatch*, June 5, 1986.

68. *T.L.J. v. Webster*, 792 F.2d 734, 739 n.4 (8th Cir. 1986).

69. Normally, an abortion controversy would fall under an exception to the mootness doctrine. Arnold explained why this case did not fall under the "capable of repetition, yet evading review" exception recognized in *Roe*: "The present case is different because there is one more essential element in T.L.J.'s lawsuit which can never be repeated: T.L.J. is now over the age of eighteen and will never again be subject to the restrictions of this statute. Her case is truly moot since there is no possibility at all of her ever again being a pregnant, unemancipated minor." 792 F.2d at 739.

70. Quoted in William C. Lhotka, "U.S. Court Warns Judges on Anti-Abortion Bias," *St. Louis Post-Dispatch*, June 5, 1986.

71. *Carhart v. Stenberg*, 192 F.3d 1142 (8th Cir. 1999), aff'd, *Stenberg v. Carhart*, 530 U.S. 914 (2000).

72. Ibid., p. 1145.

73. Ibid., p. 1150.

74. Ibid., p. 1151.

75. *Planned Parenthood of Greater Iowa v. Miller*, 195 F.3d 386 (8th Cir. 1999); *Little Rock Family Planning Services v. Jegley*, 192 F.3d 794 (8th Cir. 1999).

76. "Got One Right," *Arkansas Times*, October 1, 1999, p. 16.

77. *Stenberg v. Carhart*, 530 U.S. 914, 931 (2000).

78. *Stenberg*, 530 U.S. at 1003 (Thomas, J., dissenting).

79. "A Defeat for 'Partial-Birth Abortion,'" *St. Louis Post-Dispatch*, June 29, 2000, p. B6.

80. *Carhart v. Gonzales*, 413 F.3d 791 (8th Cir. 2005), rev'd, *Gonzales v. Carhart*, 127 S. Ct. 1610 (2007).

81. *Carhart*, 127 S. Ct. at 1616.

82. *Reproductive Health Services v. Nixon*, 429 F.3d 803 (8th Cir. 2005), vacated, *Nixon v. Reproductive Health Services*, 127 S. Ct. 2120 (2007).

83. Patricia M. Wald, "Judge Arnold and Individual Rights," *Minnesota Law Review* 78 (1993): 53.

84. Dan Balz and Ruth Marcus, "Cuomo Withdraws Name from Supreme Court Post," *Washington Post*, April 8, 1993, p. A1.

85. Ruth Marcus, "President Asks Wider Court Hunt," *Washington Post*, May 6, 1993, p. A1.

86. I discuss the NARAL opposition to Arnold in more detail in chapter 13.

87. Jo Mannies, "Rigali Exhorts Foes of Abortion to Use Clout in Election," *St. Louis Post-Dispatch*, January 23, 2000, p. A1.

CHAPTER ELEVEN

1. The debate at Yale Law School is described in chapter 1. Parts of this chapter appeared in a different form in Polly J. Price, "The Little Rock School Desegregation Cases in Richard Arnold's Court," *Arkansas Law Review* 58 (2005): 611. The author gratefully acknowledges the permission of the *Arkansas Law Review* to use this material here.

2. *Cooper v. Aaron*, 358 U.S. 1 (1958).

3. Kimberly Dishongh and Cynthia Howell, "LR Schools Stay Under Court Sway," *Arkansas Democrat-Gazette*, July 1, 2004, p. 1A. Arnold's last opinion in the case was *Little Rock School District v. Armstrong*, 359 F.3d 957 (8th Cir. 2004).

4. See, for example, *LRSD v. PCSSD, No. 1*, 921 F.2d 1371 (8th Cir. 1990); *LRSD v. PCSSD, No. 1*, 839 F.2d 1296 (8th Cir. 1988).

5. Judge Gerald W. Heaney of Minnesota was the longest-serving member of the appellate panel assigned to the Little Rock school cases. Judge Heaney, appointed to the Eighth Circuit in 1966, wrote his first opinion in a school desegregation case from Arkansas in 1967. *Kelley v. Altheimer, Ark. Pub. Sch. Dist. No. 22*, 378 F.2d 483, 485 (8th Cir. 1967). Heaney heard appeals from the Little Rock school desegregation litigation beginning in 1970 and wrote a number of opinions for the panel and the en banc court. Judge Heaney had extensive involvement in other Eighth Circuit desegregation litigation. Heaney also reflected publicly on the role of judges in desegregation cases, whereas Arnold did not specifically address the issue outside of his written opinions. Judge Heaney coauthored a book about desegregation in St. Louis and an important article on busing titled "Busing, Timetables, Goals, and Ratios: Touchstones of Equal Opportunity." Gerald W. Heaney and Susan Uchitelle, *Unending Struggle: The Long Road to an Equal Education in St. Louis* (St. Louis, MO: Reedy Press, 2004); Gerald W. Heaney, "Busing, Timetables, Goals, and

Ratios: Touchstones of Equal Opportunity," *Minnesota Law Review* 69 (1985): 735.

6. Larry Ault, "Arnold Takes Known Name to LR Hearing: Article Rates Him as Most Balanced," *Arkansas Democrat*, November 1, 1987, p. 14A.

7. Judge Donald P. Lay stated that Judge Arnold's presence on the panel was the result of random assignment, consistent with the practice of the Eighth Circuit at that time. Interview with Donald P. Lay, Judge, Eighth Circuit Court of Appeals, in Little Rock, Arkansas, May 11, 2005.

8. Anne Kornhauser, "Reagan Justice: 8th Circuit," *American Lawyer* (June 1988): 42.

9. See *Missouri v. Jenkins*, 515 U.S. 70, 101–03 (1995) (determining that absent specifically traceable segregation and discrimination, educational deficits were an inadequate justification for the district court to retain local control); *Freeman v. Pitts*, 503 U.S. at 490 ("Returning schools to [local control] at the earliest practicable date is essential to restore their true accountability in our governmental system"); *Board of Educ. v. Dowell*, 498 U.S. 237, 250 (1991) (clarifying that once a "unitary" system is established, a federal court desegregation order should end even if resegregation of schools subsequently occurs).

10. For more detailed history of the early years of desegregation in Little Rock, see Elizabeth Jacoway, *Turn Away Thy Son: Little Rock, The Crisis That Shocked the Nation* (New York: Free Press, 2007); Tony Freyer, *Little Rock on Trial: Cooper v. Aaron and School Desegregation* (Lawrence: University of Kansas Press, 2007).

11. *Brown v. Board of Education*, 347 U.S. 483 (1954).

12. *Brown v. Board of Education*, 349 U.S. 294, 301 (1955) ("The judgments below . . . are accordingly reversed and the cases are remanded to the District Courts to take such proceedings and enter such orders and decrees consistent with this opinion as are necessary and proper to admit to public schools on a racially nondiscriminatory basis with all deliberate speed the parties to these cases").

13. Ibid.

14. *Aaron v. Cooper*, 143 F. Supp. 855 (E.D. Ark. 1956).

15. Ibid., p. 860.

16. Ibid., p. 858.

17. Ibid., p. 866.

18. *Aaron v. Cooper*, 243 F.2d 361, 364 (8th Cir. 1957).

19. *Aaron v. Cooper*, 156 F. Supp. 220, 227 (E.D. Ark. 1957).

20. *Aaron v. Cooper*, 163 F. Supp. 13 (E.D. Ark. 1958).

21. *Aaron v. Cooper*, 257 F.2d 33, 40 (8th Cir. 1958).

22. *Cooper v. Aaron*, 358 U.S. 1 (1958).

23. Ibid., pp. 4, 19–20.

24. *Aaron v. Cooper*, 261 F.2d 97 (8th Cir. 1958).

25. *Essential History*, at http://www.ualr.edu/~lrsd/chap2.html.

26. See *Clark v. Board of Educ. of LRSD*, 369 F.2d 661, 665 (8th Cir. 1966).

27. *Clark v. Board of Educ. of LRSD*, 426 F.2d 1035, 1045 (8th Cir. 1970).

28. *Green v. County School Board of New Kent County*, 391 U.S. 430, 441–42 (1968).

29. *Swann v. Charlotte-Mecklenburg Board of Education*, 402 U.S. 1, 24–25 (1971).

30. "From Desegregation to Resegregation," *Arkansas Democrat-Gazette*, October 26, 2003, p. 16A.

31. See, generally, Davison M. Douglas, "The End of Busing?" *Michigan Law Review* 95 (1997): 1715 (recounting history of desegregation efforts).

32. *Essential History*, at http://www.ualr.edu/~lrsd/chap2.html.

33. *LRSD v. PCSSD, No. 1*, 778 F.2d 404 (8th Cir. 1985) (en banc), cert. denied, *Arkansas State Board of Education v. Little Rock School District*, 476 U.S. 1186 (1986).

34. *LRSD v. PCSSD, No. 1*, 921 F.2d 1371 (8th Cir. 1990).

35. *LRSD v. Armstrong*, 359 F.3d 957 (8th Cir. 2004).

36. In 1968, the NAACP sued the PCSSD to desegregate those schools. See *LRSD*, 778 F.2d at 420 (citing Zinnamon v. Board of Educ. of PCSSD, No. LR-68-C-154 (W.D. Ark. 1973)). In 1980, the NLRSD was found not to be in compliance with court desegregation orders concerning faculty and staff. See *Davis v. Board of Educ. of N. Little Rock, Ark.*, 635 F.2d 730 (8th Cir. 1980).

37. *Milliken v. Bradley*, 418 U.S. 717 (1974).

38. 418 U.S. at 744–45.

39. *LRSD*, 778 F.2d at 419.

40. Ibid.

41. Ibid., p. 427.

42. Ibid., p. 434.

43. Ibid., pp. 436–38 (Arnold, J., concurring in part and dissenting in part).

44. Ibid., p. 437 (Arnold, J., concurring in part and dissenting in part).

45. Ibid., p. 441.

46. Ibid., p. 442.

47. Ibid.

48. Ibid., p. 448 (Arnold, J., concurring in part and dissenting in part) (quoting *Milliken I*, 418 U.S. at 741).

49. Ibid. (citing *Milliken I*, 418 U.S. at 740).

50. Ibid., p. 437.

51. Ibid., p. 444 (Gibson, J., concurring in part and dissenting in part).

52. Doug Smith, "Myth about All-Black Schools Not Subscribed to by Arnold," *Arkansas Gazette*, November 17, 1985, p. 7C.

53. *LRSD*, 778 F.2d at 438 n.2.

54. See, for example, Peggy Harris, "NLR Effort Declared Victorious: Patrons Applaud," *Arkansas Gazette*, November 8, 1985, p. 1A.

55. Interview with Skip Rutherford, former Little Rock School Board Presi-

dent, in Little Rock, Arkansas, June 30, 2004.

56. *Essential History*, at http://www.ualr.edu/~lrsd/chap2.html.

57. "From Desegregation to Resegregation," *Arkansas Democrat-Gazette*, October 26, 2003, p. 16A.

58. Telephone interview with Gerald W. Heaney, Judge, Eighth Circuit Court of Appeals, June 23, 2005.

59. Interview with Roger L. Wollman, Judge, Eighth Circuit Court of Appeals, in St. Paul, Minnesota, May 10, 2005.

60. Telephone interview with Gerald W. Heaney, June 23, 2005.

61. The "Joshua Intervenors," named for Lorene Joshua, a parent with three children in the Little Rock public schools, represented black parents and students.

62. *LRSD v. PCSSD, No. 1*, 805 F.2d 815, 816 (8th Cir. 1986) (per curiam).

63. *LRSD v. PCSSD, No. 1*, 839 F.2d 1296, 1304 (8th Cir. 1988).

64. Ibid., p. 1307.

65. David Davies, "State's Tab in School Case Worrying Superintendents: Officials Outside Pulaski County Fear Decline in Assistance," *Arkansas Gazette*, February 28, 1988, p. 11A.

66. The details of the settlement plans are described in *LRSD*, 921 F.2d at 1378–81.

67. *LRSD v. PCSSD*, 716 F. Supp. 1162, 1169 (E.D. Ark. 1989).

68. *LRSD v. PCSSD*, 726 F. Supp. 1544, 1554–56 (E.D. Ark. 1989).

69. *LRSD*, 921 F.2d at 1376.

70. Ibid.

71. Ibid., p. 1383.

72. Ibid., p. 1378.

73. Ibid., p. 1386.

74. Ibid., p. 1383.

75. Liz Schevtchuk Armstrong, "Court Reinstates Desegregation Plan for Little Rock," *Education Weekly*, January 9, 1991, p. 16.

76. See *LRSD*, 921 F.2d at 1376.

77. Scott Morris, "Federal Judges Worry Whether LR Schools Have Finances," *Arkansas Gazette*, June 22, 1990, p. 1A.

78. *LRSD*, 778 F.2d at 441 (Arnold, J., concurring in part and dissenting in part).

79. *LRSD*, 921 F.2d at 1381.

80. Ibid., pp. 1381–82.

81. Ibid.

82. Interview with Donald P. Lay, Judge, Eighth Circuit Court of Appeals, in Little Rock, Arkansas, May 11, 2005.

83. Ibid.

84. Scott Morris, "Woods Steps Down from LR School Case," *Arkansas*

Gazette, July 7, 1990, p. 1A.

85. *LRSD v. PCSSD, No. 1*, 740 F. Supp. 632, 636 (E.D. Ark. 1990).

86. George Wells, "School Case Now in Wright's Hands," *Arkansas Gazette*, July 7, 1990, p. 1A.

87. Jack Bass, *Unlikely Heroes* (New York: Simon and Schuster, 1982), p. 19.

88. *LRSD*, 740 F. Supp. at 633–35.

89. Ibid.

90. LRSD, 778 F.2d at 436–37 (Arnold, J., concurring in part and dissenting in part).

91. *LRSD*, 740 F. Supp. at 365.

92. *LRSD*, 921 F.2d at 1391–92.

93. Ibid., p. 1393.

94. Ibid., p. 1392.

95. "Court OKs $129.75 Million Desegregation Settlement," *Arkansas Gazette*, August 7, 1990, p. 1A (quoting from unpublished order).

96. Richard S. Arnold, "Judge Henry Woods: A Reminiscence," *University of Arkansas Little Rock Law Review* 25 (2003): 230.

97. Ibid., pp. 230–31.

98. *LRSD*, 778 F.2d at 437 (Arnold, J., concurring in part and dissenting in part).

99. *LRSD*, 921 F.2d at 1393.

100. Editorial, "Deeper into the Legal Murk Law Logic Strikes Again," *Arkansas Democrat-Gazette*, December 31, 1994, p. 6B.

101. *Appeal of LRSD*, 949 F.2d 253, 255 (8th Cir. 1991).

102. Ibid., pp. 256, 258.

103. Ibid., p. 257.

104. Cary Bradburn, "School Appeal Heard: Settlement Changes May Go Back to Wright," *Arkansas Gazette*, September 5, 1991, p. 1B.

105. Cynthia Howell, "Appeals Panel Hears School Strike Case," *Arkansas Democrat-Gazette*, February 26, 1997, p. 1B.

106. Ibid.

107. *Knight v. PCSSD*, 112 F.3d 953, 954 (8th Cir. 1997).

108. Ibid., p. 955.

109. *LRSD v. PCSSD, No. 1*, 56 F.3d 904, 908 (8th Cir. 1995).

110. Cynthia Howell, "Williams Finds Kansas City Prickly, Too," *Arkansas Gazette*, December 7, 1996, p. 1A.

111. *Armstrong*, 359 F.3d at 961.

112. On January 3, 2002, after presiding over the case for eleven years, Judge Wright determined that it was the "appropriate time to reassign this case to another judge with minimal disruption to the parties and to allow a smooth transition." The case was reassigned to Judge Wilson by random selection. *Little Rock School District*

v. Pulaski County Special School District, 237 F. Supp. 2d 988, 995 (E.D. Ark. 2002).

113. *Armstrong*, 359 F.3d at 970.

114. Ibid., p. 959.

115. Ibid.

116. Ibid., p. 967.

117. Eva Paterson et al., "Breathing Life into Brown at Fifty: Lessons about Equal Justice," *Black Scholar* 34 (2004): 7.

118. Ibid., p. 8.

119. Gary Orfield and Susan E. Eaton, *Dismantling Desegregation: The Quiet Reversal of Brown v. Board of Education* (Harvard Project on School Desegregation, 1996), pp. 1–22.

120. *Freeman v. Pitts*, 503 U.S. 467 (1992).

121. Ibid., pp. 489, 496.

122. *LRSD*, 921 F.2d at 1386.

123. *Board of Education of Oklahoma City Public Schools v. Dowell*, 498 U.S. 237, 248 (1991).

124. *LRSD*, 237 F. Supp. at 1036–40.

125. See, for example, David S. Tatel, "Judicial Methodology, Southern School Desegregation, and the Rule of Law," *New York University Law Review* 79 (2004): 1071.

126. Ibid., p. 1074.

127. Jeffrey B. Morris, *Establishing Justice in Middle America: A History of the United States Court of Appeals for the Eighth Circuit* (Minneapolis: University of Minnesota Press, 2007), p. 197.

128. *Taylor v. Jones*, 495 F. Supp. 1285, 1296 (E.D. Ark. 1980).

129. *Taylor v. Jones*, 653 F.2d 1193, 1202–1203 (8th Cir. 1981).

130. *Dodson v. Arkansas Activities Ass'n*, 468 F. Supp. 394, 398 (E.D. Ark. 1979).

131. *Brown v. Board of Education*, 347 U.S. 483 (1954).

132. Abram Chayes, "Foreword: Public Law Litigation and the Burger Court," *Harvard Law Review* 96 (1982): 4; Abram Chayes, "The Role of the Judge in Public Law Litigation," *Harvard Law Review* 89 (1976): 1281; Owen M. Fiss, "Against Settlement," *Yale Law Journal* 93 (1984): 1073; Owen M. Fiss, "The Supreme Court 1978 Term—Foreword: The Forms of Justice," *Harvard Law Review* 93 (1979): 1.

133. *LRSD*, 921 F.2d at 1384 (citing Chayes, "Foreword: Public Law Litigation and the Burger Court," pp. 51–55).

134. Chayes, "The Role of the Judge in Public Law Litigation," p. 1309 ("School segregation, on the other hand, seemed obviously appropriate for judicial reform under the Constitution. . . .").

135. Ibid., p. 1282.

136. Ibid., p. 1297.

137. Ibid., p. 1300.

138. *LRSD*, 921 F.2d at 1383.

139. Chayes, "The Role of the Judge in Public Law Litigation," p. 1299.

140. Chayes, "Foreword: Public Law Litigation in the Burger Court," pp. 55–56.

141. Chris Heller, attorney for the Little Rock School District, e-mail to Polly Price, July 1, 2005.

142. Ibid.

143. Deborah L. Rhode, "Class Conflicts in Class Actions," *Stanford Law Review* 34 (1982): 1183.

144. Richard S. Arnold, "The Federal Courts: Causes of Discontent," *S.M.U. Law Review* 56 (2003): 767.

145. Ibid., p. 771.

146. Fiss, "Against Settlement," p. 1083.

147. Arnold, "The Federal Courts: Causes of Discontent," p. 771.

148. Ibid.

149. *LRSD*, 921 F.2d at 1377 n.2.

150. Interview with Justice Sandra Day O'Connor, February 19, 2008.

CHAPTER TWELVE

1. *Jeffers v. Clinton*, 730 F. Supp. 196, 198 (E.D. Ark. 1989), affd., 489 U.S. 1019 (1991).

2. Quoted at http://www.firstamendmentcenter.org/news.aspx?id=14098 (accessed August 15, 2008).

3. Interview with Richard S. Arnold, June 30, 2004.

4. The quotation is from Patricia M. Wald, "Judge Arnold and Individual Rights," *Minnesota Law Review* 78 (1993): 43.

5. *Jeffers v. Clinton*, 730 F. Supp. 196 (E.D. Ark. 1989), affd., 489 U.S. 1019 (1991); Noel E. Oman, "Arkansas Jurist Richard Arnold Dead at 68: Esteemed Career Spanned 25 Years on Federal District and Appellate Benches," *Arkansas Democrat-Gazette*, September 24, 2004. p. A1.

6. *Smith v. Clinton*, 687 F. Supp. 1361 (E.D. Ark. 1988), aff'd, 488 U.S. 988 (1988).

7. Charles L. Zelden, *Voting Rights on Trial* (Santa Barbara, CA: ABC-CLIO, 2002), p. 128.

8. Testimony of Professor Pamela S. Karlan, US Senate Committee on the Judiciary, *Election Law Journal* 5 (2006): 334.

9. Ibid., p. 338.

10. In a subsequent proceeding, the court granted in part plaintiffs' request for preclearance, limited to majority-vote requirements in general elections. Additionally, the court ordered that no plan of apportionment adopted by the board of apportionment for the Arkansas General Assembly after the 1990 census could go into effect until sixty days elapsed from the date of its final adoption. This opinion, too, was written by Arnold, with Judge G. Thomas Eisele dissenting. *Jeffers v. Clinton*, 740 F. Supp. 585 (E.D. Ark. 1990), appeal dismissed, *Clinton v. Jeffers*, 498 U.S. 1129 (1991).

11. Robert McCord, "State Innocent But Punished," *Arkansas Democrat-Gazette*, May 24, 1990.

12. Voting Rights Act of 1965, § 2, 42 U.S.C. §1973.

13. *White v. Regester*, 412 U.S. 755, 766 (1973).

14. *Thornburg v. Gingles*, 478 U.S. 30 (1986).

15. *Smith*, 687 F. Supp. at 1313.

16. *Thornburg*, 478 U.S. at 47.

17. Zelden, *Voting Rights on Trial*, p. 33.

18. Stephen M. Reasoner, memo to Judges Arnold and Howard, September 20, 1989. Arnold papers.

19. Richard S. Arnold, memo to Judge Reasoner, September 21, 1989. Arnold papers.

20. G. Thomas Eisele, memo to Judge Arnold and Judge Howard, September 25, 1989. Arnold papers.

21. Ibid., p. 202.

22. Ibid., p. 198.

23. Ibid., p. 211.

24. Ibid., p. 208.

25. Ibid., p. 205.

26. In a letter to civil rights lawyer John Wesley Walker, Arnold wrote: "The great point is that not only African Americans, but the whole body of the citizenry, is uplifted and improved when an institution is opened up in this way. I feel very lucky to have been part of this, and the same goes for the voting rights act cases of recent years—another example, I think, of successful affirmative action." Richard S. Arnold, letter to John W. Walker, June 22, 1992. Arnold papers.

27. Ruth Marcus, "Lawyer's Comments Present Free Speech Issue," *Washington Post*, January 8, 1991, p. A5.

28. Linda Greenhouse, "Supreme Court Roundup: Justices to Rule on Outside Comments by Lawyers," *New York Times*, January 8, 1991, p. A17.

29. Ibid.

30. "Arkansas Ordered to Alter Districts," *New York Times*, December 7, 1989, p. A28; Linda P. Campbell, "Court Tells Arkansas to Correct Racial Bias in Voting

Districts," *Chicago Tribune*, December 6, 1989, p. 11.

31. "Redistricting Ruling," *Arkansas Democrat*, December 6, 1989.

32. "Arkansas Ordered to Alter Districts," *New York Times*, December 7, 1989, p. A28.

33. "Board on Brink of Appeal," *Arkansas Democrat-Gazette*, February 14, 1990.

34. *Clinton v. Jeffers*, 498 U.S. 1129 (1991).

35. *Jeffers*, 730 F. Supp. at 279 (Eisele, J., dissenting).

36. Ibid., p. 227.

37. Ibid., p. 233.

38. Ibid., p. 228.

39. Robert McCord, "Eisele Raises Some Serious Questions about Redistricting," *Arkansas Democrat-Gazette*, February 22, 1990.

40. "Attorney Disputes Panel Ruling," *Arkansas Democrat-Gazette*, May 21, 1990.

41. *Jeffers*, 740 F. Supp. at 602 (Eisele, J., dissenting).

42. G. Thomas Eisele, letter to President Bill Clinton, April 21, 1994 (emphasis in original). Clinton Presidential Library.

43. Interview with G. Thomas Eisele, October 1, 2007, Little Rock, Arkansas.

44. *Jeffers v. Clinton*, 992 F.2d 826, 830 (8th Cir. 1993).

45. *Jeffers v. Tucker*, 835 F. Supp. 1101 (E. D. Ark. 1993).

46. *Shaw v. Reno*, 509 U.S. 630 (1993).

47. *Easley v. Cromartie*, 532 U.S. 234, 242 (2000).

48. Tony Moser, "Arkansas Case Lies at Heart of Right Over Redistricting," *Arkansas Democrat-Gazette*, February 20, 1995, p. 1A.

49. Tony Moser, "McGee Champions Concerns of Redrawn District," *Arkansas Democrat-Gazette*, February 20, 1995, p. 11A.

50. Ibid.

51. Moser, "Arkansas Case Lies at Heart of Right Over Redistricting," p. 1A.

52. *Jeffers v. Tucker*, 847 F. Supp. 655 (E.D. Ark. 1994).

53. *Shaw v. Reno*, 509 U.S. 630, 641–42 (1993).

54. *Jeffers v. Tucker*, 847 F. Supp. 655, 672 (E.D. Ark. 1994) (Eisele, J., concurring).

55. Ibid., p. 657.

56. 1990 Annual Report, United States Court of Appeals for the Eighth Circuit, "Opinions and Orders Directed to Be Entered by Judge Arnold." (Of the reported totals, seventy-two are unpublished per curiam opinions.)

57. Richard W. Garnett, "Tribute to the Honorable Richard S. Arnold," *Journal of Appellate Practice and Process* 1 (1999): 205–206.

58. Remarks of D. Price Marshall Jr., "Presentation of Portrait: Honorable Richard S. Arnold," 315 F.3d at xxxviii (June 28, 2002).

59. *Jeffers*, 730 F. Supp. at 211.

60. Ibid., p. 204.

61. Valerie Smith, "Court to Have Say in Apportionment," *Arkansas Gazette*, May 17, 1990.

62. *Jeffers*, 740 F. Supp. at 594.

63. Ibid., p. 602.

64. Richard S. Arnold, "Money, Or the Relations of the Judicial Branch with the Other Two Branches, Executive and Legislative," *St. Louis University Law Journal* 40 (1996): 22.

65. Robert A. Katzmann, *Courts and Congress* (Washington, DC: Brookings Institution Press 1997), pp. 2–3.

66. Arnold, "Money," pp. 19–20.

67. Dale Bumpers, "A Tribute to Richard S. Arnold," *Arkansas Law Review* 58 (2005): 498.

68. Interview with G. Thomas Eisele, October 1, 2007.

69. Arnold, "Money," p. 22.

70. Quoted in "Judiciary's Budget Request for FY 1997 Relates to Law Enforcement Role," Federal Court Management Report, April/ May 1996, p. 1.

71. Ibid., pp. 2–3.

72. "Judiciary Presents FY 97 Funding Request," *Third Branch* 28 (May 1996): 1.

73. C-SPAN interview with Richard S. Arnold and Gustave Diamond, March 17, 1993.

74. Henry J. Reske, "Federal Courts' Budget Blues," *American Bar Association Journal* (June 1993): 20–21.

75. Richard S. Arnold, letter to President Clinton, May 2, 1994. Clinton Presidential Library.

76. Richard S. Arnold, letter to President Clinton, June 23, 1994. Clinton Presidential Library.

77. Bill Clinton, letter to Richard S. Arnold, August 10, 1994. Clinton Presidential Library.

78. Richard S. Arnold, letter to President Clinton, November 2, 1995. Clinton Presidential Library. The statute Arnold referred to is 31 U.S.C. §1105(b).

79. Arnold, "Money," p. 24.

80. C-SPAN interview with Richard S. Arnold and Gustave Diamond, March 17, 1993.

81. Arnold, "Money," p. 26.

82. "Judge Richard Arnold: Presenting the Courts' Budget to Congress," *Third Branch* (June 1990): 9.

83. Quoted in *Third Branch* (March 1998): p. 3.

CHAPTER THIRTEEN

1. Bill Clinton, "Judiciary Suffers Racial, Sexual Lack of Balance," *National Law Journal* (November 2, 1992): 15.

2. Joan Biskupic, "Court Vacancies Await New President," *Washington Post*, November 6, 1992, p. A18.

3. Stephen Labaton, "Clinton Turns Inward in His Search for a Nominee to the Supreme Court," *New York Times*, April 6, 1993.

4. Biskupic, "Court Vacancies," p. A18.

5. Ibid.

6. Jeffrey Toobin, *The Nine: Inside the Secret World of the Supreme Court* (New York: Doubleday, 2007).

7. Ibid., p. 66.

8. Ibid., p. 77.

9. James J. Kilpatrick, "Clinton and the Courts," *Boulder Daily Camera*, November 12, 1992.

10. Jeffrey Rosen, "The List," *New Republic*, May 10, 1993, p. 14.

11. "There's No Justice: Too Bad He's So Good," *Arkansas Democrat-Gazette*, March 28, 1993, p. 4J.

12. "Who Would Get the Jobs?" *Newsweek*, October 26, 1992, p. 26. See also "Agonizing Reappraisal," *Arkansas Democrat-Gazette*, November 8, 1992, p. 4J.

13. Robert H. Joost, letter to Bernard W. Nussbaum, January 23, 1993, Clinton Presidential Library.

14. Ruth Marcus, "Babysitter Problems Sink Clinton's Second Prospect," *Washington Post*, February 6, 1993, p. A1. Judge Wood withdrew her name on February 5, only one day after major newspapers reported she was to be Clinton's nominee for attorney general.

15. Interview with Richard S. Arnold, June 30, 2004.

16. Ibid.

17. Interview with Richard Arnold, June 30, 2004.

18. Interview with Gale Arnold, November 18, 2005.

19. Interview with Richard Arnold, June 30, 2004.

20. Ibid.

21. *United States Jaycees v. McClure*, 709 F.2d 1560 (8th Cir. 1983), rev'd sub nom. *Roberts v. United States Jaycees*, 468 U.S. 609 (1984).

22. John Brummett, "Not Arnold's Time," *Arkansas Democrat-Gazette*, March 23, 1993.

23. Linda Greenhouse, "White Announces He'll Step Down from High Court," *New York Times*, March 20, 1993, p. A1.

24. Memo to Bernie Nussbaum from Ron Klain. Subject: Supreme Court Process, April 16, 1993, Clinton Presidential Library.

25. "There's No Justice: Too Bad He's So Good."

26. Ron Fournier, "Arnold Off List for High Court, Official Says," *Arkansas Democrat-Gazette*, May 22, 1993, p. 1A.

27. Terry Lemons, "LR Golf Club Now Arnold's Handicap," *Arkansas Democrat-Gazette*, May 24, 1993, p. 1A.

28. Arnold papers, correspondence (various).

29. Lemons, "LR Golf Club."

30. Ibid., p. 5A.

31. Interview with Bernard Nussbaum, June 26, 2008.

32. Ruth Marcus, "President Asks Wider Court Hunt," *Washington Post*, May 6, 1993, pp. A1, A27.

33. Transcript, National Public Radio, "All Things Considered," March 22, 1993.

34. Associated Press, *Kansas City Star*, March 21, 1993.

35. Rosen, "The List."

36. Interview with Richard S. Arnold, June 30, 2004.

37. Jeffrey Rosen, "For Arnold," *New Republic*, May 2, 1994, p. 16.

38. Stuart Taylor Jr., "Arnold: Class of the Field," *Legal Times*, April 25, 1994, p. 23.

39. Marcus, "President Asks Wider Court Hunt," p. A1.

40. Ibid., p. A27.

41. Nate Lewin, "Next Time, a Maverick Justice," *New York Times*, July 25, 1993, p. E17.

42. Richard L. Berke, "Clinton Names Ruth Ginsburg, Advocate for Women, to Court," *New York Times*, June 15, 1993, p. A1.

43. Ibid.

44. Interview with Bernard Nussbaum, June 26, 2008.

45. Interview with Richard Arnold, June 30, 2004.

46. Following intense speculation in the early months of 1994, on April 6 Justice Blackmun officially announced his intention to retire at the end of the Court's term. Linda Greenhouse, "Justice Blackmun's Journey," *New York Times*, April 7, 1994, p. 1.

47. *Callins v. Collins*, 510 U.S. 1141, 1145 (1994) (Blackmun, J., dissenting).

48. In Roe, although still recognizing limits to the circumstances under which abortions could be performed, Blackmun's majority opinion took the position that the constitutional right of privacy "is broad enough to encompass a woman's decision whether or not to terminate her pregnancy."

49. *Webster v. Reproductive Health Services*, 492 U.S. 490 (1989).

50. *T.L.J. v. Webster*, 792 F.2d 734 (8th Cir. 1986).

51. Arnold wrote: "This Court can sympathize with the ethical conflict which judges must experience when their legal duty is to act contrary to deeply held personal beliefs. The question of elective abortion arouses passionate opinions. The sharpness

of the debate has left no room for neutral moral ground in many minds. But the law on this subject cannot be disputed in the lower courts, including the Juvenile Courts of Missouri and this Court. The Supreme Court has announced that it is a woman's right to control the issue of her body up until the time that issue can live separately. This decision is the law of the land. Regardless of personal discomfort with the law, it is the duty of judges to apply it. If they cannot do so with a clear conscience, then they should remove themselves from this class of cases." *T.L.J.*, 792 F.2d at 739 n.4.

52. Stuart Taylor Jr., "For the Record," *American Lawyer*, July–August 1994, p. 82.

53. William H. Freivogel and Tim Poor, "Short List for High Court Has Four Names," *St. Louis Post-Dispatch*, April 17, 1994.

54. Steve Umin, letter to Victoria Radd, Clinton Presidential Library.

55. Jeffrey Rosen, "For Arnold," *New Republic*, May 2, 1994, p. 16.

56. Start Taylor Jr., "Arnold: Class of the Field," *Legal Times*, April 25, 1994, p. 23.

57. Ibid.

58. Ibid.

59. William J. Brennan Jr., "A Tribute to Chief Judge Richard S. Arnold," *Minnesota Law Review* 78 (1993): 1, 3.

60. Terry Lemons, "Hatch: 'Time Is Right' for Arnold on Supreme Court," *Arkansas Democrat-Gazette*, April 14, 1994, p. 9A.

61. Thad Cochran, letter to the president, April 14, 1994; Victoria Radd, letter to Senator Cochran, May 10, 1994, Clinton Presidential Library.

62. Larry Pressler, letter to the president, April 26, 1994, Clinton Presidential Library.

63. David Lauter, "Arkansan Pushed as 'Gutsy' Choice for Supreme Court," *Los Angeles Times*, April 17, 1994, p. A1. Lauter wrote: "Around the White House, some refer to it as the "guts option." Others call it crazy. At first glance, the decision in question would not appear to merit either label, for it involves nominating to the Supreme Court one of the nation's most highly esteemed federal judges, a noted legal scholar and writer whose work has been praised by admirers ranging from conservative writer William F. Buckley to liberal former Supreme Court Justice William J. Brennan Jr."

64. David Lauter, "Arkansan Pushed as 'Gutsy' Choice for Supreme Court," *Washington Times*, April 18, 1994, p. A1.

65. Ibid., p. A12.

66. This case, *Jeffers v. Clinton*, led to greatly increased black representation in Arkansas, as described previously in chapter 12.

67. Most of the withheld documents came from the files of Bernard Nussbaum and Victoria Radd. Nussbaum was White House counsel until he resigned in March 1994. Clinton replaced Nussbaum with Lloyd Cutler, who had been Jimmy Carter's White House counsel. Victoria Radd served as associate counsel

to the president with responsibility for coordinating the selection and confirmation processes for federal judges.

68. This memorandum bears the date April 25, 1994. Arnold papers.

69. Fax dated January 23, 1993, from Lynn Hecht Schafran, director, seven pages sent to Nussbaum at the Jefferson Hotel (contents withheld), Clinton Presidential Library.

70. FOIA response, request 2006-0188-F, WHORL file subject Richard S. Arnold, Clinton Presidential Library.

71. Letter to the president, signed by ninety-one federal judges, April 20, 1994, Clinton Presidential Library.

72. Scott O. Wright, senior United States district judge, Western District of Missouri, letter to President William J. Clinton, April 15, 1994, Clinton Presidential Library. The letter states: "I have been asked, apparently along with many other Judges, to sign my name to a letter endorsing Judge Richard Arnold to be appointed to the United States Supreme Court to replace Justice Harry Blackmun. My name will not be on that letter. I strongly feel that this is an appointment to be made by you and your staff and that the Federal Judges should not be involved in it."

73. Gilbert S. Merritt, letter to Bernard Nussbaum, June 10, 1993, Clinton Presidential Library.

74. Ibid.

75. Robert M. Parker, letter to William Jefferson Clinton, April 14, 1994, Clinton Presidential Library.

76. Thomas P. Griesa, letter to Mack McLarty, May 13, 1994, Clinton Presidential Library.

77. G. Thomas Eisele, letter to President Bill Clinton, April 21, 1994, Clinton Presidential Library (emphasis in original).

78. Mike Huckabee, letter to President Bill Clinton, May 11, 1994, Clinton Presidential Library.

79. A handwritten memorandum is attached to the letter from Victoria Radd to "Mr. President," undated, stating, "Lloyd thought that you might want to see this."

80. This episode is recounted in chapter 1.

81. Louis H. Pollak, letter to Lloyd N. Cutler, May 4, 1994, Clinton Presidential Library.

82. Ibid.

83. Letter to President Clinton, May 10, 1994, Clinton Presidential Library.

84. A similar letter arrived from the director of the Natural Resources Defense Council. John H. Adams, letter to Lloyd Cutler, May 4, 1994, Clinton Presidential Library.

85. Zona F. Hostetler, letter to Thomas F. McLarty, May 11, 1994, Clinton Presidential Library.

86. Diana M. Savit, letter to Victoria Radd, May 10, 1994, Clinton Presidential Library.

87. Joseph D. Shane, letter to President William Clinton, April 9, 1993, Clinton Presidential Library.

88. Lauter, "Arkansan Pushed as 'Gutsy' Choice for Supreme Court."

89. Jeffrey H. Birnbaum and Paul M. Barrett, "Clinton Has Supreme Court Short List; Judge Arnold of Arkansas Is a Favorite," *Wall Street Journal*, May 5, 1994, p. A16.

90. US Newswire, May 5, 1994.

91. Paul Richter, "Clinton Picks Moderate Judge Breyer for Supreme Court Spot," *Los Angeles Times*, May 14, 1994, p. 1A.

92. Ward Pincus, "Judge Richard Arnold to Be Treated for Tumor in Mouth," *Arkansas Democrat-Gazette*, August 9, 1993, p. B1.

93. Ibid.

94. Ibid.

95. Richard S. Arnold, letter to William Brennan, August 24, 1993. Brennan papers, Library of Congress.

96. Tony Mauro, "Disqualified by Cancer: Is That Legal?" *Legal Times*, May 23, 1994, p. 6.

97. Toobin, *The Nine*, p. 78.

98. Clinton Presidential Library.

99. Interview with Richard S. Arnold, June 30, 2004.

100. Ibid.

101. "Inadmissible: Arnold's Prognosis," *Legal Times*, May 23, 1994.

102. Ibid.

103. Interview with Senator Dale Bumpers, June 29, 2004.

104. Associated Press, "Judge Breyer Wins Senatorial Praise, But Skeptics Taking Aim at Clinton," *Baltimore Sun*, May 16, 1994, p. 5A.

105. Presidential statement on Breyer to Supreme Court, Office of the Press Secretary, May 13, 1994, Clinton Presidential Library.

106. Ibid.

107. Interview with Bernard Nussbaum, June 26, 2008.

108. Stuart Taylor Jr., "For the Record," *American Lawyer*, July–August 1994, p. 83.

109. Robert E. Tucker, letter to President Clinton, May 20, 1994, Clinton Presidential Library.

110. Sharon Joseph and Sharon Huffman, letter to William J. Clinton, May 19, 1994, Clinton Presidential Library.

111. Mauro, "Disqualified by Cancer," p. 6.

112. Ibid.

113. Frank Rich, "A Justice Denied," *New York Times*, May 19, 1994, p. A25.

114. Stuart Taylor Jr., "For the Record," p. 80.

115. Ibid., p. 81.

116. Ibid.

117. Ibid.

118. Ibid., p. 86.

119. Arnold papers, various correspondence, and interview with Richard S. Arnold, June 30, 2004.

120. Interview with Richard S. Arnold, June 30, 2004.

121. Editorial, "A Light in the Law: Richard Sheppard Arnold, 1936–2004," *Arkansas Democrat-Gazette*, September 26, 2004.

122. *Anastasoff v. United States*, 223 F.3d 898 (8th Cir. 2000), vacated as moot, 253 F.3d 1054 (8th Cir. 2000) (en banc). This case is discussed in chapter 14.

CHAPTER FOURTEEN

1. Richard S. Arnold, letter to US Representative Robert W. Kastenmeir, November 16, 1987. Arnold papers.

2. Richard A. Posner, *Overcoming Law* (Cambridge, MA: Harvard University Press, 1995), p. 111.

3. Richard S. Arnold, "Improving the Public's Perceptions of Federal Judges," *Society of Barristers Quarterly* 17 (1983): 325.

4. Ibid.

5. Bruce Rubenstein, "Controversial Cases Disappear," *Corporate Legal Times*, November 1999, p. 1.

6. Brigid McMenamin, "Justice in the Dark," *Forbes*, October 30, 2000, p. 74.

7. Ibid., p. 72.

8. Rubenstein, "Controversial Cases Disappear," p. 1.

9. McMenamin, "Justice in the Dark," p. 74.

10. Ibid.

11. William M. Richman and William L. Reynolds, "Elitism, Expediency, and the New Certiorari: Requiem for the Learned Hand Tradition," *Cornell Law Review* 81 (1996): 284.

12. *County of L.A. v. Kling*, 474 U.S. 936, 940 (1985) (Stevens, J., dissenting) ("For, like a court of appeals that issues an opinion that may not be printed or cited, this Court then engages in decisionmaking without the discipline and accountability that the preparation of opinions requires").

13. Quoted in William Glaberson, "Caseload Forcing Two-Level System for U.S. Appeals," *New York Times*, March 14, 1999, p. 1.

14. Quoted in "Controversial Cases Disappear," *Corporate Legal Times* 9, no. 96 (November 1999): 30.

15. Richard S. Arnold, "The Future of the Federal Courts," *Missouri Law Review* 60 (1995): 536.

16. Mary Ann McGrail, "A Tribute to Richard S. Arnold," *Arkansas Law Review* 58 (2005): 529.

17. Richard S. Arnold, letter to Elaine J. Mittleman, October 25, 1999.

18. Arnold, "The Future of the Federal Courts," p. 536.

19. Judicial statistics survey for the twelve-month period ending June 30, 1984, as reported by Richard Arnold. A copy of the survey, with Arnold's handwritten notations, appeared in his files.

20. Chairman's Report on the Appropriate Allocation of Judgeships in the United States Courts of Appeals, US Senate Judiciary Subcommittee on Administrative Oversight and the Courts (Senator Charles E. Grassley, Chairman), March 1999, II.h.

21. Ibid.

22. 8th Cir. R. 28A(i) (2000). The only exception recognized by this rule would involve subsequent litigation involving the same parties to the original case: "When relevant to establishing the doctrines of res judicata, collateral estoppel, or the law of the case, however, the parties may cite any unpublished opinion."

23. Steve France, "Swift En Banc Review Expected of Case Treating Unpublished Opinions as Precedent," *U.S. Law Week (BNA)* 69 (October 24, 2000): 2227.

24. American Bar Association Standing Committee on Ethics, Formal Opinion 94-386R.

25. Richard S. Arnold, letter to Judge Robert W. Pratt, January 21, 1992.

26. Richard S. Arnold, "Improving the Public's Perception of Federal Judges," *International Society of Barristers* 17, no. 3 (1983): 316. From an address delivered at the Sixth Circuit Judicial Conference, Asheville, North Carolina, July 1982.

27. "Perfunctory Justice: Overloaded Federal Judges Increasingly Are Resorting to One-Word Rulings," *Des Moines Register*, March 26, 1999, p. A12.

28. Richard S. Arnold, "Unpublished Opinions: A Comment," *Journal of Appellate Practice and Process* 1 (1999): 219.

29. Ibid.

30. Ibid., p. 221.

31. *Anastasoff v. United States*, 253 F.3d 1054 (8th Cir. 2000) (en banc). This case vacated an earlier panel decision, *Anastasoff v. United* States, 223 F.3d 898 (8th Cir. 2000).

32. Frank I. Michelman, "*Anastasoff* and Remembrance," *Arkansas Law Review* 58 (2005): 556.

33. *Christie v. United States*, No. 91-2375MN, 1992 U.S. App. LEXIS 38466 (8th Cir. 1992).

34. Quoted in France, "Swift En Banc Review Expected," p. 2227.

35. Polly J. Price, "Precedent and Judicial Power After the Founding," *Boston College Law Review* 42 (2000): 86.

36. In 2002, the Eighth Circuit referred to this practice as a "cardinal rule" of Eighth Circuit procedure. *Owsley v. Bowersox*, 281 F.3d 687, 690 (8th Cir. 2002).

37. *Anastasoff*, 223 F.2d at 900.

38. "The judicial Power of the United States, shall be vested in one Supreme Court, and in such inferior courts as Congress may from time to time ordain and establish." U.S. Const. art. III, § 1, cl. 1.

39. *Anastasoff*, 223 F.2d at 904.

40. Ibid.

41. Ibid., pp. 904–905.

42. Price Marshall, "Tribute to the Honorable Richard S. Arnold," *Journal of Appellate Practice and Process* 1 (1999): 201. The case referred to is *Ker v. Illinois*, 119 U.S. 436 (1886). Arnold's initial confusion about the spelling of "Ker" came from the misspelling in the table of contents for that volume of the Supreme Court Reports. The title is listed at the front of the book as "Kerr v. Illinois." 119 U.S. viii.

43. See, for example, Tony Mauro, "Judge Ignites Storm over Unpublished Opinions," *Fulton County Daily Report*, September 5, 2000.

44. McMenamin, "Justice in the Dark," p. 74.

45. Evan P. Schultz, "Gone Hunting: Judge Richard Arnold of the 8th Circuit Has Taken Aim at Unpublished Opinions, But Missed His Mark," *Legal Times*, September 11, 2000, p. 78.

46. Reynolds Holding, "Judges' Unpublished Opinions Uncovered," *San Francisco Chronicle*, September 24, 2000, p. 3.

47. Leonidas Ralph Mecham, letter to Richard S. Arnold, September 27, 2000.

48. Emily Bazelon, "The Big Kozinski," *Legal Affairs*, January–February 2004.

49. Quoted in France, "Swift En Banc Review," p. 2227.

50. *Hart v. Massanari*, 266 F.3d 1155 (9th Cir. 2001). In footnote 6, Judge Kozinski attributed to an article I published that "*Anastasoff*'s historical analysis has been called into question even by academics who generally agree with the result." This is incorrect. My article, "Precedent and Judicial Power After the Founding," *Boston College Law Review* 42 (2000): 81, supported Arnold's historical evidence and its interpretation, and augmented it with additional historical material that Arnold could have employed in support of his proposition.

51. Quoted in France, "Swift En Banc Review," p. 2227.

52. Richard S. Arnold, letter to Gilbert S. Merritt, September 26, 2000.

53. Quoted in France, "Swift En Banc Review," p. 2229.

54. Citations are contained in Patrick J. Schlitz, "The Citation of Unpublished Opinions in Federal Courts of Appeals," *Fordham Law Review* 74 (2005): 50.

55. Price, "Precedent and Judicial Power," p. 93; David Dunn, Note, "Unreported Decisions in the United States Courts of Appeals," *Cornell Law Review* 63 (1977): 141–45.

56. *Weisbart v. United States*, 222 F.3d 93 (2d Cir. 2000).

57. Internal Revenue Service, Action on Decision, November 13, 2000, 2000 WL 1711554 (I.R.S.).

58. *Aetna Life Insurance Co. v. Haworth*, 300 U.S. 227 (1937).

59. *Anastasoff v. United States*, 235 F.3d 1054, 1056 (en banc) (8th Cir. 2000).

60. Ibid.

61. Richard S. Arnold, letter to President George W. Bush, February 6, 2001 (announcing senior status effective April 1, 2001). The letter shows correspondence copies simultaneously sent to Chief Justice William Rehnquist and others. The announcement was also made that day to all Eighth Circuit judges. Federal judges with fifteen years of active service may retire at age sixty-five with full pay, or they can take "senior status" to continue full- or part-time work, also at full pay.

62. Kevin Freking, "Senators Fret about System to OK Judges," *Arkansas Democrat-Gazette*, May 4, 2003, p. A1.

63. Richard S. Arnold, "Judge J. Smith Henley: A Personal Reminiscence," *Arkansas Law Review* 52 (1990): 302.

64. An example is Arnold's letter to Judge Pickering: "I understand that you are to receive another hearing before the Senate Judiciary Committee next week. I sincerely hope the outcome will be favorable. I hate for you to be subjected to this sort of harassment." Richard S. Arnold, letter to Charles W. Pickering, February 1, 2002.

65. Charles W. Pickering, http://en.wikipedia.org/wiki/Charles_W._Pickering (accessed July 29, 2008).

66. Richard S. Arnold, Preface, in William D. Bader and Roy M. Mersky, *The First One Hundred Eight Justices* (Buffalo: William S. Hein & Co., 2004).

67. Ibid.

68. Tony Mauro, "Supreme Court Votes to Allow Citation to Unpublished Opinions in Federal Courts," *Legal Times*, April 13, 2006.

69. Of the many scholarly articles addressing the issue, Arnold noted an excellent study published by Mitu Gulati and C.M.A. McCauliff, "On *Not* Making Law," *Law and Contemporary Problems* 61 (1998): 157.

70. Tony Mauro, "Toward Citing the Uncitable: A First Step in What Could Take Two Years," *National Law Journal*, May 26, 2003, p. 26.

71. Owen M. Fiss and Judith Resnick, *Adjudication and Its Alternatives* (New York: Foundation Press, 2003), p. 997.

72. Mauro, "Toward Citing the Uncitable," p. 27.

73. Richard S. Arnold, "Judicial Politics under President Washington," *Arizona Law Review* 38 (1996): 479 (Isaac Marks Memorial Lecture at the University of Arizona College of Law).

74. Arnold, "Improving the Public's Perceptions of Federal Judges," p. 316.

75. The quotations are from lawyer comments in *Almanac of the Federal Judiciary, Eighth Circuit* (Prentice Hall Law and Business, 1993). These are also summarized in John P. Frank and A. Leon Higginbotham Jr., "A Brief Biography of Judge Richard S. Arnold," *Minnesota Law Review* 78 (1994): 22.

76. Interview with Sam A. Lee, March 4, 2005.

77. Pasco M. Bowman II, "Tribute to the Honorable Richard S. Arnold," *Journal of Appellate Practice and Process* 1 (1999): 190.

78. Gilbert S. Merritt, "Upon the Death of Richard Arnold: A Tribute," *Arkansas Law Review* 58 (2005): 539.

79. Ibid.

80. Richard S. Arnold, letter to Joan Biskupic, October 25, 1996.

81. Jacob Roginsky, letter to Richard S. Arnold, May 19, 2002.

82. Richard S. Arnold, letter to Dr. Jakob Roginsky, May 24, 2002.

83. Richard S. Arnold, letter to Mr. and Mrs. Eugene Lodermeier, July 3, 1997.

84. Richard S. Arnold, letter to Patricia A. Watson, January 30, 1992.

85. Richard S. Arnold, letter to Cindy Joyce Griggs, August 25, 1997.

86. Fred L. Zimmerman, letter to Richard S. Arnold, January 17, 1986.

87. "Court Upholds Inmate in Social Security Case," *St. Louis Post-Dispatch*, January 16, 1986. *Peeler v. Heckler*, 781 F.2d 649 (8th Cir. 1986).

88. Fred L. Zimmerman, letter to Richard S. Arnold, January 17, 1986.

89. Richard S. Arnold, letter to Norman A. Carlson, January 24, 1986.

90. Ibid.

91. Richard S. Arnold, letter to Fred L. Zimmerman, January 24, 1986.

92. Norman A. Carlson, letter to Fred L. Zimmerman and Richard S. Arnold, March 18, 1986.

93. The quotation is from Shakespeare's *The Merchant of Venice*, act IV, scene 1.

94. Micah 6:8 (KJV).

95. Richard S. Arnold, letter to Kletia Smith, December 5, 1984.

96. Interview with John R. Gibson, October 31, 2007.

97. Douglas E. Coe, letter to Richard S. Arnold, March 21, 2000 (thanking Arnold for reading from the New Testament at that year's National Prayer Breakfast).

98. Linda S. Caillouet, "Federal Judge Says Courts Should Look to God in Decisions," *Arkansas Democrat-Gazette*, May 2, 1998, p. 2B.

99. The Book of Common Prayer (London: Oxford University Press, 1979), pp. 71–72.

100. Frances Ross, interview with Richard S. Arnold, November 29, 1988, p. 23. This oral history transcript is on file at the Circuit Library, Eighth US Circuit Court of Appeals, St. Louis.

101. Ibid., p. 24.

102. Brennan papers, undated correspondence.

103. Richard S. Arnold, letter to Justice William Brennan, August 27, 1987. Brennan papers, Library of Congress.

104. Richard S. Arnold, letter to Justice William Brennan, October 17, 1983. Brennan papers, Library of Congress.

105. Richard S. Arnold, letter to Justice William Brennan, March 10, 1978. Brennan papers, Library of Congress.

106. William Brennan, letter to Floyd R. Gibson, January 24, 1985. Brennan papers.

107. Richard S. Arnold, letter to Jordan B. Cherrick, January 21, 1992.

108. Morris S. Arnold, "A Tribute to Richard S. Arnold," *University of Arkansas Law Review* 58 (2005): 482.

109. Interview with Jordan B. Cherrick and Abbot Thomas Frerking, July 16, 2008.

110. Ibid.

111. Linda Satter, "Portrait Ceremony for Judge Arnold Draws Legal Army," *Arkansas Democrat-Gazette*, June 29, 2002, p. B7.

112. Presentation of Portrait: Honorable Richard S. Arnold, 315 F.3d at xxxiii (June 28, 2002).

113. Richard S. Arnold, letter to Abbot Thomas Frerking, July 6, 2002.

EPILOGUE

1. *Planned Parenthood v. Rounds*, 372 F.3d 969 (8th Cir. June 21, 2004).

2. *Brown v. Luebbers*, 371 F.3d 458 (8th Cir. 2004), cert. denied, 543 U.S. 1189 (2005).

3. *Little Rock School District v. Armstrong*, 359 F.3d 957 (8th Cir. 2004).

4. Noel E. Oman, "Arkansas Jurist Richard Arnold Dead at 68: Esteemed Career Spanned 25 Years on Federal District and Appellate Benches," *Arkansas Democrat-Gazette*, September 24, 2004, p. A1.

5. Richard S. Arnold, letter to Frank Michelman, May 13, 2004.

6. Richard S. Arnold, letter to Abbott Thomas Frerking, September 13, 2004.

7. Quoted in Lawrence Piersol, "In Memoriam," *In Camera: Federal Judges Association Newsletter* 14, no. 3 (November 30, 2004), http://fja.fed.egovapps.com/egov/apps/egov/connect.egov?path=printable&id=24 (accessed August 29, 2008).

8. Neil A. Lewis, "Richard S. Arnold, 68, Judge Once Eyed for Supreme Court," *New York Times*, September 25, 2004, p. B9.

9. Jill Harrison and Elisabeth C. Yap, "A Tribute to the Honorable Richard S. Arnold," *Judicature* 88 (November–December 2004): 113.

10. Transcribed from video recording, Richard Sheppard Arnold United States Courthouse Dedication Ceremony (Government Services Administration DVD).

11. Linda Satter, "Little Rock Courthouse Dedication Draws Crowd," *Arkansas Democrat-Gazette*, September 29, 2007.

12. Editorial, "A Light in the Law," *Arkansas Democrat-Gazette*, September 26, 2004, p. 4J.

13. Ibid.

14. Richard S. Arnold, "First Draft of Obituary," May 12, 2004. Arnold papers.

15. Ibid.

16. Richard S. Arnold, letter to Connie Mack IV, September 8, 2004.

17. Antonin Scalia, "A Tribute to Chief Judge Richard Arnold," *Arkansas Law Review* 58 (2005): 542 (quoting Editorial, "There's No Justice: Too Bad He's So Good," *Arkansas Democrat-Gazette*, March 28, 1993, p. 5J).

18. A volume of Richard S. Arnold's speeches and writings, edited by D. Price Marshall Jr., is anticipated for publication.

Index

AAA. *See* Arkansas Activities Association

ABA. *See* American Bar Association

ABC (TV network), 344

Acheson, Dean, 72

ACLU. *See* American Civil Liberties Union

ADA. *See* Americans with Disabilities Act

AETN. *See* Arkansas Educational Television Network

AFL-CIO, 18, 105, 111

"Against Settlement" (Fiss), 299

Alito, Samuel, 270

Alliance for Justice, 364

American Bar Association, 355, 377
  and judicial appointments, 136–37, 171, 177–81
  on unpublished opinions, 356

American Civil Liberties Union, 51, 73, 97, 212, 237–39
  ACLU Capital Punishment Project, 81
  Lesbian and Gay Rights Project, 238

American Independent Party, 82

American Law Institute, 22

American Lawyer (journal), 347

American Nazi Party, 235

American Political Science Review (journal), 51

Americans with Disabilities Act, 346

Amnesty International, 207, 211

Anastasoff, Faye, 357, 359, 362–63

Anastasoff v. United States, 349, 357, 361, 362–63, 366

Anderson, Philip, 186, 377

Anglican Book of Common Prayer, 372–73

Antiterrorism and Effective Death Penalty Act, 220

Antitrust Law Journal, 128

Antwine, Calvert, 208–10

Arkansas
  Arnold as a political candidate, 95–122
  Arnold's legal cases in, 75–93
  Constitutional Convention, 22, 110–13, 116, 140
  and desegregation, 20, 36, 49, 100, 158, 276, 277, 279, 281, 287. *See also* Little Rock School District
  and partial-birth abortion, 268
  and preclearance provisions of the Voting Rights Act, 302–14, 315
  See also names of individual governors, i.e., Clinton, Bumpers, Rockefeller, etc.

Arkansas Activities Association, 150–58, 296

Arkansas Bar Association, 372

Arkansas Board of Apportionment, 307, 308, 312

Arkansas Chamber of Commerce, 111–12

Arkansas Conservationist of the Year Award, 92

Arkansas Democrat (newspaper), 76, 106, 139, 142, 149, 175, 274, 308

Arkansas Democrat-Gazette (newspaper), 76, 157, 328–29, 330

Arkansas Democratic State Committee, 82, 107

Arkansas Educational Television Network, 233–37

Arkansas Game and Fish Commission, 87

Arkansas Gazette (newspaper), 22, 106, 139, 156, 175, 188, 282, 309

Arkansas General Assembly, 306–307, 312

Arkansas National Guard
hiring quota for, 158–61, 296
use of in Little Rock, 276

Arkansas Power & Light. *See* Entergy Corporation

Arkansas Supreme Court, 163, 166, 207, 369

Arkansas Times (newspaper), 89

Arkansas Wildlife Federation, 87, 92

Army Corps of Engineers, 84–92

Arnold, Gale Palmer (Hussman) (wife), 38, 43, 47, 73–74, 75, 76, 118, 142, 326–27

Arnold, Janet Sheppard (daughter), 74, 145

Arnold, Janet (Sheppard) (mother), 21, 24–25, 33, 47, 107, 148, 371

Arnold, Kate Lewis (grandmother), 23, 148

Arnold, Kay (Kelley) (wife), 88, 187, 195, 378

Arnold, Lydia (daughter), 118, 145

Arnold, Morris S. (brother), 8–9, 15, 24–25, 75, 77, 79, 118–19, 199, 200, 230, 375

Arnold, Richard Lewis (father), 22–23, 24, 26, 32, 39, 75, 107, 145–46

Arnold, Richard Sheppard
childhood, 21–25

civil rights and civil liberties views, 129–34, 139, 182
desegregation, 18–20, 30, 147, 273–300, 300, 314
free speech/First Amendment cases, 225–50
right of privacy and abortion cases, 251–71
as trial judge for civil liberties, 145–69
commendations of, 7–8, 12, 15, 33, 38–39, 73–74, 92, 111–12, 134, 138–40, 179, 184–86, 225–26, 268, 270, 310–11, 321, 335–36, 337–40, 367, 379–80
death of, 378
education of, 14–15, 25–39
ethics and behavior, 351–71
federal judiciary
court of appeals, appointment to, 124, 129, 159, 171–89
district court, appointment to, 123–44, 172–73
and "not for publication" opinions, 352–63
retirement, 363–64
Supreme Court, Arnold's reaction to not being appointed, 332, 347–49
Supreme Court, considered for, 12, 142, 203, 216, 323–49
work on budgets for, 220–21, 301–302, 316–21, 325, 380
friendships, 139, 146, 379
with Blackmun, 218, 221
with Brennan, 41, 44, 48, 66, 67, 68, 71, 85, 98, 106, 134, 141–42, 184, 217–18, 300, 373–74
with Bumpers, 138
with Clintons, 12, 187, 318, 329, 334, 378
with Ginsburg, 38, 321, 332
with Lay, 181, 218
with Pryor, 106, 113–14, 139
health of, 142–43, 183–87, 327, 377–79
cancerous tumor in the mouth, 341–42
effect on his appointment to Supreme Court, 342–43, 345–47
removal of spleen, 187–88

law clerk for William Brennan, 41–70
law practice of, 71–94
as a legal scholar, 93–94, 128, 186, 227, 377
    views on unpublished opinions, 355–57
marriage and family, 38, 74, 118, 121
    divorce of Gale Hussman, 118, 121, 125, 141–42, 326
    remarriage to Kay Kelley, 88, 187
political leanings of, 13, 20–21, 29–31, 41
    effect on his judicial opinions, 314–16, 317
    as a key aide to Dale Bumpers, 120–21, 124–27
    as a political candidate, 95–122, 125
    possible attorney general for Clinton, 325–28
religious background of, 26, 34–35, 100, 185, 195, 239, 271, 326, 371–74
    Saint Louis Abbey, 374–76
sentencing, views on, 161–69, 191–223
Arnold, Thomas S. (cousin), 75
Arnold, W. H. "Dub" (cousin), 77
Arnold, William Hendrick (W. H.) (grand-father), 22, 75, 107
Arnold, William H., III (cousin), 75, 77
Arnold, William H., Jr. (uncle), 23, 75
Arnold & Arnold (law firm), 72, 75–92, 146
Arrogance of Power, The (Fulbright), 108
Association of Women Lawyers of Greater Kansas City, 179–80
attorney general, Arnold as possible, 325–28
Audubon, John, 89
Austern, Tommy, 75

Babbitt, Bruce, 345, 347
Baird, Zoe, 325
Baker v. Carr, 56–58, 101, 304
Banks, Dennis, 231, 232
Bass, Jack, 288
Batson v. Kentucky, 80, 210
Baucus, Max, 182
Beam, C. Arlen, 209, 222, 236, 255
Bell, Griffin, 124, 130, 132–34, 135–36, 145, 162, 169, 173–74, 175, 176, 177, 178–79

Bellotti v. Baird, 265
Benedictine monks, 374–76
Bethune, Edwin R. "Ed," 135
Biden, Joe, 328
Biskupic, Joan, 367
Black, Hugo, 46–47, 50, 54, 58, 59, 63, 65, 67
    influence on Arnold, 41, 47, 55, 68–69, 102, 226–28
    opinions written by, 26, 52–53, 55, 60–61, 63–64, 65, 97
Blackmun, Harry, 39, 113, 194, 200, 219, 245, 265, 333, 344
    friendship with Arnold, 218, 221
    influence on Arnold, 218–21
    opinions written by, 199, 216, 220, 230
    retirement of, 12, 203, 332
Blanton, Kenneth Ray, 77–81
Board of Education of Oklahoma City Public Schools v. Dowell, 295
Bolin, W. F., 210
Bork, Robert, 130, 324, 365
Bowman, Pasco, II, 198, 203, 232, 367
Boxer, Barbara, 341
Boynton v. Virginia, 62–64
Boy Scouts of America, 246
Bradley, Ed, 89
Brandeis, Louis, 72, 113
Branton, Wiley, 275
Braun, Carol Moseley, 341
Brennan, Marjorie, 102, 106
Brennan, William, Jr., 80–81, 96, 120, 178, 194, 199, 222, 265, 324, 333, 336, 342
    Arnold as law clerk for, 39, 41–70, 98, 132, 226, 227
    friendship with Arnold, 41, 44, 48, 66, 67, 68, 71, 85, 98, 106, 134, 141–42, 184, 217–18, 300, 373–74
    influence on Arnold, 44, 53, 55, 63, 69–70, 99–100, 132, 217–18, 226, 300, 335
    opinions written by, 101, 183, 219, 245–46, 252, 328
Breyer, Stephen, 8, 197, 325, 326, 331, 334, 339
    appointment to Supreme Court, 12, 175, 269, 323, 324, 344–46, 348
    opinions written by, 269, 270, 311

Bright, Myron, 88, 253, 255, 259, 260
Britton, John, 258
Brown, Robert, 126–27
Brown, Vernon, 192, 211–12
Brown v. Board of Education, 17–20, 35–36,
　　37, 46, 100, 275, 277, 294–95
　Yale debate about, 17–20, 296, 338–39
Buckley, William F., Jr., 18, 96, 335–36
Bumpers, Dale, 188, 344, 376
　friendship with Arnold, 138, 139, 146, 379
　as governor of Arkansas, 83, 88, 119–20,
　　124
　helping Arnold get a judgeship, 119,
　　122, 124, 127, 128, 134–36, 175–77,
　　181, 316
　as Senator, 89, 120, 124–26, 133, 290,
　　301, 317
Bunyan, John, 61
Burger, Warren E., 165, 188, 245
Burton, Harold, 48
Bush, George H. W., 188, 323–24
Bush, George W., 178, 363–64, 365

Cabranes, Jose, 331
Cache River, 84, 87–90
Callins v. Collins, 333
Camp, Frank, 81–82
Carhart, LeRoy, 268–70
Carhart v. Stenberg, 267–70
Carlson, Norman, 370
Carmichael, Stokely, 105
Carnahan, Mel, 214, 270
Carraway, Hattie, 23–24
Carswell, Harrold, 113
Carter, Jimmy, 124, 127, 130–32, 145, 175,
　　296, 338
　and judicial appointments, 129, 133,
　　135, 140, 169, 172–73, 177–78, 179,
　　180–81, 184, 324
Carter, Robert L., 56, 275
Carter, Sandy, 78
Catholic Church, 195, 239, 271, 326, 372,
　　373, 374–76
Center for Reproductive Law and Policy,
　　331
Central Arkansas Labor Council, 140–41
Central High School in Little Rock,
　　Arkansas, 273–300

Charlotte Observer (newspaper), 81
Chayes, Abram, 37, 42, 297–98, 299
Cherrick, Jordan B., 374
Christian Ministerial Alliance, 207
Christie v. United States, 358–60, 363
circuit courts. *See* courts of appeals
Civil Rights Acts, 130, 147
　Title VII of the Civil Rights Act of 1964,
　　159–61
Clark, Tom C., 43, 46, 48, 53, 58, 64, 80,
　　84
Clark v. Board of Education of LRSD, 277
Clemmons, Eric, 212–13
Clinton, Bill, 15, 99, 122, 124, 130,
　　139–40, 146–47, 172, 177, 181, 187,
　　378, 379
　friendship with Arnold, 12, 187, 318,
　　329, 334, 378
　as governor of Arkansas, 146, 187, 196,
　　201, 287, 307
　and *Jeffers v. Clinton*, 302–14
　as president, 124, 130, 310
　　choosing attorney general, 325–28
　　funding of judiciary, 318–20
　　and Supreme Court nominees, 12, 28,
　　　92, 142, 175, 269, 323–25,
　　　328–32, 336–46, 348
Clinton, Hillary Rodham, 12, 187, 325,
　　378
Clinton Presidential Library, 336–40
Cochran, Thad, 335
Coker, Frances, 18, 20
Coker v. Georgia, 163
Columbia School of Law, 107
Commission on Equal Opportunity in the
　　Armed Forces, 73
Commission on Freedom of Expression
　　(Speech Communication Association),
　　225
Committee on the Budget (for federal judi-
　　ciary), 220–21, 301–302, 316–21, 325,
　　380
Communist Party, 50, 227
　cases concerning, 58–59, 60–61
Congress. *See* House of Representatives
　and Richard Arnold; Senate and
　　Richard Arnold
Congressional Record, 126

Connally, Tom, 21–22, 43, 47
Cook, Eugene, 17–18, 19, 20
Cooper v. Aaron, 36, 49–50, 65, 69, 273,
    276–77, 290
Cornell University Laboratory of
    Ornithology, 89
Cossatot River, 84–87, 114
courts of appeals, 8, 11–12, 13, 172,
    173–75, 195, 316
  decision-making process, 157
  as source of nominees for Supreme
    Court, 324
  *See also specific courts, i.e., First Circuit
    Court of Appeals, DC Circuit Court of
    Appeals, etc.*
Covington & Burling (law firm), 72–75,
    81, 93
Cox, Archibald, 57
Craig v. Boren, 154
C-SPAN (TV network), 318
Cuomo, Mario, 331
Currie, David, 38
Cutler, Lloyd, 339, 340, 342, 344, 345

Dana Farber Cancer Institute, 342
DC Circuit Court of Appeals, 239, 249,
    324
Deacey, Thomas, 136–37
Death Penalty Resource Centers, 221
De Clerk, Danny, 140
Delamar, Kay, 88
Delamar, Nancy, 88
Dellinger, Walter, 326
Democratic Party, 23, 107
  Arnold as a Southern Democrat, 95–122
  Democratic National Committee, 177
  National Conventions, 82, 108–109
Dinwiddie, Regina, 257–59
Dirksen, Everett, 101
Dismas House in St. Louis, 369
district courts, 358
  Arnold serving on
    appointment to, 123–44, 172–73
    as trial judge for civil liberties, 145–69
  and *Jeffers v. Clinton*, 302–14, 336
  and Little Rock School desegregation,
    273–300
Dixiecrats, 29, 36, 96

Dodson, Diana Lee, 150–58
Dodson v. Arkansas Activities Association,
    150–58, 169
Dole, Bob, 328
"Don't Ask, Don't Tell," 240–41
Douglas, William O., 46, 48, 50, 53, 58,
    60, 63, 80
Drake University Law School, 356–57
Dred Scott case, 55
Drug Enforcement Agency, 317
due process clause, 46, 162, 164, 166, 168,
    243
Dym, Herb, 37

Easley v. Cromartie, 311
Eastland, James, 127, 128, 130, 133, 181
Edwards, Lindalyn, 104
Egan, Michael, 177–78
Eighth Amendment, 162–64, 166, 168,
    193, 194, 208, 214–15, 365
Eighth Circuit Court of Appeals, 11, 13,
    113, 147, 149, 156, 158, 189
  ABA and a woman appointed to Eighth
    Circuit Court, 177–81
  Arnold arguing cases in front of, 86, 88,
    89
  Arnold's appointment to, 124, 129, 159,
    171–89
    announcing retirement from, 363–64
    serving as chief judge, 189, 321
  death penalty cases, 191–223
  desegregation cases, 49, 273–300
  ethics and behavior, 351–71
  free speech and First Amendment cases,
    225–50
  on Harold Rogers's sentence, 166–68
  right of privacy and abortion cases,
    251–71
  statistics on caseload, 355
  tax cases, 349, 357–63
Eisele, G. Thomas, 112, 180, 184, 317, 338
  as district judge, 86, 145, 148, 201–202,
    203, 204, 206, 207, 210
  and *Jeffers v. Clinton*, 305, 309–11, 313
Eisenhower, Dwight D., 29, 35, 43, 49,
    65–66, 276, 365
Elders, Jocelyn, 329
Eleventh Circuit Court of Appeals, 195

"Emperor Constantine and the Christian Church, The" (senior essay by Arnold), 34
Engel v. Vitale, 97
Entergy Corporation, 187
Environmental Defense Fund, 71, 76, 84–92, 114, 137
Environmental Law Institute, 92
Environmental Law Review (journal), 128
Episcopal church, 373
equal protection clause, 28, 56, 80, 151, 154, 167, 210, 313
Exonian (newspaper), 30

Fagg, George, 215, 232, 235, 249, 259, 265, 343
Fairchild, Barry Lee, 200–208, 313–14
Fairchild, Robert, 206
Faith Baptist Church of Louisville, Nebraska, 247–49
Falk, David, 74
Farmer, James, 18, 19–20
Faubus, Orval, 96, 99, 106, 109, 124, 310
and Arnold, 95, 100, 106, 121–22
and desegregation, 20, 36, 49, 100, 158, 276, 277
Fay v. New York, 80
Fay v. Noia, 218
Federal Bureau of Investigation (FBI), 136–43
Federal Bureau of Prisons, 370
federal judiciary
Committee on the Budget, 220–21, 301–302, 316–21, 325, 380
and "not for publication" opinions, 352–63
See also courts of appeals; district courts; Supreme Court
Federal Reporter (publication), 352
Feinstein, Dianne, 341
Fifteenth Amendment, 303
Fifth Amendment, 55, 87, 102
Fifth Circuit Court of Appeals, 91, 113, 132, 209, 365
First Amendment, 16, 37, 51, 52, 65, 68, 101, 183, 252, 254
and abortion cases, 259–62
free speech and First Amendment cases, 225–50

and right of association, 241–47
vs. right of privacy, 252, 254, 257
First Amendment Center, 225–26
First Circuit Court of Appeals, 172, 324
Fisk, Robert, 329
Fiss, Owen, 299
Fitzhugh, Becky, 377
Fitzpatrick, John, 89
Floyd, Clifford, 195
Forbes (magazine), 353, 361
Forbes, Ralph P., 233–35
Forbes v. Arkansas Educational Television Commission, 233–37
Ford, Gerald, 134
Fortas, Abe, 113, 331
Foster, Lisa, 326
Foster, Vincent, 325, 326, 327, 329, 330, 331
Fourteenth Amendment, 46, 50, 52, 62, 64, 101, 219, 242
due process clause, 46, 162, 164, 166, 168, 243
equal protection clause, 28, 56, 80, 151, 154, 167, 210, 313
right of privacy and abortion cases, 251–71
Fourth Amendment, 52–53, 55, 255–56
Fourth Congressional District (Arkansas), 98–106, 113–20
Frankfurter, Felix, 42, 46, 50, 53–54, 55, 57–58, 59, 66, 67, 68, 96, 98
and Arnold, 43, 47, 69
opinions written by, 52, 54, 56
Freedom for the Thought That We Hate (Arnold), 227
Freedom of Access to Clinic Entrances Act, 258
Freedom of Information Act, 136–37, 336
Freeman v. Pitts, 295
French, John, 38–39, 43
Frerking, Thomas, 374, 375, 376, 378
Freund, Paul, 37, 38, 43–44, 98
Frost, Robert, 66
Fulbright, J. William, 24, 47, 49, 108, 109, 115, 124
Furman v. Georgia, 193
Futrell, Bill, 92
"Future of the Federal Courts, The" (lecture by Arnold), 355

Gans, Michael, 197, 206
Garrow, David, 252
Gay and Lesbian Students Association, 237–39
General Electric Company, 73
Gertz v. Robert Welch, Inc., 231
Gesell, Gerhard, 73–74, 81, 96, 120, 134
Gholson, Hunter M., 92
Gibson, Floyd, 234, 235, 249, 255, 374
Gibson, John R., 264, 265, 372
Gideon v. Wainwright, 79
Gilham Dam project, 85–87, 114
Ginsburg, Ruth Bader, 7–9, 197, 200, 216, 236, 270, 323, 324, 325, 328–29, 331–32, 341
    friendship with Arnold, 38, 321, 332
GLSA. *See* Gay and Lesbian Students Association
Goldberg, Arthur, 98
Gomillion v. Lightfoot, 56
Gramm, Phil, 320
Greenberg, Paul, 349, 380
Greenhouse, Linda, 244
Green v. County School Board of New Kent County, 277–78
Gregg v. Georgia, 164–65, 167
Griesa, Thomas P., 338
Griffin, Larry, 197
Griswold, Erwin, 35
Griswold v. Connecticut, 252–53, 257
Gunn, David, 257, 258
Gunn, George, 198

Hall, Carl D., Jr., 245
Hall, John Wesley, 201–202, 219
Hamilton, James, 326
Hand, Learned, 12, 37, 146–47, 339, 349, 380
Hansen, David R., 376
Hansen, Denny, 35
Harlan, John Marshall, 46
Harlan, John Marshall, II, 43, 46, 47–48, 54, 58, 63, 66, 67, 252
Harris, Oren, 98–99
Hart v. Massanari, 361
Harvard Law Review (journal), 38, 43, 128
Harvard Law School, 7, 15, 22, 23, 35–39, 107, 362, 378

Harvard Law Wives' Club, 38
Hatch, Orrin G., 178, 216, 328, 335
Hawke, Steve, 208
Hawkins, Marlin, 82
Haynesworth, Clement, 113
Hays, Brooks, 49
Heaney, Gerald, 88, 147–48, 160–61, 169, 184, 264, 296, 330, 358, 360
    involvement in supervision of school desegregation in Little Rock, 147, 274, 280, 283–84
Heflin, Howell, 176
Hellman, Arthur, 362
Henderson State College, 115
Henley, J. Smith, 83, 88, 89, 187, 255, 364–65
Henne, Debra, 253, 255
Henne, Robert, 253
Henne v. Wright, 253–55
Heymann, Philip, 38, 43, 70, 378
Higginbotham, Leon, 335
Hill, Paul, 258
Hlavinka, Victor, 77
Hodges, Kaneaster, Jr., 126, 133, 146
Hodgson v. Minnesota, 263–65, 271
Hoffa, Jimmy, 104, 105
Holdridge, John, 81
Hollings, Ernest "Fritz," 320
Hollingsworth, P. A. "Les," 312
Holmes, Oliver Wendell, 113, 238, 243
House Judiciary Committee, 366
House of Representatives and Richard Arnold, 98–106, 113–20
    Arnold presenting judicial budgets, 316–21
House Un-American Activities Committee, 226
Howard, George, Jr., 135–36, 140, 160, 162, 169, 175–76, 177, 180–81, 311
    and *Jeffers v. Clinton*, 305, 308, 309, 310, 311
Hubbell, Webster "Webb," 329
Huckabee, Mike, 338
Hughes, Everard, 184
Human Rights Watch, 202
Humphrey, Hubert, 95, 108, 147
Humphrey, Hubert III, 244
Hunter, Nan, 238

Hussman, Gale Palmer. *See* Arnold, Gale Palmer (Hussman) (wife)
Hussman, Walter, Jr., 76, 142, 378
Hussman, Walter, Sr., 38, 76, 111, 113–14, 118, 142
Hyman, Lester, 326

Immaculate Conception Monastery in Jamaica, New York, 373
Immigration and Naturalization Service, 317
Inter-American Foundation, 187
Interdistrict Settlement Agreement, 285–91, 292
Internal Revenue Service, 357–63
Iowa
    and partial-birth abortion, 268
    and placement of a menorah, 249–50
Iowa Girls High School Athletic Union, 158
Iowa Public Television, 235
ivory-billed woodpecker, 85, 88–89, 90
"Ivy Ode" (commencement address by Arnold), 14, 34

Jack, Wellborn, Jr., 85
Jackson, Robert, 42
Janklow, William, 231–33
Jaycees and women members, 183, 241–47, 257, 327–28, 331, 332, 340
"Jeffersonian View, A" (column by Arnold), 28–29
Jeffers v. Clinton, 302–14, 336
John Paul II (pope), 195, 373
Johnson, James D., 109
Johnson, Lyndon B., 46, 74, 95, 101, 103, 147, 296
Jones, Day, Cockley and Reavis (law firm), 43
Jones, Earl, 118–19
Jones, Henry, 185
Jones, John J. (Mrs.), 24
Jones, Nathaniel, 162
Joshua Intervenors, 284, 287, 293, 294, 298
Judicial Conference of the United States, 15, 156, 203, 357
    budget committee, 220–21, 301–302, 316–21, 325, 380

recommendation on unpublished opinions, 366
resolution honoring Arnold, 321
Judiciary Bill of 1978, 175
Junior Chamber of Commerce. *See* Jaycees and women members
Justice Department, 317

Kansas Commission on Disability Concerns, 346
Kasowitz, Moishe, 249–50
Katzmann, Robert A., 316
Keady, William C., 91
Kearse, Amalya Lyle, 331, 334, 339
Kelley, Kay. *See* Arnold, Kay (Kelley) (wife)
Kennedy, Anthony M., 8, 198–99, 219–20
    opinions written by, 236, 269–70
Kennedy, Edward "Ted," 130, 140, 181, 345
Kennedy, John F., 65–66, 67, 74–75, 96, 323
Kennedy, Randall, 256
Kennedy, Robert, 67, 97, 108
Kennedy, William, 329, 330
Ker v. Illinois, 360–61
Kilpatrick, James J., 324–25
King, Alan, 32
King, Brenda, 377
King, Martin Luther, Jr., 108, 289
Kiwanas, 243
Klain, Ron, 328
Klein, Joel, 342
Kozinski, Alex, 361, 366–67
Krauskopf, Joan M., 177–78
Ku Klux Klan, 24

Lamberg, John, 143, 183–84
Lashley, Frederick, 214–17
Lashley v. Delo, 214–17
Laws, Leonard Marvin, 219
Lawyers Committee for Civil Rights under Law, 97
Lay, Donald P., 88, 171–72, 178, 180–81, 188, 197, 230, 244, 260–61, 264, 288, 296, 330
    friendship with Arnold, 181, 218
Lee, Bruce Roy, 228–31

Lee, Sam Alston, 25
Legal Defense and Education Fund
    (NOW), 337
Legal Defense Fund (NAACP), 207, 212,
    275, 278, 284, 286, 290, 294, 298, 300,
    308
Legal Times (magazine), 334–35, 346, 361,
    366
Lesbian and Gay Rights Project (ACLU),
    238
Lewellen, Roy, 314–15
Lewis, Anthony, 121
Lewis, Tony, 64
*Liberty and Sexuality: The Right of Privacy and
    the Making of Roe v. Wade* (Garrow),
    252
"Light in the Law, A" (Greenberg), 380
Lincoln, Nebraska, ordinance restricting
    picketing, 259–60
Lindsey, Bruce, 329, 342
Little Rock, Arkansas
    Arnold serving as district judge in, 145–69
    attempts at integration, 35–36
    Cooper v. Aaron, 49
Little Rock School District, 279–81, 282,
    283, 284–85
    Interdistrict Settlement Agreement,
        285–91, 292
    resegregation in, 294–95
    supervision of school desegregation by
        Arnold, 147, 273–300, 313, 314
    and unitary status, 293
Lockett v. Ohio, 165, 215–16
Loken, James, 206, 240
London Sunday Express (newspaper), 22
Long, Huey, 24
Lowe, Lynn, 135
LRSD. *See* Little Rock School District
Lundquist, John W., 230
lymphocytic leukemia (lympho-prolific
    leukemia), 143, 184, 187–88, 341,
    347, 377–79, 381
Lyon, Philip, 185

Mack, Connie, III, 380
Mack, Connie, IV, 380
Madison Lecture (New York University),
    227, 295–96

Magill, Frank, 206, 235–36, 249, 253, 255
Magnuson, Paul, 268, 358
Mahaffey, J. Q., 33
Mapp, Dollree, 51
Mapp v. Ohio, 50–56, 67
Marcus, Jay B., 235–36
Marshall, John, 102
Marshall, Price, 314, 360
Marshall, Thurgood, 28–29, 80–81, 194,
    199, 222, 245, 265, 275, 323, 333
    opinions written by, 219, 220
Martin, Rhett, 15
Mason, Marjorie, 200, 203, 204
Mathews v. Eldridge, 168
"Matter of Justice Coalition, A," 368
Mauro, Tony, 346, 366
Mayo Clinic, 378
McCarthy, Joesph, 30, 31
McClellan, John L., 23–24, 114, 133,
    134–35
McCleskey, Warren, 219–20
McCleskey v. Zant, 219–20
McCloskey, Robert, 51, 58, 67
McCord, Robert, 309–10
McCurry v. Tesch, 247–49
McGee, Ben, 312
McLarty, Thomas F., III, "Mack," 203,
    329, 330, 341, 342–43
McMath, Sid, 112, 176, 177
McMillian, Theodore, 177, 230, 234, 235,
    255, 260, 264, 296, 330
    and the death penalty, 197, 198, 199,
        200, 209–10, 219
Mercer, George "Tiny," 196, 197
Merritt, Gilbert S., 33, 127, 177–78, 247,
    362, 367
Metropolitan Club of Washington, 182–83
Meyerson, James, 162
Michelman, Frank, 38, 43, 357, 378
Middleton, Mark E., 203
Mikulski, Barbara A., 341
Miller, Eddie Lee, 210
Milliken v. Bradley, 279, 281
Minnesota
    and access to abortion by minors,
        263–65, 330
    cross burnings in, 228–31
    Minnesota Jaycees and women members,

183, 241–47, 257, 327–28, 331, 332, 340

Minnesota Daily, 238–39

Minnesota Department of Human Rights, 242

Minnesota Law Review (journal), 335

Minnesota Supreme Court, 242, 243–44

Miranda v. Arizona, 46

Missouri
  and access to abortion by minors, 266–67, 333
  "Infant's Protection Act," 270
  and use of public facilities for abortions, 260–62

Missouri Capital Punishment Resource Center, 212

Missouri State Penitentiary, 212–13

Mitchell, George, 328, 335

Mondale, Walter, 180

Moore, H. Clay, 186–87

Moore, Michael, 185

Morgan, Henry, 157

Murphy, Diana E., 172, 181, 242

Murray, Patty, 341

NAACP, 17, 24, 28, 29, 56, 59, 162, 176, 241
  Gregg v. Georgia, 164–65
  Legal Defense Fund, 207, 212, 275, 278, 284, 286, 290, 294, 298, 300, 308
  NAACP v. Alabama, 243

Nadler, Lee, 342, 343, 348

NARAL. *See* National Abortion Rights Action League

National Abortion Federation, 364

National Abortion Rights Action League, 271, 333, 364

National Capital Area Civil Liberties Union, 73

National Coalition to Abolish the Death Penalty, 207

National Environmental Protection Act of 1969, 85, 86, 88, 90, 92, 128

National Institutes of Health, 143, 184, 187–88, 341

National Law Journal, 366

National Organization for Women, 111
  Legal Defense and Education Fund, 337

National Prayer Breakfast, 372

National Public Radio, 330

Natural Law Party, 235

Nature Conservancy, 88, 89

Nebraska
  and Faith Baptist Church, 247–49
  and partial-birth abortion, 268–70
  restricting choice of surnames, 253–55

Nebraska Supreme Court, 247–48

NEPA. *See* National Environmental Protection Act of 1969

Newman, Jon, 339

Newman, Roger, 69

New Republic (magazine), 325, 331, 334

Newsweek (magazine), 231–33, 325, 334

New York Times (newspaper), 89, 207, 244, 253, 263–64, 308, 333, 339, 346–47, 356

New York Times v. Sullivan, 226–27

New York University Madison Lecture, 227, 295–96

Nine: Inside the Secret World of the Supreme Court, The (Toobin), 21, 324

Ninth Amendment, 87, 254

Ninth Circuit Court of Appeals, 353, 361

Nixon, Richard M., 46, 96, 108, 112

NLRSD. *See* North Little Rock School District

non-Hodgkin lymphoma, 142, 341, 342, 347, 377, 381

North Little Rock School District, 279–81
  Interdistrict Settlement Agreement, 285–91, 292
  See also Little Rock School District

Nussbaum, Bernard, 325, 327, 328, 330, 332, 337, 345

O'Brien, Donald, 158

O'Connor, Sandra Day, 7, 194, 221, 245, 265, 270, 300
  opinions written by, 246, 311

Office of Management and Budget, 319

Office of Metropolitan Supervisor, 285–86

Omaha World Herald (newspaper), 180, 181

OMB. *See* Office of Management and Budget

Overton, William, 185

Palko v. Connecticut, 26

Palmer Media Group, 38, 76, 118, 141

Paltrow, Lynn, 330–31

Panetta Leon, 318–19

Partial-Birth Abortion Ban Act of 2003, 269–70

PCSSD. *See* Pulaski County Special School District

Peeler v. Heckler, 370

Perkins, Janet, 212

Phillips Exeter Academy, 19, 22, 23, 27–32, 34, 37, 75, 118

Pickens, Edward Charles, 199–200

Pickering, Charles W., 365

Pine Bluff Commercial (newspaper), 116

Planned Parenthood, 364

  Planned Parenthood of Greater Kansas City, 257–59

Planned Parenthood v. Casey, 262

Plath, Warren, 32

Plessy v. Ferguson, 28, 46

Poe v. Ullman, 252

Pollak, Louis, 18, 19, 338–39

Portrait of a Decade (Lewis), 121

Posner, Richard A., 247, 351–52, 354

"Power of State Courts to Enjoin Federal Officers, The" (Arnold), 93

Presidential Records Act, 336

Pressler, Larry, 335

Pryor, David, 315

  in Arkansas legislature, 99, 100, 104, 105, 106

  friendship with Arnold, 106, 113–14, 139

  as governor of Arkansas, 139, 146

  running for Congress against Arnold, 100, 103, 104–106, 107, 118, 121–22, 139, 315

  as Senator, 106, 114, 133, 176, 188, 344

Pulaski County Special School District, 279–81, 282, 283, 284

  Interdistrict Settlement Agreement, 285–91, 292

  teacher's strike, 292–93

  See also Little Rock School District

Purvis, Joseph, 186

"Quality of Mercy" speech, 25, 148–49, 371, 378–79

Radd, Victoria, 338, 342, 344

Rankin, J. Lee, 56

Rapp, Cynthia, 206

R.A.V. v. City of St. Paul, Minnesota, 229–30

Reagan, Ronald, 188, 193, 263, 324

Reasoner, Stephen, 305

Reavley, Thomas M., 209–10

Rector, Ricky, 208

"Red Mass," 372

Red River, 84

Reed, Howard, 330

Reed, Stanley, 48

Rehnquist, William H., 7, 42, 130, 193–94, 198, 220, 270

  appointing Arnold to present judicial budget to Congress, 301–302, 316, 320, 325, 380

  opinions written by, 262

Remembering Denny (Trillin), 34–35

Reno, Janet, 258, 327, 328

Republican Party, 29–30, 96, 135, 310

Reuther, Walter, 105

Reynolds, William L., 353

Rezneck, Dan, 44, 48, 62–63, 65, 69

Richard S. Arnold Prize for Scholarship in Free Speech, 225

Richard Sheppard Arnold Courthouse in Little Rock, 346–47, 375–76, 379

Richenberg, Richard F., Jr., 240–41

Richenberg v. Perry, 241

Richman, William, 353

Riley, Dale, 198

Roberts, John, 270

Roberts v. Jaycees, 244–47

Robinson, Tommy, 202

Rockefeller, Winthrop, 95–96, 109, 110, 124, 310

Roe v. Wade, 73, 251, 252, 260, 262, 271, 328, 333

Rogers, Harold Eugene, 161–69, 186, 221, 320

Roginsky, Jakob, 368

Roosevelt, Eleanor, 23

Roosevelt, Franklin D., 37, 42, 107, 339

Roosevelt, Theodore, 89

Root, Elihu, 71–72

Rose Law Firm, 329

Rosen, Jeffrey, 325, 331, 334

Ross, Donald, 206
Roth v. United States, 51–52, 226
Roy, Elsijane Trimble, 185, 187
Roy, James, Jr., 186
Rust v. Sullivan, 262
Rutherford, Skip, 282
Rutledge, Wiley, 18, 37

Sacks, Albert, 42
Saint Louis Abbey, 374–76
Sanderson, Lucille, 43
San Francisco Chronicle (newspaper), 361
Scalia, Antonin, 7, 38–39, 43, 198, 202,
    221, 270, 321, 378, 381
  opinions written by, 230, 264–65
Schlup, Lloyd, 213–14
Schroeder, Mary, 331
Science (journal), 89
Second Circuit Court of Appeals, 316, 339,
    363
Senate and Richard Arnold
  Arnold as aide to Bumpers, 124–27
  Arnold presenting judicial budgets,
    316–21
Senate Judiciary Committee, 181–83, 329
Seventh Circuit Court of Appeals, 247,
    351
Seward, William H., 371
Seymour, Stephanie K., 331
Shaffer, Michael, 208–209
Shaw v. Reno, 311, 312–13
Shell, Terry Lee, 145, 151, 155
Shelley v. Kraemer, 48
Shelton v. Tucker, 59
Shepard, Alan, 66
Sheppard, John L. (great-grandfather),
    107
Sheppard, Morris (grandfather), 15, 19,
    21–22, 23, 43, 47, 107, 380
Simmons, Ronald Gene, 196
Simmons, Thomas Winford, 200
Sixth Amendment, 79, 219
Sixth Circuit Court of Appeals, 127, 152,
    154, 156, 247, 362
  Judicial Conference, 356
60 Minutes (TV series), 89
Slater, Rodney, 329
Smith, Gerald, 196

Smith, John Lewis, Jr., 90–91
Smith, Lavenski R., 364
Smith, Neal, 320
Smith, Winn, 77
SNCC. *See* Student Non-Violent Coordi-
    nating Committee
Social Security Administration, 370
Souter, David, 236, 270, 321
South Dakota
  and access to abortion by minors, 265
  preclearance provisions of the Voting
    Rights Act, 303
Southern Christian Leadership Confer-
    ence, 207
"Southern Manifesto," 49
Southern Railway Company, 73
Southwestern Electric Power Company,
    76
Speech Communication Association's
    Commission on Freedom of Expres-
    sion, 225
Spidell, Linda, 253, 255
Stanley, Ivon, 195–96
States' Rights Democratic Party, 96
Steele v. City of Tallahassee, 64
Stevens, John Paul, 7, 197, 200, 265, 270,
    353
  opinions written by, 216, 220, 236–37
Stever, Donald W., 92
Stewart, Potter, 43, 46, 54, 57–58, 59, 66
Stine, Jeffrey, 92
St. James Episcopal Church in Texarkana,
    26
St. Louis Post-Dispatch (newspaper), 198, 269
St. Louis University Law School, 316
Stokes, Winford, 198
St. Paul's Episcopal Church in Wash-
    ington, DC, 373
Strauder v. West Virginia, 80
Stroud, John F., Jr., 137
Student Non-Violent Coordinating Com-
    mittee, 121
"Substantive Right to Environmental
    Quality under the National Environ-
    mental Policy Act, The" (Arnold), 93
Supreme Court, 7–9, 11–12, 13, 101–102,
    194, 218
  in 1960, 45–48

Arnold considered for appointment to, 12, 142, 203, 216, 323–49

death penalty and sentencing cases, 163, 165, 167, 168, 193, 213–17, 219–20, 333

dinner honoring Arnold, 321

due process cases, 26

equal protection and free association, 241–47, 327–28, 331, 332, 340

equal protection and gender, 154

equal protection and race cases, 48, 56, 80, 210, 218, 277–78, 279, 281, 290, 295

    Brown v. Board of Education, 17–20, 35–36, 37, 46, 100, 275, 277, 294–95, 296, 338–39

    Cooper v. Aaron, 36, 49–50, 65, 69, 273, 276–77

    Dred Scott case, 55

    Plessy v. Ferguson, 28, 46

    sit-in demonstration cases, 62–67

exclusionary rules cases, 50–56, 67

First Amendment cases, 50–56, 67, 226–27, 229–30, 231, 236–37

    Communist associations, 58–59, 60–61

and "not for publication" opinions, 353

prayer in schools, 97

right of privacy and abortion cases, 73, 251, 252–55, 257, 260–62, 263–65, 268–70, 271, 328, 333

    Roe v. Wade, 73, 251, 252, 260, 262, 271, 328, 333

Sixth Amendment cases, 46, 79

and stays of execution, 196, 197, 198–99, 200, 201, 204, 206, 219–20, 222

voting rights cases, 56–58, 101, 304–305, 307, 308, 311–13

    Jeffers v. Clinton, 302–14

"Supreme Court Change, The" (editorial by Arnold), 97–98

Susman, Frank, 333

Swann v. Charlotte-Mecklenburg Board of Education, 277–78

Swidler & Berlin (law firm), 326

Swindler, John, 196

Tatel, David, 295–96

Taylor, Corenna, 159–61

Taylor, Stuart, Jr., 334–35, 347

Taylor v. Jones, 158–61, 169

Teamster's Union, 105

Tennessee Secondary Schools Athletic Association, 158

Tennessee-Tombigbee waterway, 84, 90–92

Texarkana Bar Association, 146

Texarkana Gazette (newspaper), 21, 24, 33, 97–98

Third Circuit Court of Appeals, 335

Thirteenth Amendment, 64

Thomas, Clarence, 8, 270, 321, 365

    opinions written by, 269

Thomas Aquinas, Saint, 374

Thomas F. Eagleton Federal Courthouse in St. Louis, 375

Thornburg v. Gingles, 304–305, 307

Thornton, Ray, 82, 117–18, 120, 139

Thurmond, Strom, 36, 96

Time (magazine), 60, 124

Title IX of the Education Amendments of 1972, 151, 153

Title VII of the Civil Rights Act of 1964, 159–61

T.L.J. v. Webster, 333

Toobin, Jeffrey, 21, 324

Totenberg, Nina, 330

Tracy, Janie, 214

Tribe, Laurence, 362

Trillin, Calvin, 14, 19, 34–35

Trinity Episcopal Church in Little Rock, 373, 378

Truman, Harry, 30, 72

Tucker, Jim Guy, 199, 202, 206, 312

Udall, Walter, 61

Umin, Steve, 342

United States Jaycees v. McClure, 241–47, 327–28, 331, 332, 340

United States v. Lee, 228–31

University of Arkansas, 99, 152

    and Gay and Lesbian Students Association, 237–39, 334

    report on desegregation of Little Rock schools, 283

University of Minnesota, 238–39, 334

University of Missouri at Columbia, 177,

355
University of Virginia Law School, 93
Unlikely Heroes (Bass), 288
Uphaus, Willard, 60–61
Uphaus v. Wyman, 60–61, 67

Vance, Robert, 195
Vanderbilt University, 225
Virginia Law Review (journal), 93, 128
Voting Rights Act, 293, 321
    and *Jeffers v. Clinton*, 302–14

Wald, Patricia, 239, 249, 270, 327, 331,
    335
Walker, John W., 160–61, 287
Wallace, George, 82, 115
Wall Street Journal (newspaper), 341
Walsh, Thomas, 358
Warren, Earl, 41, 42, 45–46, 50, 51, 53, 56,
    57, 58, 60, 63, 64, 67, 102, 324
Warren, William C., 107
Washington Post (newspaper), 66, 265, 323,
    367
Washington Times (newspaper), 216,
    335–36
Waters, H. Franklin, 215, 237
Weaver, Arthur, 255–56
Webster, William H., 143
Webster v. Reproductive Health Services,
    260–62, 333
Weishart v. United States, 363

White, Byron, 323, 328
Whitewater affair, 333–34, 341
Whitmore, Jonas, 199
Whittaker, Charles Evans, 46, 48, 54, 57,
    59, 64
Williams v. Nix, 218
Wilson, William R., Jr., 293
Wolf v. Colorado, 52–53
Wollman, Roger, 268, 274, 283
Women's Bar Association of the District of
    Columbia, 340
Wood, Kimba, 325–26
Woods, Henry, 24, 155, 175–76, 293
    and Little Rock School desegregation,
    280, 283–84, 285–91, 299
World Fellowship, Inc., 60
World Wide Travel (company), 329
Wright, Scott, 267
Wright, Susan Webber, 291, 292, 293
Wyman, Louis C., 60

Yale College, 15, 22, 23, 33–35, 296
    debate on *Brown v. Board of Education*,
    17–20, 296, 338–39
Yale Law Journal, 93, 128, 299
Yale Law School Conservative Society,
    17–18
Yale Political Union, 18, 19, 34

Zimmerman, Fred L., 369–71
Zobel, Rya, 327